Social Movements and the Transformation of American Health Care

Social Movements and the Transformation of American Health Care

Jane C. Banaszak-Holl

Sandra R. Levitsky

Mayer N. Zald

UNIVERSITY PRESS

2010

OXFORD
UNIVERSITY PRESS

Oxford University Press, Inc., publishes works that further
Oxford University's objective of excellence
in research, scholarship, and education.

Oxford   New York
Auckland   Cape Town   Dar es Salaam   Hong Kong   Karachi
Kuala Lumpur   Madrid   Melbourne   Mexico City   Nairobi
New Delhi   Shanghai   Taipei   Toronto

With offices in
Argentina   Austria   Brazil   Chile   Czech Republic   France   Greece
Guatemala   Hungary   Italy   Japan   Poland   Portugal   Singapore
South Korea   Switzerland   Thailand   Turkey   Ukraine   Vietnam

Copyright © 2010 by Oxford University Press, Inc.

Published by Oxford University Press, Inc.
198 Madison Avenue, New York, New York 10016

www.oup.com

Oxford is a registered trademark of Oxford University Press

Library of Congress Cataloging-in-Publication Data
Banaszak-Holl, Jane.
Social movements and the transformation of American health care / Jane
Banaszak-Holl, Sandra Levitsky, Mayer N. Zald.
p.   cm.
Includes bibliographical references and index.
ISBN 978-0-19-538829-9; 978-0-19-538830-5 (pbk.)
1. Social medicine—United States.   2. Social movements—United
States.   3. Medical care—United States.   I. Levitsky, Sandra.   II. Zald,
Mayer N.   III. Title.
RA418.3.U6B36 2009
362.1—dc22
2009018154

1 3 5 7 9 8 6 4 2

Printed in the United States of America
on acid-free paper

Preface

Social movements are found in many countries, especially in those that allow some modicum of free speech, voluntary association, and rights to assemble in public spaces. The United States, almost from its inception, has provided fertile ground for the growth of social movements. Indeed, although social movements predate the American Revolution, it can be seen as an amalgam of many local acts of protest carried out by groups of people discontented with British rule. Over the centuries there have been a large number of movements, some aimed at changing laws and government policy, and others aimed at changing religious, social, and cultural institutions and modes of expression. There have been ebbs and flows of movements, so that some periods of time see a large number of movements with relatively large numbers of participants and other periods when there are fewer movements and little mobilization. The last several decades, roughly beginning in the early 1960s, have seen an upsurge in social movements, both in the United States and elsewhere. This upsurge has been accompanied by an increase in academic attention to social movements and their components. Scholarly debates have flourished about how to think about movements, what theories and concepts are most useful, and what methods of study should be used.

During the last half century there has also been an increasing concern with health as a personal and public matter. The public is more informed about health issues, and health institutions loom larger on the public policy agenda. The percentage of Gross Domestic Product (GDP) spent on health and medicine has more than doubled, and the absolute growth of medical and health organizations and practice has grown even faster. This growth, too, has been accompanied by a rising number of social movements, from self-help groups concerned with personal and familial experience of health-related problems, to professional movements aimed at rearranging the boundaries of specialization and of service delivery, to attempts to reconfigure the governance and financing of health care, as well attempts to influence the health-related behaviors of the population. Increasingly these movements have attracted the attention of medical sociologists, sociologists of science, and scholars concerned with specific movements, such as the environmental justice movement, and the mobilization of groups to limit tobacco usage, and specific studies of particular community conflicts around toxic environments.

One might have thought that, since health is so highly valued and supported, scholars who theorize and do research on the general topic of social movements would have put studies of health-related movements high on their agenda. But that is not the case. A search of the index of one of the leading compilation of papers using contemporary theories, that of McAdam, McCarthy, and Zald (1996) has nary a reference to the general category of health or medical movements. A later and more comprehensive volume, Snow, Soule, and Kriesi's *The Blackwell Companion to Social Movements* (2004), also does not include any reference to health or medical movements. While these volumes might reference the anti-tobacco movement, the pro-life or pro-choice movements, or movement activism around women's health, these studies do not treat these subjects as *health social movements* per se.

On the other side, scholars noted for their attention to a range of health movements and health politics issues, tended not to be versed in contemporary theories about movements. They came to their studies from their concern for health issues and other intellectual traditions, such as social studies of science, more than from a concern for social movement theory. One purpose of this book is to begin to bridge this divide.

A second purpose for bringing together these essays is to demonstrate the multiple levels of personal and public activity where a social movement perspective can be useful. Social movement and political analysis can illuminate attempts to reconfigure health institutions at the macro level of the nation state and, even, the globe. They can also illuminate more micro levels of self help groups and campaigns to change individual and household behavior.

A third purpose of the book, to illuminate the linkage of social movement analysis to recent developments in institutional theory, came into focus only late in our endeavor. As we began to think about the wider implications of the book and many of the essays, we realized that in fact we were in tune with recent efforts to move away from a largely state-centered focus upon political movements that had dominated social movement theory for the last several decades, toward a view of movements as transforming *institutions*, whether or not the state is centrally involved. Many of the papers were not written with this trend firmly in view, but are, we believe, consistent with it. We develop this linkage in both the introductory and concluding chapters.

The conference and resulting volume came about through rather fortuitous circumstances. In 1978, Mayer Zald and Michael Berger had published an article that dealt with social movements in organizations. It received little attention when it was published (see Zald 2005). More than two decades later, S. Paul Bate and Glenn Robert, social scientists in England attempting to help the National Health Service to involve its more than one million employees in efforts to improve services, read the article and contacted him. Zald ended up helping them to mount a conference in London bringing together practitioners engaged in exploratory projects using a social movement framework with a range of social movement theorists and researchers (Bate and Robert, chapter 12, this volume). Like most social movement oriented scholars, he had not previously thought about or studied health social movements.

A year or so later, Zald was sitting next to Jane Banaszak-Holl at a seminar put on by the University of Michigan's Interdisciplinary Committee on Organizational Studies (ICOS), a university-wide program bringing together faculty and graduate students interested in organizational theory. Jane is a sociologist studying health-related organizations in the School of Public Health. At the time, she had little background in social movements, but was interested in learning more, knew some of the literature on health-related movements, and had a deep background in organizational theory and research and health organizations (e.g., hospitals, nursing homes, assisted living, etc.). Zald said to her, "We ought to put on a conference on social movements and health institutions" and Jane said "Yes." They quickly developed a conference proposal and applied for funds to a variety of university units and external foundations. Sandra Levitsky joined the project after she was appointed as a postdoctoral research fellow in the Department of Sociology. Her background includes both work on social movements and health-related organizations.

The University of Michigan's ICOS and Department of Sociology became the first providers of financial support. We also received funds from the College of Literature, Science and the Arts and the Office of the Vice President for Research, the Horace H. Rackham School of Graduate Studies, and the Department of Sociology. The School of Public Health provided us with secretarial and administrative services, as did the Department of Sociology. We are grateful to all of them. We owe special thanks to ICOS, which for almost thirty years has promoted interdisciplinary work on organizations at the University.

We also want to acknowledge the wise counsel of Phil Brown in how we might structure the conference and who should be invited to it. Phil has devoted much of his career to doing research on movements and conflicts related to environmental health matters and to health movements more generally. He has trained a solid cohort of sociologists who do research in this area. John McCarthy attended the conference and gave us a critical reading of the first and last chapters. Verta Taylor has for many years been a significant contributor to the literature on social movements, the feminist movement, and health movements. She has been one of the leaders in criticizing an overly state-centric view of social movements. Her contribution here goes far beyond her coauthorship of two chapters. The authors in this volume not only responded to our editorial criticisms of their papers, but provided anonymous reviews and suggestions to other authors. Andrew Hoffman, Marie Hojnacki, Kate Kellogg, and Kelly Moore were also participants at the conference and provided valuable feedback on the conference presentations and papers. Additional reviews were provided by Cal Morrill and colleagues who reviewed the book as it was initially considered for publication. Finally, we wish to acknowledge the consistent and extraordinarily helpful work of Connie Rockman of the School of Public Health. She played a major role in making arrangements for the conference, making sure that it all came together, and in editing and putting together the final manuscript.

Contents

SECTION III. Professions and Organizations in the Transformation of Health Care and Research

SECTION IV. Culture and Legitimacy in U.S. Health Care

Contributors

Crystal Adams, Graduate Student, Department of Sociology, Brown University

Rebecca Gasior Altman, Lecturer, Community Health Program, Tufts University

Renee R. Anspach, Associate Professor, Department of Sociology, University of Michigan

Matthew E. Archibald, Assistant Professor, Department of Sociology, Emory University

Jane Banaszak-Holl, Associate Professor, Department of Health Management and Policy; Associate Research Professor, Institute of Gerontology; Adjunct Associate Professor, Organizational Studies Program, University of Michigan

Paul Bate, Professor Emeritus of Health Services Management, The Medical School, University College London

Phil Brown, Professor, Department of Sociology and Center for Environmental Studies, Brown University

Steven Epstein, John C. Shaffer Professor in the Humanities and Professor, Department of Sociology, Northwestern University

Scott Frickel, Associate Professor, Department of Sociology, Washington State University

Michael S. Goldstein, Professor, Department of Community Health Sciences and Department of Sociology, University of California, Los Angeles

Scott L. Greer, Assistant Professor, Department of Health Management and Policy, School of Public Health, University of Michigan

Beatrix Hoffman, Associate Professor, Department of History, Northern Illinois University

Elizabeth Hoover, Doctoral Candidate, Department of Anthropology, Brown University

Holly Jarman, Assistant Professor, Department of Political Science, State University of New York, Albany

Martin Kitchener, Professor of Healthcare Management and Policy, Cardiff Business School, Cardiff University

Lisa Leitz, Assistant Professor, Department of Sociology and Anthropology, Hendrix College

Sandra Levitsky, Assistant Professor, Department of Sociology, University of Michigan

Roberta G. Lessor, Professor, Department of Sociology, Chapman University

Brian Mayer, Assistant Professor, Department of Sociology, University of Florida

Sabrina McCormick, Robert Wood Johnson Health & Society Scholar, University of Pennsylvania and Assistant Professor, Department of Sociology & Environmental Science and Policy Program, Michigan State University

J. Brandon McKelvey, Doctoral Student, Department of Sociology, Florida State University

Rachel Morello-Frosch, Associate Professor, Department of Environmental Science, Policy and Management and School of Public Health, University of California, Berkeley

Constance A. Nathanson, Professor of Clinical Sociomedical Sciences and Professor of Clinical Population and Family Health, Department of Sociomedical Sciences and Department of Population and Family Health, Columbia University, Mailman School of Public Health

Maria Parries, Associate Project Manager, Department of Social Sciences and Health Policy, Wake Forest University School of Medicine

Jill Quadagno, Mildred and Claude Pepper Eminent Scholar in Social Gerontology, Department of Sociology, Florida State University

Glenn Robert, Senior Research Fellow, National Nursing Research Unit, King's College London

Laura Senier, Doctoral Candidate, Department of Sociology, Brown University

David A. Snow, Chancellor's Professor of Sociology, Department of Sociology, University of California, Irvine

Verta Taylor, Professor, Department of Sociology, University of California, Santa Barbara

Mark Wolfson, Associate Professor, Department of Social Sciences and Health Policy, Wake Forest University School of Medicine

Mayer N. Zald, Professor Emeritus, Department of Sociology and Schools of Business and Social Work, University of Michigan

Stephen Zavestoski, Associate Professor, Department of Sociology, University of San Francisco

Social Movements and the Transformation of American Health Care

1

Social Movements and the Transformation of American Health Care

Introduction

Sandra R. Levitsky and Jane Banaszak-Holl

The paradoxes of the U.S. health care system are well known: The United States spends more money on health care than any other advanced industrialized country,[1] and yet it ranks among the worst on many key indicators of health care quality.[2] Forty-seven million Americans—or 16% of the population—remain uninsured, whereas in other industrialized nations all citizens are generally covered by insurance. In the U.S. health system, many patients receive more care than they need,[3] many receive less care than medical practice guidelines prescribe, and many receive the *wrong kind* of care.[4] There are few contemporary social problems in the United States that affect more people on a day-to-day basis than the inefficiencies and inequities of the U.S. health care system. The pervasiveness of these problems—and the widespread public dissatisfaction they engender—suggests a social arena ripe for collective reform efforts.

But scholars who study social movements and American health care reform have generally disagreed about the prevalence—and effectiveness—of social movements in health care reform. One perspective sees health-related collective action everywhere: from workers' campaigns to promote occupational safety and health (see also Rosner and Markowitz 1987), the civil rights movement's claims for racial equality in health care (Quadagno 2000), and feminist challenges to gender bias in medicine (Morgen 2002), to health claims relating to abortion (Luker 1984; Staggenborg 1991), breast cancer (McCormick, Brown, and Zavestoski 2003; Taylor and Van Willigen 1996), smoking (Nathanson 1999), AIDS (Epstein 1996), disabilities (Fleischer and Zames 2000; Shapiro 1994), and environmental justice (Bullard 1993). A second perspective, in striking contrast, despairs of the *absence* of collective action: despite the rapidly growing ranks of the uninsured and underinsured and well-documented public dissatisfaction with many aspects of American health care provision, there has never been, nor does there appear to be now, a large-scale, grassroots movement seeking fundamental transformation in the American health care system (Hoffman 2003; Quadagno 2005). While the United States has seen successful movements on behalf of particular social groups or around specific issues, these demands have not coalesced into a movement for more comprehensive reform, and by some accounts may have actually *impeded* efforts to achieve large-scale reform of the American health care system.

One reason for such disparate perspectives on the role of social movements in American health care reform is that scholars who study health care reform currently lack a coherent analytical framework for studying the dynamics of change across health care institutions. Thus while there is a rich literature about health systems generally (Morone and Jacobs 2005; Scott et al. 2000; Wholey et al. 2004) and the social and political aspects of individual disease entities and disabilities (Horwitz and Wakefield 2007; Kasper and Ferguson 2002; Oliver 2006), there have been few attempts to conceptually integrate this research with contemporary theories of collective action. And while researchers have studied social movements related to specific medical illnesses or environmental threats (see, e.g., Brown and Zavestoski 2005; Epstein 1996), or considered the politics surrounding attempts to promote major changes in health insurance (Derickson 2005; Hacker 1997; Mayes 2005; Quadagno 2005; Skocpol 1997) and the delivery of services (Luker 1984; Taylor 1996), there have been few attempts to *systematically analyze the field of health care-related social movement activity* or to *connect* collective action processes across the multiple levels of the health system.

In the absence of more comparative research, we know little about the common constraints—and opportunities—that shape possibilities for social movement action within a given health institution, or how social movement reform efforts in one institution affect the possibilities for reform in other institutions. Scholars disagree about where health-related social movement activism is likely to arise and who to count as relevant social movement actors in analyzing the politics of health care reform. As a result, social movement theory has had a much smaller impact on studies of health policy change than other theoretical traditions, such as interest-group analysis (Hoffman 2003). Despite this, the extent of research on social movements in health— as we document in this volume and as the contributors have elaborated elsewhere—is substantial. The aim of this book is to demonstrate the diversity of health-related social movements and to synthesize research on these movements in ways that illuminate their effects and limitations.

In October 2007, scholars from medicine, public health, history, sociology, and political science came together for a conference at the University of Michigan on social movements and American health care institutions. The foci of the papers presented varied widely. Research ranged from micro- to meso- to macro-level analyses of health-related social movements. Some authors explicitly tied their research to social movement theory; many did not. After the conference, the editors of this volume sought a way to integrate the papers within a single analytical framework for understanding collective challenges to American health institutions. The framework we have adopted departs from the dominant paradigms in the social movement literature that focus on the state as the central source of power and the central target of social movement activism. Instead, we join a growing cadre of researchers who have adopted what Armstrong and Bernstein (2008) refer to as a *multi-institutional politics* model for understanding social movements (see also Armstrong 2002; Davis et al. 2005; Snow 2004b; Staggenborg and Taylor 2005; Van Dyke, Soule, and Taylor 2004). By conceptualizing the American health care system as being organized by and around multiple institutions—including but not limited to the state—we seek to encompass (1) the diversity of contemporary health care reform efforts and sites of activism within a single analytical framework, and (2) the full range of actors in health reform campaigns who transcend traditional social movement boundaries between institutional and extra-institutional politics, members and challengers, insiders and outsiders, and lay and expert activists. At the same time, we hope to broaden the focus of analysis from health social movements *as dependent variables* (Brown and Zavestoski 2004; McCormick, Brown, and Zavestoski 2003), to the health *institutions* that these movements seek to challenge—including the political logics, organization, and systems of meaning that sustain and reproduce dominant health paradigms and systems of health care provision. While the individual papers in this collection do not always explicitly adopt a multi-institutional orientation, we view our attempt to synthesize this work as the start of an ongoing dialogue among scholars with distinct approaches to studying the transformation of the U.S. health system.

Social Movements and Sites of Health Activism

Social movement scholars generally trace the origins of the modern social movement—conceptualized here as organized and sustained collective action on behalf of a common change-oriented goal—back to the emergence of the modern state (Tarrow 1994; Tilly 1978). As the nation-state assumed increasing legitimacy and responsibility for social order in the nineteenth century, it became the central target for those who sought to challenge the management and distribution of resources in society. Many of the most prominent theoretical frameworks for studying social movements—most notably, political opportunity and political process theory (Tarrow 1994; Tilly 1978; McAdam 1982)—continue to place the state squarely at the center of their analyses. In these accounts, the primary goal of social movements is to achieve changes in public policy to grant new benefits for constituents or recognition by authorities.

But while a state-centered view of social movements arguably remains one of the most influential approaches to studying social movements, it provides an incomplete framework for understanding the diversity of social movements—and social movement actors—seeking transformations in health institutions and systems. Many health-related social movement campaigns involve challenges to forms of political power other than the state. Health-related social movements have sought, for example, to democratize knowledge production, transform traditional assumptions and lines of inquiry regarding disease causation and diagnosis, and challenge the authority of science and medicine by promoting the personal understanding and experience of disease and disability (Brown and Zavestoski 2005;

Epstein 1996; Taylor 1996). The emergence of such movements suggests that health care reform today targets not just state institutions, but professions, corporations, hospitals, research institutions, medical practices, medical education, and the workplace.[5] Social movement models that focus disproportionately on the state as the battleground for political contestation occlude or diminish the importance of these other sites of activism.

Over the past decade, social movement scholars critical of the state-centered model have sought to expand analyses of social movements to include movements in multiple institutional arenas (e.g., Armstrong 2002; Snow 2004b; Staggenborg and Taylor 2005; Van Dyke, Soule, and Taylor 2004). We propose that this *multi-institutional* model, most recently elaborated by Armstrong and Bernstein (2008), represents a more useful way of thinking about dynamics of change in health institutions. Armstrong and Bernstein argue that society is composed of multiple—and often contradictory—institutions that are overlapping and nested. *Institutions*, according to this perspective—such as the bureaucratic state, capitalist markets, professions, religion, and the family—operate according to distinct logics or organizing principles. They are "organizationally structured, politically defended, and technically and materially constrained" (Friedland and Alford 1991: 248). Institutions are where classification and meaning systems are anchored, resources are allocated, and relationships of power and domination are reproduced.

The state, with its unique capacity to establish the rules that govern other health institutions, looms as a major institution in this model, but it is by no means the only source of authority in health systems—nor is it necessarily the most influential in all cases. Governance in the United States, with its multitiered, federated system, is achieved through a highly differentiated "state" apparatus, in which it's often difficult to know where the "state" ends and other sectors of society begin. The multi-institutional view thus builds on Foucault's (1980: 60) argument that "power isn't localized in the State apparatus and that nothing in society will be changed if the mechanisms of power that function outside, below and along side the State apparatuses, on a much more minute and everyday level, are not also changed." In this view of society as a multi-institutional system, we should expect social movements to challenge not only the state, but any social group, organization, or system in which authority is constituted (Armstrong and Bernstein 2008; Snow 2004b). And to the extent that these institutions produce and reproduce cultural meanings and classification systems—such as the medical model for addressing health problems, discussed below—we should expect social movements to challenge not just the structures and practices of these institutions, but the very legitimacy of the frames and categories they produce.

The multi-institutional politics framework thus provides a way of integrating research on social movement activity that occurs across multiple levels of the health care system. By shifting the object of analysis, we confront a set of new and important research questions: What political logics organize the health care institutions in a particular society? What forms of regulation and enforcement do these institutions use to establish and maintain legitimacy and influence? How do obstacles to reform and resources for mobilization vary across health institutions? How do changes within one institution affect other, interrelated institutions?

Social Movements and Health Activists

The multi-institutional politics view of social movement activity also substantially expands our understanding of "who counts" as relevant social movement actors in the study of health care reform. Political process and political opportunity theorists define social movement actors largely by their relationship to the state: only those "outside" the state, or who lack formal access to or influence with state officials are expected to engage in social movement activity (McAdam 1982; Tilly 1978).[6] As a result, state-centered theorists are reluctant to include state actors (whether government agencies or elected representatives) or any actor with easy access to decision-makers within the ambit of their analyses. A similar logic in research on health institutions depicts "experts" and professionals within the scientific and health care communities as *insiders* relative to social movement *outsiders*.

But research on health activism in this volume and elsewhere suggests that many collective challenges to the norms, practices, and organization of the American health care system are increasingly occurring *across* these traditional demarcations. Health-related social movements often seek to blur distinctions between experts and lay people, science and nonscience, medical and experiential knowledge (see, e.g., Allsop, Jones, and Baggott 2004; Brown et al. 2006; Hess 2004; Joffe, Weitz, and Stacey 2004; McCally 2002; Taylor 1996). Activists become "experts" by using the Internet and other resources to educate themselves about the environment, law, medicine, and science. "Experts" become activists when scientists, physicians, lawyers, and other professionals use their knowledge and skills to assist social movements and legitimize movement claims. Politicians and government agencies similarly transgress member/challenger boundaries by working in collaboration with reform campaigns to influence public policy. In all of these cases, traditional distinctions between insiders and outsiders give way to reveal a much more complex, much more diverse array of strategies, tactics, and resource exchanges than traditional social movement frameworks allow.

The multi-institutional politics model of social movements assumes that the member/challenger divide will vary across institutions and change efforts. Challengers are often structurally linked to the institutions they seek to change: they are policymakers, scientists, customers, clients, and employees with both vested interests in their home institutions and a commitment to pursuing change in those institutions (see Katzenstein 1998; Moore 1999). In this view, we should not only expect to see change initiated or encouraged by individuals who would be considered, under more traditional social movement definitions, to be "insiders," but by treating these individuals as relevant social movement actors, we raise another set of important questions (cf. Armstrong and Bernstein 2008): Which social groups can exert influence on which institutions? What gives certain individuals standing to challenge institutional norms and practices and policies? What are the particular obstacles to change faced by actors in these institutions? How do individuals who confront competing demands of institutions and political commitments respond to the stresses and contradictions of their situations? How is expertise and professional legitimacy used as a resource for social movement mobilization?

The chapters in this volume are organized into four sections. We focus on three sets of institutions as both sources of power and targets of collective action: state institutions, biomedical fields, and health-related professions. In the fourth and final section of the book we shift our attention from challenges to the structures and practices of these institutions to the systems of meaning and classification they support in American culture—specifically, the cultural dominance of the medical model for addressing health problems and its implications for social movements seeking to challenge the legitimacy of particular issues, framings, and political actors in health care reform. In what follows, we describe each of these organizing themes in greater detail.

Institutions in U.S. Health Care

The U.S. health care system, one of the largest and most complex in the world, has been characterized as a biomedical, scientifically based and corporately managed system (Clarke et al. 2003). In 2007, health care spending in the United States totaled an estimated $2.3 trillion dollars—or 16% of the gross domestic product.[7] Doctor and hospital services represented more than 50% of these expenditures; pharmaceuticals represented another 10% of expenditures (California HealthCare Foundation 2007). The complexity of the U.S. health system, with its combination of financing from the federal and state governments, private businesses, nonprofit organizations, and consumers, as well as intersecting (and sometimes competing) scientific, professional, and organizational fields, suggests that there are both multiple sites in which authority is vested, and multiple "entry points" for collective action.

The American State

The federal and state governments, by virtue of their size and their role in creating rules and allocating resources, remain a primary target of health-related social movement activity. The federal government accounts for almost a third of all health spending, largely for Medicare and Medicaid, but also for health care costs associated with the armed forces (including veterans) and the State Children's Health Insurance Program (California HealthCare Foundation 2007). State and local governments account for 13% of total health spending, approximately half of which can be attributed to the costs of Medicaid, and the rest relating to public health activity, state hospitals, and Workers' Compensation. In addition to state-run programs, American health policy is also forged in and administered by a wide range of state bureaucratic institutions, from the Occupational Safety and Health Administration and the Food and Drug Administration, to the Centers for Disease Control and Prevention and National Institutes for Health.

The United States, of course, has had a long and celebrated history of social movement activism directed at the state. Indeed, many have observed that the fragmented structure of the American political system, with its federated system and multiple points of access to decision-makers, makes the United States a particularly fertile ground for social movement activism. Volumes have been written on the question of why, despite ripe conditions for social movement mobilization, the United States has never witnessed a large-scale movement seeking fundamental transformation of the American health care system (see, e.g., Derickson 2005; Mayes 2005; Quadagno

2005). There have been five times in U.S. history in which national health care reform seemed imminent: in the Progressive era, during the New Deal, and under the Truman, Nixon, and Clinton administrations (see generally Starr 1982). None of these reform campaigns, however, were spearheaded by social movements. In each case, the contest was initiated and fought primarily by policy analysts and professional lobbyists rather than grassroots movements (Hoffman 2003). In this volume, Beatrix Hoffman provides some historical context for collective mobilization directed at large-scale federal intervention in the American health care system. Examining comprehensive health care reform efforts over the course of the twentieth century, Hoffman argues that only with the convergence of presidential leadership from "above" and social movement mobilization from "below" has major health care reform ever been achieved in the United States.

Constance Nathanson also addresses obstacles to collective action against the state in her chapter on the limitations of social movements as a vehicle for representing the health interests of poor and disadvantaged populations. Nathanson argues that in the absence of three sets of conditions—(1) the mobilization of left-leaning party and/or movement actors; (2) social, political, and/or economic crises that create opportunities for these actors to mobilize; and (3) the presence of elected officials or bureaucrats prepared to work with those actors to advance the interests of the poor— there is little hope for social movements to advance the health interests of the poor through public policy reform.

One of the primary obstacles to federal health policy reform is, of course, the complex of trade associations, insurance companies, pharmaceutical and supplier manufacturers, service providers and other interest groups that make up the biomedical industry. Historically, these actors have exerted a remarkable influence over political decisions regarding the delivery and payment for health care services in the United States (Quadagno 2005). Indeed, many commentators view the combined political influence of these groups as contributing to the defeat of every large-scale health care reform campaign at the federal level in the twentieth century (Hacker 2002; Hoffman 2003; Quadagno 2005).

The influence of these advocacy groups is derived not only from money spent on lobbying key politicians considering reform bills, but also from mobilizing the general public through publicity campaigns and targeted appeals to health consumers. During one of the first major campaigns for national health insurance in the early 1940s, for example, the American Medical Association (AMA) spent over $1 million to defeat the proposed legislation, orchestrating an elaborate public relations drive and enlisting physicians in lobbying their legislators (Hoffman 2003). Fifty years later, during consideration of Clinton's Health Security Act in 1993 and 1994, interest groups spent more than $100 million, making the bill one of the most heavily lobbied legislative initiatives in U.S. history (Center for Public Integrity 1994: 1). The Health Insurance Association of America (HIAA) alone spent more than $14 million in a now-infamous television advertising campaign featuring Harry and Louise, a fictional husband and wife who criticized the Health Security Plan from their kitchen table (Skocpol 1997:137–38). At the same time, health insurance and other companies lobbied their customers, both large and small commercial businesses, to take a direct role in opposing health reform (Quadagno 2005).

While such interest groups feature prominently in analyses of failed policy reform campaigns, social movement researchers have been reluctant to treat these organizations as social movement actors—both because of who these organizations represent and the strategies they use to advance their interests. Political opportunity and political process models assume that social movements consist of political "outsiders"—those individuals and groups with little formal access to or influence with state decision-makers. Advocacy organizations representing the insurance or pharmaceutical industries do not, therefore, fit easily into the ambit of traditional social movement definitions (but see Burstein 1999). Similarly, most social movement accounts assume that while institutional strategies may on occasion be necessary or efficacious, social movements will rely primarily on *extra*-institutional strategies to advance their interests—street protest and other forms of direct action. Movements that rely primarily on lobbying and campaign contributions to press their grievances are therefore rarely included in social movement analyses.

The chapters in this section suggest that by relying on these rigid demarcations between insiders and outsiders, institutional and extra-institutional strategies, we miss many of the key dynamics of collective action for American health care policy reform (see also Morrill, Zald, and Rao 2003). Quadagno and McKelvey, for example, demonstrate how the consumer-directed health care movement (CDHC), a loose-knit coalition of insurance companies, financial services companies, advocacy organizations, and conservative politicians, used tactics and strategies common to other social movements to successfully reshape the way health care is financed in the United States. Epstein in this volume also echoes the importance of blurring distinctions between institutional and extra-institutional politics in his analysis of reform efforts to include women, racial and ethnic minorities, children, and the elderly as research subjects in many forms of clinical research. Here the focus of contestation shifts from federal legislative institutions to regulatory institutions. Epstein documents how the effort to persuade the federal agencies of the U.S. Department of Health and Human Services (DHHS) to change its policies included not only conventional social movement actors, but also supporters from within DHHS agencies, sympathetic physicians and scientists, professional organizations, politicians, and pharmaceutical companies. Again, were we to focus only on movements of political "outsiders" in studying the politics of health care reform, we would miss many of the key actors seeking transformation of these institutions.

Finally, the American political system provides opportunities for collective action directed at state-level health care reform. Frustration with national health care reform efforts has led to a sharp increase in state-level health activism in recent years. In 2006, Massachusetts and Vermont became the first states to offer universal or near-universal health insurance coverage. As of 2008, fifteen states were considering major health reform bills (Weil 2008). In addition, federal waivers in the Medicare program that permit combining Medicare and Medicaid funds at the state level have allowed some states to reform their long-term care policies by shifting a portion of their services out of institutional settings and into home- and community-based care (Kitchener and Harrington 2004). In this volume, Jarman and Greer focus on state-level campaigns for universal health care. Comparing the campaigns in Wisconsin and Pennsylvania, two very similar states on most key dimensions, they argue that

Wisconsin is much closer to passing a radical insurance coverage expansion plan in part because, unlike Pennsylvania, it has successfully developed a strong, durable coalition that crosses traditional boundaries, incorporating within its membership not only grassroots organizations, but also organized labor, the AARP, politicians, and other political "insiders."

Biomedical Fields

Institutional fields refer to relations among a set of diverse actors all seeking to influence a common institution, whether that institution represents normative prescriptions for how social dynamics occur or is more rigidly embedded in legally sanctioned organizational forms. The process of embedding institutions in social and legal norms and developing organizational boundaries has only recently become a more dominant focus of both organizational and social movement theory (McAdam and Scott 2005; Rao, Morrill, and Zald 2000). Indeed, one of the richest descriptions of the development of health care institutions in the United States is the somewhat recent analysis by Scott and colleagues (2000) on the history of health care provision in the San Francisco Bay area. Scott and his colleagues identify three major historical shifts over a fifty-five-year period, each characterized by a different dominant institutional logic and marked by profound changes in the underlying social values, influential social actors, and networks of health delivery organizations in the area.

The study by Scott and his colleagues focuses heavily on legally sanctioned organizational actors because of the public availability of those records. Social movement researchers, by contrast, often focus on less documented contests over the development of institutional norms: contests over ideas and practices that have not yet been widely adopted or legally sanctioned. During institutionally unsettled periods, social activities become ways to negotiate the acceptability of practices and the discourse that surrounds actors' entry into acceptable social circles (Swidler 1986). Key indicators of how institutional norms become legitimized include the ascendance of social groups and their priorities in setting social agendas, favorable legal outcomes, and the dominance of organizational change processes.

The chapters in this section of the book consider four institutional field debates in which newly powerful social actors seek to challenge institutional norms and practices. Wolfson and Parries examine data on decisions regarding funding for state-sponsored research to demonstrate how support for community-action principles has increased over time. Community-action principles propose introducing community partners into the research process as partners not just in implementation but also in the design and development of research projects. This institutional practice runs antithetical to norms of scientific research that depend on the expert scientist to design and develop studies.

Kitchener's chapter uses a comparison of three historically significant changes in health delivery institutions—long-term care services, abortion services, and AIDS treatment—to argue that while conflicting institutional logics can be present for long periods of time, one mechanism for institutional change is the persistent confrontation between dialectically opposed value systems. Kitchener finds that during the hegemonic dominance of an institutional logic, resources may flow to nondominant logics but not at a level sufficient to overcome the authoritative practices.

Anspach's chapter considers how the pro-life movement, a coalition of conservative Catholics, Protestant fundamentalists, and evangelicals, used the national controversy around Terry Schiavo to redefine the field of bioethics.[8] Prior to Schiavo, a heterogeneous group of scholars based in hospitals and research centers had occupied the role of "experts" on bioethics, serving on advisory commissions and as pundits in the press. Anspach traces the movement/countermovement dynamics that unfolded during the Schiavo controversy between a group of conservative or "Christian bioethicists" who the popular press began to quote as "bioethicists," and secular bioethicists who countered by creating what is now known as the "progressive bioethics" field.

Finally, Brown and his colleagues offer a reflexive analysis of their extensive experiences studying a variety of community-based health social movements, making a case for the roles of both field analysis and policy ethnography in the study of health social movements. The authors' approach to studying institutional fields relies on a historical analysis of the lineages of health social movements, tracing the ways in which the legacies of past movements shape the expectations and beliefs of current participants.

All four of these chapters provide a rich analysis of the processes by which values, actors, and practices within distinct biomedical fields shift over time. These processes are driven by both nonlegitimated and legitimated actions of key actors and situate health-related social movements in the context of existing health delivery systems and policies.

Professions and Organizations

Key actors in the health system are clinical and scientific professionals, and we devote a section of this book to examining the professional dynamics central to health-related social movement activity. While addressing issues similar to those raised in other parts of the book, the papers in this section focus specifically on routine professional activities and professional organizations that challenge the dominant values, structures, and practices of the U.S. health system. The role of professionals in social movements is ironic given that as an elite and highly trained workforce, professionals have a vested interest in protecting—and reproducing—existing authority structures (Friedson 1986). However, as experts, they also seek to improve work practices and ensure quality within their profession. In addition, their expertise provides professionals (and social movements) with an established authoritative base from which to challenge other organized actors.

As the authors in this section elaborate, professionals can strategically combine social movement and work roles in order to push for institutional change. Frickel, for example, examines how such varied professionals as toxicologists, epidemiologists, geneticists, and physicians challenge and reconfigure the nature of scientific knowledge by participating in community environmental activism. Frickel finds that loosely configured, boundary-spanning networks—aptly named *shadow mobilizations*—act as incubators of activist cultures in science, not only increasing recruitment and strengthening ties among experts in the environmental justice movement, but also generating opportunities for institutional change in science, engineering, and public health.

Bate and Robert take this "boundary crossing" one step further by describing a project in which academics studying social movements collaborated with health care practitioners to bring about dramatic changes in patient services. Bate and Robert's chapter is unique in this volume in that it focuses on the National Health Service (NHS) of the United Kingdom. They describe a five-year collaboration in which employees of the NHS were taught the basic principles of organizing and encouraged to generate "bottom-up" ideas for organizational change.

The NHS's innovation with social movement change reflects deliberate engagement by policy leaders and hence reflects, to some extent, a "top-down" priority within the United Kingdom's centralized health system. This leads to an interesting question of whether the presence of a centralized system facilitated the quick development of these social movement activities and whether movement-driven organizational change should be encouraged as a driver of change in other countries' health systems and within the United States specifically. The U.S. system already has greater market influences on the delivery of health care services than its European counterparts, and market forces are also seen as ways to promote innovation within health care. While this volume focuses primarily on the U.S. health system, we hope that future research will draw on the tools of cross-cultural comparative analysis to identify and further elaborate the range of roles for professionals as change agents in health care delivery.

Finally, a key challenge for health-related social movements is that of contesting the legitimacy of established health professions and the health practices and approaches that they endorse. The remaining chapters in this section illuminate the processes by which social movements seek to legitimize alternative health practices or approaches to health care in contexts involving the medical professions. Goldstein's chapter explores the growing prominence of complementary, alternative, and integrative medicine (CAM/IM) practices in the medical profession. Using a meeting of academic medical leadership as a key point for studying how CAM/IM practices have become more acceptable even as allopathic medicine remains the dominant practice in the profession, Goldstein traces how representatives from just eight medical schools became major leaders in promoting the development of CAM/IM "centers of excellence" in academic medical centers. Matthew Archibald applies a macro-level lens to the phenomena of self-help movements to identify how such movements achieve sociopolitical and cultural recognition and acceptance from actors with vested interests in the institutions that organizers challenge, such as mainstream medicine and health and human services.

Culture and Legitimacy in the American Health Care System

Thus far, we have discussed the American health care system as being organized by and around multiple, nested institutions—including the state, biomedical fields, and professions. By shifting attention toward the organizing structures and political logics of the many different social groups that exercise power in the health care system, we make visible the diversity in both *sites* of health-related collective action and the *actors* seeking transformations in health institutions. But importantly, the power of these institutions is not vested solely in their structures and practices, but also through the systems of meaning and classification they support and reproduce in American culture. In this final section of the book, we examine the cultural dominance of the medical model for addressing health problems in the United States and its implications for collective attempts to establish the legitimacy of particular issues, framings, and political actors in health care reform.

Beginning in the 1980s, the study of social movements in the United States took a "cultural turn" as researchers began to focus on the ways in which movements use language, symbols, discourse, emotions, identity, and other aspects of culture to mobilize participants and achieve movement goals (see, e.g., Darnovsky, Epstein, and Flacks 1995; Johnston and Klandermans 1995; Larana, Johnston, and Gusfield 1994; Williams 2004). Seeking to "bring meaning back in" to the study of collective action (Williams 2004), researchers in this tradition shifted away from analyses of resources and structures and began examining the interpersonal processes through which individuals make sense of their circumstances, and the symbolic and meaning work done by movement activists in articulating grievances, creating consensus on solutions, and devising strategies and tactics for collective action. Social movement scholars working in the cultural tradition have also sought to understand the ways in which the "cultural environment"—systems of meaning, symbols, and classification—can facilitate and constrain opportunities for social movement action (Williams 2004).

The cultural classifications we have historically used to define social groups in the United States—citizens or noncitizens, white or nonwhite, male or female, straight or gay—affect how we distribute rights, benefits, and services (Canaday 2009; Strach 2007; Cohen 1996; Nagel 1994). In the context of American health care institutions, the relationship between systems of classification and distributional resources has largely been defined by the medical model for treatment of health problems, or the practice of identifying the underlying biological basis for health problems and applying curative treatments when possible to eliminate the risk of disease. The medical approach has proven successful in eliminating major infectious diseases—such as polio—during the twentieth century and in reducing individual morbidity and mortality from leading factors such as heart disease (Heidenrich and McClellan 2001). However, complex chronic diseases have proven less easy to address.

The medical model of disease and its causation, codified in government and private-sector practices, and legitimated and reproduced in biomedical institutions, journals, media, and universities, has emerged as what Brown and his colleagues (2006) refer to as "the dominant epidemiological paradigm." As such, the medical model implicitly confers legitimacy to those diseases that have been "discovered" or officially recognized by biomedical institutions. Social movements seeking to mobilize around health problems that lack clearly identifiable causal relationships face, in addition to all the usual obstacles to mobilization, the challenge of establishing the very legitimacy of their grievances as *health problems*.[9] Fibromyalgia, chronic-fatigue syndrome, multiple chemical sensitivity, and postpartum depression are all cases in which individuals experiencing medically unexplained symptoms have challenged medical systems reluctant to classify their conditions as officially recognized diseases in the absence of a clear etiology (Taylor 1996; Zavestoski et al. 2004). The challenges of mobilizing affected populations for reform in cases involving new or officially unrecognized diseases are illustrated in McCormick's chapter on climate-induced illnesses. Drawing on the cases of the West Nile Virus, the displacement of Alaska Natives, and heat-induced illness in Philadelphia, McCormick argues that in the absence of preexisting environmental health movements or strong scientific evidence supporting a link between ecological change and health outcomes, it is exceptionally difficult for social movements to mobilize around climate-induced illnesses.

Cultural beliefs about disease and professional authority shape the illness experience for affected populations, as well as the willingness of affected individuals to politicize their personal experiences. Much of the research on health social movements has examined the processes by which individuals with nonmedically recognized diseases come to link their individual experiences with structural explanations for their problems and a sense of collective identity. In their chapter, Taylor and Leitz trace the processes of collective identity construction and politicization among women suffering from postpartum psychiatric illness who have been convicted of infanticide. The authors document how participation in a self-help movement allowed women to draw on experiential knowledge and social support to shift blame from the mothers themselves to the medical and legal systems, encouraging their participation in collective challenges to medical and legal policy on the treatment of postpartum psychiatric illness.

To argue that the medical model legitimates certain issues, diseases, and social movement actors is not to say that it necessarily produces clear, correct, or undisputed diagnoses of health problems. Social movement scholars have long contended that collective mobilization depends in a critical respect on a shared understanding of a given problem and agreement as to what should be done to remedy it. Or, in the language of social movement framing theorists, joint action on health-related issues requires, among other things, *shared collection action frames* (see, e.g., Snow and Benford 1988; Steinberg 1999; Snow et al. 1986; Ferree et al. 2002). In their chapter, Snow and Lessor argue that *framing hazards* are often a key obstacle for health-oriented stakeholders seeking solutions to health problems. Drawing on three distinct health issues—the obesity "epidemic," work-related illnesses, and gamete transfer in infertility, Snow and Lessor elaborate four framing hazards: *ambiguous events or ailments* that do not fit neatly into an existing frame; *framing errors or misframings* based on erroneous beliefs; *frame disputes* involving competing explanations or interpretations of events; and *frame shifts* involving the displacement of one frame by another. In each case, the authors demonstrate how framing hazards dramatically increase the obstacles to health care reform.

Conclusion

By bringing together researchers with widely varying approaches to studying collective change in the U.S. health care system, this volume seeks to highlight the continuities across studies with regard to the opportunities, limitations, and effects of social movement activism in health institutions. A multi-institutional approach illuminates the diversity of challenges to institutional authorities and political logics within the health care sector. Following the 2008 election of a Democratic president and Democratic majorities in both houses of Congress, these challenges must be viewed in the context of a changing landscape of U.S. health care policy. On the one hand, a severe national—and global—economic crisis would seem to dim prospects for comprehensive transformations of the U.S. health care system—particularly in the absence of a national movement for health care reform (see the chapters by Hoffman and Nathanson). But on the other hand, an economic crisis may also provide unique opportunities for reform.

One aspect of our health care system that would benefit from such reform efforts is the urgent need for chronic care and preventive services (see chapters in this volume from Kitchener and Snow and Lessor). It is estimated that seven out of ten deaths in the United States are attributable to chronic health problems, including heart problems, chronic respiratory disease, diabetes and Alzheimer's disease.[10] These illnesses require preventative services that can hold off the disease (or at least the worst episodes of illness) and complex case management that manages symptoms addressed by a variety of clinical professionals across multiple health visits. While chronic problems sometimes need very simple approaches to care (for example, better meal options in public schools, monitoring of blood sugar and daily health for diabetics, and counseling on smoking and diet during clinic visits) clinical professionals will need to agree on a unified approach to disease management. Today this does not occur. Snow and Lessor's chapter, for example, documents how individuals approach the chronic health issue of obesity from fundamentally different reference frames, shaping both their interactions with patients and the cooperative management of patient health from multiple professionals. Political action may be needed to resolve such frame disputes and shift institutional resources to new approaches to care.

What is perhaps most notable about the current health policy environment is that mobilization for reform in health institutions is increasingly occurring not among newly developing constituencies, but among *recombinations* of existing movements and activists—as well as organizations and individuals not conventionally viewed as social movement actors. This can be seen in the mobilization to adopt more specificity in medical treatment for diverse ethnic and racial population groups (Epstein's chapter) and in the environmental justice activities of elites working on environmental health issues (see Frickel's and Brown et al.'s chapters). Indeed, McCormick's challenge to view climate change illness mobilization as social movement activity may depend on the extent to which existing environmental movement activists and disease-specific activists see themselves as part of a joint movement and are able to work together to motivate public support for these issues (see McCormick's chapter).

Within health delivery, the issue of patient safety has become a prominent policy issue partly because experts and activists have used institutional approaches developed for the dissemination of expert knowledge to share more activist approaches to improving health quality. For example, the Institute for Healthcare

Improvement (IHI), an organization leading the movement to improve patient safety and quality, explicitly makes it a priority to build collective support and action around these issues. Their mission states: "IHI works to accelerate improvement by building the will for change, cultivating promising concepts for improving patient care, and helping health care systems put those ideas into action."[11] The IHI Web site is designed in part to identify and build connections among experts, community members, health providers, and policymakers around common safety and quality issues.

It may be that the unique composition of the health care system contributes to the hybridity in social movement activity in this sector. Health care remains one of only a few sectors (with social services and education) in which a fairly balanced mix of nonprofit and for-profit organizations provide services (Boris and Steuerle 2006; Salamon 2003). Health care organizations often seek to serve a complex mix of missions that includes not just service provision but also advocacy and community building (Salamon 2003). For example, Planned Parenthood, often defined as a "feminist organization," is a primary community provider of pregnancy and reproductive services in addition to its role as an advocate for abortion and family-planning issues, and has been the home institution for women activists across decades (Whittier 1997). This blend of advocacy with service provision provides a unique role for these organizations in the policy and delivery system.

The U.S. health system is organized around multiple, overlapping institutions in which contests over authority, legitimacy, and the allocation of resources take place. Thinking about dynamics of change in health care as being organized around these nested institutions illuminates both new sites of activism and unlikely actors involved in health-related social movement activity. As the U.S. health system shows increasing signs of strain, social movements will confront new opportunities and constraints in their efforts to shape the direction of future institutional change. We hope this volume will encourage researchers to study transformations in health institutions through the lens afforded by social movement theory, with attention to the diverse ways in which collective action seeks to transform the web of relationships, resources, practices and norms that structure the U.S. health care system.

NOTES

1. In 2005, health care spending in the United States reached $2.3 trillion, or 15% of its gross domestic product (GDP). Data are from the Centers for Medicare and Medicaid Services, Office of the Actuary. In comparison, Canada, France, Germany, and Switzerland all spend approximately 10% of their GDP on health care; Japan and the United Kingdom spend around 8% (Barr 2008).

2. Among developed countries, life expectancies at birth in the United States are among the lowest and infant mortality among the highest (Barr 2008).

3. Between 2003 and 2004, for example, 22% of sick adults in the United States were sent for duplicate tests by different health care professionals (Davis et al. 2004).

4. In 46% of all cases, patients do not receive the care prescribed by national medical specialty guidelines. Another 11% of patients receive care that is not recommended and potentially harmful (Asch et al. 2006).

5. In a study of 4654 protest events related to women's rights, civil rights, gay and lesbian rights, environmental rights, peace, human rights, and other policy movements that

occurred in the United States from 1968 to 1975, Nella Van Dyke, Sarah Soule and Verta Taylor found that just under half of all protests were directed at institutions *other* than the state and/or public opinion (Van Dyke, Soule, and Taylor 2004).

6. This is not to say that the dominant social movement paradigms have assumed that movements are comprised only of the politically dispossessed and poor. To the contrary, resource mobilization and political process theorists have both emphasized the important role of individuals and groups *with* resources in the development of social movements (McCarthy and Zald 1973; McCarthy and Zald 1977). The post-1960s proliferation of social movements among the nonpoor—from the peace movement to the environmental movement to the women's and gay-rights movements—attests to the fact that even those with ample resources can feel that the state is not responding to their needs and interests.

7. http://www.nchc.org/facts/cost.shtml (accessed on September 16, 2008).

8. Terry Schiavo was an American woman who suffered extensive brain damage when she collapsed in her home in 1990. She was diagnosed as being in a persistent vegetative state and remained institutionalized for eight years. In 1998, her husband sought to remove Schiavo's feeding tube, but was opposed by her parents. What began as a family dispute over a life-or-death decision grew into a public controversy that eventually extended to Congress, the White House, and the Vatican.

9. Note that the shared experience of suffering symptoms that contradict scientific and medical explanations of disease can itself be an important source of collective identity, and a necessary, if insufficient, condition for political mobilization (Brown et al. 2004; Taylor 1996).

10. Information taken from http://www.cdc.gov/NCCdphp/overview.htm on November 5, 2008.

11. Accessed from the IHI Web site (www.ihi.org) on November 5, 2008.

SECTION I

TRANSFORMATION OF STATE FINANCING AND REGULATION

While one of the purposes of this book is to demonstrate the diversity of health-related social movement activity directed at institutions *other* than the state, we begin with the state, as the government plays a key role in establishing the legal and bureaucratic rules that regulate at least some aspects of most health institutions in the United States. The state is therefore both a familiar and important target for social movement activism.

The American political system provides multiple opportunities and venues for social movement activism. Its federated system of state and national governments—each with its own executive, legislative, judicial, and regulatory venues for pressing claims—as well as a strong cultural commitment to freedom of association and speech, voluntarism, and civic participation, have long encouraged political claims making against the state. And yet, as the authors in this section elaborate, the American political system also presents a number of formidable obstacles for social movements seeking to influence the development of public policy. Within each political venue, social movements must compete for attention and resources with other interest groups and advocacy organizations, many with considerably more resources and closer ties to policymakers. And in a context in which political influence with policymakers depends on the size and resources of social movement constituencies—as well as the scope and ambition of reform goals—social movements also face the organizational and strategic challenges of forging coalitions among diverse constituencies, and adapting goals and tactics for particular institutional forums. The papers in this section examine these and other obstacles faced by social movements seeking health care policy reform at both the national and state levels, and in both legislative and regulatory arenas.

In chapter 2, Constance Nathanson examines the challenges of mobilizing for health policies that address the needs of the poor. Nathanson argues that socioeconomic and racial inequalities in the health of Americans are both profound and largely invisible in public and policy discourse. This invisibility is the product of a political system in which the interests of poor and marginalized populations are systematically underrepresented by unions and political parties. Tracing the obstacles to mobilization faced by grassroots social movements, Nathanson foresees little success for movements that exclusively target the health of the poor, concluding instead that successful policy action to benefit the health of the poor must aim to encompass *all* Americans.

In chapter 3, Beatrix Hoffman picks up the question of why the United States does not yet have universal health coverage for its citizens. Where past explanations have focused on the role of private interest groups, the structure of government and previous policy decisions, and/ or U.S. public opinion and political culture, Hoffman examines the lack of a major social movement in support of universal health care as an explanatory factor. Tracing the historical relationship between social movements (or the lack thereof) and major attempts to reform health care in the United States, Hoffman argues that an important reason for the failure of health reform throughout the twentieth century is that health reformers have relied primarily on elite expertise rather than popular support in their campaigns. Hoffman then considers health care reform campaigns since the failed Clinton Health Security Plan (1993–94) to assess the extent to which these campaigns have relied on popular mobilization and the use of social movement rhetoric, tactics, and strategies. Hoffman concludes that while presidential leadership will be a prerequisite for any major health care reform, leaders also need the support and inspiration from strong popular movements if they are to succeed in transforming the health care system.

In chapter 4, Jill Quadagno and Brandon McKelvey challenge traditional social movement distinctions between political "insiders" and "outsiders" in their analysis of the consumer-directed health care (CDHC) movement, a loose-knit coalition of insurance companies, financial-services companies, advocacy organizations and conservative politicians. Quadagno and McKelvey argue that of all the social movement organizations that have sought to transform the financing of medical services in the United States, only the CDHC has succeeded in shifting the direction of the health care system. The CDHC movement's primary goal has been to transform patients into informed consumers by characterizing medical care as a commodity that is purchased in the same way as other market goods. Social movement theories provide few insights for understanding the success of this movement. A key argument of social movement theorists is that SMOs often operate at the margins of the political system, lacking formal representation or close ties to government officials. The CDHC movement, by contrast, consists of elite organizations with ample resources and the capacity to utilize the party system to their advantage. Despite such advantages, Quadagno and McKelvey argue, the CDHC movement shares with other social movements a desire to challenge existing health institutions and a need to devise tactics and strategies to use their resources to the best political advantage.

Holly Jarman and Scott Greer shift the focus of analysis from federal- to state-level campaigns for health policy reform. In chapter 5, Jarman and Greer consider the problem of fragmentation of the U.S. political system as a key obstacle to state-wide universal health insurance coverage. The "paradox of purity," they note, poses a difficult dilemma for reformers: groups with influence among policymakers have a better of chance of seeing their reforms enacted, but to be successful, they must adopt narrower policy goals or accept smaller reforms. Less influential groups are free to "think big," but have a greatly reduced chance of seeing their goals implemented. Jarman and Greer consider how a social movement for health reform might resolve this paradox. Their chapter analyzes the campaigns for health coverage in Pennsylvania and Wisconsin, contrasting the fragmentation of Pennsylvania activists with the coalition-building techniques developed in Wisconsin to assess how proponents of big ideas can successfully build a support base broad enough to overcome a fragmented U.S. political system.

Finally, in chapter 6, Steven Epstein considers collective efforts to transform federal health regulations guiding clinical research. Since 1986, federal laws, policies, and guidelines have either required or encouraged researchers to include women, racial and ethnic minorities, children, the elderly, and other groups within clinical research populations. New offices within the federal health bureaucracy focusing specifically on the health of women and minorities have also been established. This chapter analyzes the rise of the "anti-standardization resistance movement" that led to these institutional changes in law and policy. Epstein argues that the success of this effort depended in part on the hybrid character of the reformers' work. Specifically, the reform project was hybrid in its *formal composition* (consisting of a tacit coalition of numerous overlapping health movements); in its *social basis* (combining disease-specific activism with activism organized around social identities); in its *knowledge politics* (crossing the lines that supposedly divide laypeople from experts); in its *power politics* (encompassing ordinary people as well as elites, and biomedical outsiders as well as insiders); in its *social location* (crossing boundaries between civil society, market institutions, and the state); and in its *tactics* (combining reformist and radical approaches). While the hybrid character of the reform effort created a risk of internal conflict, Epstein argues that it also created important opportunities for the successful framing of the political project.

2

The Limitations of Social Movements as Catalysts for Change

Constance A. Nathanson

[W]hen equal protection of interests is at stake, the voluntary activity that counts is necessarily political.

—Schlozman, Verba, and Brady 1999: 427

In this paper I explore the limitations of collective action outside the polity—whether by labor unions, political parties, or social movements—as vehicles for the attainment of economic, social, and/or medical justice for the poor. This exploration assumes a particular state structure and political context, that of the United States, a country where—relative to comparable industrialized democracies—collective action in the form of social movements and other varieties of organized political advocacy plays an unusually large role in the political process. I concentrate on action by or on behalf of the poor for two reasons, both related to the focus of this volume on health-related social movements (although my examples are by no means limited to "health"). First, class and income inequalities in health in this country are profound and continuing, and are largely ignored except in narrow academic circles. Ours is not a government with a mandate to address social inequalities of illness and death. Absent collective action, these inequalities will continue to be ignored. Collective action may, as I argue, be a weak reed, but it is at least possible that analysis of its limitations will show how some weaknesses might be overcome. Second, the current last, best hope for addressing the health of the poor is some form of national health insurance. Knowledge of the circumstances under which state benefits for the poor have (or have not) been forthcoming in the past may help us in planning for the future.

Who Speaks for the Health of the Poor?

Inequalities in health across the boundaries of class, income, race, ethnicity, and other social cleavages in American society have over the last decade become a staple of public health discourse and public health research (see, e.g., Link and Phelan 1995; Phelan and Link 2005). The inverse relation between socioeconomic status and mortality along with comparable racial disparities are so well known and widely accepted among public health experts as to make its demonstration—yet again—unnecessary except to prove that the association has not disappeared since last we looked. Recently published data demonstrate its persistence across the twentieth century (Warren and Hernandez 2007). Figure 2.1 shows age-adjusted death rates by education (the only measure of socioeconomic status consistently employed in federal statistics) for the U.S. population between twenty-five and sixty-four in 2002. The death rate for persons with less than twelve years of education is more than twice that of persons with at least one year of college.[1] Death rates for African Americans are close to one-third higher than those for whites (Heron et al. 2008).

These data may be the bread and butter of American scholars of public health (literally as well as figuratively, given the recent focus of federal research-granting agencies on "health disparities"). Yet in public and political discourse they are largely invisible. Socioeconomic inequalities in mortality are not now, nor have they ever been, a public problem in the United States. In their paper aptly titled "Whose Deaths Matter?" Armstrong and colleagues show that "*who* suffers from a disease as well as

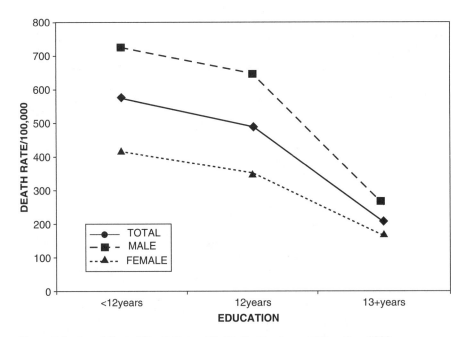

Figure 2.1. Age-Adjusted Death Rates, 25–64, By Gender and Education, 2002

how many suffer are critical factors in explaining why some diseases get more attention than others" (Armstrong et al. 2006: 729, emphasis mine). This observation is
starkly illustrated by the data presented in figure 2.2: as AIDS in the United States
shifted from a predominantly white to a predominantly black disease, HIV/AIDS
stories in the mainstream (newspaper and television) news media declined. The visibility of illness and death is not a simple function of the suffering created by those
conditions; it is socially patterned.

Differential visibility in the media, as Armstrong and colleagues point out, is
not a trivial matter: "the mass media play an influential role in the process of agenda
setting by providing one of the primary attention arenas in the public domain, by
calling attention to certain problems, and by framing what are seen as the causes of
and solutions to those problems" (Armstrong et al. 2006: 763). The mass media are
not, of course, uniquely responsible for America's stratified consciousness of illness and death. The relative invisibility of ill health among the poor (much like the
invisibility of other forms of stratification) is rooted in America's history and in its
social and political institutions (Grogan and Gusmano 2007; Massey 2007). As
Gusfield eloquently puts it, "public 'facts' are not like pebbles on the beach, lying
in the sun and waiting to be seen. They must instead be picked, polished, shaped
and packaged" (Gusfield 1975: 291). The shaping and packaging is accomplished
by social actors (individuals and groups) with interests at stake. Seldom in American
history, and only in particular circumstances (e.g., when illnesses among the poor
were construed as a threat to the larger society), have those interests included the
health of the poor (Nathanson 2007). Comprehending this blind spot requires a
brief foray into the question of how interests of the poor are represented in the
American political arena.[2]

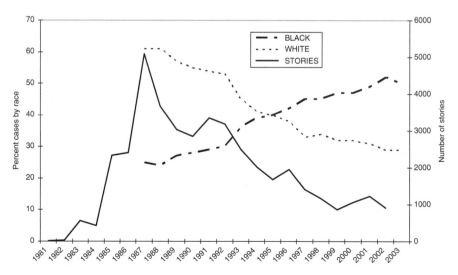

Figure 2.2. Total Number of HIV/AIDS News Stories in Selected Media Outlets and Percent
Distribution of Cases By Race and Year

Unions and Political Parties

It is a truism among American political scientists that "the poor are systematically underrepresented in the U.S. political system" (see, e.g., Grogan and Gusmano 2007: 25). In the United States historically and in other industrialized democracies, interests of the poor and disadvantaged have traditionally been represented by unions and left-wing (or in the U.S. urban- boss-dominated) political parties (see, e.g., Wilensky 2002). "Grassroots mobilization of poor and working class voters has been an important part of the American political process in the past. The New Deal coalition that gave Democrats majority support in the electorate from 1932 to the early 1970s was based on strategically placed urban party organizations and unions that could get out the vote for Democratic candidates" (Hays 2001: 234). For many and complex reasons neither unions nor our nearest approach to a "left-wing" political party (the Democrats) any longer effectively represent the interests of poor and working-class populations. Even at the peak of its power (1935 to 1946) "the labor movement never achieved the same level of prominence in the United States that it did in other industrialized democracies" (Massey 2007: 161), and it has declined steadily since that time in both numbers and militancy, to the point where unions no longer play an institutionally significant role even in determining the wage and employment conditions of American workers.[3]

The woes of the Democratic party, its fragile New Deal coalition of trade union leaders, big-city bosses, Northern liberals, and Southern conservatives fractured first by the civil rights movement and then by the Vietnam War, are all too familiar (see, e.g., Walker 1991: 23–27). As it is, the party rarely represents the interests of the poor, who are neither reliable voters nor important contributors to party coffers (Grogan and Gusmano 2007; Hays 2001; Schlozman, Verba, and Brady 1999). The result is that "citizens with lower or moderate incomes speak with a whisper that is lost on the ears of inattentive government officials, while the advantaged roar with a clarity and consistency that policy-makers readily hear and routinely follow" (Jacobs and Skocpol 2005: 1). In sum, neither unions nor political parties are currently effective representatives of the interests of the poor either in general or specifically when it comes to questions of health, illness, and medical care.

Social Movements

What, then, of alternative forms of collective action—social movements or advocacy groups organized by or on behalf of low-income populations? "The American system creates more openings for social movements to intervene in the policy process than any other liberal democratic political system and more incentives for even the most skeptical of activists to participate in the mainstream" (Rayside 1998: 13). The openings ("opportunities" is the term of art) referred to by this Canadian student of social movements are the product, first, of a federal system that offers multiple venues—social movements blocked in Washington can take their case to the state or local level with reasonable hope of being heard—and, second, of a separation of powers at the center that, again, offers multiple targets (but also limits the government's capacity to speak with one voice not only in opposition to but also in support of the voices of social movement actors).[4]

Social movements around perceived threats to life and health have been a prominent feature of American life since early in the twentieth century. Tuberculosis and infant mortality in the Progressive era and, more recently, cigarette smoking, AIDS, abortion, disabilities, nuclear power, air and water pollution, breast cancer, drunk driving and a host of other threats have sparked mobilization for change in health practices and institutions implicated in these conditions (Epstein 1996; Johnson 1983; Lantz and Booth 1998; McCarthy and Wolfson 1996; Nathanson 1999, 2007; Staggenborg 1991; Walsh 1988). The social movement form has, nevertheless, profound limitations as a vehicle for representing the health interests of poor and disadvantaged populations. The constituents of these health-related movements were comfortably middle-class, predominantly white, with concerns that seldom extended beyond the particular cause that sparked their mobilization.

Walker recognized two broad categories of social movement: first, those that "sweep through society from time to time, normally arising from the educated middle class," and, second, organizations "initiated from above" on behalf of "people usually unable to mobilize on their own because they are poor, elderly, physically or mentally handicapped, or without the capacity to represent themselves, as in the case of children" (1991: 12–13)—movements, respectively, *by* and *on behalf of* their potential beneficiaries. About the former, Walker observes,

> Successful efforts to organize such groups require a widespread perception among the potential membership that fundamental rights or crucial public goods are being threatened, and they also require that large amounts of patronage be secured, usually from business firms, trade unions, private foundations, wealthy individuals, or sometimes from the government itself.... (Walker 1991: 13)

Entrepreneurs of poor peoples' movements have found that *neither* of the two steps Walker describes—engendering "a widespread perception...that fundamental rights or crucial public goods are being threatened" or obtaining "large amounts of [sustainable] patronage"—were easy to accomplish, and political opportunities for such movements have been few and transient in recent American history. The rare examples are nonetheless instructive. They point to the major obstacles these movements confront, but also to the conditions necessary for their success.

Mobilization by the Poor

Inspired by and modeled on the civil rights movement of the 1950s and 1960s, identity-based social movements—of Hispanics, women, gays and lesbians, the handicapped—as well as more narrowly cause-based movements focused on abortion, breast cancer, and many other diseases and conditions have multiplied and flourished over the past forty years. Some of these movements (around tenants' rights, welfare rights, homelessness) were explicitly intended to mobilize the poor and dispossessed.[5] I comment on three of these movements that have been reasonably well documented: the welfare rights movement of the late 1960s and the early 1970s, the somewhat later mobilization around homelessness, and the movements against black- and brown-lung disease.[6]

The National Welfare Rights Organization (NWRO) was, by any standard, a movement of poor people, its members almost entirely black women made eligible by their poverty for the then federal-state welfare program, Aid to Families with Dependent Children (AFDC).[7] It emerged in the heady atmosphere of the1960s—"a time of hope bordering on delirium" (Cloward and Piven 1984: 591)—survived for six or seven years (approximately 1966–72), and collapsed.[8] Both the mobilization of these women and the initially positive response to their demands from local, state, and some federal officials were made possible by a remarkable—and rare—concatenation of events: the civil rights movement of the late 1950s and early 1960s, the landslide reelection of Lyndon Johnson in 1964, and the urban riots that followed the assassination of Martin Luther King Jr. in 1968. Programs funded by Johnson's "War on Poverty" brought a cadre of idealistic and energetic young people (including former civil rights lawyers and activists) to northern cities, providing "the vehicles through which the black ghettos mobilized to demand government services" (Piven and Cloward 1979: 271).[9] The movement was never large (it reached its peak of 22,000 dues-paying members in 1969) and was heavily concentrated in New York City and Boston.

Even in the short-term, the impact of the NWRO on the fortunes of poor people in America was unclear, and its long-term impact has been negligible at best.[10] The movement's collapse was the result both of events external to the movement itself and to multiple internal problems of organizational recruitment and retention. The transient legitimacy of "poverty" as a public problem ended with the Johnson administration and Piven and Cloward argue, with the decline of "black unrest" and the fear it inspired in public officials. Federally funded War on Poverty programs were shut down, and the limited foundation resources successfully garnered by the NWRO dried up, their disappearance rationalized by foundation officials on the ground that "we are no longer emphasizing poverty" (sources cited in Piven and Cloward 1979: 352). In the absence of external or indigenous financial *or* symbolic resources, without a stable base (as the black churches were for the civil rights movement), and grounded in an identity stigmatized even by many of the movement's participants, the NWRO was unsustainable.

The fate of homelessness as a social movement has been different, but no less illustrative of this form of action's limitations as a vehicle for social change in the condition of the poor. Homelessness erupted onto the public stage in the early 1980s. Poverty that walked the streets and sheltered in public spaces was—for the time being—hard to ignore: "the visible suffering of the street-dwelling poor inconveniently had no place else to go" (Hopper 2003: 175).[11] The immediate response was one of outrage and organized protest, accompanied throughout the decade of the 1980s by a voluminous scholarly literature, government reports, congressional hearings, and even legislation. "Policy initiatives did little more, [however], than expand the nation's network of shelters," and in one city after another the homeless began to mobilize (Cress and Snow 1996: 1091). In elegant detail, Cress and Snow document this mobilization and (although it may not have been their intention) provide eloquent testimony to the challenge of launching an effective social movement of the poor (Cress and Snow 1996; Cress and Snow 2000). Essential conditions—not dissimilar from those implied by Piven and Cloward's description of welfare rights organizations—were "support from nonconstituency-based facilitative organizations" (Cress and Snow 1996: 1107) and political allies. In other words, sustainable and effective organization (sustainable and effective even by Cress and Snow's quite minimal standards) demanded moral, material, and political support from groups and individuals external to the homeless themselves. This support was, and is, highly dependent on the larger political climate and on competition from other issues that emerged to command the public's attention; it was largely independent of the magnitude of the problem. Homelessness has in the present century, Hopper argues, become both domesticated and bureaucratized. "No longer cause for vocal concern, let alone outrage, it has been integrated into that cheerless diorama of unabashed wealth and relentless poverty that now passes for 'normalcy' in American cities" (Hopper 2003: 193), relegated to the ministrations of "the de-facto industry that has arisen to deal with homelessness" (Hopper 2003: 199). The few remaining activists are branded as "resurrecting defeated causes," meaning—to come full circle—the War on Poverty.[12]

Other conditions for mobilization of the poor and disenfranchised on their own behalf—in addition to a substantial investment of external material and political resources—are suggested by one of the few analyses of poor peoples' health-related social movements, Judkins' (1983) study of mobilization around black- and brown-lung disease. In the late 1960s and early 1970s social movements to protest these conditions and demand compensation were spawned in the mining communities of West Virginia and the textile-mill towns of the Carolinas. These were not spontaneous grassroots uprisings. They were promoted in West Virginia (against union opposition) by a small group of concerned physicians and in the Carolinas by students working with PIRG (Public Interest Research Group) and by Protestant and Catholic church groups. Further, both the Black and Brown Lung Associations received important financial support from federal government War on Poverty programs. Potential participants needed to be persuaded, first, that their disabilities were occupationally caused, second, that participation would produce concrete rewards (e.g., workmen's compensation), and third, that participation would not threaten the employment on which they and their families depended. Fears of employer retaliation meant that very few active workers participated in these movements. Although mobilization was successful, it was restricted to the retired and disabled, those who had the most to gain in the form of material and other (e.g., sociability) benefits from participation and the least to lose. A final, and critical, point was the presence in each of these occupation-based communities of multiple preexisting social ties, facilitating "communication, interaction, informal group structure, and trust—all of which were important...in the successful completion of the movement's goals" (Judkins 1983: 46).

I will argue below that mobilization by affected populations *on their own behalf* has become the scenario expected and preferred by contemporary public health scholars, program planners, and policy makers. My purposes in describing examples of such movements at some length have been to reinforce Walker's emphasis on "large amounts of patronage" as a principal condition for successful employment of this strategy and to point out that patronage is a highly contingent resource, heavily dependent both on the political and policy climate at the time and on the visibility—fortuitous or engineered—of the problem addressed. Judkins's case study suggests that movements of the poor and the powerless are vulnerable not only to fickle political winds that may render patronage unsustainable but also to the threat—real or perceived—of employers and other powerful elites to participants' lives and livelihoods. The tight-knit communities that sustained the black- and brown-lung disease movements represented a unique "mobilizing structure" (like black churches for the civil rights movement) difficult to duplicate on the national scale required for—say— a movement of the uninsured.

Mobilization on Behalf of the Poor

Charitable organization "initiated from above" on behalf of "people usually unable to mobilize on their own" has a long history in American civic life. The Progressive era cradled reform movements of all sorts, not least movements against diseases that found their victims primarily among the poor (see, e.g., Feldberg 1995; Klaus 1993; Meckel 1990; Skocpol 1992; Tomes 1998). Women's clubs and associations were at the forefront of campaigns against infant mortality; physicians and civic leaders created the National Tuberculosis Association, the first health voluntary association in the United States. These movement organizations—formed by educated, white middle-class reformers—essentially ignored the population (African Americans) with the highest mortality rates from these conditions. Southern blacks organized in parallel but their voices went largely unheard by the country's established medical and public health elites (Boris 1993; Nathanson 2007).

The distinction between movements *by* and *on behalf of* the less fortunate is far less clear today than it was in the Progressive era. First, movements of the poor often demand (and are accorded) representation on the boards and committees of groups that advocate on their behalf (see, e.g., Cress and Snow 2000); indeed, representation of the populations served by or of concern to these groups is more often than not mandated as a condition of foundation or government funding (Grogan and Gusmano 2007). Second, in a political climate where any and every grievance or imagined identity has become a basis for mobilization—even if only "check-book" mobilization—the "grass roots social movement" form of interest representation has become virtually a sine qua non for attention in the public and political arena (see, e.g., Quadagno 2004). Among the most striking aspects of public health commentary on HIV/AIDS in minority communities, for example, has been its heavy emphasis on the absence and/or ineffectiveness of mobilization by these communities in response to the epidemic. Taking African Americans to task, the National Commission on AIDS observed that,

> AIDS program efforts in [these] communities and in other communities of color have suffered because there has not been a united effort within the community to pressure public health authorities and other government agencies to provide resources and services. (National Commission on AIDS 1992: 33; see also Cohen 1997)

These comments and their implications go to the heart of my argument. First, the poor (and minority communities are disproportionately poor) are systematically underrepresented in the U.S. political system. Second, the Commission's remarks imply that those who are not represented—who fail to mount "a united effort within the community"—will not receive and cannot be expected to receive government "resources and services"; and, further, that the responsibility for the lack of "a united effort" lies with the affected communities themselves. If, in other words, their diseases are invisible and services and resources insufficient, the minority community has only itself to blame.

The Question of Coalitions

The picture I have painted is a discouraging one and bodes poorly for the fate of collective action for the health of the poor. I am far from alone in this pessimistic judgment. Reflecting social and political realities in the contemporary United States, current scholarship on this topic is uniformly despairing, especially when it comes to the efficacy of narrow "interest groups...focused passionately on a single issue," a characterization that describes most social movements (Wilensky 2002: 399; see also Hays 2001). In the same vein as Greer and Jarman in this volume, Wilensky and Hays advocate "broad-based mediating associations" that "spend their time bargaining with other parties about policies that can actually be enacted and implemented" rather than "pursuing maximal unnegotiable demands" (Wilensky 2002: 120). Neither Wilensky nor Hays, however, is optimistic about the prospects for such coalitions in the current state of American politics. Speaking about coalitions at the local level, Hays (2001: 227) observes that

> unless the chasms between groups are bridged by a genuine vision of the civic community in which all voices are invited to be heard, it is doubtful that the poor will ever receive more than token inclusion in the local power structure, because inclusion in the informal networks that make decisions in most communities requires a certain level of trust.

In the final section of the paper, I will come back to the question of coalitions and the circumstances under which they may—or may not—be successful in advocating for the interests of the poor.

Backlashes, Countermovements, and Competing Agendas

A political system rich in opportunities for collective action on behalf of the public's health is equally rich in openings for groups with alternative or competing agendas. These latter groups—the anti-abortion movement for example—may be deliberately organized as countermovements, but more often they are stakeholders like the American Medical Association, the National Rifle Association, tobacco-, insurance-, and pharmaceutical-industry associations organized to protect interests that often— not always deliberately—conflict with the agendas of health-related social movements. Movements by or on behalf of the poor are particularly vulnerable to oppositional movements: their redistributive (and related structural and political) implications threaten well-established groups strongly invested in maintaining patterns of resource distribution that benefit the wealthy and the powerful. These latter groups have not hesitated to take full advantage of this country's political opportunities to mobilize on their own behalf. Although "stakeholder mobilization" may, as

Quadagno points out, involve "the same processes that social movement theorists usually associate with the mobilization of politically powerless groups" (Quadagno 2004: 28), there are vast differences in material and (often) symbolic resources available to stakeholders and in their privileged access to the mainstream political arena.

Examples of this phenomenon are legion. Activist women reformers in the early twentieth century had remarkable success in building institutions for the support of mothers and children, including creation of a government bureau (the Children's Bureau) dedicated to children's health and welfare (an accomplishment unique to the United States) and passage of the country's first piece of federal welfare legislation, the Federal Act for the Promotion of the Welfare and Hygiene of Maternity and Infancy, otherwise known as the Sheppard-Towner Act (Nathanson 2007; Skocpol 1992). These were substantial achievements, generating unprecedented (and highly controversial) data on income inequalities in health among families with children and—for the first time—providing maternal and child health clinic services to poor black families in the rural South. Nevertheless, these accomplishments proved unsustainable in their original form, and they did not (as in Europe) evolve into broader state-supported benefits for mothers and children, due in important part to the implacable hostility of the American Medical Association. The AMA, designed on the federal model with branches in every state and locality as well as nationally, simply outgunned the women's groups that supported Sheppard-Towner and the Children's Bureau.

How working-class white backlash and its exploitation by conservatives politically mobilized under the aegis of the Republican party led initially to the demise of the War on Poverty (contributing heavily to the collapse of the NWRO) and, in the longer run, to a virtual shut down of agitation for an expanded welfare state has been often and eloquently described (Katz 1989; O'Connor 2001; Piven and Cloward 1979; Quadagno 1994). Quadagno's analysis is especially trenchant in two respects: first, in her identification of racism as the key to countermobilization against government programs that benefit the poor ("an anti-government ideology has generated most antagonism to the welfare state when it has been associated with racial issues" [Quadagno 1994: 196]) and, second, in her emphasis on the negative role of the labor movement, the movement that above all others would have been expected to represent the interests of the poor:

> During the War on Poverty...labor's own resistance proved to be the greater impediment to welfare state expansion. Organized labor's opposition originated in racial divisions, which make the movement hostile to programs that pursued equality of opportunity...[Among the outcomes of that opposition] was further fragmentation [i.e., weakening] of the labor movement. (Quadagno 1994:193)

The "end of welfare as we know it," marked by President Bill Clinton's signing of the Personal Responsibility and Work Opportunities Reconciliation Act of 1996 (otherwise known as Temporary Assistance for Needy Families, or TANF), was the culmination of a process begun in the late 1960s that effectively ended meaningful mobilization on behalf of the poor, at least for the foreseeable future: "A movement [e.g., the New Right coalition] that is able to win policy reforms decisively, limiting the apparent prospects for subsequent reform, is also unlikely to generate extensive and prolonged countermobilization that reaches into the political mainstream" (Meyer and Staggenborg 1996: 1636).

Circling back to health-related movements, the health insurance industry has been consistently successful over the past few decades in preventing enactment of a national health insurance program that would bring medical care to many millions of poor people. "First the American Medical Association, then organizations of insurance companies and employer groups [have been able to defeat national health plans] because they had superior resources and an organizational structure that closely mirrored the federated arrangements of the American state" (Quadagno 2004: 25). (Note that it was those same federated arrangements that accounted, at least in part, for the *successes* of women's groups in the Progressive era.) As Quadagno points out, "the institutional structure of the state in the United States channels political activities in ways that blur the distinction between the tactics and strategies" of the more as compared with the less privileged: powerful stakeholders "also manufacture grassroots protest to convince political leaders that their interests represent the public will" (2004: 40). The tactics and strategies may be the same, but the resources behind them are very different and highly skewed toward the rich, the powerful, and the politically connected.

Greer and Jarman's analysis of mobilization for health care reform (this volume) is less about countermovements—physicians are among the good guys, and there is no mention of insurance companies (or, for that matter, of the uninsured)—than about resolving conflicts internal to these movements themselves. Among their more striking observations is the persistent ambivalence of labor unions—a key player in progressive Wisconsin, a holdout in more conservative (and politically fragmented) Pennsylvania—reflecting, again, unions' broad failure to be a voice for the poor and their continued investment in a health care system grounded in private, commercial, insurance.

The political and institutional obstacles that currently stand in the way of mobilization *by the poor* are such as to cause most academic observers to discount the possibility of such a movement altogether (see, e.g. Walker 1991; Hays 2001). But, as Hays has documented in some detail, movements *on behalf* of the poor have proved almost equally vulnerable to "the [powerful] forces underlying retrenchment in social policy" that have dominated the political scene since the late 1970s (Hays 2001: 215). Where breakthroughs have occurred, they have been the result of two highly contingent sets of variables: transient political opportunities created by political or economic crises and the presence and support of friends in high places.

Politics, Opportunities, and Events

Even under the most favorable circumstances, collective action in the absence of an effective, committed state is a fragile instrument for major institutional change (see Nathanson 2007: 203–20 for an extended discussion of this point). Explaining why the United States has no national health insurance, Wilensky draws attention to a range of state as well as civil society characteristics: "electoral systems and the structure of government; the strength and character of political parties; the structure and function of major interest groups, including labor, the professions, employers, and their bargaining arrangements with one another and with government" (2002: 608). Mobilization by or on behalf of the uninsured is only one and probably not the most important of these characteristics (and is nowhere mentioned in Wilensky's treatise). Amenta and colleagues make much the same point in their discussion of the successes and failures of the 1930s Townsend movement for pensions for the aged: "Nowhere was the [Townsend] movement able to achieve both new benefits and recognition without favorable conditions in the polity" (Amenta, Carruthers, and Zylan 1992: 335). Favorable conditions are necessary, but the structure of the American state with its competing interest groups and multiple veto points makes those conditions especially difficult to realize.

The historical record suggests that in this context three sets of conditions are essential for state action to protect or advance the interests of the poor: first, the mobilization of left-leaning party and/or movement (including labor movement) actors; second social, political, and/or economic crises that create opportunities for these actors to move; and third, the presence in office of bureaucrats and/or politicians prepared to work with those actors to advance the cause. The successes of Progressive era women's movements for the health of poor women and children owed much, first, to the massive social changes of the period created by successive waves of immigration and internal migration accompanied by rapid urbanization, making the ravages of poverty and ill-health highly visible to urban reformers, and, second, to the 1904 reelection of Theodore Roosevelt to a second term, with a solid Republican Congress. Progressive women were both politically connected and astute, and their child-welfare reform program fit directly into Roosevelt's second-term agenda. He met with women reformers, sponsored a White House Conference on the Care of Dependent Children, and personally orchestrated pressure on members of Congress to create a federal children's bureau (Nathanson 2007: 214–15). The bureau came about through an ephemeral conjunction of mobilization by concerned women, political opportunity, and elite political support.

A parallel, and even more ephemeral, concatenation of events was responsible for the initial success of the National Welfare Rights Organization in getting eligible poor women on AFDC and increasing their access to available welfare benefits. The civil rights movement of the 1950s and early 1960s was both an inspiration for and a source of recruits to a new poor peoples' movement focused on economic injustice. The landslide reelection of Lyndon Johnson in 1964 made possible a set of anti-poverty programs closely aligned with the aims of the NWRO, and the assassination of Martin Luther King Jr. created an urban crisis demanding policymakers' attention.

My final example has less of crisis-based opportunity and more of elite political support. All three elements of mobilization, opportunity, and support are nonetheless present, along with a fourth element rare in the U.S. political system: an executive with the power of (more or less) unilateral action. In 1998 a consortium of hospital, union, and consumer representatives in New York State carried out a successful campaign to insure that state's uninsured adults (Cohen 2001; Nathanson 2003). Success was made possible, first, by the mobilization of a broad-based coalition that included representatives of hospital management, union members, and consumers; second, by the organizers' extensive political connections at the state level (i.e., a former Democratic majority leader of the New York State Assembly and the most politically influential union leader in the state), and third, by a series of unforeseen opportunities—a windfall of money to finance the health insurance program and weak and/or ineffectual opposition. Union and consumer groups carried out an intensive *outsider* grassroots lobbying and media campaign, complemented by the less visible but equally important work of politically connected *insiders*. Finally, executive power in New York State was heavily concentrated, facilitating the narrow targeting of individuals (the governor and the head of the state Senate, both of the same party) who did, in fact, have the power to act on the movement's demands. This is a critical point that distinguishes the state (this state, at least) from the federal political system and may have mitigated the need for a major crisis to gain policymakers' attention.

Conclusion

Poverty and powerlessness, access to health insurance, and inequalities of disease and death are interrelated (Marmot 2001; Sridhar 2005), but those relations are complex and beyond the scope of this essay. In short, close to one-third of persons with incomes below 400% of the federal poverty level (about $42,000 for a family of four in 2007) compared with 10% of individuals above that level are uninsured (Kaiser Commission 2008). Relative to whites, blacks and Hispanics are less likely to have health insurance (Kaiser Commission 2008). In turn, the uninsured have less access to medical care, are less likely to receive preventive care, and are estimated to have substantially poorer health and higher death rates from some chronic conditions as compared with the insured (Fowler-Brown et al. 2007; Kaiser Commission 2008). Death rates from infant mortality—identified by the middle of the nineteenth century as a "particularly sensitive index of community health and well-being and of the effectiveness of existing public health measures" (Meckel 1990: 5)—are higher in the United States than in many other industrialized countries with universal health insurance coverage. I argued in this essay's opening paragraph that some form of national health insurance is this nation's "last, best hope for addressing the health of the poor." There is, of course, no guarantee that universal health insurance will reduce health inequalities. There is sufficient evidence, however, for a reasonable person to so conclude, and, I continue to believe that such a program is our last, best hope. The question remains how to get there.

In a paper recently reprinted in the *American Journal of Public Health*, Hoffman argues that the failure of twentieth-century efforts to enact a national health insurance program is at least partially attributable to these campaigns lack of connection to the grassroots (Hoffman 2008 [2003]). "National health reform campaigns in the 20th century were initiated and run by elites more concerned with defending against attacks from interest groups than with popular mobilization, and grassroots reformers in the labor, civil rights, feminist and AIDS activist movements have concentrated more on immediate and incremental changes than on transforming the health care system itself" (Hoffman [2003] 2008: S69). My argument in this essay is that popular mobilization for universal health insurance—whether it is *by* the uninsured (unlikely) or *on their behalf* or both—can happen only under conditions extremely difficult to bring about.

At one level there is nothing terribly new about this message. The contingent character of social movements (and of collective action more generally)—subject to "a shifting constellation of factors exogenous to the movement itself" (Meyer and Staggenborg 1996: 1635)—has over the last decade become a virtual mantra of social movement scholars (see, e.g., Tarrow 1998; Giugni 1998). More specifically, the scope for mobilization of actions that target the state as well as their organizational form and impact are highly dependent, first, on relatively stable elements of the political structure (held more or less constant in the present instance) and, second, on largely unpredictable events, together with the interpretations and interests triggered by those events: "strategies that work in a given [political] context may simply be ineffective in other political settings and vice versa" (Giugni 1998: 7). Although I have proposed some (again, not new) elements—mobilization, opportunity, political support—that I believe are necessary for collective action to occur and to have an impact, when and where in the future these elements may come together are wholly unpredictable.

At the level of concrete prospects for meaningful political action to address health inequalities in such a way as to benefit the health of the poor, my message is unquestionably gloomy. I see little hope for the effectiveness of movements either by or on behalf of the poor *as such*—the relative ill-health of the poor is likely to remain invisible to most Americans. Clinton's action in ending "welfare as we know it" effectively put an end to "poverty" as a public problem: "When an issue is 'closed' and there is little or no opportunity to effect change in current policies, movements and countermovements are unlikely to form" (Meyer and Staggenborg 1996: 1636). More promising, perhaps, are universal welfare state policies that are not targeted toward the poor but nevertheless address their health and welfare needs. Medicare is the obvious example, but efforts to extend Medicare to other population categories have not been particularly successful (Marmor 2007: 311). As a rallying cry, "national health insurance" has the (potential) critical advantage of offering benefits to all Americans, including but not exclusively to the poor and to dispossessed ethnic and racial minorities (the "targeting within universalism" approach suggested by Skocpol [1991]). A consummation devoutly to be wished, its achievement may require not only the mobilization of a broad cross-class and cross-interest-group coalition but also a national economic crisis of massive proportions to bring that mobilization about.[13]

NOTES

1. The advent of Medicare in 1965—the one great success of President Lyndon Johnson's War on Poverty—might have been expected to narrow the inequality of death among the elderly. I have been unable to locate data for persons sixty-five and over (and consequently eligible for Medicare) parallel to those shown in figure 2.1. However, data on expectation of life (EOL) at age sixty-five by race show that the gap between blacks and whites *increased* between 1960 and 1997 from .5 to 1.7 years, due to more rapid improvement in EOL among whites (National Center for Health Statistics. 1999 (table 28, p. 139).

2. As Schlozman and colleagues point out, "when equal protection of interests is at stake, the voluntary activity that counts is necessarily political.... [C]oncern for democratic equality forces us not only to inquire how many people are bowling and whether they do so solo or in leagues, but also to ask who bowls" (Schlozman, Verba, and Brady 1999: 429).

3. Insofar as advocacy for national health insurance is a form of advocacy for the health of the poor, unions have positioned themselves so as to powerfully limit their capacity and incentive to speak out. The effectiveness of organized labor's support for national health insurance in the 1940s (i.e., the Wagner-Murray-Dingell bill supported by President Truman but derailed by the American Medical Association) was limited by "the failure of union leaders to enlist union members in the battle" (Derickson 1994: 1342–43, cited in Hoffman 2008 [2003]: S71) to the point where union-led health reform "became associated with 'union bosses' rather than ordinary workers" (Hoffman 2008 [2003]: S71). Later on, as Quadagno points out, "the spread of private health insurance in collective bargaining agreements effectively removed organized labor from the broader struggle for national health insurance and gave the trade unions a vested interest in the private welfare state" (2005: 76). Unions did play an important role in the enactment of Medicare, primarily, Quadagno argues, because for reasons of cost these bargaining agreements excluded retirees. "Thus, organized labor had an incentive to support a public health insurance program for the aged" (2004: 32).

4. The relation between state structure and the nature of political opportunities has been elaborated in work by John Peter Nettl, Theda Skocpol, Herbert Kitschelt and others. For a recent review, see Nathanson (2007: 14–17).

5. Strikingly, this history appears to have had little overall effect on what Schlozman and colleagues label "participatory stratification." "Data collected in 1967 indicate that those on the highest rung of the income ladder were three times as likely to be active members of organizations as those at the bottom. In 1990 the ratio was exactly the same" (Schlozman, Verba, and Brady 1999: 452).

6. As Greer and Jarman note, there has been relatively little scholarship on popular mobilization for health care reform—meaning, in this context, the extension of medical insurance to the uninsured who, like African-Americans, are disproportionately poor.

7. This program was abolished in 1997 and replaced by the far more restrictive Temporary Assistance for Needy Families (TANF) program.

8. My account of NWRO relies on the description and analysis of this movement by Frances Fox Piven and Richard Cloward (Piven and Cloward 1979; Cloward and Piven 1984). Although there is scholarly argument about Piven and Cloward's interpretation, their account of the facts has not been disputed (see, e.g., Gamson and Schmeidler 1984).

9. "Perhaps three-quarters of all welfare rights organizers were antipoverty workers, many of them VISTAs" (Piven and Cloward 1979: 293).

10. Piven and Cloward observe that marked increases in welfare rolls in the late 1960s were "attributed" to the NWRO, but appear to distance themselves from that interpretation. NWRO members' demands did result in increased grants to individuals. However, they also led to those same grants being "reformed" out of existence, hardly the NWRO's intent.

11. "By the mid-1980s, the number of homeless poor in the United States had outstripped anything seen since the Great Depression" (Hopper 2003: 176). Many reasons have been advanced: the end of the Vietnam War with no provision for veterans comparable to the post-WWII GI bill, the emptying of mental hospitals, and a decline in affordable housing, among others.

12. The one success of the War on Poverty was in provision for the elderly. In the United States today, "only the elderly have an extensive social safety net that protects them from the fluctuations of the business cycle and the secular economic changes that have led to declining real wages for many workers and high poverty rates for families with children" (Danziger and Danziger 2005). This safety net is the result of policies and programs (including Medicare) "enacted and/or expanded in one decade, 1965 to 1975." Keys to Medicare's success were, first, that it was framed as a benefit not to the poor but to the elderly, a nonstigmatized—even deserving—group that nevertheless included the poor elderly; second, the labor movement and

substantial numbers of seniors mobilized in support of Medicare; and third, perhaps of most importance, Medicare's supporters were able to take advantage of the large Democratic majority in Congress produced by the 1964 election (see, e.g., Marmor 2000). Nevertheless, whether Medicare has been successful in reducing health inequalities of income and education among the elderly remains unclear.

13. More pessimistically, recent experience suggests that although conditions of "massive economic crisis" increase the numbers of low-income and unemployed persons and, mutatis mutandis, the numbers without health insurance and with limited access to medical care, these conditions are unlikely to motivate political and economic elites to spend money on expanding health insurance coverage.

3

The Challenge of Universal Health Care

Social Movements, Presidential Leadership, and Private Power

Beatrix Hoffman

Does health care transformation happen from the top down or from the bottom up? In the case of universal health coverage, two of the major obstacles preventing the establishment of national health insurance in the United States have been a lack of leadership from above, and a lack of popular mobilization from below. As Constance Nathanson argues in this volume, social movements require powerful allies within the state if they are to achieve success. On the other hand, powerful leaders, even presidents, who act without the support of a popular movement have not been able to make headway against the entrenched private interests opposing health system transformation.

This chapter looks at the relationship between health care reform from above (elite reformers and the White House) and from below (social movements) throughout the twentieth century to demonstrate that only when the two came together was systemic change ever achieved. I also argue that the convergence of presidential leadership and social movement mobilization is even more crucial today because of the need for a counterbalance to the massive private health insurance industry. The public/private nature of the U.S. health care system, and especially the presence of a multibillion-dollar insurance industry, makes transforming that system extremely challenging for both political leaders and for social movements.

Health Care Reform from Above: A History of Futility

It is no coincidence that the historic attempts to establish universal health care in the U.S. are associated with presidents (Harry Truman, Lyndon B. Johnson, Bill Clinton) rather than with popular movements or movement leaders. Major health care reform efforts in the twentieth century were led primarily by elites, including those in the White House, who only rarely thought about mobilizing ordinary people's support for their cause (Hoffman 2003). The top-down nature of universal health coverage attempts has been an important reason for their failure.

Calls for state-sponsored, national, or universal health care in the United States began at the start of the last century. In 1901, the U.S. Socialist Party included "sickness insurance" in its platform for European-style social protections for American workers. Theodore Roosevelt's Progressive Party in 1912 also supported sickness insurance, which would partly cover workers' wages lost due to illness and provide them with some medical care, to be funded through contributions from workers, employers, and government. With the defeat of the Progressive Party, the movement for sickness insurance shifted to the state level. Progressive leaders in the American Association for Labor Legislation (AALL) introduced sickness insurance bills—called "compulsory health insurance" to distinguish it from German precedents—in New York and California between 1915 and 1918.

The AALL was a classic expert-led organization. Its members were primarily academic economists, social workers, and public health professionals. Although their compulsory health insurance plan actually generated considerable popular enthusiasm among, for example, industrial workers, immigrants, and suffragists, the AALL leadership chose to concentrate its efforts on winning the support of physicians, employers, and the mainstream labor movement (led by Samuel Gompers, who resigned from the AALL due to his strong opposition to compulsory health insurance). In New York, when a coalition of state trade unionists and woman suffrage leaders called a mass meeting and marched on the Capitol in support of health insurance and other labor bills, the AALL was actually taken by surprise. This street-level support came too late, and the health insurance bill (despite passage in the New York Senate) was defeated by pro-business forces in the State Assembly in 1918 (Hoffman 2001).

During the New Deal, the strongest advocates of adding health insurance to the Social Security Act were members of President Franklin D. Roosevelt's Committee on Economic Security (CES), another group of professional experts, including some members of FDR's cabinet. The CES sought to persuade FDR with expert reports, and did not look to the formidable popular movements of the time (most notably movements of industrial workers, the elderly, and the unemployed) for support. When the Social Security Act passed in 1935, it did not include a provision for medical care or sick pay. Health reformers in the Roosevelt administration continued to work for a national health act, but faced an uphill battle in the face of strong opposition from the American Medical Association. The absence of popular mobilization in reformers' favor was recognized by public health leader John Kingsbury in 1937, who asked an assembly of the National Conference of Social Work, "How can [we] expect the President and the Congress to act on a controversial issue, in the face of such vociferous and politically powerful opposition to health insurance, if there is no organized expression of public opinion in favor of it?" (Poen 1996 18).

Health reformers in the Roosevelt administration next organized a new committee to focus on medical insurance. Its title, the Technical Committee on Medical Care of the Interdepartmental Committee on Health and Welfare, could only add to the perception that health reform was a "technical" issue best handled by experts. However, when the committee called an unprecedented National Health Conference in 1938, for the first time they reached out to groups beyond the medical profession, inviting representatives of farm and labor organizations as well as the AMA to the Washington meeting. President Roosevelt (who did not attend) himself noted the shift in emphasis from private committee to public forum, writing, "I am glad that the Conference includes so many representatives of the general public. The professional experts can and, I feel sure, will, do their part. But the problems before you are in a real sense public problems" (Roosevelt 1938).

Delegates at the National Health Conference heard powerful testimony about health conditions in the nation's cities and rural areas from labor and farm leaders, as well as the standard warnings about socialized medicine from physicians. Despite reformers' celebration of the inclusion of "consumers of health care" in the proceedings, speakers came from leadership rather than the rank and file, and the meeting did not result in coordinated national advocacy by labor or farm groups on behalf of universal health insurance. Even though it continued to officially support national insurance, the labor movement overall began to turn its attention to private group health insurance and alternative forms of medical organization (like community health centers and group medical practices; Klein 2003: 150–51). Labor backed the major legislative initiative that came out of the 1938 conference, Senator Robert Wagner's national health insurance bill, but there was still no effort to organize support for it at the grassroots level.

After World War II, FDR's successor Harry S. Truman tried several times to introduce national health insurance. This time an organized advocacy group, the Committee for the Nation's Health (CNH), worked to actively support the president. The CNH was made up of the major labor federations (AFL and CIO) and led by longtime health expert Michael Davis; it was a top-down organization with little or no voice for rank-and-file workers or other health care consumers (Derickson 1994). Truman himself did little, apart from a few speeches, to sell his program to the public (Hensel 2004).

Serious grassroots mobilization instead came from the opposition. The American Medical Association ran an unprecedented campaign, funded by a $25 assessment on each of its members, to defeat Truman's national health plan. The AMA hired a professional public relations firm and directed its local branches (the county medical societies) to distribute massive amounts of literature condemning the Truman plan as socialized medicine (Quadagno 2005: 34–35). Physicians then placed the materials in their offices and thus directly into the hands of patients—a constituency the health reformers never even attempted to reach. The AMA's campaign was stunningly successful, helped along by the escalation of the Cold War, as Truman's main health advisors were condemned as Reds. Public support for national health insurance, as measured by opinion polls, dropped from 75% in 1945 to 21% in 1949, and Truman lost many congressional supporters in the 1950 election who were successfully targeted for defeat by the AMA (Poen 1979).

Throughout the 1950s, health system change came primarily through the private sector, as the employer-based health insurance system continued to expand. Federal health care programs, such as the Hill-Burton Hospital Construction Act and an indigent care program offering supplementary funds to the states, were aimed at subsidizing private and state initiatives and ensuring local rather than national control of health services (Stevens 1989). The passage of Medicare and Medicaid, while the first and only triumph for a national health coverage initiative in the twentieth century (see below), still fit the pattern of federal reluctance to intervene in or compete with private control of health care; by covering the elderly and the very poor only, Medicare and Medicaid did not threaten the system of employer benefits and private health insurance, and preserved a major role for the states.

On the other hand, some reformers saw Medicare/Medicaid as the entering wedge to creating universal insurance for all Americans. Their optimism was reflected in the flurry of national health insurance proposals put forth during the Nixon administration. In the early 1970s, it seemed that everyone—from the labor movement to the AMA—was offering their own plans for a national system; a consensus reigned that national reform was inevitable. This assumption was shattered as dozens of different proposals proliferated in Congress by 1972. The sheer number and variety of competing plans made mobilizing a unified coalition virtually impossible. When the competition finally boiled down to two major national health insurance plans in 1974—one sponsored by Edward Kennedy, the other by President Nixon—both failed to win public and congressional support. Kennedy's more comprehensive plan lost organized labor's backing because he insisted on preserving a role for private insurance companies, and Watergate ended Nixon's influence on Congress and, finally, his presidency (Quadagno 2005: 110–22).

When national health care finally resurfaced nearly twenty years later with the election of Bill Clinton, many more possibilities for popular mobilization existed. Large, well-funded and well-organized lobbying groups like the American Association for Retired Persons, the Consumers' Union, disability rights and patient groups, and child welfare organizations had grown dramatically during the 1970s and 1980s and established a permanent presence in Washington and in the media. Labor was thus no longer the only organized national group likely to support health reform. At the same time, the medical profession's opposition to universal coverage had weakened, as had that of much of American business, which found the increasing cost of employee health benefits hard to bear.

Yet the Clinton proposal for universal coverage based on an employer mandate and "managed competition" was a resounding failure. Even though the plan preserved the role of private insurance in a complex health system reorganization, the insurance industry led a massive lobbying campaign against the bill. An even bigger problem, according to Paul Starr, one of the plan's architects, was the disenchantment and fragmentation of reform supporters. "The problem was not so much that the opponents had more resources," writes Starr, "but that the supporters could not mobilize theirs. While the antagonists had great clarity of purpose, the groups backing reform suffered from multiple and complex fractures and were unable to unite" (Starr 1995). Clinton and his strategists took the support of multiple reform groups—consumers, seniors, state health care reformers—for granted, and concentrated on placating the opposition (to no avail) rather than amassing, uniting, and mobilizing public support and popular movements. This failure of mobilization can also be traced to the nature of the Clinton plan itself. A 1,300-page proposal for "managed competition" and "health alliances" could inspire little popular passion or enthusiasm, and the complexities of the plan and the bickering over its details quickly overwhelmed the single, more compelling notion of "Health Care That's Always There." The failure of the Clinton reform effort shows that presidential leadership also emerges from the nature of the reform proposal itself. The complex and technical Clinton plan returned health reform to the domain of experts and special interests and contributed to the fragmentation and weakening of its potential support base.

Social Movements Plus Presidential Power: The Case of Medicare

At one moment in the twentieth century, the power of social movements converged with presidential leadership to produce systematic, nationwide transformation in health care. In the 1960s, civil rights, labor, and a new movement of senior citizens inspired and supported two presidents who took leadership roles on health care reform. The result was the passage of Medicare and Medicaid in 1965.

Medicare represented a retreat from universal health care, since it would guarantee health insurance only for Americans over retirement age. However, it was seen as a necessary compromise by reform supporters and one with the greatest potential for political success, since it would build on the already-existing Social Security system while leaving most employer and private insurance untouched.

John F. Kennedy, who made Medicare a priority early in his administration, was the first president to not just explicitly recognize the importance of grassroots support to health reform's success, but also to participate in its mobilization. In May of 1962 he accepted an invitation from the National Council of Senior Citizens (NCSC) to address its Medicare rally at Madison Square Garden. (NCSC's chairman was Aime Forand, formerly of the House of Representatives and an early sponsor of Medicare, so this organization of retired union members still had an elite leadership). Kennedy told the 20,000 assembled, ". . . in this free society of ours the consent and may I say the support of the citizens of this country is essential if any piece of progressive legislation is going to be passed." Kennedy spent much of his speech criticizing the doctors' lobbying campaign against the Medicare bill and asking for citizens (the word he used repeatedly, but he clearly had the assembled groups of labor and retirees in mind) to throw their support behind the legislation. "I think it is most appropriate that the President of the United States, whose business place is in Washington, should come to this city and participate in these rallies," he concluded. "Because the business of the Government is the business of the people--and the people are right here" (Kennedy 1962). This was quite a departure from the political strategies of both FDR (who did not even attend the 1938 National Health Conference because he was on a cruise) and of Truman (who continued to rely on an expert rather than a popular base of support).

The mobilization of senior citizens on behalf of Medicare continued after Kennedy's assassination. "Hundreds of energetic, elderly persons crowded into City Hall" at 1964 Medicare hearings in New York, reported the *New York Times*, whose reporter was astounded by the seniors' active participation; she noted that "the elderly persons had climbed two long flights of stairs" to get to the all-day hearing (Jaffe 1964). The National Council of Senior Citizens held large rallies and organized its members to send millions of postcards to Congress in favor of Medicare legislation (Quadagno 2005: 64–75).

The role of the civil rights movement in inspiring President Lyndon Johnson's bold social reforms is well known. Movement activists were, of course, less vitally interested in medical care for the aged than they were in basic human rights and desegregation, but some civil rights organizations threw their support behind Medicare early on. One Chicago group, the African American Heritage Association, called in 1962 for a national "all-out effort" of blacks on behalf of Medicare. The National Medical Association, the organization of African-American doctors, voted to back Medicare that same year, in defiance of the AMA ("Back Medicare" 1962). It is no coincidence that Johnson succeeded in passing Medicare and the Voting Rights Act in same year (1965). In a phone call to Martin Luther King, Jr., as the civil rights leader was preparing to march in Selma, Alabama, LBJ mentioned Medicare as part of his overall civil rights agenda, including voting rights, which he planned to push through Congress (Beschloss 2001: 160).[1]

As for organized labor, the President was pressed into action not just by the traditional labor backing of national health reform (major unions offered their support for Medicare), but also by strike and protest activity on behalf of medical care for workers. The historian Robyn Muncy has found that LBJ's trip to Appalachia in the spring of 1964, where he witnessed coal miners protesting the loss of their company health benefits, helped to convince the president "of the urgency of his Medicare bill." ("Transcript" 1964; Muncy 2008: 33).

So while Johnson's landslide election victory and the 1964 Democratic capture of Congress were crucial to Medicare's passage, civil rights marches, "energetic elderly persons," and labor agitation provided the popular pressure and support needed for both JFK and LBJ to act and to succeed as health reform leaders. After Medicare's passage, LBJ credited civil rights and senior citizen leaders for their help. He invited both the director of the National Council of Senior Citizens, Lawrence Oxley, and the head of the National Medical Association, Dr. Montague Cobb, to witness the Medicare signing ceremony in Independence, Missouri, alongside former president Harry Truman. Cobb in turn praised Johnson for his continued commitment to "ending racial discrimination from American life" ("Signing of Medicare Bill," 1965; "Lauds NMA Doctors," 1965). It was clear that the civil rights leader and the president each felt that Medicare's victory would not have been possible without the other.

Governments and Social Movements Challenging Private Interests

There has not been a similar political victory for national health reform since 1965.[2] The unique convergence of presidential leadership and popular support that led to Medicare's political triumph has been replaced in historical memory by the Clinton reform's ignominious failure. And any attempt to create universal coverage today faces an obstacle that LBJ did not: the massive private insurance industry. Although private insurers also opposed Medicare, their opposition was less vociferous because the government plan did not threaten or compete with their primary market. The Clinton health policy team was acutely aware of this in 1993, and, as noted, they devoted a great deal of energy toward incorporating existing health insurance companies into their proposed system. Even so, insurance industry opposition was a deciding factor in the Clinton plan's defeat. Repeatedly, scholars of campaigns for universal health care conclude that "powerful stakeholders" played the primary role in defeating reform throughout the century (Quadagno 2005; Gordon 2003). Can national health reform ever make headway against the power of private interests, particularly the health insurance industry?

Numerous political candidates, especially Democrats, have promised to "take on the insurance and pharmaceutical industries." Bill Clinton made such a promise himself during his first campaign (Clinton 1992). Barack Obama, although his health plan, even more than Clinton's earlier one, keeps the current role of private insurers intact, promises to prohibit insurance companies from "cherry picking" and from excluding or charging higher premiums for people with preexisting conditions (Obama-Biden 2008; Families USA 2008).

But is such a challenge to private insurance prerogatives really possible, or will presidential ambitions once again founder on the reefs of interest group opposition? As another administration launches another campaign for universal health care, it is worth looking back at history to see when and how political leaders and/or grassroots groups have challenged the powerful American insurance industry, and whether such challenges have ever been successful.

Public distrust of insurance companies, and government using that distrust to regulate and police the industry, has a long history. Early in the twentieth century, a New York state investigation of the life insurance industry (the Armstrong Investigation) led to a national outcry against insurance companies' corrupt and anti-competitive practices. Labor unions and progressive leaders condemned insurance companies' lobbying power and pressed for greater government regulation of private insurance (Keller 1963). After World War II, the McCarran-Ferguson Act ensured that insurance regulation would be left primarily to the states. However, labor's post-war accommodation with the insurance industry did not end clashes between the union movement and private insurers, as unions continued to criticize private health insurance for the limitations and exclusions of its benefits for workers (Hoffman 2006; Klein 2003; Markowitz and Rosner 1991.

In the 1970s, the insurance industry increasingly came under fire for discriminatory practices. Insurance companies had always divided policyholders by factors like age, sex, race, and occupation, and set their rates according to these distinctions. The nationwide shift toward greater emphasis on social equality following the upheavals of the 1960s forced insurance companies to begin to alter these practices. A life insurance executive complained in the early seventies that his industry's "basic tools" were being challenged. "Unfortunately, the pressures on property/casualty insurers to drop ratings by age, sex, marital status and location are likely to continue to extend to the life insurance business," he warned. This change in his industry was coming about because "Over the years, the civil rights, women's rights and other social movements have begun to shift the traditional American emphasis on equality of opportunity to an emphasis on equality of result" (Greenwald n.d.).

Feminist and labor activists in the 1970s called attention to the ways private health insurance egregiously discriminated against women. For example, private plans charged higher premiums for women than for men. "Some of the oddest discrimination [in health insurance] is based on sexist myths," Olga Madar, president of the Coalition of Labor Union Women, told an audience of women unionists in 1976. "Insurance companies state that 'women have above-average claim costs, chronic illnesses, and excessive absenteeism.... You and I are termed 'clunkers....' Like old cars, we break down. We're unreliable—we're out to defraud and bankrupt the insurance industry." Madar pointed out that insurance coverage rarely included maternity care, or required longer waiting periods for maternity than other conditions. Also, exclusions for preexisting conditions, common throughout private health insurance, included a disproportionate number of disorders that were exclusive to women (Madar 1976; Patterson 1976).

Private insurance became a prime target of the burgeoning consumer movement in the 1970s and 1980s. Some victories against insurance discrimination became possible because consumer activists found support from government. States such as Michigan, Pennsylvania, and North Carolina launched investigations into insurance discrimination (Madar 1976; National Commission on the Observance of International Women's Year 1978). Consumer advocates found an influential government ally in Herbert Denenberg, the state insurance commissioner of Pennsylvania in the early seventies who became known nationwide as a "hell-raising" critic of the insurance industry. In his home state, he beat Walter Cronkite in a poll of public figures deemed "trustworthy." *Time* magazine in 1972 reported that Denenberg, a former college professor, had "ordered all the 1,157 insurance companies that do business in Pennsylvania to appoint ombudsmen to hear consumer complaints...Consumer complaints are pouring in to Denenberg's office at an annual rate of 50,000, up from 25,000 in 1971. He has conducted televised hearings and investigations on just about every topic remotely connected with insurance, from auto repairs to pension funds." Denenberg forced private health insurers to negotiate with hospitals for better prices, and repeatedly refused Blue Cross requests for rate hikes. He told *Time*, "Until insurance becomes a matter of breakfast-table conversation in this country, nothing will happen" ("The Horrible Herb Show" 1976; "They Are All Afraid" 1972).

Not much did happen. While the consumer movement did succeed in creating mechanisms for grievances and increasing state regulation of some types of non-medical insurance, particularly auto, it made little headway against discrimination in health insurance. There were a few victories for consumers, such as the Pregnancy Discrimination Act of 1978, which required insurers to treat pregnancy and childbirth the same as other covered conditions. However, private health insurers today are still permitted in most states to charge higher rates for women than for men. And exclusions of preexisting conditions are still a major feature of private insurance policies (Pear 2008).

Another wave of protest against the insurance industry came during the AIDS crisis. The AIDS activist movement is best known for its astonishing successes in drawing public attention and research dollars to the disease; its targeting of insurance discrimination is less known. Serious discrimination by insurance companies against people with HIV/AIDS led New York–based ACT UP (the AIDS Coalition to Unleash Power) to form an Insurance and Access Committee in the early 1990s. The organization used its classic street tactics to bring attention to insurance practices. In May of 1991, for example, ACT UP held a march in Washington, D.C., to protest the insurance industry's exclusions of people with HIV/AIDS. About one hundred activists marched from the headquarters of the Health Insurance Association of America to the White House, carrying black coffins draped with the names of insurance companies ("D.C. Marchers…" 1991).

The backlash against managed care during the 1990s is another example of public distrust of insurance companies. Although the "patients' rights" upsurge was never as much of a social movement as its supporters claimed, consumers did participate in transforming managed care by gravitating toward health plans with greater choice of physicians and out of network services, joining class action lawsuits against HMOs who denied care, and sharing their "HMO horror stories" with the media (Ginsburg and Lesser 1999).

Challenges to discrimination and rate hikes in insurance, and a "patients' rights" movement for people already with insurance, are not the same thing as demanding health coverage for everyone. But at times, challenges to private health insurance have been connected or led to demands for universalism. Senator Edward Kennedy during his early 1970s campaign to promote his universal health care plan was the first national politician to tap into the consumer critique of insurance industry, calling consumer representatives and "ordinary Americans" to testify at Washington hearings on his bill about their experiences with being denied private health insurance, insurance companies' refusal to pay for covered illnesses, or losing their coverage after they got sick (many of their stories were also published in Kennedy's book on the topic, *In Critical Condition*). The AIDS Coalition to Unleash Power (ACT UP) in the 1990s argued that fighting both insurance discrimination and the AIDS epidemic required fighting for national health care as well, and joined several major demonstrations demanding universal health insurance (Kennedy 1972; Hoffman 2003).

Probably the most pointed targeting of private health insurance has come in state-level campaigns for health care reform. State universal health care campaigns have taken aim at private insurers as part of their grassroots strategies. In June of 2008, for example, the California Nurses' Association, a longtime and vociferous backer of single-payer health care, sponsored a national day of protests against private insurance. Activists in California, Illinois, and several other states marched on insurance headquarters (and, in San Francisco, on the convention of the Association of American Health Plans), condemning insurance practices and demanding single-payer universal health care. Reported one activist, "In Jacksonville, passing drivers honked vigorously when they saw our signs, 'Health Care YES, Insurance Companies NO' and 'Honk if you're mad at your insurance company' " ("Fed Up With Insurance" 2008; Brown 2008). Labor unions, especially "new" unions like the Service Employees' International (SEIU), have developed campaigns to highlight the drawbacks of private insurance and the benefits of universal coverage. Michael Moore's popular film *Sicko* (2007) is also notable for its focus on private insurance companies and on the health care struggles of Americans *with* private insurance, rather than on the uninsured.

Public anger at the insurance industry has a long history and could be a potential force for popular mobilization. For national leaders intent on reforming the health care system, it will be crucial to harness grassroots anger at private insurance companies, to build on existing local initiatives, and to connect them into a nationwide movement capable of challenging a multibillion dollar industry. As insurance muckraker Herbert Denenberg said in 1972, "Powerful interest groups don't roll over and play dead for you. You have to come on with a strong argument and create intense public pressure, or else changes don't take place" ("They Are All Afraid..." 1972).

As the historical examples in this chapter have shown, in seeking health care transformation President Obama might be more likely to succeed if he proposes a plan that will mobilize and inspire his numerous supporters and channel the power of existing movements for universal health care. Although there is still no social movement for universal coverage with the nationwide visibility and influence of the civil rights or senior movements of the 1960s, grassroots activism on behalf of national health reform is far more widespread than it was at the beginning of Clinton's presidency, especially at the state level (see chapter 5 by Jarman and Greer), and citizen anger at the private insurance industry has reached new heights. To prepare for an onslaught of heavily financed opposition or co-optation, the Obama administration would be wise to place these grassroots movements at the center of its political strategy for universal health care.

This chapter has used historical evidence to show that neither change directed from the top down nor emerging solely from below has succeeded in transforming the health care system. The one instance (Medicare) in which systematic transformation was achieved occurred due to strong political leadership both inspired by, and supported by, popular movements. But history cannot provide a formula for success, especially since the nature and meaning of both social movements and political leadership have changed since the 1960s. Taking their cue from Internet groups like Moveon.org, political leaders are now literally mobilizing popular support from above. For example, as of this writing (December 2008) President-elect Obama is calling for Americans to hold "house parties" (originally an innovation of Moveon.org) to discuss health care reform. Obama's Web site, Change.gov, stated that the president-elect was "committed to health care reform that comes from the ground up—that's why this holiday season, we're asking you to give us the gift of your ideas and input." It does seem ironic that the new administration invokes the power of the grassroots even as it seeks to organize and direct it from above. Is this the end of the social movement as we know it? Are "movements" now to be organized by political leaders in a cynical ploy to seek a citizen rubber stamp for policies that are already decided? Yet Obama seems to have learned some of the lessons of the Clinton debacle in seeking to ensure popular participation in the early stages of a health reform effort. And the entire Obama presidential campaign itself blurred the distinctions between top-down leadership and popular mobilization in ways that were beneficial to both—another example of people's movements and national leaders strengthening each other.

In focusing on the relationship between presidential power and social movements, this chapter has not emphasized other contextual and historical factors in the fate of health reform. The elephant in the room is, of course, global economic crisis. Given that the sweeping reforms of the New Deal were a response to the Depression, it may be that the greatest catalyst for the creation of new social programs is neither leadership nor public support, but a destabilizing economic crisis that upsets the existing order and creates an urgent need for change. Crises also create opportunities for new social movements and visionary leaders to emerge, and thus opportunities for health system transformation.

NOTES

1. This was in marked contrast to JFK, who was criticized by civil rights advocates for prioritizing Medicare over racial desegregation; see, for example, Jackie Robinson, "Jackie Robinson Says," *Chicago Defender*, January 30, 1962, 8.

2. I do not define the Medicare Modernization Act of 2003 or the growth of State Children's Health Insurance Programs as national health reform because these were expansions of existing programs.

4

The Consumer-Directed
Health Care Movement

From Social Equity to Free Market Competition

Jill Quadagno and J. Brandon McKelvey

Since the defeat of President Bill Clinton's Health Security Plan in 1994, a myriad of social movement organizations have worked to transform the financing of medical services. The most ambitious plan, advocated by Physicians for a National Health Program, would abolish the private health insurance system entirely and replace it with a single-payer government plan (Physicians' Working Group for Single-Payer National Health Insurance 2003; Geyman 2005). Fair Share, a more modest proposal sponsored by the AFL-CIO and promoted in the states, would force large employers to cover their employees or pay into a state fund for the uninsured (Abrams 2006). Although the Fair Share movement did win a victory in Maryland, the plan was overturned in the courts. Only the consumer-directed health care (CDHC) movement, a loose-knit coalition of insurance companies, banks, advocacy organizations and conservative politicians, has seen its policy recommendations adopted by several states and inserted into federal regulations. What is CDHC and how did CDCH principles emerge as the favored conservative solution for restructuring the health care system?

Principles and Policy Options of the CDHC Movement

The central premise of the CDHC movement is that health insurance encourages wasteful consumption, because it shields patients from the actual cost of medical care. The result is an endless cycle of rising costs and reduced coverage. The solution is to make patients more cost conscious by forcing them to pay more out-of-pocket for medical services (Pauly 1968; Gladwell 2005). If patients are spending their own money, presumably they will shop more carefully and "purchase" only those services that they really need or are of proven value (Nyman 2002). As demand for unnecessary medical services declines, costs will go down, making coverage more affordable for everyone. The CDHC motto is to 'let the free market reign'.

Since the early 1990s, CDHC advocates have promoted measures to shift health care financing toward a market-oriented model. Their favored mechanism for making patients cost-conscious, other than abolishing insurance entirely, is the health savings account (HSA) coupled with a high-deductible insurance plan to cover "catastrophic" expenses. Several pieces of legislation have moved health care financing toward a consumer-directed vision. The Health Insurance Portability and Accountability Act of 1996 included a provision that allowed the self-employed and small businesses to contribute to tax-subsidized Medical Savings Accounts (MSAs), as HSAs were originally called, on an experimental basis (Hacker 2006). The Medicare Modernization Act of 2003 allowed all employees and/or employers to make tax-free contributions to HSAs, provided they were coupled with a high-deductible plan. Each year since then, the tax benefits of HSAs have become more generous and the rules for contributing funds to HSA accounts less restrictive.

Governors have also adopted the rhetoric of CDHC in reforming state health benefits. Governor Mitt Romney touted the Massachusetts Health Care Reform Plan of 2006 as a way to provide nearly universal coverage to state residents through "a single consumer-driven marketplace for health insurance for small businesses, their employees and individuals" (quoted in Owcharenko and Moffit 2006: 1). Under the administration of Governor Jeb Bush, Florida revamped its Medicaid program to "fundamentally transform relationships, responsibilities and economic incentives" and allow "market competition to inspire innovation and efficiency" (Agency for Health Care Administration 2006: 1–3).

In the 2008 presidential election, Republican Party candidate John McCain rejected the conventional view that health care reform should primarily focus on covering the uninsured. Rather McCain wanted to use the tax system to shift incentives away from employer-based coverage and instead provide tax credits for individuals to purchase health insurance on their own. His plan would "reform the system through the mechanism that has made the American economy the envy of the world—free markets and competition" (quoted in Tanner 2008: 12).

Taken together these policy choices have gradually begun to shift health care financing in both the public and private arena. To what extent can these policies be attributed to the efforts of the CDHC movement?

Explaining CDHC through Social Movement Theory

Social movement theories provide few insights for understanding the trajectory of the CDHC movement. In the ideal-typical formulation, social movements operate "at the margins of the political system rather than through existing party structures" (McCarthy and Zald 1987: 20). They lack formal representation or ties to government officials (Gamson 1990). The CDHC movement, by contrast, consists of elite organizations—insurance companies and financial institutions—with ample resources and the capacity to utilize the party system to their advantage. It has primarily sought to influence the policy process, not through public protest, but rather through the backstage tactics and strategies that are not typically considered by social movement theorists—lobbying and campaign contributions. Both have a significant effect on committee-level voting (Wright 1990; Quadagno 2005). Campaign contributions provide access to elected officials while lobbying provides the opportunity for a social movement to communicate its preferred solutions. These characteristics and tactics would seem to preclude CDHC advocates from being considered part of a social movement. Yet the CDHC movement shares with other social movement organizations grievances against the health care system, a desire to challenge the status quo, a need to devise strategies to use their resources to best political advantage and a desire to gain access to the policy process (Rochon and Mazmanian 1993).

Another problem is that there is disagreement regarding what constitutes success, because it is often difficult to determine whether a social movement has achieved its objectives (Andrews 1997; Giugni 1998; Cress and Snow 2000; Tilly 1998). Success may mean recognition from opponents or the state (Gamson 1975; Amenta, Carruthers, and Zylan 1992), securing constituent benefits, redefining public perceptions of the issues (Cress and Snow 2000), improving access, or fundamentally altering institutional arrangements (Burstein, Bricher and Einwohner 1995). Relatively few studies have examined the direct impact of a social movement on a specific policy and even in these cases the causal connection between social movement activity and policy outcomes is unclear (Amenta, Carruthers and Zylan 1992; Andrews 2001).

Like many social movements, CDHC leaders promoted their goals over years of claims-making and had multiple and changing objectives. Yet it did devise a policy agenda centered around consistent principles, it promoted legislation that supported that agenda, and it witnessed a shift in health care financing consistent with movement goals. Whether this outcome can be attributed solely or even primarily to CDHC advocates' efforts is an issue that remains unclear.

In this paper we describe the tactics and strategies of the CDHC movement, demonstrating how well-funded and well-organized elites seek to influence the policy-making process in ways that are not typically available to less connected social movements. We also show, however, that the CDHC movement depends on tactics, strategies, and a supportive political opportunity structure that are crucial for all social movements. More specifically, we argue that the CDHC movement succeeded because movement leaders proposed a plan that was consistent with a broader conservative revolution that opposed the welfare state and favored the privatization of social services. In health care the goal was to change the principles of health care financing from the social equity principle, which presumes that everyone should contribute to the cost of socially shared risks, to a model based on actuarial principles where people in the same risk class pay premiums in proportion to the likely size of their own health care costs (Keen, Light and Mays 2001).

The Consumer-Directed Health Care Movement

The Origins of Medical Savings Accounts

The CDHC movement emerged in response to a crisis in health care financing that jeopardized the profits of commercial insurance companies. The crisis was caused by rising health care costs resulting from inflationary pressures in the economy as a whole and from Medicare provisions that reimbursed physicians and hospitals for all charges with no upper limit (Quadagno 2005). As employers' expenditures for employee health benefits grew by 700 percent between 1970 and 1982, they tried to contain costs by negotiating better deals with providers and seeking a voice in health policy decisions. When these efforts failed, they turned to managed care. Between 1984 and 2000, health maintenance organizations (HMOs) and other managed-care arrangements increased their share of the private benefits market from 7 percent to over 90 percent (Scandlen 2000; Dranove 2008).

As the large HMOs gained in prominence, the commercial insurance companies that sold to individuals and small groups lost market share. Their problems were exacerbated by ERISA, the Employer Retirement Income Security Act (ERISA) of 1973. The act excluded self-insured plans from state regulations mandating that health plans include specific benefits and exempted them from federal and state taxes (Jost and Hall 2005). Following ERISA the majority of large employers became self-insured. Rather than paying premiums to insurers, they withdrew their health benefit dollars from insurance premium pools and put them in benefit trusts. Self-funding allowed companies to keep the interest on the funds in the trusts, better time payments to meet cash-flow cycles and avoid state taxes on premiums. It also liberated them from expensive state-mandated benefits that commercial insurers had to include in their plans. The shift toward self-insurance left commercial insurance companies with the less profitable business of claims processing and/or selling to small businesses that lacked the resources and administrative capacity to self-insure. Between 1965 and 1985 their market share declined from 55 percent to 35 percent. They also lost a major revenue source from interest on deposits (Goldsmith 1989).

As commercial insurers sought ways to increase profits and expand their market, they settled on a plan for a medical fund similar to an Individual Retirement Account (IRA) that would be coupled with a basic, no-frills health plan. If such a product was offered on a level playing field, employers might find it a cost-effective alternative to managed care. Yet there were numerous legislative obstacles that first had to be overcome.

The Shifting Political Opportunity Structure

Social movements operate within a particular political context. This political opportunity structure represents the system of alliances and oppositions that enhance or impede a movement's likelihood of reaching its goals (McCammon et al. 2001). In a narrow sense, the political opportunity structure consists of party politics and the configuration of elites. More broadly defined, it includes political allies and supporters, the availability of access points in the political system and the degree of elite fragmentation and conflict (Andrews 1997). The CDHC movement began slowly with a plan to reform Medicare, gained momentum as part of a larger movement to introduce greater market competition into the health care system (Jost 2007) and won its first victory when the Republican Party ascended to power in 1994 with an anti-welfare-state, pro-market agenda.

The concept of a medical IRA was first proposed by John Goodman, the president of a corporate-funded advocacy organization, the National Center for Policy Analysis

(NCPA), and Richard Rahn, chief economist of the Chamber of Commerce. In 1984 Goodman and Rahn (1984: 1) published an article in the *Wall Street Journal* arguing to privatize Medicare. Their plan would allow workers to make deposits into health bank accounts, similar to IRAs, during their working years and then use these funds to pay for private health insurance in retirement. Over the long term, Medicare would be phased out entirely. The problem was that Congress had already enacted two Medicare reform measures as part of a more general attack on welfare spending during the first two years of the Reagan administration and had experienced a political backlash as a result. Any further Medicare reform would have to wait.

Given the unfavorable political opportunity structure for Medicare reform, Goodman began a campaign to promote medical savings accounts in private health insurance. The NCPA cosponsored a series of conferences with the National Federation of Independent Businesses to spread the MSA concept and created a MSA Task Force whose members included the American Enterprise Institute, the Chamber of Commerce, the Hoover Institution and the American Medical Association (Bowen 2003). In 1990 the Task Force issued a report endorsing tax credits for funds deposited into MSA accounts. The report also called for federal legislation to allow insurers to sell basic health insurance plans that would not be subject to state regulations, mandates, or taxes (Goodman 1993). Such provisions would help level the playing field with self-insured firms. By the early 1990s, the CDHC movement had grown from a few organizations to a broader network of elites in control of large resource pools.

One of the first companies to experiment with MSAs was Golden Rule Insurance Company, a firm known for aggressive underwriting policies and battles with state regulators over insurance reform. Pat Rooney, chairman of the board for Golden Rule, initially learned about MSAs in 1990 at an NCPA conference. Rooney invited Goodman to make a presentation to his senior executives and shortly after began offering MSAs to his own employees. Rooney subsequently joined the NCPA Board of Directors, donated $60,000 yearly to the NCPA and became one of the biggest MSA promoters (Bowen 2003; Goodman 1995: 57). Within a few years other companies began offering MSAs to their employees, among them Dominion Resources, a utilities holding company, *Forbes* magazine, Quaker Oats and Wal-Mart (Rateliff 1995: 81). In 1994 Golden Rule added MSAs coupled with basic "catastrophic" health insurance plans to its product line.

Without a tax advantage, however, MSAs failed to spread in the 1990s. Even if an employer offered an MSA-type plan, employees had no incentive to choose this option over a more comprehensive health plan (Cannon 2006). What was needed was a political campaign to convince Congress to support legislation that would create a favorable tax situation for MSAs. As Goodman (1995: 51) explained: "What we ask for is a level playing field. Let us let the market decide."

To promote MSAs in Congress, Rooney formed the Golden Rule Financial Corp. and Golden Rule became one of the single largest donors to political campaigns. In 1993–94, Golden Rule donated $1,069,000, mostly to Republicans. Rooney jetted to Washington on an almost weekly basis for meetings with key members of Congress and introduced the idea of MSAs to two House Ways and Means Committee members, Representative Andy Jacobs (D-IN), whose district included Golden Rule and

Representative Bill Archer (R-TX) who had a long association with the NCPA. In 1992 Jacobs and Archer introduced H.R. 5250, a bill to grant tax exemptions to MSA deposits. In all twelve MSA-type bills were introduced that year, but none made it out of committee. Over the next few years Jacobs remained in frequent contact with Rooney to discuss tax code alterations and deregulation needed to grow the MSA market (Bowen 2003).

A Social Movement Organization (SMO) may work at the national level, but it may also develop a federated structure to organize constituents in smaller units (McCarthy and Zald 1987). With federal action blocked, the NCPA started a campaign to get MSA legislation enacted in the states, convinced that state action would pressure Congress to change federal regulations. An important ally in this campaign was the Council for Affordable Health Insurance (CAHI), an organization of insurance companies in the individual and small group markets. Many of these companies had suffered from the national trend toward managed care and were concerned that politicians from both parties appeared to view managed care as the only solution to health care inflation. By 1992, CAHI withdrew from the Health Insurance Association of America (HIAA) because of its managed care direction and initial support for President Clinton's plan, which would have put many small insurers out of business. Rooney recruited Greg Scandlen, a Blue Cross–Blue Shield employee and publisher of the *Health Benefits Newsletter*, to become director of CAHI. Over the next two years CAHI published articles on MSAs and tracked MSA activity in the states. Representatives of CAHI also traveled to various states promoting MSAs. As Scandlen explained the strategy, "The best way to get Congress to move is to get the states to move first. I think this is a far more fruitful way to lobby than hitting Congress directly" (quoted in Bowen 2003: 28).

Golden Rule also provided $10,000 to $20,000 a year to the American Legislative Exchange Council (ALEC), an organization of conservative state legislators and businesses interested in public policy who provided lobbying support for MSAs in the states. By 1994 thirteen states had enacted medical savings account laws and MSA legislation was pending in sixteen other states (Scandlen 1995: 108). In most states, these laws exempted insurance plans from state income taxes and some mandates.

Golden Rule also mobilized other conservatives to support MSAs as an alternative to the Clinton plan. After Rooney made a contribution to Phyllis Schlafly's Eagle Forum and to her anti-abortion organization, she endorsed MSAs (Dreyfuss and Stone 1996: 7). Schlafly (1996: 1) then declared, "MSAs are the best solution to all the problems connected with health care: the high cost, preserving your right to choose your own doctor, portability, job lock, uninsured Americans, gatekeepers.... Medicare going bankrupt, and even the decline in real wages." The American Medical Association, whose members were chaffing against the restrictions imposed by HMOs, also saw MSAs as a way to reinforce the fee-for-service payment system favored by physicians (American Medical Association 1995: 97).

In 1994, the political opportunity structure improved significantly when the Republicans won control of both the House and the Senate, and Representative Newt Gingrich (R-GA) became Speaker of the House. Rooney became one of Gingrich's largest donors and a charter member of GOPAC, his political action committee. In

1995 Rooney gave $25,000 to GOPAC, $43,510 to Friends of Gingrich, his campaign committee, and $20,000 to the Progress and Freedom Foundation, a Washington think tank that sponsored Gingrich's Progress Report, which was broadcast on National Empowerment Television (Common Cause 1995: 6; Dreyfuss and Stone 1996: 5). Rooney explained, "The only way you get heard in D.C. is by making political contributions." Greg Scandlen confirmed: "We've got access to the right people" (Kuntz 1995: A24). Gingrich, in turn, promoted Golden Rule in his televised college course, praised MSAs in his book, *To Renew America*, and declared that MSAs were "the most exciting option we are going to offer" (Common Cause 1995: 5).

On June 27, 1995, Representative Archer introduced H.R. 1818, the Family Medical Savings and Investment Act, to the Health Subcommittee of the Committee on Ways and Means. This legislation would exclude from gross income employer or employee contributions to an MSA as long as funds were used for medical expenses. As an additional boost to CAHI, H.R. 1818 would allow MSA funds to be used to pay for long-term-care premiums but not to finance premiums for a catastrophic plan or other types of insurance. Long-term care was a new product in the insurance market, one that could be highly lucrative, because the generation of people approaching old age had higher median income and greater wealth than any previous generation. For CAHI long-term-care insurance might compensate for their losses to HMOs (Quadagno 2005). Archer's bill would expand the long-term-care insurance market by providing a tax-subsidized way to pay for premiums.

Framing CDHC

Politics is ultimately a contest of ideas (Stone 2001), in which activists adopt frames to construct meaning for constituents, opponents, and bystander audiences (Benford and Snow 2000). Frames are central organizing ideas that define the issues, manage public impressions of movement goals and tactics, and outline the boundaries of a debate. Because of their significance, SMOs exert considerable effort in devising frames that help to put their favored solutions on the political agenda (Benford 1993). Organization leaders present frames as a way to define a situation as problematic, to identify the responsible party or structure, to articulate a reasonable solution, and to call individuals to action (Benford and Snow 2000; Gamson 1992b; Snow and Benford 1992).

Frames that are consistent with broader cultural values, what Ferree (2003) terms the discursive opportunity structure, have wider appeal than frames expressing narrow and particularistic values and more capable of adapting to a changing political environment (Rohlinger 2002). One task, then, for movement leaders is to demonstrate how their meaning constructions relate to broader cultural values.

In opening the hearings on H.R. 1818, Representative Archer (1995: 26), explained that MSAs operated through the free market and were consistent with core American values: "Freedom, choice, personal responsibility and savings." They were the antithesis of managed care. Greg Scandlen (1995: 110) agreed:

> H.R. 1818 will return our health care system to individuals by allowing them their choice of physicians, facilities and services...it will save the federal government

precious dollars in the long run by reducing health care costs without artificial controls, price caps or a new and potentially costly bureaucracy.

Similarly, Goodman (1995: 65) argued that "What medical savings accounts do is it gives people a little bit of freedom and a little bit of control over their own health care dollars so that every decision is not made by the managed care bureaucracy." The American Medical Association agreed: "Should we favor more government control over our health care dollars or more freedom for all of us as consumers of health care to make our own decisions?" (American Medical Association 1995: 97).

Diagnostic frames identify the problem, define grievances and targets of action, and distribute blame (Cress and Snow 2000). Advocates of CDHC plans used the hearings to create a new diagnostic frame. Whereas President Clinton had defined the problem as the lack of universal coverage, MSA advocates emphasized uncontrollable costs, which resulted from perverse incentives in the way health care was financed. As Goodman (1995: 50) explained:

> The traditional fee-for-service health insurance policies that most of us have grown up with cannot survive in the marketplace. A policy that allows you to see any doctor you want to see, select any test you want to have, while sending the bill to someone else cannot, will not, be affordable for most Americans.

The AMA, whose members contributed to the inflation in health care costs following the enactment of Medicare in 1965, now piously agreed (American Medical Association 1995: 98):

> Consumers are not exerting as much pressure on providers for economic efficiencies as they would if they were paying the full cost of medical care directly out of their own pockets. The result is that many prices may be higher than they otherwise would be.

The second problem identified by CDHC advocates was that the tax system discriminated against individually purchased health benefits and favored comprehensive employer plans. Every individual who testified on behalf of MSAs repeated the mantra that the playing field was not level. According to Representative Matt Salmon (R-AZ) who had promoted state legislation for MSAs in Arizona, "We have to level the playing field with other kinds of medical insurance and give the same types of tax preference to medical savings accounts we do to other kinds of coverage" (Salmon 1995: 18). Goodman, too, argued, "Because of this distortion, seven states have passed MSA legislation under their state income tax systems to create a level playing field (Goodman 1995: 51, 54).

Prognostic frames identify the solution to the problem and the means for achieving that solution (Cress and Snow 2000). CDCH Advocates of CDHC plans devised an array of prognostic claims about what H.R. 1818 would accomplish. The main theme was that MSAs would control costs. Representative Salmon declared: "Virtually every study of every company that has offered medical savings accounts has shown that health care inflation has been far less…than it has with traditional companies" (Salmon 1995: 31). These accounts would also create investment capital and fuel economic growth. According to Representative Dick Chrysler (R-MI), "A huge pool of money would be created by MSAs which would be a great resource capital for entrepreneurs" (Chrysler 1995: 17). Individuals, too, would save money because MSA type plans would create "an incentive to take better care of themselves through preventive measures" (Chrysler 1995: 16). They would also be able to accumulate wealth. As Archer argued: "There is no limit on how much can be accumulated in the medical savings account.... If you were fortunate to do a lot of good preventive maintenance and keep yourself in shape, eat right and take care of yourself" (Archer 1995: 31).

MSAs would also restore the doctor-patient relationship by making doctors "agents of patients rather than agents of third-party payer bureaucrats" (Goodman 1995:53). The AMA agreed that H.R. 1818 would improve:

> the physician-patient relationship, a relationship which has eroded by the increasing intrusion of third party payors. Unlike some traditional health benefit plans which 'manage' care by limiting access through plan restrictions, MSAs would eliminate the need for bureaucratic restraints that interfere with patient choice and the doctor-patient relationship." (American Medical Association 1995: 98)

Finally, MSAs would reduce the number of uninsured, although the causal mechanism was not specified. According to Archer: "The question has been raised about how in the world would this proposal help people who do not have insurance? And the answer is that a falling tide lowers all prices, if you think about it" (Archer 1995: 31).

Charles Rateliff, Wal-Mart senior vice president for benefits, summarized all the claims in his testimony:

> [It] will give people...more control of their health care dollars, give people an affordable way to choose higher deductible, lower cost insurance, give people a financial incentive to shop prudently...and lead to more affordability in health coverage.... [It] will improve doctor-patient relationships by removing insurance-managed care from many health services, lower health insurance costs, provide a way to pay for long-term care, promote personal savings, and most importantly, lead to a healthier America, which is what we all want (Rateliff 1995:80).

Although CDCH advocates made extravagant claims, they provided little empirical evidence to support them. For example, Missouri's law giving state tax relief to MSAs had been in place for over three years but was never mentioned. Many advocates instead relied on anecdotes, examples from single companies and personal opinions. Representative Salmon (1995: 17) used a family situation as evidence:

> About 7 years ago my last child was born....The cost, through my third party payer...was $3,500....My sister-in-law had a baby 2 months later, same hospital, same doctor, only they didn't have insurance so they paid cash, $1,500.

As evidence of public support for MSAs, Wal-Mart's Rateliff (1995: 81) proclaimed, "We have received a number of calls and letters from Wal-Mart associates around the country asking for the kind of help that Medisave could provide." Representative Chrysler (1995: 16) declared: "At my company, RCI, we use medical savings accounts as our answer for health insurance and we are proof positive that they work....After our first year of implementation, we can already say that the program has been an enormous success...our annual health care expenditures per employee was actually reduced by $600...a savings of 14.3 percent in just 1 year."

What the private sector experiments with MSAs did was give CDHC advocates "evidence" to promote their plans as successful in controlling costs. Even though the so-called evidence was unsystematic and anecdotal, their claims went largely unchallenged.

Countermovement Claims

A countermovement refers to the mobilization of sentiments in opposition to a given social movement (Zald and Useem 1987). The CDHC movement stimulated activity among social movement organizations with competing visions for health care reform. The two major critics were HMOs, represented by the Group Health Association of America (GHAA), whose market position was directly threatened by CDHC and the single-payer movement, whose advocates wanted a government-run program modeled after Medicare.

The GHAA raised numerous objections to CDHC. It opposed the mandatory linkage of MSAs with HDHC plans, fearing that this provision gave such plans a competitive advantage over managed care. The GHAA also argued that there was no need to level the playing field because, under current tax law, all employer-based coverage received the same tax treatment. H.R. 1818 would give individuals with MSA/HDHC plans an additional benefit by allowing employers to set aside tax-preferred dollars to cover *unreimbursed* medical expenses. Employees would then have "an incentive to favor these policies in preference over comprehensive coverage, such as HMOs.... The federal government is essentially picking the winners." The result would be "adverse selection against HMOs, because healthy individuals would opt for catastrophic coverage, leaving a high proportion of high-risk individuals in HMOs and "thereby increasing premium costs for those remaining in comprehensive coverage arrangements" (Group Health Association of America 1995: 112). Over the long run, "the catastrophic coverage-based MSA provisions could reverse advances in the current marketplace by providing a tax advantage to old-style, uncoordinated and inefficient health care coverage" (Group Health Association of America 1995: 114).

Advocates of a single-payer plan consisting of such organizations as Health Care Now, Physicians for a National Health Program and the AFL-CIO also attempted to mobilize against CDHC. They challenged the core principle of CDHC, that insurance created moral hazard, arguing that patients do not waste health care resources and that user fees do not reduce costs (Canadian Health Services Research Foundation 2007). They also attempted to counter CDHC claims about values with an alternative vision—that the marketization of health care would "denature fundamental human values and tear apart the ties that nurture communal life (Lown 2007: 40). Finally, they defended a single-payer plan as being "hardly analogous to the Soviet Union breadlines" but "as American as our other systems of social insurance: Social Security and Medicare" (McCanne 2006: 4).

Despite these arguments, neither countermovement was able to prevent the advance of the CDHC movement. There are several reasons why the HMOs and single-payer advocates were ineffectual. Because threats come from many directions, countermovements must focus resources on those that seem most viable. Within the large and complex health movement field, the CDHC movement was a relatively new actor, making it difficult for opponents to assess its potential risk relative to other threats. Opponents of the CDHC movement also found it difficult to frame compelling arguments against demands for a change in the tax code. While it is easy to rally troops around an issue like abortion that challenges fundamental values, it is more difficult to bring people to the barricades over tax incentives for HSAs.

Finally, the HMOs were in a particularly weak political position, because of a public backlash against managed care. Although managed-care coverage had expanded significantly in the 1990s, the HMOs' aggressive cost-containment measures had frustrated physicians who objected to restraints on their professional autonomy and angered patients who resented what they perceived as unjust rationing of medical services. After patients joined with physicians in a consumer revolt against some of the more egregious managed-care practices, Congress enacted federal mandates on hospital stays for childbirth (drive-by deliveries) and mastectomies and numerous restrictions were also enacted in the states (Quadagno 2005). As a result, HMOs had few elected officials interested in supporting their demands (Dranove 2008).

Policy Outcomes for the CDHC Movement

Many policy goals of the CDHC movement have been enacted. The Health Insurance Portability and Accountability Act of 1996 (HIPAA) is best known for its privacy provisions, but it included many other features. A series of consumer protection provisions gave employees who lost group coverage the right to convert these policies to individual coverage, prohibited insurers from charging different premiums for individuals within groups, and required insurers that operated in the small group market to guarantee renewal to any group. At Republicans' insistence, HIPAA also provided tax subsidies for MSAs for the self-employed and small businesses on an experimental basis (Hacker 2006). In a concession to the large HMOs, HIPAA did limit the amount of funds that could be maintained in an MSA account and allowed MSA withdrawals only for health-related expenses (Group Health Association of America 1995: 113).

Principles of CDHC plans have also been inserted into Medicare. When Gingrich was elected, he had promised "to rethink Medicare from the ground up." Medicare was like Soviet-style health care—"too bureaucratic, too centralized and too dominated by government" (Toner 1995: 1). Gingrich's plan would scrap existing Medicare rules, which only allowed private insurance companies to sell supplemental "Medigap" policies to seniors and instead let beneficiaries withdraw from Medicare and use their share of funds to purchase private coverage. His ultimate goal was to open the entire Medicare beneficiary market to private insurers (Ferrara 1995: A20).

The initial Republican reform bill included a provision to push Medicare beneficiaries into HMOs but did not contain an MSA option. In response to protests from CAHI, Gingrich promised to include MSAs and a pilot MSA program for Medicare beneficiaries was included in the Balanced Budget Act of 1997 (Kuntz 1995: 24). Although the pilot program represented a modest first step, the long-run plans were more ambitious. Gradually, younger, healthier Medicare recipients would choose the MSA option, leaving older, sicker beneficiaries in traditional Medicare. With the money sitting in

MSA accounts no longer available to Medicare, the government would be forced to increase spending or decrease care, creating a death spiral. As Gingrich explained: "We don't want to get rid of it in round one because we don't think it's politically smart. But we believe that it's going to wither on the vine because we think (seniors) are going to leave it voluntarily" (quoted in Dreyfuss and Stone 1996: 2).

The Medicare Modernization Act of 2003 (MMA) solidified the principles of CDHC into the private health insurance system. Its main provisions, which garnered all the public attention, included a prescription drug benefit and additional incentives for beneficiaries to switch from traditional Medicare to private managed-care plans. What was virtually ignored in the heated debates over the drug benefit was a provision that allowed an employer or employee to establish a health savings account, as MSAs were now called. These accounts had to be coupled with a high-deductible health insurance plan (HDHP) to pay for "catastrophic" care (Hacker 2006). Yearly contributions to the HSA could not exceed the amount of the deductible, originally limited to $2,250 for an individual and $4,500 for a family. The new HSAs differed from MSAs in two important ways. First, whereas MSAs were restricted to the self-employed and small employers, HSAs had no such restrictions. Second, with MSAs either the individual or the employer could make a contribution, but with HSAs both were allowed to do so (Roche 2005).

In his 2006 State-of-the-Union address, President George Bush proposed to substantially expand HSAs by increasing contribution limits to include all out-of-pocket expenses, allowing early retirees to use HSA funds to pay all insurance premiums and expanding the tax incentives. If these proposals were enacted, they would "completely level the playing field" between individually purchased insurance and employer-purchased insurance for the first time in sixty years, according to Goodman (Goodman 2006: 11). In the waning hours of the Republican-controlled legislature, President Bush signed into law the Tax Relief and Health Care Act, which included some of these proposals. It raised the allowable HSA contributions for individuals and families, gave employees the right to roll over funds from other types of employer health spending accounts into HSAs, and permitted a one-time transfer of funds from Individual Retirement Accounts (IRAs) into HSAs (U.S. Department of the Treasury 2006).

The Future of the CDHC Movement

In 2006 the political opportunity structure shifted when the Democrats swept the House of Representatives and won back the Senate. Despite this setback, HSA/HDHC plans have gained momentum. Since the new incentives first became available in 2004, HSA's share of the health care market has been steadily expanding. The major insurers already offer an HSA option and the Health Insurance Association of America has been lobbying Congress to eliminate the obstacles to expansion (http://www.ahip.org/). Most of the five thousand insurance plans offered by eHealthInsurance.com, a Web site that helps individuals find affordable coverage, include an HSA/HDHC option. Employers have also begun to offer HSAs to their employees. Between 2005 and 2006 the percentage of employers offering these plans increased from 2 percent to 6 percent (Kaiser Family Foundation 2006). By 2008 more than six million people had HSAs, up from one million in 2003 (Gateway Insurance Solutions 2008; HSA for America 2008).

The CDHC movement has also gained some new allies. The goals of the CDHC movement have become the preferred solution of many who are involved in the vast network of interest groups and constituencies that have been constructed around the existing health care system over the past seventy years and who have successfully opposed previous efforts at health care reform (Quadagno 2004; 2005). One ally is the American Medical Association, which supports tax credits and HSA/HDHC plans (American Medical Association 2006). The Republican Party has adopted CDHC as its mantra. Banks are also strong supporters. In 2005 the American Bankers Association and the American Bankers Insurance Association formed the HSA Council to increase the distribution of HSAs through banks. The council's objective is "to identify public policy hurdles and propose solutions to decision-makers in Congress" (American Bankers Association 2005). Some financial services companies, like Canopy Financial, have sprung up, focusing exclusively on the CDHC industry. Other banks and investment firms have begun offering HSAs as a product. While banks' main objective is to increase deposit income, HSA management also generates income from fees for account processing. Some insurers, like Blue Cross and WellPoint, have started handling their own banking services, blurring the boundary between banks and insurance (Werner 2007). The CDHC movement has even won support from some Democrats who represent rural areas where managed care functions poorly because of the difficulty of establishing preferred provider networks or HMOs.

Although HSA/HDHC plans were originally designed for the individual and small group market, they have been expanding among employees at large companies as well. Employers are attracted to HSA/HDHC plans because they reduce their administrative costs and make their health expenditures more predictable. A 2007 HIAA survey found that nearly half of the 4.5 million people covered by HSAs work for firms with more than fifty employees (Geisel 2007). In fact, the fastest growth is in the large group market (Wojcik 2007).

Despite the enthusiastic support of the financial services industry and insurance companies, CDHC also has many opponents. The Democratic Party as a whole favors other options, the trade unions are ambivalent, and the large HMOs are opposed. Further, the public remains wary. While younger and higher income employees may prefer these plans because of the tax advantages and lower premiums, people who hold consumer-directed plans rate their insurance lower on overall performance, are less satisfied with what they pay, would be more likely to change coverage in the future, and feel more vulnerable to health care costs (Kaiser Family Foundation 2006). Moreover, it is the target population of CDHC—wealthier, better educated, healthier people— who are most likely to have these reservations. It is unclear whether the unprecedented tax advantages of HSAs are sufficient to overcome these concerns in the long run.

Conclusion

The CHDC movement is not the typical subject of social movement research. It is an elite movement of organizations more typically classified as interest groups. Yet interest groups organized for social change share the goals, tactics, and strategies and organizational characteristics of social movements, blurring any operational distinction (Burstein 1999; Jacobs and Shapiro 2000). Thus, the focus on a social movement of elites provides an opportunity for social movement theory to explore the full spectrum of political activity and organizations that make up the health care movement field.

The CDHC movement has seen many of its objectives translated into public policy, but it would be an oversimplification to conclude that the expansion of HSA/HDHC plans is simply a product of lobbying, campaign funding, and political pressure exerted by commercial insurance companies and the financial services industry. If the CDHC agenda was incompatible with more general goals of the Republican Party, movement supporters would most likely have been unsuccessful. This is apparent from the initial support in Congress for managed care as the panacea for rising health care costs. Despite intense lobbying by HMOs, managed care's inability to contain costs coupled with the political backlash led elected officials to seek an alternative solution, creating political space for HSAs.

The CDHC movement operated in similar ways to other social movements in many respects. Advocates of CDHC wrote newspaper articles, attempted to influence party platforms and defended their proposals at public hearings. They also devised frames to diagnose the problem and identify the solution, using language that was consistent with American values. To expand their sphere of influence, they formed a coalition with groups that had strong organizational bases and ample resources, notably insurance companies and financial services companies. When the national political opportunity structure was unfavorable, CDHC advocates demonstrated flexibility by shifting the focus of activity to the states and then shifted back to the federal level when a more supportive administration was in power. Although CDHC advocates used some social movement tactics, they also employed their ample financial resources to purchase insider access. Specifically, by making large campaign contributions to sympathetic political leaders, they were able to use their lobbying activity to strategic advantage.

Our case study of an elite social movement suggests that researchers should carefully analyze the trajectories of SMOs, regardless of whether they employ traditional social movement tactics or represent the dispossessed. An in-depth analysis of the range of strategies and tactics that SMOs employ over time makes conceptual distinctions across movement types less salient. Many of distinctions between social movement organizations and interest groups rather reflect differences in outcomes or in visible strategies. These differences may also reflect the timing of research and observation as groups shift strategies and build coalitions (Ingram and Rao 2004). By recognizing the similarity among movement types, researchers can focus on repertoires of activities that change over time due to variations in resources, political opportunities, and individual movement trajectories.

NOTES

We thank Jane Banaszak-Holl, Sandy Levitsky and David Frankford for helpful comments on an earlier draft of this manuscript.

5

Mobilizing for Reform

Cohesion in State Health Care Coalitions

Holly Jarman and Scott L. Greer

Most of the time in American politics, groups seeking small objectives win. Policies change incrementally, no matter how much desire there might be for greater changes. This is why major, successful social movements are so interesting to scholars. We study them because they are the exception to the rule, big coalitions promoting big ideas that can become the foundations of major social change. As of 2008, supporters of substantial healthcare reform have been trying once again to do what they have failed to do so often: overcome the fragmentation of the U.S. political system and pass universal healthcare reform.

The problem for healthcare advocates is the "paradox of purity": groups with influence among policymakers have a better chance of getting their ideas implemented, but are incentivized to adopt narrower policy goals or accept smaller reforms. Less influential groups are free to think big, but have a greatly reduced chance of getting their goals implemented. Given these constraints, we ask how a social movement for health reform might be built. How can proponents of big ideas build a big enough support base to overcome fragmented U.S. politics and get their ideas implemented?

Fragmentation of some sort has long been cited as a reason for the American failure to pass universal healthcare coverage. Different authors note different key variables: as distinct as race, the federal system, the tax code, the weakness of unions, path dependency since the New Deal, and the power of the medical lobby (Gordon 2003; Hacker 2002; Hoffman 2006a; Mayes 2004; Morone and Jacobs 2005; Quadagno 2005; Skocpol 1997; Starr 1982). Much of the literature is occupied with efforts to create a hierarchy of the different variables: is racism more or less important than the American Medical Association (AMA), or are the courts more of an obstacle than sectionalism? But many of them can be understood through the lens of fragmentation, whether this fragmentation is political, economic, ethnic, racial, or institutional. Proponents of universal healthcare in the United States have not been able to assemble the large coalition needed to overcome this fragmentation and pass wideranging changes. As with many aspects of the American welfare state, health policy development has been hobbled by an excess of pluralism among the actors involved.

American political institutions, ridden with veto points, demand an impressive political coalition on the order of the New Deal coalition or the Republicans of 2001–6 in order to make major policies. That is because it takes a tremendous wave of support to wash over the obstacles put in the way of change. Sometimes this wave materializes, as with movements for civil rights, women's suffrage, tobacco control, or environmental protection, with substantial, long-lasting consequences for U.S. politics. But at the same time, day-to-day political struggles can be highly fragmented. Most groups find that they are better off pursuing limited, incremental policy goals. Directly, this is because the fragmentation of the American political systems makes the pursuit of limited goals more practical than wholesale transformation. Indirectly, it is because fragmented institutional politics and a fragmented society reinforce each other and create a fragmented interest-group ecology.

In health policy, this fragmentation leads to the paradox of purity: the groups that campaign hardest for universal healthcare, rather than incremental reforms, are typically the weakest. Stronger groups have more opportunities to bring about change, but are incentivized to carve out a narrow policy niche rather than promoting a broad, idealistic agenda. Rare anywhere is the interest group, party, or social movement that will defer incremental improvements in the hope of future overall change. Consider one example: labor unions. Unions, when they have good deals and the power to preserve or extend them, will face strong incentives to a focus on their members' benefits, often putting more emphasis there than on universal healthcare (Farhang and Katznelson 2005: 30; Gottschalk 1999; Hoffman 2004; Klein 2003; Hacker 2002). Such a "pork-chopping" focus on union benefits has been the bane of many union leaders and intellectuals, but it is also a rational response to the difficulty of union-led social change in the United States. When they weaken, and are less able to force political change, their interest in universal healthcare, and broader coalitions for social change, might grow (Turner and Cornfield [2007] detail the same kinds of challenges in the construction of local social coalitions around labor). Likewise, large and declining companies with unionized workforces (such as Bethlehem Steel) called for universal healthcare in the early 1990s as a way to rid themselves of their benefit costs (Swenson and Greer 2002). By the time healthcare reemerged on the national agenda in 2008, many of those employers were gone, had shed their benefits (as with most major legacy airlines), or were in the dire straits that the domestic automobile manufacturers find themselves today.

Overcoming Fragmentation, Forming Coalitions

We have painted a bleak picture so far. Accounts of America's failure to establish universal healthcare contain some depressing conclusions about the prospects for change (notwithstanding the prevalence of authors who hope to find hope amidst the ruins).

But overcoming fragmentation, whether institutionally induced or social, is clearly possible in American politics. The Bush administration shows that, with its tremendous unity of party, interest groups, and branches of government in the service of grand policies including two wars and a giant expansion of the federal government's powers and payroll (Campbell, Rockman and Rudalevige 2007; Pierson and Skocpol 2007).

The fragmented American political system encourages exchange relationships between individual interest groups and politicians (Heinz et al. 1993; Berry 1989). Groups devote financial and other resources to favored candidates at election time with the expectation that the candidate will win and support their policies more effectively once (re)elected (Hall and Deardorff 2006). This means that healthcare resources become and remain extremely dispersed. But significant, lasting healthcare reform sufficient to tackle serious deficiencies in healthcare provision does not emerge through an accumulation of transactions between individual groups and politicians. Likewise, "made to measure" plans (such as those we found in Pennsylvania), designed to purposefully minimize conflict with certain groups by avoiding policy changes that directly affect their interests, shift the costs of uninsurance from one group to another without tackling the underlying problems. To tackle these big problems, groups must change the terms of the debate.

Framing the problem that way concentrates our attention on coalitions for reform—their strength and their ability to surmount the many and varied obstacles of the American political system. According to Zald and Ash (1966), coalitions of movement organizations are distinct in that they can lead to "new organizational identities, changes in the membership base, and changes in goals." Movement organizations pool resources and coordinate strategies, but keep distinct organizational identities (335). Coalitions can form either to capitalize on new opportunities in the political system to achieve their goals (Diani 1990; Staggenborg 1986) or to respond to a threat posed by a new policy initiative (McCammon and Campbell 2002). In either case, we can expect groups to form coalitions only when they perceive that the benefits of doing so outweigh the costs. The language of resource mobilization theory is very relevant here: in order to maximize the number of people in the state who hold preferences for change and convert that into an outcome in legislatures, movements for health reform (like other social movements) must mobilize and collectivize significant resources (McCarthy and Zald 2001).

These coalitions must overcome three serious challenges that are present throughout American politics but arguably worse in the debate over universal healthcare. First of all, the complexity of the healthcare system and the high personal, pecuniary, and electoral stakes mean that a very wide variety of interests have a stake in healthcare provision. No group can affect this policy area alone. Broad-based coalitions are therefore a vital part of overcoming opposition from the many entrenched interests, both strong interests such as insurers and drug companies, but also the many weaker interests that make the health sector the densest concentration of interest groups in American politics. Second, no set of interests has been able to reform healthcare policy in one attempt. Health politics tends to be stable as well as pluralistic; amidst the hubbub of many groups, the major players are well resourced and not prone to changes of position. And repeat players usually defeat "one-shot players" (Galanter 1974) in health or any other politics. Third, healthcare reform is not a narrow political issue. Because of its cost consequences and potential effects on labor markets and insurance rates, it affects the life of every citizen in the state, regardless of insurance status. This also means that it is very complicated, with multiple and diverse veto points that require diverse political resources and tactics.

We can define the problem as surmounting interest group fragmentation by establishing a large coalition; establishing a durable presence; and having the widest possible range of tactics. These are the problems that universal healthcare advocates face in constructing support. We can then infer what they must do to overcome the problems that they face:

- Focus on the goals of reform. Create clear objectives and outcomes that transcend any one group, allowing the formation of a broad-based coalition.
- Turn frustration into momentum. Manage losses and plan for more than one cycle of protest to keep the coalition intact and moving forward. This avoids the problem of being a "one-shot" player in an interest group environment populated by "repeat players" (Galanter 1974) who develop their credibility and reputation for power over years.
- Operate inside and outside. Coordinate political and social organization in order to turn insiders into advocates (i.e., making clear links between health reform, electoral politics and public opinion).

Focus on the Goals of Reform

All social movement coalitions face a fundamental dilemma in defining what they want to achieve. In searching for objectives that all member groups find palatable, coalitions have a tendency to resort to the lowest common denominator, which may not satisfy all of the groups completely but might prevent any major splits between them. This has the advantage of creating a "broad front door" through which the coalition can recruit new activists and appeal to the wider public. But a wide entrance is also a wide exit. If politicians enact limited reforms that appear to satisfy the coalition's objectives, supporters can quickly lose interest in campaigning further, believing that they have won (Kleidman and Rochon 1997: 51).

The alternative of being too specific about a plan is also bad. A specific healthcare reform plan is a good target for opposing groups: it is much easier to publicly oppose a measure on technical grounds than it is to oppose better healthcare for citizens. Once a specific plan fails and before starting again, its supporters must slice off a segment of the plan to please its opponents. This results in a steady incremental movement toward the opposition.

A successful coalition has to mediate between these two strategies. If they set the bar too low, there is a higher risk that the coalition will be co-opted. Too high, and they risk being seen as inflexible by politicians and subsequently marginalized. Disagreements between members over objectives are also more likely. A coalition has to bait the hook enough to attract a fish, but not so much that it gets pulled out of the boat.

Turn Frustration into Momentum

Social movements are often better suited to one-shot politics. They mobilize and spread, engage in political and protest activities, and these activities often result in resistance, in which case the movement is repressed, or reform, in which case the energy behind the movement dissipates. In contrast, health policy communities contain a lot of repeat players: long-term, stable interests, with rich resources and entrenched opinions about policy. When changes in health policy occur, they tend to be incremental as one group of interests slowly loses ground to another. The losers do not dissipate, but live to fight another day.

For a health social movement to be successful, therefore, it must behave like a repeat player. Insiders must be able to wait it out. The Wisconsin coalition has learned to play the political cycle: planning for the long term, holding actions in reserve for the next cycle, and building lasting public support. To be a successful repeat player, a movement must anticipate losses and make sure that its supporters know that opposing groups are to blame in the event of failed campaigns or reforms. In the absence of substantial and secure resources, such a strategy is very important because it can turn a failure into an argument for more effort.

Operating Inside and Outside

Third, successful coalitions need insiders as well as outsiders, advocates who have credibility with the governor and state legislature who can reinforce their arguments by pointing to their supporters in the street. But how does the movement decide who will be inside the window? What skills should they have? And how will the coalition avoid co-optation? The coalition requires an organizational strategy that allows it to coordinate activities across these two arenas without being swallowed up or pushed aside.

In their discussion of labor movements, Hauptmeier and Turner (2007: 130) distinguish between *political* and *social* coalitions. In political coalitions, unions coordinate with political parties, politicians, and other actors, focusing on elections and the policymaking process. In social coalitions, unions come together with community, religious, environmental, or immigrants' rights groups and work together on a range of political, economic, and social campaigns. This implicitly counterposes political activity, focused on a narrow range of actors in relationships built on, basically, exchange, against social activity that deemphasizes exchanges with elected politicians and instead stresses the development of a power base and coalition organized around issues. A social coalition, politically engaged, is more likely to be able to draw on collective action and attract and serve diverse members over time. That, in turn, allows it to develop a durable power base that means it can be a repeat player over years while being able to change issue priorities.

Cases

We have drawn these observations from the strategies of health coverage advocates in two states: Pennsylvania and Wisconsin. They are very similar in some ways (see table 5.1). Both are relatively homogeneous industrial states with large rural populations. As a consequence of their industrial and rural economies, they have moderate unionization rates, high rates of health insurance, and expensive healthcare. They have expensive medicine, with Wisconsin's doctors paid as much as five times as the national average. They are also highly capable states (Elling 2004), and both have legislators that rank highly in political scientists' rankings of pay, resources, and

Table 5.1. State Healthcare Vital Statistics (Jarman 2007)

	Wisconsin	Pennsylvania
Median Household Income	$45,956 (whole US $46,071)	$45,941 (whole US $46,071)
Uninsured Adults under 65	13.5% (whole US 20.5%)	14.2% (whole US 20.5%)
Personal Healthcare Expenditure, %GSP	14.8%	13.3% (2004)
Commonwealth Fund Ranking	9th out of 50	15th out of 50

(Jarman 2007)

expertise (Hamm and Moncrief 2004). In other words, they are states that are capable of implementing healthcare and have relatively low numbers of uninsured citizens.

In both cases, we focus on the *how*: how did health reform advocates in each state try to build coalitions of support for their ideas? Which actions did they take that were successful and which failed? At the time of writing, advocates have not been successful either in state, but their different strategies tell us something about their future prospects. In Pennsylvania, the most powerful advocates aimed low, but hit lower. Single-payer advocates aimed high, but missed altogether. In Wisconsin, advocates constructed a coherent and substantial coalition for reform. Advocates aimed high, and while they did not hit a substantial target, they were encouraged enough to pick themselves up and try again. Their success in overcoming fragmentation and the paradox of purity laid some strong foundations for the next battle.

Healthy Wisconsin

One of the best books about Wisconsin politics is titled *Wisconsin Politics and Government: America's Laboratory of Democracy* and begins with the declaration that "The most important feature of Wisconsin's society, government, and politics during the twentieth century was its progressive nature" (Conant 2006: xv). Even if some might demur from that (and few studies of Wisconsin do), interviewees were clear that appealing to Wisconsin's sense of itself as a leader was a good political frame and tactic.

The campaign promoting the Healthy Wisconsin health reform plan certainly is good for that Wisconsin theme. It has been hailed by NGOs and policy entrepreneurs in other states as an example of how to do things right (Progressive States Network 2007) and its strategy has been emulated in Washington (through the Healthy Washington Coalition) and Michigan (the Health Care for Michigan Campaign). The Wisconsin campaign brings together a coalition of thirty-five statewide NGOs who aim to shape and increase popular support for health reform at state level. Reaching down to the roots, the campaign has mobilized activists to coordinate a series of town-hall meetings initiated by local people. Reaching up to the branches of government, popular support for the campaign has allowed NGO entrepreneurs to access important decision-makers in the senate.

Healthcare is a particularly salient issue in Wisconsin. Despite a high level of insurance in the population, or perhaps because of it, healthcare premiums in the state are the third highest in the United States and 26% above the national average. Premiums are also rising faster than the national average (by 9.3% versus 6.1% in 2006) and medical doctors' incomes are *five times* higher than the U.S. average (Bybee 2007). Wisconsin is also a swing state, hotly contested in national elections. In 2006, it had a Democratic governor and senate but a narrowly Republican house.

It became a problem and opportunity for politicians principally because of an agenda-setting move by Healthy Wisconsin activists who put local referendums on the 2006 ballot that called for the state legislature to take action on healthcare by putting forward a universal coverage plan in the next assembly term. It was a tactic led by the social movement organizations that would be key to the Wisconsin coalition, and it served multiple needs: It helped elect Democrats; it selected friendly Democrats who then owed health advocates a policy; and it created a series of local mandates for universal health-care as well as the makings of a state mandate. Eleven local referendums were held in November 2006 that asked "Should the Wisconsin Legislature pass a bill by 2008 that will assure access to quality and affordable healthcare coverage for all Wisconsin individuals and families?" The public said "yes." Public support averaged 83% of the vote and the ballots gained 280,000 votes statewide. Democratic candidates for the state senate ran on healthcare issues, with three out of the four new seats they won apparently determined by health issues. This required a level of organization (although the single innovative tactic of the referendum did much of the work on its own), which came from the organizations in the developing Healthy Wisconsin movement.

The key innovation of the Healthy Wisconsin movement has been to mould three separate coalitions, with three separate plans, into a single, flexible movement. In the best tradition of the state, the three separate coalitions chose to work together rather than compete with each other. The most remarkable thing about this is that they made the decision before a single plan was chosen. Following on from this logic, the movement stuck rigidly to a single frame from its creation until early 2007—the need for reform and the discussion of reform—never placing one plan above the others. This image is summed up by the name they chose: the Wisconsin Healthcare Reform Campaign, more commonly known as the "Big Tent" coalition. Wisconsin Citizen Action, one of the main actors in the coalition, offers "framing training" to its activists to help them strike the right tone in forums and with the media.

The movement has three big players: the Wisconsin Health Project, Wisconsin Citizen Action, and the Wisconsin state AFL-CIO, as well as a number of high-profile policy entrepreneurs from the medical professions and the state legislature. The three original plans show that the movement is indeed a big tent: the Wisconsin Health Plan, the most market-oriented of the three plans, which featured automatic enrollment combined with the creation of provider networks; the Wisconsin Health Security Plan, a single-payer model similar to the Canadian system; and the Wisconsin Healthcare Partnership Plan, created by the Wisconsin state AFL-CIO, which built on the state Workers' Compensation Program, all existed side by side. One key policy entrepreneur in Wisconsin highlighted a possible explanation:

> [T]he single payer group here, to give them due credit, has really been, [under the leadership of physician activists], less doctrinaire than in some other states. . . . [T]hey are willing to believe that passing one of the other plans would be a major step in that direction and that they should support it. (Madison, July 2007)

The Healthy Wisconsin plan is a relatively simple health reform package. It would cover all Wisconsin residents (resident in the state over twelve months) not already covered by Medicare, Medicaid, Badgercare (an existing state plan) or as a federal employee.

The package of benefits is modeled on those given to state employees (including legislators) plus mental health parity and preventative dental care for children. The plan would establish various "healthcare networks," "provider-driven, coordinated group[s] of healthcare providers comprised of primary care hospitals, and other healthcare providers and facilities, including providers and facilities that specialize in mental health services and alcohol and drug abuse treatment" (Wisconsin Citizen Action 2007). It provides two tiers of care: the costlier option provides higher quality, for which individuals pay extra. The healthcare network providing the cheapest bid will be placed in the lower tier, with other networks placed in the higher tier. There will also be a statewide fee-for-service plan. The plan would be funded jointly by employers and employees: employers would be mandated to pay 9–12% of employees' wages toward healthcare, while employees would pay 2–4% of their wages, replacing their private insurance payments. The self-employed and persons with income but no wages would pay 10% of their income up to the Social Security wage cap (Jarman 2007).

The tactics adopted by the movement (predominantly multiple town-hall meetings, a reliance on "earned" media, and working closely with legislators, especially in the state senate) have all emphasized educating the public and decision-makers about the alternatives for reform. It was these activities that brought the coalition together. When the groups backing the different plans discovered in 2005 that they were beginning to compete with each other for the location and timing of public forums, they decided to pool their resources and coordinate the forums together. Only in 2007 did they consolidate the three separate reform plans into a unified text. One interviewee explains that this strategy was deliberate. The coalition knew that the idea of general reform was much easier to promote than trying to rally around one unified plan, and so waited until the last possible moment to consolidate the three options into the single Healthy Wisconsin plan (Madison, July 2007). The result was that the process of developing the plan was deemphasized, and that deemphasized the difference in plans that had led single-payer activists, the AFL-CIO, and other groups to eschew coordination in the past.

In Wisconsin, the Democratic governor has shown some opposition to the plan, citing it as impractical, and preferring instead his own incremental SCHIP-style expansion, Badgercare Plus. Typically, the Big Tent coalition is handling this by sidestepping the governor's criticism instead of attacking it head on. When the governor tried to talk middle-ground senators into opposing Healthy Wisconsin, commenting in a local radio debate that the plan was not "real world," the coalition's main media contact responded, "the governor's doubtless talking about how conservative and disinclined to do this the state assembly is. And if we can break party unity in the Assembly then it will be real world because it will be on the governor's desk and he can make it law" (Madison, July 2007). Ultimately the legislation failed in the Republican-controlled assembly (as expected) but Big Tent advocates were confident (in April 2008) that they would be able to turn its defeat into an electoral issue that would defeat Republicans and force healthcare higher up the agenda. They recognize this as a wedge issue and are working to turn defeat into increased momentum.

The coalition fit into a larger strategy for the Big Tent coalition, one informed by national debates about both healthcare and its role in a larger progressive agenda. The source for much of the framing work was the Herndon Alliance (www.herndonalliance. org), a key part of the social movement infrastructure for healthcare advocates. The Herndon Alliance uses social movements and framing theory to craft messages for healthcare advocates. Part of their research is on the meaning of fear in healthcare debates; popular concern for healthcare is often driven by fear of losing health insurance, but that fear can turn against any plan once it becomes concrete and can be portrayed by opponents as a threat to whatever existing benefits a person enjoys.

There is a clear affinity between the demands of coalition maintenance and the project of advocating for healthcare policies that become vulnerable as soon as they become concrete. Groups might abandon a campaign for the same reasons voters might lose interest: namely, that their reading of the plan suggested that their specific needs and interests would be damaged. The policy and movement consequence was "GAC": the promise of "guaranteed, affordable coverage" [for all]. The virtue of GAC is that it avoids a specific plan that can alienate coalition members and voters, and as an added benefit leaves it to elected politicians to make the actual complicated legislative tradeoffs and reap the credit. It instead allows the coalition to concentrate on increasing pressure, such as through referendums and stunts that keep the specific call for GAC at the front of politicians' minds and even convince them that there is an electoral mandate for it.[1] It also does research that allows activists to avoid words that poll badly, according to the Herndon Alliance, including "universal healthcare" (which apparently has connotations of one-size-fits-all care).

The result is that in Wisconsin a large group of organizations have been able to develop a stable, durable coalition that can avoid being caught on internal disputes about plans. Switching the emphasis to a shared goal created the breathing space necessary for leaders (whose personal commitment to the coalition is impressive) to work on developing trust and divisions of labor between the different groups. Of course, some groups work much harder than others, and some have more resources to contribute than others (due to tax status, if nothing else). Some report that they find coalition participation useful as a justification for requests for resources to their organization's national office; participation in the Big Tent coalition is an important justification for their Wisconsin offices' budgets. Some smaller or more specialized organizations clearly value the feeling of being an insider that comes from legislative bulletins and regular meetings with major state players such as the AFL-CIO and AARP. All bring the legitimacy that comes from breadth and the knowledge about the state that are important parts of Wisconsin's coalition, which is why there is little or no call to restrict entry to groups that will agree to the coalition's overall strategy and objectives.

Prescription for Pennsylvania

Pennsylvania has fragmented, and typically American, health coverage politics. It is a geographically divided state, with two big cities separated by a mountain range. Much of the population lives outside the two big cities, in areas with distinctive economic and social ecologies of their own, from Great Lakes steel towns like Erie to colonies of Welsh miners. Fragmentation, rather than a desire to lead, characterizes its political culture. In 2000, Pennsylvania had the third-largest number of rural residents of any state in the United States (Pennsylvania Healthcare Cost Containment Council 2007). Pennsylvania is the third "oldest" state in the United States, with 14.6% of residents sixty-five or older. Furthermore, 11% of all residents are living below the poverty line. Unionization rates are roughly equivalent to Wisconsin, but unlike Wisconsin the healthcare sector was Pennsylvania's largest employer in 2005.

In national party politics, Pennsylvania is a swing state. But while the governorship and state lower chamber are competitive, the state senate is structurally Republican (Treadway 2005: 199). The Democrats in 2006 took a one vote majority in the state's house and held the governorship, but in interviews saw no prospect of senate control. As a result, any strategy requiring legislation had to be able to gain the support of at least a few Republicans (with the added difficulty in 2006–8 that the Republican leadership had control of its caucus by one vote, a problem Democrats complained made it more difficult to strike deals).

While the three coalitions in Wisconsin were molded into a single movement, opposing plans still exist in Pennsylvania. The different plans, and their different genesis, show a pair of different and very common approaches to the problem of creating change in healthcare.

Insider Politics: Governor Rendell and Representative Eachus

The first approach is that of Governor Ed Rendell, elected in 2002. A former mayor of Philadelphia, he is a very popular and nationally important Democrat whose achievements in a city with many challenges have been chronicled in a well-known book (Bissinger 1997). Rendell took healthcare reform seriously and proposed a wide-ranging health reform plan called Prescription for Pennsylvania. As proposed, this plan was a colossal undertaking, requiring forty-seven pieces of legislation, including the Cover All Pennsylvanians (CAP) program. The CAP program aimed to cover the state's uninsured by targeting small businesses that do not already offer insurance to their employees. Businesses would be mandated to pay a portion of health premiums for their employees, with those that still did not provide insurance required to pay an additional payroll tax. The plan would also expand public subsidies for healthcare. Premiums are subsidized for those with incomes up to 300% of the federal poverty level. A separate "Cover All Kids" program would expand existing benefits under the State Children's Health Insurance Program (SCHIP) to parents at up to 300% of the federal poverty level. Students would have to be insured by their universities, and students without insurance would be assessed a fine. The state would establish a set of standardized benefits packages that must accept all applicants without discrimination in cost or on the basis of preexisting conditions. Insurers would be required to spend 85% of their small business premiums on healthcare, and no more than 15% on administration or profits.

Beyond the two coverage components, Prescription for Pennsylvania stood out for the range of its concerns (a major reason for the remarkable volume of legislation it required). It did not just address coverage; it also addressed issues of interest to almost anybody concerned with healthcare. These issues included malpractice costs (a topic of great concern to doctors), banning smoking in public places, and a range of quality issues (reflecting a nationwide and global movement to reduce unnecessary treatment, and medical error, as well as the high error rates and costs of Pennsylvania). This broad agenda, and the decision to introduce it as a whole basket of bills, gave the governor the scope to trade off different values, bills, committees, appropriations, and interest groups, and frame the measures as transforming healthcare in the state.

In April 2008, an interviewee associated with the governor agreed that much of the plan was designed to demobilize opposition by leaving it untouched (as with insurance companies) or by making a bargain that could not be refused. Great effort was expended to ensure that key players were on board. The governor's office engaged in a process of "bringing all the stakeholders in" (business, labor, and consumers above all), followed by a more public campaign to promote the plan which sent Rendell on several bus tours of the state (Worden 2007).

The problem for Rendell's agenda was the Republican senate, which refused to pass legislation that would expand healthcare and increase taxes (specifically, the tax on chewing tobacco). The perfect party discipline that Democrats needed to control the house did not help, either. Passage of any legislation would require a triumph of house Democratic discipline as well as overcoming Republican party unity in the senate. Reflecting these constraints, the final plan passed by the house Democrats was not Rendell's broader prescription but ABC, "Access to Basic Care." The ABC proposal was a substantively different plan, less ambitious in terms of coverage, and requiring no new revenue. It was developed by Representative Todd Eachus, whom one interviewee called "the most powerful Pennsylvania politician you've never heard of." At the time of writing in summer 2008 its senate passage seems unlikely, despite its more modest ambitions.

Rendell's Prescription for Pennsylvania, and even more so the house Democrats' compromise, are creatures of Harrisburg politics, the politics of exchange. Their design and content reflect their proponents' anticipation of the type of reforms that could be achieved. Governor Rendell sought to expand his tactical options and potential allies in the original Prescription for Pennsylvania, while Representative Eachus removed sections of the legislation that would mobilize opposition to create a more modest plan.

The debates surrounding ABC demonstrated the Democrats' strategy: linking issues together within health reform legislation in order to bring reluctant interest groups on board. Early in his governorship, Rendell had created a state-subsidized malpractice insurance pool called MCare in response to complaints from doctors about Pennsylvania's particularly high malpractice insurance costs. MCare was due to expire in 2008, and Rendell, with the house Democrats, incorporated its renewal into the legislation to pass ABC. It was a straightforward legislative tactic intended to force the doctors to support other issues as the price of MCare. On March 27, Rendell sent a letter to the state's doctors. He concluded: "I ask for your patience... and help in ensuring that our legislators maintain their focus and attention and pass this critical piece of legislation." The gambit did not work, however. When an amended Cover All Pennsylvanians did not pass at the end of March, MCare abatement ended and some doctors in high-risk fields such as neurosurgery and orthopedic surgery faced immediate premium increases of as much as $15,000 a year (Fahy 2008).

Outsider Politics

The alternative to the classic legislative coverage expansion strategies of Rendell and the house Democratic leadership was put forward by advocates of single-payer healthcare, a small but active social movement formed around a single NGO: Healthcare for All Pennsylvania (HC4AP). Healthcare for All Pennsylvania, a 501(c) (4) organization, was founded in 2006 "to secure a comprehensive single payer healthcare system for every citizen of Pennsylvania" (HC4AP Web site, August 2007). Compared to the governor's regime, it has few resources, achieves little press coverage, and is considered by many to be an impossible proposal. One local newspaper commented that "in reality, [it] doesn't stand a chance" (Namako 2007).

Healthcare for All Pennsylvania was born of a small number of activists in western Pennsylvania who were originally energized by the national single-payer agenda of HR676, a federal universal single-payer bill put forward in the house by Representatives John Conyers (D-MI) and Dennis Kucinich (D-OH). Aware of the difficulty of promoting single-payer healthcare in the Bush years, they turned to advocating for state policy reform. Their breakthrough, and the effective start of HC4AP, came after the 2006 election when they were able to hire a director, and use his experience and the mailing lists he developed as an unsuccessful Democratic primary candidate in that year's U.S. Senate race. With this expertise and initial start, they were able to develop an activist organization. That initial start, as well as their relatively greater ambition, helps to explain some of their animus toward the "Democratic machine" that one organizer said was blocking the single-payer bill.

Perhaps because of their opposition to the state Democratic party leadership, one observer notes that they "haven't really done any formal coalition building.... Single-payer is hard enough to move but when the governor has a rival plan it gets even more interesting" (telephone interview, May 2007). The two plans are pitched as rivals on the Healthcare for All Pennsylvania Web site, which states "HR1660 vs. HR700... You're never going to get a clearer view of how—on this topic, anyway—our political class is sabotaging the welfare of the people" (HC4AP Web site, August 2007). The Healthcare for All Pennsylvania plan has received very little press attention. One organizer noted this problem. The "state media decide what can pass and cover that... a lot of activists decide if you're serious based on whether you're in the media" (telephone interview, March 2008).

Despite reports of pressure on members not to even introduce the bill, it had some life in the assembly. The Universal bill (HR1660, SB300, the Family and Business Healthcare Security Act) was backed by thirty-seven members once introduced. The governor's plan (HR700) was supported by eleven (Namako 2007). Its sponsor, Philadelphia representative Katherine Manderino, held hearings on the bill on March 16. The problem that proponents faced was a general consensus in the assembly that it would not pass; as one interviewee said, state legislators do not "come to me and say 'I had ten people in my office talking about single payer.' Instead, they say we had [the main HC4AP organizer] in my office again. That's not going to do it."

The single-payer campaign has been unsuccessful in courting the media so far, but has organized thirty-six town-hall meetings in towns throughout the state since HC4AP started to document them in March 2007, in addition to separate events held by coalitions in Pittsburgh and Philadelphia. When the two plans are presented together, however, they are seen as rivals for debate rather than alternatives for discussion.

The campaigns tripped over each other. One interviewee associated with Rendell commented that Rendell's bus trips around the state in support of Prescription for Pennsylvania were complicated by the vocal presence of single-payer activists at each event. "He's saying to them, 'we can't get any revenue at all through the senate for Prescription for Pennsylvania, so how are we supposed to do single payer?'" The HC4AP campaign, in keeping with its Web site and its organizers' roots in an insurgent Democratic primary campaign, often set itself in opposition to the governor's plan and the efforts of Democratic house leaders to keep the single-payer bill off the stage. But the interviewees not associated with HC4AP were all positive about the effect of its campaign, arguing that it contributed to public interest and education, and that it made the issue more salient for future years. In an interview with local media, Bill George, the Pennsylvania AFL-CIO's president, said that the union was indicating "soft support" for the governor's plan (Wenner 2007). To general surprise, he also endorsed the single-payer bill, pointing out to his astonished allies that the AFL-CIO had long had supported single payer on the record.

We can read this from two perspectives. From one point of view, the conventional one in studies of American health politics, there is an insider coalition-building effort that brings together the main players, and a largely symbolic social movement with very little political power but the ability to muddy the waters. While the governor tries to stitch together the minimal winning coalition of established interests, some activists work on the side. From another point of view, that of social movements, the study is of the failure to try to create a coalition that incorporates some of the key supporters. Unable or unwilling to settle on a single agenda, advocates on all sides who support universal healthcare divide their efforts, ending as rivals.

Conclusion

The main difference between universal coverage campaigning in Wisconsin and in Pennsylvania has been the structure of the advocating organizations. In Wisconsin, the coalition is built around the advocacy of universal health coverage, regardless of the preferred plan: *focusing on the goals of reform*. An intentional effort at coalition building, and a promising strategy, overcame the paradox of purity by refocusing on the shared goal and agreeing to not discuss the actual mechanisms. Building a coalition, and holding referendums, on the principle rather than a particular plan reduced their initial exposure to hostile attacks and their ability to fall out with each other. Meanwhile, the longer they worked together, the better their knowledge of each other, coordinating mechanisms, and even shared trust became.

In Pennsylvania, the paradox of purity dominates: without a social movement coalition, the single-payer advocates were frozen out and hectored what they saw as a Democratic "machine," while larger players with a commitment to universal healthcare were engaged in the politics of complex coalitions. This is a much more ordinary story of American politics, but it raises the threat that the health reforms will be nibbled to death by interest groups or blocked by political opponents such as Republicans. The removal of the revenue from Cover All Pennsylvanians might be taken as evidence of this dynamic at work.

Wisconsin's broad-based coalition has so far proved durable. Instead of dispersing after a defeat, activists have framed the defeat so as to *create momentum for future change*. In Pennsylvania, single-payer advocates persist, but have no power. Without a strategy that can overcome frustration in the senate, it is likely that sympathetic insiders will move healthcare reform further down the agenda in the future and prioritize other issues.

Pennsylvania's problems throw the advantages of Wisconsin's coalition into relief. The Wisconsin coalition was not impressive as an end in itself. Rather, it is interesting because creating a relatively large and unified coalition allowed the Wisconsin activists to effectively *mobilize different inside and outside resources*: skills, money, activist labor, geographical spread, and insider credibility. Single-payer activists, for example, were part of the coalition, with the result that it was not a vehicle for an insurgent left within the Democratic Party in the way that the Pennsylvania single-payer campaign often was.

Most social movement activity is an exercise in voluntarism: an effort to change policies through collective action. This is as true of the movement for universal healthcare as it is for any other. American politics and society create well-documented fragmentation, while proponents of reform see a need for unification.

But that is little more than a restatement of that textbook of American politics, *The Logic of Collective Action* (Olson 1965). There are always temptations to free-ride, negotiate side deals, or simply give up. Some cases of collective action, nevertheless, work and change society. This is, ultimately, why social movement theory can help us to explain the relative success and failure of movements for healthcare reform. By showing us how to understand the chances of collective action and coalition, they show us how to understand the chances of the movement for universal healthcare overcoming the obstacles that it faces.

Neither Wisconsin nor Pennsylvania has seen success or failure (but most state health plans are only under discussion at the time of writing). Both face stiff opposition and all the hurdles of institutional fragmentation, intergovernmental relations, and state politics, and both could be blown off course by national politics and policies. In both Wisconsin and Pennsylvania, businesses have resisted changes to the status quo. The main opposition to reform is very similar in each case. In Pennsylvania, the National Federation of Independent Business of Pennsylvania (the NFIB is an interesting social movement organization in itself), and the Chambers of Commerce oppose the plans. They draw on the widely held worry that Rendell's plan will violate federal law (ERISA) that allows corporations to set up large insurance schemes that disregard varying state requirements (*Philadelphia Inquirer*, October 3, 2007). Other business associations claim that the plan fails to alter the drivers of cost and so will not deliver on its claim to save money. Opposition in Wisconsin has come from similar sources: the National Federation of Independent Business, the State Chamber of Commerce (Wisconsin Manufacturing and Commerce), the Underwriters Union (who oppose community rating), and Club for Growth.

Nor is it to say that any given state plan faces a good long-term prognosis (Greer and Jacobson 2010; Jacobson and Braun 2007). Wisconsin and Pennsylvania both have balanced-budget amendments that could eventually destroy their universal coverage. Both depend on the goodwill of the federal government. But a successful state universal coverage plan, against the backdrop of a perceived national crisis, is a motive force for federal reform in itself. By showing that a policy is possible, it makes it more passable.

Our key point, though, is that the political dynamics are interesting in their divergence. In Pennsylvania, supporters of Prescription for Pennsylvania have adopted some common insider strategies: trying to construct a coalition of the most amenable major players, and leaving out an inconveniently purist ideological ally that can mobilize relatively few resources. In Wisconsin, the coalition is built around a shared goal of universal healthcare rather than the existing interest group constellation. The creation of a coalition around a shared, general goal rather than a specific plan creates management challenges but can unify a variety of actors and get them to the table, in Wisconsin and in other settings (Greer 2007: 100–12).

Their stories have implications for our understanding of the coalitions in Massachusetts and California, two states that have caught the attention of health policymakers and commentators alike. All four states have lively current campaigns for universal healthcare, and all have long records of advanced social policy. A major difference between them, though, is the degree of unity or division; in Wisconsin and to a lesser extent Massachusetts, proponents could agree on tactics, strategy, and much legislation. In California and Pennsylvania, multiple plans with multiple advocates fragment the push for universal coverage, while the ensuing complicated coalition politics also complicate the legislation.

Harder still is building support for reform at the national level. Here also, reform attempts in Wisconsin and Pennsylvania hold many lessons for advocates of a new national plan. From one viewpoint, America is strongly divided: only a handful of votes stand between the parties in Congress; only a few percentage points divide candidates in presidential elections. From another perspective, there exists a huge potential coalition for change. Providing healthcare to the American people is more challenging than it has been in many years, and the problems of uninsurance and underinsurance are vast, complex, and urgent. A large majority of Americans agree that change must happen; overall support for health reform is very high. This research shows that such consensus can be built and can be the foundation for lasting change.

NOTES

Sincere thanks go to the Americans for Democratic Action Education Fund, who funded part of this research. We would like to thank Jane Banaszak-Holl, Marie Hojnacki, Sandy Levitsky, Mayer Zald, an anonymous reviewer, and conference participants for their very helpful comments. Any remaining mistakes are our own.

1. In an application of theory to practice, one key figure in the Wisconsin movement published a book arguing that electoral mandates do exist and bind politicians (Kraig 2004).

6

The Strength of Diverse Ties

Multiple Hybridity in the Politics of Inclusion and Difference in U.S. Biomedical Research

Steven Epstein

Since the mid-1980s, an eclectic assortment of reformers in the United States has argued that expert knowledge about human health is dangerously flawed—and health research practices are fundamentally unjust—because of inadequate representation of women, racial and ethnic minorities, children, the elderly, and other groups within clinical research populations. Under pressure from within and without, federal agencies of the U.S. Department of Health and Human Services (DHHS) have ratified a new consensus that biomedical research must be routinely sensitive to human differences, especially those related to sex and gender, race and ethnicity, and age.[1] Academic researchers receiving federal funds, and pharmaceutical manufacturers hoping to win regulatory approval for their company's products, are now enjoined to include women, racial and ethnic minorities, children, and the elderly as research subjects in many forms of clinical research; measure whether research findings apply equally well to research subjects regardless of their categorical identities; and question the presumption that findings derived from the study of any single group, such as middle-aged white men, might be generalized to other groups.

This repudiation of so-called "one-size-fits-all medicine" in favor of group specificity is apparent not just in the realm of free-floating ideas. It is anchored to institutional changes—new policies, guidelines, laws, procedures, bureaucratic offices, and mechanisms of surveillance and enforcement—that are the products of collective action. New expectations are codified in a series of federal laws, policies, and guidelines issued between 1986 and the present that require or encourage research inclusiveness and the measurement of difference. The mandate is reflected, as well, in the establishment, from the early 1980s forward, of a series of offices within the federal health bureaucracy, including offices of women's health and offices of minority health. Versions of the inclusionary policies also have been adopted by the "institutional review boards" (IRBs), located at universities and hospitals across the United States—the committees that review the ethics of proposals to conduct research on human subjects. As a result, these policies affect not just those researchers seeking federal support or those companies seeking to market pharmaceuticals: they may apply, in some fashion or another, to nearly every researcher in the natural or social sciences performing research involving human beings.

In my book *Inclusion*, I analyze how this distinctive way of thinking about bodies, identities, and differences gained supporters, took institutional form as law and policy, and become converted into common sense, with various downstream consequences for doctors, patients, researchers, drug companies, and federal agencies (Epstein 2007a). My purpose in this essay is to further examine the characteristics of the "anti-standardization resistance movements" that rejected the idea that medical knowledge applies universally to a "standard human." I argue that the success of this effort, along with distinctive features of its engagement with biomedical and state institutions, can be understood through analysis of the multiple hybridity that characterized the reformers' work.

Specifically, the reform project was hybrid in its *formal composition* (consisting of numerous overlapping health movements); in its *social basis* (combining disease-specific activism with activism organized around social identities); in its *knowledge politics* (crossing the lines that supposedly divide laypeople from experts); in its *power politics* (encompassing ordinary people as well as elites, and biomedical outsiders as well as insiders); in its *social location* (crossing boundaries between civil society, market institutions, and the state); in its *tactics* (combining reformist and radical approaches); and in its *goals* (encompassing a variety of social change projects that overlapped only partially). While the hybrid character of the reform effort created a risk of internal conflict, I argue that it also created important opportunities for the successful framing of the political project.

I begin by sketching the history of this reform effort, with an emphasis on the path that led to initial successes on the part of reformers. I then analyze the nature of the political configuration that pressed for reform. In examining its hybridity, I draw connections to the work of other social movement scholars and science studies scholars, including Wolfson's (2001) analysis of "interpenetrated" movements, McCormick, Brown, and Zavestoski's (2003) depiction of "boundary movements," Frickel's (this volume) characterization of "boundary spanning" structures, Moore's (1999) analysis of social movement "mediators," and Callon's discussion of "hybrid forums" in science/society relations (Callon 2003; see also Callon and Rabeharisoa 2003). I conclude by suggesting the implications of this case for the study of health movements.[2]

The Path to Reform

Resistance to a reliance on a "standard human" in biomedicine,[3] and political pressure both for the inclusion of groups deemed underrepresented in biomedical research and for the measurement of differences across social groups, came from a diverse set of social actors who gradually came to voice a common set of complaints. Various groups, they argued, had been numerically underrepresented in clinical research and pharmaceutical drug development, and as a result, medical knowledge drew inappropriately from the study of adult white men.[4] Such tendencies were deemed problematic not only because of evidence of health disparities affecting groups such as racial and ethnic minorities, but also because of scientific evidence of relevant medical differences between men and women, between different racial and ethnic groups, and between people in different age categories. Thus reformers tied together social justice concerns about who merits biomedical attention with methodological concerns about how accurate knowledge is best attained (Epstein 2003a; 2007a: ch. 3).

While the constituencies encompassed by this political project were diverse, advocates of women's health played a special role in launching the reform wave.[5] The concern with women's health was the driving wedge for a number of important reasons. Of course, women as a class are simply the largest social category invoked in these debates, and any failure on the part of biomedicine to attend satisfactorily to more than half the U.S. population seems especially egregious. There is also a history of women's health activism in the United States going back well into the nineteenth century (Weisman 1998).

But in addition, feminist movements of the 1970s and 1980s helped create new possibilities for social change in this arena. Indeed, different political "lines" within feminism had different effects, all contributing, directly or indirectly, to the concern with research on women's health.[6] On the more left-leaning end of the movement, radical feminists and socialist feminists had promoted a thoroughgoing critique of patriarchal practices and assumptions. Activists within the feminist women's health movement had adapted this critique to address sexism within the medical profession and the health-care industry specifically.[7] The legacy of the feminist women's health movement was a deep skepticism toward the mainstream medical profession and a critique of many of its characteristic practices. These sensibilities were important not only for their direct impact on women who grew to care about the politics of biomedical research, but also because they were absorbed by many activists who became involved in organizing around HIV/AIDS or breast cancer, and whose concern with these medical conditions led them to focus on research politics and practices.

On the more moderate end of the broader women's movement, liberal feminists had pushed for the mainstreaming of women within all branches of U.S. society, with results that are consequential for the developments I describe here: because of the relative successes of this project of mainstreaming, women—at least in limited numbers—had risen into positions of prominence in government, the medical profession, and the world of scientific research.[8] As Cynthia Pearson, longtime women's health activist and director of the National Women's Health Network, observed in reference to reformers within the establishment, "this was the first generation of women who had been young adults at the time of women's liberation" (interview with Pearson). And some of these women, influenced by feminist ideals, have been especially inclined to use their positions of influence to press for reforms of biomedicine.

Once women put forward their critiques, they opened up a space of possibility that others could occupy. Racial and ethnic minorities immediately followed with arguments that they, too, were underserved by modern medicine and underrepresented in study populations. These advocates drew strength from traditions of health activism within those minority communities as well as from advocacy organizations within the women's health movement that represented the interests of women of color. In addition, here as well, the recent successes of the challenging group in gaining entry into the medical profession made a difference, as did their political organization. In the case of African American physicians, for example, their representative organization, the National Medical Association, had grown from five thousand members in 1969 to twenty-two thousand members in 1977 (Watson 1999: 154).

Advocates on behalf of children and the elderly (particularly including pediatricians and geriatricians) also joined in with similar claims soon thereafter. This sort of historical sequence—in which a common set of political demands is adopted by a series of challengers in turn—is a familiar pattern that sociologists have studied in other political contexts, such as the passage of antidiscrimination policies and hate-crime legislation (Jenness 1995; Katzenstein and Reppy 1999; Jenness and Grattet 2001; Skrentny 2002). However, all these groups faced the common problem of how to bring about biomedical change. "Biomedicine" encompasses a highly diverse set of institutions spread around the country and around the world, and reformers concerned about the politics of inclusion needed a more precise target—at least initially—if they were going to be effective. The sensible choice proved to be the U.S. federal government—specifically, the DHHS, especially the wing of it called the Public Health Service (PHS), which includes such agencies as the National Institutes of Health (NIH), the Food and Drug Administration (FDA), and the Centers for Disease Control and Prevention (CDC). Focusing on the state made sense because of the control it exerts over medical research. At the same time, as Moore (1999: 97–118) has emphasized more generally, state agencies make attractive targets because they lie within the sphere of influence of activists and politicians—more so than research centers, pharmaceutical companies, or other biomedical institutions.

Furthermore, some of the advocates of change were positioned *within* the state as DHHS employees and therefore were able to press for reform from the inside. In the 1980s, questions relating to group differences and health disparities began to surface within several DHHS agencies. The National Institute of Mental Health was perhaps the first agency to create, in 1983, a specific office devoted to underserved groups—or "special populations," as they came to be termed (Watanabe 1995). Delores Parron, the director of this office, has described special populations as "all those groups who were de facto treated as second class citizens." With some justification, Parron refers to that office as the "mother cell" that helped to inspire the creation of many of the offices for underserved groups that emerged subsequently within the DHHS (interview with Parron).

In the mid-1980s, the DHHS responded to public scrutiny and internal pressure by creating task forces to study its efforts in aiding specific communities. Both DHHS Secretary Margaret Heckler's Task Force on Black and Minority Health and the Public Health Service Task Force on Women's Health Issues, created by Assistant Secretary for Health Edward Brandt, issued reports in 1985 (Heckler 1985; Public Health Service Task Force on Women's Health Issues 1985). As Auerbach and Figert have noted in their account of the politics of women's health research in the 1980s and early 1990s, such documents had considerable strategic benefit: They "provided the 'proof'—in the form of a legitimate scientific report—that ... activists, scientists, and members of Congress needed in order to push for further reform" (Auerbach and

Figert 1995: 117). In 1986, in response to the Task Force on Women's Health Issues, the NIH, along with the Alcohol, Drug Abuse, and Mental Health Administration, issued guidelines that, for the first time, recommended the inclusion of women in research studies funded by the agencies. The two agencies extended the emphasis on inclusion the following year by issuing parallel guidelines urging the inclusion of racial and ethnic minorities. Importantly, however, these guidelines stopped short of actually *requiring* anyone to do anything, and they had no specific enforcement mechanism.

Over the next few years, a growing number of prominent women sought to bring attention to the problem of underrepresentation as well as the broader question of women's health. Women scientists such as Florence Haseltine, the director of the Center for Population Research at the National Institute of Child Health and Human Development (one of the NIH institutes), worked behind the scenes to call attention to the low profile of women's health issues at the agency. Influenced by the example of the "AIDS lobby" and breast cancer advocacy groups, Haseltine, in her words, "began to work with women who knew how to affect legislation" (Haseltine and Jacobson 1997: xiv). As a federal employee, Haseltine was forbidden from lobbying Congress, but she encouraged a lobbying group called Bass and Howes that specialized in women's issues to found a new, Washington, D.C.-based, advocacy group eventually called the Society for Women's Health Research (SWHR; interview with Haseltine). Emblematic of a new wave of women's health advocacy—more professionalized than the women's health movement of the 1970s, more focused on research issues, less critical of pharmaceutical companies, and willing to sidestep divisive issues such as abortion—SWHR explicitly took up the cause of inclusion of women in clinical research as its priority issue. The group worked to raise the issue with female legislators and others who might be sympathetic (interview with Marie Bass; "Women's Health Research" 1991; Weisman 1998: 81).

At the same time, the broad issue of women's health became a galvanizing one for women in Congress, even as the topic of health reform edged toward the top of the policy agenda in Washington (Weisman 1998, 2000). Women in Congress, especially Rep. Patricia Schroeder and Rep. Olympia Snowe, co-chairs of the Congressional Caucus for Women's Issues, seized upon the issue of inclusion as a means to bring broader attention to women's health needs. "Every time you picked up the paper, there was something," recalled Schroeder, a Democrat from Colorado, thinking of the news reports in the 1980s that trumpeted the findings of medical researchers conducting clinical studies—reports about "men eating fish, men riding bikes, men drinking coffee, men taking aspirin. And we were just wondering whether 'men' was an all- encompassing word, or whether it was truly just men" (interview with Schoeder). Schroeder had become acquainted with Florence Haseltine at the NIH, and Haseltine took the opportunity to cart her slide projector to meetings with the Caucus, teaching them the basics about the "structure and function" of the NIH (interview with Haseltine).

Schroeder, along with Snowe (a Republican from Maine), took their concerns about women's health to Henry Waxman, chair of the Health and Environment Subcommittee in the House of Representatives. Ruth Katz, who served as counsel to the subcommittee, working along with Leslie Primmer, a staff member for the

Caucus, then devised a "hook" to draw Congressional attention to the broader issue of women's health. As Katz recalled, "I said, 'I wonder if they have any rules about making sure that women are included in clinical trials?'" Upon discovering that, indeed, NIH had already implemented a policy encouraging inclusion of women and minorities in 1986, Katz proposed: "Why don't we get GAO [the General Accounting Office, Congress's own investigative agency] to take a look at the simple question of to what extent NIH is following its own rules?" (interview with Katz). Thus the focusing of congressional attention on inclusion policies—a choice that would prove consequential—came about, in some measure, as a result of a purely strategic decision about how best to attract public attention to the broader issue of women's health.

The Caucus convinced Waxman to authorize the GAO study, and the results of that investigation only confirmed the suspicions of Katz and the Caucus members—indeed, as Primmer put it, the GAO's report was "the spark that ignited the explosion of legislative action around women's health" (Primmer 1997: 303). The investigators found that the 1986 policy on inclusion had been poorly communicated even within NIH and had been applied inconsistently; moreover, "NIH has no way to measure the policy's impact on the research it funds" (Nadel 1990: 1, 5). At the June 1990 House subcommittee meeting at which the GAO report was unveiled, Schroeder declared bluntly: "American women have been put at risk" (Kolata 1990: C6).

In communicating with the media and the public, Caucus members pointed to the NIH-funded Baltimore Longitudinal Study of Aging: Its final report, based on the study of more than 1,000 men and no women, was entitled "Normal Human Aging." Another prominent, all-male study, the Multiple Risk Factor Intervention Trial examining cardiovascular disease, seemed even by its acronym—MR FIT—to suggest which half of humanity was deemed worthy of scientific attention. Other studies caught the attention of the GAO simply because of the complete absence of women in research on topics of broad public health significance. A chief culprit was the NIH-funded Physician's Health Study, begun in 1981, which had investigated the role of aspirin use in preventing heart attacks: the study had enrolled twenty-two thousand male doctors. "[NIH] officials told us women were not included in the study, because to do so would have increased the cost," commented Mark Nadel, who presented the GAO's findings: "However, we now have the dilemma of not knowing whether this preventive strategy would help women, harm them, or have no effect" (Nadel 1990: 2). Olympia Snowe, whose mother had died of breast cancer, also described for reporters a federally funded study on the relation between obesity and cancer of the breast and uterus; the pilot study had used only men. "Somehow I find it hard to imagine that the male-dominated medical community would tolerate a study of prostate cancer that used only women as research subjects," Snowe commented (Jaschik 1990: A27).

The Caucus then began pressing for legislation that would force the NIH to change its ways. Fortuitously, the NIH budget was up for reauthorization, and as Caucus staff member Primmer observed, "the need to reauthorize NIH in 1990 proved a prime opportunity to address the issue of research on women's health. In the jargon of Capitol Hill, it is known as 'having a vehicle,' and the NIH reauthorization bill provided the congresswomen with the vehicle they needed to move their legislation"

(Primmer 1997: 305). Using alternative terminology drawn from political science, Weisman noted that the need for reauthorization opened up a "policy window" for consideration of women's health issues at the agency (Weisman 2000: 215).

Congressional staff drafted a new section to be in included in the NIH Revitalization Act which obligated the NIH to ensure that women were included as subjects in NIH-funded research—transforming the NIH's existing inclusion policy from a recommendation into a requirement and giving it the force of law. As legislators began building support for these additions to the NIH Revitalization Act, African American members of Congress called for a further extension of the legislative mandate. The Congressional Black Caucus was somewhat less focused on health issues than the Congressional Caucus for Women's Issues—for example, they did not have a staff member specifically working on the topic. However, the Black Caucus had for some time kept an eye on any legislation concerning health through the activities of its "health brain trust," an advisory group of health professionals established by Rep. Louis Stokes (interview with Stokes; Cozzens and Solomon 1994). Once members of the Black Caucus expressed interest in the new NIH initiative, members of the Congressional Caucus for Women's Issues were receptive: As Schroeder recalled, "NIH actually collects from every taxpayer equally," so "when they put these studies together, they ought to be looking at what America looks like" (interview with Schroeder). Consequently, the phrase "and minorities" was added to the wording about inclusion of women in research. After many twists and turns in the story (see Epstein 2007a: ch. 4), the NIH Revitalization was signed into law by President Bill Clinton on June 10, 1993, with members of the Congressional Caucus for Women's Issues standing at his side.

As the distributor of significant amounts of taxpayers' money, the NIH bore the brunt of congressional scrutiny with regard to inclusion. By contrast, less pressure was placed on the FDA initially by reformers, both because that agency was not funding research with tax dollars, and because many politicians had motivations that cut the other way: committed to a pro-business, deregulatory agenda, they believed that the FDA already was placing too many roadblocks in the way of drug approvals, and that the last thing needed was additional bureaucracy (Baird 1999: 562). However, during the early 1990s, the FDA increasingly became a target as well. A central concern of women's health advocates was a 1977 FDA guideline that formally excluded women "of childbearing potential" from many drug trials, whether they were pregnant or not, or had any intention of becoming so, out of concern that an experimental drug might bring harm to a fetus (as, for example, the drug thalidomide had done, especially to Europeans). This exclusion of "pregnant, pregnable, and once-pregnable people (a.k.a women)"—to cite Vanessa Merton's (1993) phrasing in the title of an article critical of the FDA guideline—had clear implications for the testing of new medications.

Like the NIH, the FDA had been moving to address issues of inclusion and difference in the late 1980s and early 1990s (interview with Merkatz; interview with Temple; interview with Toigo and Klein). In 1988 the agency had requested that drug manufacturers provide analyses of subpopulation differences (by gender, age, and race/ethnicity) in new drug applications, and in 1989 the agency had called for the inclusion of elderly patients in clinical trials leading to drug approvals. However, the agency had shown little inclination to police these recommendations. Most importantly, the 1977 guideline restricting the participation of women of childbearing potential as research subjects was still on the books. Thus when Congress commissioned another GAO study in 1992, which surveyed all manufacturers of drugs that had been approved by the agency in recent years, investigators concluded that "for more than 60 percent of the drugs, the representation of women in the test population was less than the representation of women in the population with the corresponding disease." Even when women were included, drug companies typically were not analyzing the findings from clinical trials "to determine if women's responses to a drug differed from those of men." Nor were all manufacturers equally scrupulous about testing whether their products interacted with female hormones, including the hormones found in oral contraceptives (Nadel 1992: 1–3). In light of these findings, members of Congress considered taking legislative action to change FDA policies and began drafting legislation—though in this case they lacked the "hook" that was provided them, in the case of the NIH, by the fact that the agency was up for reauthorization (interview with Wood).

The Pharmaceutical Manufacturers Association took exception to congressional claims and commented instead on the "myth of too-few-women in clinical trials" ("FDA Debunks" 1992: 2–3). But, gradually, some pharmaceutical companies were moderating their positions with regard to studying women—indeed, some sensed it might be profitable to do so. By 1993 one female executive at Merck Research Laboratories had observed an "increasing interest and sensitivity within the pharmaceutical industry" to studying women and noted that several companies recently had established female health-care research departments (Goldmann 1993: 174). Companies interested in positioning themselves in the vanguard of women's health research often were sympathetic to reformers; for example, many of them became dues-paying members of the Corporate Advisory Council of the SWHR.

Meanwhile, the 1977 guideline restricting the participation of women in research continued to spark opposition from health activists. In June 1990, just days after Schroeder and Snowe held their press conference to announce the GAO study on inclusion of women in NIH studies, more than five hundred protesters blocked the streets outside the international AIDS conference being held in San Francisco, protesting the inadequate inclusion of women in AIDS drug trials (DelVecchio 1990: A11). Inside the convention center, women sprang to the stage to dramatize how researchers' interest in women with HIV seemed to extend solely to the question of how to prevent transmission of the virus to women's fetuses. "Women with AIDS can't wait till later," the protesters chanted: "We are not your incubators" (author's field notes, International AIDS Conference, San Francisco, CA, 23 June 1990).

Activists complained that when women did seek entry into many AIDS trials, they faced extraordinary obstacles. Terry McGovern, director of the HIV Law Project, a New York City–based advocacy group, described the not-atypical case of a homeless woman who tried to enroll in a clinical trial in New Jersey in 1991 for an antiviral drug she saw as her last chance for survival. The woman was told she would be eligible only if she obtained an IUD, but because of her history of AIDS-related gynecological problems, "there was no way that the doctor was going to give her an IUD." Noting that sex was "the last thing [she] was even thinking about" given her state of health, the woman showed up at McGovern's office in a rage (interview with McGovern). Some women with AIDS charged that even after they had offered to undergo sterilization, they still were told they would be unable to join the clinical trials for drugs they considered promising (Auer 1990).

In 1992, the HIV Law Project, in conjunction with a number of other advocacy groups, filed a "citizen petition" demanding that the FDA rescind its exclusionary guideline. In restricting women's participation in research, the petitioners argued, the FDA "foster[ed] and, indeed, actively encourage[d] unconstitutional gender-based discrimination" (McGovern, Davis, and Gomez 1992: 15). Significantly, the U.S. Supreme Court recently had ruled in another case where the goal of protecting women and their fetuses from harm seemed to consign women to second-class citizenship. In its 1991 verdict in *International Union, UAW v. Johnson Controls*, the court maintained that corporations could not use the risk of birth defects as justification for keeping women out of jobs they desired. The HIV Law Project's petition argued that the issue of women's participation in research was "analytically similar" to that of women's employment (McGovern, Davis, and Gomez 1992: 25).

With the citizen petition pending and the eyes of Congress upon them, it behooved the FDA to take action. Moreover, pressure for change was also bubbling up through the ranks of the agency itself, and it acquired support from FDA Commissioner David Kessler, who was appointed to head the agency in 1990 (interview with Merkatz; interview with Toigo and Klein). Reversing the 1977 restriction on women's participation, the FDA issued new guidelines in 1993 that permitted the inclusion of women even in the early phases of drug testing, provided that female subjects used birth control. Furthermore, the agency called upon drug companies to submit data on the effects of new drugs in both men and women (Food and Drug Administration 1993). In promoting the changes, agency insiders stressed the importance of "sex-specific differences" in the body's absorption of, or response to, medications.

Thus by 1993, with the passage of the NIH Revitalization Act and the replacement of the FDA's exclusionary guideline, reformers (located both outside and inside government agencies) had won two significant and unprecedented victories. Elsewhere I describe two important sets of developments that followed. First, significant opposition to these reform efforts was mounted by some clinical researchers, biostatisticians, and conservative politicians. Federal health officials within DHHS agencies then played a key role in resolving controversy between reformers and opponents through the elaboration of guidelines that spoke to concerns raised on both sides (Epstein 2007a: ch. 5). Second, the reform effort was "thickened" through the passage or adoption of a whole series of additional laws, guidelines, and policies that mandated or encouraged the inclusion of various groups and the measurement of differences across them. These included, for example, an NIH policy on inclusion of children in research, an FDA policy on geriatric labeling, and federal legislation granting pharmaceutical companies an extension on their patent protection if they went back to previously approved drugs and conducted clinical trials in children (Epstein 2007a: ch. 6). The reform effort was further strengthened by the creation of a series of offices within the DHHS and its component agencies, including offices of women's health and minority health (Epstein 2007a: ch. 6).

I have called the overall set of changes in research policies, ideologies, and practices, and the accompanying creation of bureaucratic offices, procedures, and monitoring systems, the "inclusion-and-difference paradigm" (Epstein 2006), and I have argued that this "biopolitical paradigm" constitutes a distinctive way of knowing and managing human populations on the part of both medical institutions and the state (Epstein 2007a). In short, activism resulted ultimately in a relatively successful process of institutionalization of organizational change (Zald, Morrill, and Rao 2005).[9] Here reformers played a "double-edged role" in which "they de-institutionalize[d] existing beliefs, norms, and values embodied in extant forms, and establish[ed] new forms that instantiate[d] new beliefs, norms, and values" (Rao, Morrill, and Zald 2000: 238).

The Politics of Hybridity

From the preceding narrative, it should be apparent that the politics of reform was neither a simple project nor a unified one. No one precisely set out to create a set of policies and offices regulating the inclusion in biomedical research of a diverse set of social groups. Instead, many people's strategic actions in pursuit of various individual reforms culminated in the emergence of this general approach to the problem of difference in biomedicine. No organization or leader took up the banner of biomedical inclusion on behalf of all those who ended up pursuing it, nor did everyone get together under one organizational "big tent." Representatives of the various groups covered under the umbrella of the inclusion-and-difference paradigm mostly went about their own business, sometimes borrowing one another's rhetoric or seizing common political opportunities, sometimes building on one another's successes. As I have suggested, reformers comprised a mostly "tacit" political configuration, one marked less by direct and sustained cooperation than by a certain unity of purpose that is observable mainly in hindsight: to call for increased attention by researchers to specific groups in society, and to warn against extrapolating onto those groups medical findings derived from the study of others.

How do we characterize this eclectic and tacit political configuration? It is useful to examine the multiple ways in which it might be considered to be *hybrid*:

Formal composition: First, the reform wave was propelled not by a singular or unified "Movement" but by numerous overlapping health movements. These included the women's health movement, the AIDS activist movement, the breast cancer advocacy movement, and movements promoting the health of racial and ethnic minorities. Along the way, representatives of different social interests—women, racial and ethnic minorities, children, the elderly, and so on—adopted similar strategic goals and social critiques. This is by no means unprecedented. As Swidler has observed, "many movements may invent simultaneously what seem to be common cultural frames (like the many rights movements of the 1960s or the identity movements of the 1980s)." While these kinds of convergences may reflect a "cultural contagion," they also may be "common responses to the same institutional constraints and opportunities" (Swidler 1995: 39; see also DiMaggio and Powell 1983). In other cases, however, what matters most in the creation of similar outcomes is the establishment of precedent. Once a critique is mounted and an organizational solution is engineered to address it, the path is cleared for other challengers to adopt similar analyses and call for the extension of that same solution to their own predicaments (Meyer and Whittier 1994; Jenness 1995; McAdam 1995; Katzenstein and Reppy 1999; Jenness and Grattet 2001; Skrentny 2002). In practice, the consolidation of the inclusion-and-difference paradigm has depended on both of these general processes by which similarities are forged. For example, while advocates fought more or less simultaneously for policies promoting inclusion of women and racial and ethnic minorities, the policies on behalf of children mostly followed afterward, and advocates for them gained strategic advantage by invoking the precedent that was in place.

Social basis: A different sense in which the reform movement was hybrid was in its combination of two sorts of health activism. On one hand, some of the participants were "disease constituencies"—that is, they reflected the disease-specific, "squeaky-wheel-gets-the-grease" kind of health mobilization that is perhaps especially well entrenched in the United States. In the traditional incarnation of these politics, sufferers of a disease form a national association to represent their interests, lobby sympathetic members of Congress (ideally, ones who have the disease themselves or who have a family member with the disease), and, before long, a new institute is funded within the NIH, focusing on that specific disease (Strickland 1972). In the more recent, radical variant of these politics, an activist group, such as ACT UP or one of those inspired by it, engages in highly visible and confrontational direct action protest until Congress agrees to increase NIH funding to study that disease (Epstein 1996; Anglin 1997; Kaufert 1998; Weisman 2000).

On the other hand, other key participants in the reform movement were what Brown and coauthors have called *constituency-based health movements* that focus on the health agendas of large, socially visible groups, such as those defined by gender, race, ethnicity, or sexuality (Brown et al. 2004: 52–53). Reflecting the general visibility in the United States of so-called identity politics, these are increasingly important players on the health movement scene in the United States; they press not only for changes in research practices but also for access to care, culturally sensitive care, and many other goals. Often, disease-based health movements and constituency-based health movements are depicted as alternative kinds of political formations.[10] However, in this case, not only were the two sorts of movements intertwined, but they acquired strength from complex historical feedback loops. For example, the disease-based groups of the 1980s, such as AIDS and breast cancer activists, drew inspiration and tactics from the feminist women's health movement of the 1970s (a constituency-based group), but in turn provided lessons that were picked up by the new women's health research advocates of the 1990s (another constituency-based group).

Knowledge politics: The reform effort was hybrid not just in terms of the diverse social interests that were represented within it, but also in the way that its composition traversed the boundaries between laypeople and experts. Activists without formal training in the biomedical sciences were joined by physicians and researchers who were dismayed by what they saw as biomedical business as usual. Controversy thus unfolded in the sort of space that Callon (2003: 59) has called a "hybrid forum," one in which "groups and the spokesperson who claim to represent them are heterogeneous—consisting of experts, politicians, technicians and lay people who consider themselves to be concerned" about a given issue.

Lay/expert hybrids are increasingly common in the domain of health movements and patient group activism (S. Epstein 2001, 2007b), and McCormick, Brown, and Zavestoski have proposed the term "boundary movements" to describe such blur-rings (McCormick, Brown, and Zavestoski 2003). Similarly, Frickel (this volume) uses the concept of "boundary spanning" to describe how activists and experts often become linked through ties that may cross institutions, disciplines, and cultures. Within the particular boundary-spanning movement that I describe here, notions of "race," "sex," and other forms of human difference were deployed by different actors in overlapping ways that bridged social divides. Such terms constituted "boundary objects," as Star and Griesemer have described them: objects "which are both plastic enough to adapt to local needs and the constraints of the several parties employing them, yet robust enough to maintain a common identity across sites" (Star and Griesemer 1989: 393).

Power politics: Similarly, the reform project was hybrid in terms of the political authority exercised by its various participants: it encompassed ordinary people as well as elites, and biomedical outsiders as well as insiders. Thus it is inadequate to attribute social change in this case simply to a collection of social movements, if by that we mean the "usual suspects" of groups that are disenfranchised and that mount their opposition from "outside" the mainstream political process. In fact, many of those who participated would have to be counted among the elites of U.S. society. The reform wave was pushed forward by supporters from within DHHS agencies, sympa-thetic physicians and scientists, professional organizations (such as the American Academy of Pediatrics and the National Medical Association), politicians (including members of the Congressional Caucus for Women's Issues and the Congressional Black Caucus), and specialized advocacy groups (such as the Society for Women's Health Research), and it received support from some pharmaceutical companies. Therefore it would be mistaken to understand the new biomedical policies and empha-ses as the product solely of a grassroots movement of the dispossessed.

Indeed, thinking about the composition of this hybrid political configuration should cause us to reflect critically on some of the typical assumptions about how social movements bring about change. This is not a simple story of how "outsiders" to biomedicine forced that institution to change its ways. Outsiders certainly were important to the story, but they acted in concert with well-placed members of the biomedical establishment to promote reform.

Recently, several analysts of social movements have pointed to an array of cases that suggest that this is by no means unusual—that insiders (or what Moore has termed "mediators") frequently prove central to the political processes by which institutions become forced to change (Moore 1999: 104; see also Kellogg, this vol-ume; Polletta 2004: 162–63). Scholars have provided a number of examples of stud-ies showing the significance of insiders or mediators, including my own work on AIDS activism and the role of gay physicians (Epstein 1996); Katzenstein's (1998) analysis of priests in the Catholic Church; Taylor's (1996) discussion of women doc-tors and nurses who became involved in struggles around postpartum depression; and Binder's (2002) analysis of educators who pressed for Afrocentric curricula.

Social location: In blending the efforts of experts and laypeople, and elites and nonelites, the reform effort also crossed boundaries between civil society, market institutions, and the state. Thus, the case demonstrates what Goldstone (2003: 2) has called the "fuzzy and permeable boundary between institutionalized and non-institutionalized politics," and it underscores the risk, described by Skrentny (2002: 7), "[of assuming that] social movements are discrete entities that exist *outside* of government" (see also Jenness 1999; Meyer, Jenness, and Ingram 2005).

As Wolfson noted in his analysis of a comparable case, the tobacco control movement, too often analysts of social movements tend to see the state simply as a movement's "target," "sponsor," or "facilitator," or as the provider or denier of "opportunities" for activism. But in many cases, "fractions of the state are often allied with the movement in efforts to change the policies of other fractions." In such cases—for which he has proposed the label "interpenetration"—"it is hard to know where the movement ends and the state begins" (Wolfson 2001: 7, 144–45). Though not using the term, analysts have revealed state/movement interpenetration to be a defining characteristic of a number of national health-advocacy groups in the United States in their formative relationship with specific branches of the National Institutes of Health (Fox 1989; Talley 2004: 58). A recent example is the intimate relationship between the Genetic Alliance (a super-group of genetic support groups) and the NIH's Office of Rare Diseases, established in 1993 (Rayna Rapp, personal communication).

Tactics: Yet another marker of the diversity of the movement was its encompassing of both reformist and radical approaches to social, political, and biomedical change. Styles of activism and organizing varied considerably—between, say, the AIDS activist who, at a noisy protest outside the FDA in 1988, held up a mock tombstone reading, "As a person of color I was exempt from drug trials" (Bull 1988: 3); and NIH scientist Florence Haseltine's description of how she began working with Pat Schroeder on the inclusion issue:

> And then one day I was [returning home from] a meeting, and I saw Pat Schroeder sitting in first class. And fortunately I had upgraded. So I just sat next to her. . . . And Pat and I talked, and she said, "how many gynecologists are there [working at the NIH]?" And I said, there are three permanent ones . . . and there are 39 veterinarians. And she was aligned [with us] from then on. (Interview with Haseltine)

Literally but also metaphorically, some advocates rode in "first class" while others traveled in "economy." However, since no members of this loose collection were obliged to agree on tactics, these differences in social location proved a form of strength.

Goals: Finally, the hybridity of the reform effort is evident in the wide assortment of goals pursued by specific contributors. For example, female members of Congress who promoted the greater representation of women in medical research presented their demands under the rubric of a wide-ranging "Women's Health Equity Act" which, among other things, called for the creation of a research center on infertility and Medicare coverage for screening mammography (Primmer 1997: 307–9). However, the common characteristic that united the individuals and groups that constituted the tacit political configuration was a concern with research underrepresentation and the biomedical scrutiny of differences. Out of this interest, which cut across individuals and organizations, the policies and practices that I call the inclusion-and-difference paradigm gradually fell into place.

Conclusion

It is rarely an easy matter to explain why a social movement succeeds in achieving its goals (or even how "success" should be defined; Giugni, McAdam, and Tilly 1999). In the case I describe, a hybrid reform project has significantly affected U.S. society, politics, and culture, as well as its biomedical institutions.[11] Certainly some of the successes of reformers in raising their concerns can be attributed to broader circumstances. By the 1980s, in the wake of several decades of struggles in the United States for equality and civil rights by women, racial minorities, and others, and in a climate where commitment to some notion of multiculturalism was taken for granted by at least some sectors of the public, political demands couched in the language of equity and social justice on behalf of important groups in U.S. society were likely to attract attention. Still, there was no guarantee that such demands would be seen as "making sense" in the specific domains of medical research and pharmaceutical drug development.

Therefore, it is important to attend to the particular characteristics of the reform project in order to fully understand their successes in framing the debate and institutionalizing their demands. Elsewhere I point to a number of factors that help explain the power of reformers to achieve their goals (including what I call their "multirepresentational politics" and their facility with "categorical alignment work" [Epstein 2007a: 88–93]). But in addition, I would argue that the power of this political configuration was enhanced by its hybrid character and its traversing of boundaries. Because membership spilled across the normally recognized divides between state and society, experts and the laity, science and politics, "insiders" and "outsiders," and the powerful and the disenfranchised, opponents of a reliance on a biomedical standard human were well positioned to address multiple constituencies and speak credibly and authoritatively in diverse public and private arenas. To be sure, a hybrid composition might have been a source of tension and internal division, but because there was no formal coalition that required explicit agreement on a program or platform, such dissent did not really arise as a problem (Ghaziani 2008). Instead, these advocates of social change benefited from the "strength of diverse ties,"[12] through which they could position themselves as collectively representing the better part of the U.S. population.

Many commentators have noted the flourishing of lay expertise in the domain of health in recent years, including the rise of patient groups organized in relation to many conditions, illness categories, and social constituencies (for a review see Epstein 2007b). Scholars also have observed the tendency toward "marriages, mergers, and traffic among these organizations" in recent years (Rapp, Heath, and Taussig. 2001: 392) as well as the diffusion of "shared values and norms across condition areas" and the emergence of a common discourse across groups (Allsop, Jones, and Bagott 2004: 745). Such developments may well herald the increasing salience of hybridity, as I have described it, within the landscape of health politics—at least in the United States. Elsewhere, by contrast, a logic of claims-making organized around multiple, particular identities may find little political traction. For example, medical research policies such as those encompassed within the inclusion-and-difference paradigm would be nearly inconceivable in a country such as France, given the reigning ideology of "republican citizenship"; indeed, the French government does not collect data on race or ethnicity and has proclaimed (remarkably) that "France is a country in which there are no minorities" (DeZwart 2005: 138–39). Thus the whole strategy for the pursuit of equity and social justice that I described here, and that was especially facilitated by hybrid forms of political organization, itself presupposes particular histories of conceiving of social identities, group rights, and the relations between political actors and the state.

Even within the United States, it is difficult to say with precision exactly when hybridity of the sort I have described here is likely to emerge, or under what circumstances it will prove politically efficacious. However, my analysis suggests that, at present, hybridity may pose strategic advantages for health movements or other social movements that engage with scientific experts—at least when, as in the case described here, hybridity implies a loose coordination of efforts and frames among diverse actors, rather than a requirement for explicit agreement on political ideology and analysis. More specific claims about the efficacy of hybridity would require careful consideration of a range of examples drawn from the broader domain of health politics. Indeed, we would benefit from close comparative analysis of cases such as the one I have analyzed here—including comparison across cases within a single country as well as comparisons across national contexts. Through the logic of comparison, we can better understand how and whether hybridity emerges as a practical accomplishment, how hybrid political configurations hold themselves together over time, and what kinds of social, political, cultural, and medical changes their efforts help bring into being.

NOTES

This work was supported by an Investigator Award in Health Policy Research from the Robert Wood Johnson Foundation as well as by grant no. SRB-9710423 from the National Science Foundation's Ethics and Values Studies program. Any opinions, findings, and conclusions or recommendations expressed in this material are those of the author and do not necessarily reflect the views of funding agencies. I am grateful to Mayer Zald, Jane Banaszak-Holl, Sandra Levitsky, David Frankford, an anonymous reviewer, and the participants at the conference on "Social Movements and the Development of Health Institutions" for useful feedback on a previous draft.

1. The categorical terms used in this article are meant to represent the terms employed by the actors I studied, in all the ambiguity of everyday usage. On the history of the biomedical reliance on age, sex, and race categories, see also Hanson (1997). Additional categories also have been incorporated within the inclusion-and-difference paradigm to a lesser degree. For a discussion of attempts to obtain recognition of sexual orientation as an important variable in medical research, see Epstein (2003b).

2. Data for the larger project of which this article is a part were obtained in accordance with a strategy to juxtapose perceptions and trace actions across multiple "social worlds"

(Clarke 1990), including those of clinical researchers concerned with recruiting "underrepresented groups," pharmaceutical companies, federal health officials promoting the health of "special populations," politicians, and health advocacy organizations. Data have been obtained from seventy-two semi-structured, in-person interviews in and around Boston, New Haven, New York, Baltimore, Washington, Atlanta, Ann Arbor, Chicago, Denver, Boulder, San Francisco, Los Angeles, and San Diego. Those interviewed included past and present NIH, FDA, and DHHS officials; clinical researchers; pharmacology researchers; biostatisticians; medical-journal editors; drug-company scientists; women's health advocates and activists; bioethicists; members of Congress; congressional aides; lawyers; representatives of pharmaceutical-company trade associations; experts in public health; and social scientists. Additional primary data sources include documents and reports from the NIH, the FDA, the CDC, the DHHS, and the U.S. Congress; archival materials from health advocacy organizations; materials from pharmaceutical companies and their trade organizations; articles, letters, editorials, and news reports published in medical, scientific, and public-health journals; and articles, editorials, letters, and reports appearing in the mass media.

3. The material in this section of the chapter is drawn from Epstein (2007a). For a more general discussion of the "standard human," see Epstein (2009).

4. As I describe in Epstein (2007a: ch. 2), the claim that medical research previously had focused on adult white men to the exclusion of other groups was in fact an oversimplification of a complex history. Here my point is simply to identify the arguments and collective action frames put forward by reformers.

5. On the movement to include women as subjects in clinical research, see also DeBruin (1994); Johnson and Fee (1994); Rosser (1994); Auerbach and Figert (1995); Hamilton (1996); Narrigan et al. (1997); Primmer (1997); Eckman (1998); Weisman (1998); Baird (1999); Eckenwiler (1999); Schiebinger (1999: 14–15, 107–25); Weisman (2000); Corrigan (2002).

6. The following discussion borrows the accepted understandings of distinctions between radical feminism, socialist feminism, and liberal feminism in the 1970s and afterward (see, for example, Echols [1989]).

7. For introductions to the feminist women's health movement in the United States, see Ruzek (1978); Auerbach and Figert (1995); Avery (1996); Treichler, Cartwright, and Penley (1998); Weisman (1998); Clarke and Olesen (1999); Grayson (1999); Morgen (2002); Murphy (2004).

8. On the role of educated, middle-class women in recent health advocacy, see also Kaufert (1998: 303).

9. In speaking of relative success, I mean in relation to addressing activists' stated concerns. In Epstein (2007a: ch. 8), I take up the important issue of just how well these concerns were translated into substantive change. Elsewhere I also consider the multiple downstream *consequences* of the rise of the inclusion-and-difference paradigm, not all of which were intended by its proponents (Epstein 2003b, 2004, 2007a, 2008).

10. For a review of recent thinking on this issue, see Epstein (2007b).

11. Again my goal here is not to evaluate these effects, which I think are double-edged (see Epstein [2007a]).

12. My thanks to David Snow for suggesting this phrase—which is, of course, a play on the title of an influential article by Granovetter (1973)—as the title for my essay.

Interviews (Affiliations Were Those Held By the Person at the Time of the Interview)

Bass, Marie. Bass and Howes (lobbying agency). Interviewed in Washington, D.C., 12 April 1999.

Haseltine, Florence, M.D., Ph.D. Center for Population Research at the National Institute of Child Health and Human Development, NIH. Interviewed in Rockville, Md., 19 April 1999.

Katz, Ruth, J.D., M.PH. Yale University School of Medicine (formerly counsel to Health and Environment Subcommittee, U.S. House of Representatives). Interviewed in New Haven, Conn., 21 April 1999.

McGovern, Terry, J.D. HIV Law Project. Interviewed in New York, N.Y., 10 May 1998.

Merkatz, Ruth, Ph.D., RN. Pfizer (formerly with Office of Women's Health, FDA). Interviewed in New York, N.Y., 9 March 1998.

Parron, Delores. Deputy Assistant Secretary for Planning and Evaluation, Office of Program Assistance, DHHS. Interviewed in Washington, D.C., 8 August 2000.

Pearson, Cynthia. Executive Director, National Women's Health Network. Interviewed in Washington, D.C., 19 March 1998.

Schroeder, Patricia. Former U.S. Representative (D-Colorado). Interviewed in Washington, D.C., 18 March 1998.

Stokes, Louis. Former Member of U.S. Congress. Interviewed in Washington, D.C., 16 August 2000.

Temple, Robert J., M.D. Associate Director for Medical Policy, Center for Drug Evaluation and Research, FDA. Interviewed in Rockville, Md., 11 August 2000.

Toigo, Teresa, R. Ph.D, M.B.A. Office of Special Health Issues, FDA (and Richard Klein). Interviewed in Rockville, Md., 12 April 1999.

Wood, Susan, Ph.D. Associate Director for Policy, Office on Women's Health, DHHS. Interviewed in Washington, D.C., 13 April 1999.

SECTION II

THE REORIENTATION OF INSTITUTIONAL FIELDS

Every institution is embedded in an institutional field, the relatively organized set of organizations and practices and beliefs shaping the discourse and practice toward the core object and norms of the institution. When we first think about health-related institutions we are inclined to think about hospitals and doctors and nurses, medical schools, pharmaceutical companies, and so on. But each of these are part of the institutional field for some of the others. The Federal Drug Administration (FDA), an agency operated by the government, would also be part of the medical field. To the extent that we are concerned with the funding and practices of the FDA we are concerning ourselves with part of the field of health. We would be less inclined to think of behavior in the family to be part of the institutional field, but it is obvious that individual and family behavior has an impact on our health, and professional and state policy often focuses upon efforts to change such behavior. Similarly, agents of the state inspect agricultural products and regulate what is considered safe and unsafe in food production. They are part of the field of public health, which for some purposes can be treated as overlapping the field of health institutions, broadly conceived. It is important to note that social movements can be part of the field of health-related institutions, and also can be treated as institutional objects themselves. That is, they are shaped by expectations, norms, and practices of the participating actors and organizations, as well as other organizations in the society such as police, courts, educational organizations, professions, community groups, and other social movement actors that they engage with.

It is also important to note that fields need not be homogeneous; several different logics and orientations may exist. Indeed, the existence of movements aimed at changing practice is one index of contestation in the field.

Phil Brown and his collaborators have been major contributors to the study of health social movements. In "Field Analysis and Policy Ethnography" (chapter 7 this volume) they focus upon the most recent developments in their approach to them. First, they elaborate on how they intend to study institutional fields of health social movements. They usefully introduce a historical dimension to fields, emphasizing the lineage of where the health social movement comes from relative to other social movements and, we might add, other professional and organizational developments. For instance, the environmental justice movement develops out of both the environmental movement and the earlier civil rights movement. That legacy influences the expectations and beliefs of current participants. Similarly, the movement for breast cancer awareness has roots in the feminist movement. After showing how they intend to study fields they turn to a methodological development in their work, the writing of policy ethnographies. Brown's group has long had a focus upon action to achieve movement goals, as well as analysis of the movement per se. The policy ethnography helps them to be reflexive as they untangle the activities of movements, themselves as participants, and others in the development of policy. It also adds descriptive richness to the study of movement process and movement outcomes.

In chapter 8, Mark Wolfson and Maria Parries discuss the institutionalization of community action in public health. To say that some kind of activity is "institutionalized" means that it has become "routine," a relatively stable and fixed part of supported and required behavior. Here they mean that community action has become supported and mandated in the public health—funded programs of the U.S. government. Social movements have been deeply intertwined with the public health profession and state policy. Wolfson and Parries discuss the adoption, standardization, and dissemination of community action in its several forms (e.g., community organizing, community coalitions, and community-based participatory research). They are able to chart the dramatic increase in the funding of community action methods, using a database of federally funded biomedical research.

Where Wolfson and Parries examine the institutionalization of community action–related federal projects, Martin Kitchener presents in chapter 9 one of the first attempts to use social movement studies to extend institutional theory so that it can frame processes by which resource-poor actors initiate new structures within fields of healthcare organizations. Using insights from studies of countermovements, political opportunity structures and social processes, a series of propositions are derived and illustrated using three case studies of institutional change driven by health reform movements. The framework rests on the understanding that multiple belief systems (logics) within healthcare fields ensure that institutional arrangements will be challenged, sometimes by reform movements. Such efforts are supported by five political opportunity structures: organizational fields that are centralized and immature, an open policy context, a decentralized state, neighboring fields of reform activity, and journalistic standards of balanced reporting. Health reform movements are enabled by three factors: networked forms of leadership, the development of equivalent capacities to countermovements, and leaders framing an array of arguments. Finally, the framework suggests that successful reform processes are likely to be slow, highly contested, and result in the new structure being accommodated alongside aspects of the traditional arrangements.

In the final chapter in this section, Rene Anspach (chapter 10) examines how a social movement/countermovement focus illuminates the attempt by some members of the religious right to change the orientations and assumptions of mainstream bioethicists. The mainstream of bioethics had developed in the last half century. Although discussion of ethical issues in medicine date at least back to Hippocrates in the fourth century BCE, bioethics as a specialized academic topic, combining medical choices and analysis, and as an explicit part of hospital and general practice is a fairly recent development. Anspach shows how the conflict over whether Terry Schiavo should be taken off of life-support provided a window for the religious right to challenge the then-current standards of when someone's life could be terminated. They did it by using a variety of tactics including use of the media, court battles, and demonstrations—tactics used by many movements. But they also set up alternative curricula and founded institutes and used the discourse of bioethics. In turn, mainstream bioethicists developed tactics that mirrored those used by the religious right. In the end, the assumptions of an academic sub-discipline had been put in political play.

7

Field Analysis and Policy Ethnography in the Study of Health Social Movements

Phil Brown, Rachel Morello-Frosch, Stephen Zavestoski, Laura Senier, Rebecca Gasior Altman, Elizabeth Hoover, Sabrina McCormick, Brian Mayer, and Crystal Adams

Introduction

This chapter presents new analytical and methodological approaches to studying social movements. We develop two theoretical concepts, "field analysis" and "policy ethnography," and explore how each contributes to the study of health social movements. Field analysis is a qualitative approach through which social movements can be situated within multifaceted social and institutional spheres that include diverse strategic allies and coalition partners. The social and institutional spheres we consider include government, academic, scientific, as well as public and nonprofit civic organizations. Policy ethnography, which employs field analysis as one analytical tool, combines organizational and policy analysis with ethnographic observations and interviews, and has a policy goal in mind. In some cases, those carrying out policy ethnography are themselves acting in the policy realm. These methods move beyond simplified notions of researcher and subject, and acknowledge the contributions that researchers themselves may have on social movements and policy outcomes.

Before describing these methods in more detail, we first define health social movements and acknowledge how their unique features prompted methodological innovation. Health Social Movements challenge political power, professional authority, and personal and collective identity. For purposes of discussion, Health Social Movements can loosely be grouped into three categories, though we have found, too, that most movements blur these distinctions in interesting ways. *Health Access Movements* seek equitable access to health care and improved provision of health care services, such as movements seeking national health care reform. *Constituency-Based Health*

Movements concentrate on health inequalities based on race, ethnicity, gender, class and/or sexuality differences. The women's health movement is a prime example of a constituency-based movement. *Embodied Health Movements* address disease, disability, or illness experience by challenging science on etiology, diagnosis, treatment, and prevention, such as the breast cancer movement. By extension, the same categories could be used to think about health social movement organizations, or HSMOs, as well. Our starting point for this definition of health social movements draws from Della Porta and Diani's (1999) articulation of social movements as "informal networks based on shared beliefs and solidarity which mobilize around conflictual issues and deploy frequent and varying forms of protest."

For a decade, the Contested Illnesses Research Group (CIRG) centered at Brown University, whose members represent the disciplines of environmental and medical sociology, science studies, environmental health science, anthropology, and epidemiology, has focused on health social movements dealing with environmental health (for details on the CIRG's history, see Senier et al. 2006). Since the late 1990s, group members have met weekly to discuss field experiences, write collaboratively, and think broadly about our substantive topics of interest. The CIRG sought to address the dearth of knowledge regarding movements that address health, and to improve understanding of the multiple realms that play a role in policy change. Our first empirical cases were controversies over contested environmental illnesses: asthma, breast cancer, and Gulf War Illnesses (Brown et al. 2003; Mayer, Brown, and Linder 2002; McCormick, Brown, and Zavestoski 2003; Zavestoski et al. 2002). We then expanded our range to include coalitions with environmental health and justice activists, environmental health scientists, and social scientists. Later work examined scientific research and activism around chemicals in household air and dust, and in human bodies, where we studied human biomonitoring, the field of environmental health science that characterizes environmental pollutants in human tissue samples and blood, urine, or other bodily fluids.

We examine HSMs, much as any researcher might assess SMs, by looking first at antecedents and concurrent movements. To study a movement's antecedent and concurrent movements is to situate it within a complex web of other social actors and institutions. For example, we argue that we can better understand the manner in which activists in the environmental breast cancer movement engage with science by looking at how AIDS activists a decade earlier demanded greater participation in research decisions about the design of clinical trials (McCormick, Brown, and Zavestoski 2003). Another example can be found in how feminist recognition of male supremacy in the civil rights movement led to the second-wave women's movement (Evans 1979). This plotting of social movements is a strategy to examine a movement's self-awareness. Different groups or actors identify with certain people, leaders, and perspectives, so that when they need advice or historical lessons, they look at the experience of antecedents to learn how issues were framed, allies sought, strategies and tactics devised. In other cases, incongruencies between movement constituents may result due to differing assumptions, experiences, motivations, and knowledge. By addressing these characteristics, we can learn how movements develop, since a movement organization's own hindsight often provides inadequate data and memory.

We have also studied organizations and the broader disease and exposure issues that define their mission, as well as cases where social movements were involved in seeking research, compensation, and public policy. In all these cases, disease suffer-ers-turned-activists and their lay and professional allies challenged public and scien-tific understanding of diseases and conditions. These social movement groups offer a strong critique of contemporary science, medicine, and policy by emphasizing how ideological and political-economic factors shape medical research and treatment to systematically overlook the contribution of environmental (largely chemical) factors in disease etiology. Often the production of this new scientific knowledge was used as a form of "data judo" (Morello-Frosch et al. 2005) to reshape debates about the regulation of chemicals in the policy and regulatory arenas, and hence the policy focus became increasingly important in our research.

In contesting diseases and conditions, activists often seek to reshape or overturn a shared set of entrenched beliefs and practices about disease treatment and causation embedded within a network of institutions, including medicine, science, government, health charities/voluntaries, charitable organizations, and the media. We term this network the *dominant epidemiological paradigm* for a given disease. Activists chal-lenge the dominant epidemiological paradigm by working to shift lines of scientific inquiry and to refocus regulatory and policy attention on critical issues that had pre-viously been overlooked or ignored (Brown et al. 2001b). These HSMs challenge scientific and medical authority and professional dominance inherent in the domi-nant epidemiological paradigm. For example, scientists may be asked to weigh in on questions that are virtually impossible to answer scientifically (either because data do not exist or because studies required to answer the question at hand are not feasible). Many scientists, especially if they accept the dominant epidemiological paradigm, may frame political, moral, or ethical questions in scientific terms, in effect limiting participation of lay people. This scientization of contemporary issues delegitimizes questions that cannot be framed in scientific terms (Morello-Frosch et al. 2006). Health Social Movements may respond to these situations by marshaling resources to conduct their own research and produce their own scientific knowledge. In doing so, they democratize the production of scientific knowledge and then use that trans-formed science as the basis for demands for improved research on disease etiology, treatment, prevention, and stricter regulation (McCormick 2007).

Citizen-science alliances (CSAs) are the most central vehicle for this kind of col-laboration. Citizen-science alliances are lay-professional collaborations in which citizens and scientists work together to develop and examine research questions of mutual interest and importance. These citizen-science alliances both contribute to new knowledge as well as challenge, and sometimes change, scientific norms. Citizen-science alliances may be citizen-initiated, professionally initiated, or created through a joint-affinity model where lay and researcher interests are aligned. Community-based participatory research (CBPR) programs are the most inclusive type of CSA because this research model involves all affected parties and all poten-tial end-users of the research, including community-based organizations, public health practitioners, and local health and social services agencies. The most demo-cratic community-academic collaboration occurs when there is a grassroots move-ment, since this makes it more likely that community groups will initiate and/or play key roles in the scientific process, as opposed to simply participating as advisors. More comprehensive citizen involvement in research often occurs as the social problem becomes more public and the social movement gains strength and momentum. Citizen-science alliances are significant in HSMs because they are often the most successful approach toward integrating science and advocacy. At the same time, CSAs offer a way to improve the scientific world's understanding of activism and policy, and to boost the activist world's awareness of the need for scientific knowledge that can impact policy.

New Methodological Tools

We have developed two sets of methodological tools—one for examining our combined study of participation in these movements, and another for thinking about the significance of these research collaborations for the broader discipline of sociology. First, we have found policy ethnography useful because much of our work takes a community-based, participatory approach to working with communities and activists. For example, it is important to us that we translate technical and empirical findings into tools that support communities' efforts to promote environmental justice, worker health and safety, and challenge toxic contamination. Thus, for us, policy ethnography has drawn us, as researchers, into policy work, in addition to studying it. Second, we have sought to develop field analysis as both a tool for studying movements and for understanding the impact our research has on the field. In one key example, we have sought to link the environmental breast cancer and environmental justice movements, two historically distinct movements with parallel concerns about the role of chemical and industrial exposures in human health. Our research connects activist organizations that had not previously collaborated to conduct scientific research, and simultaneously led us to a broader notion of how multiple movements coexist and mutually alter a single field of action.

These experiences led us to develop further a multisited approach to ethnography (Marcus 1995), a model that allowed us to connect diverse sites of contestation and activism. In so doing, we addressed numerous limitations we found when using a more traditional ethnographic approach to studying social movements. By going beyond a traditional state-centered approach, we learned that activists needed to challenge a multiplicity of power structures, and we therefore had to expand the set of actors and institutions we examined. We also found that activists were increasingly grappling with science, so we had to extend our ethnography into the labs and field research settings of the scientists who were central to the movements being studied. Finally, our emphasis on the embodiment of symptoms, conditions, and diseases with either known or putative environmental causation led us to seek an integration of personal illness experience with broader social action.

Field Analysis

A social movement has a boundary far larger than we might expect, and it is a shifting boundary. Field analysis is an approach that situates social movements in their lineage from other movements, and in their multifaceted social and institutional worlds, which include diverse strategic allies and coalition partners who may have conflicting perspectives or ideologies. Our perspective on these boundaries is both conceptual and theoretical, and is tied to our methodological approach of policy ethnography, described in the next section. Field analysis stems in part from Raka Ray's (1999) "fields of action," Maren Klawiter's "cultures of action" (1999), Meyer and Whitter's (1994) "social movement spillover," and Clarke's (2005) "social worlds."

Our approach to field analysis also draws on field theory, which has been used in the social sciences to explain how relationships shape the behavior of social movement organizations and actors (Martin 2003). In this tradition, the analysis of fields maps the dynamic relationships between actors in a particular social space. This approach is perhaps best developed in the work of Bourdieu (1984), who uses the concept of "field" to understand how actors struggle within a shared space to appropriate power and capital in their efforts to monopolize authority. Bourdieu's "field" is a network of individuals and groups defined by the influence they have on one another. By understanding the whole network, one can determine how a particular actor might affect change or control future outcomes. For example, Bourdieu (1985) sees intellectual fields as matrixes of institutions, organizations, and markets in which actors compete for recognition for their ideas and work. Competition among actors in the field is thus not only a means of acquiring prestige within the field but also constitutes the field itself (Dezalay and Garth 1995). Field analysis thus lends itself not only to considerations of how competition and conflict constitute the field, but also how actors cooperate in shaping the field. This analytic approach also highlights the rules that govern relationships where various organizations, both inside and outside the movement, interact to produce a complex set of relationships, and how those rules and relationships change over time.

Field analysis is also important in explaining the actions of organizations involved in a particular field. DiMaggio and Powell (1983) extended Bourdieu's notion of field to organizational field, where groups assemble into an institutionalized arena of social life. Similarly, Scott and Meyer (1992) examine the development of sectors to see how a set of organizations interact to shape institutional norms. In the examination of social movements, Armstrong (2002) has explored how collective action creates new fields of political and cultural debate that define what strategies and tactics are available to actors within that field. Social scientists have used this approach in studying epistemic communities (Haas 1992; Knorr Cetina 1999) and transnational issue networks (Keck and Sikkink 1998); it has informed our own work on coalitions among diverse actors from the labor and environmental movements (Senier et al. 2007; Mayer, Brown, and Senier 2008). Focusing our attention on fields and relationships helps us understand how movements grow and interact as they compete for legitimacy in science and science policy and cooperate to attain mutually important goals.

Field analysis also helps social movement organizations, or SMOs, situate themselves within a broader movement. It is likely that any SMO has a story about the movement's history that may not reflect the complexity of its organizational origins. There will always be some disconnect between these organizational-level stories and how the SMs and SMOs really emerged. One reason is that as time passes, events occur that can lead actors to reconstruct history. As well, one SMO may simply not see the entirety of the field, and hence not understand the place of other SMOs in that movement. Also important is that SMO stories will be dependent on the place of an SMO within an SM, especially if that SMO differs from other organizations within the same movement, based on race, class, gender, or other key factors. Another complexity that field analysis can uncover is the evolution of themes, goals, concerns, and strategies of an SMO, which emerge and change over time. This continual change is also what allows new SMs and SMOs to emerge.

The diagram below illustrates how to apply a field analysis approach to understanding the origins and networks of a social movement field, in this case for the Patient Rights/Radical Psychology movement (figure 7.1). In the middle circle are the various groups and organizations that comprise a broad, multiorganizational movement, not all of whom might understand their linkages with each other. On the left are social movement influences, a variety of movements that impact the Patient Rights/ Radical Psychology movement, sometimes consciously and at other times indirectly. On the right are influences from the mental health system. There too, involved parties and organizations may not necessarily grasp their impact on that movement. It is difficult to diagram temporal elements in this movement, since many antecedent influences continue to impact the Patient Rights/Radical Psychology movement.

The set of groups, individual actors, and movement organizations constitute a *movement field*. Because movement growth and generation is a continually unfolding process, the movement field may need to be remapped periodically at various points during the research process. Indeed, the very process of working out such a map

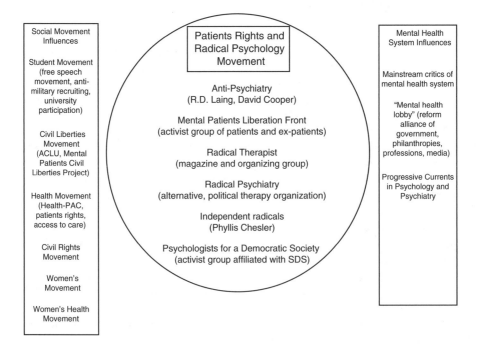

Figure 7.1. Field Analysis Model for Patients' Rights/Radical Psychology Movement

offers us the opportunity to examine historical connections that we might otherwise not imagine; diagramming a particular antecedent might, for example, dredge up connections to other legacies, some relatively indirect. This process additionally helps examine the movement field of a given antecedent.

By applying field analysis techniques we can also understand the complex social and institutional worlds in which many contemporary health social movements operate. For example, social movement organizations often participate in diverse arenas and with strategic allies and coalition partners that hold conflicting goals, perspectives, or ideologies. Analyzing fields of action can reveal the potential for political opportunities or strategic partnerships that have yet to materialize. For instance, by knowing the possible players in the field, we can hypothesize what likely coalitions or forms of noncoalition cooperation (e.g., temporary cosponsorship of a rally or press conference) may emerge from within a field. By sharing this information in the practice of community-based participatory research, we may inform these groups' policy advocacy work. Additionally, we can understand how groups might choose to recruit from related groups in the movement field. Or, field analysis can help us understand changes in strategy and tactics and enable us to discern the development of new movements.

Support groups, HSMs, and their allies in government, philanthropy, and professional bodies, are not mutually exclusive, and we do not know enough yet about how membership in multiple groups may influence the direction of a social movement group or the constitution of the overall movement field. No matter which form of action we are considering (for example, the oft-considered dichotomies of patient support groups and health social movements), participation in any arena of action is a question of degree as much as kind. For instance, a support group might verge toward a more activist stance at certain times. We can think about this in terms of a spectrum of possible actions and activity, rather than such forms being mutually exclusive. By extension, this means that participation in any of these forms may overlap with participation in another: a cancer patient may belong to a self-help support group and may also participate in an event sponsored by a health social movement, such as the Race for the Cure, or even a more radical movement, such as a Safe Cosmetics Rally organized by Breast Cancer Action. The literature so far has been silent on micro-level processes of mobilization that lead people to adopt several of these various forms of action in combination, and how individual-level behaviors and participation in multiple groups may contribute to the formation of collective identities and broader movement networks.

Field analysis can extend even further to include broad networks of many types of actors, organizations, and ideas. For example, we are in the earliest phases of understanding interpenetration (Wolfson 2001) of movement groups with government agencies and professionals and their associations, and think this is a fruitful direction for new research.

Policy Ethnography

Policy ethnography is a form of extended, multisited ethnography that studies social movements by including organizational and policy analysis alongside ethnographic observations and interviews, and that operates with a policy goal in mind. For clarification, we define "policy" to include institutional policy, science policy, as well as state, national, and international lawmaking. In some cases, those carrying out policy ethnography are themselves acting in any one of these policy realms. We have found that ethnography is the best way to conduct HSM research, because it allows for a combination of interviews, observations, and document analysis that let us enter into the daily life of HSMs. In this way, our ethnographic approach follows in the tradition of much social movement scholarship that examines movements on the ground and in specific locales. However, in studying social movements related to health, we discovered that traditional ethnography was insufficient for this task, because HSMs are so tightly interwoven with the medical and scientific realms they challenge (Frickel and Gross 2005).

We devised policy ethnography at a time when many other similar ethnographic applications were being developed. Burawoy and his students (Burawoy et al. 2000) developed the extended case method to push ethnographic work beyond its traditional bounds. In this method, they use participant observation to situate everyday life in its extralocal and historical context, thus extending it beyond the immediate site of study. At the same time, they use a reflexive approach that is based on the intersubjectivity of researcher and subject of study. Individual research sites, even when redolent with rich description and analysis, cannot convey larger trends in a complex, interdependent world (Gille and O'Riain 2002). Any ethnography of a single cultural formation is implicitly a study of the larger system in which that single formation exists. The researcher's knowledge of the micro level affects her understanding of the macro level, and vice versa. Hence, the ethnographer must trace a cultural formation across diverse sites while simultaneously developing the interaction of the macrosocial context with those specific sites. Rapp similarly (1999) speaks of multisited ethnography as an "endeavor to break the connection of space, place, and culture," because there are no clear boundaries to the research sites, the people who populate them, and the places from which those people came. Taking all this into account, we sought to identify interconnected locales that make up environmental and health social movements without being tied together in a formal organizational form, and the boundaries of which are continually in flux.

Policy ethnography combines (1) ethnographic interview and observation material, (2) background history on the organizations we study, (3) current and historical policy analysis, (4) evaluation of the scientific basis for policy-making and regulation, and in some cases (5) our group's engaging in policy advocacy through ongoing collaborations. Our approach acknowledges and responds to important developments in social movement theory and research that find social movements do not just confront singular authority structures, but rather the multiple, interconnected authorities of policy structures and science (Zavestoski et al. 2004; Myers and Cress 2004). Using these multiple categories of data, we shift our analytic focus between three tracks of analysis. We move between analysis at the micro- (personal experiences and interactions), meso- (organizational and institutional factors), and macro-level (government structures and political-economic forces). Throughout, we focus on the spaces and boundaries *between* science, policy, and civil society, because health problems and solutions are defined and debated through interactions and exchanges among these sectors rather than any one sector in particular. Policy ethnography operationalizes the conceptual ideas of boundary work we have explored, in which hybrid movements blur the boundaries between lay and expert forms of knowledge, and among activists, scientists, and the state (Brown et al. 2004; Gieryn 1999; Star and Griesmer 1989).

Much ethnographic work on illness experience has been valuable in uncovering the ways people recognize and cope with various components of disease and illness. As we first began to study contested environmental illnesses, we found that there was something larger at work, too—a collective illness experience, and ultimately a politicized illness experience (Brown et al. 2004). Since collectivized and politicized experiences often led to a push for policy change, we found it necessary to incorporate policy into what might be considered a "basic" illness ethnography. We expect that this will be broadly applicable to many other illnesses that are not environmentally induced, since politicization and economic control, and challenges to this, are widely involved in illness experiences. For example, we argue: how can one study reproductive rights, silicone breast implants, or childhood obesity without a thorough policy consideration? Hence, for a substantial number of medical concerns, policy ethnography may in fact be the logical historical development of ethnography as it applies to this field of study. As we note, many researchers have been working on transformations of the ethnographic method, and we do not mean to claim credit for the explosion of methods and broadened scope of ethnographic inquiry. We do not believe, however, that anyone has yet systematized it as an approach tailored to the study of social movement organizations or applied it to the analysis of movement fields in quite the same way as we have in our work.

Policy ethnographies engage: (1) multiple perspectives from the vantage point of (2) multiple sectors, (3) across multiple issue areas or cases, and (4) multiple phases of mobilization. Our approach to policy ethnography is thus a "multi-sited ethnography" (Marcus 1995), and it is also "multi-sighted," in that we consider the vantage of multiple social groups and stakeholders, since policy affects and involves diverse groups.

Engagement with Multiple Perspectives

Multiple groups may hold different views toward illness, treatment, and prevention, and our approach works to first identify and characterize these different standpoints. In our work on the environmental breast cancer movement, we see a perspective on breast cancer etiology and prevention that diverges from views commonly held by the biomedical establishment, which attributes the disease to genetics or lifestyle factors. In contrast, activists in the environmental breast cancer movement press for more research into the influence of environmental exposures on disease incidence. Our "multi-sighted" approach works to document these diverse perspectives and to locate them within broader discursive and political trends in policy and science. As this example suggests, the contested nature of illness means diverse groups often have dissimilar positions, even if they share concerns over the same disease or operate in the same organizational or movement fields. This is also evident in the case where environmental health and environmental justice organizations disagreed over the value of monitoring women's breast milk for contaminants, compared to other biological samples like blood serum, during deliberation over the California biomonitoring bill (Brenner 2003).

When illness, its etiology, or treatment is not contested, policy debates involve less conflict, because there is greater consensus on how to resolve a given problem. In this situation, different parties are more likely to have similar approaches to policy. When illness is contested, however, policy involves greater conflict. This follows from our understanding of the dominant epidemiological paradigm: conflict arises because professionals and authorities holding the established perspective on health effects have become accustomed to not being challenged by lay persons (Brown et al. 2001a). Health Social Movements force them to take challenges seriously.

Engagement with Multiple Sectors

With the increasing involvement of science and social movements in policy-making, understanding the history of, progression of, and influences on health-relevant policy also requires researchers to span multiple sectors: government, science, academia, broad public opinion, media, SMs, and SMOs. In studying this field, researchers observe as much in policy chambers as in scientific laboratories or conferences, as well as at street-corner protests and diner counters where social movements and publics call for, challenge, and deliberate proposed policy solutions. This is what we mean by saying that policy ethnography engages the articulation between science, policy, and publics. This necessitates that our work be multisited as well, as we travel to and among the spaces where policy, science, and publics intersect. In our study of the breast cancer movement, we observed how policy-makers allocated money for etiological research, sat bench-side with breast cancer scientists, entered surgical suites as patients underwent mastectomies, and marched alongside survivors and women living with breast cancer at public rallies (McCormick, Brown, and Zavestoski 2003; McCormick 2009; Brown et al. 2006).

More important, however, is not just the need to move *between* disparate sectors. Studying health social movements also leads researchers into interesting and new *hybrid* spaces where the work of science, policymaking, and social change take place. Science is increasingly being conducted outside laboratories; policy is formulated beyond policychambers; and as a consequence, social movement groups often move across multiple sector boundaries (i.e., as conveyed in concepts like boundary work and interpenetration). For example, when studying human burdens of chemicals, Altman (2008) found herself in many such boundary-crossing spaces. She observed a social movement organization's press conference at the Maine statehouse about chemical body burden, where nonprofits and legislators together pushed for a state ban on a class of brominated flame retardants; she watched community organizers pack glass specimen collection jars in the offices of Alaskan environmental health and justice organization; and she attended science-intensive discussions held by a journalist at a rural Appalachian high school auditorium.

Engagement with Multiple Cases

In addition to studying multiple perspectives and moving between sectors, in many instances, we also opt to study these issues across multiple cases. Doing so allows us to tease out the influence of different contextual factors such as social movement fields, lineages, or political-economic relations on social movement behavior. As we discuss here, cases can vary by issue, by context, or by temporal difference in stage or phase of movement or policy formation.

Multiple sites were helpful in examining how a variety of environmental breast cancer movement groups differed. While as an aggregate, those groups differed from mainstream breast cancer groups on the matter of environmental causation, within the environmental breast cancer movement they differed in terms of how much they worked with local, state, and federal agencies, strategy and style of work, and with what other kinds of allies they collaborated. Had we only studied the single group in the initial research proposal, we would have missed seeing critical, yet nuanced differences among these groups. More importantly, we might not have been able to adequately understand the broader SM in which these SMOs were situated (McCormick 2009).

Multiple sites can also be selected for their contextual differences. For example, Altman (2008) examined public involvement in biomonitoring science across the life-cycle of a toxic chemical: from where chemicals are produced, to where they are consumed, to where they ultimately accumulate as discarded wastes. This tripartite case-study model borrows the idea of life-cycle analysis used in the field of industrial ecology, but develops how the political-economic, scientific, and social contexts differ between sites in ways that influence the conduct and interpretation of biomonitoring science. Widener (2007) used a similar approach. She examined controversy over the construction of an oil pipeline across Ecuador by looking at contests where the pipeline started, where it terminated, and where it was politically controlled and financed.

Of particular note is that in both of these examples, Widener and Altman examined not just the differences between cases, but the *interrelationship* among them. For Widener, her cases were linked by the oil pipeline. Similarly, for Altman, her cases were linked by the flow of toxics from cradle-to-grave through industrial release, commercial distribution, and global fate and transport. While the sites may differ in mobilization capacity, what is even more important is that they have very different mobilization contexts, each with a unique set of exogenous political-economic factors in play. These factors combine to produce different social relations, discourses, debates, and stakes for the public groups that contest exposures there. Altman, for example, examined the relationship between science and policy in each site as one of the key factors setting the conditions for social relations and mobilization. In sites of production, regulation and toxic torts are two of the most common avenues for redress and remediation. These are also highly organized arenas where there are standards and protocols for incorporating and interpreting scientific evidence about human exposure. These, in effect, set the rules of the game for the debates and contests that ensue. However, struggles over chemical body burdens later in the life cycle, in what she terms sites of chemical consumption and persistence, exposures result from unregulated exposures or from gaps in the regulatory system. Here, rules for incorporating science and power are not well established, and there is more room for affected parties to define not just what the science means, but also to define the rules by which science is used in decision-making. Altman's examination of multiple sites also reinforces the call for true pollution prevention in public policy. Only by knowing the complexities of fate and transport of toxic substances through their life cycle can we adequately regulate them and move to toxics use reduction and more effective chemical screening and regulation.

Covering Multiple Phases of Mobilization

Finally, policy ethnographic work can also be multi-phasal, in which we examine disease contestation and HSMs at different stages of mobilization or social movement formation. We have studied Gulf War illnesses, which became a less active topic in scientific research and policy-making until the 2008 federal Research Advisor Committee report the "scientific evidence leaves no question that Gulf War illness is a real condition with real causes and serious consequences for affected veterans." Returning to our earlier study offers an opportunity to demonstrate how a dominant epidemiological paradigm evolves.

Policy Ethnography as Public Sociology

We draw on past–American Sociological Association (ASA) president Michael Burawoy's definition of public sociology, which was later adopted/endorsed by the ASA Task Force on Institutionalizing Public Sociology. As Burawoy notes, public sociology is "a sociology that seeks to bring sociology to publics beyond the academy, promoting dialogue about issues that affect the fate of society" (2004: 104). The Task Force extended this definition: "to include a more comprehensive view of public sociology as including both the 'traditional' and 'organic' public sociologies. As framed by Burawoy, traditional public sociologists do not necessarily interact with their 'publics.' Writing op-ed pieces, making research reports available to broader groups of users, and just documenting, questioning, and analyzing the social world are forms of public sociology" (ASA Task Force 2005). This broader definition encompasses all sociologists who "work in close connection with a visible, thick, active, local and often counter-public" (Burawoy 2004: 7).

Although it is not an automatic transition, by virtue of studying movement organizations already inclined to gathering information, conducting research, and partnering with scientists, we found our ethnographic involvement often lead to research-based collaborations with the same groups we studied. For example, one of our early fieldsites, Alternatives for Community and Environment, an environmental justice group working on asthma, suggested we give feedback on our observations to their staff. This, in turn, led to a collaboration that yielded a research proposal and a series of environmental ethics forums. The Boston Environmental Hazards Center, our research site for Gulf War illnesses, asked one of us to be on the science advisory board for a research project they were proposing. Another research site, where we were studying toxics reduction, the Precautionary Principle Project, asked one of us to be a workshop facilitator at their 2002 international conference on the precautionary principle. When the Precautionary Principle Project later transformed itself into a broader group, the Alliance for a Healthy Tomorrow, they asked us to collaborate on developing and performing a pesticide awareness survey, to work on a project to examine environmental factors in autism, and to participate in meetings to develop communications projects with scientists. Through the asthma research and through a project on labor-environment coalitions, the Boston Urban Asthma Coalition and Massachusetts Coalition for Occupational Safety and Health asked us to evaluate a program to provide safer cleaning alternatives for custodians in the Boston Public Schools. After we conducted long-term observations and interviews there, Silent Spring Institute asked us to collaborate on a research project to demonstrate a long historical legacy of community involvement in health research, which would help justify the continuation and strengthening of community participation in current research on environmental factors in breast cancer. This was part of a chain of events that led us to partner with Silent Spring Institute and Communities for Better Environment in a major funded project that links breast cancer advocacy with environmental justice activism.

When policy ethnography transforms itself into actual participatory collaboration, it adds another layer of complexity to the movement field—at this point, policy ethnography needs extra attention to reflexivity in order to recognize these mutual influences. One feature is how our presence enables our partners to realize things that would be otherwise inaccessible or invisible to them. For example, in discussions with our collaborators from Silent Spring Institute (SSI), one of the staff stated, "Of course it makes sense to have a sociologist on the team if you're interested in social change," though at the time, science-social science collaborations were sparse. She noted that when we shared our analysis of SSI's work and impact with SSI staff and board members, it allowed them to see themselves in a field of actors that is much larger than just their one group. At the same time, we better grasp and fine-tune our understanding of that organization by being their partners, rather than merely studying them. Ongoing, reiterative, reciprocal relationships are beneficial for all involved parties. This imposes unique ethical considerations as well, including raising issues of how researches work with and protect organizations and communities, as well as individuals.

In our work, we research answers to policy-relevant questions and assist strategic dissemination of knowledge in order to affect policy. Policy includes not just public policy (typically legislation, regulation, judicial involvement), but also science policy, policies of health care institutions and practitioners, and policies of professional associations. Our engagement in a policy world means that we make our work accessible to the public and to the organizations that represent them. In our green cleaners project, for example, we produced a report for the lead organizations with whom we collaborated (Senier, Mayer, and Brown 2005). In Altman's study of biomonitoring conducted by Alaska Community Action on Toxics and their community and scientific partners, she prepared a brochure on environmental reproductive health that would help them in their organizing and scientific work (Altman 2006).

Sometimes we begin with one form of policy orientation and find it shifting in midstream. In our project, "Linking Breast Cancer Advocacy and Environmental Justice," we tested air and dust in Richmond, California homes, in a fenceline community next to the largest oil refinery west of the Mississippi River. We initially believed that our findings would be useful both as part of a national effort to intro-duce more precautionary chemicals policy, and as part of the local neighborhood's efforts to limit the refinery's emissions. Thus, in our research, we worked collabora-tively to develop and evaluate models for results communication (Brody et al. 2007; Altman et al. 2008). While our project was underway, the refinery sought a large expansion that would include burning much dirtier crude oil. The city's hearings on this were occurring in the same time period as our second community meeting, where we provided aggregate data to residents about chemical pollutants detected in house dust as well as indoor and outdoor air samples. The neighborhood people attending the meeting saw our work as expressly valuable for their efforts against the refinery expansion, and they drove the discussion of the data in that direction. As a result, one of our team members (Morello-Frosch 2008) prepared a major report to the city's permitting commission, which helped to reopen what initially seemed like a done deal for the refinery. In addition, we also detected the highest dust and blood levels of brominated flame retardants found in the United States, a likely consequence of California's strict flammability standard (Zota et al. 2008). This work has the poten-tial to support academic and labor activist efforts to motivate policy changes that would ban the use of halogenated flame retardants in the state (Blum 2007). These examples are cases of citizen-science alliances that found scientifically relevant find-ings, and that help us understand the most effective routes to citizen/science engage-ment. Inspired by the work of sociologists and advocacy scientists who seek to enhance the relevance and reach of their research (Krimsky 2000), policy ethnogra-phy advances our efforts to understand and cultivate social change. While much of what we work on is community-based participatory research, we also do community-engaged outreach and service. This is not collaborative CBPR, but is still designed to give voice and aid to the communities it is involved with. For example, through our Community Outreach Core of Brown University's Superfund Research Program, one way we assist community groups facing toxic waste contamination is through inter-vention with state agencies and legislators.

We believe it is necessary to include policy analysis in an ethnographic approach to contested illnesses and related subjects because the contestation is inseparable from the policy issues such as official diagnostic recognition, treatment, reimburse-ment, research appropriations, and legislation. For example, asthma organizing is intimately tied to demands for better regulation of air pollution, and environmental breast cancer organizing is tied to demands for more comprehensive chemical reg-ulation and/or bans. Further, the notion of interpenetration tells us that policy-makers are indeed part of some HSMs, and hence it would not make sense to examine those movements without looking at those actors as well (Wolfson 2001). While valuable research on HSMs can take place without the types of alliances we develop, we argue that all research needs to examine whether it serves particular ideologies or interest groups. For those who are engaged or collaborating with communities and/or activists, it is always important to leave space and time for reflexive analysis. As we have done, researchers need to explore their interaction with partners, and how the partnership affects all involved parties. They also need to reflect on whether they are able to step outside the partnership, in order to bring a sociological perspective to the causes and consequences of the HSMs they study.

Our experience has showed us that community partners constantly seek the perspective and guidance of this view from outside.

Conclusion

Our discussion about the many facets of HSMs and health SMOs informs us that we cannot separately address science, activism, and policy: all are part of the same phenomenon and need to be addressed together. There are many nonhealth SMs and SMOs that do not engage with science, and these may not appear to require the same level of engagement with science. But there is a larger expanse of movements involved with science than we might have expected. In examining the interactions between HSMs and their components, we have developed our field analysis approach, and to study those HSMs, we have put forth a policy ethnography method; field analysis, we have found, leads toward policy ethnography by identifying the universe of actors and activities we need to examine. With our larger framework, we find it useful to put special emphasis on entire social movements, and entire fields of movements, rather than only on social movement organizations.

There are both scholarly and policy outcomes of our work. For social movement scholarship, studying field analysis can contribute to three levels of attention. At the macro level, it can inform us about how SMs develop, change, and are changed by their interaction with the broader environment. At the meso level, we can study the substance of collective action and collective identity itself, gaining an understanding of the broad societal effect of the diversity of strategies and tactics within one multibranched movement. For example, the environmental breast cancer movement simultaneously works on toxics reduction and chemical regulation, while also challenging researchers and funders to pay attention to environmental causation. At the micro level, we understand how movements give capacity and legitimacy to individual experiences that may be invisible to isolated people. Microanalysis can also show how and why individuals participate in the initiation of collective action.

In looking at policy outcomes, policy ethnography helps us understand how SMs and SMOs select allies and make strategic choices. Taking a multisited approach can explain a diverse range of choices among the environmental breast cancer movement. Local groups on Long Island were more likely to link up with status quo allies, including Republican lawmakers, while more radical groups like Breast Cancer Action took direct action such as demonstrations and challenges to mainstream breast cancer organizations (Brown et al. 2006). A multisited approach to biomonitoring can show diverse political strategies, ranging from anticorporate litigation in the mid-Ohio Valley, conflict in Alaska with the Army Corp of Engineers and the state health department, to legislation in Maine in which activists are strongly allied with legislators and select business interests (Altman 2008).

Other scholars have analyzed social movements in ways that mirror our field analysis and policy ethnography approaches. We codify one such approach here to guide others interested in the study of social movements, and to offer legitimation of evolving modes of ethnographic inquiry. Though they stem from our specific experience with health social movements, we find these methods are widely applicable to many other social movements.

NOTES

We thank Alison Cohen, Alissa Cordner, Mercedes Lyson, Ruth Simpson, and Rebecca Tillson for helpful comments on the manuscript.

8

The Institutionalization of Community Action in Public Health

Mark Wolfson and Maria Parries

Introduction

The relationship between states and social movements has been a fixture in social movement theory and research. This relationship has been conceptualized in a number of ways. First, the state is often an explicit target of movements. Movements deploy a variety of strategies and tactics to gain state recognition and concessions (Tilly 1978; Gamson 1990). Second, the state represents a system of opportunities and constraints that movements must negotiate. This conception focuses on structural features of political systems that are related to their degree of permeability by "outside" agents, such as social movement actors and organizations (McAdam, Tarrow, and Tilly 2001). Finally, the state has been conceived as a facilitator or repressor of movements (Gamson 1990; Barkan 1984; Jenkins and Eckert 1986; della Porta 1996).

These conceptions have come under strain in the past five to ten years. It is widely recognized that each of them captures part of the reality of the relationship between states and social movements. However, these three perspectives also miss a critical dimension of that relationship. Increasingly, analysts have painted a picture of overlapping interests, and active cooperation and interplay, of state and movement actors and organizations. For example, in a case study of the tobacco-control movement, the relationship was described as follows: "Subdivisions of the state are often active participants—even collaborators, and sometimes instigators—in the movement's efforts to obtain desired changes in public policy" (Wolfson 2001: 188). The study of Health Social Movements (HSMs), in particular, has shown that "insiders...frequently prove central to the political processes by which institutions become forced to change (Epstein 2007a: 88; also see Epstein 2010; Frickel 2010; Moore 1999; McCormick, Brown, and Zavestoski 2003).

There is a need for research—and the development of theory—on the confluences of the work of state actors (and other "insiders") and social movements. In this chapter, we seek to illustrate an example of the incorporation of a group of practices that is often the domain of social movements—what we will call "community action"—into the field of public health.

Community Action in Public Health

Public health, as a profession and as a key function of the state, has been deeply intertwined with social movements. It began as the "Public Health Movement," promoted by reformers concerned with the unsanitary and unhealthful conditions associated with industrialization and urbanization in mid-eighteenth-century England and other Western countries (Szreter 2002, 2003). And, over its history, it has been allied with, borrowed from, and informed a number of widespread social movements, including breast cancer (Casamayou 2001), environmental health (Brown 2007), drinking and driving (McCarthy and Wolfson 1992), and tobacco control (Wolfson 2001).

The roots of public health are in changing environmental conditions that affect the health of entire communities. The classic example is the response to an 1854 outbreak of cholera in the Broad Street neighborhood of London. Using what was later to become known as "shoe leather" epidemiology, John Snow traced the source of the outbreak to contaminated water from a public pump on the corner of Broad Street and Cambridge Street. Snow persuaded the Board of Guardians of the local authority—St. James Parish—to remove the pump handle. By the end of the month, the epidemic, which had killed 616 Londoners, had ended (Johnson 2006; Summers 1989).

More generally, public health advocates, as well as those from the closely allied emerging field of social medicine, focused largely on the social and environmental conditions that gave rise to ill health in urbanizing communities in Western Europe and the United States (Brown and Fee 2006).

Not surprisingly, the challenge confronted by workers in the field of public health—changing community social and environmental conditions related to health and illness—bears a marked similarity to the challenges faced by social movements that seek structural change. How can individuals be mobilized to support change efforts? What strategies and tactics can be deployed to support structural changes? How can the attention of the public and potentially sympathetic elites be captured?

We argue that a number of social movement strategies and tactics have been incorporated into the field of public health. What we will call "community action"—deliberate efforts to change these conditions, bounded in space—has come to be an essential element of public health efforts (also see Israel et al. 1998; Minkler 2005). This phenomenon has important implications for students of social movements, in that it speaks to issues of the relationship between movements and the state, the strategic and tactical repertoires of movements, and movement impacts.

In the following sections of this chapter, we discuss community action efforts—including community organizing, community coalitions, and community-based participatory research—that have been directed to a wide range of public health problems.

Community Organizing

Community organizing is an important example of such community action efforts. Beginning in the late nineteenth century, "mobilization of the forces of the community for the control of [tuberculosis] was first undertaken in the United States" (Rosen 1958). In 1941, the American Public Health Association published a monograph entitled Community Organization of Health Education (APHA 1941). In more recent times, community organizing has become an important and accepted part of the "tool kit" of public health, reflected in textbooks (Bracht 1999; Minkler 2005), professional training, and journal articles (Brown 1983; Freudenberg and Trinidad 1992; Cheadle et al. 2001).

Minkler and Wallerstein, in what is often regarded as a seminal text, define community organizing as "the process by which community groups are helped to identify common problems or goals, mobilize resources, and develop and implement strategies for reaching the goals they collectively have set" (2005: 26).

Community Coalitions

Community coalitions are another vehicle—or way of conceptualizing—community action to promote public health. A contemporary definition of a coalition, from the substance abuse arena, is: "a vehicle for bringing together community sectors to develop and carry out strategies to reduce substance abuse problems" (Callahan 2007).

The use of such coalitions in public health promotion has been extensively treated in the research and practice literature of public health (Butterfoss et al. 1995; Zakocs and Edwards 2006). They have become central to many government- and foundation-funded, broad-scale initiatives to reduce the harms associated with the use of alcohol, tobacco, and illicit drugs. These include Fighting Back, the American Stop Smoking Intervention Study, A Matter of Degree, and Reducing Underage Drinking through Coalitions.

Fighting Back was a $71 million initiative funded by the Robert Wood Johnson Foundation (Jellinek and Hearn 1991; Zakocs and Guckenburg 2007). The goal of Fighting Back was to use community coalitions as a vehicle for reducing the use of illegal drugs and alcohol by developing a unified, community-wide system of prevention, treatment, and aftercare. Grants were awarded to coalitions in fifteen cities to implement this approach. In order to provide training, technical assistance, and support to Fighting Back coalitions, and coalitions nationwide, RWJF provided over $16 million to support a national organization, Join Together, which is based at the Boston University School of Public Health.[1]

Other national initiatives that have used an approach based on community and/or statewide coalitions include the National Cancer Institute's American Stop Smoking

Intervention Study, and the RWJF initiatives A Matter of Degree, (which focused on high risk drinking by college students), and Reducing Underage Drinking through Coalitions (Manley et al. 1997; Weitzman et al. 2004; Wagenaar et al. 2006).

In 1992, many coalitions focused on substance abuse coalesced into the Community Anti-Drug Coalitions of America (CADCA). The development of CADCA was promoted by the President's Drug Advisory Council, to "respond to the dramatic growth in the number of substance abuse coalitions and their need to share ideas, problems, and solutions" (CADCA 2007).

The Community Anti-Drug Coalitions of America 2007 National Coalition Registry includes more than 1,400 local organizations. In order to be listed, these organizations must (1) report that they have a mission focused on solely, or in part, on "Alcohol, Tobacco and Other Drug Issues," and (2) have at least two community partner organizations as members of the coalition. CADCA's National Coalition Institute provides training and technical assistance to local coalitions in "best practices in community problem solving."

Most recently, a number of federal agencies concerned with substance abuse have explicitly adopted an approach that involves funding local coalitions to address alcohol, tobacco, and illicit drug use. These include the Substance Abuse and Mental Health Services Administration's Drug Free Communities Program, and, to a lesser extent, its Strategic Prevention Framework State Incentive Grant Program and the Office of Juvenile Justice and Delinquency Prevention's Enforcing Underage Drinking Laws Program (Battelle 2008; Wolfson et al. 2006; Substance Abuse and Mental Health Services Administration 2006).

Community-Based Participatory Research

In recent years, "Community-Based Participatory Research" (CBPR) has emerged as an overarching framework for classifying projects that involve a "partnership" between community members and researchers (Israel et al. 1998). A recent evidence review of CBPR published by the Agency for Healthcare Research and Quality defined CBPR as "a collaborative research approach designed to ensure and establish structures for participation by communities affected by the issue being studied, representatives of organizations, and researchers in all aspects of the research process to improve health and wellbeing through taking action, including social change" (Viswanathan et al. 2004).

The concept and language of CBPR has diffused widely in public health practice and in the practices of several funding agencies. This is reflected in a spate of recent textbooks, articles, course syllabi, and training institutes (Israel et al. 2005; Viswanathan et al. 2004; Cashman et al. 2008). Moreover, recent funding solicitations issued by the National Institutes of Health and Centers for Disease Control and Prevention have incorporated a CBPR framework.[2]

As shown above, there are many examples of the incorporation of community action approaches into public health. However, to our knowledge, no one has used systematic data to explore (1) trends in these approaches over time within public health, and (2) variations in these trends across different types of community action. We use data from a database of federally funded biomedical research to explore these trends. Of course, research is not a perfect indicator of patterns of practice. However, research both provides models for practice and reflects patterns of practice—albeit imperfectly. Moreover, federal research is well documented in an existing database that covers a thirty-five-year span, affording the opportunity for a first look at patterns of community action over time within the health field.

Data and Analysis

The analyses reported below use data from the Computer Retrieval of Information on Scientific Projects (CRISP) database of federally funded biomedical research. This database includes biomedical research projects funded by the National Institutes of Health, Substance Abuse and Mental Health Services Administration, Health Resources and Services Administration, Food and Drug Administration, Centers for Disease Control and Prevention, Agency for Health Care Research and Quality, and Office of the Assistant Secretary of Health (see http://crisp.cit.nih.gov/). We conducted a search using the following terms: *Coalition, Community Organizing, Community Organization, Community-Based Participatory Research, Participatory Research, Advocacy, Partnership, Community Based Public Health, Community Based.* The search identified grants in CRISP that contained one or more of these terms in the grant title or abstract, to which we will apply the shorthand label "Community Action" research grants.[3] Grants with multiple instances of these search terms were treated as a single grant for the purposes of overall counts (figures 8.1 and 8.2). When comparative trends across search terms are presented, each grant may be counted multiple times, depending on the number of search terms present (figures 8.3 and 8.4).

Figure 8.1 shows trends in funding over the thirty-six-year period for which CRISP data are available (1972 to 2007). There were thirty-one grants with a title and/or abstract that contained one or more of these terms in 1972. The number of new grants awarded grew to forty-two in 1974, dropped to nine in 1975, and then fluctuated between nine and twenty-seven in the late 1970s and early and mid-1980s. The year 1988 marked the beginning of a period of steady growth in Community Action grants, which grew from 21 to 269 in 1994, more than a ten-fold increase. The number of these grants remained high in 1995 (230), and then dropped in 1996 to 84. However, from 1997 on, there has been steady and rapid growth in the number of these grants awarded, increasing to 1,359 in 2007.

While the data depicted in figure 8.1 demonstrate a large numeric increase in community action grants, federal investment in the NIH and biomedical research as a whole increased dramatically during this period (Ruzek et al. 1996). Figure 8.2 again shows the trends in funding community action grants from 1972 to 2007, but this time measured as a percentage of all grants in the CRISP system. These trends closely mirror those depicted in figure 8.1: steady growth in the late 1980s and early 1990s, surging to a peak of .5% of all grants in 1994.[4] The percentage of grants declined slightly in 1995 (to .42%) and sharply in 1996 (to .13%), but has shown dramatic growth since then, increasing each year to a peak of 1.89% of all grants in 2007.[5]

Figure 8.3 shows trends by search term (note that these search terms are not mutually exclusive). Although not evident because of the scale of this graph, the

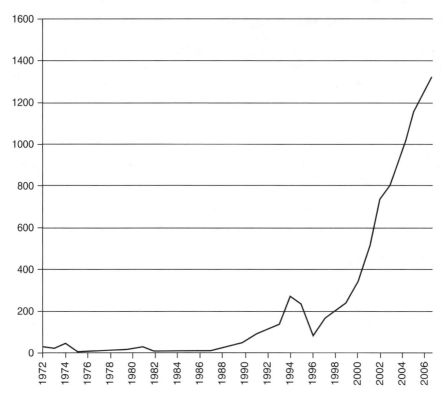

Figure 8.1. Number of Biomedical Research Grants Involving Community Action, by Year (1972–2007)

Data are from the NIH CRISP database. Search terms included: Coalition, Community Organizing, Community Organization, Community-Based Participatory Research, Participatory Research, Advocacy, Partnership, Community Based Public Health, Community Based.

underlying data show some interesting trends in the early years of the time series. "Community Organization" was the most common search term on which there were "hits" from 1972 through 1974 (57 out of the 98 community action grants awarded during this period, or 58%).[6] This shifted to "Advocacy" during the 1975–1981 period, representing 66 of 106 grants (62%).

Most striking are the key words underlying the dramatic surge in community action grants in 1993, 1994, and 1995. In 1993, when 134 community action grants were awarded (increasing from 102 the previous year), the "Coalition" and "Partnership" terms accounted for 36 and 57 of these grants, respectively (or 27% and 43%). Similarly, these two terms accounted for large shares of the community action grants awarded in 1994 (72 for Coalition and 150 for Partnership out of 269 grants awarded [27% and 56%]) and in 1995 (24 for Coalition and 158 for Partnership out of 230 grants awarded [10% and 69%]).

The subsequent years marked the continued ascendancy of the Partnership model, accounting for much of the growth in community action grants during the late 1990s

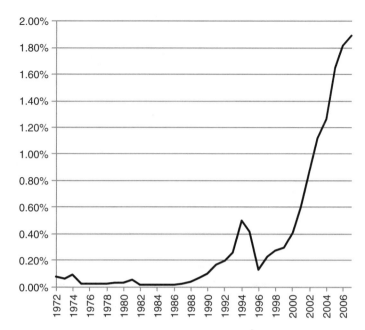

Figure 8.2. Biomedical Research Grants Involving Community Action, as a Percentage of All Grants (1972–2007)

Data are from the NIH CRISP database. Search terms included: Coalition, Community Organizing, Community Organization, Community-Based Participatory Research, Participatory Research, Advocacy, Partnership, Community Based Public Health, Community Based.

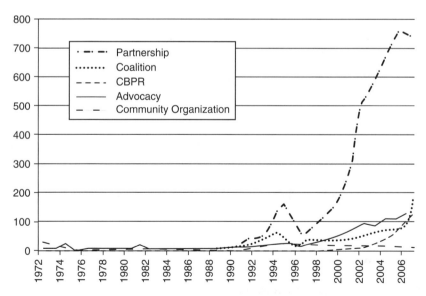

Figure 8.3. Biomedical Research Grants Involving Community Action, By Search Term and Year (1972–2007)

Data are from the NIH CRISP database. Search terms included: Coalition, Community Organizing, Community Organization, Community-Based Participatory Research, Participatory Research, Advocacy, Partnership, Community Based Public Health, Community Based.

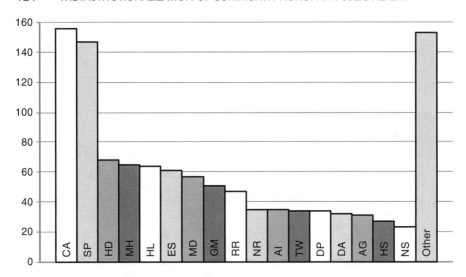

Figure 8.4. Biomedical Research Grants Involving Community Action, By Institute/Center/ Office (2007)

Data are from the NIH CRISP database. Search terms included: Coalition, Community Organizing, Community Organization, Community-Based Participatory Research, Participatory Research, Advocacy, Partnership, Community Based Public Health, Community Based.

and thus far in the 2000s. As of 2007, the Partnership term was reflected in 731 of the 1359 community action grants (54%). Participatory Research (or Community Based Participatory Research) also increased dramatically (from 5 grants in 2000 to 164 in 2007). Finally, there has been steady growth, and a recent upswing, in grants using the Coalition keyword (from 15 in 1996 to 86 in 2006 and 209 in 2007).

Figure 8.4 breaks down community action grants made in 2007 by funding agency.[7] The greatest numbers of these grants were made by the National Cancer Institute (156), the Center for Substance Abuse Prevention (147), the National Institute of Child Health and Human Development (68), the National Institute on Mental Health (65), the National Heart, Lung, and Blood Institute (64), the National Institute of Environmental Health Sciences (61), the National Center on Minority Health and Health Disparities (57), and the National Institute of General Medical Sciences (51).[8]

Discussion

Grants involving what we have characterized as community action grew dramatically over a 35-year period, from 31 in 1972 to 1,359 in 2007. Remarkable growth is also evident when these grants are examined as a percentage of all federal biomedical research grants, increasing from .08% in 1972 to 1.89% in 2007—more than a twenty-fold increase.

We also found marked shifts in the particular "flavor" of community action—as reflected in the search term found in the title or abstract of the grant—over time. "Community organization" was the most common term during the 1972–74 period, shifting to "advocacy" from 1975–81. There was a surge in community action grants in the early 1990s, largely accounted for by grants that involved the "coalition" and "partnership" terms. "Partnership" grants continued to grow during the late 1990s and through 2007, representing 54% of community action grants in the final year for which we have data (2007). "Participatory research" (or "community-based participatory research") also increased dramatically since the year 2000, and "coalition" grants also experience an upsurge in 2006 and 2007.

Of course, it is clear that there is imprecision in our search process using the CRISP database. Some of the grants may not involve what a knowledgeable observer would characterize as "community action" (while we conducted some "spot checks" by reading the titles and abstracts of the identified grants, we did not undertake a systematic validation effort). Conversely, it is likely that some grants that could be characterized as community action were not captured by our keywords. Nevertheless, we believe that the evidence from CRISP, as well as the trends in government- and foundation-funded initiatives and professional literature and training discussed above, illustrate the central role that community action to change social conditions has come to play in public health practice.

The observed trends in the "types" of community action—as captured by keywords—raise a number of questions. Do the changes in the most popular terminology—from "community organization" in the early 1970s to "advocacy" in the late 1970s to "coalitions" and "partnerships" in the early 1990s and "partnerships" again in the late 1990s through 2007—with more recent surges in "participatory research" and "coalitions"—represent substantive shifts in approach, or simply changes in nomenclature? The extent to which these terms actually reflect important differences in practice is a topic that is actively discussed in the field (e.g., Israel 1998) and is an important area for future research.

Another key question is how community action approaches came to be incorporated within public health research and practice. As mentioned earlier in this chapter, community action has long historical roots in public health. But the growth in community action that we observed in our data, starting in the 1970s and continuing to this day, cannot be explained by examples of such approaches earlier in the century. Some authors have argued that citizen participation in solving community problems experienced a tremendous upsurge during the War on Poverty, most evident in the Community Action Program (Piven and Cloward 1971; Moynihan 1969). Others have argued that the emergence of this form predated the War on Poverty, surfacing earlier in the 1950s in such efforts as the Mobilization for Youth project (Helfgot 1981). Regardless of the sequence of emergence, writers on this subject have proposed explanations that revolve around the "professionalization of reform" (Moynihan 1969), or social control (Piven and Cloward 1971). An alternative—or perhaps complementary—form of explanation is that community action may be viewed as an important outcome of social movements, such as the women's health movement.

Another important question is what happens to social movement strategies and tactics—such as community action—when they are imported into a heavily state-sponsored, evidence-based field? The demands and constraints of public health may require that these strategies and tactics be reformulated in ways that can be described in research protocols, approved by university institutional review boards, measured, and pass muster with NIH peer review committees and institute staff (see Brown et al. 2008). Do these demands lead to the weakening, and even vitiation, of otherwise effective practices (see Lipsky and Smith 1989; Gronbjerg 1991)?

Finally, an important question is the extent to which incorporation of community action into public health is a distinctly U.S. phenomenon. It is striking that key texts on many of these approaches have few if any mentions of contemporary applications in other countries (e.g., Minkler 2005; Israel et al. 2005). Whether community action in public health is an example of American exceptionalism is an important topic for future research.

The incorporation of community action into public health adds to the emerging literature on the fluidity of the boundaries between states and social movements. This includes work on the active involvement of state actors in movements, as well as the dissemination of movement framings, strategies, and tactics into nodes of the state (Epstein 2007, 2009; Frickel 2009; Moore 1999; McCormick et al. 2003). The dramatic increase in the use of community action methods in public health reflected in federally funded biomedical research raises a number of important questions for the fields of public health and social movements.

NOTES

Support for preparation of this chapter was provided in part by grants from the National Institute on Alcohol Abuse and Alcoholism (R01 AA14007-2), the Office of Juvenile Justice and Delinquency Prevention (2002-DR-FX-0001), and the Robert Wood Johnson Foundation (044123).

1. A lively debate has taken place over the past several years on the impact of Fighting Back—see Hallfors and colleagues (2002) and Hingson and colleagues (2005).

2. These include calls for research on Health Promotion Among Racial and Ethnic Minorities, Patient Oriented Research, and Reducing and Eliminating Health Disparities.

3. See Wallace and Hurlstone (2003); Hughes and Liguori (2000); and Portnoy and colleagues (2007), for other examples of researchers using CRISP to track trends in biomedical research funding.

4. Note the scale used in this figure, which ranges from 0% to 2%. Community action grants, while numerically significant, represent a small fraction of the total biomedical research enterprise in the United States.

5. The CRISP system does not include information on the amount of individual grants, so we were unable to conduct a parallel analysis of trends in community action grants in terms of dollar amounts.

6. For the purposes of the analyses presented in figure 8.3, the search terms "Community Organization" and "Community Organizing" were lumped together. The combined counts are labeled as "Community Organization" in the figure.

7. The institutional codes used in figure 8.4 are as follows: CA=National Cancer Institute (NCI), SP=Center for Substance Abuse Prevention (CSAP), HD=National Institute of Child Health & Human Development (NICHD), MH=National Institute of Mental Health (NIMH), HL=National Heart, Lung and Blood Institute (NHLBI), ES=National Institute of Environmental

Health Sciences (NIEHS), MD=National Center on Minority Health and Health Disparities (NCMHD), GM=National Institute of General Medical Sciences (NIGMS), RR=National Center for Research Resources (NCRR), NR=National Institute of Nursing Research (NINR), AI=National Institute of Allergy and Infectious Disease Extramural Activities (NIAID), TW=Fogarty International Center (FIC), DP=National Center for Chronic Disease Prevention and Health Promotion (NCCDPHP), DA=National Institute on Drug Abuse (NIDA), AG=National Institute on Aging (NIA), HS=Agency for Health Care Research and Quality (AHRQ), NS=National Institute of Neurological Disorders and Stroke (NINDS).

8. Other institutes and centers with twenty or more "community action" grants are the National Center for Research Resources, National Institute of Nursing Research, National Institute of Allergy and Infectious Diseases, the Fogarty International Center, National Center for Chronic Disease Prevention and Health Promotion (which is a component of the Centers for Disease Control and Prevention), National Institute on Drug Abuse, the Agency for Health Care Research and Quality, and the National Institute of Neurological Disorders and Stroke.

9

Social Movement Challenges to Structural Archetypes

Abortion Rights, AIDS, and Long-Term Care

Martin Kitchener

Introduction

Social movement researchers and institutional analysts of organizations have long shared an interest in systems of beliefs and values (logics) and the motivated action (agency) of reformers (Davis et al. 2005). The two scholarly traditions have, however, conceived of relations between logics and agency rather differently. While social movement researchers recognize that prevailing logics, or frames, present significant barriers to social reform, they have shown that new systems of beliefs can motivate the change efforts of disadvantaged actors (Snow 2004a). In contrast, a central understanding of institutional analysts is that within "fields" of related organizations, a dominant logic tends to restrict opportunities for change by underpinning a template, or "archetype," of prescriptions concerning what constitutes legitimate organizational form and behavior (Greenwood and Hinings 1998: 295).

Although institutional analysts have recently given more attention to agency and the implications of multiple field logics, they have generally provided accounts of a new logic and archetype being imposed, top-down, by powerful actors (e.g., state agencies) relatively quickly, and with little reported *resistance to change* (Brock, Powell, and Hinings 1999). With little consideration of social movement studies, the pursuit of new archetypes by less powerful field actors remains under-studied, under-theorized, and leaves unattended the interesting phenomenon of *resistance for change* (Spicer 2006).

This chapter presents the first attempt to explicate the potential for social movement studies to provide empirical insights and theoretical leverage for analyses of the promotion of new archetypes by grassroots health reform movements. The chapter is structured in four main sections. The first argues that while archetype analysis has proved useful for the study of change in healthcare fields, it offers limited capacity to analyze bottom-up and contested processes. Section two draws from social movement studies to suggest that weaknesses of archetype theory may be addressed through the consideration of movement-countermovement dynamics, political opportunity structures, and institutional process. The third section draws from three case studies of institutional change driven by health reform movements to introduce a new conceptual framework of research propositions concerning the bottom-up promotion of new archetypes in healthcare fields. The paper concludes with an assessment of this framework for future work.

The Archetype Approach to Studying Field Dynamics

Some of the main contributions to institutional theory have emerged from analyses conducted at the level of organizational fields defined as communities of organizations "that partake of a common meaning system and whose participants interact more frequently and fatefully with one another than with actors outside of the field" (Scott 1994: 207–8). In a seminal example, DiMaggio and Powell (1983) report that mimetic, coercive, and normative forces combine to produce templates of what constitutes legitimate organizational structure and action. In fields of professional organizations, legitimacy (which can be conceived as congruence within professionals' beliefs and values) is vital for survival (Friedland and Alford 1991). In such contexts, organizational templates become taken for granted as a result of interactions among factors including: organizations' desire to copy organizations with high degrees of legitimacy and the stabilizing influence of professional norms. Especially in healthcare fields, this tendency toward similarity of organizational form (isomorphism) arises less from managerial concerns for efficiency, and more as a means of displaying legitimacy to facilitate organizational survival.

In a leading institutional approach to studying change in organization fields, Greenwood and Hinings (1993) advocate the specification and tracking of "archetypes" which are analytical abstractions of the core normative and structural elements of a field's institutional framework. More specifically, archetypes are conceived as coherent sets of formal structures and operating systems that are underpinned by a logic specifying appropriate approaches to organization. The archetype approach to analyzing institutional change first identifies archetypes within an organization field and then traces movement between archetypes along three main "tracks" of change: (1) inertia, or relative stability; (2) proposals for new archetypes that fail to become institutionalized (unresolved excursions); and (3) new archetypes that become institutionalized (transformations).

When compared with alternative approaches to studying healthcare field dynamics, the archetype approach offers a number of advantages including a socio-historical perspective, a concern for process (through the examination of tracks of change), and the specification of transformational change as the institutionalization of all three components of a new archetype: logic, structures, and systems (Brock, Powell, and Hinings 1999; Reay and Hinings 2005). Despite this potential, applications of the archetype approach in studies of professional fields including healthcare have typically produced accounts of new archetypes emerging quickly, often under five years, from transformation processes that are driven by powerful actors such as state agencies or corporate elites (Brock, Powell, and Hinings 1999). In one example, an early application of the archetype approach in a healthcare field studied the "top-down" introduction of a new market system into the field of British National Health Service (NHS) hospitals in 1991 (Kitchener 1998). In common with applications in other fields, the analysis of movement between archetypes (see table 9.1) proceeded through three main stages.

First, the "traditional" archetype of NHS hospital organization was specified in terms of a coherent configuration of structure, systems, and logic. This was termed

Table 9.1. The NHS Directly Managed Unit and Trust Hospital Archetypes, c. 1991

	Directly Managed Unit Hospital Archetype	Trust Hospital Archetype
Logic	Collaboratively organized hospital care, free at point of delivery.	Competitively organized hospital care, determined within quasi-market. Market relationships to "promote efficiency. "
	Structural adjustment based on incremental increases in funding.	Transformation.
	Sharp management-staff boundaries, professional autonomy, pluralistic politics.	Blurred managerial-staff boundaries, attempts to reduce professional autonomy, pluralistic politics.
	A budget surplus will reduce next year's resources, patient care generates expenses, successful professionals consume resources, regulation largely determines service-mix, in-house provision of services.	A contract surplus will increase next year's resources, patient care generates revenue, successful professionals budget consumption, markets determine service-mix, contracting-out of services.
Systems	Each directly managed hospital's income is largely derived from health authorities. Cross subsidies for e.g., teaching and community services. Poor information systems	Each Trust's income is largely derived from contracts with health authorities, GP fund holders and the private sector Increased need for market information
	Asset base is managed externally, salaries/staffing are fixed short-term, closures and changes of use are subject to formal consultation.	Asset base is managed internally. There is no requirement for a Trust to consult on closures or change of use.
Structure	Sector—hierarchical and functional, based upon vertical communications.	Sector—flatter more organic structures, network communications, based upon contract specifications.
	Internal—professional collegiate and administrative hierarchy.	Internal—networks, clinical directorates market-customer based.

the directly managed unit (DMU) archetype because it was based on the logic of bureaucratic hospital control culminating in the responsible minister of government for health. Second, the model of hospital organization envisaged in reform legislation was presented as a new configuration of logic, structures, and systems. This was named the Trust archetype because all hospitals were required to incorporate the word into their titles to signal their continued not-for-profit status within the new logic of market-based "co-ordination." The third stage of the analysis traced the movement between the two archetypes. In contrast to previous accounts of one arche-type replacing another, it was reported that a hybrid archetype emerged to combine new market structures with the traditional bureaucratic logic. While it was recog-nized that such incongruence between organizational logic and structures might be resolved, it was warned that such "schizoid" archetypes are unstable (Greenwood and Hinings 1993).

Limitations of Archetype Analysis in Healthcare Fields

Despite the advancements to knowledge of healthcare field dynamics that have emerged from archetype analysis, two main limitations persist. First, little attention has been given to exploring the implications of organization fields being structured systems of social positions within which "institutional wars" rage over logics and resources (Hoffman 1999: 352). As early as 1983, DiMaggio suggested the use of the word "field" in the dual sense in which Bourdieu (1975) uses the French term "champ" (battlefield) to signify both: (a) some commonality of purpose, and (b) a theatre of strategy and conflict over logics. A lack of attention to the inherent conflict within fields has meant that archetype studies tend to produce accounts of "punctu-ated equilibrium" whereby lengthy periods of stability (inertia) are broken either by internal powerful elites or by exogenous shocks (Delbridge and Edwards 2007). Greater concern for countervailing field logics within archetype theory would encour-age the reassessment of periods previously labeled as equilibrium to periods of con-certed institutional maintenance (Lawrence and Suddaby 2006). It may also help illuminate the role of logics in endogenous change, for example, by enabling change agents to creatively resist for change and propose new archetypes (Friedland and Alford 1991; Thornton, Jones, and Kury 2005; Townley 2002; Seo and Creed 2002; Greenwood and Suddaby 2006).

Second, while the notion of institutional entrepreneurship has been coined to refer to the activities of actors who try to leverage resources to create new archetypes (DiMaggio 1988; Rao, Morrill, and Zald 2000; Dorado 2005), archetype studies have concentrated on the leadership of powerful actors, such as the state and large corpo-rations (Reay and Hinings 2005; Greenwood and Suddaby 2006; Lawrence and Suddaby 2006), or new field entrants (Leblebici et al. 1991). The role of disadvan-taged (resource-poor) field participants remains understudied even though it is recog-nized that in fields such as healthcare that have been traditionally dominated by providers and the state, dominated actors, such as consumers, "attempt to usurp, exclude and establish monopoly over the mechanisms of the field's reproduction and the type of power effective in it" (Bourdieu and Wacquant 1992: 106). The next section explores the potential for social movement studies to frame ways that less powerful field participants draw from logics to resist for change by mobilizing new archetypes.

Extending Archetype Analysis through Social Movement Studies

As institutional theorists give increasing attention to issues of change and agency, some have begun to investigate what can be learned from studies of social movements defined as "collective enterprises seeking to establish a new order of life" (Blumer 1969: 99). The starting point for this exploration is recognition that some social movements attempt bottom-up institutional transformation by introducing new organizing templates into organizational fields (Jenkins and Perrow 1977; Davis and Thompson 1994; Schneiberg and Soule 2005). The primary concern of this chapter is with exploring how this occurs (Hensmans 2003; McAdam and Scott 2005). This venture is timely given both (a) Tarrow's (1998) assertion that Western societies are now "social movement societies" in which movement activity has become an important vehicle of social change, and (b) calls for social movement researchers in healthcare fields to develop "integrative, and even interdisciplinary, approaches to the study of multi-layered and complex health social movements" (Brown and Zavestoski 2005: 12). Conceptually, the project is aided by the fact that the two research traditions share a concern for logics. As noted earlier, while logics within archetype theory provide underpinning organizing principles (Freidland and Alford 1991), for social movement analysts frames are seen to form the glue between challengers providing "justification, direction, weapons of attack, weapons of defense, inspiration and, hope" (Blumer 1995: 73).

At a general level of comparison, the social movements and archetypes literatures concur that while processes of bottom-up institutional change will vary across contexts, common characteristics include attempts to mobilize resources (legitimacy, finances, etc.) and political support by the "framing" of issues (DiMaggio 1988; Snow 2004; Rao, Morrill, and Zald 2000). While archetype studies have traditionally offered little further elaboration of bottom-up and contested change processes, social movement research has made considerable headway in explaining how forms of social change develop from nonelites developing frames for organizing and introducing new institutions that serve as mobilizing strategies (Clemens 1993, Schneiberg and Soule 2005; Schneiberg and Clemens 2006; Schneiberg, King, and Smith 2008; Schneiberg and Lounsbury 2008; Stryker 2000). This stream of work directs attention to three issues of relevance to studies of archetype change in organizational fields: movement-countermovement dynamics, political opportunity structures, and institutional process.

Movement-Countermovement Dynamics

While early social movement studies concentrated on single movements against the state, increasing attention has been given to the interplay between opposing movements (Tarrow 1998). The basis for this work is the understanding that, by advocating change, social movements necessarily create the conditions for their own opposition among those who share objects of concern but who draw from countervailing logics to make competing political and resource claims (Gale 1996). This sometimes takes countermovement form and once a countermovement is mobilized, conflict ensues in which the state may occasionally intervene on one side or the other (Zald and Useem 1987: 247–53).

In analytical terms, the labeling of participants within an institutional process as movement or countermovement rests, to some extent, on the timescale of study. In the case of the U.S. abortion rights struggle, for example, it is typically held that the "pro-choice" movement secured the *Roe v. Wade* decision, which then sparked the "pro-life" countermovement aimed at reversing the decision. Taking a longer timeframe might lead to the labeling of pro-choice activity as a countermovement to a movement that developed the extant institutional framework. Recognizing this difficulty, here, a group proposing transformation of an existing healthcare archetype is conceived as a reform movement. Challenge to that movement comes from a countermovement. Because the prevailing logic and archetype in most healthcare fields is supported, at least to some extent, by the state, this labeling of reform movements and countermovements is largely consistent with Arno Mayer's view that the state is the enemy of, and countermovement to, reform movements. However, as each of the cases presented later show, successful health reform movements generate supporters (sometimes even activism) within government agencies. Contra Mayer, this suggests a more ambiguous and complex role of the state that may include dynamic elements of support for health reform movements.

Political Opportunity Structure

Institutional analyses and social movement studies use a number of terms to refer to the historical structure of sociopolitical opportunities and constraints that influence the emergence of change processes (McAdam 1982; Gamson and Meyer 1996; Dorado 2005). Here, we use the social movement term "political opportunity structure" to emphasize that while certain conditions and events may encourage reform movements to propose new field archetypes, they do not determine it. Rather, as Hoffman (1999: 366) argues, field-level change emerges through the way in which "events are socially constructed through a contest over meaning among the players." While it is recognized that relatively stable opportunity structures (e.g., political processes) and more volatile characteristics (e.g., elite alignment) vary between fields, it is generally accepted that the "success" of social movements in aggregate has altered the structure of political opportunity for subsequent challenges (Quadagno 1992).

Institutional Change Process

Social movement studies of institutional change strategy tend to concentrate on two component processes: mobilization and framing (Clemens 1993, Schneiberg and Soule 2005; Schneiberg and Clemens 2006; Schneiberg, King, and Smith 2008; Schneiberg and Lounsbury 2008; Stryker 2000). In both social movement studies and institutional theory, mobilization refers to challengers' attempts to expand the material resources aligned with the proposed institutional change such as formal organization structures and funding flows (Maguire, Hardy, and Lawrence 2004). Similar to the institutional theory notion of "theorization" as the political process of seeking legitimacy for a *normative* "conceptual destination" (Greenwood and Hinings 1996: 1040), the social movement concept of "framing" refers to the "collective processes of interpretation, attribution and social construction that mediate between opportunity and action" (McAdam, McCarthy, and Zald 1996:2). In practice, this process involves various activities including: positing the failures of the prevailing arrangements, aligning the interests of aggrieved constituencies, diagnosing causes, assigning blame, and demonstrating the ways in which the new institutions provide solutions to these problems (Bourdieu 1975; DiMaggio 1988; Rao, Morrill, and Zald 2000).

Studies of Field Transformation Driven by Reform Movements

From among the institutional theory and social movements literatures, three studies present excellent cases of movement-countermovement dynamics within processes of organizational field change: (1) Kitchener and colleagues' (Kitchener and Harrington 2004) analysis of U.S. long-term care provision; (2) Maguire and colleagues' (Maguire, Hardy, and Lawrence 2001) study of Canadian AIDS treatment; and (3) Staggenborg's (1993) analysis of the U.S. pro-choice struggle. Although none of these cases use an analytical framework that combines archetype and social movement studies, insights from each influenced the development of the framework presented in the next section. Thus, as background to the introduction of the new conceptual framework, the three focal studies are summarized briefly below.

Kitchener and colleagues' (Kitchener and Harrington 2004) historical study of the mature field of U.S. publicly funded (Medicaid program for the poor and disabled) long-term care services is a rare example of the application of archetype theory to a case of field-level change driven by a social movement. The focal process centers on the iterative mobilization and framing efforts of the fragmented movement of elderly and disabled consumers. The traditional archetype of long-term care in the United States is shown to rest on a logic of professional power and autonomy that supports the state-level administration of services provided in residential facilities (e.g., nursing homes) under the control of physicians. The reform movement has long demanded more state (Medicaid) funding for services provided in home and community-based settings that allow greater independence for consumers. These demands have been consistently resisted and challenged by a countermovement comprising state agencies and the increasingly corporate provider industry that has a powerful political lobby. For more than fifty years this intensive institutional maintenance activity (which other analyses may have labeled as inertia) has frustrated the reform movement and led both sides to use militaristic metaphors including the term "war."

After basing its early demands for reform on claims about consumers' civil right to independence, the long-term care reform movement has increasingly drawn on consumerist (choice) and cost-efficiency arguments. The movement has received growing elite support through, for example, the *Olmstead* Supreme Court ruling that states' restriction of home care services to public program participants constitutes illegal discrimination. Increasingly, but at a slow pace, home and community-based care has secured a larger proportion of total public long-term care expenditures, and this has supported the growth of a field of service provider organizations such as home care agencies.

The Canadian case reports an institutional study (but not an archetype analysis) of the attempts of a social movement to alter the structure and operation of the emerging field of HIV/AIDS provision within the context of a more centralized state than the United States of America. Between the early 1980s and late 1990s, the state collaborated with service providers and the pharmaceutical industry to establish a template of AIDS provision that was characterized by limited services and restricted information exchange with consumers. From the inception of the field, the demands of loosely connected consumers for enhanced services and mandated consultation were ignored or resisted by a countermovement comprising the state and industry. In response, the consumer groups developed a tighter-linked movement that increased political lobbying activity and attracted increasing support among elite groups including the press. In a landmark outcome in 1997, the establishment of the Canadian Treatment Advocates Council transformed the field structure. This new and influential body was funded by the state and industry with a mandate to convene regular consumer-industry consultations on issues including service development, new treatments, and clinical trial design and results.

Staggenborg's (1933) social movement study of the U.S. pro-choice struggle reports that it arose from the framing and mobilization efforts of reformers based around a belief system that stresses women's civil right to have access to safe and legal abortion services. Following that reform movement's success in the 1973 *Roe v. Wade* Supreme Court case, an organizational field of women's health services providers developed from the movement's logic to include hospital units and clinics. Contesting this institutional framework and its underpinning logic, a countermovement developed around a politicoreligious belief system that denies the morality of abortion. This logic forms the basis of intense framing and mobilization activity that has secured legal victories including the 1976 Hyde Amendment prohibiting Medicaid funding of abortions, and the 1989 *Webster* ban on the use of public facilities for counseling.

Conceptual Framework

This section combines the resources from the institutional and social movement literatures that were introduced above to derive a conceptual framework of research propositions concerning reform movements' pursuit of new archetypes in healthcare fields. In addition to the social movement concepts and empirical insights introduced earlier, some inspiration for the conceptual framework is drawn from Meyer and Staggenborg's (1996) framework for studying movements and countermovements. Three main extensions to that work are offered here. First, additional propositions are derived from the institutional analysis literature. Second, propositions from the original framework are restated to specifically address the focal issue of bottom-up sponsorship of new field archetypes. Third, justifications for the propositions are refined from the studies summarized above.

The starting point for this conceptual framework is the understanding that in all healthcare fields, the existence of multiple belief systems (logics) will ensure that the prevailing institutional framework (archetype) will derive opposition (Friedland and Alford 1991; Brown and Zavestoski 2005). While not unique to healthcare fields (but to a greater extent than in commercial fields), the plurality of logics in healthcare fields—arising from the conflicting interests of various occupation groups, consumers, and other agents—present opportunities for grassroots reformers to mobilize their claims for resources to support new archetypes (Friedland and Alford 1991). This phenomenon can create conditions under which reform movements mobilize "upstart" institutional forms with less fear of losing legitimacy (Shortell et al. 2000).

Whereas challenges to prevailing archetypes can emerge "top-down" from elite groups such as the state and corporations (Useem and Zald 1982), this framework concentrates on change processes initiated by disadvantaged movements of reformers. In most Western nations, prevailing archetypes in healthcare fields are, to some extent, developed and sustained through support from the state (e.g., funding and service provision agencies) and professions. From social movement studies, while it is expected that all such archetypes will attract opposition, not all will generate grassroots reform movements proposing new archetypes. Thus, the first component of our framework examines the political opportunity structures supporting this particular form of institutional process.

Opportunity Structures for Reform Movements' Pursuit of New Archetypes

Social movement studies suggest that the emergence of reform movements proposing new archetypes in healthcare fields is influenced by interactions among a number of political opportunity structures including: field structure, policy context, state structure, and reporting standards.

Field Structure. One of the key factors shaping the potential for reform movements to mobilize new healthcare archetypes is the structure of the organizational field. As indicated by the comparison (albeit limited) presented between the long-term care, AIDS and pro-choice cases above, the relative speed of the Canadian process suggests that a centralized field may present a more conducive political opportunity structure for reform movements, than does a decentralized field such as that of long-term care in the United States. Presumably, this is because a centralized field presents a united force against change.

In addition to being centralized, the Canadian AIDS field was emergent (immature) when compared with the fields of U.S. long-term care and U.K. hospitals. This may suggest that proposals for a new archetype are more likely to succeed in immature fields than mature fields that tend to have "stable and broadly acknowledged centers, peripheries, and status orders" and are therefore less likely to embody change and diversity (DiMaggio and Powell 1983: 156; Dorado 2005; Maguire, Hardy, and Lawrence 2004). The availability of elite support (e.g., government and industry) is a critical political opportunity structure for movements in all fields including healthcare (Tarrow 1998). This point is well illustrated in D'Aunno and colleagues' (1991) study of the development of drug treatment centers in the United States in which the support for state and federal government agencies was shown to be critical. Whereas in the American pro-choice struggle the Catholic Church helped to generate and support the countermovement, Canadian anti-abortion activists have received less attention and are disappointed with the lack of similar support, which results from factors including the relationship between the Church and Canadian government (Cuneo 1989). Until recently, the lack of elite support for consumer demands for expanded access to home care is one of the main reasons for the slow progress of that campaign in the United States.

According to standard organization theory, fields tend to develop from relative decentralization with little elite support into more centralized entities with increasing elite support (DiMaggio and Powell 1983). Thus, to some extent the issue of elite support may be seen to confound the notion of centrality and maturity being distinctive comparative dimensions of fields. However, it is possible for decentralized fields to be mature with stable archetypes (e.g., U.S. long-term care) and for centralized fields to be immature with unsettled archetypes (Canadian AIDS).

Proposition 1. The successful promotion of a new healthcare archetype by a reform movement is more likely to occur in centralized and immature fields.

Policy Closure. While this framework holds that the existence of any healthcare archetype is likely to provoke challenge, archetypes may be protected to some extent by a widespread consensus that they are not currently vulnerable to political contest (Meyer and Staggenborg 1996). If such an aura of "policy closure" exists, dominant archetypes are less likely to be challenged, because it is known that judgments about the possibility of success influence support among potential reformers. For example, while recent extensions to restrictions on cigarette smoking in many countries creates the potential for reaction by countermovement (pro-smoking) activity, the potential for this is mitigated by a situation of perceived policy closure in which the pro-smoking lobby is considered to have a diminishing impact.

Proposition 2: The pursuit of a new healthcare archetype by a reform movement is less likely when allies of the prevailing archetype successfully promote an image of policy closure.

State structure. The openness of prevailing archetypes to opposition from reform movements is influenced by the nature of state structure. Specifically, states with federal structures, such as the United States, are more likely to face movement-countermovement conflict than are more unitary governments such as Britain and France (Meyer and Staggenborg 1996). The basis for this is that unitary states face fewer potential challenges over policy implementation than in federal states where political authority is divided, both among branches of government and among national and regional governments. This fragmentation of authority provides a political opportunity structure for the development of alternative logics, archetypes, and allegiances. Support for this view is given by the fact that most reported studies of grassroots advocacy for institutional change in healthcare fields are based on cases from the federal United States (Scott 2001; Brown and Zavestoski 2005).

Proposition 3. The promotion of a new archetype in a healthcare field by a reform movement is more likely to occur in states with decentralized governance.

Spillover. While it is generally believed that the "success" of social movements in aggregate has altered the structure of political opportunity for subsequent institutional reformers, the concept of "social movement spillover" (Meyer and Whittier 1994: 277) draws attention to the fact that reform logics established in one field may present nascent challengers in a neighboring field with a condition of possibility. The U.S. long-term-care case shows clearly that the reform movement drew significant inspiration from (and influenced) both broader civil rights activity during the 1960s, and the deinstitutionalization movement in the neighboring mental health field.

Proposition 4. The promotion of a new archetype in a healthcare field by a reform movement is more likely to occur in fields neighboring similar activity.

Journalistic Standards. When the media cover "institutional wars" in organizational fields, journalistic standards of balanced reporting encourage the reporting of the reform movement and its logic (Gitlin 1980). As reported in the cases of U.S. pro-choice, Canadian HIV activism, and U.S. long-term care, this balancing process can lead to coverage that both emphasizes conflict and presents a political opportunity structure for reform movements to mobilize alternative archetypes. While balanced reporting is an expectation within most Western democracies, variations do exist, and the expectation is not yet realized in nations such as China.

Proposition 5. The promotion of a new archetype in a healthcare field by a reform movement is more likely to occur in contexts of higher journalistic standards of balanced reporting.

The Process of Reform Movements' Pursuit of New Archetypes in Health Fields

Institutional and social movement studies of change processes variously highlight issues of leadership, structure, and strategy.

Leadership. While the need for reform movement leadership is recognized widely, there is a tension between a perceived need for heroic leaders (who charismatically envision, energize, and enable) and the problems arising from a "cult of personality." Increasingly, successful healthcare movement leadership is seen as a process involving multiple, yet networked activities including: constructing and framing the logic, identifying political opportunities, mobilizing support, and linking adherents with potential recruits (Rao, Morrill, and Zald 2000).

A key basis of leaders' legitimacy in other areas of society is affiliation with a dominant power (e.g., prestigious firms), and this can encourage the development of heroic leadership roles. In sharp contrast, legitimacy for the leaders of healthcare reform movements more typically arises from social positions that engender respect from diverse stakeholders including consumers of services and sympathetic government officials (Maguire et al. 2001; Brown and Zavestoski 2005). Given the long-term nature of the struggle to introduce a new archetype into a healthcare field, all of the focal case studies show that movement leaders must mobilize wider political support through negotiations, bargaining, and compromise to lock stakeholders into a stable and enduring coalition. Thus, the role of movement leaders is not to "direct" but to create a receptive context for change through strategic framing: "collective processes of interpretation, attribution and social construction that mediate between opportunity and action" (McAdam and Scott 2005: 17). For example, Arndt and Bigelow (2000) show how executives in the field of U.S. hospitals use "impression management" techniques to theorize the adoption of new practices against prescriptions for the adoption of managerial practices that have come to dominate political rhetoric and discourse.

> Proposition 6. The promotion of a new archetype in a healthcare field by a reform movement is enabled by a network approach to movement leadership.

Structure. The "organizational repertoire" (Clemens 1993) of a reform movement proposing a new field archetype will be restricted, especially in the early days, by limited resources (e.g., finance and expertise). Three main organizational forms of social movements have been identified: (a) formal organizations, (b) the organization of collective actions, and (c) connecting structures or networks (Tarrow 1998: 123–24). Given the requirements for sustained action and the development of collective identity (and not withstanding the perils of goal displacement, routinization, and conservatism), the grassroots pursuit of a new field archetype may require reform movements to adopt a formal structure or network form. Whatever structural form a reform movement adopts, it has been noted that over time they develop similar organizational competencies to their countermovement. For example, as the home care movement in the long-term care field engaged in legal action at the state and federal level, it developed a legal capacity (of aligned lawyers) to match that of those aligned with the traditional archetype (e.g., the powerful institutional-provider lobby).

> Proposition 7. The promotion of a new archetype in a healthcare field by a reform movement will involve the movement developing equivalent capacities to their countermovement.

Strategy. As noted earlier, the grassroots proposal of a new healthcare archetype will likely encounter resistance and take years to achieve. As the AIDS and long-term-care cases show, to sustain their movements and develop relationships with potential supporters, reformers need to frame their demands to changing external circumstances. For example, when the efficiency of public services rose to the top of the policy agenda in the 1970s and 1980s, the home care reform movement began framing their archetype as presenting a cost-effective means of delivering long-term care, which also preserved consumer independence.

In the presence of strong resistance to a reform movement's proposal for a new field archetype, there are likely to be numerous "frame disputes" both within the movement and with the countermovement (Benford 1993; Snow 2004). Within the fragmented home care movement, for example, there have been fierce disputes between the elderly and younger disabled on: (1) the relative importance of campaigning on the basis of independence or cost efficiency, and (2) priorities for extended access to various services such as consumer-directed care, attendant care, job-supports, and devices.

In contrast to fields in which movements are based on limited, often economic, concerns (e.g. smokers' rights and whaling), movements proposing new archetypes in healthcare fields are more likely to arise when opposition is framed as being based on broader systems of social values (logics) such as the right to independence or access to care. Examples of this include the cases of abortion, HIV/AIDS care and consumers' demands to remain independent of residential care facilities. Additionally, campaigns that begin on economic grounds (e.g., logging) but which become associated with larger value debates (e.g., local culture and environmentalism) are more likely to involve the reform movement sponsoring a new archetype.

Although movement activism for a new field archetype will initially be based on perception of the most direct means toward policy influence (Downs 1957), movements have a limited "tactical repertoire" to select from (Allsop, Jones and Bagott 2005). A requirement for success in the longer term is that they tactically innovate and escalate (Tilly 1993, McAdam 1982). One common tactic when faced with setbacks or slow progress in one arena is to shift efforts to new arenas of conflict. Thus, in the long-term-care case, when the originating federal legislation for public funding (Medicaid) offered little support for home care, the movement directed to other arenas including attempts to expand home care access through state-level policy. After slow progress in that arena, advocates initiated legal action that led to Supreme Court ruling in the *Olmstead* case that states' failure to provide access to Medicaid HCBS constituted discrimination under the Americans with Disabilities Act.

> Proposition 8. The promotion of a new archetype in a healthcare field by a reform movement requires leaders to frame an array of arguments that translate to the interests of diverse stakeholders and match the current political economy.

Process

The third concern of this framework is the under-researched theme of new archetype change process in terms of pacing and form (Amis, Slack, and Hinings 2004). The prevailing characterization of the S-shaped diffusion curve (new archetypes are first recognized, then accepted by relatively few actors, and then taken for granted more broadly) is overly simplistic because it ignores issues of power and countermovement resistance. Lawrence, Winn, and Jennings (2001) suggest that there will be distinct temporal patterns of archetype diffusion depending on whether "influence" or "domination" power is relied upon. Influence, the form of power most usually associated with reform movements, "works" more slowly than domination by actors aligned with prevailing archetypes. This is because of the reliance of influence on shifting the costs and benefits of different behavioral patterns while dominance relies on changing the range of behavioral choices available to actors in the field.

Given the likelihood of resistance from interests associated with the prevailing archetype who wield domination power, the AIDS, long-term-care, and pro-choice cases demonstrate that processes of grassroots pursuit of new archetype are likely to be protracted, iterative, and contested when compared to the rapid transformation processes (less than five years) reported in the archetype studies (Brock, Powell, and Hinings 1999). Although the outcomes of reform movements are typically modest, it has been argued that institutional resistance can help change happen by energizing and encouraging imagination (Palmer 1997).

> Proposition 9. The influenced-based promotion of a new archetype in a healthcare field by a reform movement is likely to be slow (taking at least ten years), iterative, and highly contested.

Form of Transformation. While the archetype approach defines field-level transformation as the institutionalization of a new archetype, this does not require the replacement of existing institutions that are reported in some institutional analyses (Biggart 1977). Rather, the logic and structures of an insurgent archetype can become "sedimented" on top of the logic and structures of the existing configuration (Cooper et al. 1996). Because many healthcare fields have highly developed sets of interlocking practices and stable relations among organizations, when new archetypes are institutionalized, they are most likely to be either: (a) accommodated alongside the existing archetype (Reay and Hinings 2005), or (b) sedimented upon the traditional archetype. After a lengthy period of institutional war, the sedimentation of new archetype may stabilize the field or it may produce a "schizoid" archetype that is unstable (Greenwood and Hinings 1993).

> Proposition 10. The promotion of a new archetype in a healthcare field by a reform movement may result in the replacement of the prevailing form but is more likely to result in either: (a) accommodation alongside the existing archetype, or (b) sedimentation upon the traditional archetype.

Conclusions

In extending the capacity of archetype theory to frame the promotion of new institutional arrangements by disadvantaged field participants, this chapter provides a response to the question of what institutional theory and social movement theory can learn from each other (McAdam and Scott 2005; Brown and Zavestovski 2005). The resulting conceptual framework comprises a (nonexhaustive) set of ten related research propositions to guide subsequent empirical research and theory building. The starting point for this framework is the understanding that in healthcare fields, the existence of multiple belief systems (logics) ensures that the prevailing institutional framework (archetype) will derive opposition. More specifically, the plurality of logics in healthcare fields—arising from the conflicting interests of various occupation groups, consumers and other agents—presents opportunities for institutional reformers to mobilize new archetypes comprising a new combination of logic, operating structures, and systems. While such an attempt at transformational change is typically instigated "top-down" by elite groups such as government agencies, this framework concentrates on the potential for it to be generated "bottom-up," from reform movements.

The conceptual framework introduced here contains three sets of propositions. The first concerns the opportunity structures under which reform movements in healthcare fields emerge to propose an alternative archetype. It is argued that five contextual features support such reform efforts: organizational fields that are centralized and immature, an open policy context, a decentralized state, neighboring fields of reform activity, and journalistic standards of balanced reporting.

The second set of propositions addresses the structures and strategies that arise when reform movements mobilize a new archetype in healthcare fields. It is suggested that such efforts are enabled by three factors: networked forms of movement leadership, the development of equivalent capacities to the countermovement, and leaders framing an array of arguments that fit with both the diverse membership, and current political context.

The final set of propositions refers to the nature and timing of processes emerging from reform movements' pursuit of new healthcare archetypes. It is proposed specifically that successful processes will be slow (taking at least ten years), iterative, and highly contested, and will most likely result in either: (a) accommodation of the new archetype alongside the existing archetype or, (b) sedimentation upon the traditional archetype.

The primary concern of this framework is archetype change driven by reform movements in healthcare fields. The applicability of the framework beyond that realm will rest on judgments concerning the uniqueness of both healthcare fields, and health social movements. The critical feature of healthcare fields in this framework is the ongoing (rather than more sporadic) existence of countervailing systems of beliefs and values (logics) that generate reform agency. While plural logics are known to characterize other organizational fields such as education and the arts, this feature is less typical in commercial fields, such as manufacturing, that tend to be dominated by a single (typically capitalist enterprise) logic (Brock, Powell, and Hinings 1999). In the framework presented here, a critical feature of health social movements is their mobilization around a relatively broad set of beliefs and values concerning health (e.g., the right to maintain independence while receiving long-term care) that transcend a single issue, such as demanding wheelchair access to hospitals (Brown and Zavestoski 2005). The framework presented here is, therefore, most likely to be relevant to cases that present similar field and movement characteristics.

The investigation of the propositions presented in this framework (in healthcare or other settings) will require longitudinal studies of bottom-up processes of archetype change that vary in terms of characteristics such as interests, logics, and countermovements. Specifically, attention must be given to how the tactics of each side evolve, how alliances and form and shift, and how frames are manipulated by both sides. Comparative studies of similar conflicts (abortion, long-term care, and HIV/AIDS) in different organizational fields (countries, regions etc.) would also present the opportunity to investigate the role of state structures in enabling or discouraging bottom-up archetype change.

The early stage of empirical and conceptual work on the issue of bottom-up archetype reform processes presents the opportunity to use a wide range of research methods to advance knowledge. Analyses of institutional process in social movement research and archetype studies have both typically adopted qualitative historical and case-study approaches. These demonstrate that institutional processes can be well researched using combinations of archival research, participant observation, and interviewing. Following a research tradition in historical sociology, it may be fruitful to qualitatively consider the research propositions in the conceptual framework presented here. To this end, content analyses of materials produced by opposing movements can illuminate particular frames and constructions of key issues and perceptions. Analyses of media accounts could also be used to examine issues including the relative influence of opposing movements on public discourse.

In part due to researchers' concern for process, and in part due to a lack of appropriate datasets, there has been relatively little use of quantitative analysis in archetype analysis. As the number of reported cases of reform movements promoting new field archetypes increases, the potential for cross case analysis increases and this may be aided by the use of event data coded from secondary accounts (e.g., newspapers and journals) to help reveal patterns of mobilization and conflict. Pursuit of these directions may lead to the development of comparative case datasets that allow analysis using techniques such as quantitative comparative analysis (Ragin 1999).

It is hoped that the multidisciplinary research agenda proposed in this chapter provides a platform from which to advance theoretical and empirical knowledge of the interesting, and increasingly pervasive, phenomenon of *resistance for change* (Tarrow 1998; Spicer 2006). Because the framework was developed from both institutional theory and social movement literatures, it offers potential for generating contributions to both research traditions. For institutional analysts, the line of enquiry proposed here envisages two streams of related activity. First, the conception of fields as battlegrounds in which institutional wars rage over logics (Bourdieu 1975; DiMaggio 1983; Hoffman 1999) provides a basis for endogenous explanations of change and encourages the reassessment of periods previously labeled as equilibrium to periods of institutional maintenance (Lawrence and Suddaby 2006). Second, the framework presents a way of conceptualizing the ways that disadvantaged field participants attempt to gain greater control over the mechanisms of field reproduction and the type of power effective in it (Bourdieu and Wacquant 1992). For social movement researchers, this framework introduces the archetype approach to studying healthcare field dynamics as means of addressing the need to develop interdisciplinary approaches to the study of complex health social movements and their impact on organizational fields (Brown and Zavestoski 2005).

10

The "Hostile Takeover" of Bioethics by Religious Conservatives and the Counter Offensive

Renee R. Anspach

How, why, and with what effects does a social movement lay claim to an issue or field? What happens when social movements compete for control over social problems and professional jurisdictions? These questions are the focal points of this paper, and I will begin to answer them, using the controversy over Terri Schiavo's fate as an illustrative case. In many ways, the Schiavo case was a defining moment in the history of bioethics. Never before had a family dispute over a life-and-death decision assumed the proportions of a public controversy of this magnitude, reverberating in the halls of Congress, the White House, and the Vatican. The Schiavo controversy was also a defining moment in the history of the pro-life movement, a coalition of conservative Catholics, Protestant fundamentalists, and evangelicals most widely known for its opposition to abortion. With the Schiavo case, its first large-scale mobilization around an adult patient, the pro-life movement pursued a broader agenda that now included end-of-life decisions.[1]

At stake in the Schiavo case, however, was a very different conflict over what the field of bioethics was to become and who could call themselves "bioethicists." Over the past three decades, a heterogeneous interdisciplinary group called "bioethicists," based in hospitals and research centers, had come to occupy the role of experts on ethics, some serving on advisory commissions or as pundits quoted in the press. For mainstream bioethicists, who saw themselves as *the* experts on ethics, it came as a surprise—and not a pleasant one at that—to find a new group of "conservative" or "Christian bioethicists," quoted as "bioethicists" in the popular press. Some mainstream bioethicists viewed this development as an unwelcome, "hostile takeover." This metaphor is, however, somewhat overdrawn, since mainstream bioethics continues to thrive and has not actually been *taken over* at all. But it does capture the way

144

many mainstream bioethicists reacted to the sudden realization that they were not alone. Surely, many believed, a response was necessary.

Drawing on the work of Zald and Useem (1987) and Rao, Morrill, and Zald (2000), I explore the movement/countermovement dynamics between the new, conservative bioethics and mainstream bioethics, using the Schiavo case as an example. In order to understand these dynamics, some descriptive scaffolding is necessary. To this end, I first provide a brief overview of the field of bioethics—as it existed before the Schiavo case. Next, I give a brief chronology of the Schiavo case and discuss the impact of religious conservatives on the public discourse on the case. In the third section, I analyze how religious conservatives came to mobilize successfully around the Schiavo case. Finally, I examine how secular bioethics has mounted a counteroffensive and created what is now known as "progressive bioethics." In the conclusion, I discuss the implications of these events for the study of social movements and health.

This article is based on several sources of data. The account of the Schiavo case is based on articles in the popular press that appeared at the time. To reconstruct the events that occurred when the case was only of local interest, I examined articles in the *Tampa Tribune* and the *St. Petersberg Times*. Most information about the Schiavo case after it had gained national attention is drawn from 182 articles mentioning the Schiavo case that appeared in the *New York Times* between 2001 and 2006. I also examined several Web sites belonging to think tanks and activist organizations. Because this is a small, exploratory study, it is based primarily on articles in a single newspaper. Had this been a larger project, I would have triangulated among several newspapers and collected oral histories from activists. It is clearly impossible to draw inferences about how other newspapers would have depicted the case. However, as one of America's three largest-circulation papers with a national readership, the *Times* plays a part in the construction of public ethical problems (see Anspach and Halpern 2000).

I read these articles from three distinct standpoints. First, I read them as *primary sources*, to assemble an account of the events that unfolded in the Schiavo case. A second reading was more analytic: I used the articles to examine activists' strategies, tactics, and response to opportunities. Finally, I read the 182 articles in the *New York Times* as *texts* to explore the language journalists used in framing the Schiavo case and to determine which activists and experts were quoted. The overview of bioethics in the next section is based on historical accounts of the field as well as my own observations.

Bioethics Before Schiavo

So far, I have suggested that the Schiavo controversy was also a conflict over who should be included within the boundaries of bioethics. I use the term "bioethics" to refer to that field which takes as its subject matter the ethical dimensions of biology and medicine. Whether the topic is defining death or deciding who is to receive an organ transplant or be taken off life support; bioethicists examine the principles, norms, or precepts on which medical decisions are or should be premised (Anspach 1993; Jonsen 1998).

Forty years ago, neither the term "bioethics" nor the field itself existed. In fact, not until the 1970s did bioethics emerge. While historical accounts differ, scholars have identified several catalysts for the beginning of bioethics: the erosion of trust in medicine as it became increasingly bureaucratic (Rothman1991); the proliferation of new social movements that promulgated a "culture of rights," many of which attacked medicine (Starr 1982; Halpern 2004); demands for regulating medical research in the wake of exposes of abuses (Rothman 1991; Jonsen 1998); and conflicts among patients, professionals and social movements over life-and-decisions (e.g., Rothman 1991). Moreover, the emphasis in bioethics on individual rights, such as patients' right to refuse treatment, had deep cultural resonance. The idea of experts in ethics had potential appeal to groups on all sides of the political spectrum: philosophy students demanding more relevant subject matter; increasingly restive medical consumers; and physicians seeking moral guidance or expert validation of their decisions. As activists on the right or left threatened to take decisions out of the hospital and into the courts, physicians undoubtedly saw the benefit of "experts on ethics" who could mediate between patients, professionals, and the courts, thereby protecting the vestiges of autonomy from impending deep incursions by social movements and the state.

Pressure from social movements and the state, then, became part of a broader opportunity structure for the emergence of bioethics. These developments opened a "market niche" or a jurisdiction for "experts on ethics," a niche that was quickly filled by theologians seeking a place in the secular world (Jonsen 1998), academic philosophers seeking to apply their skills to actual problems, and other philosophers facing a shrinking academic job market and seeking careers outside the academy. Some of the early bioethicists were invited into medical settings by physicians, and others perceived a potential market for their expertise. Although most of the founders of bioethics had degrees in philosophy and theology, the field became increasingly secularized (Jonsen 1998; Evans 2002).

Since its inception, the field of bioethics has expanded exponentially both in numbers and influence. In 1977, there were only two centers of bioethics: the Hastings Center, established in 1969, and the Kennedy Center at Georgetown University, which opened in 1971 (Jonsen 1998). By 2007, the NIH listed more than thirty bioethics centers, most affiliated with universities and many affiliated with medical centers (http://bioethics.od.nih.gov/academic). Interdisciplinary from its inception, bioethics has become increasingly diverse. Today's bioethicists are trained not only in philosophy or theology but also in medicine, nursing, or the social sciences—a trend that is increasing.

Over time, bioethicists came to play a wide variety of roles in an increasingly broad array of settings. To name just some of the roles of today's bioethicists, they include: research, teaching, and writing; consulting in hospitals (clinical bioethics); advising the state on health issues (policy bioethics); and communicating with the media (public intellectuals; for related discussions see DeVries, Dingwall, and Orfali n.d.; DeVries et al. 2006). There have been limits to this diversity, however. Most of those trained in theology were liberal Catholics or represented mainline Protestant denominations (Evans 2002)—a pattern that would change with the Schiavo case.

As the field has developed, bioethicists have steadily acquired the accoutrements of a profession: a large professional association and several journals. After some debate about credentialing, beginning in the late 1990s, several university centers began to issue master's degrees, and Ph.D. programs have also emerged (DeVries, Dingwall, and Orfali n.d.). Given the steady progression of these moves to professionalize, it would seem that the next logical step would be to institute licensure, to control entry into the profession. However, licensure remains controversial and has not been established (DeVries et al. n.d.). Thus, bioethics has not yet attained closure, or exclusive jurisdiction, and can be seen as a case of "incomplete professionalization"—a fact that will later prove significant.

The Schiavo Case: A Brief Summary

In the early morning of February 25, 1990, Michael Schiavo was awakened by a thud. He found his twenty-nine-year-old wife Terri, collapsed on the floor. Although the paramedics were able to resuscitate Terri, she did not regain consciousness and was unable to eat without a feeding tube. Within a year, Terri received the diagnosis of persistent vegetative state. Despite some recent controversies, most neurologists agree that patients in a persistent vegetative state are "awake but not aware"—that is, they can respond to stimuli but lack consciousness or the ability to communicate (The Multi-Society Task Force on Persistent Vegetative State, 1994). A brief summary of the events surrounding the Schiavo case is presented in table 10.1.

Over the next four years, Michael Schiavo and Terri's parents, Robert and Mary Schindler, had a close relationship and were optimistic that Terri could regain consciousness. For example, Michael Schiavo took Terri to U.C. San Francisco for a highly experimental procedure that proved unsuccessful (Goodnough 2005c).

In 1992 and 1993, he successfully sued Terri's doctors for malpractice for failing, he argued, to diagnose an eating disorder that led to her collapse. It was at this point that his relationship with the Schindlers began to deteriorate, though the causes of the falling out are in dispute. Michael Schiavo claimed that the Schindlers wanted to share the malpractice money, but the Schindlers said that the dispute concerned Terri's treatment and prospects for recovery. Indeed, by 1994, Michael had concluded that Terri could not recover, while her parents remained optimistic. He also had just won a substantial settlement, and the Schindlers were suspicious of his motives for wanting to stop treatment (Goodnough 2005c).

Between 1998 and 2002, Michael Schiavo and the Schindlers were embroiled in protracted and bitter litigation in the Florida courts. Michael filed petitions with the Pinellas-Pasco court for permission to have Terri's feeding tube removed, arguing that she would not have wanted to live without hope of recovery. Her parents contested these petitions on three grounds, which they were to use throughout their lengthy legal battle. First, they argued that their daughter, a devout Catholic, would never have wanted to violate the Church's prohibition of euthanasia. Second, they petitioned the court to have Michael removed as Terri's guardian on the grounds that as a confirmed "adulterer" who was dating other women, he should not be entrusted to make decisions on her behalf (Goodnough 2005c; Sommer 2002a). Finally, the Schindlers challenged the diagnosis of persistent vegetative state and called witnesses who testified that Terri was in a "minimally conscious state," a condition with

Table 10.1. The Schiavo Controversy: A Brief Chronology

February 25, 1990	Terri Schiavo collapses
1990–93	Close relationship between Schindlers and Michael Schiavo
	Optimism: Michael takes Terri to UCSF for experimental treatment
	Michael enters nursing program
1992–93	Michael successfully sues for malpractice
1993	Falling out between Terri's husband and parents
1998–2002	Michael Schiavo and Schindlers take case to court. Michael petitions to remove feeding tube; Schindlers dispute account of Terri's wishes, Michael's motives, and Terri's prognosis
2002	Schindlers and doctor make and edit videotape
2003	Parents seek publicity, hire Randall Terry
	Feeding tube removed on orders from Judge Greer
	Fla. Legislature passes "Terri's Law," authorizing Jeb Bush to intervene; Bush orders tube reinserted
Sept. 2004	Fla. Supreme Court finds "Terri's Law" unconstitutional
2005	
March 18	Feeding tube removed third time on orders from Greer
	Vatican denounces decision; massive protests, vigils
March 20	Congress passes Palm Sunday Compromise, transfers jurisdiction over case to federal courts
	Motions to reinsert tube denied in federal courts
March 23	Gov.Bush appeals for delay to present new evidence from William Cheshire; Fla. Supreme Court rejects appeals
March 30	Terri dies; 800 mourners at mass
June 15	Autopsy results show evidence of massive damage
	Bush orders investigation of abuse allegations;
	Prosecutor declines to pursue case

a better prognosis. The Schindlers and Dr. Hammesfahr, a neurologist, made a six-hour videotape of Terri Schiavo that was presented as evidence and viewed by thirty-three expert witnesses. However, three neurologists testified on behalf of Michael Schiavo that Terri was in a persistent vegetative state and highly unlikely to recover. Judge Greer ultimately ruled that in favor of Michael Schiavo (Smith 2005; Sommer 2002b; Levesque 2002).

These acrimonious battles, which unfolded over a four-year period, received little coverage in the national press. However, in 2003, the Schindlers, frustrated by numerous defeats in court, began to publicize their cause and asked pro-life activist Randall Terry, founder of Operation Rescue, to serve as their spokesperson (Kirkpatrick 2005). Terry Schiavo's brother Bobby Schindler was a featured speaker at a National Right to Life Committee conference (Goodnough 2005c). What had once been a family feud had become a national controversy.

In September 2003, Terri's feeding tube was removed on orders from Judge Greer. Faced with five days of prayer vigils in the street, broadcasts on the religious radio and thousands of e-mails pleading with them to come to Terri's rescue, Florida legislators passed Terri's Law, authorizing Governor Jeb Bush to intervene in the case (Goodnough 2003a, 2003b). Bush, a religious conservative, ordered Terri's feeding tube reinserted. However, Michael Schiavo, supported by the ACLU, mounted a series of challenges in the courts, and ultimately the Florida Supreme Court found Terri's Law unconstitutional (Goodnough 2003c, 2003d; 2004a; 2004b; Newman 2005).

The Schindlers filed new motions to forestall removal of the feeding tube so that the Department of Children and Family Services could investigate "anonymous" allegations that Terri Schiavo had been abused. Ultimately, however, Judge Greer ordered Terri's feeding tube to be removed on March 18, 2005. That day, the Vatican denounced the decision "to pull the plug as if we were talking about…a broken…appliance" (Rosenthal 2005).

It was at this point that Ken Connor, Governor Bush's lawyer and an active member of the pro-life movement, began to lobby U.S. representatives and senators for congressional action in the Schiavo case. Several members of Congress, including former heart surgeon Bill Frist and Tom DeLay, watched the video of Terri, which by now had been edited to 4.5 minutes, and ardently supported the cause (Stolberg 2003b). On March 20, Congress passed the "Palm Sunday Compromise," which transferred jurisdiction of the Schiavo case to the federal courts. President Bush, who had interrupted his Texas vacation to sign the bill, proclaimed that "it's always best to err on the side of life" (Hulse and Kirkpatrick 2005; Kornblut 2005). But when federal courts denied the Schindlers' requests to reinsert the feeding tube, it became apparent that congressional efforts had failed (Goodnough and Liptak 2005).

On March 23, 2005, Governor Bush filed a new motion to present new evidence in state court from Dr. William Cheshire, Jr., a sleep researcher at the Jacksonville Mayo Clinic and a Christian bioethicist, who had reviewed the tapes and concluded that Terri was in a minimally conscious state. When the 2nd District Court of Appeals rejected Bush's appeals, he concluded there was little more he could do (Goodnough and Liptak 2005).

Meanwhile protestors, consisting of conservative Catholics, fundamentalist Protestants, and disability rights activists held a vigil, reciting the Lord's Prayer and singing "Amazing Grace." A rumor spread through the crowd that Terri had made sounds interpreted as "I want to live" (Goodnough 2005a, 2005b). Some carried signs warning Jeb Bush not to "be a Pontius Pilate." (Lyman 2005a; 2005b) On March 30, Terri Schiavo died, more than fifteen years after her collapse in 1990. More than eight hundred mourners attended the mass, overflowing into the street (Associated Press 2005b).

Two weeks later, the medical examiner reported the autopsy findings, all of which were consistent with a diagnosis of persistent vegetative state. Terri Schiavo had suffered extensive brain damage; her brain had withered to half its size; and she was blind (Grady 2005). Governor Bush then ordered the state prosecutor to investigate the circumstances surrounding Terri Schiavo's cardiac arrest, noting that the autopsy report suggested a possible gap between Terri Schiavo's collapse and the time of Michael Schiavo's call to 911. Only when the state attorney general found no evidence of criminal activity did the governor declare the case closed (Herbert 2005; Associated Press 2005a).

What is the sociological "moral" of the Terri Schiavo story? On the one hand, the story can be seen as ending in a resounding defeat for conservatives. After all, Terri Schiavo died, leaving some influential politicians embarrassed. On the other hand, when viewed sociologically, an altogether different story emerges. Of the millions of

Americans who die each year in today's hospitals, many do so because somebody made a decision to forego life-sustaining treatment. Patients or families and professionals usually reach a consensus, and prolonged disputes seldom occur (Schneider 2005). Of the decisions to stop treatment, only a minority involves conflict *within* the family (Breen et al. 2001). These disputes, when they do occur, are usually resolved within days or weeks at most (Curtis et al. 2005). Only a small number of conflicts—estimated to be as low as 3–4 percent—are prolonged, though the Schiavo case, which lasted twelve years, remains an anomaly (Burt 2006). Of the small number of cases involving protracted intra-family conflict, only a fraction reaches the courts (Anspach 1993). Of the cases that reach the courts, only one other case, the case of Baby John Doe, reached the White House. Given these facts, the statistical probability of a case reaching state legislators, a governor, Congress, the White House, and the Vatican, as did the case of Terri Schiavo, must be infinitesimally small. It is also remarkable that this conflict persisted for twelve years, even after district, appellate, and federal courts had ruled against the Schindlers. These anomalies can be explained in part by the dogged determination of the Schindlers. But more important, the case attests to the power of social movements to transform a private dispute into a public issue.

In a recent paper, Anspach and Halpern (2008) compared media discourse in the *New York Times* on Terri Schiavo to that on Nancy Cruzan, who ten years earlier had been given a diagnosis of persistent vegetative state. We found that even in a liberal paper such as the *Times*, religious conservatives had a subtle but discernable impact on how Schiavo's condition, the warring families, and the case itself were depicted. Most notably, whereas *Cruzan* was framed as a right-to-die case, *Schiavo* was framed as a right-to-life case or a contest between the right to live and the right to die (Anspach and Halpern 2008).

A second finding concerned the activists who gained media exposure. Whereas in *Cruzan*, both pro-life activists and representatives of right-to-die organizations were mentioned or quoted in the *Times*, right-to-die activists rarely appear in media accounts of *Schiavo*. Activists supporting the Schindlers, including religious conservatives and, less often, representatives of disability rights organizations, were most likely to be mentioned or quoted, as table 10.2 shows—and the pattern is striking (Anspach and Halpern 2008).

A third finding concerns the experts who were quoted or characterized as bioethicists, presented in table 10.3. As was the case in *Cruzan*, articles in the Schiavo case quoted well-known bioethicists, most affiliated with hospitals, the Hastings Center, or university-affiliated bioethics centers. However, in accounts of the Schiavo case, some affiliates of conservative think tanks were quoted and identified as bioethicists. Consider, for example, "William L. Saunders, Director of the Center for Human Life and Bioethics at the Family Research Council" or "Wesley J. Smith, author of books on bioethics" (Stolberg 2003a). These references suggest that the a new kind of bioethicist had appeared.

Many religious conservatives viewed their newly found visibility—as activists and as ethicists—as a reaction to mainstream bioethics and the right-to-die movement that had dominated media accounts of end-of-life issues.[2] For anti-euthanasia activists, the Schiavo case provided an opportunity to reverse what they viewed as

Table 10.2. Which Activists Are Cited?*

Nancy Cruzan	
Kind of Activist/Organization (number)	Number of Articles Citing
"Right-to-Die" Activists (4)	10
Pro-choice Activists (1)	1
Right-to-life Activists (10)	15

Terri Schiavo	
Kind of Activist/Organization (number)	Number of Articles Citing
Supporting Michael Schiavo	
Political action committee (PAC) (1)	2
ACLU (1)	2
Communist organization (2)	2
Right-to-die organization (2)	3
Supporting the Schindlers	
PACS (3)	8
Think tanks (2)	9
Christian broadcast networks (2)	3
Right-to-life organizations (2)	4
Organizations organized around Terri Schiavo (4)	10
Evangelical church-affiliated (2) Organizations	2
Catholic organizations (2)	3
Disability rights organizations (3)	4
Legal advocacy groups (1)	1
Unaffiliated clergy (2)	2
Unaffiliated activists (3)	3
Author of books on bioethics (1)	1

* This table lists the organization with which the activist is affiliated, the number of activists in parentheses (), and the number of articles in which the activists are cited in *New York Times* stories on Nancy Cruzan and Terri Schiavo. The table contains the same information as is presented in Table I in Anspach and Halpern (2008: 50–51), but the information is presented quite differently.

victories of the right-to-die movement and mainstream bioethics: the Supreme Court's recognition of a right to die in the Nancy Cruzan case and the passage of Oregon's Death with Dignity Act (Filene 1998), which permitted physician-assisted suicide (Chin et al. 1999). It also provided an opportunity to break what was viewed, with some justification, as mainstream bioethicists' monopoly of media attention and their claim to be the exclusive authorities on ethical issues. The remarkable success of this movement in achieving these goals demands sociological explanation.

The Schiavo case, then, presents us with several sociological questions: What enabled conservative activists to bring the case to the highest reaches of Congress, the White House, and the Vatican? How were they able to persist in the face of repeated defeat in the courts? How did they establish a presence in the media? Finally, what happened to bioethics? As the next section shows, religious conservatives were able to accomplish the three objectives of social movements: to avail themselves of

Table 10.3. Who Is Cited As a Bioethicist?*

Bioethicist	Affiliation	Number of Articles in Which Cited
Mainstream Bioethicists		
Arthur Caplan	Director, Center for Bioethics, University of Pennsylvania	4
R. Alta Charo	No Affiliation Given	1
Kenneth W. Goodman	Ethics Professor, University of Miami, Co-Director, Florida Bioethics Network	2
Nancy Dubler	Professor of Bioethics at Montefiore Medical Center, New York City	1
Ezekiel Emanuel	Chair of Department of Clinical Bioethics at NIH	2
Robert Veatch	Professor of Medical Ethics, Georgetown University	1
Bruce Jennings	Senior Research Scholar at Hastings Center	1
Courtney S. Campbell	Professor of Medical Ethics, Oregon State University	1
Daniel Sulmasy	Franciscan Friar, Medical Doctor, Chairman of the Ethics Committee, St. Vincent's Hospital, Manhattan	1
Joseph Finns	Chief of Medical Ethics, Division of New York Presbyterian/Weill Cornell Hospital	1
Diane Meier	Professor of Medical Ethics at Mt. Sinai School of Medicine	1
Rabbi Leonard A. Sharzer	Doctor and Bioethicist, Jewish Theological Seminary of America	1
Robert Walker	Director of Division of Medical Ethics and Humanities, University of South Florida College of Medicine	1
Conservative Bioethicists		
William L. Saunders, Jr.	Senior Fellow at Family Research Council Director, Center for Human Life and Bioethics, Family Research Council	1
Wesley J. Smith	Author of books on bioethics	1
William Cheshire	Director of Lab at Jacksonville Mayo Clinic, Director of Biotechnology Ethics, Center for Bioethics and Human Dignity	2
Burke J. Balch	Director of Powell Center for Medical Ethics, National Right to Life Committee	1
Samuel Gregg	Director of Research at Acton Institute For the Study of Religion	1

* A computer search was performed on the articles in the *New York Times* relating to Terri Schiavo, using the terms "bioeth/*" and "medical ethics."

opportunities in the environment; to mobilize resources strategically; and to frame issues persuasively (Rao, Morrill, and Zald 2000).

From Activists to Experts: Mobilization of Religious Conservatives

Opportunities and Networks

The movement to keep Terri Schiavo alive did not emerge in isolation from the rest of society. In fact, the timing of this movement illustrates the central insight of political opportunity theory: that the emergence, trajectory, and fate of social movements are shaped by features of the social context. These features can include, for example, resources, historical precedents, and, most notably, changes in the political environment (for discussions of political opportunity theory, see Meyer and Whittier 1994; McAdam, McCarthy, and Zald 1996).

New political regimes can create a favorable climate for some social movements to take shape. With the election of Jimmy Carter, a "born-again Christian," in 1974, elite evangelical Christians gained access to centers of power (Lindsay 2006). The close alliance between a Republican administration and Christian *conservatives*, however, began with the election of Ronald Reagan in 1980, when prominent Christian conservatives such as Surgeon General C. Everett Koop were appointed to key positions.

This newly found presence of religious conservatives in the White House set the stage for the only other large-scale mobilization of religious conservatives around end-of-life issues: the case of Baby John Doe. In 1983, in Bloomington, Indiana, a baby was born with Down syndrome and an obstruction of the throat. The parents decided not to treat him, and when the courts upheld their decision, pro-life activists, disability rights groups, the courts and the Reagan administration became embroiled in a national controversy. Ultimately, Congress passed a law that requires Child Protective Service agencies to investigate "infant abuse" (withholding treatment) and mandating aggressive treatment except of babies already dying. The case also put in place what would become one of the *Schiavo* case's most notable features: the alliance between pro-life and disability rights activists and the partial convergence of pro-life and disability rights discourse. To the extent that it created an alliance that would later be pivotal, the case of Baby Doe can be seen as a dress rehearsal for *Schiavo*. (For discussions of Baby Doe, see, for example, Guillemin and Holmstrom 1986; Anspach 1993).

Just as the case of Baby John Doe was the "child" of the Reagan administration, so was the movement to "save" Terri Schiavo the "child" of the close, symbiotic relationship between President George W. Bush and religious conservatives. Bush had been elected for a second term, and Republicans had gained a substantial majority in both houses of Congress. Even more important was the increasing power of social conservatives and their growing influence on the Republican Party. The relatively new alliance between former adversaries, conservative Catholics and evangelical Protestants, had become a potent force in American politics (Goodstein 2005).

Politicians, including the president, the governor of Florida, and many members of Congress were indebted to the socially conservative base that had elected them. Given this relationship, Bush chose Leon Kass, a noted conservative bioethicist, to head his Council on Bioethics. Consider Kass's widely-circulated memo:

> The purpose of this memo is to outline a bold "offensive" bioethics agenda for the second term.... New biotechnologies challenging human freedom, equality, and dignity are arriving at an accelerating pace, especially in the domains of assisted reproduction and genetic manipulation. And yet there are currently no boundaries or protections in federal law to help us confront the challenges they pose.... We have today an administration and Congress as friendly to human life and human dignity as we are likely to see for many years to come.... (quoted in Hinsch 2005: 6; see also Weiss 2005)

It is difficult to imagine a more powerful illustration of political opportunity theory than Kass's memo. As sociologists have observed, activists assess the probability of success and are much more likely to commit resources to social protest movements when they anticipate a political victory. Context—in this case, the alliance between religious conservatives and the Bush administration—creates powerful incentives for mobilization.

Also important was the role of the Vatican in creating discursive opportunities, a role which extended beyond the Schiavo case. In 1968, Pope John Paul II reshaped the cultural context of the right-to-life movement when he proclaimed the Church's commitment to a "culture of life" which, he said, is being threatened by a "culture of death," manifested in birth control, abortion, and euthanasia. Thus, by promulgating the idea of a "culture of life," the Vatican expanded the discursive opportunity structure of religious conservatives (Ferree 2003; Koopmans and Olzak 2004). Support for a "culture of life" became a rallying point for conservative Catholics, evangelical Protestants, and President Bush, and served to broaden the pro-life movement's political agenda (Kirkpatrick and Stolberg 2005).

Vatican policies also affected the Schiavo case more directly. Prior to 2004, Catholic theologians were divided over the ethical status of the feeding tube. For some theologians, feeding tubes constituted "extraordinary" medical treatment, which, like respirators, could be withdrawn when the burdens of treatment outweighed the benefits. For others they were a form of basic care, food and sustenance to which all patients were entitled (Johnson 1990). In a 2004 address, Pope John Paul II settled the issue, proclaiming that "the administration of food and water, even by artificial means, always represents a natural means of preserving life not a medical act" (Goodstein 2005). Writing in the Vatican media, officials went beyond formulating general policies when, in a move that is rare if not unprecedented, they lent their support to the Schindlers' cause and explicitly condemned Judge Greer's decision to allow Terri Schiavo's feeding tube to be removed.

But mobilization is not just about opening political opportunities: equally important is the closure of other opportunities, the "push" factors. Consider, for example, the case of Randall Terry, organizer of the Schiavo protest. Terry is influenced by theologian Franklin Schaeffer, who viewed "secular humanism" as a threat to the social fabric (Schaeffer and Koop 1979). Terry is openly committed to reconstituting society along theocratic lines—gay marriage, abortion or euthanasia, prayer in the schools, and creationism interest him only so far as they serve this broader agenda. For Terry, the Schiavo case was a "crack in the wall," a chance to begin a broader program of social change. But Terry's personal fortunes also had changed. After the right-to-life movement failed for a decade to overturn *Roe v. Wade*, Terry turned to more militant tactics. As the founder of Operation Rescue, he is credited leading the "direct action" wing of the pro-life movement whose militant protests outside abortion clinics sometimes turned violent. By the mid-1990s, as Faye Ginsburg (1998) notes, Operation Rescue and other direct-action organizations were all but dead after a series of legal challenges by pro-choice organizations, government investigations of their finances, and the erosion of their credibility by widely publicized murders. Terry had left Operation Rescue and had turned his energies to cofounding Right March.com to counter MoveOn.org (Kirkpatrick 2005). He was, however, an activist without a cause. For Terry, the Schiavo case was the cause he needed, an outlet for his prodigious talents as an organizer and a chance to increase his visibility. While his actual motives cannot be established, the Schiavo case was the moment in which Terry's political and personal opportunities converged.

The Schiavo case also illustrates the importance of social networks to political mobilization. When the Schindlers called upon Randall Terry to publicize their cause, they were able to activate an array of organizations that were politically astute, well-funded, and interconnected. Many of these organizations had become involved in "culture of life" issues in the years before *Schiavo*, galvanized by the movement to legalize assisted suicide and by their perceived defeat in the *Cruzan* case. Terry immediately enlisted the support of William Green and Philip Sheldon, cofounders of Right March.com. Sheldon is the son of Lou Sheldon, who had founded the large and influential Traditional Values Coalition. A key turning point in the *Schiavo* case for Jeb Bush was his choice of prominent conservative attorney Kenneth Connor to represent him. Connor, former president of the conservative Family Research Council, had ties to Washington. When the court set a deadline for removing Terri Schiavo's feeding tube, Connor called on Representative David Weldon, a Florida Republican senator whom Connor had known for years. Weldon turned to fellow Florida Republican Mel Martinez, Connor's former college roommate, to help sponsor a bill he had crafted with the assistance of the National Right to Life Committee. Equally important were the decisions of House Leader Tom DeLay and Senate leader Bill Frist. Before drafting the "Palm Sunday Compromise Bill" that members of Congress had interrupted their vacations to support, Frist conferred with neurologist and Christian bioethicist William Cheshire, one of the few physicians who questioned Terri's diagnosis (Kirkpatrick and Stolberg 2005). Activists, then, were embedded in vertical ties that extended from street protests to the White House.

Also important was the coalition of religious conservatives and disability rights groups—a coalition that dates from the 1983 Baby Doe case. This alliance created a bridge to the opposition, as activists could now reach across party lines and rally some Democrats to their support. For example, Democratic Senator Tom Harkin, author of the Americans with Disabilities Act, lobbied for the bill and enlisted the support of several Democrats. The bill passed without strong opposition (Kirkpatrick and Stolberg 2005). In addition to disability rights activists, supporters of the Schindlers were able to enlist the support of Jesse Jackson, Al Sharpton, and Ralph

Nader. Faced with a Republican majority in Congress as well as strong, well-organized and, in some cases, bipartisan support for the bill, few Democratic members of Congress were willing to expend their meager political capital on the Schiavo case.

Isomorphic Strategies

Opportunities afforded by a politically conservative climate are only part of the Schiavo story. In fact, the success of any social movement ultimately depends on activists' ability to recognize and avail themselves of opportunities and exploit them strategically. Thus, the Schiavo case is a story of strategy and tactics within the pro-life movement as well as social forces outside it, of agency as well as structure, of narratives as well as networks.

Supporters of the Schindlers deployed a wide array of strategies and tactics, from prayer vigils to lobbying politicians to filing legal briefs. Some of these strategies were borrowed from the left. As Rao and his colleagues (2000) note, this tendency of social movements to appropriate their opponents' tactics is characteristic of movement-countermovement dynamics. Loosely borrowing from DiMaggio and Powell's (1983) neo-institutional approach to the study of inter-organizational fields, I refer to these tactics as isomorphic strategies rather than isomorphic processes or pressures in order to emphasize the agency of activists who consciously deployed them as weapons in the culture wars.

In the Schiavo case, activists engaged in what could be termed *discursive isomorphism* as they borrowed and reframed the language of the opposition. For example, a long-standing strategy of religious conservatives was the use of civil rights discourse to refer to the fetus, newborn infant, or, in this case, Terri Schiavo. One activist described the case as a "grave human rights violation" (quoted in Goodnough 2005a; see also Goodnough 2005d); others spoke of discrimination against the disabled. Unlike symbolic inversions, in which activists turn epithets into marks of pride such as "queer" or "black power" (see Anspach 1979), in this case they appropriated the language of the left and extended its meaning by transposing it to a different context. For those who accept the personhood of the embryo, the newborn infant, or Terri Schiavo, these frames are logical extensions of concepts; for the opposition, they are mere metaphors (see, for example, Macklin 2006). In reclaiming and reframing the language of civil and human rights, conservative activists demonstrate the deep and broad cultural resonance of the individual-rights discourse. But more to the point, they also illustrate the ability of religious conservatives to extend the rhetorical reach of their arguments by recasting them in a language resonant with audiences located across the political spectrum.

Other strategies resemble the classical mimetic isomorphism described by DiMaggio and Powell (1983), in which activists strategically emulate their rivals' organizational forms. Perhaps the most important instance of this isomorphism is the establishment of conservative bioethics. Beginning in the late 1990s, a number of well-funded conservative think tanks made bioethics a central part of their agenda. For instance, the Family Research Council now has a Center for Human Life and Bioethics. Other conservative think tanks, such as the American Enterprise Institute, which had focused on economics and foreign policy, incorporated bioethics into their programs. These organizations expanded to embrace a wide range of issues, from abortion to assisted suicide, stem cells, and cloning (Eisenberg 2005; Hinsch 2005; Scott and Tong 2005). To be sure, some of these organizations were founded before Terri Schiavo's case had become a public issue. However, the *Schiavo* case galvanized these groups and provided them with a rallying point. Developing a new bioethics is not difficult in a field that issues credentials but does not license.

Conservative bioethics can be based in colleges as well as think tanks, and training programs in the new bioethics have emerged. For example, the Center for Bioethics and Human Dignity, based in Trinity University in Deerfield, Illinois, holds conferences, educational workshops, and programs, all designed to train practitioners in Christian bioethics (http://cbhd.org). Although conservative bioethicists are somewhat overrepresented in its syllabi, the Center's training program is indistinguishable in *form* from mainstream bioethics programs throughout the country.

Although some conservative bioethicists refer to themselves as "Christian bioethicists," not all conservative bioethicists are Christian. In fact, some of the leading proponents consider themselves part of the neo-conservative movement and are Jewish. In addition to Leon Kass, these writers include Kass's former student Yuval Levin; William Kristol, editor of *The Weekly Standard*; and Eric Cohen, editor of *The New Atlantis*. Levin and Cohen are affiliated with the Bioethics and Public Policy Program, which publishes *The New Atlantis* and is itself part of the Center for Ethics and Public Policy, an ecumenical think tank "dedicated to applying the Judeo-Christian moral tradition to critical issues of public policy" (http://www.eppc.org/default.asp). Despite different religious beliefs, conservative bioethicists use a similar language, centering on a belief in the equal dignity of human beings. This belief in human dignity leads them to protect all lives, from "disabled" fetuses in utero, to embryos in the laboratory, to "profoundly disabled" human beings such as Terri Schiavo.

The new bioethics transgresses and effaces the boundary between experts and activists that bioethicists had long worked to establish. It also expands religious conservatives' *protest repertoire*. By adopting the title of "bioethicist," Christian activists could capitalize on mainstream bioethicists' long-standing credibility with the press. Creating the new conservative bioethics allowed its practitioners to speak as experts to the mass media, to say nothing of enhancing their public credibility.

Finally, as the Schiavo case unfolded, activists made extensive use of *tactical isomorphism*, borrowing opponents' tactics that had proved successful. In fact, the very conservative organizations that repudiated "secular humanism" and some concomitants of modernity proved remarkably adept at turning the tools of modernity to their own ends. Conservative activists found that the Internet provided a potent weapon in the culture wars. After MoveOn.org had proved successful during the mid-term election, Randall Terry and Philip Sheldon established a conservative counterpart, Right March.com. Web sites could mobilize thousands of Americans with the click of a mouse. The Web could be used for lobbying, and Florida legislators found their computers jammed by tens of thousands of e-mails urging them to help keep Terri alive. For example, www.Terrisfight.org reportedly raised forty thousand signatures on a petition to Jeb Bush. For organizations such as Voice for Terri, Right March.com, and the TraditionalValuesCoalition, the Web proved to be a powerful fundraising tool.

Visitors to these Web sites found video clips of Terri, scathing indictments of Michael Schiavo, and pleas to "Help Save Terri's life," all used to raise money for the campaign to keep Terri alive and other conservative causes (Kirkpatrick 2005a; Kirkpatrick and Schwartz 2005; Goodnough (2003e; 2003f).

Words, Images, and Spectacular Politics

The Internet (as well as television) provided a forum for what I call "spectacular politics," or the use of visual drama and images. Through the spectacle, collective action frames become embodied in action rather than mere words. Thus viewers could witness hundreds of protestors from all parts of the country converging on the hospice where Terri Schiavo lay dying. Picket lines, prayer vigils, and attempts to cross picket lines to "give Terri water" created a visual spectacle that fed the media's hunger for drama (Kirkpatrick 2005a; Hilgartner and Bosk 1988). Perhaps the most memorable examples of embodied, spectacular politics are the images of Terri Schiavo smiling and following a balloon on the Web and the nightly news.

Through pictures, images, and words, the Schindlers and their supporters *personalized* and humanized Terri, inviting us to see her as a sentient being who smiles, suffers, and desperately clings to life. Her parents described looking on helplessly as their daughter is cruelly and unnaturally starved to death, increasingly "resembling a concentration camp survivor" (Schwartz 2005), while, in the words of one activist, "they can't even give her a cool sip of water" (Brother Paul O'Donnell, quoted in Goodnough 2005b). This spectacular politics and evocative, emotive language is usually the exclusive prerogative of activists, rather than experts.

With the development of conservative bioethics, the repertoire of religious conservatives expanded to include the language of expertise. Consider, for example, this statement by William L. Saunders, Jr., Director of the Center for Human Life and Bioethics at the Family Research Council, who noted that "the idea of building a culture of life is a Catholic articulation, but it echoes in the hearts of many people, evangelicals and others" (quoted in Goodstein 2005). The tone of this statement does not differ from that of other bioethicists quoted in the popular press. Thus, a broad protest repertoire allowed religious conservatives to use both the language of embodied suffering and that of expertise, images as well as words.

To summarize: the Schindlers and religious conservatives were able to accomplish the three tasks of social movements. First, they availed themselves of opportunities opened by the Bush administration and called upon social networks that reached to the White House. Secondly, they were able to mobilize participants, often drawing on the tactics of their opponents. Finally, as cultural entrepreneurs, they deployed words and images that depicted Terri Schiavo as a sentient person. At the same time, the role of conservative bioethicist gave them the credibility and legitimacy that allowed them to speak authoritatively to the press. Although they managed to move politicians, religious conservatives were unable to persuade the courts, which ruled against them. Although they were able to dominate the pages of the *Times*, they were not able to persuade large segments of the American public, which continued to support Michael Schiavo. Perhaps the most enduring legacy of the *Schiavo* case is its impact on the field of bioethics, an issue I pursue in the next section.

From Experts to Activists: Bioethicists and the Counter Offensive

Counterthemes and Images

It would be highly misleading to suggest that only religious conservatives mobilized words and images to promulgate a point of view. Juxtaposed against religious conservatives' language of embodied suffering were the counterthemes of their opponents: liberal bioethicists, supporters of Michael Schiavo, and many physicians. In this latter language, the voice of science, medicine, and expertise, removing the feeding tube does not constitute killing but is a purely medical decision to let nature to take its course. Consider, for example, this feature-length article, entitled "Neither 'Starvation' Nor the Suffering It Connotes Applies to Schiavo, Doctors Say," in which the reporter uses a resolutely clinical language to tell a story about dying:

> Once doctors stop providing the nutrient paste and fluids that flow through the feeding tube, death usually comes in about two weeks. As the days pass, organs begin to shut down, starting with the kidneys. Toxins build up in the body, and the patient slips into what is known as a uremic coma. The balance of electrolytes is upset, disrupting the electrical system that drives muscles. The heart eventually stops. In the case of Ms. Schiavo, experts say, the potential for discomfort is nonexistent because higher functions like consciousness... were destroyed 15 years ago.... (Schwartz 2005).

Just as Christian activists used the language of embodied suffering to personalize Terri Schiavo, here the writer uses the language of science to *depersonalize* her. In fact, the characters in this mechanistic story are organs and biological processes: kidneys, toxins, electrolyte balances, and, eventually, the heart. In this language of medicine, Terri Schiavo's body becomes a trope, the body as machine, that differs dramatically from the language of activists, which depicts an embodied, suffering person (for a related discussion of competing discourses, see Schwartz 2005; for a discussion of framing, see Benford and Snow 2000). Language, no less than the spectacle, is used strategically.

Religious conservatives were not alone in their use of images. Looming in the background of the Schiavo case was another image, evoked by the previous passage: the tropes of the right-to-die movement, in which a body lies haplessly, lingering and held hostage to medical technology that is out of control. Since the Schiavo case did little to change public opinion, it may have been the latter image, of the body as hostage, rather than the image of Terri following the balloon, that was etched in the popular collective memory.

Policing the Boundaries of Bioethics

For several mainstream bioethicists, the Schiavo case brought the sudden realization that they faced a new competitor. They responded to the challenge of conservative bioethics in two ways: First, they challenged their competitors' legitimacy through boundary-work. In a now-classic formulation, Gieryn (1983) and Gieryn, Bevins, and Zehr (1985) show how professionals attempt to demarcate boundaries between themselves and potential "usurpers" by distinguishing their own scientific goals, methods, epistemology, and expertise from those of their ostensibly nonscientific competitors (783). Similarly, bioethicist Ruth Macklin (2006) draws sharp, invidious distinctions between the professionalism, epistemology, and rhetorical style of mainstream and conservative bioethics. Unlike mainstream bioethicists, who work in universities and publish in scholarly journals, conservative bioethicists are, Macklin notes, public intellectuals and journalists who work in think tanks and publish in "magazines" such as *Commentary*. This difference between scholarship and journalism allows conservatives to flout academic conventions by using "*sweeping generalizations* (italics mine)... without *supporting evidence* or *citations*" (41). Second, conservatives use *rhetoric*, "metaphors and slogans" instead of "*reasoned arguments*" (38). Macklin's third contrast is epistemological: conservative bioethicists endorse an "intuitionist epistemology" that appeals to intuitions, moral sentiments, and *emotions* (e.g., "repugnance" for cloning) rather than careful analysis of evidence, *rational* argument and dispassionate discourse. Other bioethicists view themselves as committed to science and conservatives as standing in the way of *progress* (see Moreno and Berger 2007). By drawing these binary distinctions between academics and journalists, emotion and rational argument, and rhetoric and reason, mainstream bioethicists attempt to police the boundaries of their jurisdiction.

Isomorphism Redux: The Birth of Progressive Bioethics

Blindsided by conservatives' newly found visibility in the Schiavo case, several leading mainstream bioethicists, such as Jonathan Moreno and Arthur Caplan, have argued that mainstream bioethicists must themselves become politicized in order to compete with their challengers. Thus, a second response to the conservative challenge is the creation of "progressive bioethics." At a 2005 meeting in Washington, D.C., several prominent bioethicists met to launch a social movement to counter conservative bioethics and oppose its positions on issues ranging from embryonic stem cells to national health care (Check 2005). Like conservative bioethicists before them, these mainstream bioethicists appropriated their adversaries' strategies and transgressed the activist/expert divide. They did so by affiliating with another isomorphic countermovement: the Center for American Progress, a Washington think tank directed by former Clinton chief of staff John Podesta and partly funded by George Soros to serve as a counterweight to the conservative think tanks that were proliferating. Not only did these progressive bioethicists emulate their competitors' organizations, but they also emulated some of their tactics. For example, a speaker at the conference, Glenn Magee, founder of the *American Journal of Bioethics*, discussed how progressives, like conservatives, could develop blogs, which had the capacity to reach large numbers of readers and journalists. In short, just as conservative activists were able to expand their credibility as public intellectuals in think tanks, so are progressive bioethicists using think tanks and blogs to expand their protest repertoires by embracing activism—a repertoire that now can include emotive images and spectacular politics.

The fate of this newly politicized progressive bioethics is unknown, but there may be some barriers to its success. A first is a potential gap between progressive bioethicists and the political left. To be sure, during the 1990s some bioethicists were invited to serve on Hillary Rodham Clinton's ill-fated committee on national health care.

However, the Democratic Party has yet to put the *concerns* of bioethics on its radar screen. With the exception of California's stem-cell initiative, Democratic candidates have focused on national health care and Social Security—issues that concern Democratic voters—rather than gene therapy or end-of-life decisions.

This gap between progressive bioethics and the broader left may arise from an historical tension within progressivism itself. In a recent commentary, Charles Bosk (2007) criticized progressive bioethics for its lack of attention to social justice and cautioned that early twentieth-century progressivism culminated in eugenics. In fact, classical progressivism was founded on two principles that were sometimes in conflict: a commitment to social justice and a potentially elitist belief in the power of science, technology, and experts to ameliorate social problems. When the two principles collided, the latter sometimes prevailed. It would be exaggerating to accuse progressive bioethics of a complete neglect of social justice. However, the following mission statement, while mentioning "social, political, and economic issues," places science and technology front and center:

> Rather than decry progress as inherently dangerous, the Progressive Bioethics Initiative embraces the promise of science to improve our lives with a critical optimism that understands that science must be guided by our values.... We understand government must regulate science so that it proceeds within our existing ethical framework, without needlessly restricting scientific progress or ignoring the value of scientific fact. (http://www.americanprogress.org/projects/bioethics)

This faith in the "promise of science to improve our lives," grounded in the Enlightenment's grand narrative, portends an emphasis on science and technology, stem cells, and gene therapy housed within a larger progressive movement focused on income redistribution and the living wage, Social Security, and national health care. Thus, unless they broaden their agenda, progressive bioethicists may find a more receptive audience among mainstream scientists, with whom their concerns resonate, than in the Democratic Party or the Center for American Progress.

Third, sharp differences of opinion among liberals and the left may prevent them from coalescing around a broad-based progressive bioethics agenda. Despite deepening fissures within Christian conservatism around environmental stewardship and social justice, religious conservatives offer a moral philosophy that addresses many bioethical issues, from cloning to decisions at the end of life. The Schiavo case resonated with many neoconservative commentators and Washington lobbyists as well as street organizers. By contrast, the left is deeply divided over many bioethical issues, from cloning and embryonic stem cells to assisted suicide. Many feminist groups, for example, have opposed the unchecked use of technology to medicalize reproduction and take a dim view of the growth of some medical technologies. Recently, a feminist group, Hands Off Our Ovaries, managed to form a coalition with anti-abortion groups to oppose California's stem-cell initiative. Their concern is not with the sanctity of embryonic life or the power of technology to alter the traditional family. Rather, they are concerned with public funding of private biotechnology, its potential for misuse, and the risks of some new technologies for women (www.handsofourovaries.com). These divisions within the left portend future alliances around single issues cross-cutting political ideologies, rather than a broad-based, cohesive progressive bioethics movement.

Concluding Remarks

Whither Bioethics?

I conclude with some thoughts about the implications of this paper for the bioethicists who study moral life and the sociologists who study them. Although sociologists have been notoriously loathe to make predictions, I will venture some conjectures about the future of bioethics. First, conservative bioethics is here to stay. Even if mainstream bioethicists were to institute licensing, there is little that they could do to exclude their conservative counterparts. Second, although they may never reach a consensus, conservative bioethicists will come increasingly to resemble their counterparts in terms of institutional affiliation and socioeconomic status. Today bioethics is bifurcated into two camps, one located in research institutes and elite universities and the other located in think tanks and small colleges (Hinsch 2005)—a situation that is likely to change. Recently D. Michael Lindsay (2006) has noted a steady growth of an evangelical elite over the past three decades, which now includes intellectuals more likely to have been educated in Harvard or Yale than in small bible colleges. While many evangelical intellectuals are currently affiliated with think tanks, divinity schools in Ivy League universities have begun to be somewhat more open to their ideas (Lindsay 2006: 217). Thus as mainstream bioethicists affiliate with think tanks and some conservative Christians affiliate with elite universities, bioethics may come to consist of two increasingly similar rival groups, who will often cross paths and may even find themselves working in close proximity.

These considerations suggest that both varieties of bioethics should enter into dialog, rather than competing for legitimacy. For mainstream bioethics, this would mean nothing more than returning to its roots. As Daniel Callahan (1996, 2006) has observed, among the founders of bioethics were liberal Joseph Fletcher, originator of situation ethics, "who never said no," and conservative Paul Ramsey, "who usually said no." At the heart of early bioethics, Callahan goes on to note, was a debate about the potential pitfalls of technology—a debate that has given way to a new orthodoxy about the benefits of scientific progress (Callahan 1996, 2006). Thus, rather than treating their rivalry with conservative bioethics as a Manichean struggle between progress and backwardness, reminiscent of the Scopes trial, mainstream bioethicists might consider the promises—and pitfalls—of technology as an open question to be debated. For mainstream bioethicists, returning to their roots would mean continuing a conversation with conservative bioethics that has just begun (see Moreno and Berger 2007). It would also mean acknowledging very real divisions *within* the left around some of the same issues. A conversation between mainstream and conservative bioethics might expose issues that both groups give short shrift, which, if Bosk (2007) is correct, include social justice.

Beyond Bioethics

The battle for bioethics provides a powerful illustration of more generic social processes. It shows, for example, how movements and countermovements emulate each others' discourse, tactics, and organizational forms and how these dynamics can reconfigure fields. However, this paper suggests four additional topics for future research on social movements and health care institutions. Sociologists should:

Explore Cyberspace and the Blogosphere

For both conservative and progressive bioethics, much of the "action" took place online. While it is commonly acknowledged that the Internet has transformed American politics, its effect on social movements has not been well studied. Because it is one of the most effective tools for reaching the 55 percent of Americans who own computers (Horrigan 2008), the Internet can become a powerful resource. The Web makes it possible for activists to circumvent the gatekeepers that constrain them. Movement activists can reach large audiences directly without having to compete with other activists for media exposure or airtime (Hilgartner and Bosk 1988). Bioethicists can promulgate their ideas without the constraints of peer review. Because it allows the use of images as well as words, the Web also can be a powerful tool for mobilization. For activists in the Schiavo case, the Internet was a highly efficient fundraising tool that enabled them to generate vast lists of prescreened, prospective donors. Finally, Web sites can form linkages to large numbers of other sites, the Web can provide a vehicle for the formation of social networks. To be sure, medical sociologists have studied how self-help groups, cancer survivors, such as cancer survivors (Pitts 2004) or groups organized around contested illnesses (Barker 2005) have used the Internet. Much remains to be learned, however, about the role of the Internet in collective action. Within a decade, it is possible that the site of civil society will have moved from coffee houses and the media to the Web, the blogosphere, and e-mail.

Analyze Boundary Crossings

Running through this paper and others in this volume is a common leitmotiv: social movements repeatedly transgress the border between activism and expertise, producing hybrid forms in the process. Among health-related social movements, examples of this hybridization abound: activists can become experts (Epstein 1996) and, conversely, experts, like the progressive bioethicists in this study, can morph into activists (Moore 1996). By comparing these cases, we can begin to identify the social conditions under which such boundary crossings occur. For example, Moore's (1996) work on scientists who embraced activism between 1955 and 1975 shows us *who* are most likely to become activists (they tend to be biologists, to be younger, and to work as academics where they are exposed to campus protests); *when* they are likely to politicize (when social movements raise critical questions about the ethical uses of science or when activists enter the profession); and *how* they are likely to do so (by establishing advocacy groups that allow them to retain their identities as both professionals and protectors of the public interest).

Less is known, however, about the social conditions that lead activists to become experts. Because professions create powerful institutional barriers, such as licensure, to protect their jurisdictions from incursions by outsiders, this kind of hybridization is less likely to occur. The best-known case of such boundary crossings is described in Epstein's (1996) study of how AIDS activists played a significant role in developing treatments by persuading researchers to alter their research designs. These activists carried out clinical trials, attended conferences, and participated in powerful research groups. By contrast, conservative bioethicists have not gained full legitimacy in the eyes of mainstream bioethics. However, they have gone father in actually taking on professional roles.

These cases differ in the extent to which activists assumed expert roles and the extent to which they gained recognition by the mainstream disciplines. However, taken together, they suggest hypotheses about who, when, and how activists become experts. In each case, activists had considerable cultural capital—they were white, relatively affluent, and highly educated. Most conservative bioethicists, like the first bioethicists, held advanced degrees in law, medicine, or theology—credentials that gave them enough credibility to speak as experts to target audiences. The cases also suggest when activists are most likely to adopt expert roles. In the case of bioethics, a change in political administrations provided conservative ethicists with political opportunities and access to centers of power. In the case of AIDS activism, the urgent need to find treatments for AIDS may have made members of the medical establishment more open to alternatives. An important factor is the nature of the barriers between professional jurisdictions and the public since activists are more likely to cross porous boundaries and less likely to cross those that seem impermeable. Because mainstream bioethics had not attained "closure"—that is, because it issued credentials but had not instituted licensing—its borders were quite permeable. Finally, both Epstein's analysis and this paper address the questions of how activists became experts. The most important strategy of the AIDS activists was to become so knowledgeable about AIDS that experts would take them seriously. Conservative bioethicists emulated the discourse, tactics, and, most important, the organizational forms of their adversaries, developing conservative bioethics programs that issue credentials and establishing bioethics programs in think tanks.

Explore Hybrid Organizations

Think tanks are quintessentially hybrid organizations—research institutes often linked to political causes that combine activism with expertise (Eisenberg 2005; Hinsch 2005; Scott and Tong 2005). They have provided an environment in which public intellectuals can flourish outside the academy. Both conservative and liberal think tanks provided settings in which bioethicists were able to promulgate political positions without relinquishing claims to expertise.

In the last three decades, think tanks have proliferated rapidly, steadily growing from about seventy in 1970 to about three hundred in 2005 (Scott and Tong 2005). Think tanks vary along a continuum in the extent to which they adopt a nonpartisan identity or have a particular political orientation. Some critics distinguish between nonpartisan think tanks such as Rand and the new think tanks that proliferated during the past decades, which have an explicit political identity. The latter, critics suggest, cross the line between research and advocacy (Scott and Tong 2005). Political think tanks, according to their critics, allow their fellows to give political advice to policy makers' political processes while retaining their nonprofit status (for a discussion of these issues, see Scott and Tong 2005). The role of think tanks in political mobilization merits further study. What is needed, then, is a systematic account of hybridization processes as well as the hybrid institutions in which these processes take place.

Problematize Concepts

The present paper raises yet another issue. This paper began as a story of hybridization, of activists who became experts and experts who embraced activism. However, a more complicated issue soon surfaced. For example, to prepare the tables in this paper, it was necessary to decide who is to be counted as an activist and who is to be coded as an expert. Answering this question was difficult because *the very definition of "expert" or "activist" is itself contested.* This problem is even more acute in the case of policy bioethicists who engage in normative discourse, testify before Congress, and speak to the press, and whose activities sometimes overlap with those of activists. The problem of distinguishing activists from experts also occurs in discussions of think tanks. Some critics contrast think tanks devoted to nonpartisan research from those that engage in advocacy (Scott and Tong 2005). But a closer look reveals numerous problems in distinguishing research from activism. Can a think tank that engages in military research actually be said to be apolitical? Since all think tanks engage in the work of knowledge production, how do we decide that some are involved in advocacy? There are no objective criteria for deciding where to place the hypothetical line of demarcation between research and advocacy, activism and expertise.

In short, the term "expert" may be what philosopher W.B. Gallie calls an "essentially contested concept," open to dispute each time it is used and applied (quoted in Bosk 1979). It is also a politically contested concept, for how we distinguish experts from activists often depends on our own political assumptions. These considerations call for new concepts that transcend the canonical distinctions between activism and expertise. In the interim, more research is needed that examines how people actually distinguish activists from experts, and researchers from advocates, in contemporary political contexts. At the very least, we need to be more reflexive and self-conscious about our use of concepts that have fuzzy edges and are politically contested.

NOTES

I would like to thank the editors of this volume, Kelly Moore, Ray DeVries, Sydney Halpern, and Scott Kim for their suggestions.

1. For purposes of clarity, I am referring to the movement among religious conservatives as a movement and the response of mainstream bioethics as a "countermovement" or "counter-offensive." These labels are somewhat arbitrary. In fact, conservative activists saw their movement as a "counter revolution" against the right-to-die movement, mainstream bioethics, and the courts.

2. My use of the term "isomorphism" differs from that of DiMaggio and Powell (1983) in three ways. A first contrast concerns what is being borrowed. Like DiMaggio and Powell,

I discuss borrowing organizational forms (mimetic isomorphism), but I also emphasize borrowing language and tactics. Second, this paper treats isomorphism as a set of consciously chosen strategies, rather than as a response to pressures or forces. Third, there is some difference in the "engines" or drivers of isomorphism. For DiMaggio and Powell, these include uncertainty, coercion, and a quest for legitimacy. The activists here are also motivated to emulate their opponents by a quest for legitimacy, but their principal motive is to appropriate weapons shown to work in order to trump their opponents.

PROFESSIONS AND ORGANIZATIONS IN THE TRANSFORMATION OF HEALTH CARE AND RESEARCH

Clinical and scientific professionals and health care organizations are central to the social movements that arise in the U.S. health system, and we devote a section of this book to examining the role of these organizations in health-related social movement activity. While addressing issues similar to those raised in other parts of the book, the papers in this section focus specifically on routine professional activities and formal organizations that challenge the dominant values, structures, and practices of the U.S. health system. The role of professionals in social movements is ironic given that as an elite and highly trained workforce, professionals have a vested interest in protecting—and reproducing—existing authority structures (Friedson 1986). Characteristic of the multi-institutional basis for authority within health care, professionals act as a cultural authority central to the reproduction of cultural meaning and classification.

Likewise, health service organizations are a central part of the delivery of care to individuals and play a leading institutional role, particularly since both federal and local governments transfer substantial amounts of money to service providers for their activities. At the same time, the nonprofit missions of many service providers encourage advocacy activity and the mobilization of new institutional claims. In many cases, both health care professionals and organizations use mobilization tactics to improve work practices and insure adherence to quality standards under attack from other interests in the health care sector. Expertise embedded within the professions and organizations provide the established authoritative base from which to challenge other organized actors.

As the authors in this section elaborate, professionals can strategically combine social movement and work roles in order to push for institutional change. These issues are addressed explicitly by Scott Frickel's examination of how professional networks operate in the environmental health and justice movements and Michael Goldstein's consideration of professional involvement in the movement to bring complementary and integrative medicine into medical education. Paul Bate and Glenn Robert offer a new perspective on how institutions can engage their employees, and specifically professionals, in social movement activity within the care setting to improve work practices; they describe how this activity is currently occurring through the National Health Service in the United Kingdom. Finally, Matthew Archibald takes an ecological perspective to evaluate the extent to which organized social movement activity is supported by legitimacy claims in various media sources. Each of these chapters is described in more detail here.

Frickel describes how professionalization in environmental health and justice (EHJ) has been occurring under the radar through "shadow mobilizations"—semiformal networks of health scientists and medical professionals that flexibly intersect with activists. Using data from thirty-two in-depth interviews with scientists, medical professionals, and EHJ organizers, this chapter defines and develops the concept of shadow mobilization as an alternative route to movement professionalization. Movements for environmental health and justice are commonly described as grassroots phenomena but are different from more mainstream environmental and health movements, in which professional advocacy has centered in large organizations staffed by legal, scientific, and public health experts. The paper considers the role that invisibility, secrecy, and temporality play in the formation of loosely coupled networks of expert activists. These networks span knowledge institutions and sectors (university, state, and industry) as well as the cultural and class divisions ostensibly separating experts and at-risk communities.

Goldstein describes how the prior personal experiences—political, physical, and emotional—of individual physicians were instrumental in the introduction of complementary and integrative medicine (IM) into medical school facilities and curricula. Goldstein applies parallel arguments to those used in past research on patient-driven movements, which has emphasized the effects of personal experiences on involvement and leadership for those at risk for or affected by a particular condition or disease in the study of professionally driven movements. From eight of the medical schools currently belonging to the Consortium of Academic Health Centers for Integrative Medicine, fourteen individuals, including five deans and nine other IM advocates, attended a key organizational meeting during the summer of 1999. Goldstein has interviewed a number of these participants on the extent to which attendees conceptualized their actions at the time of the meeting as part of a social movement and the degree to which personal experiences of participants were significant factors in their participation. The chapter findings indicate that most participants were conscious of being part of a social movement and recalled this as quite important. Additionally, many respondents reported self-perceptions as "wounded healers" and saw movement participation as a means to address this status.

Bate and Robert's chapter translates social movement theory into a change intervention designed to improve patient services. The chapter describes how the authors' team from University College London came together with the English National Health Service (NHS) staff in a unique five-year collaboration to apply social movement principles to the challenge of bringing about major health care reform. This collaboration has gone through five stages on its journey from concept to implementation, including: (1) *evidence gathering and literature review*, identifying themes related to movement development; (2) *practitioner-academic fora*, including seminars, conferences, and workshops exploring the relevance and application of social movement ideas to healthcare reform; (3) *field testing*, including developing and testing a change intervention within four pilot NHS organizations; (4) a *launch*: "going live" with a revised model based on learning from pilot sites to a larger group of twelve NHS organizations with an identifiable "cause"; and (5) *evaluation* with participant feedback and telephone interviews with a sample of those who attended events to ascertain what happened after they returned to their organizations and took initial steps towards implementing plans. Bate and Robert's chapter critically considers the relevance and utility of social movement theories and concepts for practitioners, a comparison between the social movement lenses and theories of organizational change commonly used by health providers, and discussion of practical issues arising during implementation of the social movement activity within a large formal organization.

Matthew Archibald's chapter focuses on the challenges health social movements face in their efforts to achieve legitimation—sociopolitical and cultural recognition and acceptance—from actors with vested interests in the institutions organizers challenge, such as mainstream medicine and health and human services. Using the case of the self-help movement, this chapter explores how health social movements simultaneously challenge institutional authority in medicine and health care while seeking the approbation of those interests. Prior analyses of the histories of national self-help organizations reveal that despite their vaunted opposition to mainstream health care practices they actively seek recognition from a number of institutional authorities. This chapter considers multiple sources of legitimation for self-help organizations and whether sympathetic actors are positioned in a variety of disparate fields, including medicine, academia, politics, and popular media. To understand how these actors shaped self-help, Archibald examines longitudinal trends in targeted fields of influence and asks three related questions: (1) Are some sources of legitimation more important than others? (2) Do these have differential effects in self-help specialty niches? and (3) How do these effects impact niche growth? Results confirm that medical, academic, political, and popular legitimation make unique contributions to the self-help movement, that the importance of each varies dramatically by specialty niche, and that legitimation has a differential impact on niche growth.

Overall, these chapters address a range of questions about the resources that support social movement activity from within health professions and formal health organizations. Together they raise additional questions about how dominant professional and organizational authorities can also be tools for mobilizing others through their influence on social legitimacy, role as network connections, and advocacy for new institutional interests. These professional and organizational actors simultaneously provide valuable service in the production of health services and hence offer a link between existing service provision and potentially new ways to structure health care.

11

Shadow Mobilization for Environmental Health and Justice

Scott Frickel

For over a quarter century, citizen demands for "environmental justice" and more recently "environmental health justice," have energized place-based political struggle in rural and urban settings across the United States (Gibbs 2002). Although widely varied, these conflicts typically involve citizen groups or a coalition of community groups and "grassroots support organizations" (Tesh 2000) organized against industrial polluters and the various governmental organizations charged with the regulation, disposal, and management of environmental hazards (Cable and Cable 1995; Szaz 1994).

While the rights-based discourse adopted by the environmental justice movement (EJM) locates its political demands squarely within U.S. civil rights law (Cole and Foster 2001), community-level outcomes often turn on the technical merits of activists' claims regarding the existence of environmental contamination and the various impacts those hazards have on individuals and communities. The question of impacts, and particularly health impacts, depends further on the generation of credible evidence regarding chemical fate, transport, and bioavailabilty, as well as the length, frequency, and routes of exposure. In such contexts, toxicologists, epidemiologists, geneticists, physicians, and other health experts can influence community outcomes by reconfiguring the production and circulation of strategic forms of scientific knowledge (Allen 2003; Brown 2007; Fischer 2000). To maximize that potential, it is necessary to gain a better understanding of whether and how those "expert activists" are organized. Existing research has focused almost exclusively on the roles that individual professionals play in various local settings, but has yet to engage broader sets of questions concerning the structure of expert activism and the dynamics of expert mobilization and recruitment.

This chapter offers a framework for studying the structure and dynamics of expert activism in EJM. I develop the concept of "shadow mobilizations" in describing the loosely configured, boundary-spanning networks that tie variously positioned environmental health professionals to contaminated communities, to social movements, to the state, and to one another. Drawing on interview and biographical data from EJM expert activists and organizers, I argue that shadow mobilizations hold significance in social movement theory as incubators of activist cultures in science, organizing and reproducing environmental justice-oriented expertise in at least three interrelated ways: they thicken strategic ties across expert communities; they increase the recruitment potential of experts into EJM; and they generate opportunities for institutional change in science, engineering, and public health. The potential for shadow mobilizations to spur institutional change "upstream" in environmental health and allied fields as well as impact struggle on the ground is conditioned by political, organizational, and temporal logics that push the networks underground and insulate vulnerable expert activists from reprisal by professional opponents, industry and the state. Consequently, the analysis of shadow mobilizations has implications not only for social movement research on protest inside social institutions (e.g., Katzenstein 1998) and network theories that highlight the structural position of key actors (e.g., Burt 1992), but practical and political implications for activists and scientists as well.

Knowledge Politics in Environmental Justice

The environmental justice movement's relationship to environmental health science is complex. On one hand, the movement presents a broad challenge to the social authority of scientific knowledge. This challenge is materialized most explicitly in a variety of community-based research strategies developed within the movement to identify environmental hazards, document their deleterious effects, and mobilize that evidence in pursuit of movement demands (e.g., O'Rourke and Macey 2003). On the other hand, the outcomes of local struggles are often dependent on the regulatory regimes that structure environmental assessment and on the knowledge practices and disciplinary commitments that feed mainstream environmental health research (Frickel 2004b). Even when community groups are successful in generating their own data and getting regulatory decision-makers to consider seriously the evidentiary basis of their claims, the legitimacy of EJM "street science" (Corburn 2005) will likely be judged on how closely that knowledge conforms to the expectations of environmental health professionals and the assessment standards set by regulatory bodies (Allen 2004; Ottinger 2007).

The significance of EJM's structural dependence on mainstream science is sharpened further by the social gulf separating toxic communities from the professional community of environmental health experts. Class, occupational, and cultural differences mean that scientists and community activists do not typically live in the same neighborhoods, have access to similar economic and educational opportunities and resources, or hold common expectations of political representation and procedural justice. Scientists and community activists also tend not to share a common language for describing and assessing health threats posed by environmental hazards. A common result of this social divide—noted repeatedly in the literature if rarely examined systematically—is mutual distrust (Bullard 1993; P. Evans 2002). In such contexts, where cultural differences, resource disparities, and unequal political access can hamper communication and thwart social change efforts, expert activists allied with the goals and strategies of EJM represent a thin, yet crucial, conduit linking two vastly dissimilar social worlds.

What Is the Structure of Expert Activism in EJM?

Launched by Brown's (1987) study of "popular epidemiology" in a community anti-toxics campaign in Woburn, Massachusetts, a sizeable body of case-study research on community-based expert activism has developed in recent years. In general, these studies celebrate expert activists as individuals who are uniquely motivated by strong values of political and social justice to "do what's right" despite countervailing professional norms and institutional pressures to focus on research and grant-getting and to otherwise remain above the fray. Against those pressures and under threat of professional and occupational sanction, expert activists are credited with taking on a number of critical functions within EJM. These include translating technical information into language nonexperts can more easily understand; assisting in the design of community-oriented research projects; analyzing and organizing community-generated data; and representing community interests in court, the media, town council meetings and other political and educational fora. In these ways and more, the success or failure of community efforts to seek and attain redress for environmental injustice often seem to hinge on allied experts' skillful provision of technical knowledge, professional connections, and experience with regulatory bureaucracies.

Boiled down to essentials, case studies repeatedly express four related ideas about the context and nature of expert activism in EJM:

1. The institutions of academic and industrial science and medicine are generally unsympathetic to the claims of EJM activists.
2. Expert activism is an individual choice that is accompanied by associated risks to one's professional status, reputation, employability, and the like.
3. Because those risks are high, activism in EJM is a path that few qualified experts willingly follow.
4. The long-term involvement of those committed few have importantly conditioned what modest successes the movement to date has achieved.

While somewhat oversimplified, these ideas point to the potential significance of expert activism in shaping organizing strategies and protest tactics in EJM. For the movement, they suggest the value of increasing expert participation in EJM and pursuing ideological and organizational change "upstream" in the environmental professions. For social movement scholars, these ideas also prompt new questions—for example, about the hybridization of movements and the impacts of movements on the cognitive structures of science—that promise to push scholarship in new directions. Both goals will require research that moves beyond the case study to investigate the structure of expert activism.

The sole survey to address the topic to date highlights this need. Cable, Mix, and Hastings (2005) asked thirty-five EJM activists to describe their groups' collaborations with academics. Study respondents reported knowing about "a few" university-sponsored neighborhood health studies, admitted to the "occasional" provision of technical support from experts, and had no interactions with "traditional researchers conducting studies in contaminated communities" (68–70). While the study lends some credence to the commonly held notion that formidable institutional barriers separate academic researchers and contaminated communities, empirical support for this and related claims remains thin: the experts referred to by survey respondents are identified mostly as social scientists, not the engineers, chemists, public-health specialists, and medical professionals featured so prominently in existing research.

That literature, based almost entirely on case-study analysis, contains several distinct biases—for example, toward studying those experts who are highly committed to EJM, who identify with and maintain ongoing relationships with support organizations and community groups, and who do not shy away from public controversy. As a result, little is known about expert activism that is inspired by relatively modest expressions of commitment or identity investment. Extant scholarship also says less than it might about experts' involvement with the grassroots that is sporadic or even "one shot," or that is brokered by other actors. And we have limited understandings about the impacts of less overtly contentious forms that expert activism can take "under the radar."

This restricted view of expert activism in EJM is a methodological artifact generated by one or a combination of three tendencies: to bound cases organizationally, focusing on the work of support organizations (e.g., Brown et al. 2006), but missing extraorganizational dynamics; to bound cases temporally, focusing on specific episodes of conflict (e.g., Roberts and Toffolon-Weiss 2001), but overlooking important work that occurs during periods of relative quiet; or to bound cases biographically, focusing on the efforts of specific individuals (e.g., Allen 2003), but not the dynamics of expert networks. Of course, such limitations are simultaneously the hallmark strength of the case-study approach, in which a clearly demarcated research context permits in-depth investigation of specific context- and time-delimited processes. Yet the nearly singular dependence on the case study as a research strategy has begun to yield increasingly fewer returns on researchers' collective investments, repeatedly tapping an important but overly narrow segment of a more diffuse and complex phenomenon.

What may prove to be most distinctive about the experts portrayed in existing research is not their activism per se, but the intensity and public visibility of their activism. The celebrated experts of environmental justice may not be the rare few, so much as the visible few. Those who are less visible may or may not understand their position in a larger network of expert activists. These at least are empirical questions to be born out or not by research. The challenge is to develop analytic strategies that bring expert activism in all its variability of form and impact more fully into the light.

A Relational Research Strategy

My own efforts to develop an institutional analysis of expert activism begin with the basic premise that professionals' engagement with EJM is complex. It takes many forms, across a range of social settings and time frames, and can have widely varying impacts, negative as well as positive. I assume also that experts themselves make up a diverse population. They come to EJM for different reasons and from different places—not just university settings, but hospitals and clinics, government, private businesses, social movement organizations, and even industry. Experts also bring with them different combinations of interests and skills. Some contribute a great deal, others far less. Additionally, I resist the assumption that, all else being equal, more expert activism is better than less. Like any long-term relationships, those between experts and community groups can grow stale and ossify with time, but a quick telephone call or text message by a new acquaintance to the right people at the right time—and nothing more—can set serious changes in motion. And sometimes, what seem like good ideas simply fail to generate momentum. We need definitions and frameworks that can accommodate this level of complexity of action and diversity of actors.

Accordingly, I define expert activism as action by professionals that is coordinated with or in support of environmental justice community groups and support organizations and that is intended to further specific or general movement goals. I define expert activists as those professionals who contribute to EJM directly through involvement with community-based protest, or indirectly through expert networks that in one way or another intersect EJM. These definitions are framed broadly to make room for a potentially wide spectrum of activities, roles, career trajectories, and institutional settings, all of which may vary along several dimensions including relative visibility, duration, organization, and level of contention. What matters, I argue, is not the particular forms expert activism takes or who occupies those particular roles, but the quality of relationships formed through activism and the shape and dynamism of the networks that result from those interactions.

A main advantage of a relational approach lies in providing additional analytical perspective to each of the four ideas that comprise what I earlier called the restricted view of expert activism. If the institutions of science and medicine constrain expert activism, these institutions also provide opportunities for tactical innovation and expert recruitment. If activism in professional contexts entails substantial risks, when necessary experts can also find lower-risk ways of getting involved. While visible expert activists seem to be few and far between, we should also investigate whether others are working behind the scenes or in places that are less visible to outsiders. Rather than assume that expert activism is a net benefit for community groups, research should study experts that drift away and expert-led projects that fail. And so on. The point is to develop frameworks for investigating a fuller spectrum of connections linking experts and expert communities to EJM.

The rest of this chapter outlines such a framework. It is informed by thirty-two in-depth interviews that I conducted with scientists, engineers, public health specialists, medical professionals, and environmental justice organizers between 2002–6. All of the experts I interviewed were actively engaged in EJM at the time of the interview, and all of the organizers I interviewed had active ties with multiple experts. It is a small but diverse sample. The experts I interviewed live in various regions of the U.S. and come from a variety of scientific, engineering, biomedical, and public health backgrounds. Most work in research universities or medical schools, but a few are employed in government and in the private sector as physicians with clinical practices or as small-business owners. One was employed by a large pharmaceutical company. They ranged in age from their early thirties to early sixties, some of them entering their professions as activists, but most coming to activism as experts. All but a few were men. Some of the organizers I interviewed also had advanced degrees but most did not. The environmental justice and community groups they represented concentrate in the Texas and Louisiana Gulf region, but the other two coasts and the Midwest are represented as well. Perhaps the most distinctive commonality among all the interviewees is their ability and willingness to provide me with names of other expert activists—about fifty people, whom I have yet to interview—and the surprising fact that only a few of the names I have collected through this snowball method are duplicates. In other words, the community of expert activists in EJM would seem to be larger, more diverse, and more networked than expected based on research to date. I call this still-amorphous network a "shadow mobilization" and turn now to a sketch of its basic features.

Shadow Mobilizations

Shadow mobilizations are networks of experts—primarily public health researchers, environmental scientists and engineers, and medical professionals—that "interpenetrate" EJM and form important linkages between community and support organizations, national social movements, and the state.[1] Shadow mobilizations are dynamic relationship structures that organize and reproduce expert activism. They are incubators of activist culture in science that channel technical information and other resources into grassroots conflicts, but can also channel political critique, local knowledge, and organizing strategy "upstream" into environmental health fields. In this way shadow mobilizations can operate as mechanisms for institutional change in science.

Shadow mobilizations are related although not directly analogous to academic-based scientific/intellectual movements (SIMs), which have been broadly defined as "collective efforts to pursue research programs or projects for thought in the face of resistance from others in the scientific or intellectual community" (Frickel and Gross 2005: 206). In some contrast to SIMs, shadow mobilizations straddle academic and other knowledge systems, garnering resources and power through cross-disciplinary ties and ties to at-risk communities. Also, shadow mobilizations do not create new knowledge fields per se, but generate new ways of producing, organizing, and using expert knowledge in communities that traditionally lack access to experts and expert knowledge. To be sure, the professional communities that are both the target and outcome of SIM insurgencies can also provide infrastructure, resources, and identities that shadow mobilizations require. But unlike SIMs, shadow mobilizations are not likely to achieve institutional stability as either a distinct community of knowledge workers or as a formally constituted knowledge movement. One reason is because of their dependence on existing knowledge structures, but another is that unlike SIMs, shadow mobilizations tend not to be organized around coherent and ongoing intellectual projects. Instead, shadow mobilizations embody diffuse goals that correlate loosely with abstract theories of social justice, the knowledge interests of individual expert activists, and time-sensitive opportunities for community-level political engagement.

In that sense also, shadow mobilizations are not merely subsidiary components of EJM or constituency-based health social movements. They find their organizational center of gravity in diverse professional communities and knowledge institutions, not grassroots networks or formal social movement organizations. Their importance in EJM, then, derives not from strong ties to professional academic and political organizations as SIMs and the mainstream environmental movement do, but from the connective opportunities or "weak ties" they generate for communication and coordination among experts from different fields and between expert communities and EJM (Granovetter 1973). Three key features of shadow mobilizations are their boundary-spanning structure, their anchoring in diverse professional organizations, and their relative social invisibility.

Boundary-Spanning Structures

Shadow mobilizations span organizational, professional, and cultural boundaries. They are hybrids structured and held in dynamic tension by expert-local ties as well as ties among experts. *Expert-local ties* link professional communities to the EJM grassroots. Such ties exist in abundance among the experts and organizers interviewed for this study, with every expert citing active relationships with one or more community group, and every organizer acknowledging ongoing working relationships with multiple experts. The qualities of expert-local ties have received careful attention in existing research in part because they tend to bridge class and cultural differences and thus generate strategic channels for information provision as "weak ties" (Granovetter 1973). For example, one expert described his experience working for a state agency involved in a landfill contamination controversy:

> My primary role...was to sort of describe as the eyes and ears and eventually the nose of the community during the cleanup. I was the person, none of the community members were allowed to go on site, but I was allowed to. So during the actual clean up of the land fill, I was there most days, not every day, but most days. And I would write reports. A lot of what I did was write up a daily log of what happened on the site. That would be written and given to the residents. And then I would also give an oral report. That was my primary role.[2]

This expert describes what has come to be understood as a typical pattern, of activist experts unblocking information log-jammed in state bureaucracies or hidden away in corporate research offices so that it flows more freely from professional domains into local communities. Conversely, strong ties generated, for example, by local activists with some technical expertise but lacking connections to larger professional communities would presumably not permit the same breadth of information provision.

But information flows the other direction as well. Experts told me how much they have learned from working with community members, whose more intimate knowledge of their local environment, the industrial history of those places, and the patterns of community life provide epistemological advantage that outside experts do not have (Corburn 2005). This sort of lay-to-expert learning arms expert activists with experiences and knowledge about the unintended consequences of knowledge systems and for instigating changes to those systems in scientific and policy arenas. One example comes from a medical professional who described the pivotal nature of his "on-the-job" education as a volunteer with an environmental organization conducting community-based water quality monitoring projects.

> So we would identify where that [pollution] source would be, [and] a local secondary school actually did the water analysis in their lab. We taught them how to do it so that their results would be validated with the state health department. And then we could document where certain areas were clean enough, the shell fish bed could be reopened. That was the idea. That turned out to be an interesting mix of research at a community level with the watershed association training lots of people to do this. So I would go out on Sunday morning to do a water collection with maybe a clam digger. He had a lot of interest in getting these shell fish beds reopened as well, because that was his source of income. I remember one guy who lived off in the woods... with his family and that's how he supported himself.

The physician quoted here eventually translated his introduction to community-based environmental health research first into a new public health degree from an elite university and then into a career of expert activism in EJM. Here we see that the experiential value that experts may gain from working with communities is not limited to specific epistemological insights gleaned from local knowledge—for example by drawing on a clam digger's familiarity with a river to identify the point source of *E. coli* contamination—but can be generally life-reorienting as well. This example is illustrative of other interviewees who told me that community-based research was instrumental in their identification of and commitment to a larger political project (EJM), and that precipitated the politicization of their professional identities.

Community-based research projects or social protest that draws official and public attention to a contaminated site can also provide strategic advantages to expert activists engaged in contentious remediation projects. As the state expert quoted above told me,

> So I got to work for kind of everybody that was involved in the task force and the clean up,... and on the health study [that followed] and a lot of the other work and I had my fingers in a lot of different pies. Got to meet a lot of the attorneys who were involved in different ways... there were a lot of federal agencies that came in and out.... So I got to see it through a lot of layers.

In addition to gaining technical insight into the specifics of contamination and remediation at the site in question, this expert—a toxicologist—gained valuable political insight about how regulators respond to community demands and sociological insight about how bureaucracies gather and use information. Perhaps even more important, he met and established relationships with other concerned professionals—relationships that formed in a contaminated community but that continued beyond the particular controversy. Others I interviewed related similar, if somewhat less intense, experiences, illustrating how community-based protests function as "micro-mobilization contexts" for expert recruitment into EJM (McAdam 1988a) as well as establishing conditions for the generation of ties among experts situated in diverse fields and institutions.

Expert-expert ties represent the organizing capacity of shadow mobilizations within a diverse professional population whose training, structure of employment, and professional commitments and identities have traditionally been barriers to political organizing. Professional ties within and across expert communities are commonplace, although we would not expect to find the same densities or the same qualities of ties linking expert *activists* to one another. We can also distinguish the intraprofessional activist ties characteristic of SIMs from the more diverse interprofessional ties that signal shadow mobilizations. Indeed, this study finds that cross-professional networking among expert activists engaged in EJM is common, if not well understood, and that such efforts generate ties linking experts from different fields across academic, government, NGO, and even industry sectors. These professionally heterogeneous networks provide a level of resource diversity and potential for cross-disciplinary collaboration that SIMs are less likely to enjoy. Strong evidence for the existence of such networks lies in the fact that every expert I interviewed provided me with names of several other people they identified as expert activists, making clear that these expert activists are not working in isolation. Beyond this general statement, there are a number of reasons how, why, and with whom expert activists make these connections.

Clearly, local communities that are sites of environmental justice conflict are one important context in which expert activists meet and form relationships, as we have already seen. Conferences and government advisory committees are two other venues that bring different types of experts together to discuss ideas and issues of mutual concern. For example, when I asked one expert how he had met another expert with whom he now works closely, he told me,

> I got invited to this meeting and it just turned out that [name] was there as well. There were people there from around the country who had come in for a one-day meeting on reproductive health stuff. A whole bunch of non-profit activists. And [name] and I have both laughed about it a number of times since, because we both agree that it was one of the worst meetings that either of us had ever attended. But, it was where a number of us met each other for the first time....folks whom I've continued to work with over the years.

A similar account by an NGO-employed environmental health specialist speaks to the synergies that can emerge among experts working together across disciplinary and institutional lines. This instance involved a government advisory panel on children's health protection "made up of industry, academia, public interest, medicine, pediatrics. Its got a wide swath of folks, but all of whom know something about children's health. Even the industry people do." This person described the panel's efforts to advise the agency on a proposed utility rule limiting mercury emissions and the panel members' response at having their recommendations twice ignored by agency officials:

> [P]eople on the committee are pissed. And I don't mean people like me. I mean the guy from [chemical corporation]....[He will not] talk about pesticide issues...because that's what he works on, but on this issue he's willing to stand up and say 'this administrator is not listening to children's health experts and that is not acceptable.' And is willing to be pretty hard-nosed. So we wrote a third letter to the agency, which industry

people from [pharmaceutical corporation], from [energy corporation], wanted to strengthen. So, in my view, that's an example of how [industry experts] under certain circumstances [are] willing to stand up and speak truth to power.

These accounts demonstrate how organized events facilitate happenstance meetings among experts and the ongoing work and collaboration that can evolve from them.

Other interviews speak to the importance of existing friendship, collegial, and even business relationships in extending expert-expert ties. One example involves a series of invited workshops organized by an environmental health NGO to bring experts and EJM organizers together to discuss specific topics. In drawing up the invitation lists, the science director of that organization told me that, "we would invite friends, people we knew from the [city] area, because most of these meetings were held here.... We brought in people like [name]...and others who were, who knew the topic really well, had expertise." Other experts described reconnecting to former graduate-school colleagues or advisors. A molecular biologist who founded an environmental justice organization after finishing his Ph.D. and while working on a postdoctoral fellowship told me he began the organization with "a couple of my buddies from graduate school." This same person acknowledged that he also continued to seek advice from his graduate school mentor—advice on political organizing as well as on the technical issues pertaining to his environmental justice-oriented research. The frequency with which the interviewees stressed the importance of preexisting collegial or other ties is itself instructive. While expert recruitment into EJM can generate new ties, as in our earlier examples, these later examples suggest that transforming the quality of existing ties is another way to extend—or perhaps thicken—expert-to-expert linkages. Such new and newly transformed ties are two of the ways in which shadow mobilizations represent the interpenetration of EJM into environmental health and related knowledge domains.

Another indicator of interpenetration is found not in ties, but in the frequency with which individual experts migrate across the employment sectors that feed shadow mobilizations. Career trajectories among the experts interviewed for this study indicate some evidence for a "revolving door" of employment. In much the same way that members of Congress and top military officials shift between government positions and industrial lobbying jobs, it seems not uncommon for expert activists to migrate between academic, government, and NGO positions. While different people interviewed for this study navigated these opportunities in different ways, each example demonstrates how moving across employment sectors and forming new relationships in the process cumulatively deepens the interpenetration of EJM into environmental health sciences.

Anchoring Organizations

The fine structures of shadow mobilizations, constituted from social ties described above are, much like SIMs, anchored institutionally in professional organizations. Unlike SIMs that rise and fall within the academy and associated disciplinary societies, however, shadow mobilizations are tied into but not subsumed by those academic organizations. Grassroots support groups along with "activist" academic departments and politicized sections of professional associations bring a measure of organizational stability to networks that otherwise tend toward dynamic instability as provisionally networked individuals shift into and out of the movement.[3] The variety of organizational actors provides shadow mobilizations with a diverse set of resources that nourish and sustain these expert networks.

Grassroots support groups assist local environmental justice groups, in part by "mobilizing members, running meetings, using scientific data, talking with the media, pressuring policy makers, and dealing with stress" (Tesh 2000: 3). Another key aspect of support these groups provide to communities is helping local activists connect with experts who may be in positions to provide technical assistance. This type of support can come in a variety of forms that may include identifying researchers with relevant expertise, making initial contacts, and facilitating meetings between experts and local groups—sometimes on a case-by-case basis, and sometimes by organizing conferences that bring these actors together. The physician quoted earlier describing a conference at which he met many of his future activist colleagues noted that the meeting had been convened by a support group that "had some money left over from a grant…and wanted to bring some people together at the end of their grant year to discuss reproductive health issues and the environment." Putting local activists and experts together is often a difficult task, for many reasons, but overcoming barriers is facilitated when the organizers of grassroots support groups understand how scientific culture works. Roughly half of the EJM organizers interviewed for this study held advanced degrees in science, engineering, or public health. For some, recruiting and organizing experts was a major part of their duties. One interviewee, for example, estimated that he had recruited about two hundred experts over the years.

Another function that grassroots support groups can perform is bringing research ideas to scientists. A pharmacologist interviewed for this study described one organizer with a doctorate in zoology as someone who "puts people together. He also just as valuably puts ideas together." The pharmacologist continued,

> So he'll see something, he'll come to me and say, 'the stuff you're talking about with [topic], have you ever thought about that in [different context]? That's a place where there's a lot of change going on.' And you start to think about it for the first time. So he plants these ideas that are totally outside a discipline.

In some cases, those ideas become laboratory experiments that in turn reorient scientific attention toward topics that had previously received little notice. The research that evolved out of the above exchange examined the role of a class of environmental chemicals on obesity and was eventually published in *Nature*. This may be an atypical example, but it illustrates a more general point that grassroots support groups act as conveyors of ideas that can refocus or redirect knowledge practices in environmental health sciences.

Academic departments whose faculties take an "activist" or social justice-oriented approach to training are another type of organization that anchors shadow mobilizations. I asked all the expert activists I interviewed about their educational backgrounds and several described their graduate training in terms of the political values imparted by department faculty and curriculum. In describing the social significance of the training she received in the community health program at U. C. Berkeley's School of Public Health, one expert explained that

> A lot of public health is about teaching people how to have safe sex and to not smoke, and especially when you do health education, which is the piece of the field that I was in, most health education programs in schools of public health in this country are all about individuals' behavior.... But Berkeley wasn't at all. Berkeley was focused on media advocacy and systemic change.... And if you look at the Bay Area community, you see graduates from that program all over the place, doing really progressive social change in departments of health.

I am not aware of research that examines the role that activist departments play in social movements (but see Zald and McCarthy 1975), but the emphasis that this and other interviewees placed on their graduate-school training suggests that the topic deserves attention. In addition to providing social justice-oriented training to their graduate students, these departments promote activism on their campuses and in their communities, and provide employment opportunities for expert activists. These service roles may run counter to administrative goals and strategies, as illustrated by the fact that the Dean of Public Health at U. C. Berkeley combined the community health program described above

> with behavioral science and created something called the Division of Community Health Sciences. And within two years she [the Dean] eliminated the entire division.... So the whole community perspective of the school got lost because that was the body of students who cared about community health. They were gone. And there was a mass exodus of the faculty.

This progressive department's fate serves as a cautionary reminder that administrations facing budget pressures may be more likely to find reasons to cut politically contentious organizational units in universities than those that project more conformist identities on and off campus.

Politicized sections of professional societies are a third organization type that channels resources to EJM via shadow mobilizations. The American Public Health Association (APHA) is a professional society whose annual meetings tend to be populated by advocacy-themed panel sessions and keynote addresses and where health movement activists often participate as panel members or invited speakers. Within APHA, some sections are seen as more activist than others. For example, one interviewee noted that "the Occupational Health Section at APHA is really activist because it comes out of the labor movement." This same expert described the APHA Environment Section as a more contested terrain between "old guard sanitarian industrial hygienists, who are not political and do not want to get the boat rocked, and the newer generation of environmental health activists and policy people who really want to talk about mercury policy and energy policy." When asked to identify the more progressive actors in this section, this expert named only two who held academic faculty positions. The others worked in nonprofit organizations, environmental foundations, and government agencies. The institutional heterogeneity that is represented among experts who shape the section's discourse and programmatic agenda illustrates the boundary-spanning diversity of shadow mobilizations in microcosm.

Like activist departments, the authority of professional societies and sections that earn "activist" reputations may be limited relative to other societies that steer away from visibly political programs. For example, the APHA Environment Section progressives' hold on power is tenuous, at best. "The minute the eight or ten of us [activists] are not paying attention," my informant noted, "the Environment Section [will] start putting out sessions on vector control and, oh God." Another expert I spoke to about APHA expressed the opinion that the society has low credibility in the medical profession because its program is driven by "NGOs and politics" rather than by "basic science" and for that reason little if any important research on public health actually gets reported at these meetings.[4] Empirically accurate or not, this claim raises the question of whether the role that APHA conferences play as shadow mobilization venues also extend to other professional societies in the health and biomedical sciences.

Overall, these examples underscore the strategic importance of anchoring organizations in holding shadow mobilizations together. They connect experts to at-risk communities, they train and employ expert activists, and they provide venues for experts to exchange ideas, discuss research and political strategy, and shape professional discourse. Yet if grassroots support organizations, activist departments, and politicized sections of professional societies lend stability to an otherwise unstable expert network, we should not take the survival of those organizations for granted. As contested organizations, small nonprofits can easily fail to capture a vital funding stream, academic units can disappear when they cause more trouble for university administrators than justified by the money they bring in, and the leaders of politicized professional organizations can be toppled by revolts from the center. Their formal diversity is an advantage, to be sure, but as organizational anchors in shadow mobilizations, professional organizations may not hold in rough seas. Another way to avoid the tempest of political reaction is to swim in the relative calm beneath the waves.

Under the Radar Activism

Because "epistemic authority" in science is so often posed in formal opposition to professionals' political commitments (Gieryn 1999), whatever politically contentious goals that experts may seek to achieve in science can often be accomplished creatively through relatively conventional forms of collective action (Frickel 2006). Where those goals tend toward more contentious modes of engagement, as in forming citizen-scientist alliances in EJM, cultures of expert activism are more likely to develop when those networks remain hidden from view. There are at least three dimensions to shadow mobilizations' relative social invisibility.

The first involves *secretive action*. One way that secrecy shapes the organization of shadow mobilizations is through contacts in government agencies and in industry that provide opportunistic information to trusted experts joined to EJM. Not surprisingly, the identities of these government and industry "moles" are closely guarded. None of the several interviewees who mentioned these secretive contacts would provide names, choosing instead to discuss those relationships anonymously. One such account involved a local doctor whose collaboration in a community blood study sponsored by a chemical company gave him access to information about worker health that was being kept from the workers themselves. The doctor leaked that information to local environmental justice organizers. Another interviewee described occasional telephone calls from a "friend" inside EPA who would occasionally alert my informant to agency decisions that had time-sensitive significance for the grass-roots support group she directed. Several others corroborated this person's experience with government or industry informants.

Another form that secrecy takes in shadow mobilizations are closed-membership communications networks that expert activists use to share sensitive information and discuss confidential planning strategies with trusted others. In my interviews I was alerted to the existence of two such lists, but again without being granted access. The activists who maintain exclusive access to those lists—in this case both were organizers with science backgrounds—serve important gate-keeping and security functions, effectively designating who are shadow organizers and decision-makers.

A second dimension of the relative social invisibility of shadow mobilizations involves *advisory action* that occurs largely as a consequence of the networks' structure. Earlier I noted the role that graduate-school advisors continue to play in providing information and advice to former students who have joined EJM. The role of these advisors in shadow mobilizations is not so much hidden by conscious design, as it is hidden as an indirect result of network structures. The relative invisibility of these experts is derived from the fact that their advisory roles place them "backstage" relative to their more visibly activist protégés; it is the quality of their connections into the network, more than an intent to remain hidden, that makes their participation in shadow mobilizations less obvious. If these experts are less than centrally connected into EJM, their impact is by no means marginal or trivial. One interviewee gave an account of behind-the-scenes activism, here referring to a university professor

> ...who is probably the pre-eminent UV open path monitoring guy in the world making all of our standards and QA cells and all these things. And we just call him up and we say, 'hey, we need some help with this stuff, can you help us design it?' and he is so happy to give us that information and wants to do it so badly, that he will spend hours working with us to develop these things. And that's the network that's out there. It's there. It exists. It's not just him.

This example, among others, describes experts indirectly connected to EJM through former students and professional colleagues—people who may not think of themselves as activists, but who nevertheless contribute to a movement whose cause they believe in.

Expert activism can also remain hidden from broader view when it takes place within bureaucratic organizations that shield workplace activities from those outside. Thus a former federal government employee related her role in informally negotiating interoffice funds transfers that facilitated assistance to contaminated communities.[5] The informal nature of these deals kept knowledge of the transfers from agency officials, who may not have willingly given formal approval, and the bureaucratic contexts of the deal-making ensured that few in EJM had direct knowledge about backstage expert activism occurring inside the state on the movement's behalf.

Shadow mobilizations also operate under the radar through *episodic action* as a consequence of network dynamism. One aspect of this dynamism involves the fluidity of expert participation in EJM. Several organizers I interviewed had worked with numerous experts over the years, most of whom would come and go in fairly short order. "Obviously you'd have a range," one organizer told me.

> Some people who've worked with us for 20 years and some percentage who'd do one thing and that was it. But people tend to do these things for a while, a couple of years. Then they moved on, did something different, changed in different ways, any number of things.... There were always things that [came up and] people move on.

As this observation suggests, those experts who remain in the fight for the long term—and are most visible because of that commitment—are not the norm. Brief episodes of expert activism seem far more common. In the aggregate, the high rate of expert turnover decreases the overall visibility of shadow mobilizations.

In addition to expert churning, the temporal logic of protest is another aspect of network dynamism that nudges the experts of EJM out of sight, if not intentionally underground. Community-based environmental justice conflict often involves protracted, sometimes decades-long, struggles in a social environment shaped by limited resources and limited political opportunities. When opportunities do emerge, community groups and support organizations need to act swiftly and decisively, often with little lead time for planning. Such conditions can mean that experts are most useful to movement actors in highly specific ways, times, and places. One organizer expressed the opinion that scientists are only useful if they arrive at media events on time and say the right things in front of the cameras.[6] The on-again/off-again pace of protest may not conform to professional schedules, especially those governed by academic semesters. Or scientists may not be willing to make public preliminary research results in the timely manner that community groups may require (Allen 2004). Such incongruities in the temporal logics of protest and research can result in missed opportunities and lower visibility for expert activists—even those who have every intention of being seen.

Conclusion

This chapter begins to investigate the structure and dynamics of expert activism in EJM through an analysis of "shadow mobilizations." These highly dynamic boundary-spanning networks tie variously positioned environmental health professionals to contaminated communities and to one another. Suspended between the state and civil society, I argue that shadow mobilizations represent new and important forms of expert political organization. They organize and reproduce activist culture in science by thickening strategic ties across expert communities and increasing the recruitment potential of experts into EJM, thereby generating opportunities for institutional change upstream in environmental health sciences. That potential, however, is conditioned by political, organizational, and temporal logics that render the networks less publicly visible and partially insulate vulnerable expert activists from negative sanction or reprisal.

While preliminary, the argument sketched here draws critical attention to a number of assumptions embedded in the case study literature. Most significantly, research on shadow mobilizations challenges the view that expert activism in EJM is exceedingly rare. In contrast, much strategic collective action undertaken by environmental health experts on behalf of the movement seems to be hidden from view. For some experts, their low-profile activism is intentional. Where the stakes are high, secrecy becomes a necessary and effective strategy. For other expert activists, however, the relative lack of public visibility may result unintentionally from their network position, one or more ties removed from the grassroots. Moreover, many experts indirectly connected to EJM seem to have shorter term or discontinuous commitments to the movement. Like volunteers in other domains, these experts come and go as opportunities and interests permit, and as the rhythms of their professional lives and the cycles of protest in EJM sporadically coincide. In the aggregate, this churning process also contributes to keeping shadow mobilizations below the radar of public (and political) awareness. It is these structural features of shadow mobilizations, more than presumptions about professional risks to individual reputations and livelihoods that help explain what makes the experts of EJM paradoxically more common and more difficult to see.

This argument bears several implications for sociological research on networks, social movements, and science, as well as for activist practice and environmental policy. One set of implications concerns network theory and the nature of the ties that constitute shadow mobilizations. If, as in Granovetter's (1973) classic formulation of the problem, expert activists of EJM truly represent weak ties to the movement, this implies that their primary function is mainly limited to facilitating the transfer of information and technical skills from environmental health professions into grass-roots protest, as most existing research seems to demonstrate. However, if expert activism is more widespread than typically claimed, as the present analysis suggests may be the case, a more extensive set of ties connecting professional fields and the EJM grassroots may instead represent a largely untapped resource for mobilizing expertise. To the extent relational analysis aids in understanding whether and how the experts of EJM can be organized as a more cohesive and potentially more effective force for social change, the density of hidden and visible network resources may imply a different source of weak-tie strength. Future research on shadow mobilizations needs to better clarify the nature of these networks and network ties. For example, does expert churning represent a source of network instability as this study suggests? Or are there yet-to-be- identified mechanisms for expert replacement that maintains network stability even as individuals enter and exit in seemingly ad hoc fashion? Answers to these and other questions about the relationship between network structure and network dynamics can influence social movement practice by helping activists develop strategies for organizing expertise.[7]

Another of this study's implications concerns the interpenetration of EJM and environmental health professions and the analysis of protest inside social institutions and organizations (Katzenstein 1998; Raeburn 2004; Van Dyke, Soule, and Taylor 2004). Commonly described as a movement built on grass-roots community networks, this study suggests that EJM is professionalizing. In contrast to more mainstream environmental and health movements, however, where professional advocacy has centered in organizations staffed by legal, scientific, and public health experts, professionalization in EJM may be occurring largely, although not exclusively, under the radar. In this sense, shadow mobilizations may represent both an alternative route to movement professionalization and a means of importing contentious politics and collective action into the environmental health sciences. One set of questions that follow from this line of thought concerns the nature of protest in science and the relationship between the forms and outcomes of expert activism. Is disruptive protest effective inside science? In a study of the 1970s-era SIM that created genetic toxicology, I argued that conventional behavior pointed toward contentious goals can have "deceptively profound changes in the institutions that produce and certify knowledge" (Frickel 2006: 207). Additional research will be needed to assess whether conventional practices among EJM's expert activists produce and distribute similarly contentious results across a range of environmental health fields. A related line of investigation might examine the distinct forms that expert activism takes in those fields, specifically attending to the relationship between shadow mobilizations that channel contentious ideas into science and the emergence of insurgent SIMs that take up those ideas in challenging the scientific status quo. As this chapter suggests, there are both important differences and similarities between SIMs and shadow mobilizations. These might be more clearly disentangled through the comparative analysis of expert activism.

Finally, results of this study suggest important implications for science and pubic health policy. Transformative changes in environmental health sciences toward capital- and technology-intensive knowledge domains—such as bioinformatics, genomics and proteinomics—are placing knowledge practices and expertise at an ever-greater institutional remove from EJM community activists (Shostak 2004). At the same time, environmental health policy is moving toward more inclusive decision-making (Epstein 2007a), exemplified by the promotion of community-based environmental justice research at the National Institute of Environmental Health Sciences and other federal regulatory and research agencies (http://www.niehs.nih.gov/research/supported/programs/justice/). The technocratic and democratic impulses embodied in these changes are countervailing and their impacts on the mobilizing potential of the environmental health science work force will have important ramifications on the expression of expert activism in EJM. In policy contexts then, as well as theory and practice, clearly there is more to expert political organization and activist cultures in environmental health science than meets the eye.

NOTES

I thank an anonymous reviewer, the editors, conference participants, and colleagues in the Sociology Faculty Research Colloquium at WSU for instructive feedback on earlier versions of this paper.

1. On interpenetrated social movements, see the chapters by Epstein and Wolfson, this volume.

2. I have removed all names and identifying markers contained in the interview transcripts to protect the anonymity of people quoted in this paper.

3. I describe this "churning" dynamic and its implications later in the chapter.

4. Author's field notes (December 12, 2005).

5. Personal communication with anonymous informant (June 8, 2007).

6. Personal communication with anonymous informant (June 6, 2003).

7. I thank Jane Banaszak-Holl and an anonymous reviewer for pointing out some of the parallels between shadow mobilizations and network theory noted here.

12

Bringing Social Movement Theory to Healthcare Practice in the English National Health Service

Paul Bate and Glenn Robert

Even though there is a history of connection and overlap between the Social Movements (SM) and Organization Studies (OS) fields, recent years have seen an increase in the pace and density of these boundary crossings (Davis and Zald 2005: 336). For example, there have been two recent books bringing together SM and OS scholars (Snow, Soule, and Kriesi 2004; Davis et al. 2005), the purpose of these purely scholarly exchanges being to apply and develop theory in new ways and in new contexts and directions. In addition to this, articles have begun to appear with increasing regularity in mainstream OS and management journals, some directly addressing social movements as an organizational phenomenon (Crotty 2006), others using insights from the SM literature to explore a variety of OS issues from new perspectives; for example, how activist groups influence corporate social change activities (Berry 2003; Kozinets and Handleman 2004; den Hond and De Bakker 2007), stakeholder and shareholder mobilization and activism for change (Rowley and Moldoveanu 2003; Rehbein, Waddock and Graves 2004), and the role of leadership in mobilizing collective resistance and grassroots change in the workplace (Zoller 2007).

This chapter, in contrast, is about a boundary crossing of a very different kind, not between academics from different disciplines but between academics and practitioners, in this case practitioners in healthcare organizations. Rather than focusing on theory development per se, the work described here has relocated social movement theory to an action research setting, transposing it into an organizational change intervention aimed at bringing about dramatic improvements in services to patients (and the experience of staff providing those services). The chapter relates how academics and policymakers came together with healthcare staff in a unique five-year collaboration to apply social movement theory to the challenge of bringing about major reform within the English National Health Service (NHS).[1] The central question the chapter addresses is whether it is possible to apply knowledge from SM research to help create or—perhaps more accurately—unleash movement-like dynamics by means of problem- and change-driven activities and processes aimed at improving, indeed transforming, healthcare services.

In recounting the story of this change attempt we shall also be seeking to (a) describe and critique the design process through which movements' ideas were refined down into a practical approach to organizational change which was then piloted and tested by various NHS teams *in vivo*; and (b) evaluate and reflect upon the relevance and utility of a social movements paradigm within a healthcare organizational change context.

Background and Context

Academic Context

For more than a decade accusations of "disconnected" (Bennis and O'toole 2005) or "disengaged" (Van de Ven and Johnson 2006; Van de Ven 2007) scholarship have been leveled against organization and management theorists, the major criticism being that in turning increasingly inward on their theoretical world, OS scholars have turned their back on the "real-world" needs of organization practitioners. The specific criticism is that most of the work carried out under this disciplinary banner is irrelevant or unusable in any practical way—what Rynes and colleagues (2001) refer to rather grandly as the "knowledge utilization problem." While a major talking point today, this problem is not new: as long ago as 1988, Porter and McKibbin noted that business-school scholars had become indifferent to the concerns of management practitioners: "Most business school professors are purposely aiming their research reports toward their academic brethren and...do not *care* whether such publications are comprehensible to practicing managers, or not" (1988: 167).

The logical response to these accusations, which has found growing support in a number of quarters, lies in closing the "translational gap" between academic research and practitioners (Khurana and Marquis 2006) and the conversion of "theoretical knowledge into practical applications" (Bate 2005; Hambrick 1994; Bartunek 2004)—what Van Aken (2004) and others refer to as "actionable knowledge." Action research is certainly no stranger to organization and management studies but in this case (partly inspired by the sentiments surrounding movements) we wanted to go one step further, beyond "applied" or even "action research" to what elsewhere we have described as "activist research" (Bate 2005). The distinguishing feature of activist research in the social sciences is that it involves a commitment to *doing something* with the knowledge one has acquired through research (the concept of a knowledge intervention), of trying to "make a difference" and improve things for the better (Stanford 2008), in our case services to patients.

So much for the OS academic context for this paper, but what of the SM context? This is similar and different to the former, similar because we found the same disconnection between SM theory (and theorists) and SM practice (and practitio-ners), but different in that, unlike OS, this issue has attracted little comment or criti-cism from SM scholars themselves. Initially, we were somewhat perplexed by this: the whole nature and rationale of social movements is that they are about "action," so why is the writing so biased toward the theoretical, and fellow scholars, and not movements' practitioners or improvement activists?[2]

Differences between OS and SM research apart, the context of our paper is the desire to draw attention to and suggest ways of closing the translational gap between scholars and practitioners in *both* fields, the potential attraction being work of greater relevance, utility, and practical value to people in organizations and social move-ments, but also two fields that are theoretically and empirically richer as a result of this cross-fertilization.

Healthcare Context

The healthcare context for our work is the English NHS, a 1.3 million person organi-zation desperate for new ways of thinking and approaching healthcare change and improvement. In 2000, amidst mounting criticism of the quality of the services it was providing, the NHS embarked on a major program of change and reform. In a lan-guage often more reminiscent of a social movement than a national policy program, the Labor Government's NHS Plan (Department of Health 2000) called for a "revolu-tion in quality and a step change in results," for "radical action" to bring about "radi-cally reformed services"—big transformational change around the "cause" of dramatically improving healthcare in England. It also had the same scale ambitions as a movement, being described at the time as "the largest concerted systematic improvement effort ever undertaken, anywhere, in any industry" (Berwick 2003).

However, despite the bold words, it became evident quite early on to those leading it that the "revolution" would not be achieved through the normal repertoire of NHS improvement methods and approaches, these being the "continuous improvement" methods typically found in the Total Quality Management (TQM) and business process reengineering literatures. While capable of delivering gradual incremental improve-ments to the system over time, these were not suited to the scale, pace, breadth, and depth of change envisaged in the Plan. The NHS view at the time was very much that "radical times" called for "radical remedies." This is what lay behind the search for new theory, methods, and practices in the change/improvement arena, which in turn led to our involvement and subsequent exploration of the social movements field.

Our Story

With the two contexts above in mind, our story begins in 2002 when Helen Bevan, a leading healthcare-improvement practitioner in the NHS, asked the authors of this chapter to conduct an initial review into different theories of large-scale change. As we wrote together at the time (Bate, Robert, and Bevan 2004):

> Most ideas that underpin contemporary healthcare improvement initiatives are derived
> from planned or "programmatic" approaches to change (Pettigrew 1998)... However,

there is another so far unused research base in the social and political sciences that offers an entirely different perspective on how large-scale change occurs. This is social movement theory (McAdam, McCarthy, and Zald 1996; Strang and Jung 2002 [2005]; Crossley 2002), which seeks to explain "why collective episodes [such as movements and protests] occur where they do, when they do, and in the ways they do?" (Smelser 1962)

Below we describe in turn the five broad phases that our subsequent collaboration has since gone through, moving from original concept to eventual implementation in mid-2007.

Evidence Gathering, Literature Review, and Dissemination

This first phase, which began in fairly traditional fashion, comprised secondary and then primary research to identify key themes and issues relating to how movements, particularly organizational movements, form and develop.

Literature Review

Our work started with a conventional systematic literature review, initially taking in the broad sweep of different kinds of large-scale-change literature (OD, complexity and chaos theory, generative change and social movement theory). In 2002–3, our first sweep of the social movements literature—a review of 147 books and articles—resulted in a conceptual report (Bate, Bevan, and Robert 2004) based on three different schools of thought in social movements theory (collective behavior and social movements, resource mobilization and political process theories, and New Social Movements) and a classification of six different types of factors we identified as influencing movement formation and development (rational, emotional, social and normative, behavioral, organizational, and leadership). As stated at the time, this review had four objectives:

1. to explore "social movements" as a new way of thinking about large-scale systems change;
2. to assess the potential contribution of applying this new perspective to NHS improvement;
3. to enrich and extend NHS thinking in relation to large-scale, system-wide change; and
4. to begin to establish an evidence base to support the emergence of an improvement movement in the NHS.

Our final report was widely disseminated and, we believe, helped to put "social movements thinking" on the NHS change agenda for the first time.

Significantly, as we read subsequent material we increasingly began to ask "what is this saying or implying in terms of 'must do's' for creating a movement or unleashing movement-like dynamics?" Drawing on the "design principles" idea found in the design sciences like architecture and indeed medicine itself (which pride themselves on not having seen the same disconnection between research and practice and which were therefore an obvious exemplar for our work [Bate and Robert 2007; Bevan et al.

2007]), we embarked upon what was to become more of a "translational literature review." This involved not only noting what the literature said (key themes, hypotheses, and issues) but wherever possible translating this knowledge into more practical "design rules," heuristic statements in the form of "if you want to achieve Y in situation S, something like X might help" (Plsek, Bibby, and Whitby 2007). These were to become hypotheses that we could pilot and test, and concepts that practitioners could begin to play and work with ("play" again being important to the innovation process in the design field).

"Authentic Voices"

The project then progressed to some primary research as we began a search for "authentic voices" in the NHS in order to capture the experiences of people who had been directly involved in trying to improve some aspect of health or social care using a movements mindset (whether explicitly or implicitly).[3] We came across and were alerted to numerous examples of movements-based approaches to change in the NHS (for example "see and treat" in emergency care, the hospice movement, self-help movements such as Age Concern and Braintalk, the AIDS movement, community-regeneration projects, the UK "Children's Crusade," and what later became one of our video documentaries, "The Early Psychosis" movement in mental health).

This first research phase in all its forms was crucial to people's later willingness to give the approach a try, as we could show them that this "new" approach to large-scale change was supported by a wealth of primary and secondary evidence—important to people brought up on the notion of evidence-based medicine (EBM)—as well as providing real-life examples to which they could directly relate as healthcare professionals.

"Breaking the Silence"

The story then took an unforeseen, but lucky, twist: early in our search one of us read a paper from as long ago as 1978 (Zald and Berger 1978) which, as later described by one of its authors, had been "greeted by stillness, indeed silence" at the time of its publication (Zald 2005). Only much later would this paper be resurrected as a precursor of contemporary work that uses concepts drawn from social movement and collective action theory to analyze change in organizations and industries. The paper argues that the political processes within organizations have many parallels to those found in society and politics at large and that we can, therefore, move the whole apparatus of political sociology into organizations to explain the forms and dynamics of protest and conflict in organizations. Upon reading the paper in May 2002 we e-mailed Zald, explaining our interest and asking for any advice or pointers he could give to empirical studies or ongoing research in this area that we may have missed. He generously replied and it transpired that the timing of our enquiry had been fortuitous; he had just been one of the conveners of a conference of leading scholars at the University of Michigan on the relationship of organization theory to social movement theory, and kindly provided us with full access to the conference papers. Prompted by these communications and papers our collaboration eventually came to include a colloquium between NHS practitioners and leading social movement academics in London in 2004, which would turn out to be a watershed event in the unfolding story, and strong testament to the value of joint practitioner-academic exchanges of this nature.

Practitioner-Academic "Fora"

The next step in the translational process thus involved exposing the key findings from our initial review of the social movement literature to policymakers and practitioners and asking them to reflect upon and begin to develop and apply them to the practical challenges of effecting change within the NHS. We did this by means of a series of seminars, conferences, and workshops to explore social movement ideas and their relevance and application to healthcare reform. These included, for example, the presentation in July 2002 of our initial thoughts to a very senior group of NHS leaders, posing three questions (the last of which led directly to the two-day colloquium between academics and practitioners referred to in the previous section):

1. How do these ideas resonate with your own experiences and views of leading improvement in the NHS?
2. What relevance does this approach to thinking about large-scale change have for the NHS?
3. What questions and issues would you want to pose to leading social movements academics? What is the problem you would want to set for them?

The outcome of these discussions is described more fully elsewhere (Bate, Robert, and Bevan 2004) but the overall conclusion reached was that those leading and implementing modernization in the NHS might indeed benefit from considering the change task from the alternative perspective of social movements, as distinct from the usual OS, TQM, and change management perspectives.

What was the wider subsequent reaction? Wherever we went people were intrigued and excited, if a little skeptical, the reasons they gave being that this new perspective (a) challenged the current NHS taken-for-granted approach to improvement, (b) offered something that felt new and different, and (c) seemed to address the unprecedented scale and pace of change with which the NHS was struggling. Of particular significance in this regard was the observation (Zald, Morrill, and Rao 2002) that most of the big changes in society and the way we live over the last several decades had come by way of social movements rather than through the rational planned change programs so beloved of organizations.

At this point, and as a brief aside to our story, it is timely to reflect on the fact that much of the skepticism we encountered at this early stage came from the threat SM thinking was seen to pose to the organization itself (and hence why senior managers particularly were sometimes highly suspicious of it and its advocates). The perception of threat is not without foundation: social movements (particularly newer ones) are indeed based on a nonhierarchical, consensus-based model of organization, and associated with the taking away of formal organization or organization constraints, hence nineteenth century Spiritualists advocating "no-organizationizm" and suffragist Lucy Stone comparing organizations to Chinese footbinding, declaring that

Table 12.1. How Does Organizational Logic Differ from "Social Movements' Consciousness"?

The Logic of Organization/Authority	The Consciousness of Mobilization and Social Movements
Formal Ties	Informal Ties
Hierarchical	Equal and Fraternal
Bureaucratic	Communal and consensus based
Centralized	Devolved
Led from the Top (the privilege of the powerful)	Participative and Led from the Bottom (the privilege of the less powerful)
Coercive	Voluntary
Legitimate authority	Empowered
Rational	Emotional
Planning/Order	Action/Emergence

The Power of One, the Power of Many Handbook (adapted from Bate, Bevan, and Robert 2004).

she had "had enough of thumb-screws and soul-screws never to wish to be placed under them again" (Clemens 2005). In sharing our initial findings with practitioners it became clear that the two approaches to organization and change (mechanistic and generative) are very different (table 12.1), and indeed seemed almost hostile to each other:

Not surprisingly, given these contrasts, a good deal of the discussion in these early fora centered upon whether it was necessary for the organizational activist to choose between the two approaches ("either-or") or whether they could be combined or reconciled in some way ("both-and"). This is an issue that never found true consensus among the practitioners with whom we worked, although the official line from the NHS has always been that they do complement each other. The only point on which there was broad agreement was that organizational context for movements differed in important ways from the wider social context, sometimes being more constraining (for example, the fear of losing one's job and career was more immediate and real), and sometimes more enabling (for example, many professional networks and communication systems already existed and did not need to be set up from scratch).

Returning to our story: there was now a significant pause. People—including ourselves—were enthused and intrigued but unsure what to do next; we suspected that "movements" would probably remain as an idea on the NHS drawing board. Then in 2006 the idea of bringing social movement thinking to NHS improvement and change was resurrected (by Helen Bevan), and the authors were asked to work directly with some NHS pilot sites to help translate the thinking into practical advice that could be implemented in the organizational context of the NHS. The design sciences once more came to our aid in suggesting a way forward and pointing us in the direction of the obvious: that the point had been reached where "proof of concept" was required. As with any kind of design prototype, what was now needed was a test flight of our movements model in a real-life—but closely managed—organizational setting. The problem was that such a model did not actually exist. We now had to set about building it.

Model Building and Field Testing

So, in late 2006, we set out to develop and test a change model/intervention based on social movement theory with four pilot NHS organizations from both primary and secondary care, three of them staff-led initiatives, the fourth a patient-led initiative. This third phase of model building and field testing was characterized by early flirtations and failures as we struggled to articulate the model and give the evidence and ideas some kind of form. This was in part a consequence of our decision to abandon the usual linear, planned "*n*-step"—first you do this and then that—model of change (Collins 1998) so beloved of management consultants (who had actually been brought in at this point to help with the design and implementation and were advocating exactly this kind of approach) and focus instead on ways of liberating the kind of generative "spiraling" change dynamics (Beck and Cowan 1996; Cacioppe and Edwards 2005) typically found within social movements. As part of this decision, pilot sites were given maximum freedom to (as we said at the time) "find their own way up the mountain" with the aim of developing "ground up" some broad "design principles" (Bate 2007; Alexander 1979; Lidwell, Holden, and Butler 2003) as opposed to externally imposed change "stages" or "steps." What we were seeking were some "design principles": evidence-based, tried-and-tested solutions and approaches that had worked for movements and which now might work for the pilot site teams.

Teams from the four pilot sites worked for six months on a total of ten separate projects, and we supported them in this with a series of monthly training days consisting of some limited formal inputs on SM and SM thinking as well as sharing opportunities between the sites, and on-site support and advice. In our work with the sites it was clear that the generative approach with its emphasis upon liberating energies and mobilizing staff at the grassroots level and as free of hierarchical control as was possible had struck a chord with the practitioners:

> I think there's certainly more freedom. I don't mean it's not organized but there's more opportunity to probably think outside of the box and be a bit different.

> With some project deadlines you feel that they are put on you and forced, and I think this is trying to get around all that and being about us wanting to bring about the change ourselves. This isn't the usual "death by project management."

> Well it went from a group that had never met before in January to them wanting to meet in the evenings once a week because they were so enthused about the whole thing. It was incredible how this happened.

> We just talked about things we could do and it was quite infectious. People were saying we could do this, we could do that and the ideas were brilliant.

Although there was more than sufficient here to suggest "proof of concept," the level of achievement had left something to be desired. When we came to characterize each of the projects across the four sites at the end of this pilot phase we concluded that the vast majority were still more like traditional NHS improvement projects than movements, although a small number of these had acquired certain movement-like dynamics. Perhaps unsurprisingly, the best example was the patient-led group that had acquired many hallmarks of a movement, and considerable mass and momentum behind a number of deep-seated grievances its members had chosen to work on (hospital-acquired infection, transport problems, destruction of community, and so on).

We reflected on this slightly disheartening outcome and concluded that one of the reasons was the lack of personal connection between individual staff and the chosen goals of their projects, and resolved to address this when we came to launching the approach more widely. Then, based on the accumulated learning from the first two phases (successes and failures)—and after much iteration and discussion—we extracted five principles[4] upon which our change intervention would be built:

—frame to connect with hearts and minds

—energize and mobilize

—organize for impact

—making change a personal mission

—keep forward momentum

Launch

From the evidence gathered through the literature review, "authentic voices," and field testing we now began to (a) prepare early drafts of materials and toolkits, (b) find and brief internal facilitators, and (c) recruit and brief sites for a "launch" event, which was to be called *The Power of One, The Power of Many. Three Days in July.* Appendix 1 details the major concepts we addressed under each of the five principles.[5] A handbook was produced with supporting materials to reinforce the key concepts and exercises as they were introduced to the participants.

Participants comprised teams of three or four volunteers from twelve NHS organizations who, over three days in the summer of 2007, were taken through each of the five principles—effectively a crash course in SM "thinking"—using a combination of:

—formal taught inputs

—specially made films of real-life stories as examples (some from our "authentic voices" and field test sites)

—fiction (such as an excerpt from a film of a John Grisham story to illustrate the power of framing) and imagery

—voting handsets (to test the consensus around the room on various issues and viewpoints)

—case studies from the social movement literature (for example, a timeline of the antismoking movement, and McAdam's [1988] description of how middle-class teenagers were recruited to "Freedom Summer")

—team and group work

—posters, post-its, wall charts and rollerboards

—a minimal use of PowerPoint!

Building on the learning from the field-test sites, we briefed each of the twelve teams in advance to prepare to bring to the event a "cause" (as opposed to a "project")

that they wished to work on by means of the following request: *"As you know, during the three days we shall be asking you to work on your 'cause'—something you really care about. In preparation for this we would like you to go out and spend a day observing an area or activity that is likely to be affected by your cause.... And ask yourself what is really going to make a difference here?"* At the event, core teams of physicians, nurses, and managers from the twelve organizations then came together on the neutral ground of a conference center in order to learn about movements and work on their cause. The causes brought by the participants included transforming the patient experience, mobilization of physicians and clinical teams, radically revised ways of working, and so on. After a brief introduction explaining what we meant by a "social movement" and how a movements approach was different from the traditional programmatic approach to change within the NHS, much of the work on day one was devoted to refining (and where necessary reframing) these causes as part of the first principle.

Principle 1: Framing to Connect With Hearts and Minds

Our first principle drew heavily on Snow and colleagues' (1986, 1988) seminal work on framing in movements but also Feldman (2007) and Westen's (2007) more recent writings on "framing the debate" (and its decisive importance) in American politics. Participants were introduced to the idea that frames have a number of important roles in relation to the turning of opportunity into action, and this was illustrated by means of film excerpts and contemporary healthcare examples. Exercises to support this principle also included asking the teams to reframe a current NHS organizational challenge (in this case the "18 week minimum wait" for treatment—an issue that participants agreed had been poorly framed by senior NHS leaders) to make it irresistible for people to join; to refine and reframe their own cause; and to think about how they might hook various groups of people (believers, sympathizers, ambivalents, antagonists, and the disaffected) into their cause using a variety of framing strategies (see appendix 1).

Principle 2: Energize and Mobilize

The second principle was concerned with getting people to "step off the pavement" and move from bystander to participant. We introduced a spectrum of participation—moving through from "engagement" to "commitment" to full blown "mobilization," and suggested that mobilization at the organizational level was concerned with rallying and propelling people to take joint action for the purpose of realizing common goals. The task here was to unleash or unlock organizational energy (Loehr and Schwartz 2003; Bruch and Ghoshal 2003)[6] and "discretionary effort" (a concept from the Human Resource Management discipline which refers to people being willing to give more than what they are formally contracted to give) as necessary steps toward mobilization. This principle also highlighted the importance of narrative and story-telling in the mobilization process (Bate 2005); a practical workshop was run to help participants draw on the power of stories with regard to their own causes (similar workshops were run on patient and caregiver involvement, and organizational energy). We also suggested to the participants that attention-grabbing spectacles, pictures and images—funny and serious—could have a similar effect to stories in moving and mobilizing people. Amongst a number of other exercises, we shared with participants lessons on how to mount successful campaigns (adapted from Hirschhorn 2002). The application of a campaign-based approach to organizational change and improvement was illustrated by video-based case studies of the US Institute for Healthcare Improvement's (IHI) recent, and well respected, "100,000" and "5 Million Lives" Campaigns. The teams were then given time and support to develop their own campaign-based approaches with the aim of building mass around their own causes.

Principle 3: Organize for Impact

"Organize, organize, organize" was Saul Alinsky's (1971) famous call for radicals, echoed more recently by Snow and colleagues (Snow, Soule and Kriesi 2004:10):

> There is absolutely no question about the fact that social movement activity is organized in some fashion or another. Clearly there are different forms of organization and degrees of organization (e.g. tightly coupled vs. loosely coupled)…But to note such differences is not grounds for dismissing the significance of organization to social movements.

Under this—our third—principle, we introduced participants to the need for a core structure and a distributed model of leadership (i.e., leadership at every level). We asked them to consider who needed to be in their core team, and who were their "bridge leaders" and their local organizers. Then, using James Jasper's (2004) concept of strategic dilemmas (among other things), we presented the teams with a series of key organizational choices based upon the social movements literature (for example, questions as to the manner and degree to which their "movement" needed to be organized, the optimum size and scale of their "movement," and whether they needed to work with or against the system). Finally, we suggested that movements typically position themselves and their tactics at a point along the spectrum from moderate/reformist action to extreme/disruptive action and that the choice of tactical positioning depended on a number of factors. The teams were asked to consider which tactics (from the specific examples we presented) would be most appropriate for their cause and local organizational context.

Principle 4: Making Change a Personal Mission

Under our fourth principle we shared with participants the profile of an organizational radical, drawing heavily upon the notion of "tempered radicals": change agents who work inside organizations by rocking the boat just enough but not so much that it turns over and takes everyone down with it! (Meyerson 2003; Meyerson and Scully 1995). Personal qualities and characteristics highlighted from our literature review and case studies and shared with participants included authenticity, energy, passion, impatience, self-belief, self-doubt, persistence, stamina, "chutzpah,"[7] and finally, "quiet courage."[8] Using these as referents, participants were then invited to draw up their own "organizational radicals CV" and share these with the wider group.

Personal risk is an issue that we also advised would need to be considered both for themselves and others that they might recruit and mobilize for change. As Kleiner (1996) has pointed out, organizational heroes can so easily end up being recast as heretics and villains, and left to languish in some corporate backwater, their careers effectively over:

> Modern heretics are not burned at the stake. They are relegated to backwaters or pressured to resign. They see their points of view ignored or their efforts undermined. They see others get credit for their ideas and work. Worst of all, they see the organization thrive as a by-product of their efforts, while the point of their heresy, the truth they fought to bring to the surface, is lost. (228)

Here, the challenge we posed to participants was to find a way of minimizing the risk, or at least perception of it, since it is self-evident that people are much less likely to join or participate in a movement when the risks in their doing so are high—echoing Strang and Jung's concern that "[w]hether individuals can be mobilized for risky forms of collective action with unclear pay-offs is highly problematic" (2005: 308). We suggested among other things that understanding the context (and knowing how to use it, for example, Alinsky's [1971] "schmoozing the community") could help one to manage such risks and stay out of danger.

Principle 5: Keep Forward Momentum

Change initiatives in the NHS are normally discussed in terms of "spread and sustainability," but this time we suggested to participants that the term "momentum" from the social movement literature might be a better concept because it dealt more directly with the issues of mass and energy. We illustrated growth and decline in momentum (with case studies such as the "Slow Food" and antiwar movements in the United States) and suggested that the notion of "unstoppable momentum"— something on the move that is difficult to stop, that can "keep going in the absence of external forces"—is also a helpful one in the light of how hostile or unreceptive the organizational context might be for a change intervention. This was particularly significant here because much NHS thinking and received wisdom is concerned with how to create "receptive contexts" for change; however, with this social movement concept, the question changes to how to create something that will survive and grow *despite* the lack of organizational or wider environmental support? We proposed nine common failure modes (see appendix 1) associated with loss of momentum in movements, relating each back to one of our four earlier principles and suggesting how to avoid falling foul of these.

Evaluation

So how relevant and useful did our healthcare practitioners find these social movement theories and concepts for their own change/improvement efforts? The evaluation of the three-day event comprised (a) detailed feedback from participants at the event itself, and (b) telephone interviews with a sample of those who had attended some two–three weeks after the event to ascertain what had happened since they had returned to their organizations and taken the first steps toward implementing their campaign plans.

At the end of the three days we asked participants for their comments and views on specific elements of the event (for example, the examples and illustrations used, the ideas and concepts etc.). The concepts underpinning the three days were clearly credible with the participants and it was also evident that they had been mobilized and energized by the event itself. The practitioners, with few exceptions, had connected emotionally, cognitively, and intellectually with SM thinking during the three days. Not only had it "rung bells" and "pushed buttons" for them (their phrases), it had also brought back what, for them, had faded or been missing in the NHS during the past ten years of top-down, target-driven change, namely the emotional, community, and values dimensions of change. They commented positively on several aspects of the approach including, firstly, (to paraphrase) the generation of change from the grassroots level upward, which they thought would bring more energy and drive to the change effort. Secondly, they particularly liked the idea of framing, which shifted the focus from the well-worn concept of "communication" to how to "define" the issue so that it becomes important, meaningful, and attractive to all those who need to be involved—not just managers who make decisions about developments and funding, but also the staff and clinicians who have an idea for change or improvement and believe strongly that it should be achieved for reasons that are vitally important to them, their colleagues, and their patients. Thirdly, they appreciated that the "social movement approach" was not about abandoning structures and frameworks that give organization and robustness to change processes (for example, analysis, review, implementation and evaluation) but of using them in a different way, not so much for planning or control purposes, but for mobilizing staff and sustaining momentum within the change effort.

A common issue for participants after the event has been how to link or position their cause with regard to established organizational structures and processes, and where (if anywhere) one went to get "permission" or legitimacy for the work. Some felt that placing it outside the hierarchy as a local "grassroots" activity was right, whereas others felt that to have any impact in the organizational contexts within which they were working they needed to have more senior people involved (or at least explicit senior "buy in"). Certainly there did appear to be a sense of disconnect between many of the causes and the formal structures and change agenda of the local organizations, and we resolved that a good deal more thought would need to be given in future events to how an SM approach can be situated and embedded within the "normal" organization, if at all. Of course, such uncertainty as to the "impact" of a SM approach is not only felt in this novel context of organizational change; as Den Hond and De Bakker (2007) point out SM research itself often does not know the outcomes of activist groups' efforts in great detail, and such outcomes are notoriously difficult to measure.

On the positive side, one of the more interesting pieces of feedback was that teams were not only "doing" change and improvement in a different way, but also "thinking" about it in a different way—there appeared to have been a mindset change that in the longer term may be one of the more significant benefits of this work. For us, this was a particularly pleasing discovery since from the outset we had stuck doggedly to the radical pedagogy of Paulo Freire (1972) and others that, from a movements point of view, change is: (a) a frame of mind not just a set of methods and tools; (b) that "revolutions begin in transformations of consciousness"; and (c) a matter of learning to question answers rather than answer questions—or as Quinn (1996) has since put it, "we reinvent ourselves by changing our perspective."

Set backs and difficulties apart, the evaluation was sufficiently positive for the work to continue and for the NHS sponsor to organize and support three more events during 2008. Not only will teams bring their local causes as before, they will now be expected to become facilitators and champions of the SM approach, following the surgeon's mantra of "see one, do one, teach one."

Discussion

Looking back over our journey, we end this chapter by reflecting on four fundamental questions in turn:

—How successful was this attempt at translational research? Can practitioners in healthcare organizations meaningfully blend the "social dynamics" perspective of social movements with the rational, programmatic, systems perspectives that tend to dominate in healthcare thinking (and that they are used to), or are the paradigms incommensurable at the level of action?

—How different are these conceptual lenses from the conventional ones currently being deployed in healthcare organizations to view and think about change and improvement, and are there any grounds for thinking they might be any better or more effective?

—How generalizable is the learning from this work in the NHS? Are those who attended the event largely self-selecting and focusing on "causes" that are already well established in the discourse of the health service at large? If so, could such an approach apply equally well to less established activities and thereby bring nascent interests to the foreground? And is such "movement" activity unique to the NHS or can other health systems learn from this model? How much adaptation would need to take place in transferring the model outside of the NHS?

—And finally, will the social movements process set in train through the organizational intervention we have described grow and spread, and if so, in what direction and on what scale? Or will it follow the path of so many of the previously "promising" change ideas and projects with the NHS and simply wither away? In short, will the much-vaunted "service revolution" actually occur?

With regard to the first of these questions, we are conscious that in the process of translation a huge amount of material from our original review of the social movements literature found its way on to the cutting room floor. So, what, if anything, did the practitioners miss out on? Could the content of the three days have been better? We were sometimes surprised at what the project leader—or "editor"—did cut out, (in particular material on community activism and local politics and further inputs around framing tactics). Later, when questioned, she said that she had cut the bits that would not "sell"—i.e., would not have credibility with practitioners—either because they were not in her view ready for them, or that these elements were already obvious and well known and did not need to be restated. This comment is interesting, firstly because "believability" (or "acceptability") was given priority over the more usual translational research criteria of "relevance" and "utility" (see introduction), and secondly because it underlines the importance of framing "movements" itself in a way that will get the attention and interest of practitioners. Our hypothesis would be that if anything is framed in too radical or "off-centre" a way it will run the danger of losing credibility and *scaring people off*; on the other hand, if it is framed in too conventional a way it will lose its edge and appeal and *turn people off* (or just fails to switch them on). Clearly the positive reaction to the event from the participants would suggest our editor achieved something approaching the right balance, but we would ask did she "normalize" it too much—particularly the language of movements? On one side some participants agreed that using social movements language in its undiluted form ("activists," "radical," "campaign" etc.) in an organizational context was not the best way to frame the ideas: people back in their organizations mocked it (and you), were confused by it, or associated it with other things (including bowel movements, the first thing that apparently comes to mind if one works in health care!). Others argued that such language should be used up-front; the SM approach is different so acknowledge this and be prepared for some eyebrows to be raised. In the light of these comments, our tentative guidelines for translational research in the change arena would be:

- Much about such teaching is not about change methods at all but about enabling people to think differently about what they do and how they do it, and to apply themselves in different ways. If language is the frame of thought (the accepted idea that "we think through language") we will only think differently, about change or anything else, if the language is different. In this case people will only "think movements" if the language of movements is retained in some form (if not in its entirety);
- Do not debunk conventional thinking but extend it while making it safe for people to "let go" by allowing them to keep one foot where it is; provide a bridge back, a safety net. If one can be bilingual or multilingual in everyday life why not in organizational life as well? By the same token it could be argued that one does not have to give up the language of programmatic change in order to speak the language of movements. It depends on the audience, the "cause" and the context in which one is speaking;
- Provide ample space for personal translation and customization, hence the emphasis on design principles not detailed steps; innovation not imitation. The "script" for change (i.e. the frame or language in action) will never be the same, and so part of the skill of framing is to find an appropriate narrative or form of words to suit the different situations, events and audiences that change agents will inevitably encounter as they work.

Secondly, how different is the social movement lens from conventional approaches to organizational change? Is it a question of "either-or" or "both-and"? And does it have to be all or nothing? Our view as change researchers is that in many ways the paradigms are incommensurable and if we try to integrate or balance them we may end up merely repackaging traditional OD and systems theory as social movements.

On the other hand there may be a hybrid which simply accepts the contradictions and tensions as part and parcel of the change process, a view shared by many of the NHS leaders themselves, accustomed as they were to the plurality of models and perspectives found in professional organizations like theirs. On the related question, "does it have to be all or nothing?" the answer depends on what one is ultimately hoping to achieve. Here again, practitioners were divided. Some decided to play it safe, taking the view that "movements" represented, for the NHS at least, a new way of thinking about and "doing" change and improvement, something to add to the armory of tools of the change agent, but not a movement in the bigger and literal sense of the word (*movements as a paradigm or method*), while others believed that this idea could go much further, leading to the emergence of a "real" healthcare movement, an "Improvement Movement" of up to a million people, with the same dynamics and scale as any movement would have; in other words, a social movement organization (*movements as an institution*). There is something of a parallel here with recent SM research by den Hond and de Bakker (2007), who ask how the different tactics (in the context of activist groups seeking to influence corporate social change activities) and campaigns regarding individual firms can build up to what they term "field-level" change? We ask ourselves a similar question and our view is that the first of these (*movements as a paradigm or method being employed in individual organizations*) is now already a reality in a few parts of the NHS, whereas with the second (*movements as an institution seeking field-level change*) it is simply too early to say.

Our third reflection concerns the generalizability of the work to date with particular focus on the profile of those who attended the three-day event (and the "causes" they brought), and on the applicability of the model to health systems in other countries. Those who attended the three-day event were recruited (using the term "change activists") by means of a senior executive sponsor in the parent organization who was asked to:

—identify a priority challenge to focus on (for example, impending organizational change, safer patient program, improving staff morale, changing a patient service, reducing waiting times)

—conduct team and individual "insight" surveys to "take the pulse" on current energy levels and personal styles of working

—commit key people to attend the three-day NHS Change Activist's Event

—spread the approach through communication and team workshops across the organization following the event, and

—give feedback and insight via e-mail and scheduled calls immediately following the event, and then four weeks later.

Clearly, the approach was therefore predominantly one of "selecting" participants to work on an already predetermined organizational "cause." With hindsight we would view this approach as misguided. Certainly in the future we would recommend starting the process by allowing participants to self-select and have much greater involvement in choosing their causes.

With regard to the second issue we have written elsewhere about the social movement characteristics of organizational change efforts in the US healthcare context (Bate, Mendel and Robert 2008), albeit in the field of HIV care where, of course, the

AIDS movement has been an especially strong and pervasive influence. Nonetheless we found that:

> delving into the quality journey of the AIDS Treatment Centre…has illustrated the utility of a movement and mobilization perspective to sustaining quality and service improvement. This perspective includes the role of social movements in providing impetus, support and resources for high-quality care and improvement…as well as the potential of movement processes for introducing and implementing change within healthcare organizations.

More broadly, we would also note the adoption of campaign-based approaches to quality and service improvement in hospitals across the United States, perhaps best exemplified by the IHI's "100,000" and "5 Million" Lives campaigns, which—as already referred to—were used as case studies for our "Three Days in July" event. Indeed, the CEO of IHI, Don Berwick, has argued that "we no longer have a campaign; we have a movement."

And so to our final question: what of the future? We paint first a pessimistic scenario with five possible pitfalls or risks. Firstly, that we may be helping to create hopes and expectations that will not be met—a scenario that some participants may already be experiencing:

> We recognize that there may be consequences for the Trust in adopting an approach that encourages commitment and energy to causes that are dear to people's hearts, in an environment where there is very little growth money and many, often conflicting, priorities. We may have to anticipate recommendations arising that cannot be met, and then have to manage the disappointments that this may cause. (Participant)

Secondly, that this attempt to bring social movement thinking to healthcare improvement efforts will gradually run out of energy and become "yet another program" or "yet another initiative" along with the many other previous fads and fashions in management that have come and gone in the NHS, especially in the change management domain. Our view is that this may well happen if the NHS does not put an infrastructure around the movements work, one that not only continues to resource the initiative (which is currently happening) but also provides opportunities for participants to communicate and to meet regularly in order to build their "activists' community." In other words, without some facilitation of such "co-operation and collaboration among different activist groups" (den Hond and de Bakker 2007) that are seeking similar goals, the potential collective impact across the NHS as a whole may be largely dissipated? Thirdly, that participants have been provided with the "know-how" but still not the "knowing-how"—that is to say, they lack the necessary tools and skills to do change the "movements way." On this point it has already been resolved that there will need to be more on the "how" at future events—the issue of implementation and what makes a movement successful (or not). Fourthly, that the "revolution will be put down": those in control will feel so threatened by it that they will subvert or oppose it. Certainly the experience of some participants is that it has already caused "stresses on people who are naturally more reserved and traditional about how to achieve change and improvements" (participant). Finally, that the community will become a nonconforming enclave of harmless oddballs on the edge of the NHS (like the Berkeley activists in the 1960s who were branded "freaks and kooks" in order to discredit them and render them impotent).

Again it is too early to say how likely any of the above scenarios might become reality but all of them are risks. However, in the spirit of social movements, we end with the optimistic scenario of a still small but nascent healthcare activist community and a bottom-up, "radical-led" NHS reform process living the five principles (as opposed to doing programs or planned interventions), characterized by an ability to work with multiple perspectives especially around power and change issues, bridging with the NHS wider "values" program, and reinvigorating the previously disconnected and disaffected with energy and commitment; in short, a healthcare reform movement that is not only possible but already happening. Interestingly, recent research from a purely OS perspective, undertaken in the NHS, revealed how widespread the distribution of change agency was in a case study of a successful quality improvement initiative. The authors (who also advocated for the "resilience of an approach that does not depend on one individual, or on a small project team") concluded that the:

> traditional response to such untidiness in an organizational context is to advocate structure...however, the flexibility created by ambiguity and blurred boundaries [in the case study] may have contributed to the effectiveness of service improvement in this context...Given the complexity of the context and the pace of structural and role changes, understanding how to operate effectively in such a fluid setting may be of more value than knowledge of conventional change management methods. (Buchanan et al. 2007)

Perhaps, soon, SM and OS scholars will be having many more conversations together concerning the change competencies best suited to the context of healthcare organizations, and exploring the potential impact that both their fields, working together, may have on practitioners beyond the traditional beneficiaries of leadership-development programs.

Undoubtedly, some of the teams we have worked—and are working—with will not succeed in getting their movement off the ground or coalescing with other teams into a bigger movement; in fact the odds are that they will not (just as is the case with the high failure rate associated with "real" social movements), but that would not necessarily mean the effort has all been wasted. The key thing will be whether the individuals who have attended any of the events we have described now think differently about change and have adopted more of a "social movement mentality." This is undoubtedly the case: "programs" and "plans" no longer hold complete sway and in have come "energy," "mass," "passion," "commitment," "pace," "momentum," "spread," and "longevity." The language of change is itself changing, and because language is the primary cultural form, it is likely the culture of the organization will also begin to change.

Conclusions

We have presented this ongoing collaboration as a real-life case study in doing translational, ambidextrous, boundary-crossing research. Markides (2007) argues that there can be a virtuous or synergistic combination of both theory and practice, and that cooperative action research does not have to be atheoretical or nonrigorous. Our experience would strongly accord with this. Sadly (and ironically), however, many of these debates about research into practice remain theoretical (even idealistic) rather than real. Just like those practitioners that we have tried to expose to social movements thinking, so too Markides argues, do academics have to move from being bystanders into being participants, stepping off the pavement and being prepared to meet the practitioners half way. Our experience of trying to do just that is that it offers excitement and satisfaction through seeing academic work actually having an influence on practice, in this case on improving the quality of healthcare.

NOTES

The authors are grateful to Helen Bevan and Jo Bibby for their support during our long collaboration, originally with the NHS Modernization Agency, and latterly with the NHS Institute for Innovation and Improvement. The learning captured from this project is entirely due to the commitment and efforts of the four field-test sites and participants from the twelve organizations who attended the three-day event. The authors are grateful to Mayer Zald and Jane Banaszak-Holl for their helpful comments on an earlier draft of this chapter.

1. Throughout this chapter the pronoun "we" is used to refer to this collaboration, which included the two authors in the role of academic partners to the NHS Institute for Innovation and Improvement (formerly the NHS Modernization Agency). Helen Bevan and Jo Bibby led the work on behalf of the NHS Institute. A wider reference group comprising NHS leaders and managers provided ongoing advice to the project.

2. One notable exception is William Gamson at Boston College who—with Charlotte Ryan—founded "The Movement/Media Research and Action Project (MRAP)" over twenty years ago. MRAP's mission is to strengthen progressive local, national, and global social movements that are working toward social justice and inclusive, participatory democracy. The project focuses on the interface of movements and media in particular, working with underrepresented and misrepresented communities to: identify and challenge barriers to democratic communication; develop proactive strategies and messages; and build ongoing communication capacity (see http://www.mrap.info/index.html for further details). Although several other leading social movement scholars were deeply engaged in movements in the 1960s and early 1970s when they were students, they have subsequently done little action research or attempted to apply their own concepts and theories (Mayer Zald, personal communication).

3. The notion behind this drew on the "movement to end child abuse and neglect" in the United States, a coalition of more than thirty national health and child-abuse organizations and over three thousand individual members committed to mobilizing two million authentic voices (survivors) and supporters across the country (National Call to Action 2007).

4. Originally—and for some time—we were working on seven principles: making change a personal mission; framing to connect with hearts and minds; organizing for impact; mobilizing and activating; getting results and taking action; handling the politics; and keeping moving. Eventually we settled on the five principles in the order shown above.

5. It is not possible in this chapter to faithfully report on all of the detailed content of this remarkable three days; readers are encouraged to contact the NHS Institute for Innovation and Improvement for further information (http://www.institute.nhs.uk/).

6. Which addressed the issue of how to move people from "unmobilized" nonactivist zones (comfort zone—"free rider"; resignation zone—"victim"; aggression zone—"sniper") to the positively engaged, activist zone (passion zone—"activist").

7. In other words, nonconformist but gutsy audacity and based on a phrase used by the "Industrial Areas Foundation" (1990), a movement formed by Saul Alinsky in the 1940s that continues as a living-wage, housing movement in the US today: "We do it with chutzpah." Alinsky himself was regarded as the embodiment of chutzpah.

8. To illustrate this point one of the examples we gave was Rosa Parks, the activist who helped ignite the U.S. civil rights movement, of whom the commonly held perception is as the "seamstress who refused to sit at the back of the bus." But Kohl (2005: 10) writes that "to call Rosa Parks a poor, tired seamstress and not talk about her role as a community leader and civil rights activist as well, is to turn an organized struggle for freedom into a personal act of frustration."

Appendix 1

Five Principles: Major Concepts Used at "The Power of One, The Power of Many" Three-Day Event (adapted from event handbook)

1. Framing to connect with hearts and minds
   a. Key factors in framing; what makes a good frame?
   b. Key steps for successful framing:
      i. have a cause
      ii. connect with a range of stakeholders
      iii. frame to connect with people's emotions (hearts)
      iv. frame to connect with people's logic (rational thinking/minds)
      v. bridge and link diverse groups
      vi. employ a range of strategies appropriately (words, stories, anecdotes and slogans; visual images; humor and irony; performance and spectacle)
2. Energize and mobilize
   a. Key steps for successful mobilizing:
      i. unleash and harness energy
      ii. draw on discretionary effort
      iii. tap into patient energy
   b. Build commitment and connection:
      i. develop mobilizing narratives
      ii. "Authentic Voices"
      iii. "Hot housing"
   c. Build mass:
      i. recruitment (including network connection and cultivation)
      ii. campaigns
3. Organizing for impact
   a. Why think about organization?
   b. Key approaches:
      i. build a distributed leadership model
      ii. get the strategy right
      iii. get the tactics right

4. Change as a personal mission
   a. Key approaches:
      i. be an organizational radical
     ii. have the right characteristics
    iii. manage risk and minimize danger
     iv. understand the context
5. Keep forward momentum
   a. Key approaches:
      i. mitigate against common failure modes:
        —loss of resonance (see framing)
        —lack of time (energize and mobilize)
        —membership trickles away (energize and mobilize)
        —loss of key individuals/leaders (organizing)
        —lack of co-ordination (organizing)
        —self-destructive group behavior (organizing)
        —stand-off between movement and wider organization and current agendas/priorities (organizing)
        —old ways of thinking and behaviors reassert themselves (change as a personal mission)
        —not being able to see possibility of success (change as a personal mission)

13

Complementary and Integrative Medicine in Medical Education

The Birth of an Organized Movement

Michael S. Goldstein

Social Movements and Medicine

Studies of changes in health care and the medical profession have increasingly utilized a social movements approach. This perspective first emerged about fifty years ago in the work of Bucher and Strauss (1961), who recognized that professions were not homogeneous entities, but collections of subgroups that are in a constant state of flux as they vie for recognition, respect, and resources. Viewing these subgroups as social movements within a broader profession can be a fruitful for understanding how and why professions change.

Frickel and Gross (2005) set out criteria by which scientific/intellectual movements within a profession can be identified and differentiated from mere trends or changes that are constant in all social institutions. A true social movement sets out a coherent core set of beliefs that pose a significant challenge to the dominant way in which the profession carries out its work. The movement challenges received wisdom in the field, and its efforts encounter conflict and resistance from more traditional elements in the profession. Such movements do not exist merely on the intellectual or conceptual level, or in the actions of like-minded individuals. Rather, a movement requires organized collective action by networks of people who act politically (i.e., to change social institutions) by recruiting others and establishing their views within the reality of professional life and practice. Finally, scientific/intellectual movements are "episodic"; they have beginnings and endings that can often be specified in terms of real events in the world (206–8).

However, most scholars who have employed the concept of a social movement to examine changes within the healthcare system have been not been primarily concerned with health professionals. Rather, they have focused on groups such as patients and their family members, who seek to bring about change from outside of the medical profession. For example, Brown and colleagues (2004) have used the term "embodied social movements" to describe health movements characterized by the way in which the personal experiences of the participants in the movement (typically those who have personally experienced a particular disease or condition) are central to the challenge that the movement brings to existing medical knowledge and practice. In Brown's view, "what sets embodied health movements apart from other movements is less *that* they challenge science, but *how* they go about doing it. Activists in embodied movements often judge science based on intimate, firsthand knowledge of their bodies and illness" (2004: 56). These firsthand experiences are crucial to supporting a sense of collective identity and shared values that reinforce an "oppositional consciousness" to the dominant biomedical understanding of health, illness, and disease. In their efforts to alter how illness is understood, embodied health movements "attempt to reconstruct the lines that demarcate science from nonscience, as well as demarcating good science from bad science" (2004: 63). The requisite of having personally experienced an adverse situation or condition would seem to be a clear line of demarcation between embodied health movements and scientific/intellectual movements. However, in our view, the lack of attention to interpersonal relationships as formative influences on scientific/intellectual movements makes the assumption of a clear separation between these two types of movements premature.

This paper deals with the ongoing efforts to incorporate complementary, alternative, and integrative medicine (CAM/IM) in the curricula and research agenda of American medical schools. The paper begins by demonstrating that these efforts truly qualify a scientific/intellectual movement as set out by Frickel and Gross. Next, the paper looks closely at a single event that took place at the very beginning of the movement: an organizing meeting out of which grew the most influential organization in the movement. Our goals in examining this single brief episode are to: (1) illustrate the value of examining a formative event in understanding the history of a scientific/intellectual social movement; (2) to examine the extent to which the concept of an embodied health movement can offer a useful complement for understanding scientific/intellectual movements of the sort that occur within medicine itself.

The Changing Role of CAM/IM within the American Healthcare System

There is no standard or fully agreed upon definition of either CAM or IM. Some scholars have delineated the field by creating lists of techniques not "commonly" used by conventionally trained physicians or taught in American medical schools (Eisenberg et al. 1993, 1998), while others have attempted to specify sets of therapeutic beliefs or practices as the defining characteristics of the field (Kaptchuk and Eisenberg 2001; Goldstein 1999). Over the past several years, developments (described below) both within and outside of medicine have made an agreed upon definition of the field even more problematic. Yet, despite this ambiguity, it is clear that the use of CAM/IM within the United States is growing, especially among those dealing with chronic conditions and those seeking to enhance their health (Astin 1998; Eisenberg et ala 1998; Goldstein 2004). The attention of sociologists and others to this development has been directed primarily toward understanding the motives of patients and prospective patients for using these approaches. Additional medical literature is concerned with assessing the efficacy of these approaches for dealing with clinical problems. Relatively less attention has been paid to how physicians themselves have become more involved with integrating CAM/IM into health care.

The hostility of American organized medicine toward CAM/IM goes back to the "Flexner Report" of 1910 (Flexner 1910), which sought to eliminate all techniques and practices that were not grounded in the emerging western bioscientific perspective from the realm of true medicine (Starr 1982). The subsequent development of accredited medical schools and governmental licensure for physicians largely succeeded in eliminating a wide array of "nonscientific" practitioners from being defined as part of medicine. Yet, the countless forms of healing that were excluded (herbalism, homeopathy, psychic healing, nutritional therapies, etc.) never really disappeared. Although disregarded and dishonored by most physicians and the state, they continued to be used throughout the nation's history by large segments of the population (Kaptchuk and Eisenberg 2001; Rothstein 1985; Kessler et al. 2001).

Over the past few decades a number of factors have led to a reemergence of these approaches to healing under the rubric of CAM/IM. These include the recognition that the dominant biomedical model is of limited value in dealing with many chronic conditions that affect the aging population; the impact of globalization and immigration, which have made Americans more aware of non-Western approaches to healing (such as acupuncture and Ayurvdea); a growing dissatisfaction with approaches to healing that disregard the importance of the mind on the body (including the role of the placebo effect), the value of prevention, and the value of spirituality in enabling people to respond to illness; a heightened awareness of how qualities of the healer (personality, values, personal experiences such as burnout, alienation, etc.) can affect outcomes; growing concern for the serious side effects brought about by many conventional medical and surgical therapies; and the growing amount of research that indicates many alternative therapies may be useful in dealing with symptoms.

These developments, which taken together comprise a manifold challenge to many elements of the healthcare system, have occurred within a broader intellectual climate that is increasingly receptive to CAM/IM. This climate is marked by recognition of the biomedical model's limits for dealing with chronic problems; increased concern for dealing with symptoms such as pain and functional limitations arising from chronic conditions; and an acceptance of the role behavioral and psychological interventions can have in dealing with symptoms (Goldstein 1999). Equally important is that the broader socio-political environment of health care has shifted dramatically over the past several decades. The power of physicians and the organizations that represent them has greatly diminished. Health care is increasingly seen as a commodity to be sold for a profit by corporations and other "third-party payers" who are frequently responsive to consumer demand for access to CAM/IM. Their willingness to offer CAM/IM is enhanced by the (largely untested) view that CAM/IM interventions are less costly than conventional care. Even the government, largely in response to the lobbying of consumers and a handful of legislators, has become more open to

CAM/IM. Over the objections of many in the medical community the Office of Alternative Medicine was created in the National Institutes of Health (NIH) in 1991. In 1998 it grew into the National Center for Complementary and Alternative Medicine that now controls an annual budget of more than 121 million dollars and fosters more than 176 million dollars of additional research in other parts of NIH (National Center for Complementary and Alternative Medicine 2008) A White House Commission on Complementary and Alternative Medicine was formed in 2000. In 2005 the prestigious Institute of Medicine issued a 330-page report on CAM that called for a significantly greater expenditure of funds for the study of CAM/IM and how it can best be integrated into mainstream health care, along with recommendations for training all health professionals about CAM/IM (Institute of Medicine 2005).

Given these developments, it is not surprising to find that conventionally trained physicians and other health professionals are more involved with CAM/IM. One reflection of this interest is that in November of 1998 the American Medical Association devoted the entire contents of all its major journals to articles about CAM/IM. Today over half of all family physicians consider many CAM/IM modalities as legitimate forms of treatment and almost two-thirds report referring to a CAM practitioner in the past twelve months (Berman et al. 1998; Milden and Stokols 1998). Currently many hospitals offer both in and out patient CAM/IM services (Institute of Medicine 2005).

Yet within the context of these changes academic medicine has lagged behind. For example, by 1995, when about two-thirds of family practitioners had either used or referred their patients for some type of CAM/IM, only one-third of the 125 accredited American medical schools offered *any* course work on CAM/IM. While the number of medical schools offering such courses grew to about 60 percent in 1998 and about 80 percent in 2003 (Barzansky and Etzel 2003), most offered only elective courses attended by relatively few students (Brokaw et al. 2002). Clearly, not all medical schools have been equally committed to integrating CAM/IM into their curricula, and research has shown that academic physicians are less likely than physicians outside of academia to believe both that their patients use CAM/IM and these techniques can be useful (Rosenbaum et al. 2002). Academic medicine is often viewed as highly receptive to clinical innovations, but the basis for its relative lack of receptivity to CAM/IM is not well understood. In part, this hesitancy may reflect CAM/IM's stigmatized status among many academic physicians, especially those most committed to a dualistic biomedical view of health and illness, as well as academia's highly specialized approach to care that often neglects the needs of the chronically ill to manage symptoms. A more widespread and robust incorporation of CAM/IM into medical education has the potential to raise the level of acceptance of CAM/IM techniques and approaches among medical students and physicians, as well as to influence their behavior as clinicians in terms of the techniques they use, and the referrals they make to other providers.

Despite the overall limited receptivity of academic medicine to CAM/IM, some schools were considerably more committed than others. Currently, those schools that are most committed, and which offer the most extensive array of courses, clinical experiences and research projects in CAM/IM are the forty-one schools that make up the Consortium of Academic Health Centers for Integrative Medicine (CAHCIM). The

Consortium defines its mission as helping to "transform medicine and healthcare through rigorous scientific studies, new models of clinical care, and innovative educational programs that integrate biomedicine, the complexity of human beings, the intrinsic nature of healing and the rich diversity of therapeutic systems" (CAHCIM 2008). While other organizations, such as the American Holistic Medical Association, represent practicing physicians who consider themselves "alternative" or "holistic," and some medical specialty and subspecialty groups now make some effort to include information about selected aspects of CAM/IM in their programming, CAHCIM is the sole organized entity that represents the movement's efforts to bring CAM/IM into medical education. In carrying out its mission CAHCIM has intentionally set out to avoid defining the field as limited to specific therapeutic techniques (CAM), or a specific set of beliefs about how health care might be delivered (IM). Rather, the goal has been to achieve maximal inclusiveness by emphasizing: (1) the importance of rigorous research for evaluating any approach to healing, and (2) the importance of mind-body interactions, and other aspects healing, such as quality of life, that have an impact on all healing modalities.

The Consortium emerged from a series of meetings, the first of which was held in the summer of 1999 in Kalamazoo, Michigan. This meeting has been continually viewed as a seminal event within CAHCIM. For example, CAHCIM's Web site describes the meeting as "historic" and goes on to note that the experiences at the meeting led to the vision that the group still holds as "essential" and a "core value" (CAHCIM 2008). Thus, by the time of that initial meeting the integration of CAM/IM into conventional medical practice was well underway. However, this integration was just starting to be reflected within the curricula of American medical schools. Representatives from eight medical schools attended. Most of these medical schools were ones where CAM/IM was already relatively well established as evidenced by the fact that many had successfully sought federal funding from OAM to establish "centers of excellence" on CAM/IM or related areas. The faculty member representing each school (one school was unable to have a representative attend due to last-minute scheduling problems) attempted to persuade its dean (or associate dean) to accompany them to Kalamazoo to discuss the future of CAM/IM and medical education. Only five of the schools succeeded in bringing a dean. In total fourteen individuals attended the meeting; five deans and nine IM advocates (a single school sent two faculty members). One measure of CAHCIM's success is its growth. Within a year after its formation in 1999 it had increased its membership from eight to eleven medical schools, and it has continued to grow since that time. It currently (2008) has forty-one member schools, including some of the most prestigious in the nation. Within academic medicine, it is the group most representative and emblematic of CAM/IM, and its annual research conferences, publications, curricula material, and policy reports are widely known and frequently cited.

The research reported on here is based on an attempt to interview as many of the participants in that 1999 meeting as possible, with the specific goal of answering two research questions:

1. To what extent did the attendees conceptualize their actions at that time as being part of a social movement? This includes seeing the meeting itself as part of a movement strategy, the extent of the attendees prior contact and experience with

other attendees, the expectations they brought to the meeting, their actions during the course of the meeting, as well as their conscious appreciation of being movement participants and what precisely that meant to them.

2. To what extent did the participants understand their own identity as participants in a social movement directed toward changing their profession's standards for doing science as being, in some significant way, a response to their own personal experiences that fostered an oppositional approach toward the dominant medical paradigm?

Methodology

A review of material on the CAHCIM Web site as well as contact with some of the attendees yielded a list of the fourteen target respondents: nine IM faculty leaders from seven medical schools, and five deans/chancellors. Each of these individuals was contacted by letter, e-mail, follow-up e-mail, and, when necessary and possible, by phone. All of the IM faculty members were interviewed. However, only two of the five deans were willing to be interviewed (one refused, and two others did not respond to repeated requests to be interviewed.) The interviews were conducted by phone, using a semistructured interview schedule. The interviews lasted between twenty-five minutes and fifty minutes with a mean length of thirty-five minutes. The interviews were conducted between July 16 and September 24, 2007. All interviews were tape recorded. Respondents were guaranteed anonymity, and all personal identifiers have been removed from any quotations and descriptions. In addition, two of the respondents offered to provide documentary materials from the meeting that were useful in understanding what occurred.

The interview began with questions (and flexible probes) that asked the respondents to describe what in both their personal and professional lives they believed were significant factors leading up to their presence at the meeting. Details regarding the respondents' experience and training in CAM/IM prior to 1999 were also elicited. Respondents were then asked about the extent and nature of their prior relationships with other attendees at the meeting. This was followed by questions regarding the expectations they had about what would take place at the meeting, including probes (used as needed) about specific outcomes they wanted to occur, strategies they expected to employ to bring about these outcomes, as well as their recollections of any conflicts or disagreements that occurred at the meeting. Finally, the respondents were asked if, at the time of the meeting, they felt that they had been participants in a social movement within medicine, (and, if so,) how that movement could be described, and why they had come to be active within it.

After all the interviews were complete, the audio transcripts were transcribed and reviewed for completeness. Multiple reading of the interviews transcripts using a grounded theory approach (Glaser and Strauss 1967) yielded a set of key words/phrases/themes in the responses. These themes were used as the basis for assembling narrative quotations that could be used to explain the categories and develop a coherent sense of how the respondents understood their presence at the meeting and what had brought them to positions of leadership in the movement. All the interviewing was conducted by the author. The Institutional Review Board of the University of California, Los Angeles approved the procedures used in this research.

Results

In what follows, we first present the results in terms of information from the respondents about the meeting itself: How well did the participants know each other prior to the meeting? How were the goals of the meeting understood by both the organizers and other participants at the meeting? What type of interaction took place at the meeting? Next, we present our findings about whether the respondents perceived their presence at the meeting as being part of a social movement, and, if so, how they understood the goals of that movement. Finally, we describe the personal narratives the respondents offered to explain how they came to be involved with CAM/IM. Here we describe their responses in terms of prior personal experiences with health and illness, spirituality, nonmedical training, feelings of personal isolation, and alienation from conventional medicine, as well as factors more directly associated with the values of CAM/IM.

How Well Did the Participants Know One Another Prior to the Meeting?

Most of the participants were acquainted with one another before the meeting began. Six of the nine advocates said they had been familiar with "all" or "almost all" of the others. One had only "very limited contact with a few of them at professional meetings," while two had even more restricted contacts ("minimal at best"; "virtually none. I only knew one other person there"). Although two of the six reported extensive contact with other attendees, the other four who reported that these prior relationships had been limited to contact at professional meetings. The most common point of contact had been meetings of program directors of the "Centers of Excellence" funded by the Office of Alternative Medicine (now the National Center for Complementary and Alternative Medicine) at NIH.

The Goals of the Meeting as Seen by the Organizers

The consensus among the respondents was that the meeting had come to pass through the efforts of a single individual. He concurred:

> The meeting was my idea.... I thought that this [CAM/IM] is so important, and that work was already being done at so many institutions. I knew the chancellors and CEOs of the biggest places. So there was no need to reinvent things everywhere. I thought let's get these people [medical school administrators] and give them a crash course in IM.... By bringing the deans together we could deal with any backlash. We could show the deans what their own faculty were doing to push the envelope of medicine. They were training house staff and medical students. And they weren't just using CAM which substitutes one modality for another. They were re-recognizing the sacredness of the

doctor-patient relationship, and how it is enhanced by mindfulness.... And I thought I would also be getting my friends together and training them in mindfulness. Those were all very personal motives...that's how it developed.

When asked what expectations he had for the meeting, the organizer answered, "the original intention was ignite some sort of social movement to transform medicine and reconnect it with its roots." It is certainly noteworthy that the convener of the meeting understood his actions in the context of forming a social movement.

Two other participants, who had worked with the leader, corroborated how the meeting was planned. One said:

X was the key. He knew Y and Z (two influential medical school deans). X wanted to support the deans who were already helping IM at their schools. So he got Fetzer to give the use of the facility. He had an existing relationship with them too. And he got me to do the day to day organizing. X did the initial one or two phone calls. He had the concept. Then I said I'll do it. He was just too busy.

The other stated:

We wanted to start a dialogue that included administrators, and we wanted to initiate an academic consortium to bring the field into the spotlight, to give IM an academic legitimacy because the field had so much political baggage at the time. So our goals were to get a consensus statement on what the field was about, and why it was important for academic medicine to address it, and to include the potential upside for incorporating mind-body medicine in academic medicine.

The goals of the meeting as described by these three organizers match the goals for the meeting as described in the invitation letters that went out to the invitees. The letter clearly stated the preliminary nature of the meeting, the desire to educate the deans about CAM/IM and support them, along with the need for free and open dialogue. The agenda also specified that one session would be devoted to "(1) Is there something here worth pursuing collectively beyond this meeting? (2) Is a consortium on integrative and mind-body medicine a good idea? (a) annual meeting or semiannual? (b) rotating to different host institutions? (c) additional institutions to be invited? (d) funding?" In that regard, part of the closing session was set aside to "appoint officers/coordinators for next meeting."

Goals of the Meeting as Seen By the Attendees

In contrast to the views of the organizers, almost all the other attendees stated that the meeting was intended simply to allow people get to know each other and provide an opportunity for the participants to learn what was happening at schools other than their own. The consensus was that organizational matters were never intended to be addressed. The difference in memories about the goals of the meeting between the organizers and the attendees is striking.

This was a preliminary meeting. There were no firm expectations of what would happen.... It was just remarkable that administrators at that level with there.... We just wanted to be credible with them, be reasonable so we could build in our own institutions, you know, bring the administrators on board.

There were no goals at all; an open agenda...it was just information exchange. There was no organization—what became CAHCIM—on the agenda. Forming an organization would have been premature.... There were debates: Was scientific medicine so flawed that it couldn't evaluate CAM/IM? Was the medical school curricula too ossified to be meaningfully changed? Just debates, not disagreements. That sort of thing.

No, I really didn't have any expectations. It was just for discussion. I came just to be together, share experiences... It wasn't until 2001 that we talked about an organization and got cohesive.... This was about the "being side" not the "doing side"... the meeting was about people's authentic voice. We just wanted the deans to be there.

There were really none [goals]...just the feeling of potential. I had no knowledge of a formal agenda. The product only became clear as we met.

The two deans also recalled no specific goals for the meeting.

It was just talk about how we see things. There ware definitely no organizational goals. There was no idea it would lead to CAHCIM... From the standpoint of today, obviously it was a social movement. But that term was not used at the meeting. The key was getting us, the deans, involved. That was most impressive. I was shocked that other deans were there.

The other dean said: "I had none [expectations] really. I was just fascinated by the topic. Intuitively it seemed like the right thing to do. I thought I could learn a lot."

Aside from the organizers, only a single attendee recalled a more specific set of goals:

It was to get a movement started in academic medicine. There was already a movement around holistic and then alternative and then integrative medicine in North America that went back to the 1960s. The movement was already very big, but there were almost no physicians involved. It was lay people, nurses, psychologists. The public was demanding that MDs be more open minded.... There were no specific goals at the start of the meeting but three emerged from the meeting: to link the schools, enroll the deans in the movement, and to enlarge the group.

What Happened? Interaction at the Meeting

In large part, memories of being at the meeting, as well as the respondents' desire to talk about it, revolved considerably more around the nature of the interaction at the meeting than around the substance of what was discussed. All the participants had strong and positive memories of being there and how different this meeting was from other meetings and conferences they had attended. X, the organizer, said "I ran the meeting as if it was a mindfulness meditation retreat with rules for enhancing dialogue and being non-judgmental... You don't talk to them [the deans] about IM. You give them direct experience and enhance community with those who are involved."

One of the IM advocates who assisted X in putting the meeting together agreed.

So the focus was on planning a meeting that was more experiential than cognitive. Should we start out with guided imagery, sit in a circle, meditate? This was all planned in advance. We brought candles and didn't know if we would use them. We decided no, that would be too much for them. Then when the electricity went out, it was like a sign from above, divine intervention.... It was the "open heart" not the academic model. The participants were hungry for this. It, the hunger, was more palpable among the deans.

Almost without exception, the other participants concurred about the atypical quality of interaction at the meeting and the impact that it had on all who were there.

I believe that all change comes from personal relationships, and that was the breathtaking thing about this meeting. For example, Y [one of the deans] was new to the field but open. He had never experienced the experiential-mindfulness stuff. He was moved by it. X was amazing. He showed that we could do business in a different and better way. One night the electricity went out. It was dark, there was no air conditioning. We lit candles. It was a tribal feeling, intimate, like we were around a campfire.... When the lights came on we were on a different level.

There was a different atmosphere; more hugging... that was happening all the time.... It all came down to relationships. Without relationships it doesn't go forward. We were able to talk about hopes and aspirations. Why we went into medicine in the first place.

The experiential component, for some it was different or unique.... The lack of electricity with no air conditioning in record heat was important, an opportunity. There was no option of giving a Power Point or going back to your room to watch TV. That was the evening everything happened. We sat around, took off our shoes and had a real conversation. Personal experience is so important. People say evidence shapes attitudes. But personal experience can be incredibly powerful.

The deans who responded had varying recollections of what had happened and its significance. One said: "The experiential aspects of the meeting, the yoga, shoes-off stuff. That was optional. It didn't impress me much." The other stated:

X was brilliant. He forged a ground where everyone felt comfortable.... It was special. The place, the setting out in the woods, isolated but a rustic sort of luxury. When the power went out it was a bonding experience in the candlelight. It was so easy for people to deal with each other. It brought the best our in everybody. Conversations were in a quasi-Buddhist sort of thing, starting with pillows and gongs; all kind of things I wasn't familiar with. All the deans were a bit quizzical.... The whole environment isolated us from the outside world and gave us intimacy within....

The degree to which the participants' descriptions of interaction at the meeting reflect some important substantive dimensions of CAM/IM itself (the use of personal interaction, personal history, and narrative as tools to bring about change; the value of eastern therapeutic techniques) that the movement sought to bring into conventional medicine is striking.

Did the Participants Identify as Members of a Social Movement?

At least in retrospect, all of the IM advocates agreed that they themselves and the other faculty attendees identified as members of a social movement. Typical responses

to being directly asked included: "Yes, very much. We were comrades in arms."
"Absolutely." "We all did or quickly came to feel that way." "Yes, it was powerful."
Both deans had a different view. One responded,

> Oh, not in those terms at that time. From the standpoint of today, yes. But then the key
> was simply the fact that the deans were there. It was the Eisenberg article. [Eisenberg
> et al. published two widely cited articles in major medical journals (1993, 1998) that are
> often credited with sensitizing conventional physicians to the growing use of CAM in
> the United States.] Patients were already doing this, using CAM, and we had to know
> about it.

What Were the Goals of the Movement?

The respondents were consistent when they described the goals of the movement.
The clear majority of the faculty (seven of nine) defined the movement in terms of
bringing medicine back to its roots as a profession that recognizes the importance of
mind-body interactions, as well as the value of the doctor-patient relationship. Most,
but not all, differentiated between CAM (the use of various specific therapeutic techniques that were seldom used by conventional physicians) and IM (an approach to
healing that emphasizes mind-body interactions and the relationship between doctor
and patient, independent of any specific therapeutic technique.)

> It goes back a long time, to the roots of medicine. Today the science of medicine is
> spectacular, but the art of medicine has been lost.

> It's things that were part of medicine, but that the system had lost: to reconnect with the
> lineage of healing; to go back to the roots of medicine. That is what is powerful; reclaim-
> ing traditions of healing and healthy communities.

> The movement was to move from emphasizing the techniques of CAM to the whole
> person point of view: body-mind-spirit or the bio-psychosocial model...to give people
> options where there is evidence. It was about the importance of relationships with
> patients and colleagues. In essence it was getting away from alternative therapies to
> something more essential.

> Conventional medicine was breaking down. Medicine had lost the human touch. It had
> to acknowledge enormous consumer demand. Doctor-patient interaction, which is
> important to the healing process and a source of great import to the healing profession,
> had eroded in the era of managed care. All this had to be remedied.

One of the deans put it this way: "This was going to be the beginning. They
wanted IM to be called medicine. They wanted to bring medicine back to its roots."

Personal Narratives of Being a Movement Leader: Why Was I There?

We wanted to know what the respondents themselves saw in their own personal histories, besides their training or knowledge about CAM/IM, as being responsible for
being early leaders in the movement. The sharing of personal stories was an important
part of the meeting, and one that was planned for by the organizers who were acutely

aware of the impact it could have on the group. Almost all the respondents, both faculty and deans, stated that being able to tell their stories and hear the stories of the other participants had a major impact on themselves and was a key factor in the success of the meeting.

> Everyone had a personal story that drew them to IM. We all shared them.... This is very different than in most of medicine where most people make choices in ways that are less personally meaningful. You know, I had an opportunity to do this, I was offered a fellowship in that, or just at random, or some sort of administrative action; you've been re-assigned to whatever clinic. This was different. It wasn't just a job. Something had drawn these people in; gave them a passion. They needed that because at the time there were so many negatives, stigmatization in what they were doing.

One of the deans described it this way: "People mostly spoke about their own journeys to IM...[offers detailed account of his own journey to IM]....Everybody had a story....Everyone had a subjective passion for being there."

Based on earlier research (Goldstein et al. 1985, 1987) we expected the respondents' personal history of illness, and/or spirituality would be important dimensions of their stories. This did not prove to be the case.

Prior Experience with Illness/Health

Although six of the nine faculty reported that their own use of CAM/IM prior to becoming clinicians had been a factor in their involvement in the movement, none of the accounts was highly specific, and only two individuals alluded to specific serious and/or chronic conditions, only one of which (allergies) clearly preceded entering medical school. While most of the respondents reported that they used techniques such as meditation, self-hypnosis, or yoga for purposes of health enhancement, stress reduction, or personal transformation, these were typically initiated during or after medical training.

Spirituality

A number (five of nine) of the attendees did speak about spiritual experiences such as meditation, yoga, or martial arts, but only one mentioned religion or religious experience as a factor in their CAM/IM involvement. The timing of these activities relative to the respondents' medical training, and their involvement with CAM/IM, varied, and was not always clear. Again, none mentioned these experiences as being central to their involvement. Even the case of X, the meeting organizer, is ambiguous on this point. He has been widely known for his involvement in meditation, which many would consider spiritual in nature. Yet his own comment ("I avoid the word 'spiritual,' it's divisive."), combined with the other motivations he offered for his involvement, preclude considering spirituality as a major motivation for him.

Despite the limited impact of personal health and spirituality in the narratives of the participants, other personal factors appear to have played a consistent and important role in their involvement with CAM/IM. Chief among these factors was the prevalence of earlier nonmedical training, as well as a strong sense of personal isolation and alienation.

Nonmedical Training

Fully two-thirds of the faculty had professional training in a field outside of medicine prior to becoming a physician or joining the faculty of a medical school. Each had trained in a different area prior to having become involved with CAM/IM. What seemed to be important was that the training offered a coherent alternative intellectual perspective on health/illness. Just having this experience and bringing it into the context of medical education seemed to have a major impact on the respondents.

> For me my training in botany, which was so unusual for an MD, was so crucial. In botany it is the whole plant, the complexity, not just the specific purified chemicals that is important. That experience led me to connect on a personal level with so many things that were happening [in IM.]

> I went to med school at age 35. First I got a Ph.D. at Berkeley. When I arrived it was "the summer of love." So when I went through that Ph.D. coming to California, it was a personal transformation. There was a huge interest in health and wellness all tied into the stuff from the 60's.

> I had a broader background; not just medical education. I was in nursing and public health; had administrative experience to go along with my clinical experience.

Personal Isolation

For most of the attendees, it was a sense of personal isolation within medicine, and a sense of alienation from medical training and practice, rather than experiences that took place before becoming physicians that were the most significant factors in their involvement with CAM/IM. Almost all the respondents touched on the theme of isolation in explaining their own involvement, as well as the involvement of the other attendees.

> We were all rebels...being a seeker was so important. We were looking for more.
> We were visionaries...my whole wiring was to bring change to something. I've known I was like this since 3rd grade. It was just a matter of figuring out what I was going to change.

> Everyone there was unique. They had vision and passion.

There is no question that these individuals felt, both then and now, that they were special. But that very sense of being unique also led them to feel isolated or alone in medical school and later in practice:

> The people who came to the meeting were isolated individuals. They had no collegial support. Academic medicine wasn't represented in the broader alternative medicine movement. That movement was growing rapidly and there was very little response from academic medicine.

> All of us were "lone rangers" looking to network with others like ourselves. No one was communicating [with each other].

Just having the meeting was significant in itself because it promoted connections and communication between us. . . . We were hungry for this. The feeling was palpable.

The mindset was very much "comrades in arms." It was so reassuring to find others with similar views.

What is true for me, and I think for some of the others, is that it was a connection to something outside of ourselves. We were connecting to something. . . .

Alienation from Medical Training and Practice

Perhaps the most common theme, and the one most strongly articulated among the faculty narratives, was that of having been hurt in some way by medical training or the practice of medicine. The "wounds" that remained after these experiences were often offered as an explanation for their early and intense involvement in the CAM/IM movement.

It's all based on things that were part of medicine but that the system has lost. To reconnect with the lineage of healing; go back to the roots of medicine . . . everyone comes into the healing professions with a desire to serve. But the system isn't easy on that. The rites of passage take it out of lots of people. Why wasn't it lost for these people? I don't know. It's the wounded healer. Even the most intact person is wounded a bit. It was the desire to heal that was my motivation.

We were all people who were unhappy with the limitations of their training or practices, feeling a bit lonely, and who sought out other avenues. My path? In my heart I wanted more, more holism for myself as well as for my patients. That's why I went into medicine in the first place. . . . We talked about what it was people were trying to do. Let people talk about their hopes and aspirations; why they went into medicine in the first place. And the deans, they felt they could let down their hair, be just people. . . . They really enjoyed being back close to their healing roots, not just focusing on the bottom line.

They were all there because they had been blown away by some prior experience; the total inadequacy of medical education; you know some experience that makes a young doctor feel like they have to change things. Like when Z talks about her chief resident telling her not to cry in front of the family.

For me it was my own view of the world: what's important, what are we doing, what is each person's mission . . . I mean what is it all about. I was a cardiologist. The people come in, you give them good care, change their medicines . . . but the people are dying . . . hello . . . you want me to up your ACE inhibitors and increase your diuretics, but actually you're dying. Is that the best use of our time together here? . . . I'm going to talk to you about the end of life, but not the end of your life. I mean standard care is great. Here are the documents; do you want to be resuscitated and so forth. But I'm not going to talk to you about what is important: you don't have much time, who do you want to see, who do you want to apologize to, what's important to you about dying. . . . Myself and the others at the meeting had a different view of what does it mean to practice medicine. In standard cardiology we are nice to people, but we don't engage them in a holistic way about who they are, where they are going and what would be the best way for them to spend their time.

People talked about pain and suffering in medical education. The personal pain of being leaders yet being limited in their ability to change the system. The need to reconnect the heart back to medicine and re-engage the human and humane parts of medicine. People's stories focused on what they'd done to students; trampled them, beaten the humanity out of them. For example, I remember B telling what he felt like standing at the door and not going in when he had nothing else to give a patient. We thought, we are all in positions of power and influence in medicine. Maybe we can make a difference if we do this differently.

Other Motivating Factors

In addition to the motivations mentioned above, the respondents offered an array of other reasons for their involvement. Not surprisingly, almost all spoke at some length about holism; the philosophy that stresses the unity of body, mind, and spirit. Five of the nine faculty specifically mentioned that international travel was something that they felt had been influential in bringing them to active participation in the movement. Each of the five felt that seeing a variety of healthcare systems and ways of healing in the context of other societies had a deep impact on their own views of how healing should be understood. In most instances, these experiences occurred subsequent to medical training. None of the respondents mentioned an underlying political perspective as part of what brought them to their roles in the movement, although some did offer politically tinged comments on problems in the American healthcare system.

Both deans described prior experiences that they felt were not typical of other medical school deans. One noted that he "always had an interest in the social sciences. I was a psych major in college and got a masters degree in it after I graduated. I was quite different than all the other first-year med students who had majored in chemistry." The other dean said:

> I was raised to think that kindness, compassion, caring is fundamental to being a human being. That's just how my parents raised me.... I had a tremendous responsibility as the head of XYZ medical center, the hospital, the medical school, the nursing school, etc. I just had an insight, profound to me, of the need to couple the science and technology with more humanistic forms of care. This was very important. I felt compelled to bring this into the mainstream of care since I felt that this was what care was all about.... Why did I feel that way? Honestly, I don't have a clue. But, I can tell you that my father was an immigrant who was the sole proprietor of a retail store. It was his business. This sense of total responsibility was embedded in me ... I am stubborn. I will not be impeded by taking on difficult things.

Discussion

The recollections of participants at this 1999 meeting of CAM/IM advocates and medical school deans offers some insights about the functioning of social movements among medical professionals. Although the broader alternative medicine movement was large and well developed by 1999, change within academic medicine lagged behind. In order for the efforts directed at bringing CAM/IM into academic medicine to be considered a scientific/intellectual movement requires that the challenge the movement presents to the dominant paradigm be carried out in an organized manner, by a collective entity that has a discrete beginning (Fickel and Gross 2005). The Consortium is that entity. The particular meeting studied here was instrumental in eventually elevating and enlarging the role of CAM/IM in medical schools. The organization that emerged from the meeting is now ten years old and has a membership of over forty medical schools. It is the preeminent organization for American academic physicians who are concerned with CAM/IM.

Our findings clearly indicate the meeting was the outgrowth of the vision of a single individual. It is rare that we have the opportunity to "be present" at the very earliest stages of the development of a movement organization and observe the influence that a single person can have. In this case, the atypical nature of the interactions at the meeting and the correspondence of his stated goals with the eventual founding of CAHCIM indicate that the influence of a single individual was quite substantial. It was not only his intellectual concerns, but his emotional and personal identity that led to his efforts to bring about the meeting. From the start this key individual conceptualized his activities as fostering a social movement. He consciously chose to utilize techniques (drumming, subdued lighting, meditation, etc.) that would heighten the emotive quality of the meeting and make it more likely that the participants' experiences would be similar to those found in support and/or consciousness-raising groups. In addition, both he and the handful of others who assisted him were quite conscious of the way in which use of personal narratives or stories of the attendees could be used to facilitate his goal of having the participants come to feel an emotional identification with the movement. It is also of some interest that, while the organizers saw the meeting as a conscious attempt to foster a movement organization, almost none of the attendees were aware of this. Nor were most of the attendees aware of or able to accurately recall the stated goals of the meeting, which had been openly presented in the invitation letter and articulated by the organizers.

A second conclusion concerns the role that group interaction may play in the development of a social movement within a profession. Reports of intense emotional interactions among health movement participants are not unusual. However, most of these accounts describe interactions among patients, their families, or other nonprofessionals outside of medicine. The structures and processes by which these emotional interactions take place (support groups, online journals, etc.) are an essential feature of many embodied health movements. Our findings indicate that the intense interactions associated with participant bonding can be equally important for developing cohesion in social movements that arise inside of medicine. The mechanism for producing this cohesion appears to be quite similar to that found in many embodied health movements: giving the participants the opportunity to tell their stories in a respectful and welcoming environment. In addition, the theme of personal suffering (in their medical education and training) and the subsequent questioning of conventional medical approaches that it produced, which was at the heart of the stories told by many of the professionals was markedly similar to the stories of suffering from chronic illness and the subsequent questioning of medicine that are commonly reported by patients and their families in embodied movements. As in most support and consciousness raising groups, these opportunities for emotional interaction do not occur randomly or spontaneously. Rather, the movement leaders intentionally build them into the structure of the setting.

Embodied health movements engage in "boundary work," which is an attempt to distinguish good science from bad (Brown et al. 2004). In doing so the movement redefines the basis for expertise in a certain area. Expertise within an embodied movement arises largely from personal experience and interacting with others who have had similar experiences. Typically, the experiences related by participants in embodied health movements revolve around the stories that those with a specific disease or condition tell each other concerning their diagnosis, treatment, and the way the larger society deals with them. Here we find professionals engaged in a health- related social movement who do not suffer from a common set of symptoms or diagnoses. Yet we do find a common set of experiences and bonding interactions that define who can be an expert about CAM/IM. While the specific content of these experiences varied, there was a common theme: the psychological distress, dissatisfaction, and alienation from being a conventionally trained and practicing physician. At the meeting, these commonly held themes comprised the core of an "oppositional consciousness" to the dominant biomedical understanding of health and illness that is the hallmark of an embodied health movement. Thus, it is clear that the concept of "embodiment" and the insights it offers to our understanding of how health-related movements develop, can enrich our knowledge about scientific/intellectual movements that arise inside, as well as outside, of the medical profession.

The term "wounded healer" has its origin in the Greek legend of Asclepius, the physician who used his knowledge of his own wounds to create an ideal environment for treating others at Epidaurus (Rousselle 1985). It is this sense of utilizing one's own personal wounds or experience as a basis for healing others that was the most frequent, and often the most intensely felt, reason why our respondents felt they had become active in the movement. Many had, in some way, been deeply affected by their prior experiences of not being able to be the healer they wanted to be. In a sense, involvement in CAM/IM was a "solution" to this dilemma. Many of the participants felt this "wounding" experience was the basis of a common identity with their fellow attendees. In many ways this "wounded healer" narrative appears to function in a similar manner to the narratives of illness that are central in many embodied health movements. It offers the common first-hand experience that unites the participants.

Our conclusions must be tempered by the limitations of the study. The findings are based on a small group of individuals who were participating in a single event in the life of a health- related social movement. Most of the information we gathered comes from self-reports of events that occurred years in the past and is therefore subject to recall problems. Our sample is limited to individuals who were invited to attend this very restricted event on the basis that the organizers viewed them as "leaders" in the field of CAM/IM. We have no information from other individuals who were unable or unwilling to attend, or, more important, from individuals who were also "leaders," but not acquainted with or judged to be "leaders" by the conference organizers. Therefore we must be very careful about drawing general conclusions from our results.

Despite these caveats, the movement to bring CAM/IM into conventional medical schools is an example of a movement seeking to reconstruct the boundaries of science. We have offered an example of an important event in the life of the movement which shows that the leadership had a clear oppositional consciousness to the dominant biomedical paradigm. This consciousness was deepened and strengthened by the collective identity that their presence at this meeting facilitated by providing an opportunity for them to interact and coalesce around first hand, emotional experience. Leadership and participation in movements among professionals working in healthcare institutions may be heavily influenced by personal, nonprofessional factors that are similar to those that influence nonprofessional movement participants. In this instance, the changes sought, and to some degree successfully attained, by the movement have the potential to influence the attitudes and clinical behavior of a growing segment of American physicians.

The movement to promote complementary, alternative and integrative medicine offers some fundamental challenges to "business as usual" for the American healthcare system. Until relatively recently, academic medicine has been more resistant to inroads from CAM/IM than other parts of the healthcare world. The formation and success of CAHCIM offer an indication that a social movement arising from within academic medicine has begun to make some inroads to changing this situation.

NOTES

I am deeply grateful to each of the respondents. Their willingness to share their time and provide their recollections and thoughts are what made this paper possible. I hope that what I have written presents their views in as fair and representative manner possible.

14

Sources of Self-Help
Movement Legitimation

Matthew E. Archibald

Health social movements bring about social change by challenging the authority of dominant interests in medicine and health care (Brown et al. 2004; Brown and Zavestoski 2004). To mobilize constituents, activists must demonstrate that their mission, its organizations, and its activities align with the sociopolitical and cultural (or identity) interests of constituents (Armstrong 2002). Challenger movements must demonstrate that they possess a moral justification for their program of change equivalent to that of their detractors and in doing so seek to acquire not only material support but legitimacy—sociopolitical and cultural recognition and acceptance (Scott 2003). Paradoxically, sources of legitimation, particularly for health movements, are controlled by actors with vested interests in mainstream health and health care. As Epstein (1996) and others in this volume, and elsewhere, have shown, health movements are dependent on their antagonists to a striking degree. How then do health social movements acquire legitimacy to foster social change from their adversaries who are invested in preserving the status quo?

Current research in health social movements sheds light on this question by theorizing a number of ways activists and institutional actors[1] interpenetrate movements (Wolfson 2001) and create hybrids that blur the boundaries between lay and expert forms of knowledge, overcoming organizational and political divisions between them (Brown et al. 2004; McCormick, Brown, and Zavestoski 2003). The specific conditions under which these interpenetrated or boundary movements emerge and develop vary widely but one important precursor is elite discord—movements can and do take advantage of rifts among elites in order to win converts to their cause and secure formerly inaccessible institutional resources (Meyer 2004). Declining professional autonomy and authority has led to elite discord in the field of medicine and competition among professionals (Scott et al. 2000), providing fertile ground for the rise of alternative medical practices (Ruggie 2004).

The self-help movement and its organizational actors—member-designed psychotherapeutic organizations of people who experience a common illness or condition, ranging from alcoholism to cancer—is one such alternative. Self-help arose within the context of structural transformation in the authority of physicians and the jurisdictional disputes among healthcare elites that followed, by creating alliances and networks with sympathetic professionals (Archibald 2007; Katz 1993; Taylor 1996). Although popular support for health movements like self-help is important, constructing alliances and cultivating links to institutional actors through strategies reliant on "intentionally porous organizational, epistemological and political boundaries" is crucial (Frickel 2004a: 269). The answer to how a health social movement such as self-help simultaneously challenges institutional authority in medicine and health care while seeking its approbation, is that institutional fragmentation creates multiple sources of legitimation and a broad range of sympathetic (and potentially co-optable) actors.

Legitimating authority is therefore not a single generic process but a varied set of actors, rules, and practices governing recognition in institutional domains (Scott 2003). Likewise, social movements consist of shifting clusters of organizations, networks of individual supporters, institutional allies, alternative institutions, submerged networks and other cultural groups (Staggenborg 2002; Whittier 2002). Struggles between movements and institutional authorities can take place in any number of specific-issue domains and involve relatively autonomous actors, issues, and processes (Burstein 1991; Burstein, Einwohner, and Hollander 1995; Schwartz 2002). Different social movement actors will use different tactics and rely on different authorities for resources and legitimation depending on their goals (Burstein, Einwohner, and Hollander 1995). Movements in multiorganizational fields are therefore likely to find themselves pursuing disparate goals as various actors challenge particular antagonists for access to resources, and sociopolitical and cultural authority.

How this happens is of compelling interest to health movement scholars because failure to elicit authoritative support can derail collective efforts to bring about social change. As research in this volume demonstrates, there are many routes by which health social movements finesse institutional authority and achieve public recognition. For instance, Taylor and Leitz (chapter 16, this volume) show how networks of activists and their professional allies, including attorneys and health officials who testify as expert witnesses, generate cultural and legal support for women who have killed their children because of their postpartum depression. Similarly, Frickel (chapter 11, this volume) investigates how semiformal networks of professionals and environmental health and justice organizers operate together to bring about environmental reform. Other chapters describe how the overlapping context of health social movements includes alliances between unlikely partners, frequently bridging antipathetic groups (Anspach chapter 10 and Brown et al. chapter 7, this volume). Sympathetic professionals and internal reformers can finesse institutional authority and garner legitimacy for their causes by working within organizations, as Goldstein (chapter 13, this volume) show.

Building on this research, I explore the ways in which medical, social science/academic, political, and popular sources of legitimation influence the self-help movement. The self-help movement strives for (formal and informal) change in healthcare systems by engaging in political advocacy (e.g., National Alliance for the Mentally Ill), providing a well-known set of alternative healthcare beliefs and practices, and fostering a new social identity linked to membership in the movement (e.g., cancer survivor, recovering addict). Self-help consists, in part, of a long-lived population of national organizations that emerged during the transformation of health care in the United States during the 1960s and 1970s and remains a critical actor in the broader healthcare movement to this day. Constituents disillusioned with the dominant healthcare system can design their own service delivery mechanisms in the form of the self-help group with no professional or legal interference (Borkman 1991; Katz 1993; Powell 1994; Riessman and Carroll 1995). Self-help, like other change-oriented movements, is self-mandating in this respect. Yet, examination of historical accounts of self-help reveals that like other challengers, its advocates use organizational resources to acquire sociopolitical and cultural recognition and acceptance (Rice 1996; Taylor 1996; Taylor and Leitz chapter 16, this volume). While recognition by medical, social science/academic, political, and popular actors contributes to the growth of self-help, and different types of self-help groups rely on different combinations of authorities for legitimation (Archibald 2007), the relative importance of various types of legitimation, their differential effects across self-help specialty niches (i.e., based on members' conditions, their stigma, and the authorities who preside over the institutional domains that are contiguous to them) and their impact on niche growth, remain understudied. Rather than examine legitimation for a single case (see, e.g., Katz 1993; Rice 1996; Taylor 1996), I investigate longitudinal patterns in the sources, timing, and impact of legitimation over the history of the movement from 1955–2000.

First, I discuss the rise of self-help and sketch the four main sources of its legitimation. Second, I examine longitudinal changes in the amount of legitimation provided by medical, social science/academic, political, and popular actors. This illustrates the ways in which the four different sources of public recognition vary among themselves in their recognition of self-help. Third, I analyze the trajectories legitimation takes in three kinds of specialty niches—self-help specialty areas in medical self-help (e.g., cancer, neurology), social welfare self-help (e.g., family, reproduction, abuse) and institutionally independent self-help (e.g., grief, loss, anonymous groups). In analyses of these niches, I examine trends over the forty-five-year period and compare the sources of legitimation for each domain. The central question is how important are the different kinds of authorities for groups comprising the niche? If we envisage each specialty niche contiguous to its institutional counterpart, then it is expected that recognition will derive from parallel authorities. Medical self-help will be legitimated by medical authorities, and groups with a social welfare focus will be recognized by political actors, since the state itself provides contiguous services. Groups with a social welfare focus will also rely on health and human services professionals who have social science/academic credentials. Independent behavioral groups will depend largely on popular acclaim. Moreover, sources of legitimation should impact differentially on growth within the domains. For instance, medical recognition for self-help groups in the medical niche should influence growth in the niche to a much greater degree than social science/academic, political, and popular legitimation. Results indicate, however, that this is not always so. In the medical example, political recognition influences growth of the niche to a much greater extent than medical legitimation. I discuss this and other findings in the concluding section.

The Evolution of Self-Help

The self-help movement arose during a period of radical change in American health care. Decreasing medical-professional hegemony, increasing rationalization within the healthcare system (Scott et al. 2000), and privatization in health and human services (Wolch 1996) during the 1970s and 1980s contributed to the rise of health social movements and grassroots organizations. Self-help emerged along with social practices such as group psychotherapy and community-based health and human services, which persisted into the 1990s when a variety of health social movements achieved prominence including the breast-cancer movement, AIDS activism, and the women's health movement (see Brown et al. 2004; Klawiter 2004).

Self-help consists of a wide range of social movement and movement-affiliated actors. Many engage in socio-legal and political change (e.g., National Alliance of the Mentally Ill, Depression After Delivery, and the National Sudden Infant Death Syndrome Foundation) while others are social movement—affiliated associations that indirectly foster political and institutional reform (e.g., Mended Hearts and Epilepsy Concern: see Kriesi 1996). Like many health social movements, organizational members benefit from an identity derived from movement specialties (e.g., cancer survivors, recovering addicts, parents without partners). Their primary purpose is to address members' healthcare issues by overcoming the social stigma of otherness which attaches to a social group whose members possess a degraded status (such as the disabled and chronically ill). Self-help is designed to address personal stigmatizing conditions or problems, ranging from medical disability to behavioral dysfunction, in a public but intimate face-to-face group setting. Groups renegotiate identities and seek legal and social change in areas such as physical disability (National Amputee Foundation), cancer (Reach to Recovery), and alcoholism (Alcoholics Anonymous). Self-help blossomed during the 1970s and early 1980s as social movements' aims shifted from overt contention with state authorities to quality-of-life and identity issues (Armstrong 2002; Gamson and Meyer 1996). Stabilization followed in the 1990s during which time national self-help organizations encompassed tens of thousands of local meetings and chapters and participation was estimated at around twenty-five million (Davison, Pennebaker, and Dickerson 2000). For comparison's sake, the number of American workers who were union members in the 1990s hovered around 16.5 million (World Almanac 1996).

Sources of Self-Help Legitimation

Legitimation consists in sociopolitical and cultural recognition and acceptance of forms of collective behavior and related practices (Scott 2008). Legitimation facilitates self-help movement growth by making creation of self-help organizations the norm for organizing certain kinds of healthcare delivery systems. Eventually this form becomes taken for granted as *the way* to organize services.

Like most health social movements, sources of self-help legitimation are varied because the domain is a large multiorganizational field. Some sources are internal insofar as health social movements are self-mandating: they derive their legitimacy from the experiential authority of their members and recruit others based on the putative validity of this authority (Turner 2004). Self-help, like other embodied health movements, places primary importance on the legitimacy of members' illness experience (Brown et al. 2004). Movements also derive legitimacy from alignment with norms based on the right of individuals to form groups aimed at collective self-determination (Boli and Thomas 1999) which includes exercising the right to engage in dissent with regard to healthcare services. The latter frequently entails the construction of alternative knowledge claims that resist, even delegitimate, institutional authority (Stryker 2002).

Self-help is at the vanguard of movements that strive to wrest authority from mainstream health experts by positing oppositional knowledge claims. Advocates note that professionals have "monopolize[d] definitions, diagnosis and treatment of problems people face" and neglected "their clients' self-understanding, self-management and self-reliance," resulting in clients' increased "dependency and passivity" (Katz 1993: 71). Yet, the rebuff of medical authority and state-sponsored health and human practices is only partial. For example, even prior to recognition of alcoholism and drug addiction as diseases by the American Medical Association, groups such as Alcoholics Anonymous sought validation of their brand of treatment from physicians, medical authorities, and political figures (White 1998). Although self-help maintains its autonomy with regard to mainstream health care, its members often find their way to self-help through health and human services' systems, as well as hospitals, private medical practices, and the courts. Consequently, clinical professionals, social workers, public administrators, psychologists, counselors for drug courts, and other allied healthcare professionals foster recognition of self-help and promote it through their practices.

The case of Parents Anonymous provides an example. In the early 1960s, an alliance of radiologists, pediatricians, and psychiatrists discovered the syndrome of child abuse and publicized it in a Journal of the American Medical Association article entitled "The Battered Child Syndrome" (in Pfohl 2003). This fueled the so-called "reporting movement" aimed at uncovering, identifying, and prosecuting cases of child abuse. In response, an abusive parent, Jolly K., under the urging of her case worker, formed Parents Anonymous to create a therapeutic rather than medicolegal solution to child abuse. In this organization, members are encouraged to make behavioral changes that foster positive family relationships. Institutional connections with famous individuals (e.g., James Avery, Dennis Franz, Bob Goen, Catherine Hicks, Craig Nelson, Phylicia Rashad, Jacklyn Zeman, and Lucy Johnson) provide legitimacy for Parents Anonymous as does a board of directors that includes a social worker, a child-welfare-foundation director, and a former State Commissioner of Human Services. In addition, recent medical research has studied Parents Anonymous and these studies are highlighted in the organization's own publications.

The case of The National Alliance for the Mentally Ill (now called the National Alliance on Mental Illness—NAMI) offers another glimpse into legitimation processes. This organization was founded in 1979 by families of patients discharged from mental institutions in the 1970s (Katz 1993). Some of the constituent groups included Parents for Mental Recovery (founded in 1972), Parents of Adult Schizophrenics, Alliance for the Mentally Ill of Dade County, and the California Association of Families for the Mentally Disabled. In 1979, a University of Maryland professor studying support groups for those with mental illness helped organize a conference attended by 284 people representing 59 groups from 29 states (Katz 1993). Some of the money for the conference was provided by the Department of Education. The MacArthur Foundation donated $100,000 for a national office. Considerable political activity accompanied the founding of the national office and popular recognition followed increased access to the political system. In 1981, *Women's Day* reported favorably on NAMI and later that year the *New Yorker* serialized a story written about one woman's struggle to come to terms with schizophrenia. Books and movies with famous actors playing mentally unbalanced but heroic characters, such as *One Flew Over the Cuckoo's Nest*, demystified mental illness.

In 1983, a prominent psychiatrist, E. Fuller Torrey, appeared on the *Donahue Show* to laud the work of NAMI and turned over proceeds from his book on mental illness to the organization. Torrey's unconditional support for NAMI reflects the activities of an organizer engaged in boundary spanning between mainstream and alternative sectors. The connection with the medical community is essential for sufferers of mental illness because most require its resources (e.g., medication, counseling, professionally regulated housing). The linkage with mainstream health care is so important, in fact, that while the majority of NAMI board members must be patients or families of patients (a defining feature of all self-help organizations), twenty-two psychiatrists sit on its advisory council.

Although hostility between actors pursuing mainstream and alternative practices creates grounds for contentious relationships in the mental-health sector (as elsewhere), individuals and groups also cross boundaries and negotiate alliances in order to acquire resources and legitimacy for their causes. The National Alliance for the Mentally Ill is structured to act as a social movement organization as well as a support group, and therefore its access to political resources such as those held by the Department of Education and the MacArthur Foundation is more developed than that of other self-help organizations. Cooperation between various groups with an interest in the mentally ill and local and state bureaucracies has been powerful enough to mobilize a large number of constituents and launch national campaigns with substantial financial success. Recognition in mainstream circles has been essential for NAMI's growth, which rose to 1,200 local chapters by the end of the twentieth century (NAMI 2007).

Legitimating Authority and Specialty Niches

Self-help is situated in a multiorganizational field that consists in part of specialty niches of organizations addressing medical, behavioral, psychological and general status problems (Powell 1987). These niches are shaped by resource use, institutional authority, and broader cultural norms about the collective identity of the chronically ill. By definition, self-help groups are specialists whose service provision is aimed at a population with a special set of needs such as breast cancer, bipolar disorder, autism, or gambling.

Naturally, the movement is sustained by its constituents but other relevant contributors of resources and legitimation for these niches are medical practitioners and allied healthcare professionals (covering psychologists, social workers, counselors, institutional administrators) as well as their political counterparts in local, state, and federal government. Institutional authorities control access to resources and favor some movement organizations and networks over others. Alliances between movement actors and co-optable, sympathetic professionals can determine the success of the movement. Some niches have more of these kinds of authorities than others. The question about which interests dominate depends on how well individual and organizational actors are integrated into institutional contexts, since different institutional authorities allow constituent actors greater or lesser autonomy in carrying out their activities (see, e.g., Meyer 2004; Rao, Morrill, and Zald 2000; Schneiberg and Soule 2005).

It is expected that medical and professional (and political) elites will be important for self-help organizations depending on how closely groups' services depend on medical and professional expertise, and support from political authorities. Families that deal with genetic illnesses such as Monosomy 9p, for example, may have little understanding of resources available to help them cope with medical situations that arise and need information and support from professionals with expertise in this area. Thus, self-help niches with groups that require the expertise of mainstream medical authorities will be more likely to rely on this type of authority than others. Likewise, specialties in the area of, for instance, reproductive health or family (such as Parents Anonymous) are more closely positioned between medicine and the domain of health and human services, the latter of which is provided by the state. Political and legal mobilization (Burstein 1991) is therefore crucial for social welfare groups (see Taylor and Leitz's discussion of imprisoned mothers, chapter 16, this volume) and political authorities should have an important impact on self-help in the domain of social welfare. In addition, depending on need, social welfare groups will be more likely to rely on social science/academically credentialed health and human services experts to legitimate their activities and practices.

Significantly, there are self-help specialty groups that are not contiguous with any obvious institutional authority or, whose organizational mandates outright reject institutional linkages. Anonymous twelve-step self-help groups, for example, have organizational barriers in place to distance them from both medical and social welfare professionals. Their organizing principles mandate that they remain nonprofessional and maintain no formal alliances (Alcoholics Anonymous 2005). These groups therefore will rely more heavily, although not exclusively, on popular legitimation than that made available by professionals in medicine or health and human services or political authority (see Katz 1993).

Self-Help Database

To examine these relationships I use data from a recently created database that includes life histories of all 589 active national self-help organizations in the United States between 1955 and 2000 (Archibald 2007). It contains year-by-year records that cover organizational founding date, organizational dissolution and changes in name, legitimation, and organizational resources. The database was constructed from several sources. Major sources of data are: the *Encyclopedia of Associations* (Gale Research Co.), covering the years 1955–2000; the *Self-Help Sourcebook* editions 1–7 (White and Madara 2002), the *IRS Exempt Organization Microrecord Files*, the *Congressional Information Service, Index Medicus-Medline, Sociological and Psychological Abstracts*, the *New York Times Index*; *American Medical Association*; *Bureau of Economic Analysis-U.S. Department of Labor*; *Association of American Medical Colleges*.

The *Encyclopedia of Associations* was used to select cases and contains historical information on all self-declared national membership organizations, including voluntary associations providing health and human services. Only member-controlled self-help organizations that identified themselves as "self-help" and those providing peer-to-peer support groups, networks, meetings, chapters and the like, were selected. These were compared with White and Madara's listings (2002) and IRS microfiles, both supported case selection from the *Encyclopedia* consistently. The database contains information on the three different types of self-help specialty groups (i.e., medical, social welfare, and independent), and four types of legitimating authorities (i.e., medical, social science/academic, political, and popular).

Measuring Specialty Niches

Self-help groups provide the *Encyclopedia* with information for classification into two domains: medical or social welfare (health and human services). Based on Powell (1987) I divide these two domains into eighteen organizational subpopulations. Classifying self-help into these specialty groups clarifies the link between members' conditions, their stigma, and the authorities who preside over the institutional domains that are contiguous to them. Since legitimation is a function of the extent to which institutional domains are more or less controlled by established authorities, I examine professional affiliation—the extent to which the specialty groups border either medical or social welfare institutional domains—and collapse the specialty niches into three spheres of (external) influence: medical, social welfare, and independent. The point is to develop a continuum of authoritative dominance ranging from physicians to social workers and other allied healthcare professionals to niches that are entirely independent of institutional control.

Medical self-help consists of populations of organizations addressing:

—cancer

—neurology (e.g., pain, sleep, stroke, paraplegia, head injury, fatigue)

—gastroenterology

—eye, ears, nose, and throat

—disease, infections, autoimmune disease, diabetes

—hormones, genetics, metabolic growth and development

—skin, burns, facial reconstruction

—respiratory, circulatory, and pulmonary illnesses

These specialties included groups such as Autism Network International, National Amputees Foundation, Alliance for Lung Cancer Advocacy, Support and Education.

Social Welfare self-help consists of populations of organizations addressing

—family/relationship (e.g., marriage, divorce, adoption, widowhood)

—reproduction, children (e.g., high-risk pregnancy)

—abuse, violence (e.g., incest, self-mutilation, destructive relationships)

—status (e.g., sexuality, women, race/ethnicity, gender dysphoria)

—some nonindependent addiction, grief, mental illness, and disability groups

These specialties included groups such as Depression After Delivery, Adoptees in Search, and Cesarean Prevention Movement, American Assembly of Men in Nursing.

Independent self-help consists of populations of organizations whose organizational mandates limit interference by all institutional actors. They mostly address behavioral issues such as

—alcohol, drug addiction

—other addictions (e.g., food, sex, gambling, codependency)

—grief (e.g., loss, death)

—mental illness (e.g., obsession-compulsion, depression)

—other anonymous (e.g., shoplifting, prostitution)

These specialties included groups such as Alcoholics Anonymous, Rational Recovery, Debtors Anonymous, Nicotine Anonymous, The Compassionate Friends.[2]

Measuring Legitimation: Self-Help Database Sources

Medical professionals, social science academics, popular opinion leaders, and politicians are institutional authorities who contribute to self-help's growing reputation through their recognition of it as a legitimate provider of health care. I use recognition of self-help as an indicator of legitimation (see Rao 1994) in order to investigate expansion of the movement.

Table 14.1. Variables and Definitions for Specialty Group Niches and Sources of Legitimation, National Self-Help Organizations, 1955–2000

Variables	Definitions
Specialty Group Niches	
Medical	Cancer, neurological, eye/ears/nose, disease, hormone, etc.
Social Welfare	Family/relationship, gender, sexuality, abuse, etc.
Independent	Alcohol, drugs, grief-anxiety, mental illness, 12-step, etc.
Sources of Legitimation	
Medical Legitimation	References in medical literature
Social Science/Academic Legitimation	References in social science/academic literature
Popular Legitimation	References in the *New York Times*
Political Legitimation	Congressional appearances and testimony

In the following analyses of legitimation rates, medical legitimation is measured by counts of articles during every year referencing each of the 589 self-help organizations from 1955–2000. Articles were compiled by the National Library of Medicine's *Index Medicus-Medline*. This index contains articles in 4,300 periodicals ranging from the *New England Journal of Medicine, Journal of the American Medical Association*, and *International Journal of Psychiatric Medicine*, to the *Journal of Consulting Clinical Psychology*. Locating these records involved a search by name of each self-help organization over the period of its existence. For some organizations such as Alateen (circa 1957), the search covered a forty-three-year period. For other organizations, such as Depression After Delivery (circa 1985), the task involved a seventeen-year search. I measure social science/academic recognition of self-help in the same way by counting articles contained in journals in the *Sociological* and *Psychological Abstracts*. These databases provide access to 3,800 scholarly journals, including the *American Sociological Review, American Journal of Sociology, Psychological Bulletin, Psychological Assessment*, and *Journal of Community Psychology*.

In addition, I assess popular recognition of self-help using counts of articles from the *New York Times*. Media coverage of the entire forty-five-year period required access to a journal that retained records of its articles over that time period, while also providing electronic access to search for almost six hundred names multiplied by forty-five years. The *New York Times* was well-suited to this purpose. To the extent that a newspaper such as the *Times* publishes major stories and reports, and identifies meeting times and places, self-help achieves a great deal of popular support.

Lastly, members of congressional committees generate political legitimation for self-help through the relationships and alliances they develop. Self-help activists meet with politicians, appear before Congress and other legislative bodies, give expert testimony on medical and social welfare policy debates, lobby for fiscal support, and seek legal reform. Political authorities can then generate political legitimation for self-help organizations. I measure political legitimation by references to appearances and testimony in congressional hearings of each of the 589 self-help organizations active at one time or another in the United States. The task was facilitated by *Congressional Universe/Congressional Information Services*. The *CIS* subject index includes all regularly produced publications including hearings, testimony, and reports of such political bodies as the House Interior and Insular Affairs Committee, Department of Labor, Department of Health and Human Services, Department of Education, and Related Agencies for Appropriations.[3]

Since there will be a rise in the amount of recognition self-help achieves simply because of increases in the sheer volume of organizations, adjusted rates are used to depict trends in the "average" legitimation rate over time. For each time period, I divide legitimation counts by number of extant self-help organizations.

Another question that arises is whether or not recognition of self-help entails a favorable assessment. As Brown et al. (2001b) caution in their study of the breast-cancer movement, the media is just one of many actors involved in shaping the field by enhancing or depreciating issues and actors (see also Hughes and Griffiths 2003)

In constructing this dataset, I examined journal articles, newspaper accounts, and congressional reports closely to gauge the degree to which articles were approving of self-help or not. Close inspection of articles showed that references tended to be either neutral (e.g., reporting the outcome of a study) or positive (e.g., praise for an organization's skill in serving a marginalized population such as the mentally ill). The *New York Times*, for instance, operating under the principle of fair and balanced coverage, tended to promote self-help even though it incorporated the occasional dissenting voice in its stories.[4] Individual organizations usually referred to these opportunities for publicity in their own autobiographical histories. These histories typically referenced journal articles, newspaper accounts, and congressional testimony as a sign of the efficacy, importance, and legitimacy of the organization. For example, the headline "Troubled Millions Heed Call of Self-Help Groups" in the *New York Times* July 16, 1988, typifies articles in the popular press publicizing the availability of thousands of support groups across America in the 1980s and 1990s.

Nonetheless, skeptical accounts of self-help do appear, largely in books and occasionally in magazine articles published in the 1990s. Commentary by Greenberg (1994), Kaminer (1992), Peele (1989), Rapping (1996), Rieff (1991), and Wagner (1997) have all generated a good deal of critical and ideological hostility aimed at self-help.

Measuring Specialty Niche Growth

Lastly, I assess specialty niche growth using the number of self-help movement organizations in each niche at each of the forty-five time periods. Following previous research, the growth (or density) of self-help population niches is measured by the cumulative total of active organizations at time *t*, net dissolutions (Carroll and Hannan 2000). In analyses with legitimation, I lag legitimation one year behind niche growth to limit the reciprocal influence of density on legitimation.

Public Recognition: Evidence from Self-Help Data

Trends in figure 14.1 depict the unfolding of self-help legitimation over a forty-five-year period. Based on previous founding rate analyses, I collapse periods into fifteen-year aggregates; 1955–1970 represents the emergence or youth of the movement; 1970–1985 represents self-help's adolescence; and 1985–2000, movement maturity (see Archibald 2007). Figure 14.1 shows the adjusted legitimation rates for self-help for the four public domains. Examining these rates, it is obvious that legitimation is contingent on domain.

In the earliest years, all adjusted legitimation rates show similar peaked increases and decreases through the mid 1970s. The jagged peaks of the earlier periods suggest that taking account of population size, legitimation varies widely, with averages spiking and declining regularly until the 1970s. Medical legitimation and to a lesser extent, social science/academic legitimation, peaked in the 1970s, declined, and then rose from the 1980s through the end of the century. The overall pattern is consistent with the view that movements experience cycles of burgeoning and declining activity (Tarrow 1998).

Why does there seem to be a change in linear trends around the 1970s? Self-help advocates argue that the phenomenon took off during the 1970s because of popular

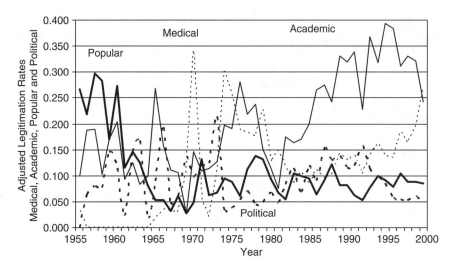

Figure 14.1. Adjusted Legitimation Rates for Self-Help Organizations, 1955–2000

disillusionment with mainstream health care (Katz 1993). Clearly, political and popular legitimation did not contribute much to recognition in the 1970s. On the other hand, medical and social science/academic domains show a marked increase in legitimation of self-help. In fact, one of the contributing factors to the increase in medical legitimation was the steady acceptance of the disease model of addiction accompanied by medical recognition of addiction organizations such as Alcoholics Anonymous (White 1998). The data provide mixed support for self-help proponents' suggestion that self-help "took off"—became more legitimate—during the 1970s.[5] In medical and social science/academic domains recognition did increase considerably.

Political legitimation as well moves in a cyclical fashion over time. The cycles in political legitimation can be explained in that state support of mainstream and alternative health care and human services has always been divided. On the one hand, the National Institutes of Health (NIH) encompass several divisions funding complementary and alternative medical research. This includes the National Center for Complementary and Alternative Medicine that began with a budget of $2 million in 1992 and in 2002 had a budget of $104.6 million. A number of universities are funded by this budget including Columbia, Harvard, and Stanford (Ruggie 2004). On the other hand, The Omnibus Reconciliation Act (OBRA) of 1981 began the devolution of public policy by reducing federal spending for public programs and consolidating social welfare programs. In spite of welfare state devolution, federal healthcare spending grew rather than declined during devolution in the 1980s and 1990s (Smith and Lipsky 1993). While it is thought that reduction in governmental involvement in health and human services should increase private entrepreneurial activities, prior self-help research shows that self-help began to decline rather than grow during the 1980s (Archibald 2007). Moreover, Surgeon General Everett Koop's 1987 recognition of self-help followed reduction of federal spending for public programs and the consolidation of social welfare programs under OBRA. The drop in political legitimation rates following Koop's 1987 Workshop lends some credence to claims that state pro-motion of self-help was largely a rhetorical strategy (see, e.g., Borkman 1991). The state's interest in self-help seems therefore to be ambivalent at best.

As noted, the pre-1970s adjusted rates for medical, social science/academic, and political legitimation are very different from popular rates. Why is popular legitima-tion high to begin with while medical, social science/academic, and political sources start low and then increase? Sympathizers in the press are likely to have been much more attuned initially to self-help relative to the size of the phenomenon than medi-cal, social science/academic, or political sources because their production standards and temporal framing for observing and explaining social phenomena differ from those of the sciences.[6] Medical, social science/academic and political legitimation are slower to emerge than news stories about self-help because professional journal articles and congressional appearances are based on institutional logics—practices and beliefs governing appropriate action (Scott 2008)—which determine when and how issues such as self-help achieve prominence that differ significantly from those of the press.

For instance, stories in the press in the 1980s, when self-help reached its largest size were filled with glowing recognition of the individual and civic good provided by voluntary community-based groups such as Compassionate Friends, AA, and Friends in Adoption. They were "news." The medical counterpart to these advertise-ments for self-help can be seen in a research study conducted in May 1994 and pub-lished in the *Journal of the American Optometric Association* (Maino et al. 1994). Its headlines were less dramatic than the announcement of a deluge of millions of self-help constituents. Instead, it pointedly explored "Ocular Manifestations of Sotos Syndrome" (and the role of Sotos support groups). Much of the recognition and legitimation in medical and social science/academic domains, as evidenced in the cases above, entails appraisal, proper categorization or recategorization, and analysis of outcomes of a serious illness, stigma, or problem. For instance, the *International Journal of Psychiatric Medicine* (Peindl et al. 1995) examined the "Effects of Postpartum Depression on Family Planning International" in 1995 (referencing DAD) and the *Journal of Consulting Clinical Psychology* (Yeaton 1994) was inter-ested in "The Development and Assessment of Valid Measures of Service Delivery to Enhance Inference in Outcome-Based Research" by "Measuring Attendance at [DAD] Self-Help Group Meetings."

Political legitimation has similar exacting standards. Political appearances are likely to involve a much higher expectation of self-help accountability than stories in the press because group spokespersons become experts providing legal testimony before congressional committees such as the House Committee on Appropriations, the Committee on Aging, and the Committee on Commerce.

Public Authorities and Self-Help: How Trends Affect Specialty Niches

Like figure 14.1, figures 14.2, 14.3 and 14.4 depict burgeoning public recognition of self-help movement subspecialty niches over its forty-five-year history. The graphs

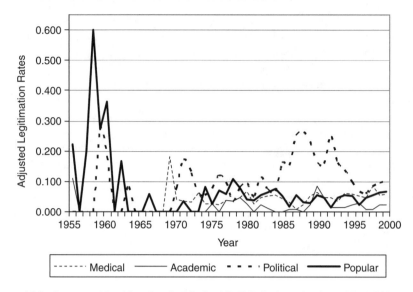

Figure 14.2. Sources of Legitimation for Medical Self-Help Organizations, 1955–2000

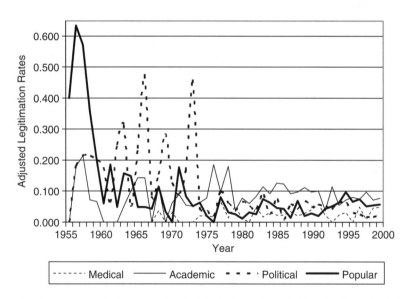

Figure 14.3. Sources of Legitimation for Social Welfare Self-Help Organizations, 1955–2000

show the relationship among the different sources of public recognition and medical, social welfare, and independent specialty groups. As I emphasized in the discussion of figure 14.1, the four sources of legitimation show remarkable variation over the history of the population. Figures 14.2, 14.3 and 14.4 address the central question: Where do different types of self-help get their legitimacy? On the basis of the three graphs in total, the answer to the question is that legitimation is differentially

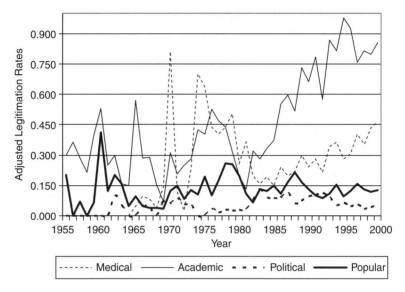

Figure 14.4. Sources of Legitimation for Independent Self-Help Organizations, 1955–2000

allocated among niches. Differences can be highlighted by comparing the trajectories within and between subspecialties.

For medical self-help, the graph in figure 14.2 shows that this type of group derives its legitimation from political authorities, especially during its mature years, 1985–2000, although even during the middle years, political legitimation dominates medical, social science/academic, and popular recognition. It then accelerates dramatically in 1985. The marked decline in political legitimation in the late 1990s indicates that fewer medical organizations were being called to testify before Congress, and here recognition by medical authorities begins to rise slightly. The dramatic decline in political legitimation may be due either to a slackening of interest or because political connections had already generated as much support on the part of Congress as possible, signaling the beginning of abeyance with regard to this niche. I expected that physicians, specialists, medical researchers, and others would be key allies in medical self-help organizations, such as the Myasthenia Gravis Foundation, Mended Hearts, or Epilepsy Concern, but they are not. Self-help's challenge to mainstream medical hegemony is met by resistance, or at minimum, indifference, on the part of medical professionals.

Figure 14.3 shows the relationship between the four legitimating authorities and social welfare groups. For social welfare (family and reproductive) self-help, while political legitimation is high during the early years (1950s–early 1970s), social science/academic recognition predominates from adolescence through the mature phase of the movement. Where political recognition drove medical self-help, social science/academic recognition is generally the legitimating source of authority for social welfare groups. Another interesting pattern emerges for the social welfare groups: the influence of medical legitimation is almost nonexistent.

Figure 14.4 shows a markedly different pattern of relationships. While medical and social welfare self-help emerge supported by considerable media acclaim in the popular press, the field of independent self-help (including Alcoholics Anonymous and other well-known self-help organizations) receives only a minimal average amount of recognition in mainstream media. Academic legitimation supersedes it and rises steadily throughout the niche's expansion. The burgeoning of social science/academic legitimation is followed, surprisingly, by medical legitimation. Academic recognition is of overwhelming importance for independent groups followed by medical legitimation, while popular and political legitimation remain low. That political legitimation remains low is not surprising because the niche includes anonymous twelve-step groups and others whose rules preclude involvement in political affairs per se. That medical recognition rises during adolescence for this group of behaviorally oriented organizations is somewhat surprising in that organizations in this niche have clear boundaries regarding relationships with institutional authority. However, the rise in medical legitimation is probably due to increasing medical recognition of drug and alcohol addiction as a disease. Addiction groups make up the majority of this independent subspecialty area (Alcoholics Anonymous 2005). Still, it was expected that this niche would achieve greater recognition from popular sources rather than institutionally constrained ones, like professionals writing in social science/academic journals, and it did not.

Table 14.2 approaches the question of the importance of legitimating actors from another angle by examining the (lagged) impact of legitimation on growth of the three speciality niches. If previous figures 14.2 to 14.4 are any indication of the impact of legitimation on specialty niche, different patterns of growth should emerge. To investigate these relationships, I ran polynomial regressions of growth rates on first-, second- and third-order terms for each type of legitimation (e.g., medical legitimation, medical legitimation squared, and medical legitimation cubed) because both speciality niche growth, as well as legitimation, are nonlinear (Gujarati 2003).

For medical self-help, political recognition (as well as popular acclaim) has a strong impact on growth of the niche, while for independent self-help, social science/academic legitimation and (not surprisingly) popular legitimation have the strongest impact. The latter is consistent with hypotheses but contrasts with what might be expected given the trends in figure 14.4, where popular legitimation tended to stabilize

Table 14.2. Bayesian Information Criterion Model Fits for Regression of Specialty Group Niche Growth on Sources of Legitimation

Sources of Legitimation[a]	Specialty Niche Growth		
	Medical	Social Welfare	Independent
Medical Legitimation	291.02	296.03	219.66
Social Science/Academic Legitimation	292.98	307.7	263.19
Political Legitimation	300.92	297.53	256.07
Popular Legitimation	309.83	307.83	268.07

[a] Each variable set contains first, second, and third order terms lagged one year.

after the late 1970s. Academic and popular recognition have about the same impact on growth in the sector, even though the niche witnessed a notable rise in social science/ academic legitimation in late adolescence which continued through the end of the century. For social welfare, the two strongest influences on growth are social science/ academic and popular legitimation. These results are consistent with expectations, although political legitimation should have a stronger relative effect than it does. Popular legitimation has such a strong impact on social welfare legitimation because these groups were often written up in the press during the movement's emergent phase (see figure 14.3).

Conclusion

The longitudinal study of legitimation and healthcare provision is central to under-standing the dynamics of health movements such as self-help and strengthens the link between social movement frameworks and social studies of science. This research builds on case studies of healthcare boundary movements by answering fundamental questions about how professional, political, and popular legitimation of alternative healthcare delivery shapes the movement. The point of mapping the expansion of public recognition is not just that it indicates the extent to which it has become a popular method for engaging in healthcare support, although this is true, but to demonstrate that the mix of institutional authorities fostering recognition serves as a mechanism that drives changes in the system and, ultimately, leads to self-help being taken for granted (i.e., institutionalized). Knowing the source of self-help recognition helps us understand how movements will develop strategies for persuad-ing institutional authority presiding in those domains of the credibility of their causes. When self-help organizations acquire medical, social science/academic and political capital they are better able to mobilize resources, increase their chances of survival and promote the goals of the movement (Archibald 2007). Since challenger move-ments must demonstrate that they possess a moral justification for their program of social change equivalent to that of their antagonists, sociopolitical and cultural rec-ognition and acceptance goes a long way towards meeting this goal.

Paradoxically, garnering elite sociopolitical and cultural recognition has a certain piquancy for social movements, when we consider the extent to which they threaten prevailing social and cultural institutional orders (Fligstein 1998; Gamson and Meyer 1996). A strategy of cultivating institutional allies and other nonmovement sources of legitimation then is risky at best. The cost of external legitimation may be goal displacement, co-optation and member disillusionment (McAdam 1999). The acqui-sition of external legitimation is therefore anomalous insofar as the movement gains recognition from its opponents by seeking alliances with some of them while attempt-ing to avoid co-optation itself. Since self-help's legitimation depends on recognition by audiences in already institutionalized fields such as medicine and politics, the struggle for it yields an oppositional culture that tenuously spans mainstream institu-tions and the movement's own alternative organizations and practices. Some of the legitimacy proffered by medical and social science/academic authorities is surely a function of professional boundary-spanning strategies and therefore a token of exchange by which some occupational groups try to dominate others by aligning themselves with self-help. To investigate this possibility, research should use this data to inform a multiple case-study approach examining the dominant occupational trends in each of three of the professional orders I have presented here.

The results of this study supports this view in that legitimating authority is not a single generic entity but a varied set of actors, rules, and practices governing recognition of self-help. They show that different sources of legitimation have different effects on groups depending on the specialty niche. Where it was expected that medical groups such as Reach to Recovery or Associated Blind would rely exclusively on mainstream medicine and the healthcare industry for justification, this is not so, largely because mainstream medicine remains hostile to many kinds of alternative practices (Ruggie 2004). It is perhaps not surprising that medical self-help itself is indebted to political authorities for recognition since the state has become the largest player in health and health care (Scott et al. 2000). In contrast, independent groups such as Gamblers Anonymous and Al-Anon find legitimation in social science/academic circles, and secondarily in medical circles but not politics. In fact, recognition from medical authorities was observed more often for independent groups than for medical self-help, although it had little influence on specialty growth overall. While I had expected the near complete autonomy of "independent" self-help—addiction, compulsive behavior, grief and (some) mental illness—because their mandates prohibit professional interference (Alcoholics Anonymous 2005), findings showed that, to the extent that recognition depends on alliances between organizations and healthcare professionals, independent groups needed recognition by boundary-spanning allied-healthcare professionals, such as addiction counselors, more often than they needed recognition by physicians in mainstream medicine and their political counterparts. At the same time, social welfare self-help, groups largely devoted to family and reproductive issues, did experience early critical political support (which was then overshadowed by social science/academic recognition). Social welfare groups' domain of care—reproduction, abuse, family and status issues—finds its counterpart in state-managed health and human services, and many of these groups may have served early on as sites for off-loading of state services. In classic social movement fashion, openings in the political environment provide the chance for social movements to link with external allies in order to legitimate new forms of collective action and integrate them with the prevailing institutional order (Rao, Morrill, and Zald 2000). Here the state is target, facilitator, supporter, and sometimes proponent of social movements.

The answer to the question about how health social movements challenge legitimating authority is that self-help-movement actors situate their project in a field that includes both alternative and mainstream health care. A common perception of social movements as static, centralized entities is replaced with the view of movements embedded in multiorganizational fields (McAdam and Scott 2005; Snow 2004b). Here the logic of strategic action permits activists and institutional actors to cross boundaries and to construct alternative knowledge used to challenge the hegemony of mainstream healthcare delivery. The result enhances the legitimacy of the movement and contributes to its expansion. The study of legitimation of health movements in multiorganizational fields provides a context for understanding how the shifting matrix of forms of healthcare delivery represents different logics governing individual and organizational movement sectors. It also highlights the role organizational dynamics play in expansion of the civil sector, broadly construed, an ongoing expansion that is bound to see new movements and organizational forms arise in this century in the same way the last century witnessed the dramatic growth in alternative health care.

NOTES

This research was supported by a National Science Foundation Grant (62-5041).

1. In this chapter, I use "institution" to refer to rules, norms, and scripts for behavior including conventions and practices, knowledge, and strategies which characterize a particular domain of social activity such as the economy, politics, religion, science, medicine, and even popular culture (Scott 2008).

2. To further refine the measurement of "independent niche," I stipulate that groups with any professional affiliation are classified as social welfare and not independent. In addition, groups addressing physical disability, autism, retardation self-select as health and human services groups. Analyses shows that they do retain their autonomy from medicine, have few professional linkages, and function as independent groups. Most were started as groups of parents with children with disabilities in the 1950s who found themselves marginalized by mainstream health care (Katz 1993).

3. In some sense, measures of congressional appearances, lobby efforts and interactions with elites represent alliances between self-help and political authorities (see Bergman's 1986 discussion for example). Since these alliances produce legitimacy, I use them in these analyses as indicators of legitimation. Elsewhere, I have used them as measures of self-help-political affiliation.

4. One of the limitations of this study is that at the time of data gathering (1997–2000), it was impossible to obtain and code the hundreds of articles for strength of support or hostility towards self-help. A sample of articles, however, revealed that very few were critical of self-help and these tended to maintain a stance of scientific neutrality. Books about self-help, not included in these counts, are a different matter. See below.

5. This underscores the importance of investigating longitudinal trends that may not emerge in single case studies.

6. Thanks to an anonymous reviewer for this point.

SECTION IV

CULTURE AND LEGITIMACY IN U.S. HEALTH CARE

The chapters in this final section of the book focus on collective attempts to challenge the cultural meanings and systems of classification that sustain and reproduce the power and legitimacy of American health institutions. Many health-related social movements target not only institutionalized structures and practices, but the identities, beliefs, categories, and modes of thought that shape how we view health problems—and solutions. In the United States, health benefits and services are allocated and distributed according to a particular understanding of the relationship between classification of disease and treatment. According to the *medical model* for the treatment of health problems, the underlying biological basis for health problems must first be clearly identified and then curative treatments applied to eliminate the risk of disease. As the "dominant epidemiological paradigm" (Brown et al. 2006), the medical model confers legitimacy to those diseases that have been officially "discovered" or recognized by biomedical institutions. But in doing so, the medical model poses formidable obstacles to those constituencies seeking to mobilize around complex chronic diseases that lack a clear etiology, unexplained or poorly understood medical symptoms, and alternative or oppositional understandings of health problems. The chapters in this section seek to elaborate the challenges faced by health-related social movements in constructing, promoting, and legitimizing these oppositional understandings of health issues.

In chapter 15, Sabrina McCormick examines the conditions that lead to the emergence of "climate-induced illness movements" (CIIMs). Climate-induced illnesses, which include illnesses caused by vector-borne transmission, urban temperature and air pollution, and extreme weather events, are rising in number and in scope in the United States, but citizen responses to the proliferation of these illnesses have been hampered by the difficulty of establishing disease causation, identification, and treatment. Focusing on three cases—West Nile Virus, the displacement of Alaska Natives, and heat-induced illness in Philadelphia, McCormick finds that pre-existing movements and the formation of "boundary organizations"—or hybrid institutions that embody both science and politics—may serve as catalysts for the formation of CIIMs. But scientific challenges, such as the lack of cause-effect relationships between environmental and disease phenomena or limitations of localizing macro-level models, hamper the ability of movements to successfully link environmental outcomes to health in their mobilization efforts. As a result, CIIMs generally emerge when there is a preexisting environmental health movement or strong scientific evidence supporting a link between ecological change and health outcomes.

Cultural beliefs about disease also shape the illness experiences of affected populations and their willingness to politicize their personal experiences by connecting them to structural explanations for their grievances. In chapter 16, Verta Taylor and Lisa Leitz trace processes of collective identity construction and politicization among women suffering from postpartum psychiatric illness who have been convicted of infanticide. Joining a recent stream of research suggesting that self-help and consumer health movements can be a significant force for change in both the cultural and political arenas (Whittier forthcoming; Brown and Zavestoski 2005; Klawiter 1999; Taylor 1996; Allsop, Jones, and Baggott 2004), Taylor and Lietz examine one such movement, a pen-pal network of women incarcerated for committing infanticide. The network is part of a larger self-help movement that emerged in the mid-1980s to challenge medical and legal practices related to the treatment of postpartum psychiatric illness. Taylor and Leitz show how a sense of collective identity fostered by the pen-pal network triggered a profound emotional transformation in participants, allowing them to convert shame and loneliness into pride and solidarity, and encouraging their participation in efforts to change how the medical and legal system treat postpartum psychiatric illness.

Finally, in chapter 17, David Snow and Roberta Lessor examine the challenges to social movements posed by unclear, incorrect, or disputed diagnoses of health problems. Social movement researchers generally agree that collective action requires, among other things, shared *collective action frames*—or common understandings of a given problem and proposed collective solutions (Snow et al. 1986). In this chapter, Snow and Lessor conceptually and empirically explore how *framing hazards* can encumber the efforts of medical practitioners and other health-oriented stakeholders to deal with various health problems and issues. Drawing on three distinct case studies—the obesity "epidemic," work-related diseases, and gamete transfer in infertility—they elaborate four types of framing hazards or vulnerabilities: *ambiguous events or ailments* that do not fit neatly into an existing frame; *framing errors or misframings* based on erroneous beliefs; *frame disputes* involving competing explanations or interpretations of events; and *frame shifts* involving the displacement of one frame by another. The authors conclude by considering the implications of framing hazards for collective attempts to prevent or remedy health problems more generally.

15

Hot or Not?

Obstacles to Emerging Climate-Induced Illness Movements

Sabrina McCormick

Climate-induced illnesses are rapidly becoming one of the most important public health issues of this century (Haines et al. 2006). These illnesses, such as vector-borne disease, heat-induced illness, and injury from extreme weather events are rising in number and in breadth in the United States (Balbus and Wilson 2000). Although their existence and magnitude is increasingly well-established by epidemiologists (Houghton et al. 2001), they have been infrequently addressed by policymakers (Morgan et al. 2005). Public reactions to climate-induced illness have varied by disease group or illness risk and have been shaped by prior social movements. While in some cases, there has been almost no sustained response in civil society, other cases have resulted in the formation of new networks, collaborations, and actions to address impacts.

In this paper, I review the varying social responses to climate-induced illnesses and discuss new and often under-recognized related movement activities, which I call Climate-Induced Illness Movements (CIIMs). These movements arise to connect illness to changing climatic conditions. I focus on the conditions under which such movements emerge, with particular attention to related obstacles. I use three cases to explore these developments—West Nile Virus, displacement of Alaska Native people, and heat-induced illness in Philadelphia—to argue that conditions fostering emergence include a preexisting movement and especially environmental justice organizing, and that obstacles relate largely to scientific uncertainty and impediments to framing.[1] Scientific obstacles are partially caused by illnesses related to climate change being new, or at least newly reaching extreme levels, indeterminately linked to environment, and frequently affecting isolated populations without histories of social movement formation. CIIMs also have difficulties with "framing" (Snow and Benford 1992), such as frame transformation and diagnostic framing.

Obstacles and Catalysts to CIIM Formation

Citizen responses to illness take multiple forms ranging from the smallest support group to massive social movement contestation. A diverse range of such develop-ments has been reviewed extensively in the sociology of health and illness and social movement literatures. The type of response to any illness has depended on a number of factors such as unavailability of a diagnosis, lack of access to proper treatment, and ability of disease group to gain access to resources (Brown and Zavestoski 2004). The case of Climate-Induced Illness Movements articulates two obstacles to health social movement (HSM) formation—scientific uncertainty and framing impedi-ments. Climate change may lead a range of social responses. They may trigger a short-term community or government response. Alternatively, climate events may lead to social movement organizing based on a collective challenge, social solidarity, and sustained interaction to challenge the powerful institutions they believe are responsible (Tarrow 1998). In the following sections, I outline some of the factors that shape CIIMs.

Conditions for Movement Emergence

There are several factors shaping when and how a CIIM emerges, such as history of social movement organizing in that area, the ability to link climate to health, and the multiple types of organizations and actors available to support movement formation. Social movement research has shown that preexisting social movements engender future activism (McCarthy and Zald 1977). In this case, environmental, environmen-tal health and environmental justice movements would be logical precursors. There has also been a growing amount of social movement activism focused on climate change, especially related to mitigating greenhouse gas emissions and ecological effects. Moser's (2007) study of the climate change movement describes the mem-bers of civil society and state governmental leaders who are interested in addressing multiple, intersecting concerns about security, oil dependence, and war. She argues that this movement has become firmly entrenched in public awareness and political discussion, citing its greatest successes as the introduction of legislation regarding the reduction of greenhouse gas emissions. Paradoxically, while this movement may engender CIIMs, it may also limit their emergence. CIIMs are different from the broader climate change movement in that they must also bring together concerns regarding health to demonstrate the affects of climate change on humans. In some ways, this innovation in framing represents a frame resonance problem, where a group has difficulty transitioning from one frame to another.

In other cases, health social movements (HSMs) have more generally engaged in processes of creating overlapping movement frames that both draw attention to an illness phenomenon and an additional set of concerns such as social justice, racial inequality or the necessity for consumer justice (Hess et al. 2007). In the case of CIIMs, environmental justice activists have played a larger role than the mainstream environmental movement in drawing attention to the human impacts of climate change (Dorsey 2007). They provide frames, resources, and tactics that can be lever-aged in new ways. For example, EJ activists have long been concerned about inner-city asthma rates due to exposure to urban air pollution. This argument can be extended to climate change since rising temperatures speed the catalyzation of such pollutants and lead to more "bad air" days. This environmental justice framing is unlike the mainstream climate movement that has focused on melting polar ice caps, sea-level rise, and other environmental processes without always making the human effects of those processes apparent. The usage of multiple frames can help connect new groups or maintain the consistency of movements across periods of latency and resurgence (Marullo 1996). Introducing the frame of climate change may also function to globalize EJ struggles across multiple contexts, ultimately expanding the geological reach of this new frame. These framing processes can also lead to multiple points of recognition regarding power inequalities in unhealthy exposures and health care. Preexisting movements more generally, and EJ activism specifically, also provide access to political opportunities often cited as a source of movement emergence (Tarrow 1994).

Alliances between public health officials, some scientists and environmental justice activists have also played a role in engendering new, powerful arguments about resolving climate-induced illness. Some have recommended immediate political action to account for the illness outcomes of minority communities. This is in part because there is significant agreement between these activists and the scientific community regarding these health impacts of climate change. This development reflects Tesh's (2000) finding that lay and scientific arguments often overlap in significant ways, and assist in the creation of an important "public paradigm" (McCormick, Brown and Zavestoski 2003) where citizens use scientific findings to reshape politics.

Climate-Induced Illness Movements may also form boundary organizations (Guston 1999) and boundary movements (McCormick, Brown and Zavestoski 2003). Boundary organizations are institutions that embody both science and politics. Critical components in boundary organizations are hybrids, or social constructs such as conceptual or material artifacts, techniques or practices, and organizations that encompass both scientific and political elements (Miller 2001). The composition, principles, and practices of these organizations fundamentally shape health outcomes since they are the locus of related political decision-making. Social movement actors also often insert their interests in these institutions. Like boundary organizations, boundary movements blur distinctions between activists and scientists, or movement and nonmovement actors.

Collaborations between state public health institutions, nonprofit networks of concerned health practitioners and scientists and other political organizations reflect boundary organizations and movements. These movements mediate science, lay perspectives and policy in understanding how the health impacts of climate change. Multiple types of social movement actors are likely to engage in climate-induced illness movements due to the very nature of climate events. These actors may include political representatives themselves, such as has occurred in other health social movements (Wolfson 2001). These movements may be initiated or led by nontraditional social movement actors like scientists, medical experts, or political representatives. Their interests may also play out in multiple boundary organizations. For example, the International Research Institute for Climate Prediction attempts to create concrete applications of climate models to policy (Agrawala, Broad, and Guston 2001), similar to policy incursions made by activists. Institutional change may also result as movement concerns are introduced, connecting ecological change with human health. Institutions dealing with ecological concerns are often not well connected to those that deal with health and illness. Such political organization and fragmentation may function to allow those most affected by climate-induced illnesses to fall through the cracks. However, in some cases this disjuncture is being overcome as the integration of these concerns is occurring through workshops held by the Centers for Disease Control on health and climate change and institutions like the National Aerospace Administration offering funding so that their satellite data can support end-users to understand health effects.

Climate-Induced Illness Movements have begun to develop boundary movements that facilitate resource exchange between diverse social actors. The formation of boundary movements and organizations is critical to overcoming scientific obstacles in particular. In this case, participating groups include environmental justice activists, scientists, and medical practitioners. Scientists provide the evidence that links environment to health. Health practitioners legitimate the tangibility of these outcomes as illnesses are seen in their practice. Activists translate these problems to a broader level through public framing and activism.

Obstacles to Movement Emergence

There are two main obstacles to the emergence of CIIMs, scientific uncertainty and hindrances to framing. These two factors are often intertwined in that movement framing may depend on scientific findings or related medical thinking. Social movements incorporate science into their agendas and efforts to gain credibility, to develop and test new hypotheses that support their perspectives, and to change expert-based policy (McCormick 2007). Health social movements have frequently engaged in such work due to the interrelationship between scientific findings, medical knowledge, and treatment. However, the case of CIIMS demonstrates that even in instances where ecological conditions have clearly induced illness onset, there are challenges to linking climate change to the disease.

Scientific Uncertainty

Scientific and medical uncertainty has long played a role in engendering movement activism or slowing activist success. In the case of AIDS activism, scientific findings were both used and challenged by social movement actors in framing the illness. Epstein (1999) detailed some of the first, and most intimate, movement usage of science and medicine in that case. Activists concerned about AIDS and HIV were some of the first to gain specific roles in government reviewing and granting of health research by gaining access to agencies and institutions in order to inform and shape research. This opened the credibility arena to create, in Epstein's words, "multiplication of the successful pathways to the establishment of credibility and diversification of the personnel beyond the highly credentialed" (1999: 3).

In other cases, scientific or medical challenges have limited activism (McCormick 2007). Activism related to Medically Unidentified Disease Phenomenon (MUPS) has shown that the lack of a diagnosis can both stimulate and limit movement formation and success (Zavestoski et al. 2004). Veterans who suffered from Gulf War–Related Illnesses (GWRI) whose symptoms were diffuse and disconnected from any etiology initiated organizations and contestation in order to gain recognition and benefits but had limited effectiveness in part due to little scientific understanding of the causes of GWRIs (Zavestoski et al. 2002). In the case of fibromyalgia, a disease whose diagnosis criteria were only recently established and are still far from well-situated in medical expertise, illness sufferers have formed very little social contestation although online support has grown (McCormick and D'Ottavi 2001). These cases demonstrate the importance of scientific knowledge that links symptomology to disease criteria that is then adopted by medical experts in practice.

The challenges that health social movements face when there are multiple, seemingly unconnected symptoms can be extended to CIIMs. In some cases of climate-induced illnesses, disease phenomena are new and are therefore difficult to identify. In addition, the geophysical processes that engender climate-induced illnesses are incompletely understood. Climate models represent the most ubiquitously important type of climate research, but are themselves quite uncertain (Sundberg 2007). Scientific uncertainty has played a critical role in shaping the pace for the understanding and acceptance of global warming (Ingham et al. 2007). There has been a parallel uncertainty determining when and how illnesses emerge. Applying global models to the sub-regional level is a particularly vexing technical issue (González-Rouco et al. 1999), as is establishing a causal connection between specific environmental shifts and the incidence and prevalence of illness (McMichael and Martens 2002). These represent some of the difficulties activists have in linking health outcomes to climate change.

Hindrances to Framing

Social movement framing is central to movement formation and success. There are a number of related challenges that hinder CIIM emergence. They include threats to ontological security that result in a lack of quotidian disruption, obstacles to frame transformation and diffusion, and lack of diagnostic framing. Norgaard (2006) claims that movements dealing with climate change have difficulty framing because they threaten individuals' ontological security. Discussing the threats linked with climatic developments invoke feelings of helplessness and guilt that lead people to hold information about climate at a distance. Social movement theorists have argued that "quotidian disruption" (Snow et al. 1998) where routine practices and assumptions are interrupted leads to social movement formation. However, Norgaard's research demonstrates that this disruption can be difficult to invoke for populations that have not yet felt any impacts of climate change. Consequently, the concept of quotidian disruption does support a rationale for why environmental justice activists would be the leaders of CIIMs, since they perceive themselves as already affected by the impacts of climate change.

Frame transformation (Benford and Snow 2000) and frame resonance are also useful concepts to explain obstacles to CIIM emergence. Thess concepts explain how newly introduced movement frames may be antithetical to current paradigms and practices, and therefore more difficult to implement. Since remedying climate-induced illnesses means replacing a traditional biomedical approach with a public health approach, activists may encounter obstacles to frame transformation. For example, West Nile Virus has been linked to climate change by some scientists and therefore movements, but framing it as linked to climate change encounters obstacles to frame transformation because the illness is deeply embedded in a biomedical framework centered around diagnostic procedures and individual-level prevention. In a similar vein, CIIMs may have difficulty achieving frame resonance, or a congruency between movement actors and those they hope will arise to affect change. This is in part due to the lack of connection made between global warming on the international scale and local impacts sustained by communities.

Another framing problem relates to the difficulty with diagnostic framing, where problem identification is linked to attribution of blame. Identifying an illness as climate-induced implies legal governmental responsibility for address (Warner 2008). However, it is virtually impossible to link a certain polluter to the health impacts on a specific population. In other cases in which this has been possible, new systems of entitlement have emerged where there is insufficient care for affected groups (Petryna 2004). Groups who feel that they are affected by climate change, including the Alaskan village of Kivalina, which is being displaced due to sea-level rise, have begun to leverage lawsuits against oil companies that make the largest contribution to greenhouse gas emissions. That case is currently pending, and other cases have already been struck down. Therefore, the attribution of responsibility component of diagnostic framing has not been effectively elaborated by movement actors.

Social Movement Formation and Climate-Induced Illness

In the following section, I review social, governmental, and medical responses to three cases of climate-induced illness. Climate-induced illnesses are multiple and diverse. They include short-term outbreaks that have only a brief history of precedence, such as West Nile Virus or Hantavirus. Other climate-induced illnesses have a long-term history of medical understanding, treatment, and debates over causes, like asthma. Social responses have been similarly divergent. There has been little social movement contestation of West Nile. Unlike vector-borne illnesses, which have affected few people in the United States, dislocation due to extreme weather events has been a major problem in multiple locales, and the initial stages of a social movement response have arisen. Asthma movements are some of the most well addressed, with activism taking place in multiple American cities for some years. Asthma movements and the EJ organizations in which they are sited represent the historical background from which an overall climate-induced illness movement framework is emerging.

Vector-Borne Disease

West Nile Virus (WNV) has historically been endemic to Africa, but appeared in New York City in 1999, engendering local concern and a public health response (Nash et al. 2001). Local governments sprayed pesticides and distributed 300,000 cans of DEET to cut down on the number of mosquitoes, the vector for the disease (Asnis et al. 1999). Resultant exposures were later argued to potentially harm humans, wildlife, and hydrological resources (Sharpe and Irvine 2004). In the United States, healthcare practitioners and communities in areas where new vector-borne diseases emerge lack knowledge of these illnesses or how to prevent them. The lack of current expertise is the unhappy consequence of past success: such diseases have not been seen in the United States for many decades. Most vector-borne diseases, like malaria that mainly inhabited the southeast, were eradicated by the 1930s (Sachs and Malaney 2002). Public health officials have "a poor sort of memory" recalling past effective measures (Stevens 1989).

Communities in which outbreaks occurred were divided on how to enact preventive measures; while some fully supported widescale spraying of pesticides, others were concerned about possible toxicity issues (Tickner 2002). Activists argued against spraying and the usage of malathion in particular. For example, the No Spray Coalition formed in the New York area:

> To oppose New York City's mass spraying of Malathion and Pyrethroids by helicopter and truck...the No Spray Coalition has become expert in the dangers of pesticides and presenting alternative and non-toxic methods for dealing with mosquitoes.... (www.nospray.org)

This organization leveraged a local lawsuit against the New York City government in order to stop spraying. Beginning in 2000, the No Spray Coalition brought suit against the city for widespread pesticide applications in the wake of the 1999 outbreak, charging that the city's "indiscriminate" spraying was itself a danger to public health and ineffective. The ensuing series of cases was brought to a close in 2007 when No Spray and New York City signed a "Stipulation of Agreement and Order" in which No Spray agreed to discontinue legal action, and the city agreed to pay No Spray's court and legal fees, as well as paying $80,000 to a group of five nonprofit organizations conducting "environmental projects" around the city, including environmental education, water-quality monitoring, and mosquito-breeding habitat reduction. In addition, a series of "good faith" meetings between the Coalition and the NYC Department of Health were convened.

West Nile presents important issues of scale in disease phenomena, medical or governmental response, and resultant contention. While the problem is inherently local, much of the public health response is directed on the federal level from the CDC. When the disease was initially "discovered" in 1999 and 2000, local concerns translated to the federal level so that in 2001 the CDC recommended to localities that they only spray as a last resort. This development reflects how, even without a sustained movement response, some level of porosity took place between community-based concerns and federal-level decisions. As such, concerns raised by one community may result in different disease prevention methods in another. Future attempts to manage illness emergence may present more questions in this vein, as the disease expands and crosses state boundaries. Based on last year's 4,269 cases, even more are forecasted for 2007 and the situation is being called a potential "epidemic" (Grady 2007).

Another emerging disease linked to climate change that has recently become more common is the Hantavirus. It was found in the southwest in 1993 after a disperse group of people were infected around the Four Corners region. Consequent investigation and study by multiple government agencies resulted in its diagnosis (Khan et al. 1996). Although investigators thought that the illness was new to the United States at that time, they have since realized that it has previously existed in twenty-one states since 1959. In addition, Native tribes in the area report the virus in their folk tales, indicating it has long been of consequence (Parker 2007).

After the Hantavirus was "discovered," scientists began campaigns to study those affected and quickly generated a partially effective vaccine. As a result of immediate concerns about the virus, the CDC began a national survey to track emerging diseases (Dawson 1995). The media also covered stories about Hanta well, with over seven hundred articles in newspapers discussing the illness between 1993 and 1995. During those years, there was a rapid rise in the incorporation of vector-borne disease in popular culture and other media outlets with the publication of the scientific best seller, *The Hot Zone* (1994) and the movie *Outbreak* (2004). Corporate groups that would benefit from such treatments and other preventive activities became involved in the debate. D-Con Rodenticides, a company selling products that extinguish deer mice, the main vector for Hantavirus, published an informational pamphlet approved by the CDC and distributed to local groups (*Chicago Sun-Times* 1995). The National Pesticide Management Association, a large nonprofit representing the pesticide industry, also published information about the importance to use pest management methods to prevent Hanta. Although government organizations have dedicated more resources to identifying the disease, media coverage has been vast, and corporate groups are involved in the debate, little has been done by nongovernmental groups.

Although when they were first discovered there was no connection between West Nile and Hantavirus, scientists have more recently linked them directly to climate change. Connecting disease outcomes with climate change has been constricted by scientific approaches that examine ecological shifts unconnected to disease trends. Scientific studies that examine the emergence of vector-borne diseases, and these two in particular, had been done at a more macro level, utilizing geosensing data regarding land-cover use and rainfall patterns. Experts indicted that the Hantavirus outbreak was caused by El Niño events in both 1993, then again in 1997. During these periods, increased rainfall fostered mouse reproduction (Hjelle and Glass 2000). In order to monitor a potential outbreak of the disease, scientists use landsat data to track the growth of vegetation that would foster rodent reproduction. While this data is sufficient to convey basic land-cover data, it cannot collect the detailed analysis, like soil quality, necessary to predict the likelihood of Hantavirus risk (Glass et al. 2000). The emergence of West Nile has also been linked to changes in rainfall patterns and droughts generated by global climate change (Patz et al. 2000). Drought conditions caused stagnant water in sewers and unused swimming pools that became breeding grounds for mosquitoes (Wilogren 1999).

While recent scientific advances have linked changing ecological conditions probably caused by climate change to the emergence of West Nile and Hantaviruse, this information has yet to reach local communities who might use these findings to demand improved surveillance or prevention methods. In addition, the small numbers affected may be limiting citizen responses. In both cases, few citizen groups have arisen and there is no framework linking disease emergence to climate.

Extreme Weather Events and Displacement

A vast amount and type of research has examined the social responses to disasters, but little has allowed for the presence of social movement responses (Oliver-Smith 1996). In addition, while epidemiological and public health research has explored the health impacts of disasters such as extreme weather events (Campbell-Lendrum and Woodruff 2006) and other researchers have evaluated the organizational capacity for management (Boin et al. 2005; Sims 2007), little research has linked these two topics. Emergent movements may play an important role in generating improvements in these conditions and changing the outcomes of future cases.

Displacement of coastal Alaskan Inuit communities due to melting permafrost and storm surges is widely accepted as an outcome of global warming (Epstein and Mills 2005). Such displacement has had massive health ramifications for those communities. They include: nutritional decline as hunters are unable to reach fishing or catching locations that are now surrounded by thin, instead of thick, ice; water contamination caused by dropping water tables and mixing of sewage of fresh water; and increased exposure to organic pollutants stored in frozen sediment and released with warming (Tenenbaum 2005).

Alaska is a shifting terrain of movement activity around climate health issues. Movement responses began there in the mid-1990s and largely centered around the secondary human impacts of melting permafrost, such as damaged infrastructure and hindrances to hunting. More recently, they have begun to focus on toxics that are being released as permafrost melts and are increasing as temperatures shift globally. Activities around erosion and displacement have been generated in Alaska because these impacts have taken place there more significantly and earlier than anywhere else in the United States. Nine coastal communities are now in the process of considering how to deal with displacement. Four of them are already being forced to evacuate, causing serious public and governmental debate about costs for relocation. Massive inter-institutional confusion is occurring since there are multiple federal agencies that share responsibility for the costs, but few of them are actually willing to provide financial support (GAO 2003).

Despite the lack of political opportunities for Native communities, Alaskan Inuit are organized in tribal councils that provide a preexisting social network that can be used to formulate a new movement. The Alaskan Federation of Natives represents these tribes and has begun to demand address of climate health impacts. The organization states:

> Erosion, accelerated in recent years by a series of near-catastrophic storms, has given rise to public health, safety and welfare concerns in many communities. In more graphic

terms, erosion has exposed sewer and septic systems, jeopardized community water lines, and rendered unusable road systems that serve as escape routes. The impacted communities are in need of assistance to rebuild/restore infrastructure and to undertake preventative measures to mitigate erosion damage from future storms. (AFN 2006)

In 2007, a lawsuit was leveraged by one of these communities, the Village of Kivalina, against several oil companies in order to gain compensation for their losses. This case is currently in process.

Several other organizations have formed to address the effects of global climate change on their locales. They have addressed health or toxics in the past, but that have shifted their agenda to include climate change. The Alaskan Community Action on Toxics based in Fairbanks has examined human impacts of toxics since it was founded in 1997. Its work uses an environmental justice approach through which to view the disproportionate impacts of toxic contaminants on Native populations. The organization has only recently begun to consider climate change as a subject of import as data is being generated that shows climate change will increase the toxic load in Arctic areas (Tenenbaum 1998).

Scientific activity examining changes in Inuit territories has also grown recently, a portion of which has involved local communities in the gathering of indigenous knowledge about climate change impacts (Alaskan Native Science Commission 2005). These projects that bring communities together and generate consolidated findings about warming impacts have the capacity to shape communities outside of these studies. One of the Native organizations that focuses on health impacts is called Native Science. It primarily manages research relationships between Native Alaskan communities and outside researchers. Founded in 1994 and based in Anchorage, the organization is supported by or linked with some of the most powerful government agencies and nongovernmental foundations such as the Department of Energy and the Henry J. Kaiser Family Foundation. Universities from all over the world have collaborated with the group to generate new studies and draw attention to the human impacts of climate change in Native communities.

Collaboration between Native peoples and scientists draws a collectivity of knowledge that might otherwise be informal or unconsolidated. For instance, at the 12th Annual Alaska Tribal Conference on Environmental Management, cosponsored by the U.S. EPA and the Alaska Native Tribal Health Consortium in October 2006, a session was held in which individuals from many locations discussed and mapped out climate impacts on their communities, many of which impact health like thinning ice that hinders hunting (Altman 2007). Clearly, by engaging with researchers and accessing related resources, Native peoples have been able to draw attention to issues that may have been sidelined otherwise.

One of the largest organizations not based in Alaska that assists those communities is the Indigenous Environmental Network (IEN). Founded in 1990 then expanded to a functioning organization in 1995, indigenous peoples throughout the United States work in this organization. The main office is located in Minnesota and two of its field offices are in Alaska, one in Fairbanks and the other in Anchorage. Leaders in those locations address environmental health and climate issues, amongst others. The Network uses a clear EJ framework to protest the disproportionate burden of environmental and environmental health burdens on Native communities. At first the organization worked solely in the United States, but it has expanded to form coalitions with and support indigenous and EJ struggles in other parts of the world.

The group allies itself with the environmental justice movement and has been a formal leader in the EJ movement's platform about climate issues. In this sense, there is a direct relationship between responses to displacement of Alaskan Natives and the illness burden on urban populations caused by global warming. While the network is not substantiated by a multitude of organizations, the activists working in these groups have long-term commitments to overlapping issues and are some of the most well known in the environmental justice community.

Asthma and Heat-Induced Illness

Climate-induced illnesses that have generated the greatest public concern include asthma and heat-induced illness. Climate models reflect that asthma will be exacerbated as air pollution patterns shift, especially in cities. In the same settings, increased heat and urban heat islands result in heat waves that have killed tens of thousands of people in cities around the world (Poumadere et al. 2005). Heat-induced illness disproportionally affects minorities, the poor and the elderly (O'Neill et al. 2005). The most striking example of this in the United States was the 1995 heat wave reported on by Klinenberg (2002), who argued that the social structural contexts of elderly African Americans shaped mortality trends in an ecologically driven phenomenon. This is not dissimilar from the pattern of asthma rates that follow spatial distributions. Both of these groups of illnesses are projected to rise in urban contexts, such as New York City (U.S. Global Research Program 2000), where asthma and environmental justice movements have existed.

The link between asthma rates, untenable urban conditions and air pollution was scientifically asserted in the 1990s by a series of studies including the Six Cities Study that linked asthma and cardiopulmonary malfunction with PM10 fine air particles. Even before climate change entered the scientific and activist agenda, these rates put asthma on the agenda of urban environmental justice movements. Movements that address disproportionate rates of asthma in inner-city communities have grown largely in cities such as Los Angeles, New York, and Boston (Brown et al. 2002; Loh and Sugerman-Brozan 2002). Several locations in New York City have witnessed burgeoning movements regarding asthma since the mid-1990s. El Puente and Community Alliance for the Environment in Brooklyn have connected local residents with healthcare workers who can help them find treatment and protested the siting of an incinerator in their Brooklyn neighborhoods (Corburn 2005). Both organizations were founded around 1995 and have since generated new local studies and policies. Similarly, uptown in Harlem, West Harlem Environmental Action has addressed a vast range of environmental and environmental health problems. One of their main foci has been linking transportation emissions with increased asthma rates in areas where bus parking and waste facilities exist. On the opposite coast, in Los Angeles, similar communities of African Americans and Latinos have come together to push polluters to better regulate in order to decrease asthma rates.

Although these movements have existed for over ten years, and during a time when climate activism was arising, they did not connect their struggles to climate change for some time. Rather, they stayed locally focused by targeting polluters in the community and resultant air pollution. It is likely that their localized approach has been caused by the struggles they have faced in simply changing the paradigm of asthma. All of these organizations have struggled against a "blame the victim" approach to asthma which claims that dirty homes, cockroaches, and poor housing are the causes of heightened rates in those areas (Brown et al. 2005). They have generated new science in order to make their link to environmental causes credible (Kinney et al. 2000). The science that relates these local findings to asthma has surfaced even more recently and been more abstract than the reports local EJ activists have generated. These movements are a central part of EJ activism, of which other organizations have linked local phenomenon to global warming.

Climate-Induced Illness and Environmental Justice Movements

Asthma movements are one part of environmental justice activism that has created the strongest and broadest climate-induced illness movement. Concerns about the impacts of climate change have broadened both the discourse used by EJ movements, as well as the organizational networks themselves. These groups are predominately concerned about how climate-induced illness will disproportionately affect poor and minority populations. The vast majority of EJ groups challenge the siting or practices of local polluting sources (Bullard 1990). They often coconstruct locally based science to prove toxic exposure (Allen 2003). However, by nature of the phenomena, their address of climate has been driven by local communities and linked to the trans-local, national, or international levels. As a result, introducing climate concerns to the EJ movement has the potential to both shape politics and the environmental justice movement itself. For the EJ movement, reorienting environmental justice to encompass an issue that is geographically diffuse and involves multiple scientific actors may change the structure and/or practices of the movement.

Leaders interested in climate health concerns are some of the most well-known in the EJ movement, such as Beverly Wright, director of the Deep South Center for Environmental Justice, and Tom Goldtooth, executive director of the Indigenous Environmental Network. They codirect one of the few organizations dedicated solely to environmental justice concerns that center around climate change called the Environmental Justice and Climate Change Initiative. The Initiative is a network of twenty-eight organizations based across the United States that includes such groups as WEACT, Communities for a Better Environment, and the Native Village of Unalakleet. Health is central to its agenda. Its homepage states:

> Climate change harms the health of communities of color and Indigenous Peoples. Communities of color and Indigenous Peoples are burdened with poor air quality and are twice as likely to be uninsured than whites. Yet, these communities will become even more vulnerable to climate-change related respiratory ailments, heat-related illness and death, and illness from insect-carried diseases.

Groups proposing a climate justice agenda have now burgeoned in California, New York, Alaska, Michigan, Illinois, South Africa, India, and the United Kingdom. They include indigenous organizations in rural areas, like Indigenous Environmental Network in Minnesota or the Black Mesa Water Coalition in the Navajo Nation, and urban-based coalitions such as West Harlem Environmental Action in New York City. In November, 2000, environmental justice groups from the United States, Africa, and Latin America met at the Hague to hold a conference about climate justice. Hosted by Redefining Progress, an organization based in California, speakers were from other organizations from the United States, such as the Environmental Justice Resource Center at Clark Atlanta University, Southwest Workers Union, Southwest Network for Environmental and Economic Justice, and Washington Association of Churches and Community Coalition for Environmental Justice-Seattle. The following year, the U.S. delegates to the World Conference Against Racism released a consensus statement that claimed:

> People of color, Indigenous peoples and workers bear a disproportionate health, social, and economic burden of a society addicted to a fossil fuel economy. As such, they are the first victims of government inaction, corporate abuse, and negligent public policy.

Environmental justice groups developed a new "Climate Justice Framework" in 2004 and 2005. It was composed of ten points such as the need to make polluters accountable, participation of affected people in policy-making and inclusion of inequalities in planning for climate change health outcomes (Cordova et al. 2005). The framework was developed through two workshops that outlined its goals and that resulted in "The Climate Justice Declaration" (Dorsey 2007). These workshops and the consequent declaration brought together principals from environmental justice and climate activism to emphasize how climate change would result in adverse health outcomes, and how such illnesses would be exacerbated by lack of access to health care and mitigation measures, disparities in health insurance coverage, and increased susceptibility of inner-city communities and communities of color.

Prestigious academic institutions have also utilized the framework's language and approach in developing new studies. It has also been used internationally as a way to frame the global burden of greenhouse gas emissions generated by developed nations (Parks and Roberts 2006; Pettit 2004). This discourse developed by environmental justice organizations has been used to unite diverse communities, including those outside the EJ movement.

Other Movement Groups and Boundary Actors

Scientists and medical practitioners have also begun campaigning regarding the health impacts of climate change. These are nontraditional movement actors who can be conceptualized as tutoring members of a boundary movement (McCormick, Brown, and Zavestoski 2003). Groups not historically considered social movement organizations have joined in with the environmental justice movement to promote discourse and action to prevent public health impacts of climate change. The American Medical Student Association and Physicians for Social Responsibility have created new campaigns both about mitigating climate impacts and the illnesses climate change generates. Both groups draw attention to health inequalities and the disproportionate burden on poor people and people of color. In fact, these groups leverage a very similar discourse about environmental justice as the EJCC. While most of the organizations' activities are focused on policy change and reducing greenhouse gas emissions through such groups as the Medical Alliance to Stop Global Warming, their primary concern is about illness outcomes, and they utilize networks of healthcare providers to generate activism.

While the medical community has begun new campaigns, researchers have also become activists themselves as they testify before government hearings and assist local communities in understanding the health impacts of climate change. Paul Epstein (2001), one of the most well-known American climate health researchers and who codirects the Center for Health and the Global Environment at Harvard University, has offered testimony at several government hearings and made statements for the media. For example, in July 2007, Epstein was featured on National Public Radio's "All Things Considered" making an analogy between earth and humans, that both must be treated immediately if they are ill in order to prevent complications. Many of these researchers are not only interested in advancing new study, but also engendering new activism amongst their colleagues. Professor of Public Health at Johns Hopkins University Cindy Parker gave a teleconference to the Collaborative on Health and Environment, a group which links activists, medical practitioners, and scientists regarding the health implications of climate change and what must be done about them. She said:

> The debate about whether global environmental change is real is now over; in its wake is the realization that it is happening more rapidly than predicted. These changes constitute a profound challenge to human health, both as a direct threat and as a promoter of other risks. We call on health care providers to inform themselves about these issues and to become agents of change in their communities.

Through these sorts of statements and activities we can see the shifting landscape of CIIMs and the types of outcomes they may be able to achieve as they gain strength.

Impediments to Climate-Induced Illness Movements

Scientific Uncertainty and Discursive Formation

The formation of HSMs depends on the recognition that there is an illness and linking that illness with a discourse or set of grievances. In the case of most CIIMs, illness outcomes could be framed in the terminology of climate change, inequality, or need for better prevention and treatment. Such discursive action on the part of lay populations generally depends on previous scientific conclusions. However, scientifically linking climate change to human health outcomes is a difficult and debated process. In addition, research about health impacts is generally disconnected from that regarding climate change exhibited in models.

There are a number of scientific uncertainties that hinder the development of a discourse about health-related climate impacts. Most climate work is based on empirically observed weather or climate conditions and illness outcomes, the study of past events, identifying sensitivities and dose-response relationships for specific illnesses, and assessing what portion of a disease response can be attributed to a particular event (Bernard et al. 2001). Scientific consensus has supported both the existence of climate change and the broad-level impacts it will have on health but less consensus exists regarding exactly how those impacts will play out on the local level. There is little agreement about how many cases of new illnesses will appear or even how to measure mortality. For example, mortality rates during extreme heat events could be caused by preexisting illnesses, and hence not attributed to climate change (WHO 2003). In addition, the lack of clear definitions regarding what constitutes a threatening heat level makes it difficult for public health officials to know when to begin assessing heat-related death rates. More specifically, constructed models are not directly linked with health and also do not account for local context (Campbell-Lendrum and Woodruff 2006). Global models can, at most, currently be translated to the regional level.

Possibly the biggest challenge is to project long-term climate change with potential health outcomes. For example, there is a range of potential extreme weather events that are difficult to calculate. While climate models have recently improved and are able to account for a vast number of variables, they are still only indicative rather than predictive (McMichael, Woodruff, and Hales 2006). Temperatures may change radically or slightly. For example, in the New York area, temperature increases projected for the 2050s range from 2.6 to 6.5 degrees Fahrenheit (Metropolitan East Coast Assessment 2000).

Climate-Induced Illness Movements may react in a variety of ways to scientific uncertainty. Uncertainty may make such movements more difficult to form because it delegitimizes claims on the part of affected populations. Alternatively, activists may make claims about the need for more scientific research that they consequently use as a basis for credibility. For example, the EJCC and another organization in California, Redefining Progress, developed a report on the relationship between African Americans and climate policy that argued:

> [T]here is a disproportionate burden on African Americans from heat deaths; floods, fires, and other climate-related disasters; tropical storms like Katrina and Rita; and economic disruption of various sorts. (Hoerner and Robinson 2008: 5)

This report developed scenarios for the social, health, and economic costs to African American populations, and based on this analysis, argued for specific policies that would affect climate change. Similarly, some climate justice organizations provide scientific reports about the impacts of climate change as a resource to educate their constituents, therefore connecting the abstract concept of climate to their daily lives.

Another possibility is that such movements ignore scientific uncertainty entirely and instead use their own, embodied knowledge to make arguments. This has been true in other cases of embodied health movement activism. Contestation regarding West Nile Virus largely centered around exposure to the pesticides sprayed in response to the vector. Activists used accounts of increased asthma rates in neighborhoods where pesticides had been sprayed without scientific evidence or research findings to support their claims. Locally, they focused less on long-term underlying causes of WNV expansion and return year after year, although on the national and international climate justice platform West Nile has been used as an example of the health costs of climate change.

Making the Leap to Health: Frame Transformation and Diagnostic Framing

The initial framing of climate change was congruent with the environmental movement, which is most generally focused on habitat, green space, and nature, rather than on human life. Therefore, CIIMs face the challenge of shifting the framing of climate change to humans on the one hand, and also face obstacles in shifting from a biomedical disease paradigm to one of climate. There are two main underlying framing problems in this process: frame transformation and diagnostic framing.

Climate-Induced Illness Movements may encounter problems of frame resonance in creating concern about health when the vast majority of concern has been focused on environmental conditions. There is a traditional distinction between environment and health, between which there is little interaction (Kroll-Smith and Lancaster 2002). Remedying this disconnect means replacing a biomedical approach focused on the individual body (Mishler 1981) with a public health approach concerned with population health. In addition, it means localizing previously global models about environment within the human body. Therefore, connecting the rise of new illness to localities without seeing visible ramifications of climate change is very difficult. For those groups that are able to overcome this difficulty, they render the invisible visible by making disembodied climate change an embodied experience. This process is something common to health social movements since the body is the point of interest, reflection of broader phenomenon, and site of resistance.

Climate-Induced Illness Movements represent the ways in which HSMs may also face issues of diagnostic framing, where problem identification is linked to attribution of blame. The predominant frame constructed by national-level social movement organizations (SMOs) concerned about climate change is one in which responsibility is placed on humans for the destruction of natural resources, such as the ozone layer and animal populations. For example, the National Resources Defense Council, one of the "Big Ten" environmental groups, claims that: "global warming is already affecting the world we know, endangering polar bears, shortening ski seasons and creating more intense storms." However, environmental justice and other groups have shifted the frame to include the human impacts of climate change and to emphasize the need for participatory decision-making about how to deal with these climate impacts. This has been difficult, in part, because climate-induced illnesses are often framed by the media as mysterious, such as the case of vector-borne diseases.

Health has been leveraged as a part of several initial lawsuits regarding the impacts of climate change and their remedy. For example, in 2007 the Village of Kivalina, one of Alaska's Native communities being displaced by erosion linked to climate change, began a lawsuit against a group of oil companies for their losses. The loss of habitat and property was raised in addition to the multiple health impacts to that community and many others around the world that climate change will affect. Much criticism has been raised against this suit, particularly because it is difficult to scientifically link these companies specifically to the impacts being sustained in Alaska. This and the other obstacles to CIIMs demonstrate that connecting health to climate change has potential gravity and promises to be slowed by a number of obstacles.

Conclusions

The health impacts from impending climate change represent some of the most pressing public health needs of this century. However, these impacts have not been the primary focus of most organizations concerned about climate change. Connecting tangible illnesses to climate change generates concern especially amongst either those already impacted, or those who give care to affected populations. In many cases, it is difficult at this stage to generate a CIIM. There is little broad-based awareness of the health effects of climate change and historically a general disregard for adaptation that is only shifting very recently. Without the help of scientists who have data that link climatic changes to health and lacking evidence that links polluters to specific disease outcomes, CIIMs may emerge very infrequently. This reflects their difficulty with framing. The challenges that CIIMs face in formation reflect challenges characteristic of other HSMs as well.

Because of this initial stage of CIIM formation and research on CIIMs, this chapter raises more questions than it answers. Questions about how climate change may shape the environmental justice movement are rife for further examination. Of equal importance is how movements will make abstract science, which is the basis for most arguments about climate, concrete or embodied. Finally, the focus on health and health inequalities highlights the disjuncture between agencies that address root environmental issues, like air pollution, the destruction of wildlife habitat, and others, and those that answer human health needs. Therefore, even other uncertainties remain about how climate-induced illness movements may generate new political institutions and practices that simply have never existed, since climate change is a new phenomenon. Further research should more thoroughly explore cases of climate-induced illness to understand how they can be addressed better and how such movements are distinct to an unprecedented state of hotter human affairs.

NOTES

1. This research is based on qualitative data in the form of documents, Web sites, ethnographic observations, informal interviews, and scientific literature. I reviewed Web sites and documents by environmental justice, environmental, academic, and medical organizations concerned about climate change. Using MEDLINE, I also conducted an in-depth analysis of scientific and medical literature regarding the health impacts of climate change. Keywords included "climate change," "health," "illness," "heat," "vector-borne disease," and displacement. I also conducted a media analysis of major newspapers using Lexis/Nexis from 1990 to the present, searching for the portrayal of health issues, as well as the scientists and activists quoted in these articles. These bodies of data were contextualized in ethnographic observations of activist and academic meetings about climate change. Informal interviews were conducted with relevant experts and activists at these meetings.

16

From Infanticide to Activism

Emotions and Identity in Self-Help Movements

Verta Taylor and Lisa Leitz

Over the past two decades support groups and networks mobilized around a shared bodily condition, psychological problem, or victimization experience have become pervasive in American society. Social movement scholars working in the political process and contentious politics traditions have tended to overlook health and self-help movements because their actions purportedly do not constitute a force for political and institutional change. A stream of recent research suggests, however, that self-help and consumer health movements, many of which originated in earlier protest campaigns such as the women's, gay and lesbian, disability rights, AIDS, and mental health movements, have been significant forces for change not only in identity and public opinion, but in the healthcare industry and the legal sector (Taylor 1996; Klawiter 1999; Klawiter 2008; Allsop, Jones, and Baggott 2005; Brown and Zavestoski 2005; Crossley 2006; Archibald 2007; Epstein 2007a; Whittier forthcoming).

Although self-help movements share many of the attributes scholars associate with social movements (Katz 1993; Wuthnow 1994; Taylor 1996; Archibald 2007), the self-help repertoire represents a displacement of protest from the economic and political realms to other institutional arenas such as medicine, mental health, law, religion, and education. Social movement scholars continue to debate whether collective challenges that do not target the state can rightly be considered under the rubric of social movements (McAdam, Tarrow, and Tilly 2001). Over the past decade, however, a less state-centered conceptualization of social movements has emerged rooted in what Armstrong and Bernstein (2008) describe in a provocative article in *Sociological Theory* as a "multi-institutional politics" approach (Zald and Berger 1978; McCarthy and Wolfson 1996; Armstrong 2002;

Cress and Myers 2004; Van Dyke, Soule, and Taylor 2004; Staggenborg and Taylor 2005; Jasper 2006). The political process model is based on a Marxist conception of power that views domination as organized by and around the economic and political structures of society with culture playing a secondary role. This leads to a narrow conception of politics. Contemporary approaches to power, influenced by European New Social Movement theory (Giddens 1991; Touraine 1981; Melucci 1996; Katzenstein 1998; Crossley 2002) and contemporary cultural theory (Bourdieu 1977; Foucault 1977, 1980; Fligstein 1991; DiMaggio and Powell 1991; Sewell 1992; Armstrong and Bernstein 2008), hold that in late modern societies power is more multidimensional and is both symbolic and material. Conceiving of power as structurally and culturally based justifies a more inclusive definition of social movements by connecting shifting repertoires of contention mobilized around identity classifications and distribution to the multidimensional nature of power in modern society.

We adopt David Snow's (2004b: 11) definition that views social movements as collective challenges to cultural as well as material systems of authority. In this paper, we examine a self-help movement that has been a significant force for cultural and political change by challenging medical knowledge and practice, mobilizing constituents to obtain research funding, changing legal regulations and laws, and fostering public discussion about postpartum depression. Our analysis focuses on a Pen-Pal Network of women incarcerated for committing infanticide who, by virtue of participation in a self-help movement, come to define their actions as being the result of postpartum psychiatric illness. We will show how participation in the movement allowed women to minimize their shame and emotional distress and to shift blame for their actions to the medical and legal systems, enabling them to remake their identities as mothers. The network is part of a larger self-help movement that emerged in the mid-1980s focused on providing support and direct services to women who suffer postpartum psychiatric illness and on changing medical and legal policy and practice related to the treatment of postpartum psychiatric illness (Taylor 1996).

The core of self-help is social support and an emphasis on experiential as opposed to professional knowledge. In this paper we show how the social networks and the solidarity that form among self-help participants in the process of getting and giving support and formulating an experiential definition of postpartum depression to explain the reasons they killed their children foster a sense of injustice and righteous anger, which are necessary for movement mobilization. One of the reasons that social movement scholars have failed to take self-help movements seriously is that they have been deemed "expressive" and oriented to personal change, rather than "instrumental" and directed at structural transformation. Rather than dismiss the significance of self-help because of its emotionality, we aim to show that emotion is fundamental to the politicization of self-help participants. A great deal of the mobilization work of self-help movements is "emotion labor" (Hochschild 1983) that involves channeling, transforming, legitimating, and managing participants' emotions to bring them into alignment with the movement's claims.

Theoretical Links between Emotions and Identity

In the last decade, there has been a flurry of scholarship in search of an empirically grounded explanation of the common emotional patterns associated with social protest and social movements (Taylor 1995a; Goodwin, Jasper and Polletta 2001; Einwohner 2002; Benford and Hunt 1992; Flam and King 2005). In our view, a theoretical understanding of how emotions operate in social movements requires that social movement scholars make greater use of middle-range theories and empirical research by scholars in the field of emotions (Klein and Taylor 2007). In this analysis, we link theories of emotion that focus on the way emotion confirms and affirms individual identity with collective identity approaches to social movements that consider the strategic deployment of identity as vital to understanding social movements engaged in struggles that occur in culture and everyday life (Giddens 1991; Gamson 1992a; Taylor and Whittier 1992; Melucci 1995; Bernstein 1997; Snow 2001). Self-help movements contribute to the reconstruction of social identities by mobilizing around collective identities that translate negative and stigmatized emotions and identities imposed by dominant groups and classificatory schemes imbedded in modern institutions, such as medicine, psychiatry, and the criminal justice system, into positively valued self-definitions (Whittier forthcoming; Morrison 2005 Taylor 1996). Sociologists interested in emotions have documented the significance of emotions for the construction of self and identity (Stryker 1987; Howard and Callero 1991). According to affect control theory (Smith-Lovin and Heise 1988; Smith-Lovin 1990, 1995), emotions act as messengers that signal to the self whether events confirm or disconfirm identities. The theory predicts that, because the character of a person's emotions is determined by his or her identity, people construct events in ways that corroborate their own and others' identities so as to create positive emotions. Particularly relevant to the study of social movements is the way sociological models of emotion address the matter of nonnormative identities. Affect control theory postulates that occupying stigmatized, deviant, or marginal identities gives rise to strong negative emotions, such as shame, guilt, and fear, which can set into motion a search for new ways to characterize the self (Smith-Lovin 1990; Scheff and Retzinger 1991; Britt and Heise 2000).

Whereas affect control theory helps us understand the process by which self-help participants accept, negotiate, and resist emotional states perceived as nonnormative, social movement theory directs our attention to the collective processes involved in the construction of new emotional framings, labels, and identities (Taylor 2000a; Polletta and Jasper 2001; Blee 2002; Hunt and Benford 2004). Social movement scholars have demonstrated that the construction of a collective identity among participants is essential to the mobilization of social movements. Further, in modern societies participation in social movements is becoming a key factor in the ongoing social constitution of personal identities and biographies (Giddens 1991). Taylor and Whittier define collective identity as a "shared definition of a group" or a sense of "we" (1992: 105, 110) and suggest that it entails an ongoing process of negotiating and framing a group's commonalities. Numerous studies have shown that participants engage in considerable emotion labor in order to merge their personal identities with the collective identity of a social movement community (Taylor and Rupp 1993; Snow and McAdam 2000; Klandermans and de Weerd 2000; Dunn 2004; Whittier forthcoming). In this paper, we draw upon insights from this body of work to understand the role that emotion plays in the politicization of self-help activists.

The Pen-Pal Network of Women Who Have Committed Infanticide

In the 1980s the American public knew very little about postpartum depression. That changed, however, after a *Phil Donahue Show* about a woman imprisoned in the Muncy State Correctional Institution in Pennsylvania for killing her one-month-old son by dropping him off a bridge into a creek while suffering psychotic symptoms of postpartum illness. What most viewers who saw the program did not know is that Donahue's guests were part of a submerged network of activists mobilizing to demand that the medical establishment recognize the emotional problems that some women experience after the birth of a baby as a distinctive medical and psychiatric condition (see Taylor 1996 for a fuller description of the postpartum self-help movement). Over the next two years, widespread media attention to postpartum illness related to infanticide fueled the growth of two national social movement organizations, Depression After Delivery (DAD) and Postpartum Support International (PSI) that have brought public and professional awareness to postpartum-related psychiatric illnesses. These organizations operate through support groups; produce newsletters, publications, and conferences; and are involved in a myriad of tactics aimed at legislative, policy, and legal change, challenging cultural ideas about what constitutes normal motherhood, and transforming medical and psychiatric practices.

The movement originally mobilized among networks of feminists with clear connections to the women's movement of the late 1960s and 1970s. In 2006, DAD, the more grassroots of the two organizations, merged with PSI. Over time, PSI, headquartered in Santa Barbara, California, has evolved into a professional social movement organization with a largely paper membership base that relies largely upon a paid staff and stable funding to influence policy and public opinion on behalf of its constituency (McCarthy and Zald1973). Professionalization has allowed the movement to survive and gain legitimacy with medical professionals and policy makers. The movement has also acquired legitimacy through celebrities who have gone public about their experiences with postpartum psychiatric illness (see Lerner 2006).

The Pen-Pal Network we focus on here is part of this larger movement. The network emerged in 1990 when the leaders of DAD and PSI were deluged by letters from women serving time in prison for postpartum-related infanticide reaching out for emotional support and for legal and psychiatric assistance. To respond to these requests, the founder of PSI modeled a support group for imprisoned women on pen-pal networks she had been involved in as a child. She mailed a letter to each of the imprisoned women who had written PSI and DAD, and within a month she received nine letters from women wanting to be included in the network. Prison life made the traditional pen-pal model impractical, however, because most prisons do not allow inmates to correspond directly with other inmates. In order to get around this, PSI established a Pen-Pal Network Newsletter that summarizes letters women write to a coordinator and this newsletter is, in turn, mailed to all the women in the network. The newsletters contain information about the network members' welfare, progress on their trials, appeals, and parole decisions, legislative and psychiatric developments concerning postpartum illnesses and infanticide, and summaries of recent research and professional conferences on postpartum psychiatric illness.

The Pen-Pal Network actively recruits participants. When cases of postpartum-illness-related infanticide receive media coverage, members of the Pen-Pal Network and the network coordinator write encouraging the women to join. Some women also discover the Pen-Pal Network through the web site of Postpartum Support International, and others are referred by attorneys, family members, and friends. Since 1990 the network has had six coordinators, and most have themselves experienced postpartum psychiatric illness. The coordinators are women outside prison walls, and their role is to correspond with women in prison, manage the newsletter, mail materials to prisoners, family members, and attorneys, and maintain lists of attorneys and health officials to testify as expert witnesses in court cases.

Since its inception, between nine and thirty-five women have participated in the Pen-Pal Network at any given time. As is typical of social movements, women move in and out of the network. When we conducted the survey in 2002, sixteen women were involved, but by summer 2007 the network included thirty women. They ranged in age from twenty-three to fifty. Most participants are white, although members of nearly every racial minority have been represented in the group. At the time we surveyed the network, twelve participants were white, one was biracial and one was Native American. Prior to the crime, eleven were married, and they had an average of 2.2 children. Half reported a preprison household income of less than $25,000, and only one reported an income of more than $100,000. Less than a third (six) of the women worked outside the home, primarily in a range of low-paid occupations. In terms of education, three women had college degrees, and another eight of the fourteen women had some college or technical-school training.

Thirteen women in the network were charged with murder. Half of the cases went to trial, and only half of the women had access to a private attorney. About half used a postpartum psychiatric defense, although the majority could not afford to mount a full insanity defense with expert witnesses. Seven were serving life sentences, three with no option of parole. Five were engaged in some type of appeal at the time of the survey. Although all of the women had undergone a psychiatric evaluation, typically the examination did not take place until several months after they were arrested. Four women volunteered that they had been sexually or physically abused prior to their crime.

As part of the movement's strategy to bring about change, the Pen-Pal Network provides women the opportunity to promote, manage, and express emotions that resist and oppose the stigmatized identity of a purposeful killer. There are two main categories of emotions expressed in the context of the movement: the *emotions of guilt*, which include grief, shame, and loneliness; and the *emotions of resistance*, which include righteous anger, moral outrage, and love. Our analysis will demonstrate that women's involvement with the network allows them to embrace a collective identity that overcomes their shame and isolation by defining them as reasonable mothers; provides medical and legal explanations for their actions that evokes righteous indignation over the institutional treatment of infanticide linked to postpartum psychiatric illness; and supplies identity accounts that complicate and redefine the emotion norms of conventional motherhood (Taylor 1996, 2000a).

Data and Methods

Our analysis is based on individual-, organizational-, and cultural-level data obtained primarily through field research conducted between 1985 and 2007. We used qualitative procedures to organize, code, and analyze all of these sources of data. Individual-level data include an open-ended survey of participants in the Pen-Pal Network conducted in 2003 and letters of participants in the Pen-Pal Network written to each other and to the network coordinator since the network's inception in 1990. We mailed open-ended surveys to sixteen participants in the Pen-Pal Network serving time in prison for killing their children, and fourteen were returned (n =14, response rate = 87.5 percent). The questionnaire explored demographic data, stories of women's crimes, disposition of their legal cases, their participation in the Pen-Pal Network, and their personal feelings and identities. The survey data were coded for these themes and analyzed qualitatively. We also analyzed more than three hundred letters from over thirty participants in the Pen-Pal Network written to Postpartum Support International (PSI), Depression After Delivery (DAD), and the first author by women serving prison sentences for committing infanticide. We coded the emotions conveyed in women's letters and used them to develop in inductive theoretical understanding of the emotional transformations associated with collective identity construction.

Organizational-level data about collective identity construction and the tactics of the Pen- Pal Network were obtained from PSI and Pen-Pal Network newsletters published from 1990, when the Pen-Pal Network was first established, to 2007. The PSI newsletter is published quarterly, and the Pen-Pal Network newsletter is sent only to imprisoned women who are members of the Pen-Pal Network. Additional organizational-level data was derived from multiple key informant interviews with Jane Honikman, founder of Postpartum Support International and the Pen-Pal Network, and Nancy Berchtold, founder of the now-defunct Depression After Delivery. We also draw upon participant observation of the two social movement organizations between 1987 and 1995 by the first author (Taylor 1996).

To obtain information about cultural representations of maternal infanticide, we examined media coverage of the cases of all of the women in the Pen-Pal Network. A Lexis-Nexis search elicited more than three thousand newspaper and magazine articles, editorials, and opinion pieces. We used these data to obtain additional details about the crimes and disposition of the legal cases and to develop an understanding of the cultural depictions of the women and their crimes. In addition, we analyzed transcripts of television appearances by members of the Pen-Pal Network.

Collective Identity

Getting and giving support is the heart and soul of self-help. Women's interactions in the Pen-Pal Network through the newsletter and personal correspondence allow them to construct solidarity and a collective identity in spite of the fact that they are incarcerated and geographically separated.[1] Our analysis draws on Taylor's previous writings on collective identity (Taylor 1989; Taylor and Whittier 1992), which suggest that there are three components to collective identity: boundaries, consciousness, and negotiation. We turn now to a consideration of how each of these components allows us to understand the role that emotion plays in the construction of collective identity among members of the PSI Pen-Pal Network.

Boundaries

Boundary work is a central task in collective identity construction, and it entails constructing both a collective self and a collective other (Taylor and Whittier 1992; Hunt and Benford 2004). The construction of a positive identity requires both a rejection of the classificatory schemes, codes, and stigmatized identities of the dominant society and the creation of new-self affirming identities.

Infanticide has a long history in most societies. Most scholars hold that the specific patterns associated with child killings in different societies are a reflection of societal variations in the construction of motherhood and parenting (Oberman and Meyer 2008; Meyer and Oberman 2001). Beginning in the late nineteenth century, a medical model of infanticide began to emerge in Western Europe and Canada in which child killing came to be understood as a response to social and demographic processes that altered the practice and meaning of motherhood. In the United States, however, neither the courts nor medical experts have embraced the medical model of infanticide as fully as in France, England, and Canada. In England, for example, the British Infanticide Act of 1922 recognizes infanticide as a distinct form of homicide linked to the effects of pregnancy, birth, and early motherhood on the emotional and mental status of the mother. Women who are able to demonstrate that they suffered from a postpartum mental disorder at the time they killed a child are charged with manslaughter instead of murder and most receive probationary sentences and psychiatric care rather than prison sentences.

The United States presents a stark contrast. The criminal justice system has only rarely accommodated a postpartum psychiatric defense, and women whose postpartum psychiatric illness results in infanticide are treated poorly by the legal system and stigmatized in the media (Spinelli 2003, 2005). The case of one of the women who participated in the Pen-Pal Network is fairly typical of the judicial handling of infanticide. A single women living in rural Ohio, she was working at a minimum-wage job after her husband walked out of their marriage when she became pregnant. With no family support, unemployed, and on welfare, she gave birth to a son, but the father, an alcoholic, took no responsibility for the child. She had two daughters from her previous marriage, and in the three years prior to giving birth, there had been three suicides in her family, including her mother, plus the unexpected death of her father. On the morning she killed her son by slitting his throat, she was suffering paranoid delusions. She imagined that people were following her, hiding in her home, and were going to kill her and her son. She writes in a letter to the Pen-Pal Network:

> I had been experiencing people following me for months, traveling behind me in cars, hiding in the closets of my home, peaking through the curtains from outside my windows, and following me in grocery stores. They were going to kill us both by stabbing us with knives and scissors. I felt I had no choice but to take the life of my son and mine as well before these people entered the bedroom to kill us. I was protecting him from screaming with the pain of having that happen to him. I couldn't stand the thoughts of him crying. Not because the sound of his crying bothered me, but because I loved him so much, it hurt me when he cried.

In a classic case of what psychiatrists define as "altruistic suicide" because her motivation for killing her son was to protect him from greater harm (Resnick 1969), she then attempted suicide by cutting her own throat and setting fire to her house to speed up her own death. Her ten-year-old daughter came home, found her, and reported the murder to a neighbor, who called paramedics who then revived the woman. She was diagnosed as insane at the time of the crime by five psychiatrists. Tried before a judge without a jury, she was charged with aggravated murder and aggravated arson, was found not guilty on both of those counts but guilty of murder, and sentenced to fifteen years to life. She was a model prisoner visited regularly by her two older children and grandchildren, but despite several appeals, served twenty years and was released at the age of sixty-one. Her time was reduced by four years largely as a result of appeals to the Adult Parole Authority of the State of Ohio by legal and psychiatric experts and researchers affiliated with Postpartum Support International and the Pen-Pal Network.

Medical, sociological, and psychological research describes the strong stigma attached to postpartum psychiatric illness (McIntosh 1993; Dennis and Chung-Lee 2006). Major newspapers wrote more than one story about half of the fourteen women who responded to our survey, and two of the cases received enormous attention, generating hundreds of articles in the national media and feature stories and covers of *Time* and *Newsweek* magazines. The case that received the widest media coverage during this period was that of Andrea Yates, who drowned her five young children in a bathtub, was convicted of first-degree murder in 2002 and sentenced to life in prison. Her conviction was later overturned on appeal. A Texas jury then ruled Yates not guilty by reason of insanity, and she was committed to a high-security mental health facility where she remains, sharing a cell with another woman who committed infanticide. Although news stories frequently make reference to mental illness, specifically postpartum depression and psychosis, the headlines and stories nevertheless depicted the women as "monsters," "baby killers," "killer moms," "evil," and "cold-blooded killers with the icy will to slaughter their children."

To kill one's own child is the antithesis of ideal motherhood. An article in *Time Magazine* describes how these women's actions defy the expectations of maternal caring, proclaiming that "when an apparently normal mother suddenly snaps and kills her newborn child, it elicits an almost primal horror."[2] Women in the network approach the media with deep misgivings because, according to one of the network coordinators, "they've all had their (negative) fair share as a result of their own personal circumstances." Participation in the Pen-Pal Network allows women the latitude of expressing the guilt, shame, and intense grief they experience as a result of their actions and to overcome their isolation by connecting with other women who have experienced a similar fate. Through supportive communication, often referred to as "a lifeline" or "life saving," the women in the network develop a sense of "we" that centers around the shared experience of postpartum mental illness that led to what they typically refer to as the "loss" of their children, their negative portrayal in the media, and the injustices they believe they have suffered in the courts and criminal justice system.

Both the survey data and women's individual letters to the coordinator of the Pen-Pal Network reveal that, despite the fact that they are behind prison walls, participation in the network allows women to forge strong bonds of friendship and solidarity with women who are, as one woman put it, in "similar situations, so little explanation is required." Women's correspondence frequently refers to the "abuse" they have suffered in the media, the legal system, and in prison, and the Pen-Pal Network uses a variety of tactics to build solidarity among women in prisons, including writing encouraging notes to each other and the use of expressions such as "stay strong," and "keep your head up." One woman who tried unsuccessfully to kill her son and was charged with attempted murder explained that the women in the Pen-Pal Network are "all an extension of my immediate family … I feel that I am not alone with what I go through and feel." When another woman serving a life sentence for killing her child first received an information packet and letter of support from PSI, she wrote, "I got your card tonight and about cried. I have been praying for someone like you and your organization to come along. It is so good to know that I am not alone."

Women's correspondence is sprinkled with expressions of love, concern, and compassion, which allows participants to create a sense of community built on shared affection with other women who have undergone the same experience (Rupp and Taylor 1987; Taylor and Rupp 2002). At the end of 2001, a woman serving time wrote to the network members, "I want to wish my fellow Pen-Pal Network ladies the merriest of holidays and always remember that 'you are not alone! And to my PSI family—I love you and thank you for all you do for everyone." Most of the women express the view that only someone who experienced postpartum psychosis and killed a child can truly understand what they have experienced. Women who form a connection with other women serving prison sentences for committing infanticide express mistrust and fear about discussing their crimes with other prisoners because, as one member of the Pen-Pal Network explained, "so many of them talk about what they hear or read and it's hard to learn to trust." In some prisons women serving sentences for infanticide are referred to by other inmates as "baby killers."[3] A line of demarcation is even drawn between the network and family members: One woman explains:

> I know how special and precious my family is, but they don't understand what I am going through. They think they do, but they don't. They can't. No one can.... When I said no one could understand I was wrong. Support groups understand. The women in the Network of Pen Pals understand. My true healing began when I was put in contact with these women.

The solidarity that forms between women who are bound mainly through written correspondence is evident in the letter of one woman who wrote to the network describing her sadness when Susan Hickman, one of the leading experts on the relationship between postpartum illness and infanticide, died in 1998. She writes:

> My heart is saddened and I cried yesterday morning when I read of her passing. I feel as though I know her, though I never met her, though I met her through the information I was given on PPD/P as one of the articles was all about her. I was able to relate to her and all the others I read about. I feel a bond with each and every one of them.

Working collectively with others allows women who have been defined by the state as deserving of punishment for the crime of infanticide not only to express emotions of guilt but to create narratives that suppress unwanted emotions and evoke more pleasurable emotions of love, compassion, and friendship.

Consciousness

Affect control theory (Smith-Lovin and Heise 1988; Smith-Lovin 1990; 1995) predicts that feeling bereft leads individuals to try to change the way they feel. Participation in the Pen-Pal Network provides women convicted of infanticide an opportunity to engage in emotion work to transform their discredited identities into valued ones. To do this requires not only rites of affirmation and expressions of solidarity that foster new emotions, but collective resources that allow participants to remake their identities as mothers (Schrock, Holden, and Reid 2004).

Critical to this process is the formation of group consciousness that imparts a larger significance to the collectivity. Group consciousness is constructed through the Pen-Pal Network's talk, narratives, framing processes, and emotion work, all of which provide women an opportunity to construct new narratives indicative of a more emotionally satisfying story: victimization. Two frames bind women together and generate oppositional emotions: a *medical frame* that justifies their actions on the basis of postpartum psychiatric illness, and a *legal frame* that attributes their imprisonment to an unjust judicial system.

The network's affiliation with the larger postpartum self-help movement supplies a medical frame (Snow et al. 1986; Snow and Benford 1992) for the inappropriate negative emotions—depression, guilt, shame, anxiety, and fear—experienced by a significant number of new mothers that are rarely acknowledged in dominant representations of motherhood (Taylor 1996). Women in the Pen-Pal Network receive the newsletter of PSI, which summarizes recent research and conference presentations that discuss the medical basis of postpartum psychiatric conditions and promote medical strategies for the treatment of these conditions. Since 1952, the *Diagnostic and Statistical Manual of Mental Disorders (DSM)*, the official handbook of mental illness, has excluded psychiatric illness connected to childbirth as a distinct diagnostic category. After more than a decade of campaigning by professionals and researchers affiliated with DAD and PSI, the most recent edition makes reference to postpartum onset in connection with depressive, bipolar, and brief psychotic disorders (American Psychiatric Association 2000). This condition is limited, however, because DSM-IV specifies that it has to occur within four weeks of delivery.

In their letters to the network, it is common for incarcerated women to recite statistics on the prevalence of postpartum psychiatric illnesses and to decry the lack of public awareness of the condition, as a letter from a woman who served twenty-five years for killing her son illustrates: "I wish to become a part of this organization in order to help inform society of the symptoms of this illness, so it can be recognized and treated before a tragedy occurs that causes it to have to go into the court of law." All of the women who completed the survey explained their killings using medical and psychiatric diagnostic terms, and the overwhelming majority indicated that they had no intention of killing their children, except in those cases where the act was motivated by altruistic considerations. Debra Gindorf, who killed her two children in order that they would not survive her own multiple suicide attempts, explained in a media interview: "I know it's the illness that did this, not Debra Gindorf, not their mommy."

Women's lack of agency in attributing their actions to postpartum illness is striking. When pen-pal women refer to the deaths of their children, they express intense grief, but avoid any reference to their own role in the killings, using phrases such as "the tragedy," "the consequences of PPD and PPP," "the results of this illness," and "the loss of my child to this illness." Typical is the explanation of one woman who wrote in a letter to the network: "It is possible to be so stressed, so overworked, and so overrun that it takes a toll on one's mental capacities and one comes to the state of mind I was in when this tragedy happened." That this woman understood her behavior to be the result of a medical condition is clear when she goes on to state that "it is possible that through medication and proper therapy, and a strong desire for a person to get well, this tragedy could have been prevented." Another woman wrote in a letter to the network: "I really am understanding that my son's death wasn't truly my fault, but sometimes that is a little difficult to fully accept. I have a lot of healing to do through the PPD and abuse from this tragedy."

It is important to emphasize that the women are not unwilling to accept responsibility for their actions. Just the opposite; they use repentant language, making frequent reference in their letters to "dealing with my crime" and "facing what I did." Participation in the Pen-Pal Network provides, however, a medical and scientific explanation of their actions that allows women to offload their guilt, intense grief, and shame, and to maintain their identities as mothers. Typical of the kinds of letters written by women to the network is a letter from a woman sentenced to sixty-three years in prison for killing her son; at the time she wrote she was engaged in an appeal based on postpartum psychosis: "Any and all advice you can find will benefit me greatly, both legally and therapy-wise. Your material has eased my confusion, guilt, and isolation and I thank you from the depth of my heart."

The medical frames provided by the postpartum depression self-help movement (see Taylor 1996) also allow women in the Pen-Pal Network to build a collective oppositional consciousness around their unjust treatment by the criminal justice system. The medicalization of their crimes contributes to a collective understanding that the responsibility for their children's deaths lies, in part, with the failure of society to recognize the connection between postpartum psychiatric illness and child killing. The use of an insanity defense and the standards for insanity vary widely among states in the United States (Perlin 1997). Although the cases of some women in our study have been instrumental in revising case law with respect to the insanity defense (Prejan 2006), most of the women in the Pen-Pal Network did not use an insanity defense because they did not receive a psychiatric diagnosis at the time the killing occurred, they lacked sufficient resources for a protracted legal battle, or they were unaware of the network of legal and medical experts associated with PSI whom they could all upon for advice. Even when it was later introduced in appeal, an insanity defense rarely resulted in a "not guilty" verdict. The coordinator of the Pen-Pal Network indicated that, for the most part, only women with significant financial resources had been able successfully to mount an insanity defense.

In their letters, members of the Pen-Pal Network express strong oppositional emotions over what one woman described as "how lame our medical and judicial systems are in not only handling infanticide due to post-partum mood disorders, but meeting[*sic*] out compassion towards those of us who are trying to survive the loss of both our children and our freedom." Women convicted of child killing receive differential treatment in prison. A woman serving a life sentence expressed moral outrage over this:

> I still have one child alive, I have missed the last 10 years of his life. We have an active mother's support group here (in prison), but due to my particular crime I can't have my son participate! How is this helping family unity? Also, because of my crime, I am not allowed to participate in our Dog Training Program. Makes me feel less than human, almost like a slap in the face.

Another woman wrote of her "outrage" upon reading about the life sentence handed out by the Philadelphia court system to another "helplessly sick woman," and yet another describes members of the Pen-Pal Network as having been "railroaded by the legal, judicial (system) because of a radical change in our hormones and lack of understanding given to birth."

As a measure of the emotional transformation that occurs by virtue of women's participation in the Pen-Pal Network, a woman penned a letter after watching a November 8, 2001, *Oprah Show* on which Deborah Sichel, a member of PSI, appeared in support of Andrea Yates' insanity defense. She writes: "I am truly 'revived.' Today is the first time that I didn't get 'depressed' on the anniversary (11-11-1995) of M____'s death." Responding to another women's recent life sentence for killing her child, a member of the Pen-Pal Network wrote:

> I truly feel that sexism in the justice system has been demonstrated in this case. Postpartum psychosis is a woman's issue and women must stand united about it to open men's eyes. Wouldn't it be different if men suffered from such a diagnosable illness?

That these women are "doing the time" instead of "letting the time do you," as the expression goes among prisoners, is fairly evident: she ends her letter with the P.S. "Please inform me if I can help make a change for the better!" These expressions of oppositional emotions are encouraged by participation in the Pen-Pal Network. The politicized emotions of the Pen-Pal Network emerge, in part, from its roots in the women's movement and the strong feminist influence that legitimizes the expression of anger and criticism of male-dominated institutions (Taylor 1996).

Negotiation

Remaking the self through the redefinition of the self, the strategic use of identity, and the public deployment of emotion are the core of self-help. Scholars of social movements view collective identity as an interactional accomplishment that is the product of negotiations between participants in social movement networks and organizations and relationships with a movement's allies, opponents, and bystanders, including the media (Gamson 1992b; Gamson 1995; Whittier 1995; Melucci 1996; Snow 2001; Hunt and Benford 2004). As Bernstein (1997) has argued, identity-oriented movements achieve change through two types of identity work: *identity for education* that challenges the dominant culture's perception of the group, and *identity for critique* that challenges the values, identity categories, and practices of the dominant culture.

Previous work by scholars such as Whittier (forthcoming; 2001), Kemper (2001), Dugan (2005), and Dunn (2004) demonstrates that social movement participants often use emotions strategically in their attempts to resist negative definitions imposed by the larger society and to generate the sympathy of bystanders and authorities. In her research on the child sexual abuse movement, Whittier (2001) found that activists display different emotions and engage in different kinds of emotion work in internal movement contexts than they do when they are dealing with external targets, such as the media, medical and legal institutions, and the state because of variations in what she conceptualizes as the emotional opportunity structure.

Thus far, we have focused on the emotional expressions and strategies used by members of the Pen-Pal Network within the context of the movement where participants are encouraged to express both emotions of guilt, shame, and loss, and emotions of resistance, such as moral outrage, righteous indication, and love, that promote solidarity and healing. In keeping with the movement's emphasis on the deployment of identity to educate others about postpartum conditions, when members of the Pen-Pal Network make public appearances in the media, or allow their stories to be told in criminal cases, public conferences, movement publications, and in connection with the enactment of legislation, they avoid emotional displays that might evoke opposition. The Pen-Pal Network steers them toward a simple retelling of their story, which frames their actions in terms of maternal grief and loss and psychiatric illness rather than providing a complex account of the legal and social injustices they have encountered, their failure to receive adequate treatment by the medical establishment, and their resulting anger and moral outrage.

During the early stages of the movement, between 1986 and 1990, women who committed infanticide and/or their husbands, along with medical professionals and activists affiliated with the postpartum support movement, made thirty-four appearances on nationally syndicated television programs and news broadcasts including the *CBS Morning Show, Good Morning America*, the *Today Show*, 20/20, *Hour Magazine, Larry King Live*, and the *CBS Evening News*, as well as on local and national talk shows including *Geraldo, Phil Donahue Show, Joan Rivers Show, Morton Downey Jr. Show*, and *Salley Jessy Raphael*.

One woman who made dozens of media appearances was Angela Thompson, a registered nurse, who typically appeared with her husband Jeff, a police officer.

Angela was charged with first-degree murder for killing their son, Michael, but was acquitted by reason of insanity. Believing Michael the devil and her husband Christ (a common delusion), she drowned her baby, meticulously wrapped him in a blanket, placed him in a box, and buried him in the garden with mothballs (which she believed to be Rosary beads) around his grave to "expunge the world of the devil." Angela was treated for one month in a psychiatric hospital and spent four months out on bail awaiting the results of the trial. In none of her public appearances did she deploy oppositional emotions by expressing anger or moral outrage at the medical and legal systems. Rather, hers and other women's emotional displays when they told their stories were structured by what Whittier (2001) terms the emotional opportunities of the context. The societal stigma surrounding infanticide is not conducive to the expression of oppositional emotions, such as anger and indignation. The following statement by Angela Thompson from a January 22, 1991, *Oprah Winfrey Show* titled "Baby Killers" illustrates this:

> As a mother you can only imagine the tremendous guilt and grief I felt when I woke up from the delusions. I remember pounding my fists on the wall in disbelief screaming, "my son, my son, how could I have done this?" I couldn't understand how someone like me who always wanted to have children, to rear children, could do something like this.

More recently, three members of the Pen-Pal Network—Paula Sims, Debra Gindorf, and Tammy Eveans—serving no-parole life sentences in the Dwight Correctional Center spoke out about their grief. Although they admit that telling their stories might spark more hatred than pity because the public may think they are using "postpartum psychosis as a convenient excuse for their crimes," all three women indicate that they poisoned, drowned, or smothered their children not because they did not love or want them, but because "they were victims, too—of postpartum psychosis, the rarest and most severe form of postpartum mental illness." Paula Sims admits, "I don't expect people to forgive me. I haven't forgiven myself, but I'm being punished for being mentally ill." Like so many women in the Pen-Pal Network, these women still embrace their identities as mothers. Tammy Eveans suffered postpartum psychosis after the birth of all three children, suffocating two as infants and her oldest as a three year old: "There's not a day that goes by that I don't think about my kids," she says. "If I ever get out of here, the first place I'd want to go is the cemetery." She adds that if she doesn't get out of prison, "I know I'll see them again someday. And the first thing I'll tell them: 'I love you.'"[4] Both the print and electronic media continue to report sensational cases of infanticide related to postpartum illness, and recently two celebrities, Brooke Shields and Marie Osmond, have spearheaded the movement's public-awareness campaign by publishing books on their personal experiences with postpartum depression.[5]

Despite being incarcerated, members of the Pen-Pal Network are able to engage in a variety of tactics to bring about change. They form support groups in prison that both educate pregnant women about postpartum illness and allow at least some women who have committed infanticide to form a collective identity inside prison walls. They frequently write letters to members of Congress and elected state officials. For example, one woman's letter to the network makes reference to writing President Clinton urging him to promote legislation to prevent the deaths of future children. Characterizing postpartum psychosis and postpartum depression as "a national health issue," she goes onto say that when she reached out for help before she killed her child, the "doctors did nothing to help me except make fun of me and send me home." The women urge PSI to initiate advocacy projects, such as the "Free Deborah Gindorf Campaign," that petitioned judicial bodies for parole and governors for clemency for women prosecuted for postpartum infanticide. In May 2009, this long-running Pen-Pal Network campaign succeeded when Illinois Governor Pat Quinn commuted Gindorf's life-sentence, and she was paroled after serving twenty-four years in prison. Members of the Pen-Pal Network also provide advice to women and their attorneys about how to draft appeals, clemency petitions, and parole paperwork. Women even engage in high-risk activism with respect to their own legal trials in order to raise awareness about postpartum illness. Recently, one member of the network went forward with a trial because she wanted to publicize postpartum psychiatric illness, in spite of her lawyer's strong objection that the state where she resides does not recognize postpartum psychiatric illness as grounds for an insanity defense and that the publicity would likely lead to a longer sentence. The judge determined that this woman's decision to use her trial as a social movement tactic was itself an indication of insanity and committed her to a state mental institution.

The public-awareness campaign to frame and reframe child killing as linked to postpartum psychiatric illness has done more to stimulate the growth of the postpartum support group movement than perhaps any other tactic, and postpartum-related infanticide also has been at the forefront of PSI's lobbying for legislative and legal changes for the prevention and treatment of postpartum illness. With the support of a Democratic senator from New Jersey inspired by the first lady of New Jersey's personal battle with postpartum depression, PSI is lobbying for U.S. Senate passage of "The Mom's Opportunity to Access, Help, Education, Research, and Support for Postpartum Depression (MOTHERS) Act" (S. 324). The House version of this bill (H.R. 20), which passed in March 2009, was first introduced in 2003 as the "Melanie Stokes Postpartum Depression Research and Care Act." It was named after a pharmaceutical sales manager married to a physician in the Chicago area who committed suicide after the birth of her child. Both bills would expand research funding for postpartum psychiatric illness, increase public awareness, and assure psychiatric screenings for new mothers. In at least five states (New Jersey, California, New York, Texas, and Washington), PSI has successfully lobbied for legislation that increases awareness of postpartum illness among the general public, the medical community, and/or correctional officers. In at least two of these states, California and Texas, the legislation was the direct result of high-profile infanticides. In California the heightened awareness of postpartum psychosis resulting from Angela Thompson's infanticide case resulted in legislation, and the Texas law is named the Andrea Pia Yates Bill to commemorate one of the highest profile cases of multiple infanticides in American history.

Through their participation in the PSI Pen-Pal Network, women who have committed infanticide reconstruct their own identities while strategically deploying identity for education and critique to challenge public policy, medical and judicial practices, and cultural definitions and meanings of motherhood by bringing to light the serious emotional problems experienced by some new mothers. The medical frame, solidarity, and emotional transformation that result from the collective identity constructed by the Pen-Pal Network provide an alternative space where women can reclaim the idea that they are good mothers. Many of the pen-pal women work for change in the name of their children. The explanation of one woman's motivation for participating in postpartum awareness campaigns is typical: "I hope to be able to bring something good out of this for children, in memory of my son, John." In a later letter, she elaborates: "The more society is informed of this illness, the less chance of this happening to another infant. My son's life will be meaningful through the process of educating others and saving the lives of other infants." In their narratives, women redefine themselves as "good mothers," not only to the children they still have, but to the ones they once had.

When members of the network heard about Andrea Yates' drowning her five children, many wrote her to provide support. They also reach out to women in their own prisons, urging them to join the network. One woman who heard about another prisoner who had committed infanticide on her cell block wrote:

> There are probably many more like her here that are too afraid to be known. Oh, if they could only realize they are *not* bad people—that they were mentally ill—*not* criminals. I can never forget where I came from. Thus I have a greater love for people and a deeper compassion for women who *have walked* in these same shoes (her emphasis).

Conclusions

Since the 1980s, we have witnessed in the United States the surge of powerful expressions of collective identity in the form of self-help movements that make contradictory claims. They challenge the wide-ranging forms of control used by institutions of the therapeutic state at the same time that they co-opt therapeutic discourse to obtain access to the benefits and services of medical institutions (Polsky 1991; Giddens 1991). The Pen-Pal Network we describe here is typical of the self-help repertoire of collective action that emerged in the historical moment of the 1980s, which saw the dismantling of the U.S. social welfare state engineered in the wake of the New Deal, the expansion of the medical system, and the professionalization of grassroots self-help movements that spun off from the feminist, civil rights, ethnic, and gay and lesbian movements of the sixties. It is remarkable that this form of collective action has received so little attention from scholars of social movements. Self-help movements share the fundamental features scholars associate with a social movement—solidarity, temporal continuity, strategic action, the use of noninstitutionalized tactics, and the quest for social change.

In the introduction to this paper, we attribute the neglect of research on self-help movements, in part, to the state-centered bias of the political process and contentious politics approaches to social movements. In modern societies, culture and identity play a central role in power and resistance. To ignore self-help and medical movements that both appropriate and challenge therapeutic discourse and practice to define collective identity would be to overlook a considerable amount of collective action that has been a significant force for change in U.S society. Some scholars may take issue with the fact that we define the Pen-Pal Network as a social movement because of its relatively small size. Although size is one of the ways social movements signal support for their claims, we agree with scholars such as Melucci (1996), Castells (1997), and Goldfarb (2006) who have argued that the submerged networks of civil society where solidarity, resistance, and change is hatched slowly outside the nests of power should be as interesting to scholars of social movements as the mass-based movements that preoccupied researchers in the 1970s and 1980s.

The existing body of theorizing and research on social movements has a great deal to offer scholars interested in self-help and medical movements. It is our view, however, that these movements may require students of social movements to rethink some of the assumptions underlying general social movement theories about the size, targets, organization, tactical repertoires, and outcomes of social movements that rely on the politics of recognition and visibility (Bernstein 1997; Fraser 1997; Whittier 2007). In this paper, for example, we illustrate how the study of self-help and medical movements can contribute to theoretical advances in understanding the role that emotion plays in collective identity construction in social movements. Starting with the premise that empathy and support are fundamental to the self-help repertoire led us to theorize the significance of emotions for the construction of collective identity and social movement tactics. The field of social movements only recently has acknowledged the centrality of emotions to social protest and political contention, and studies of self-help movements have been at the forefront in nudging the field in this direction (Taylor 1995a; Taylor 1996; Gould 2001; Whittier 2001).

Emotions are an integral part of the personal and collective identities associated not only with self-help, support, and health advocacy groups, but all social movements (Melucci 1995). Our research demonstrates that the emotional transformation associated with participation in self-help movements and the public sympathy generated by the emotion work of self-help activists in the reconstruction of stigmatized identities and their collective representation are key to understanding the politicization of self-help. While several scholars have called for the reincorporation of emotions into the study of social movements, much of this work fails to draw adequately on the body of theory and research by scholars interested in the structural, cultural, and interactional processes that give rise to emotions and their expression. This paper seeks to bring about a greater synthesis of these two fields of sociology by combining affect control theory, which is concerned with individual's experience, expression, and management of emotions, with collective identity theory that accentuates the collective processes involved in the formation and collective representation of a movement identity.

NOTES

1. Debate about whether collective actors are able to construct collective identity without face-to-face communication has centered primarily on internet organizing and online chat groups. Although some researchers have argued that online participation does not contribute to the construction of collective identity (Ayers 2003; Allee 2007), a growing body of research has found that the internet facilitates the maintenance of an existing collective identity and that the internet can also be an especially useful tool for identity construction within geographically disparate (Drentea and Moren-Cross 2005) and marginalized groups such as transgender people (Broad 2002; Shapiro 2004) and white power activists (Dobratz 2001; Futrell and Simi

2004). Similarly, Rupp (1997) has shown that letters were important to the maintenance of collective identity in women's groups that were unable to meet face-to-face, such as international women's organizations between the two world wars.

2. Anastasia Toufexis, "Why Mothers Kill Their Babies: Severe Distress Affects Some Women in the Months after Giving Birth," *Time Magazine*, June 20, 1988, 81, 83 (quotation on 81).

3. Lori Rackl, "'It's the Illness that Did This...Not Their Mommy': Illinois Women Locked up for Killing Kids Hope Change in Attitude on Postpartum Depression Could Free Them," *Chicago Sun Times*, July 27, 2006, 22.

4. All of the quotations in this paragraph come from Rackl (2006).

5. Brooke Shields, *Down Came the Rain: My Journey Through Postpartum Depression* (New York: Hyperion, 2005); Marie Osmond with Marcia Wilke and Judith Moore, *Behind the Smile: My Journey Out of Postpartum Depression* (New York: Warner Books, 2001).

17

Framing Hazards in the Health Arena

The Cases of Obesity, Work-Related Illnesses, and Human Egg Donation

David A. Snow and Roberta G. Lessor

The resolution of health-related problems is almost always, short of raw-boned coercion or appeals to divine intervention, contingent on some joint, cooperative action involving at least two or more individuals working together to deal with the designated problem. It may be preventative, in the case of an individual receiving Hepatitis A or B shots before traveling to certain parts of the world, or it may be corrective, in the case of an individual securing a prescription of some variant of Cipro for diarrhea or a urinary tract infection. In both instances, the problem-resolution effort involves people working cooperatively—a physician, nurse, and patient in the first case, and a physician, druggist, and patient in the second. Such cooperative action is contingent on a number of factors, not the least of which is a shared understanding of what the issue or problem is and agreement as to what should be done to remedy it. In other words, in the language of the framing perspective associated with the study of social movements, such joint action requires, among other things, shared diagnostic and prognostic frames, or the willingness of some actors to accede to the framings of other actors because of their presumed expertise or authority, and sufficient motivation for all actors to act in concert. We would argue that shared frames, or what has been called frame alignment, is a necessary condition for dealing with health-related issues and problems institutionally, nationally, and globally. But achieving such frame alignment and acting accordingly are no small tasks, as they are often the shoals upon which medical and health care initiatives and interventions become stuck and falter. Consider, for example, the Surgeon General's ongoing efforts to curtail smoking by highlighting how it "increases the risk of lung cancer" in contrast to the cigarette industry's framing smoking as "pleasurable."

In this paper, we begin to explore conceptually and empirically various framing problems, which we conceptualize as framing hazards that encumber the efforts of medical practitioners, the health care system and other health-oriented stakeholders to deal with various health problems and issues. We identify four framing hazards—ambiguous events or ailments, framing errors or misframings, frame disputes, and frame shifts—and then examine how they have operated in relation to three quite different health issues: the so-called obesity epidemic, work-related illnesses, and human egg and gamete transfer in infertility. We then assess the implications of our analysis of framing hazards for mobilization efforts to prevent or remedy health problems. Toward this end, we begin with a brief overview of framing theory and an elaborated conceptualization of what we mean by frame hazards.

Framing, Frames, Frame Hazards

Grounded in the interactionist and constructionist principle that meanings do not naturally or automatically attach themselves to the objects, events, or experiences we encounter, but arise, instead, through interpretive processes, the concept of frame designates interpretative structures that render events and occurrences subjectively meaningful, and thereby function to organize experience and guide action. Within sociology, the concept is derived primarily from the work of Erving Goffman (1974), which is beholden in part to the earlier work of Gregory Bateson (1973). For these scholars, as well as others who use the concept analytically, frames provide answers to such questions as: What is going on here? What is being said? What does this mean? And I how should act or respond?

Frames do this interpretive work by performing three core functions. First, like picture frames, they *focus attention* by punctuating or bracketing what in our sensual field is relevant and what is irrelevant, what is "in-frame" and what is "out-of-frame," in relation to the object of orientation. Second, they function as *articulation mechanisms* in the sense of tying together the various punctuated elements of the scene so that one set of meanings rather than another is conveyed, or, in the language of narrativity, one story rather than another is told. And third, frames often perform a *transformative function* by reconstituting the way in which some objects of attention are seen or understood as relating to each other or to the actor. Examples of this transformative function abound, not only in the context of social movements as in the transformation of routine grievances or misfortunes into injustices or mobilizing grievances, but also in relation to health and medicine as in the deeroticization of the sexual in the physician's office, the reconfiguration of aspects of one's biography as commonly occurs in health-related self-help groups like Alcoholics Anonymous and Weight Watchers, and when patients diagnosed with a chronic illness such as cancer reassess their biographies in an attempt to identify what in their pasts might have rendered them vulnerable to this dreaded disease. Given the focusing, articulation, and transformative functions of frames, it is arguable that how we see, what we make of, and how we act toward the various objects of orientation that populate our daily lives depends, in no small part, on how they are framed.

The analysis of frames and associated processes has been conducted in relation to various activities and social categories (e.g., advertising, face-to-face interaction, gender, talk) in a variety of domains of social life (e.g., culture, organizations, politics, public policy). To date, however, the most systematic application and development of frame analysis within sociology can be found in the substantive study of collective action and social movements.[1]

Used in the context of social movements, the idea of framing problematizes the meanings associated with relevant events, activities, places, and actors, suggesting that those meanings are typically contestable and negotiable and thus open to debate and differential interpretation. Framing, in relation to social movements, thus refers to the signifying work or meaning construction engaged in by movement adherents (e.g., leaders, activists, and rank-and-file participants) and other actors (e.g., adversaries, institutional elites, media, and countermovements) relevant to the interests of movements and the challenges they mount in pursuit of those interests.

Various sets of actors are typically involved in social movement framing processes. It can be argued that framing in this context can best be understood as embedded in a discursive field in the sense that the framing occurs in relation to other sets of actors (e.g., targeted authorities, social control agents, countermovements, media, bystanders) discussing and debating the issue. Discursive fields are thus constituted by various sets of actors interested in the event or issue being discussed and who may be differently positioned organizationally and hierarchically, and thus in terms of where they stand in relation to the events or issues.[2] Furthermore, discursive fields can vary in terms of the extent to which they are emergent or highly structured or organized, and the extent to which they are consensual or contested. For example, the discursive field that surfaced in relation to the French riots that occurred in the fall of 2005 was emergent and contested, whereas the discursive field associated with the Iraq war is contested but quite organized. Within these fields, the various frames arise and change through interactive, recursive processes.

As our point of departure, we assume that framing in the context of health and medicine shares many of the characteristics of framing in the context of social movements and related collective action. Not only is framing in relation to health embedded in discursive fields involving numerous actors, but those fields are often contested ones. Additionally, framing in the context of health, just as in social movements, is often encumbered by various framing problems that we call hazards. Such framing hazards or vulnerabilities threaten the prospect of frame alignment—that is, the linkage or conjunction of individual and organizational/institutional interpretative frames (Snow et al. 1986). Inasmuch as concerted problem-solving is contingent, in part, on interpretive alignment regarding the diagnosis and prognosis of some problem, then framing hazards constitute impediments to concerted collective action, whether that action is associated with advancing the claims and interests of a social movement or health policy initiatives.

There are numerous hazards or vulnerabilities that can encumber framing efforts, and thus the prospect of preventative or corrective joint action. Expanding on the work of Goffman (1974), we discuss four such framing hazards: ambiguous events and/or ailments; framing errors or misframings; frame disputes; and frame shifts.

Ambiguous Events and/or Ailments

The first hazard is an *ambiguous event* or *happening* or *ailment* that does not fit neatly into or under the interpretive canopy of an existing frame. Goffman suggested that there are two kinds of ambiguity: "one, where there is question as to what could possibly be going on; the other as to which one of the two or more clearly defined possible things is going on" (1974: 302–3). The "difference," as he puts it, is "between vagueness and uncertainty" (1974: 303). Both kinds of ambiguity are omnipresent in medicine, especially in the case of diagnostic puzzlements of the kind chronicled over the past several years in the *New York Times Magazine* (see, for example, Sanders 2006).

Framing Errors or "Misframings"

A second set of hazards is comprised of various *framing errors* or *misframings*. One subset, which Goffman accents, is based on erroneous beliefs "as to how events at hand are to be framed. Instead of merely stopping short to try to figure out what is happening, the individual actually lodges himself in certitude and/or action on the basis of wrong premises" (Goffman 1974: 308). Examples of this kind of misframing abound. Consider, for example, the case of puerperal sepsis, or "child-bed fever," the contagious disease that killed significant percentages of women in English hospitals in the early nineteenth century. In 1843, Oliver Wendell Holmes saw that the women delivered outside of hospitals by midwives did not become septic yet those delivered by physicians became septic and died. When he suggested that perhaps the dreaded condition was caused by the unwashed hands of physicians, his ideas were met with derision by obstetricians of the time. Or consider the way in which pellagra, a disease of malnutrition, was dealt with in the early 1900s. In 1912, a Pellagra Commission was formed to search for the cause and cure of the disease. A prominent member of the committee—C. B. Davenport—was convinced the disease was hereditary because it was found exclusively among the very poor and was common in prisons and mental asylums. In 1914, however, malnutrition was found to be the actual cause of the disease, but in the Pellagra Commission's final report, issued in 1917, the disease was still explained as a hereditary one that infected people of presumably inferior breeding stock. Moreover, the Commission's verdict was accepted for the next two decades and by 1929 the disease was responsible for some six thousand deaths annually. This was a colossal misframing that was not jettisoned until after the Depression, when the fact that many previously self-sufficient people became malnourished prompted the government to change its diagnostic framing of the cause of pellagra.

In addition to such misframings prompted by the persistence of erroneous beliefs, there is another set of framing errors that result not so much from misguided beliefs as from mistakes that undermine the prospect of frame resonance—that is, the correspondence between or alignment of proffered frames and those of the constituents or targets of the framing efforts.[3] Such framing vulnerabilities indicate that affecting resonance is a precarious enterprise and ongoing challenge, whatever the context.

Frame Disputes

A third set of framing hazards are constituted by what Goffman called "frame disputes." Goffman notes that in many situations

> An appreciable period can elapse when there is no immediate potential agreement, when, in fact, there is no way in theory to bring everyone involved into the same frame. Under these circumstances one can expect that the parties with opposing versions of events may openly dispute with each other over how to define what has been happening. A frame dispute results. (1974: 322)

Within the context of social movements, such disputes have been examined primarily in terms of intramovement disagreements—that is, as disputes among various actors within social movement organizations (SMOs) and social movement industries (McCarthy and Zald 1977). Because movement frame disputes can arise in relation to problem diagnosis and prognosis and the challenges of participant motivation and frame resonance, it is reasonable to assume that frame disputes are ubiquitous within social movements (Benford 1993). The same also holds, we would argue, within the health and medical arena. Additionally, just as movement frame disputes have been found to have both detrimental and facilitative effects with respect to movement interests and goals (Benford 1993; Haines 1996; Jessup 1997), we would expect frame disputes within health and medicine to have both detrimental effects, as when problem resolution is delayed because of unnecessary disagreements, and facilitative effects, as when debate spurs further, productive research.

Frame Shifts

A fourth type of framing hazard is what we call *frame shifts*. By frame shifts, we have in mind a displacement of one frame by another. It is not a transformation of an existing frame but the ascendance of a different one due to a change in the grounds on which the displaced frame was based. In the study of social movements, such frame shifts or displacements are typically preceded by new, often unanticipated, events or the confluence of a number of events (see Ellingson 1995; Noonan 1995; Rothman and Oliver 1999). We suspect frame shifts are prevalent in the various institutional domains of social life, but we would hypothesize that vulnerability of dominant frames in different institutional sectors to displacement is partly contingent on the extent to which the framings are empirically based and thus falsifiable. In institutional sectors in which the empirical grounding of dominant framings is not so relevant, as with religion, we would expect relatively few frame shifts. Instead, we find historically a plethora of rancorous frame disputes that often lead to sectarian factionalization. In contrast, in institutional domains wherein systematically derived empirical evidence and the principle of falsifiablility are the coins of the realm and thus the referential basis for frame claims, as in science, we would expect more frequent frame shifts. Given that health and medical initiatives rest in no small part on scientific inquiry, we would also expect frequent frame shifts within this institutional arena.

In the reminder of the paper, we examine and elaborate these framing hazards in relation to obesity, work-related illness, and egg donation in the treatment of infertility.

Obesity, Frame Disputes, Ambiguity, and Misalignment

At first glance, the problem of obesity in the United States would not appear to be one that would stimulate frame disputes. After all, do not the epidemiological/CDC statistics suggest overwhelmingly that America is confronted with an "obesity epidemic?"[4] Consider, for example, the following summary statement of statistical trends on obesity in the United States:

> In 1991, only four states had obesity prevalence rates above 15%. Today, 20 states have rates of 15–19 percent; 29 states have rates of 20–24 percent; and one state reports a rate of more than 25 percent. Indeed, in our contemporary culture, nearly two out of three adults are either overweight or obese. Among adolescents, the prevalence of overweight has nearly doubled over the last two decades.

The framing of the obesity problem as a crisis was constructed by staff of the Academy for Educational Development in Washington, D.C., working in conjunction with the CDC, for a report, titled "Overview of the Obesity Epidemic," for a one-day workshop in July 2006 exploring the application of social movement theory to overweight and obesity prevention in the United States. The purpose of the workshop was "to create a process for identifying and positively directing a social movement toward ... ultimately reducing overweight and obesity among all age groups in the United States" (Academy for Educational Development 2006). Why the need for such a social movement? Because, to paraphrase a CDC official helping to lead the workshop, the science behind the epidemic and the relevant facts are understood, but we do not seem to be very good at controlling and reducing the problem, which, according to the lead sentence of the overview report, is unquestionably of epidemic proportions (Academy for Education Development and CDC 2006: 1).

There are, we think, at least two frame-related problems encumbering the effort to control the growing overweight and obesity problem: one is associated with frame disputes; the other entails various misframings that generate ambiguity and pit scientific frames against identity-group frames. Turning first to the frame disputes, a number of research scholars from different disciplines have argued in a series of papers that "the so-called obesity epidemic (is) a highly contested scientific and social fact" (Saguy and Riley 2005: 869, Saguy and Almeling 2005; Campos et al. 2005).[5] They base that contention on the observation that there are at least three strikingly different framings of obesity, each of which frames fatness differently and attributes it to different causes, and each of which is associated with one or more sets of actors. One frame is dubbed "the antiobesity frame" or the "obesity as risky behavior frame." From the vantage point of this frame, which is the dominant one in the United States, obesity or fatness is seen as a serious and escalating illness, one of epidemic proportions, but an illness and health risk that is preventable if only people would change their unhealthy lifestyles by making healthy food choices and engaging more regularly in exercise. Here attention is focused on the illnesses presumably linked to obesity, such as cardiovascular disease, diabetes, and cancer, and the role of the victim—the fat person that is—as a causal agent in the process.

Somewhat different than the illness/risky behavior frame is the more recent "disease frame," which views obesity, or the tendency toward it, as a heritable genetic or hormonal disposition. Here the attributional locus of the diagnostic frame shifts from the individual to forces or factors beyond the individual's control, thus exempting those burdened with excessive weight from personal responsibility.

Standing in sharp contrast to the obesity as risky behavior frame is the "fat acceptance" or "fatness as body diversity frame." For the proponents of this frame, fatness is seen as a form of diversity and a core identity not unlike race, gender, disability, and sexual orientation. And this is especially so for proponents of this frame that subscribe to the disease frame's attributional focus on genetics. Thus for those who frame fatness as a form of diversity, "diversity training, greater social tolerance, and less discrimination on the basis of size are needed" (Saguy and Riley 2005: 873).

We do not take sides here. Rather, we want to suggest that when the same issue or behavioral phenomenon is not only subject to differential framing, but two or more of the competing frames posit strikingly different assessments of the issue or behavior, the prospect of effectively dealing with the problem diminishes considerably. Moreover, in the case of obesity, we suspect that the various sets of actors within the obesity discursive field is greater than the four sets that Saguy and Riley (2005) identify—anti-obesity researchers, anti-obesity activists, fat-acceptance researchers, and fat-acceptance activists. Certainly another set of actors within the field is the loosely coupled set of critics that target the fast food industry, such as Eric Schlosser and his *Fast Food Nation* (2001) and Morgan Spurlock and his "Super-Size Me" documentary. While these authors might be construed as anti-obesity activists, they step outside of the illness/risky behavior frame by targeting the fast food industry as the source of blame. And, not surprisingly, such targeting invites executives and proprietors within the fast food industry into the fray in order to defend themselves and redirect causal attention back to the fat individuals themselves.

Table 17.1 summarizes the key actors in the obesity discursive field and highlights the bases for the disputes. We could go on and describe these sets of actors more fully, but the analytic point should be clear: a crowded and contentious discursive field reduces the likelihood of frame alignment, thus reducing the prospect of dealing effectively with the designated problem or issue.

A second framing hazard flows from this increasingly congested and contested discursive field: ambiguity of the kind when faced with two or more plausible alternatives. When confronted with such ambiguity, it is easy to be overcome by a sense of puzzlement as to what to do. And this uncertainty today is fed by the seemingly endless reports of new and often contradictory findings regarding the do's and don'ts of eating, diet, and weight control.[6] Because of the frame disputes within the obesity discursive field, and the flow of often-conflicting reports and directives from the medical institution, there is also the risk of misaligning or mistargeting the diagnostic, prognostic, and motivational frames. For example, framings that are resonant with teenagers are less likely to be equally resonant with their parents, and vice versa. Similarly, we might expect that other sets of relevant actors, such as community

Table 17.1. Frame Disputes in Obesity Field

	Illness Frame	Disease Frame	Acceptance Frame	Fast Food Frame
Diagnostic Frame				
• Problem	Life Styles and Eating Habits	Disease	Stigmatization of Fatness	Too Many Fast Food Choices
• Attribution	Individual/Victims	Genetics or Body Chemistry	Medicine, Media, Film Industry	Fast Food Industry and Advertizing
Prognostic Frame	Change in Individual Behavior	Gastric Bypass	Tolerance, Diversity Training	More Healthy Food Choices

elites, are likely to require even somewhat different framings. The point is that the obesity field is a crowded one, and that doing something about the issue is contingent not only on relatively consensual scientific framings of the problem, but ongoing consideration of the degree of resonance between audience targets and the various framings. To do otherwise is to guarantee that the framing efforts will fall on deaf ears, which appears to have already happened for many citizens.

Frame Disputes and Misframing in Relation to Work-Related Ailments of Flight Attendants

To further illustrate the relevance of the concept of framing hazards to understanding health-related issues, we explore frame disputes and misframing in the case of flight attendants and focus on the process through which they became disputants, coming to frame their health problems as work related. And, in doing so, we identify a number of conditions that are presumably necessary in order for clusters of individuals within a discursive field to find their voice and develop an oppositional or counter frame. Here, rather than focusing on how frame disputes may retard the process through which a serious problem comes to be addressed and resolved, we focus on how frame disputes can arise that neutralize erroneous misframings.

The career development of women flight attendants and the related process of their coming to recognize work-related health problems is an excellent illustration of frame disputes and misframing in occupational health. In the mid-1950s, most "stewardesses," as they were then called, became unionized. However, in exchange for unionization, airline companies imposed work rules that forced retirement when women married or became thirty-two years old, conditions of work that continued until they were challenged in court in 1968 (Lessor 1984b). In a short-term job, flight attendants paid comparatively little attention to the connection between the conditions of their work and the various ailments they experienced. There were no challenges to the frame held by the airline companies that viewed any emergent health problems as due to the predominantly female constitution of the work force. Airline company doctors framed the health issues observed in cabin attendants ("stewardesses") as a result of the individual's constitution, or even as typical of the young "neurasthenic" female (McFarland 1953). By the end of the 1970s, however, a short-term job had become for many a long-term career, and unionized flight attendants were now framing health problems they experienced on the job as work related. They compiled their own statistics on bladder and upper respiratory infections, back and foot troubles, menstrual irregularities and other gynecologic symptoms, and on spontaneous abortion, sleep disturbances, and depression, problems that were widely acknowledged among women cabin attendants (Lessor 1984a). The company's earlier individualistic or "neurasthenic female" frame, which flight attendant union activists would come to see as a form of erroneous misframing and thus "blaming the victim," directed attention to individualistic treatment solutions. Moreover, the company's framing the issues in this way had underscored the logic of the short-term employment policies. While the age barrier had related to economics and marketing (Lessor 1984a) rather than health, terminating employees prior to their developing health problems also supported company economic interests.

So what happened? What were the conditions that congealed to move flight attendants from the sidelines to the center of the discursive field? Why or how did they find their voice, which had been relatively mute, and come to frame their situation contentiously?

The first condition facilitating the involvement of the flight attendants was their *increasing temporal connection* to the discursive field in which the dispute occurred. Given that the "stewardesses" previously did not have a stake in long-term employment and were therefore not particularly motivated to think in terms of careers, they did not as a group dispute the company's individualistic, victim-blaming frame or move toward developing a counter frame of their own. When the average time on the job for stewardesses was two or three years, and the job was defined as fun with an opportunity to see the world before one "settled down," no one was disputing the company doctor's claim that young women's constitutions were not really strong enough to avoid developing certain health problems. The general point is that if one is not in or on the field where there is a basis for dispute, or if one is just passing through it, there is little cause for developing a competing frame. And in addition to being present long enough to develop a new consciousness about careers, the women were also on the job long enough to develop work-related health problems.

A second condition that facilitated the development of a counter frame among flight attendants was *increasing interaction and identification with others who were equally impacted*. For flight attendants, this interaction began to occur after they had established their right to a job beyond the age of thirty-two, they began to see themselves as having a career, with the prospect of seniority, and they began to interact with others in their cohort who shared a similar experience. It is notable that that women who saw health problems as arising from working conditions and as important issues to be addressed were also women who saw themselves as pursuing a career (Lessor 1985). There were women who had put in a number of years on the job, but who did not necessarily see it as their career. Ironically, there were some who saw it as "short-term" work in spite of their years of service, and thus were not particularly motivated to support the union and other collective efforts to change working conditions that impacted their health.

A third condition that not only helped flight attendants find their collective voice, but also contributed to the framing of their situation health-wise was *the influence of social movements that were extraneous or only indirectly related to the health issues* in question (Lessor, 1984a). More specifically, social movements of the 1960s and 1970s provided a rights frame that functioned as a kind of "master frame" (Snow and Benford 1992) for a variety of movements during this era. The civil rights movement, which functioned as the mother lode for the rights frame, was an influential resource in aiding flight attendants to declare their rights as workers and to successfully challenge the company rules that demanded retirement at age thirty-two. The women's movement similarly provided strong new language with which to attribute health problems to the work environment and *not* to female weakness. Partly as a result of these external influences, or what Meyer and Whittier (1994) have called "social movement spillover," the group Stewardesses for Women's Rights (SFWR) was formed, and one of its top priorities was to address the health issues of women whose workplace was 37,000 feet in the air.

Flight attendant activists did more than collect statistics on the incidence of problems such as sinus infections and miscarriages; they also began collecting data on the work environment. A health committee that one of us studied discussed a range of dehydration-related health problems (bladder infections, frequent colds, sinus infections) in relation to the occurrence of zero humidity one hour into a flight. At that time, only one company, the Australian carrier *Quantas*, humidified its planes. Often the flight attendants went beyond collecting data on incidence of problems by also concerning themselves with identifying causes. One example is provided by SFWR members working with the engineering department at Arizona State University in conducting a study that demonstrated radiation exposure received by commercial airline cabin personnel. The flight attendants wore dosimeters to detect exposure to radioactive cargo. Later, working jointly with the Airline Pilots Association, SFWR flight attendants presented congressional testimony that resulted in legislation limiting the carrying of such cargo (Unselman and McKlveen 1975; Lessor 1985). The women's movement probably had yet another indirect influence. Company physicians who had taken a "personal troubles" view of health problems of women workers would soon hesitate to attribute health problems to "feminine weakness," seeking instead to highlight more gender-neutral individualistic explanations for ill-health on the job.

A fourth condition affecting the collective mobilization and vocalization of flight attendants was the realization that *individual efforts alone are not particularly effective*. Once again, flight attendant experiences during this period are particularly instructive. Some of the individual strategies were provided by the companies, such as training sessions in how to lift and move heavy items in safe ways to avoid back injury. Health activists criticized these individualistic strategies and demanded that the 250-pound food and drink carts be designed to move more easily, perhaps with battery-operated motors, pointing out that the aisle of an airplane is on a slant, and that 250 pounds is even heavier when being pushed uphill. Many of the individual strategies had been initiated by the women themselves, such as carrying aboard their own drinking water (this was before the ubiquitous presence of bottled water in plastic containers) to maintain hydration and avoid the drinking water held in the plane's tanks; the water was "protected" from bacterial contamination with the addition of chemicals, which did not enhance the taste and which therefore discouraged drinking a sufficient amount. In addition, many flight attendants did not trust the purity of the water. Other strategies involved making "secondary adjustments" (Goffman 1961) to circumvent airline company rules for flight attendant appearance that the women felt interfered with health. One such frequent measure was to change into comfortable shoes once out of sight of ground supervisors checking for the neat appearance of carefully groomed women in high heels. The flight attendant health activists and union leaders would eventually press collectively for changes in working conditions that had necessitated their individual strategies.

In this case, we see that a frame dispute is beneficial to the victims of the misframing being challenged. The case also illustrates that contestants sometimes have to be mobilized and moved from the sidelines or margins to the field of play by finding their voice and articulating an oppositional or counter frame to what has been promulgated. In the case of the flight attendants, we have identified and elaborated four conditions that congealed in time and space to facilitate that joint process. We suspect some of these conditions hold for other cases as well, but that remains an empirical question that invites further research.

Frame Shift and Frame Misalignment in the Transformation of Human Egg Donation

In 1995, a Corona, California, couple, Debbie and John Challender, went public with the story of their ovarian eggs, taken from Debbie during infertility treatment, being given to another woman. The Challenders were the first couple to speak out in the press, in an article that won a Pulitzer Prize for the *Orange County Register* (June 8, 1995), catapulting the story onto a national stage and sparking widespread outrage. The Challenders were one of dozens of couples who alleged that their gametes (eggs *or* embryos) had been stolen by the physicians at U.C. Irvine's Center for Reproductive Health and donated without their consent to other women. Dozens of lawsuits were filed against the physicians and against the university, numerous hearings were held by state legislators such as Tom Hayden, and outrage was expressed on television, in radio talk shows and print over what was characterized as an assault on parental rights. Prior to these startling charges, for over ten years the U.C. Irvine Center for Reproductive Health (UCI-CRH) had enjoyed a reputation in the top tier, even number one, among centers for assisted reproductive technology (ART).

What happened to change the view of the CRH from that of a medical setting that made parental dreams come true to one that turned dreams into nightmares through deceit, lies, and "theft"? One can leave to the psychologists and lawyers the imputation of motive and guilt; indeed, the physicians involved long ago fled the country to avoid prosecution. However, we believe that the notion of framing, and particularly the concepts of frame shifts and frame misalignment, can shed light on the context and misunderstandings that led to this unfortunate medical situation to occur.

The UCI-CRH case is an illustration of how technological innovation produced new ways of framing egg donation. Even while certain changes rendered previous frames for egg donation obsolete, various actors continued to operate within these frames. In addition, as new frames arose, drastic misalignment occurred that led to severe emotional, social, and legal consequences.

The Cooperative Frame

Egg donors in the 1980s in university medical centers in Europe, the United States, Japan, and Australia were themselves infertility patients undergoing treatment. Eggs and embryos could not be frozen, and donation involved an immediate transfer between women. The donor was always a woman who could produce plenty of eggs but who usually had blockages preventing the eggs from traveling through the fallopian tubes to the uterus. The recipient was a woman who at a young age had ceased to produce eggs (diagnosed as having "premature ovarian failure" or POF). The donor would undergo in-vitro fertilization, after having been given drugs to stimulate oocyte production that often resulted in thirty or more eggs. Since neither eggs, nor embryos created in the laboratory with the addition of sperm, could be frozen, only a maximum of four embryos could be immediately created and implanted in the donor. Women rarely chose to have the eggs they could not use discarded; rather, most women were commonly supportive of donating their extra eggs to a woman who could not produce her own or to donating the eggs to further infertility research. The routine consent forms that patients signed included these specifications.

Although medical and drug treatment was expensive, no patient was "paying" for eggs. Women who were themselves undergoing infertility treatment were sympathetic to helping another woman, and expressed optimism for others. A typical comment was provided by a patient, who said, even after her failed IVF attempt, that she hoped that the two women to whom she had donated eggs would be more successful.

The Ownership Frame

In 1990, when embryo freezing finally became possible, the meaning of eggs and embryos changed. Eggs produced with hyperstimulation of ovaries went from being something a woman did not want to waste and was happy to share to being property that she could keep.[7] The technology would advance even further when the freezing of eggs themselves became possible, further solidifying the notion of property.

The ownership frame was enhanced by other corollary frame changes in both recipients and donors. The recipient was no longer seen in a "premature ovarian failure" frame but rather, in a "poor responder" frame. Such diagnostic language "medicalized" the recipient as a legitimate candidate.[8] The framing of women as "poor responders" had the further effect of legitimizing the techniques for older women and rapidly increasing the potential pool of consumers. At the UCI-CRH, in 1989 the average age of recipients was thirty-six years and by the last six months of 1991, the average age was forty-one. The age of women seeking egg donation continued to rise, and was mirrored nationally, although not internationally, in other ART centers doing egg donation.[9]

A New Donor Frame: The Recruited Donor

The "patient as donor" frame was replaced by the "recruited donor" frame. As the numbers of would-be recipients increased and as the number of women donating extra eggs suddenly decreased, another source of eggs had to be found. A recruited donor could be a woman who was not undergoing her own infertility treatment and therefore not needing her own eggs. Technology made recruited donors possible in that embryo freezing made the prospect of egg extraction in a single menstrual cycle more productive. The donor's eggs could be harvested, combined with the sperm of the recipient's husband, and the resulting embryos frozen for several tries at pregnancy during more than one menstrual cycle.

A Competition and Marketing Frame

One frame remained constant however, and that was the competition frame among assisted reproductive technology centers. At meetings of the American Fertility Society and at other regional sessions, papers and posters emphasized "success rates," in spite of constant talk about the difficulties of measuring "success." Success at numbers of pregnancies and numbers of live births were constantly debated, yet the statistics produced were treated as real. The competition among university centers was intense and the drive to be rated number one in the world and to stay there was enormous. Even the high numbers of patients who left with no pregnancy in every one of the major centers did not interfere with the determination of physicians to plunge ahead, nor did it interfere with the expectations of the potential recipients of treatment. The high earnings were a further marker of success, demonstrating that because expectations of success were so high, a great many patients put their fate and their fortunes in the hands of the physicians.

Frames Misaligned

The Center for Reproductive Health in the first half of the 1990s had all the qualifications of a "going concern" with hundreds of new recipients, now framed as "poor responders," anxious for a pregnancy. Medical residents and research fellows from around the world crowded the laboratories and operating rooms. *Recruited donors* abounded, as the women who produced eggs went from being "patient donors" to "mother donors" drawn from women who had finished their childbearing (Lessor et al. 1993), and ultimately to nulliparous "paid college student donors" who could produce even larger amounts of eggs due to their youth. In many cases, patient recipients themselves became "owners" of eggs and embryos: a donor's eggs were fertilized with the sperm of the husband of the recipient patient and the resulting embryos were then frozen and stored by the couple for future use. In some cases the sperm as well as the egg were donated to create the embryo, causing comments about the "embryo with four parents." The vats were filled with thousands of sticks of frozen embryos saved for an indefinite future. In many cases, even after the recipient and her husband achieved the long-awaited pregnancy, the embryos lived on in the freezer. Later still, another technological barrier was broken and unfertilized eggs could be frozen, leading to even greater stores of gametes in waiting.

A few short years earlier, no eggs waited in freezers for a hypothetical future, because it was impossible to possess them. Donated eggs were not property as well because no one paid for them. A heartsick John Challender would not have, as he reported in 1995, cried daily and spent every sleepless night imagining "his children," as he thought of his wife's "stolen" eggs. With the help of the UCI-CRH, the Challenders had produced their long-awaited second child. And like most of the patients existing in the "ownership frame," they stored their remaining gametes. The physicians, operating in the old "cooperative frame," spurred on by the "competition frame," appropriated the eggs. And the records show that the woman to whom the Challender eggs were given gave birth to a child. While cooperative frame donors would have been pleased, in the now misaligned ownership frame, the Challenders were devastated.

This case illustrates not only the need in medical settings for agreement on framing, but also how those conditions can generate misalignment, particularly when technological innovation moves at a rapid pace.

Conclusion

In this paper, we have examined various framing hazards that have encumbered health policy and medical initiatives and implementation in relation to the so-called obesity epidemic in the United States, work-related ailments among flight attendants, and egg donation in infertility. The framing hazards examined included ambiguity of the kind that surfaces when confronted with two or more relevant alternatives, misframings associated with erroneous beliefs or misjudgment, frame disputes among the various sets of actors embedded in a discursive field, and frame shifts entailing the displacement of one frame by another. Not only did we find evidence of two or more of these hazards operating in each of the cases examined, but, even more significantly, we saw how they can impede the advance of health care initiatives and policy. In the case of the obesity problem, we have seen how escalating frame disputes among the various sets of actors constituting the obesity discursive field generates ambiguity and uncertainty that is compounded by contradictory framings issued from within the scientific community itself, and this confusion, in turn, can lead to misalignment. The obesity frame disputes also demonstrate again how science-based frames and identity-group-based frames (fat-acceptance proponents) are often at loggerheads, and how the resultant conflict can retard the implementation of policies based on the science claims.

In the case of the flight attendants, we saw how their evolving counter frame to that of the airline industry and its physicians led to a frame dispute, but one that was a welcome corrective to the latter's misframing of flight attendant health problems. Thus, here, in contrast to the obesity case, we see how a frame dispute can facilitate the advancement of health care. We also noted that mobilizing and activating those who are relatively mute within a discursive field is a contingent enterprise based on the intersection of a number of conditions that we suspect hold for other voiceless actors in other discursive fields.

Finally, turning to the scandal involving the issue of egg and embryo transfer in relation to infertility, we found that the conflicts and tensions were due in no small part to frame shifts and the misalignment of the evolving frames that were stimulated by technological advances for preserving and disseminating gamete donations. Additionally, we found that while certain changes rendered previous frames for egg donation obsolete, various actors continued to operate within these frames, thus generating dramatic and consequential misalignments when new frames emerged.

Taken together, these observations suggest two general conclusions. The first is that framing processes appear to matter greatly within the health and medical arena of social life just as they do in the contexts of social movements and politics. And the second general conclusion is that those in the business of health care and the promotion of health care initiatives should be on the lookout for ways to align competing frames rather than dismiss them, especially when each frame may highlight a set of factors that also contribute to the problem. Returning to the case of obesity, for example, it is now understood that there are multiple pathways to and causes of obesity. As summarized earlier in table 17.1, some contributing factors may be genetic or hormonal, others may be lifestyle based and subcultural in origin, and still others may be associated with the overly abundant availability of fat-laden food choices promulgated by the fast food industry. Rather than frame each of these alternative sets of contributing factors in a way that makes them incommensurable, far better to seek alignment by developing a "master frame" (Snow and Benford 1992) that incorporates the scientifically credible diagnostic and prognostic elements of the competing frames. To do otherwise increases the odds of continued frame ambiguity and disputes and thus the failure of any single frame-based corrective initiative.

NOTES

1. For a review of this theorizing and research, see Benford and Snow (2000); Snow (2004a)

2. See Snow's (2008) elaborated discussion of discursive fields.

3. See Snow and Corrigall-Brown (2005) for a discussion of four common framing mistakes or errors within the context of social movements.

4. See Centers for Disease Control (CDC) 2004 Web site reports on obesity.

5. See also Campos's *The Obesity Myth* (2004).

6. For a critical discussion of such reports, typically based on epidemiological, correlational studies, see the *New York Times Magazine* September 16, 2007, cover story, titled "Unhealthy Science" and subtitled "Why can't we trust much of what we hear about diet, health and behavior-related diseases?" (Taubes 2007).

7. Another influence on eggs and embryos becoming property may have been the Baby M case and the Anna Johnson surrogate motherhood cases. In both cases the court ruled that the surrogates had entered into a property agreement with the biological father, agreeing to surrender the baby the surrogate was carrying because it was part of the property agreement. The old definition of birthing as determining motherhood was thrown out the window.

8. Diagnostic language such as premature ovarian *failure* and *poor responder* casts recipients in a rather dismal light. Feminist critiques of demeaning language aside, it should be pointed out that in addition to first being "pathologized," "recipients" were later seen as part of the problem in that they "seized" stolen eggs or embryos.

9. The late-life childbearing frame was further strengthened by demographic trends detected in the 1990s: a greater number of women who had encountered workplace barriers to childrearing and had deferred childbearing, a rise in the number of marriages of older women to younger men, a greater percentage of people being married, albeit "serial marriages," greater affluence, and a desire among couples to produce a child in a second or third marriage. While a more familiar case with men, the reproductive technology was now making this change possible for women.

18

Conclusion

The Shape of Collective Action in the U.S. Health Sector

Verta Taylor and Mayer N. Zald

The purpose of this volume has been to make visible the range and many forms of social movement activities, largely in the United States, that attempt to change or channel aspects of health care institutions. From self-help and disease-oriented patient groups, to groups organized to combat toxic environments, to movement-like activities of mobilized professionals, to coalitions of groups organized to change national policies, social movement–like groups interact with and sometimes come into conflict with other movements, professions, and interest groups. They join forces with activist scientists, and attack corporate interests; yet at other times they may coalesce with professional groups and representatives of established interest groups (Frickel and Moore 2005). In some instances, the common-sense distinction between interest groups and movements will make little sense, as both may use similar tactics; so-called interest groups may mobilize on the streets and encourage their constituencies to write to their legislators, and representatives of movements may lobby legislators. Our intent has been to show the varied nature of these movements and to think about their effects and limitations. We also wanted the opportunity to think about the relationship of modern social movement theory to the study of health movements. In the past and still today, students of health movements have written important and interesting papers without finding it useful to use the language and insights of contemporary social movement theory. For their part, many contributors to contemporary social movement theory rarely, if ever, refer to the literature on social movements related to health care. Some of the papers in this volume are couched in the language of contemporary social movement theory as they might be applied in an institutional setting and some are not. Later in this chapter we will suggest how developing this linkage might facilitate our understanding of health social movements and also contribute to expanding and modifying contemporary conceptualizations and theories of social movements.

In this volume we have shown that movements exist and attempt to influence health care at many levels. On the most macro level, movements interact with professions, political parties, labor unions, insurance industry lobbyists, the pharmaceutical industry, managed care organizations, and a variety of other groups to establish or forestall national- and state-level plans to authorize large new programs, such as national health insurance, or more limited national programs, such as funding building programs and modifying existing programs, such as Medicare, Medicaid, and Veteran's health care benefits. Movements also develop around alternative specializations and different systems of diagnosis and treatment. At this level, movements attempt to reshape professions, organizations, and modes of delivery of service. Movements also develop around the way we think about, understand, and experience disease and other health-related phenomena; they use and create emotions, identities, and ways of framing disease and health-related issues to politicize the illness experience (Taylor 1996; Klawiter 2004; Brown 2007). Finally, larger social movements in the United States concerned with inequalities of race, gender, ethnicity, class, and sexuality spillover (Meyer and Whittier 1994) to the medical sphere, addressing issues of unequal access and health equity (Epstein 1996, 2007a).

To say that health movements may have impact at many levels is not to say they always achieve their intended effects. Nor is it to say that movements are the most important drivers of change in health institutions. As we noted in the first chapter, demographic trends, technological changes, scientific understanding, the growth and decline of economic resources, the market-based nature of health care, the cultural, economic, political power, and expertise of the medical profession, and the agendas and opportunities of political parties and elites must be seen as major drivers of change or resistance to change. Over the past fifty years, social movements have, nevertheless, played a major part in the medicalization of all sorts of human maladies and conditions—from childbirth and depression to gender identity disorder and erectile dysfunction—and this has contributed significantly to the expansion of the biomedical complex in U.S. society (Conrad 2007). In this chapter we first expand on some of the issues raised in the introduction to the volume. Then we show how concepts from contemporary social movement theory can be used to analyze institutional movements, and, in particular health-related movements.

American Exceptionalism

As we noted in the introduction to this volume, the health care system in the United States is permeated by social movements to a much greater extent than in most other developed nations, although some kinds of health social movements may be found in many other nations. This abundance of movements characterizes the United States as a whole in comparison to most developed nations. It is also the case that the United States has been a welfare state laggard, and that has included its historical reluctance to develop a national health insurance system or a single provider system guaranteeing universal access to medical services. The explanation of these two kinds of "American Exceptionalism," a hesitant welfare state and an abundance of movements, entail each other. That is, aspects of the larger socio-political context create the efflorescence of movements and at the same time have restrained the possibilities of developing a comprehensive welfare state. The United States as a welfare state laggard is explained in the same way as the foundational question for American political sociology "Why No Socialism in the United States?" (Sombart [1906] 1976) is explained. There is a vast literature that attempts to explain American exceptionalism (see Lipset 1996; Wilensky 2002; Archer 2007). Of the main factors usually cited are the difficulties of developing a relatively unified and solidary working class, partly related to ethnic and racial antagonisms and also to the splits and ideological differences between mass industrial unions, which organized by industry and enrolled all blue-collar workers in a company, and craft unions, which organized by occupation. A second major factor is the deep distrust of centralized government reflected in the founding documents of the U.S. federal system and carried forward to this day. Still today, after almost every other developed country has scaled back the extent of state ownership of major industries and espouses a commitment to market capitalism, while maintaining a more comprehensive welfare state, in the United States the charge of "socialism" is raised and fears of "bureaucracy" are used against attempts to provide universal health insurance. Moreover, since the United States developed a large role for private welfare and health provision including hospitals, whether through churches, nonprofit organizations, or profit-making firms, the demand for federal action was muted by the presence of these alternative sources of supply of welfare and health provision. When federal support was supplied it tended to be sought for narrow program definitions and funded by grants and contracts to public agencies in local communities, state agencies, and nonprofits.

At the beginning, too, the United States encouraged voluntary associations, unmediated by or barely controlled by governmental policy. Here, both through our ties to dissenting religious groups and to Protestant denominations and to our commitment to both freedom of association and freedom of speech, the ground was ripe for an efflorescence of private associations and social movement and religious movement expression. Associations were also encouraged by the rapid spread of migrants across the continent; organizing community functions was a self-organizing process. The development of a two-party system also contributed to the proliferation of social movements, because the parties were so heterogeneous that the political claims of aggrieved citizens were not easily represented by a party; indeed, different parts of a party might well be opposed to each other on significant programs. While there is some reason to believe that in recent decades many nations have developed a larger movement sector (see Meyer and Tarrow 1998), the United States continues to be more movement prone than many developed nations. And the fractionation of authority across different levels of government, and across the public, private, nonprofit divides, provides multiple targets and levels for collective action.

The United States has a specific cultural context related to the limits and opportunities for state action (Pieterse 2008). It also has cultures of belief related to definitions and etiologies of health and illness and to what kinds of individual treatment and public health interventions are treated as orthodox or heterodox (Rosenberg 2007).

The Biomedical Complex: Culture and Organization

All institutional complexes are potentially subject to the pressures of social movements (Snow 2004b; Van Dyke, Soule, and Taylor 2004). The structure of power in families; inequalities in the workplace; the operation of the military; the limit or expansion of religious authority; the regulation of the media and entertainment; the system of local, state, and federal taxation; the acquisition of human capital in education—in other words the exercise of power in any institutional arena—becomes a potential site of political and movement contestation (Schneiberg and Lounsbury 2008).

But we believe the health care complex in U.S. society provides more targets for social movement–related action than most institutional complexes. It does so for at least four reasons. First, more than most institutional arenas, the medical sector engages a wide range of professionals and professional specializations. As professions and professional segments change or attempt to change, they threaten what may be relatively stable practices, which then come up for renegotiation. Second, the organization of medical knowledge around disease classification reconfigures the lives of patients, linking them to a system of power that objectifies and alienates them from the larger society (Foucault 1980). Sickness, however, is experienced in diverse ways, which leads to medical contestation. Third, the cultural authority of the male-dominated U.S. medical profession, which consolidated economic and political power by transforming women's atypical thoughts and behaviors into sickness of the mind or body (Smith-Rosenberg 1972; Oakley 1979; Wertz and Wertz 1989; Lunbeck 1994) has given rise to women's movements challenging medical authority and male control (Morgen 2002). Finally, the corporatization of health care coupled with cutbacks in public financing (Rosner 1982) aggravated inequalities of race, gender, and class in health care, making issues of medical access and the relative mix of public rather than private funding for health care contested ground.

The above analysis would suggest a kind of continuing Hobbesian interprofessional war over diagnoses and funding. But in fact the institutional complex is much more stable than that. That stability comes from the continued dominance of the biomedical model of Western medicine, traditions of educating various professions and technicians that define authority relations, a dominant emphasis, at least in the United States, on the search for effective medical and surgical technologies and intervention and less emphasis upon alternative modes of treatment and of public health policies, the corporatization of U.S. health care, and a political system that has entertained proposals for major reform of financing health care, but has not, at the federal level, succeeded in changing that system. Also vital to the stability of the biomedical complex are the moral ideas of medicine that create a tension between the biomedical reductionism inherent in the "disease as entity" way of thinking about sickness and the idea that medicine is a caring enterprise (Rosenberg 2007). Medical historian Charles Rosenberg (2007) argues that disease-based and reductionist thinking about illness, which led to the bureaucratization of the health care system, the definition of fields of medical specialization, the nature of everyday medical practice, and treatment protocols and compensation policies, is ultimately responsible for how the United States came to be in its current medical predicament.

Health systems follow what Carolyn Hughes Tuohy (1999) calls an "Accidental Logic." The health care system is path dependent: the directions of change are shaped by the balance of commitments to funding arrangements, to professional prerogatives, to the roles of the state, and markets that have developed over time. No master plan or design determines how each component relates to each other. Tuohy examines the ways in which Canada, the United States, and the United Kingdom have developed their medical systems. Each of the three nations has been affected by the same long-run trends, the growth of new technologies and therapies, changes in professions, and demographic trends, yet each has developed different ways of funding, governing, and organizing health care. For instance, in England what we would call family doctors have no access to hospitals; the patient is served by the specialized consultants attached to particular hospitals. The salaries and facilities of family doctors are set through a different process than is used for setting consultants' fees. Thus, political issues and movement emergence develop around different axes in the United States than in England. Or, to give another example, Canada restricts private practice to a greater extent than the United Kingdom. Social movements emerge in response to the specific national, regional, and local context. New issues and alternatives arise, as sectors of the health care system are subject to stress and change as a result of the changes in the political, economic, and social context (Abbott 2005).

Combining Social Movement Theory and Institutional Analysis

In this volume we have used a multisite, multilevel approach to social movement analysis. We depart from what has become the dominant focus of social movement analysis for the last several decades, the focus upon state-centered movements (Tilly 1979; McAdam 1982; McAdam et al. 2001). Instead, we view social movements more broadly as networks and organizations in a variety of institutional settings where groups contend over ideas, practices, identities, and resources. Contention takes place in nonstate authoritative bodies, such as professions and corporations (see Raeburn 2004; Davis et al. 2005), and even in markets, where new products and modes of treatment may be promoted with the enthusiasm and sense of identity and difference typically associated with movement mobilization (see Rao 2009). Social movements and contentious interaction are endemic to U.S. society (Taylor 2000).

Over the past decade, social movement scholars critical of the state-centered model have argued that this approach to social movements ignores many post-1960s social movements that target the sphere of civil society, as well as movements that have pursued cultural and mobilization goals, rather than strictly political goals (Bernstein 1997; Binder 2002; Myers and Cress 2004; Staggenborg and Taylor 2005). Between 1968 and 1995, for example, the civil rights, gay and lesbian, and women's movements were more likely to direct their appeals to public opinion and nonstate institutions, such as educational, religious, and business institutions (Van Dyke, Soule, and Taylor 2004). To capture the multiple sites and targets of contention. David Snow (2004b) offers a more inclusive conceptualization of social movements as "collective challenges to systems or structures of authority." Drawing from the body of scholarship that, over the past decade, has sought to expand the conception of social movements to encompass movements in multiple institutional arenas, Armstrong and Bernstein (2008) propose a "multi-institutional politics approach" to social movements that synthesizes recent multisite, multi-institutional approaches to movements. We believe that it is useful to propose an institutional-centered approach to movements, which extends the insights and concepts of contemporary theory usually applied to political movements to understand social movements in a variety of venues. The women's movement, for example, targets the subordination of women in a wide range of institutions, including medicine, the workplace, the media, education, the law, and more (Staggenborg and Taylor 2005). Each of those settings has a structure and set of practices and ideologies specific to the particular institutional sphere. More to the current case, institutions differ in the way authority is buttressed by tradition and normative practice. The logic of action of an institutional field is dictated by the cognitive and normative definitions of the institution as they relate to available technologies and practices used to realize institutional performance. As the institutional order is challenged from within, by participants whose actions and identities come into conflict with the institution's culture and activities, or from without, by elements of the larger institutional field, or by changes in the general societal/cultural context, claims may be made to change the system. These aggregated claims represent institutionally aggregated collective action. In the remainder of the chapter we attempt to spell out the implications of the health care system for institutional movements, especially in the United States. We examine how the structure and cultural logic of the health care system creates a context for movement emergence and action. At the same time, we will be emphasizing the value of this approach for expanding the use of social movement analysis, particularly for understanding health care institutions.

An institution is a complex of roles, norms, and practices that form around some object, some realm of behavior in a society that is identified by members of the society as having some coherence, belonging together, as contrasted with some other set of roles, norms, and practices around a different realm of behavior. Institutions have a history and current norms and practices are touched by the past, but are subject to change. These histories are an important component of the context for analyzing the movement issues that develop. Institutions vary enormously in their size, complexity, rate of change, and openness to dissent. Because they may be complex, institutions may actually be seen as made up of several institutional arenas, each of which may be subject to institutional analysis, though they overlap in practice. That is, there may be several focal components with different but overlapping structures, habitual practices, and normative expectations.

At any point in time, one could focus microscopically on a very narrow range of practices and behaviors or draw back to focus upon large macroscopic issues to understand how the institutional context structures social movement dynamics. For instance, as far as health movements are concerned, in the United States, one could focus upon the movement to reduce the hours that hospital residents are expected to work. This movement was a response to claims that the inherited system of training residents led them to be over-burdened and sleepless, thus prone to making errors

(Kellogg 2007). The movement met a great deal of resistance from residents who believed that the new system meant a diminution in the continuity of care, because residents had to hand off cases at an arbitrary "end of shift." It also met resistance because it challenged an image of heroic medicine, of the doctor as having enormous stamina and ability to see a problem through to its end. Focusing macroscopically, one might examine the episodic history of attempts to transform the major forms for funding patient care in the United States (Hoffman 2003, and Hoffman this volume, chapter 3). Where at the microscopic level we would examine the interaction of residents and staff at the floor and specialty level of hospitals, the macroscopic involves focusing upon the interaction of parties, politicians, insurance companies, professional associations, pharmaceutical companies, hospital corporations, labor unions (Fantasia 1989; Lopez 2004), and organizations, such as the American Association of Retired Persons, that represent the elderly.

Different institutional levels of the health care system obviously entail different kinds of change efforts. The organizational form and the tactics of social movements are a response to the configuration of power in the arena in which collective action emerges. The collective actors involved in health movements vary from networks of people of different statuses and genders interacting in meetings at the micro level, or support groups of parents of children with leukemia to local citizen alliances collaborating with scientists to raise concerns about environmentally related illnesses and federated social movement organizations trying to affect the positions of major parties, politicians, and interest groups with respect to the treatment of breast cancer or HIV/AIDS. The tactics used by health movements also vary: from the interpersonal expression of support for or against the new residency hours rules or the personalized political strategies of breast cancer activists who refuse to have breast reconstruction at the microscopic level, to national advertisement campaigns, public demonstrations, lobbying efforts, and use of mass media for the more macroscopic changes. We will have more to say about tactics, targets, and forms of mobilization below.

Key Concepts

Let us lay out some of the key concepts and definitions that are often used in social movement analysis, and suggest how they might be used to examine the dynamic relationship between health movements and the practices of medicine, science, and public health that they challenge.

Movements and Interest Groups

Social movements are often contrasted with interest groups. The former are composed of groups and individuals with little formal access to decision makers and little influence. They use a variety of tactics, including street protest, to gain attention for their claims. A quintessential movement might be the civil rights movement or the feminist movement. Interest groups, on the other hand, are believed to be more stable and have easy access to decision makers; they rely on lobbying and direct contact with legislators and officials. The quintessential interest group might be the insurance industry or the American Medical Association. Historically, sociologists studied movements, while political scientists studied interest groups.

In the modern era, the distinction has become less useful (Burstein 1999). A movement may be made up of people with resources and access, and yet be dissatisfied with their ability to affect policy. Such was the case with the modern neo-conservative movement for a period of time, although in the last two decades the new right has gained access to the political process. On the other hand, the larger organizations in the environmental movement, such as the Nature Conservancy or the Sierra Club, may largely work through lobbying and educational campaigns, eschewing public protest. Moreover, movement campaigns that mobilize large numbers of organizations and individuals may be mobilizing organizations and groups that often function like typical interest groups, largely working for benefits for their own members, but also occasionally mobilizing for issues of "justice" or "rights" that apply far beyond their own members. Associations of workers, nurses, and doctors may coalesce around a social policy issue, such as national health insurance. Taken separately, one could analyze each of the groups as an interest group, but as they coalesce around a large but contested issue, they take on the dynamics of a social movement.

Fields of Contention

The institutional field in which a social movement mobilizes includes a large array of actors held together by common cultural understandings, practices, and rules, but it may also be driven by conflicting logics and beliefs about how practices and roles tied to the institution ought to be enacted. Much of an institutional field may be relatively stable and, at least for a given period of time, noncontentious. The institutional field includes the groups and organizations that bear on and influence the structure, norms, and practices of the institutional arena. The Federal Drug Administration, state departments of health, professional associations, medical journals, schools of medicine, pharmaceutical companies, and hospital corporations are all part of the health care institutional field. So, too, are patients and their families seeking medical care. The field or part of the institutional field becomes contentious when groups and organizations develop conflicting views of the norms, practices, processes, and forms of the institution. Movements to change aspects of health care institutions may focus on a relatively small part of the overall institutional field, or they may have broader agendas, such as changes in disease classifications and increases in research funding for particular diseases, that have implications across a large array of actors and groups. For instance, for some time there has been a political movement waged to change the mission of the FDA to include the regulation of tobacco. Allied on one side are various organizations and professional groups who believe that the use of tobacco and the marketing of it present a health hazard; on the other side are groups who oppose the spread of government power, and those who profit from tobacco, tobacco farmers and end-product producers, the cigarette companies. The contentious field includes legislative and administrative agencies that have jurisdiction over aspects of the FDA and tobacco usage and production. The policy issue is important and may have ramifications beyond the particular case, but yet is a small slice of the overall health care field. A movement to transform the funding base of patient care might well have implications for almost all health care providers and patients, and thus mobilize many groups and organizations, each with their own concerns about how the change would affect them.

The student of institutional movements would focus upon "fields of contention" (Ray 1999; Crossley 2006; Brown 2007; Klawiter 2008) to understand the dynamics of health movements. The field of health movements, according to Phil Brown and his collaborators (this volume, chapter 7) includes all the movements and groups that are mobilized to press for change, even though some may have conflicting ideologies. A broader definition of a field would include the agencies, organizations, and countermovements that resist or aid the movement, and these actors need not necessarily be movements. In this usage, a field of contention is a structured arena of conflict that includes all relevant actors to whom a social movement might be connected in pursuing its claims. In the health arena, this would include other social movements vying for disease recognition and access to the medical system; professional associations struggling to maintain authority over medical knowledge and practice; scientists, health researchers and epidemiologists debating the causes of illness; consumer groups trying to gain access to the health care system; hospital corporations; health maintenance organizations; the pharmaceutical industry and other groups with an interest in health care markets; state and government regulatory agencies: and political parties that arbitrate the interests of all of these parties. The concept of field of contention calls attention to the fact that in modern society social movements target a wide range of institutions, both governmental and nongovernmental, and that every arena of struggle has its "own logic, rules, and regularities" (Bourdieu and Wacquant 1992: 104).

Political and Discursive Opportunity

Any attempt to understand the broader forces that contribute to the emergence of social movements requires attention to questions about how power and resources are distributed in an institutional sector, as well as to the cultural beliefs, normative frameworks, and discourses that provide meaning and stability in the institutional sector. The various positions and organizations within an institutional field make up a field of power and authority. Power and authority are derived from traditional understandings of how positions are meant to relate to each other, from the rulings of superordinate groups or statuses, from beliefs about expertise and technical competence, and from everyday practices. In the biomedical complex, the regime of power is reinforced by the standardized education and licensing of physicians and other health professionals, scientific authority, the structure of hospitals, managed care, the policies of health insurers, and the federal health bureaucracy. One aspect of an institution that structures the context of political action by both challengers and authorities is the how open or closed it is to challenges. Are there avenues and openings for pressing claims for change, or is the field closed? What are the dynamics and contradictions within an institutional field that lead parts of the field to become more or less receptive to the claims of social movements?

Institutional boundaries are vulnerable to political contestation, new practices, and even the development of new institutional logics (Clemens 1997; Friedland forthcoming). Political opportunities are created by changes in the structure of a field that make it more conducive to supporting the aims of movement actors. The corporatization of health services that began during the late 1980s and the countervailing power of health corporations, health maintenance organizations, consumers, and payers have eroded the authority of physicians (Starr 1982; Light 1993). Increased fragmentation of the health care system, brought about by specialization, privatization, and the market orientation of health delivery systems (Scott et al. 2000) has provided openings for social movements. Windows of opportunity for groups seeking to transform health care policy are also created by law and state policy. Dramatic changes in state policy and funding for family planning, birth control, and abortion that occurred during the 1960s and 1970s supported the early growth and spread of the health clinic sector of the women's health movement (Morgen 2002). Scientific discoveries that dramatize new procedures and definitions of diseases can also shape the contours of social movements. Historical changes in practices of detection, diagnosis, and treatment of breast cancer that gradually defined breast cancer from an either/or condition to a disease continuum, placing large numbers of asymptomatic women at risk for the disease, facilitated the formation of the new social networks, solidarities, and identities that created the breast cancer movement (Klawiter 2008).

If the bureaucratization and corporatization of health care would seem to make the biomedical complex resistant to change, the soaring faith in medical and therapeutic approaches to human problems that underlies the moral economy of U.S. health care, provides the opposite impetus (Polsky 1991; Conrad 2007; Whittier 2009). Social movements have played a significant a role in the medicalization of human problems and the increase of medical jurisdiction over people's bodies and interior worlds along with medical and health care professionals and markets (Conrad 2007). The past four decades have seen a proliferation of movements struggling to legitimate a host of new illnesses, such as the gulf war syndrome, adult attention-deficit/hyperactivity disorder, anorexia, chronic fatigue syndrome, postpartum depression (Taylor 1996), post-traumatic stress disorder (Scott 1990), obsessive compulsive disorder, and Alzheimer's disease (Fox 1989). Social movements have also played a major role in the introduction of alternative treatment protocols for diseases, such as HIV/AIDS (Epstein 1996), breast cancer (Klawiter 2008); postpartum depression (Taylor 1996); asthma (Brown 2007), and other diseases promoted by grassroots groups. To the extent that medical knowledge is consistently articulated around disease entities (Rosenberg 2007), the cultural logic of the health care system, which is structured around the introduction of new disease classifications and treatment modes, provides a discursive framework around which scientific and intellectual movements and patient and consumer movements are able to mobilize (Ferree 2003). Somewhat paradoxically, movements that help create new disease entities and protocols for their treatment also contribute to medical jurisdiction over people's bodies and make it difficult for patients whose symptoms do not fit neatly into the medical model to advance their interests and needs.

Patterns of inequality, embedded in broader social, political, and economic structures, must also be considered as factors that affect possibilities for groups to articulate and mobilize around social movement identities (Taylor and Whittier 1992). Virtually all institutions in U.S. society are structured to reproduce social inequalities of gender, race and ethnicity, class, and sexuality. These inequalities intersect and operate at every level of the biomedical institutional complex, including in the hierarchy of medical specializations and occupations (Lorber 1984), differential access to health care (Willie et al. 1995; Bird and Rieker 2008), the federal government's health research apparatus (Epstein 2007a), the ways of classifying people into disease categories (Klawiter 2008), and everyday medical practice (West 1984). The women's, civil rights, gay and lesbian, and environmental movements that emerged our of the 1960s and 1970s cycle of protest have spawned a wide variety of subsequent movements (Meyer and Whittier 1994; Epstein 1996; Taylor 1996) and the effects of these movements have spilled over to influence the frames, mobilizing structures, collective identities, movement culture, and tactics of health movements (Epstein 1996; Taylor 1996; Klawiter 2008).

Mobilizing Structures

Scholars of social movements have long recognized the importance of mobilizing structures for understanding the trajectory of social movements (McCarthy and Zald 1977; Tilly 1984; McAdam, McCarthy, and Zald 1996). By mobilizing structures, we mean the formal organizations, associations, networks, and informal structures of everyday life where collective action is generated that serve as the building blocks of social movements (McAdam 1982; Gould 1991). A variety of factors influence the different structural configurations through which social movements mobilize, including national and political contexts (Kriesi 1996; Rucht 1996); historical protest cycles (McCarthy 1996); and activist frames about the appropriateness of particular mobilizing structures (Clemens 1996; Polletta 2002). The student of institutional movements would add to this list institutional context because the organizational and cultural logic of a particular institutional arena influences the structural forms through which a movement mobilizes in the same way that the characteristics of the modern state configured the social movement as a repertoire of contention (Tarrow 1994).

The frameworks provided by the health care system—specifically medical discourse and practice that centers around disease categories and treatment—make it likely that health care movements will mobilize, at least in part, through self-help and support groups that are structured to provide treatment and emotional support (Taylor and Van Willigen 1996; Klawiter 2008; Taylor and Leitz this volume, chapter 16). Formally organized advocacy groups also play a critical role in health movements seeking access to the health care system. Moreover, as Wolfson and Parries (this volume, chapter 8) demonstrate, the National Institutes of Health have encouraged the development of advocacy groups by funding programs and projects of health care organizations that require community participation. The advocacy groups parallel the structure of the biomedical complex and the therapeutic state that have incorporated therapeutic requirements into state bureaucracies and regulatory agencies that determine individuals' access to medical benefits by virtue of identity categories (Whittier 2009). Finally, because health care movements often grow out of preexisting social movements, such as feminism, the gay and lesbian movement, civil rights, Chicana/o activism, and other movements with a participatory democratic structure, grassroots health movement organizations are often organized loosely and collectively to mimic the structure of prior movements (Taylor 1996).

The mobilizing structures that propel health movements, then, range from more formally structured national organizations and associations to more loosely structured local networks, such as direct action, self-help, and support groups. The women's health movement, for example, mobilized through formally structured advocacy groups, such as the National Women's Health Network, National Black Women's Health Project, National Asian Women's Health Organization, and the National Latina Health Organization, as well as through feminist health clinics and radical feminist collectives such as the Boston Women's Health Collective, creators of the bible of women's health, *Our Bodies, Ourselves* (Morgen 2002; Davis 2007). These different organizational configurations were effective in mobilizing a broad-based movement. Large-scale organizations succeeded in organizing ambitious campaigns directed at policy changes, and local women's health clinics and collectives generated grassroots and public support. The campaign to win health benefits for domestic partners in American corporations was waged primarily by gay employee networks spawned by the larger gay and lesbian movement that diffused from one corporation to another, eventually forming interorganizational linkages that allowed the movement to win domestic partner benefits in hundreds of Fortune 1000 companies (Raeburn 2004). The Aids Coalition to Unleash Power (ACT UP), which was instrumental in mobilizing the larger AIDS treatment movement, was composed of decentralized, collectively structured, local chapters that used street theatre and dramatic performances of embodied protest, such as "die ins" to win public attention to HIV/AIDS (Epstein 1996).

Broad-based health movements, such as the breast cancer movement, HIV/AIDS movement, environmental health justice movement, women's health movement, disability rights movement, and psychiatric consumer movement, mobilize through a variety of overlapping organizations and networks. The hallmark of most health movements, however, is hybrid organization (Taylor 1996; Epstein 2007a; Whittier 2009), or mobilization structures comprised of expert activists. For this reason, Phil Brown (2007 considers health movements as "boundary movements" or "hybrid movements" because they blur the boundaries between lay and expert forms of knowledge and between activists and the state. In the field of social movements, there is a significant body of research that demonstrates that variations in the forms of organization adopted by social movements that target the state are related to movement success (Gamson 1975; Staggenborg 1991). We expect this is also the case with movements in health care, and there is some evidence that hybrid organizations have proved effective in making medical policy more inclusive (Epstein 2007a) and in winning recognition for contested illnesses (Taylor 1996; Brown 2007; see also Frickel this volume, chapter 11).

Framing and Collective Identity

Institutional fields are structures of symbolically constituted power arrangements and practices, and social movements, in turn, consist largely of practices linked to symbolic production. An institutional approach requires attention to the ways that institutional sources of meaning or the discursive context shapes the symbols, values, beliefs, and icons of social movements in a particular field of contention (Snow 2004a; Friedland forthcoming). All social movements are engaged in a struggle to propose new frames or interpretations of problems that resonate with the beliefs and practices of adherents, constituent organizations, and other actors in a field of contention (Snow and Benford 1992; Snow 2004a; see also Snow and Lessor this volume, chapter 17). Social movements also seek to create new interpretations of subjects through the construction of collective identities that categorically redefine marginalized and stigmatized groups in more favorable ways and foster solidarity and collective consciousness (Melucci 1989; Polletta and Jasper 2001; Taylor and Whittier 1992; see also Taylor and Leitz this volume, chapter 16). Myra Marx Ferree (2003) argues that alternatives closest to the dominant logic of an institution are more likely to prevail than radical alternatives. Moreover, it is important to note that a frame that favors one definition of a problem may freeze out another. McCormick (this volume, chapter 15) argues that the dominant framing of global warming has subordinated a frame of climate change as the cause of the spread of climate-related diseases.

In health social movements, the reframing of illness is central to collective identity construction for two reasons. First, the etiological uncertainty of disease generates multiple explanations for patient's symptoms, which can then be debated among physicians, scientific experts, and laypersons and experts (Brown et al. 2004; Cable, Shriver, and Mix 2008). Second, "medical work," as Monica Casper and Marc Berg (1995) argue, is a principle locus for the construction and reconstruction of bodies and subjectivities and the health care system is a "crucial site of control over bodies and lives." Sociologists have long recognized that illness is a stigmatized personal identity, a failure, if you will, to meet normative role expectations (Parsons 1951; Gerhardt 1989). The good patient accepts illness as a disempowered role, while the bad patient resists the sick role identity and may even claim to know more than medical professionals about the causes of his/her illness and how to direct their care (Morrison 2005). When individuals' experience of illness is at odds with medical and scientific explanations and practices, they may adopt a collective identity around a disease and set of causes that reframes and politicizes their illness experience (Taylor 1996; Klawiter 2008). Phil Brown describes the process of transforming an individual disease into a social movement focused on health and social inequalities as a *politicized illness experience* (Brown 2007: 30).

Research on the disability rights movement (Anspach 1979; Groch 2001), social movements in mental health (Taylor 1996; Morrison 2005; Crossley 2006), health movements mobilized around asthma, environmental health issues, breast cancer, and Gulf War–related illnesses (Brown 2007; Klawiter 2008) demonstrate the centrality of framing processes to the formation of collective identity in social movements mobilizing to repudiate and challenge medical and scientific understandings of diseases. Through the process of collective framing, all of these social movements have allowed individuals to turn the personal identity of illness into a collective identity, which allows participants to resist the stigma of illness, to arm themselves with medical and scientific knowledge to use in conflicts with medical providers, to develop alternative and frequently more socially based explanations of their illness, and to resist unnecessarily dangerous treatments. Professions, too, not only medicalize "unacceptable" behavior patterns, explicating their connections to good health, but also justify authority relations and economic arrangements as beneficial to health care institutions, medical practice, and ultimately to patients.

Not all health movements, however, are based on contested illnesses and disease categories. Collective challenges to medical and public healthy policy are also mounted by movements pursuing such aims as equitable access to health care through national and state health care reforms, extension of health insurance and drug benefits to the uninsured or underinsured, containing health care costs through the total privatization. Framing in relation to these kinds of health movements is embedded in discursive fields comprised of numerous actors, including agents of the state (Ferree 2003). The collective frames used to justify health movements engaged with the state mirror the therapeutic state's use of discourses of illness and health (Whittier 2009), but also draw upon core American values about "freedom, choice, personal responsibility, and savings" (Quadagno and McKelvey this volume, chapter 4). The AARP, for example, advocated for Medicare Part D supplemental drug coverage by framing it as a public-private or market-based model. Gray Panthers, a more radical social movement organization among the elderly, have denounced the legislation on Part D on the grounds that it undermines traditional Medicare by converting it into a private industry using taxpayer subsidies.

Some health movements are constituency based and concerned with health inequality resulting from race, ethnicity, gender, class, and sexuality differences. These movements are often spin-offs from earlier broad-based movements, such as the women's, civil rights, environmental, and gay and lesbian movements, as well as countermovements such as the anti-abortion movement and the Christian right (Meyer and Whittier 1994). Health access movements frequently borrow from the master frames that shaped the orientations and strategies of earlier movements and countermovements to justify their claims. For example, the language of gender and power is pervasive in women's self-help movements, serving as a framework to punctuate and explain a host of problems that trouble women (Taylor 1996). Similarly, movements promoting the health of racial and ethnic minorities, the elderly, and children draw upon master frames borrowed from earlier mobilizations, such as underrepresentation, health disparities, and biological differences, to justify their claims (Epstein 2007a). The debate over a petition to change the emergency contraceptive Plan B from prescription-only to over-the-counter status demonstrates the role that social movement framing plays in disputes over the introduction and legalization of new drugs and treatments (Kimport 2005). Participants in the Food and Drug Administration's hearings to review the petition drew upon gendered frames, with proponents echoing claims about women's empowerment and patient autonomy borrowed from the women's and reproductive rights movements. Paternalist and life-at-conception frames that originated in countermovements such as the anti-reproductive rights movements and the Christian right were used to justify opposition to the petition.

Just as health care is a discursive terrain in which contests over meaning occur (Steinberg 1999), so too are other institutional fields. Institutional fields are both sustained and challenged through debate over contested issues, events, and identity classifications in which actors have different stakes. It is because institutional power is both culturally constitutive and culturally constituted that framing and collective identity processes are critical to understanding the trajectory of institutional movements.

Tactical Repertoires in Institutional Contexts

The tactics used by social movements range from conventional strategies of political persuasion, such as lobbying, petitioning, and voting; confrontational tactics such as marches, strikes, boycotts, blockades, and demonstrations that disrupt day-to-day life; and cultural forms of political expression such as rituals, street theatre, identity deployment, and cultural practices of everyday life. Sarah Soule and her collaborators (Soule et al. 1999; Van Dyke et al. 2001) propose a useful typology of social movement tactics that distinguishes between *insider tactics* and *outsider tactics* to accentuate the wide range of tactics used by virtually all social movement actors to press their claims.

Institutional movements develop *insider* and *outsider* tactics that mirror institutional rules and practices suitable for employment in relation to the elements of the institutional field most likely to give leverage in pursuing or resisting particular changes. In many instances, the tactical repertoires of institutional movements parallel the tactics used by political movements. Professional groups may strike, organize petitions, and use courts and legislative bodies to press their claims. Patient and consumer groups may coalign to create organizations to lobby physicians, corporations, and the government for the redefinition of disease categories. For example, social movements as wide ranging as nuclear workers seeking to link their illnesses to environmental exposure (Kroll-Smith et al. 2000; Cable, Shriver, and Mix 2008) to intersex activists challenging the health care system over the management of gender assignment and gender surgery (Preves 2005) have used lay understandings of their conditions to challenge expert forms of knowledge.

Segments of professions may start new professional organizations or lobby extant groups to change health care policies or programs. Some institutional movements may even resemble elite-driven campaigns, as senior personnel identify with a movement's goals and use their positions, authority, and expertise to press for change. Such would seem to be the case with the movement to reduce medical errors, which has used dramatic cases of error and statistical assessments of aggregate case analyses to pressure medical chiefs of staff to place the problem of medical error on organizational agendas. To some extent we might expect institutional movements to operate through quiet voice, as demands for change and perceived opportunities are pressed through *insider tactics* that rely upon routine communication channels, such as journal articles, committee reports, conferences and interpersonal communications where activists engage in what Tom Burns called "micro-politics" (1961).

Micro-politics may also have an edge of resistance and hostility even while it is conducted with quiet voice if participants perceive their actions and attitudes to be resisted by those who represent authority or control important resources and incentives (Morrill, Zald, and Rao 2003; Ewick and Silbey 2003).

But institutional movements need not be quiet. Where large stakes appear to be at risk and institutional segments have the resources and status to resist intimidation, visible internal movements may develop, as when a medical staff organizes to pressure the executive officers of hospitals to represent their interests. Health movements also originate among patient and consumer groups with a deep sense of mistrust of government and institutional authorities, and these types of movements have often resorted to *outsider* tactics, including street demonstrations, direct action, boycotts, and even threats of violence. Public demonstrations, such as the "Race for the Cure" promoting breast cancer awareness and treatment and boycotts of drugs and products that pathologize menstruation remain part of the battery of tactics of national and local women's health movements (Staggenborg and Taylor 2005). ACT-UP has embraced direct action and civil disobedience campaigns, die-ins and other forms of street theatre, eye-catching graphics, and in-your-face queer-positive politics in its struggle to promote public awareness of HIV/AIDS, obtain access to experimental drugs, and demand a coordinated national policy to respond to the disease (Gamson 1989). ACT-UP demonstrations have halted trading at the New York Stock Exchange, blocked the Lincoln Tunnel, and shut down the offices of the Food and Drug Administration. Finally, in extreme cases, health movements have resorted to the use of violence. In the 1980s, the anti-abortion movement took up arms to shut down abortion clinics by murdering and wounding abortion doctors, clinic staff, and clients (Simonds 1996).

Institutional movements adapt their tactics to the logic, or the rules, practices, and discursive context, of the institutional field. Three tactical innovations associated with embodied health movements are worth brief mention because they illuminate how the repertoires of contention used by institutional movements do not conform to the narrow definition of politics, tactics, goals, and targets associated with the state-centered political process model (Taylor and Van Dyke 2004; Armstrong and Bernstein 2008). The first strategy is *self-help* or mobilization around a shared experience or problem, experiential knowledge as an alternative or supplement to professional knowledge, and mutual support that fosters unconditional acceptance and new ways of providing services (Taylor 1996; Archibald this volume, chapter 14). The cornerstone of self-help is patient-controlled health care through support groups and alternative health clinics that destigmatize illness, provide alternative treatments, politicize health care, and empower individuals. *Coming out*, or a politics of visibility (Taylor 1996; Bernstein 1997) is a second tactic used by embodied health movements. Nancy Whittier (forthcoming) defines coming out as "a movement strategy that includes public framing of the group through strategic identity disclosure, internal group definitions of collective identity, and emotion-laden individual transformations of identity." Health movements deploy identity strategically to empower people disenfranchised by the disease classifications, reimbursement policies, and practices of health institutions. Finally, embodied health movements use various forms of *lay knowledge*, including popular epidemiology and bibliotherapy, both to challenge and to coopt the institutional discourse and power of the biomedical complex that has an interest in denying the social and environmental causes of illness (Taylor 1996; Brown 2007; Cable, Shriver, and Mix 2008).

Repertoires and tactics of protest are the theoretical building blocks of all the major theories constructed to understand social movements and other forms of contentious politics. Some research based largely on political movements suggests that *outsider* tactics are more effective than *insider tactics* in achieving policy change (Piven and Cloward 1979; Gamson 1990), but does the distinction between *outsider* and *insider* hold up in institutional movements that mobilize in multi-institutional fields of contention? Moreover, the use of outsider tactics that conflict with sanctified norms of institutions may be counterproductive. Imagine the response of politicians and public opinion if doctors and nurses conducted strikes that jeopardized patient care. Attention to variations in the tactical repertoires of institutional movements is essential for understanding what kinds of social movement tactics are the most effective for producing enduring impacts on institutions.

Conclusion

In this volume we have brought together essays that span the range of movements that impact upon health institutions, especially in the United States They range from papers examining movements that address the overall funding and definition of individual responsibility for making decisions about funding health care to papers showing how a self-help movement aimed at helping mothers imprisoned for life for killing their own children used the language of psychiatric illness to understand their actions. This understanding both changed their own self-perceptions and raised implications for social policy. In bringing together these articles we hope to have contributed to a merger of social movement and institutional theory that is fruitful for both. We believe the synthesis is a fruitful one. Institutional theory is bolstered by having a well-developed approach to social change being applied to understanding institutional change; social movement theory is advanced by focusing upon an institution that has been only rarely and incompletely analyzed as the site for social movement analysis. It is worth noting that some of the papers are explicitly tied to contemporary social movement theory, while others are not. Below we comment further on this.

Although not explicitly stated, many of the papers and the underlying assumption of the editors has been that social movements are beneficial to improving health care and health policy. But, of course, such an assumption may be unwarranted, or at least requires empirical examination. Movements may have little impact on and can sometimes actually impede good research and good medical care. Has the demand for research on breast cancer, to the neglect of research on heart disease of women, been helpful to women? Has the mobilization of parents against the vaccination of children because of an asserted link between vaccination and autism been useful or has it deflected attention, energy, and money from more important lines of research on autism? It would be easy to list dozens of instances where movements have led to unproductive or distracting lines of research and practices. That said, it would be a mistake to ignore the study of health-related movements. We simply can not understand the directions of change without at least some attention to the contribution that movements are making to the ongoing dialogue about a multitude of health care issues.

There are often contradictory interests and logics in complex institutions, and that is especially true in the case of health care; the multiple professions and specializations, the complexity of organizations and the interconnections of industries all contribute to a push and pull among interests. An overriding logic has to do with the empowerment of professions as dominant as they use expertise in the management and treatment of illness. But patient-oriented movements and the new sources of information they promote (e.g., on the internet) operate with a contradictory logic, seeking to empower patients vis-à-vis the experts. Certainly one of the long-term trends in U.S. health care is the growing voice of patient interests. At the same time, although medical knowledge and expertise continue as a dominant logic, the role of insurance and pharmaceutical companies, managed care, state agencies, and regulatory bodies are powerful constituents in the health care field. There is no evidence that that trend will decline.

This book has been predicated on the notion that social movement analysis can be useful for understanding institutional transformation. Although the field of social movement theory and research has matured considerably in the last several decades and its concepts and precepts rest increasingly on a solid base of empirical research, much analysis of what we think of as social movements is not guided by mainstream social movement theory and research but by general political and social science concepts, by other specializations such as the social studies of science, and by concepts developed in the process of studying health movements. In part, we think that may be because so much of social movement theory has been oriented toward political movements, whereas the student of health movements often has been concerned with the particular configuration of practice and mobilization around a specific health-related issue. As social movement theory and research moves more toward examining movements related to institutions, it should become more useful to students of health movements. The reverse is also true; the growth of an institutionally oriented social movement theory will be richer for having a range of institutions, especially ones so large and important to human well-being.

It is also our goal to draw on the articles in this volume and other literature on health movements to join other scholars who are calling for an institutional approach to social movements (Young 2002; Armstrong and Bernstein 2008; Cable, Shriver, and Mix 2008; Friedland forthcoming). We do this by showing how the main precepts of social movement theory can be used to illuminate the characteristics, trajectory, and significance of health movements in the United States. It is important to keep in mind that institutional movements operate in institutional fields of contention, and they also target the state because of the nature of the therapeutic state. We think social movement theory can contribute further to the understanding of institutional movements.

References

Abbott, Andrew. 1988. *The System of Professions*. Chicago: University of Chicago Press.
———. 2005. "Linked Ecologies: States and Universities as Environments for Professions." *Sociological Theory* 23 (Sept.): 245–74.
Abrams, David. 2006. "Wal-Mart forced to Pay More for Health Benefits." *The Capital* January 13.
Academy for Educational Development. 2006. Social Movement Analysis Conference Agenda. Washington, D.C.: AED, July 6.
Academy for Educational Development and Centers for Disease Control. 2006. Overview of the Obesity Epidemic. Washington, D.C.: AED.
Agency for Health Care Administration (ACHA). 2006. Florida Medicaid Reform: Application for 1115 Research and Demonstration Waiver, August 30.
Agrawala, Shardul, Kenneth Broad, and David H. Guston. 2001. "Integrating Climate Forecasts and Societal Decision Making: Challenges to an Emergent Boundary Organization." *Science, Technology & Human Values* 26(4): 454–77.
Alaska Federation of Natives. 2006. "Federal Priorities." Anchorage, Ala.
Alaskan Native Science Commission. 2005. "Southeast Alaska Regional Meeting Report." Anchorage, Ala.
Alcoholics Anonymous. 2005. New York: A.A. World Services.
Alexander, Christopher. 1979. *The Timeless Way of Building*. Oxford: Oxford University Press.
Alinsky, Saul. 1971. *Rules for Radicals*. New York: Vintage Books.
Allee, Kegan. 2007. "Drag Kinging and the Creation of Cybernetworks." Paper presented at The American Sociological Association's Annual Meeting, New York, N.Y.
Allen, Barbara. 2003. *Uneasy Alchemy: Citizens and Experts in Louisiana's Chemical Corridor Disputes*. Cambridge: MIT Press.
———. 2004. "Shifting Boundary Work: Issues and Tensions in Environmental Health Science in the Case of Grand Bois, Louisiana." *Science as Culture* 13: 429–48.
Allsop, Judith, Kathryn Jones, and Rob Bagott. 2005. "Health Consumer Groups in the UK: A New Social Movement?" In *Social Movements in Health*, ed. Phil Brown and Stephen Zavestoski, 57–76. Oxford: Blackwell Publishing.
Altman, Rebecca Gasior. 2004. "Biographical Disruption and Local Anti-Toxics Activism." M.A. thesis, Department of Sociology, Brown University.
———. 2006. "Body of Evidence: Reproductive Health and the Environment." Report published by Collaborative on Health and the Environment—Alaska and Alaska Community Action on Toxics.
———. 2008. "Chemical Body Burden and Place-Based Struggles for Environmental Health and Justice: A Multi-Sited Ethnography." Ph.D. diss., Department of Sociology, Brown University.

———. 2008. Gasior, Rachel Morello-Frosch, Julia Green Brody, Ruthann Rudel, Phil Brown, and Mara Averick. "Pollution Comes Home and Gets Personal: Women's Experience of Household Chemical Exposure." *Journal of Health and Social Behavior* 49(4): 417–435.

Amenta, Edwin, Bruce Carruthers, and Yvonne Zylan. 1992. "A Hero for the Aged? The Townsend Movement, the Political Mediation Model, and U.S. Old-Age Policy, 1934–1950." *American Journal of Sociology* 98 (September): 308–39.

American Bankers Association. 2005. "Bankers Form Health Savings Account Council." http://www.theabia.com.

American Medical Association. 1995. Statement of the American Medical Association before the Health Subcommittee, Way and Means, House of Representatives (June 27): 97–100.

American Psychiatric Association. 2000. *Diagnostic and Statistical Manual of Mental Disorders DSM-IV-TR*. 4th ed. Washington, D.C.: American Psychiatric Association.

American Public Health Association. 1941. *Community Organizing for Health Education*. Cambridge, MA: The Technology Press.

American Sociological Association Task Force on Institutionalizing Public Sociologies. 2005. "Public Sociology and the Roots of American Sociology: Re-Establishing Our Connections to the Public: Interim Report and Recommendations to the ASA Council." Available from http://pubsoc.wisc.edu/. Accessed September 24.

America's Health Insurance Plans. 2008. "Health Plans Offer Comprehensive Reform Proposal." http://www.ahip.org/content/pressrelease.aspx?docid=25126. Accessed December 29.

Amis, John, Trevor Slack, and C. R. Hinings. 2004. "The Pace, Sequence, and Linearity of Radical Change." *Academy of Management Review* 47(1): 15–39.

Andrews, Kenneth T. 1997. "The Impacts of Social Movements on the Political Process: The Civil Rights Movement and Black Electoral Politics in Mississippi." *American Sociological Review* 62(5): 800–19.

———. 2001. "Social Movements and Policy Implementation: The Mississippi Civil Rights Movement and the War on Poverty, 1965 to 1971." *American Sociological Review* 66:71–95.

Anglin, Mary K. 1997. "Working from the Inside Out: Implications of Breast Cancer Activism for Biomedical Policies and Practices." *Social Science & Medicine* 44:1403–15.

Anonymous. *Bioethics and Public Policy Program, Center for Ethics and Public Policy*. Online. Available at http://www.eppc.org/default.asp.

———. Bioethics Resources on the Web: Academic Centers and Programs. Online. Available at http://boethics.od.nih.gov/academic.

———. Center for Bioethics and Human Dignity, Trinity University. Online. Available at www.cbhd.org.

———. Hands Off Our Ovaries. Online. Available at http://www.handsoffourovaries.com.

———. Progressive Bioethics Project, Center for American Progress. Online. Available at http://www.americanprogress.org/projects/bioethics.

Anspach, Renee. 1979. "From Stigma to Identity Politics: Political Activism among the Disabled and Former Mental Patients." *Social Science and Medicine* 13A: 776–83.

———. 1993. *Deciding Who Lives: Fateful Choices in the Intensive-Care Nursery*. Berkeley and Los Angeles: University of California Press.

———, and Sydney A. Halpern. 2008. "Cruzan to Schiavo: How Bioethics Entered the 'Culture Wars.'" In *Bioethical Issues, Sociological Perspectives*, ed. Barbara Katz Rothman, Elizabeth M. Armstrong, and Rebecca Tigger, 33–64. Oxford: Elsevier.

Archer, Bill. 1995. Testimony of Rep. Bill Archer (R-TX) before the Health Subcommittee, Way and Means, House of Representatives (June 27): 26–27.

Archer, Robin. 2007. *Why Is There No Labor Party in the United States?* Princeton: Princeton University Press.

Archibald, Matthew E. 2007. *The Evolution of Self-Help.* New York: Palgrave Macmillan.

Armstrong, Elizabeth A. 2002. *Forging Gay Identities: Organizing Sexuality in San Francisco, 1950–1994.* Chicago: University of Chicago Press.

———, and Mary Bernstein. 2008. "Culture, Power, and Institutions: A Multi-Institutional Politics Approach to Social Movements." *Sociological Theory* 26(1): 74–99.

———, Daniel P. Carpenter, and Marie Hojnacki. 2006. "Whose Deaths Matter? Mortality, Advocacy, and Attention to Disease in the Mass Media." *Journal of Health Politics, Policy and Law* 31(4): 729–72.

Arndt, Margarete, and Barbara Bigelow. 2000. "Presenting Structural Innovation in an Institutional Environment: Hospitals' Use of Impression Management." *Administrative Science Quarterly* 45(3): 494–522.

Asch, Steven M., Eve A. Kerr, Joan Keesey, John L. Adams, Claude M. Setodji, Shaista Malik, and Elizabeth A. McGlynn. 2006. "Who Is at Greatest Risk for Receiving Poor-Quality Health Care?" *New England J. of Medicine* 354:2617–19.

Asnis, D., R. Conetta, and G. Waldman, et al. 1999. "Outbreak of West Nile-like Viral Encephalitis: New York." *Centers for Disease Control, Morbidity and Mortality Weekly Report* 48(38): 845–49.

Associated Press. 1993. "Doctors Confirm One Oregon Case of Mystery Illness." *New York Times,* August 11.

Associated Press. 2005a. "Florida Closes its Investigation into Collapse of Schiavo." *New York Times,* July 8.

Associated Press. 2005b. "Schiavo Dies, Ending Bitter Case over Feeding Tube." *New York Times,* April 1.

Astin, John. 1998. "Why Patients Use Alternative Medicine: Results of a National Study." *Journal of American Medical Association* 279:1548–53.

Auer, Lisa. 1990. "Developing a Clinical Research Agenda for Women." *PI Perspectives* October 9.

Auerbach, Judith D., and Anne E. Figert. 1995. "Women's Health Research: Public Policy and Sociology." *Journal of Health and Social Behavior* 35:115–31.

Avery, Byllye Y. 1996. "Breathing Life into Ourselves: The Evolution of the National Black Women's Health Project." In *Perspectives in Medical Sociology*, ed. P. Brown, 761–76. Prospect Heights, Ill.: Waveland Press.

Ayers, Michael D. 2003. "Comparing Collective Identity in Online and Offline Feminist Activists." In *Cyberactivism: Online Activism in Theory and Practice*, ed. Martha McCaughey and Michael D. Ayers, 145–64. New York: Routledge.

"Back Medicare, Afro-American Group Pleads." 1962. *Chicago Daily Defender*, June 26, 6.

Baird, Karen L. 1999. "The New NIH and FDA Medical Research Policies: Targeting Gender, Promoting Justice." *Journal of Health Politics, Policy and Law* 24(3): 531–65.

Balbus, John M., and Mark L. Wilson. 2000. *Human Health and Global Climate Change: A Review of Potential Impacts in the United States* Arlington, VA:.Pew Center on Global Climate Change.

Barkan, Steven. 1984. Legal control of the southern civil rights movement. *American Sociological Review* 49:552–65.

Barker, Kristin. 2005. *The Fibromyalgia Story: Medical Authority and Women's Worlds of Pain.* Philadelphia: Temple University Press.

Barr, Donald A. 2008. *Health Disparities in the United States: Social Class, Race, Ethnicity and Health.* Baltimore: Johns Hopkins University Press.

Bartunek, J. M. 2004. "Is Design Science Better at Creating Actionable Research and Knowledge than Action Research Is?" Symposium at the Annual Meeting of the Academy of Management, August 6–11, New Orleans.

Barzansky, Barbara, and Sylvia Etzel. 2003. "Educational Programs in U.S. Medical Schools, 2002–2003." *Journal of American Medical Association* 290:1190–96.

Bate, S. Paul. 2005. "Ethnography with 'Attitude': Mobilizing Narratives for Public Sector Change." In *Organizing Innovation: New Approaches to Cultural Change and Intervention in Public Sector Organizations*, ed. M. Veenswijk, 105–32. Amsterdam: IOS Press.

———. 2007. "Bringing the Design Sciences to Organization Development and Change Management." Special issue, *Journal of Applied Behavioral Science* 43(1): 8–11.

———, Helen Bevan, and Glenn Robert. 2004. "Towards a Million Change Agents. A Review of the Social Movements Literature: Implications for Large Scale Change in the NHS." Leicester: NHS Modernization Agency.

———, Peter Mendel, and Glenn Robert. 2008. *Organizing for Quality. The Improvement Journeys of Leading Hospitals in Europe and the United States.* Oxford: Radcliff Publishing.

———, and Glenn Robert. 2002. "Studying Health Care 'Quality' Qualitatively: The Dilemmas and Tensions Between Different Forms of Evaluation Research Within the UK National Health Service." *Qualitative Health Research* 12(7): 966–81.

———, and Glenn Robert. 2007. "Toward More User-Centric OD: Lessons from the Field of Experience-Based Design and a Case Study." *The Journal of Applied Behavioral Science* 43(1): 41–66.

———, Glenn Robert, and Helen Bevan. 2004. "The Next Phase of Health Care Improvement: What Can We Learn from Social Movements?" *Quality & Safety in Health Care* 13(1): 62–66.

Bateson, Gregory. 1973. "A Theory of Play and Phantasy." In *Steps to an Ecology of Mind*, 177–93. New York: Ballantine Books.

Battelle. 2008. Interim DFC Program evaluation findings report. Battelle Memorial Institute. 12-15-2008.

Beck, Don, and Christopher Cowan. 1996. *Spiral Dynamics: Mastering Values, Leadership and Change.* Oxford: Blackwell.

Benford, Robert D. 1993. "Frame Disputes within the Nuclear Disarmament Movement." *Social Forces* 71:677–701.

———, and Scott Hunt. 1992. "Dramaturgy and Social Movements: The Social Construction and Communication of Power." *Sociological Inquiry* 62(1): 36–55.

———, and David A. Snow. 2000. "Framing Process and Social Movements: An Overview and Assessment." *Annual Review of Sociology* 26:611–39.

Bennis, Warren, and James O'Toole. 2005. "How Business Schools Lost Their Way." *Harvard Business Review* 83(5): 96–104.

Bergman, Abraham. 1986. *The Discovery of Sudden Infant Death Syndrome: Lessons in The Practice of Political Medicine.* New York: Praeger.

Berman, Brian, Betsy Singh, Susan Hartnoll, B. Krishna Singh, and David Reilly. 1998. "Primary Care Physicians and Complementary-Alternative Medicine: Training, Attitudes and Practice Patterns." *Journal of the American Board of Family Practice* 4:272–81.

Bernard, Susan, and Michael A. McGeehin. 2004. "Municipal Heat Wave Response Plans." *American Journal of Public Health* 94(9): 1520–22.

Bernard, Susan, Jonathan Samet, Anne Grambsch, Kristie Ebi, and Isabelle Romieu. 2001. "The Potential Impacts of Climate Variability and Change on Air Pollution—Related Health Effects in the United States." *Environmental Health Perspectives* 109 (suppl. 2): 199–209.

Bernstein, Mary. 1997. "Celebration and Suppression: The Strategic Uses of Identity by the Lesbian and Gay Movement." *American Journal of Sociology* 103:531–65.

Berry, Gregory R. 2003. "Organizing against Multinational Corporate Power in Cancer Alley: The Activist Community as Primary Stakeholder." *Organization and Environment* 16:3–33.

Berry, Jeffrey M. 1989. *The Interest Group Society*. New York: HarperCollins.

Berwick, Don M. 2003. "Improvement, Trust, and the Healthcare Workforce." *Quality & Safety in Health Care* 12(6): 448–52.

Beschloss, Michael. 2001. *Reaching for Glory: Lyndon Johnson's Secret White House Tapes, 1964–1965*. New York: Simon and Schuster.

Bevan, Helen, Glenn Robert, S. Paul Bate, Lynne Maher, and Julie Wells. 2007. "Using a Design Approach to Assist Large-Scale Organizational Change: '10 High Impact Changes' to Improve the National Health Service in England." *The Journal of Applied Behavioral Science* 43(1): 135–52.

Biggart, Nicole. 1977. "The Creative-Destructive Process of Organizational Change—The Case of the Post Office." *Administrative Science Quarterly* 22(3): 410–26.

Binder, Amy. 2002. *Contentious Curricula: Afrocentrism and Creationism in American Public Schools*. Princeton: Princeton University Press.

Bird, Chloe E, and Patricia P. Rieker. 2008. *Gender and Health: The Effects of Constrained Choices and Social Policies*. Cambridge: Cambridge University Press.

Bissinger, Buzz. 1997. *A Prayer for the City*. New York: Random House.

Blee, Kathleen. 2002. *Inside Organized Racism: Women and Men in the Hate Movement*. Berkeley and Los Angeles: University of California Press.

Blumer, Herbert. 1969. *Symbolic Interactionism*. Englewood Cliffs, N.J.: Transition.

———. 1995. "Social Movement." In *Social Movement: Critiques, Concepts and Case Studies*, ed. S.M. Lyman, 60–83. London: Macmillan.

Boin, Arjen, Paul 't Hart, Eric Stern, and Bengt Sundelius. 2005. *The Politics of Crisis Management: Public Leadership under Pressure*. Cambridge: Cambridge University Press.

Boli, John, and George Thomas. 1999. "INGOs and The Organization of World Culture." In *Constructing World Culture*, ed. John Boli and George M. Thomas, 13–49. Stanford, Calif.: Stanford University Press.

Boris, Eileen. 1993. "The Power of Motherhood: Black and White Activist Women Redefine the Political." In *Mothers of a New World: Maternalist Politics and the Origins of Welfare States*, ed. Seth Koven and Sonya Michel, 213–45. New York: Routledge.

Boris, Elizabeth T., and C. Eugene Steuerle. 2006. "Scope and Dimensions of the Nonprofit Sector." In *The Nonprofit Sector: A Research Handbook*, ed. W. W. Powell and R. Steinberg, 66–88. New Haven: Yale University Press.

Borkman, Thomasina. 1991. "Introduction." *American Journal of Community Psychology* 19(5): 643–50.

Bosk, Charles L. 1979. *Forgive and Remember*. Chicago: University of Chicago Press.

———. 2007. "Either Way the Political Culture Loses." *Society* 44(4): 45–47.

Bourdieu, Pierre. 1975. "The Specificity of the Scientific Field and the Social Conditions for the Progress of Reason." *Social Science Information* 14:19–47.

———. 1977. *Outline of a Theory of Practice*. Cambridge: Cambridge University Press.

———. 1984. *Distinction: A Social Critique of the Judgment of Taste*. Cambridge: Harvard University Press.

———. 1985. "The Market of Symbolic Goods." *Poetics* 14(April): 13–44.

———, and Lois J. D. Wacquant. 1992. *Invitation to Reflexive Sociology*. Chicago: University of Chicago Press.

Bowen, William J. 2003. "Policy Innovation and Health Insurance Reform in the American States: An Event History Analysis of State Medical Savings Account Adoptions (1993–1996)." Ph.D. diss., Florida State University.

Bracht, Neil. 1999. *Health Promotion at the Community Level* (revised edition). Newbury Park, CA: SAGE.

Breen, Catherine, Amy D. Abernathy, Katherine H. Abbott, and James A. Tulsay. 2001. "Conflict Associated with Decisions to Limit Life-Sustaining Treatment in ICU's." *Journal of General Internal Medicine* 16:283–89.

Brenner, Barbara. 2003. "BCA Withdraws Support for Breast-Milk Biomonitoring Program." *Breast Cancer Action Newsletter* 75 (Jan./Feb.).

Britt, Lory, and David Heise. 2000. "From Shame to Pride in Identity Politics." In *Self, Identity, and Social Movements*, ed. Sheldon Stryker, Timothy J. Owens, and Robert W. White, 252–70 Minneapolis: University of Minnesota Press.

Broad, K. L. 2002. "GLB + T?: Gender/Sexuality Movements and Transgender Collective Identity (De)Constructions." *International Journal of Sexuality and Gender Studies* 7(4): 241–64.

Brock, David, Michael Powell, and C. R. Hinings. 1999. *Restructuring the Professional Organization: Accounting, Healthcare and Law*. London: Routledge.

Brody, Julia Green, Rachel Morello-Frosch, Phil Brown, Ruthann A. Rudel, Rebecca Gasior Altman, Margaret Frye, Cheryl C. Osimo, Carla Perez, and Liesel M. Seryak. 2007. "Is It Safe? New Ethics for Reporting Personal Exposures to Environmental Chemicals." *American Journal of Public Health* 97:1547–54.

Brokaw, James, Godfrey Tunnicliff, Beat Raess, and Dale Saxon. 2002. "The Teaching of Complementary and Alternative Medicine in U.S. Medical Schools: A Survey of Course Directors." *Academic Medicine* 77:876–81.

Brown, E. Richard. 1983. Community Organization Influence on Local Public Health Care Policy: A General Research Model and Comparative Case Study. *Health Education Quarterly* 10(3–4):205–233.

Brown, Jenny. 2008. "Health Care for America Now: Which Side Are They On?" *MRZine*, October 7, http://www.monthlyreview.org/mrzine/brown100708.html. Accessed November 19.

Brown, Phil. 1987. "Popular Epidemiology: Community Response to Toxic Waste-Induced Disease in Woburn, Massachusetts." *Science, Technology, and Human Values* 12:78–85.

———. 2007. *Toxic Exposures: Contested Illnesses and the Environmental Health Movement*. New York: Columbia University Press.

———, and Stephen Zavestoski. 2004. "Social Movements in Health: An Introduction." *Sociology of Health and Illness* 6:679–94.

———, and Stephen Zavestoski. 2005. "Social Movements in Health: An Introduction." In *Social Movements in Health*, ed. Phil Brown and Stephen Zavestoski. Oxford: Blackwell.

———, Brian Mayer, Stephen Zavestoski, Theo Luebke, Joshua Mandelbaum, and Sabrina McCormick. 2005. "Clearing the Air and Breathing Freely: The Health Politics of Pollution and Asthma." *International Journal of Health Services* 34(1): 39–63.

———, Sabrina McCormick, Brian Mayer, Stephen Zavestoski, Rachel Morello-Frosch, Rebecca Gasior Altman, and Laura Senier. 2006. "A Lab of Our Own: Environmental Breast Cancer Causation and Challenges to the Dominant Epidemiological Paradigm." *Science, Technology & Human Values* 31:499–536.

———, Rachel Morello-Frosch, Julia Green Brody, Rebecca Gasior Altman, Ruthann A. Rudel, Laura Senier, and Carla Perez. 2008. IRB challenges in multipartner community-based participatory research. Last accessed December 15, 2005. http://www.researcheth-ics.org/uploads/pdf/x-IRB-paper%206-16-07%20rev.pdf.

————, Stephen Zavestoski, Theo Luebke, Joshua Mandelbaum, Sabrina McCormick, and Brian Mayer. 2003. "The Health Politics of Asthma: Environmental Justice and Collective Illness Experience in the United States." *Social Science and Medicine* 57:453–64.

————, Stephen Zavestoski, Brian Mayer, Sabrina McCormick, and Pamela S. Webster. 2002. "Policy Outcomes of Environmental Health Disputes." *Annals of the American Academy of Political and Social Science* 584(1): 175–202.

————, Stephen Zavestoski, Sabrina McCormick, Joshua Mandelbaum, Theo Luebke, and Meadow Linder. 2001a. "A Gulf of Difference: Disputes Over Gulf War-Related Illnesses." *Journal of Health and Social Behavior* 42:235–57.

————, Stephen Zavestoski, Sabrina McCormick, Joshua Mandelbaum, and Theo Luebke. 2001b. "Print Media Coverage of Environmental Causation of Breast Cancer." *Sociology of Health and Illness* 23(6): 747–75.

————, Stephen Zavestoski, Sabrina McCormick, Brian Mayer, Rachel Morello-Frosch, and Rebecca Gasior Altman. 2004. "Embodied Health Movements: New Approaches to Social Movements in Health." *Sociology of Health & Illness* 26(1): 50–80.

Brown, Theodore M. and Elizabeth Fee. 2006. Rudolf Carl Virchow: medical scientist, social reformer, role model. *American Journal of Public Health* 96(12): 2104–2105.

Bruch, Heike, and Sumantra Ghoshal. 2003. "Unleashing Organizational Energy." *MIT Sloan Management Review* 45(1/Fall): 45–51.

Buchanan, David, Rachel Addicott, Louise Fitzgerald, Ewan Ferlie, and Juan Baeza. 2007. "Nobody in Charge: Distributed Change Agency in Healthcare." *Human Relations* 60 (7): 1065–90.

Bucher, R., and A. Strauss. 1961. "Professions in Process." *The American Journal of Sociology* 66:325–34.

Bull, Chris. 1988. "Seizing Control of the FDA." *Gay Community News*, October 16–22.

Bullard, Robert. 1990. *Dumping in Dixie: Race, Class, and Environmental Quality*. Boulder, Colo.: Westview Press.

————. 1993. *Confronting Environmental Racism: Voices from the Grassroots*. Boston: South End Press.

Burawoy, Michael. 2004. "Public Sociologies: Contradictions, Dilemmas, and Possibilities" *Social For*ces 82:1603–18.

————, Joseph A. Blum, Sheba George, Zsuzsa Gille, Millie Thayer, Teresa Gowan, Lynne Haney, Maren Klawiter, Steve H. Lopez, and Sean O'Riain. 2000. Global Ethnograpy: Forces, Connections, and Imaginations. Berkeley and Los Angeles: University of California Press.

Burns, Tom. 1961. "Micropolitics: Mechanisms of Institutional Change." *Administrative Science Quarterly* 6 (Dec.): 257–81.

Burry, John Jr. 1995. Testimony of John Burry Jr., Chairman and Chief Executive Officer of Blue Cross and Blue Shield of Ohio before the Health Subcommittee, Way and Means, House of Representatives (June 27): 101–107.

Burstein, Paul. 1991. "Legal Mobilization as a Social Movement Tactic: The Struggle for Equal Employment Opportunity." *American Journal of Sociology* 96:1201–25.

————. 1999. "Social Movements and Public Policy." In *How Social Movements Matter*, ed. Marco Giugni, Doug McAdam, and Charles Tilly, 3–21. Minneapolis: University of Minnesota Press.

————, Marie Bricher, and Rachel Einwohner. 1995. "Policy Alternatives and Political Change: Work, Gender, and Family on the Congressional Agenda, 1945–1990." *American Sociological Review* 60:67–83.

————, Rachel L. Einwohner, and Jocelyn A. Hollander. 1995. "The Success of Political Movements: A Bargaining Perspective." In *The Politics of Social Protest: Comparative*

Studies of States and Social Movements, ed. J. Craig Jenkins and Bert Klandermans, 275–95. Minneapolis: University of Minnesota Press.

Burt, Robert A. 2006. "Law's Effect on Quality of End-Of-Life Care: Lessons from the Schiavo Case." *Critical Care Medicine* 34 (11 Suppl.): S348–54.

Burt, Ronald S. 1992. *Structural Holes: The Social Structure of Competition*. Cambridge: Harvard University Press.

Butterfoss, Frances Dunn, Robert M. Goodman, and Abraham Wandersman. 1995. Community coalitions for prevention and health promotion. *Health Education Research* 8(3): 315–330.

Bybee, Roger. 2007. "The Wisconsin Way." *American Prospect*, March 29.

Cable, Sherry, and Charles Cable. 1995. *Environmental Problems/Grassroots Solutions: The Politics of Grassroots Environmental Conflict*. New York: St. Martin's Press.

Cable, Sherry, Tamara Mix, and Donald Hastings. 2005. "Mission Impossible? Environmental Justice Activists' Collaborations with Professional Environmentalists and with Academics." In *Power, Justice, and the Environment*, ed. D. N. Pellow and R. J. Brulle, 55–75. Boston: MIT Press.

Cable, Sherry, Thomas E. Shriver, and Tamara L. Mix. 2008. "Risk Society and Contested Illness." *American Sociological Review* 73 (June): 380–401.

Cacciope, Ron, and Mark Edwards. 2005. "Seeking the Holy Grail of Organizational Development. A Synthesis of Integral Theory, Spiral Dynamics, Corporate Transformation and Action Inquiry." *Leadership & Organization Development Journal* 26(2): 86–105.

CAHCIM (The Consortium of Academic Health Centers for Integrative Medicine). 2008. http://www.imconsortium.org/cahcim/home.html. Accessed February 22.

California HealthCare Foundation. 2007. *Snapshot: Health Care Costs 101*. Oakland, Ca. HealthCare Foundation.

Callahan, Daniel. 1996. "Bioethics, Our Crowd, and Ideology." *Hastings Center Report* 26(6): 3–4.

———. 2006. "The Emergence of a Politicized Bioethics." Panel in *Bioethics and Politics: Past, Present, and Future*, Washington, D.C.: Center for American Progress. www.americanprogress.org/transcriptforbioethicsconference.

Callahan, Daniel. 2007. "Images, Arguments, and Interests." *Society* 44(4): 22–25.

Callahan, Jane. 2007. Best practices in community problem solving. Presented at the CADCA National Coalition Institute Missouri Department of Mental Health, Spring Training Institute, May 2007. Online. Available: http://www.dmh.mo.gov/ada/provider/CallahanJaneMo.Dept.ofMentalHealthSpringTraining2007BestPractices.ppt. Accessed December 15, 2008.

Callon, Michel. 2003. "The Increasing Involvement of Concerned Groups in R&D Policies: What Lessons for Public Powers?" In *Science and Innovation: Rethinking the Rationales for Funding and Governance*, ed. A. Geuna, A. J. Salter, and W. E. Steinmueller, 30–68. Cheltenham, U.K.: Edward Elgar.

———, and Vololona Rabeharisoa. 2003. "Research 'in the Wild' and the Shaping of New Social Identities." *Technology in Society* 25(2): 193–204.

Campbell, Colin, Bert A. Rockman, and Andrew Rudalevige, ed. 2007. *The George W. Bush Legacy*. Washington D.C: CQ.

Campbell, John T. 2002. "Ideas, Politics and Public Policy." *Annual Review of Sociology* 28:21–38.

Campbell-Lendrum, D., and Rosalie Woodruff. 2006. "Comparative Risk Assessment of the Burden of Disease from Climate Change." *Environmental Health Perspectives* 114(12): 1935–41.

Campos, Paul. 2004. *The Obesity Myth*. New York: Gotham Books.

————, Abigail Saguy, Paul Ernsbrerger, Eric Oliver, and Glenn Gaesser. 2005. "The Epidemiology of Overweight and Obesity: Public Health Crisis or Moral Panic." *International Journal of Epidemiology* 35(1): 55–60.

Canaday, Margot. 2009. *The Straight State: Sexuality and Citizenship in Twentieth Century America*. Princeton: Princeton University Press.

Canadian Health Services Research Foundation. 2007. "Myth: User Fees Would Stop Waste and Ensure Better Use of the Healthcare System." *PNHP Newsletter* (Spring): 54–55.

Cannon, Michael F. 2006. "Health Savings Accounts: Do the Critics Have a Point?" *Social Science Research Network Working Paper Series No. 569*. Social Science Research Center.

Carroll, Glenn R., and Michael T. Hannan. 2000. *The Demography of Corporations and Industries*. Princeton: Princeton University Press.

Casamayou, Maureen Hogan. 2001. *The Politics of Breast Cancer*. Washington, D.C.: Georgetown University Press.

Cashman, Suzanne B., Sarah Adeky, Alex J. Allen, Jason Corburn, Barbara A. Israel, Jaime Monano, Alvin Rafelito et al. 2008. "The Power and the Promise: Working with Communities to Analyze the Data, Interpret Findings, and Get to Outcomes." *American Journal of Public Health* 98(8):1407–1417.

Casper, Monica, and Marc Berg. 1995. "Constructivist Perspectives on Medical Work: Medical Practices and Science and Technology Studies." *Science, Technology, and Human Values* 20 (Autumn): 395–407.

Castells, Manuel. 1997. *Power of Identity: The Information Age: Economy, Society, and Culture*. Cambridge: Blackwell Publishers.

Center for Public Integrity. 1994. *Well-Healed: Inside Lobbying for Health Care Reform*. Washington, D.C.: Center for Public Integrity.

Cheadle, Allen, Edward Wagner, Mary Walls, Paula Diehr, Michelle Bell, Carolyn Anderman, Colleen McBride et al. 2001. The Effect of Neighborhood-Based Community Organizing: Results from the Seattle Minority Youth Health Project. *Health Serv.Res* 36, no. 4:671–689.

Check, Erika. 2005. "US Progressives Fight for a Voice in Bioethics. Nature.com, October 12.

Chicago Sun-Times. 1995. Hantavirus Brochure. Chicago, Ill.

Chin, Arthur E., Katrina Hedberg, Grant K. Higginson, and David W. Fleming. 1999. "Legalized Physician-Assisted Suicide: The First Year's Experience." *New England Journal of Medicine* 340:577–83.

Chrysler, Dick. 1995. Testimony of Rep. Dick Chrysler (R-MI) before the Health Subcommittee, Way and Means, House of Representatives (June 27): 16–17.

Clarke, Adele. 1990. "A Social Worlds Adventure: The Case of Reproductive Science." In *Theories of Science in Society*, ed. S. E. Cozzens and T. F. Gieryn, 15–42. Bloomington: Indiana University Press.

Clarke, Adele E. 2005. *Situational Analysis: Grounded Theory after the Postmodern Turn*. Thousand Oaks, Calif.: Sage.

————, and Virginia L. Olesen, eds. 1999. *Revisioning Women, Health, and Healing: Feminist, Cultural and Technoscience Perspectives*. New York: Routledge.

Clarke, Adele E., Janet K. Shim, Laura Mamo, Jennifer R. Fosket, and Jennifer R. Fishman. 2003. "Biomedicalization: Technoscientific Transformations of Health, Illness, and U.S. Biomedicine." *American Sociological Review* 68:161–94.

Clemens, Elizabeth. 1993. "Organizational Repertoires and Institutional Change: Women's Groups and the Transformation of U.S. Politics, 1890–1920." *American Journal of Sociology* 98(4): 755–98.

———. 1996. "Organizational Form as Frame: Collective Identity and Political Strategy in the American Labor Movement." In *Comparative Perspectives on Social Movements: Political Opportunities, Mobilizing Structures, and Cultural Framings*, ed. Doug McAdam, John D. McCarthy, and Mayer N. Zald, 205–26. Cambridge: Cambridge University Press.

———. 1997. *The People's Lobby: Organizational Innovation and the Rise of Interest Group Politics in the United States, 1890–1925*. Chicago: University of Chicago Press.

———. 2005. "Two Kinds of Stuff. The Current Encounter of Social Movements and Organizations." In *Social Movements and Organization Theory*, ed. G. F. Davis, D. McAdam, W. R. Scott, and M. N. Zald, 351–65. Cambridge: Cambridge University Press.

Clinton Campaign Brochure. 1992. www.4president.org/brochures/billclinton1992brochure. htm. Accessed November 15.

Cloward, Richard A., and Frances Fox Piven. 1984. "Review: Disruption and Organization: A Rejoinder to William A. Gamson and Emilie Schmeidler." *Theory and Society* 13(4): 587–99.

Cohen, Cathy J. 1996. "Contested Membership: Black Gay Identities and the Politics of AIDS." In *Queer Theory/Sociology*, ed. S. Seidman, 362-94. Cambridge: Blackwell Publishers.

———. 1997. *The Boundaries of Blackness: AIDS and the Breakdown of Black Politics*. Chicago: University of Chicago Press.

Cohen, Eric. 2005. "How Liberalism Failed Terri Schiavo." *The Weekly Standard* 10(26): April 24.

———. 2006. *Conservative Bioethics: The Search for Wisdom*. Hastings Center Report.

Cohen, Rima. 2001. "From Strategy to Reality: the Enactment of New York's Family Health Plan Plus Program." *Journal of Health Politics, Policy, and Law* 26:1375–93.

Cole, Luke W., and Sheila, R. Foster. 2001. *From the Ground Up: Environmental Racism and the Rise of the Environmental Justice Movement*. New York and London: New York University Press.

Collins, David. 1998. *Organizational Change. Sociological Perspectives*. London: Routledge.

Common Cause. 1995. "Politically Insured, Doctor Recommended: Health Insurance and Doctors Give Nearly $50 Million in PAC and Soft Money Contributions During Last Decade." *Common Cause News*, December 1. http://www.ccsi.com/~comcause/news/medical.html.

Conant, James K. 2006. *Wisconsin Politics and Government: America's Laboratory of Democracy*. Lincoln: University of Nebraska Press.

Congressional Universe/Congressional Information Services, 1955–2000 (CIS subject index).

Conrad, Peter. 2007. *The Medicalization of Society: On the Transformation of Human Conditions into Treatable Disorders*. Baltimore: Johns Hopkins University Press.

Consumerwatchdog.org. 2008. "President-Elect Obama: Continue to Oppose Mandatory Purchase of Junk Health Insurance." http://www.consumerwatchdog.org/patients/articles/?storyId=24046. Accessed December 29.

Cooper, David. J., C. R. Hinings, Royston Greenwood, and John L. Brown. 1996. "Sedimentation and Transformation in Organization Change: The Case of Canadian Law Firms." *Organization Studies* 17(4): 623–47.

Corburn, Jason. 2005. *Street Science: Community Knowledge and Environmental Health Justice*. Cambridge: MIT Press.

Corrigan, Oonagh P. 2002. " 'First in Man': The Politics and Ethics of Women in Clinical Drug Trials." *Feminist Review* 72:40–52.

Cozzens, Susan E., and Shana Solomon. 1994. "Women and Minorities in Biomedical Politics: Case Studies in Democracy?" Paper presented at Annual Meeting of the American Sociological Association, Los Angeles, August.

Cress, Daniel M., and Daniel J. Myers. 2004. "Authority in Contention." In *Authority in Contention*. Vol. 25, *Research in Social Movements, Conflict, and Change*, ed. Daniel J. Myers and Daniel M. Cress, 279–84. Oxford: JAI Press.

Cress, Daniel M., and David A. Snow. 1996. "Mobilization at the Margins: Resources, Benefactors, and the Viability of Homeless Social Movement Organizations." *American Sociological Review* 6 (December): 1089–109.

Cress, Daniel M., and David A. Snow. 2000. "The Outcomes of Homeless Mobilization: The Influence of Organization, Disruption, Political Mediation, and Framing." *American Journal of Sociology* 105 (January): 1063–104.

Crossley, Nick. 2002. *Making Sense of Social Movements*. Buckingham: Open University Press.

———. 2006. *Contesting Psychiatry: Social Movements in Mental Health*. New York: Routledge.

Crotty, Jo. 2006. "Reshaping the Hourglass? The Environmental Movement and Civil Society Development in the Russian Federation." *Organization Studies* 27(9): 1319–38.

Cuneo, Michael. 1989. *Catholics Against the Church: Anti-Abortion Protest in Toronto, 1969–1985*. Toronto: University of Toronto Press.

Curtis, J. Randall, Ruth A. Engelberg, Marjorie D. Wenreich, Sarah E.Shannon, and Patsy D. Treece. 2005. "Missed Opportunities during Family Conferences about End-of-Life Care in the Intensive Care Unit." *American Journal of Respiratory and Critical Care Medicine* 171:844–49.

"D.C. Marchers Fault Insurance Industry's Approach to AIDS." 1991. *The Washington Post*, May 14, B2.

D'Aunno, Thomas, Robert I. Sutton, and Richard H. Price. 1991. "Isomorphism and External Support in Conflicting Institutional Environments: A Study of Drug Abuse Treatment Units." *Academy of Management Journal* 34:636–61.

Danziger, Sheldon, and Sandra K. Danziger. 2005. "The U.S. Social Safety Net and Poverty: Lessons Learned and Promising Approaches." Paper presented at the Conference on "Poverty and Poverty Reducation Strategies: Mexican and International Experiences," Monterrey, Mexico.

Darnovsky, Marcy, Barbara Epstein, and Richard Flacks, eds. 1995. *Cultural Politics and Social Movements*. Philadelphia: Temple University Press.

Davis, Gerald F., and T. A. Thompson. "A Social Movement Perspective on Corporate Control." *Administrative Science Quarterly* 39 (1994): 141–73.

Davis, Gerald F., and Mayer N. Zald. 2005. "Social Change, Social Theory, and the Convergence of Movements and Organizations." In *Social Movements and Organization Theory*, ed. G. F. Davis, D. McAdam, W. R. Scott, and M. Zald, 335–50. Cambridge: Cambridge University Press.

Davis, Gerald F., Doug McAdam, W. Richard Scott, and Mayer Zald, eds. 2005. *Social Change, Social Theory, and the Convergence of Movements and Organizations*. Cambridge: Cambridge University Press.

Davis, Karen, Stephen C. Schoenbaum, Anne-Marie J. Audet, Michelle M. Doty, and Katie Tenney. 2004. *Mirror, Mirror on the Wall: Looking at the Quality of American Health Care Through the Patient's Lens*. New York: The Commonwealth Fund.

Davis, Kathy. 2007. *The Making of Our Bodies, Ourselves: How Feminism Travels Across Borders*. Durham, N.C.: Duke University Press.

Davison, Kathryn P., James W. Pennebaker, and Sally S. Dickerson. 2000. "Who Talks? The Social Psychology of Illness Support Groups." *American Psychologist* 55:205–17.

Dawson, Jim. 1995. "Beating Disease: Are We up to the Challenge?" *Star Tribune*. Minneapolis, Minn.

DeBruin, Debra A. 1994. "Justice and the Inclusion of Women in Clinical Studies: A Conceptual Framework." In *Women and Health Research: Ethical and Legal Issues of Including Women in Clinical Studies*, ed. A. C. Mastroianni, R. Faden, and D. Federman, 127–50. Washington, D.C.: National Academy Press.

Delbridge, Rick, and Timothy Edwards. 2007. "Reflections on Developments in Institutional Theory: Towards a Relational Approach." *Scandinavian Journal of Management* 23:6191–205.

della Porta, Donatella. 1996. Social Movements and the State: Thoughts on the Policing of Protest. In *Comparative Perspectives on Social Movements.*, eds. McAdam, Doug, John D. McCarthy, and Mayer Zald, 62–92. New York: Cambridge University Press.

della Porta, Donatella and Mario Diani. 1999. *Social Movements: An Introduction*. Oxford, UK: Blackwell.

DelVecchio, Rick. 1990. "500 Protesters Block Market Street Traffic." *San Francisco Chronicle*, June 23.

Den Hond, Frank, and Frank De Bakker. 2007. "Ideologically Motivated Activism: How Activist Groups Influence Corporate Social Change Activities." *Academy of Management Review* 32(3): 901–24.

Dennis, Cindy-Lee, and Leinic Chung-Lee. 2006. "Postpartum Depression Help-Seeking Barriers and Maternal Treatment Preferences: A Qualitative Systematic Review." *Birth* 33(4): 323–31.

Department of Health. 2000. *The NHS Plan: A Plan for Investment, A Plan for Reform*. London: The Stationery Office.

Department of Health and Human Services. 2001. *Healthy People 2010: Understanding and Improving Health*. Washington, D.C.: Department of Health and Human Services.

Derickson, Alan. 1994. "Health Security for All? Social Unionism and Universal Health Insurance, 1935–1958." *Journal of American History* 80(4): 1333–56.

DeVries, Raymond, R. Dingwall, and Kristina Orfali. *Regulating Professions: The Profession of Ethics and the Ethics of Professions*.

DeVries, Raymond, Leigh Turner, Kristina Orfali, and Charles Bosk. 2006. "Social Science and Bioethics: The Way Forward." *Sociology of Health and Illness* 28:665–77.

Dezalay, Yves, and Bryant Garth. 1995. "Merchants of Law as Moral Entrepreneurs: Constructing International Justice from the Competition for Transnational Business Disputes." *Law & Society Review* 29:27–64.

DeZwart, Frank. 2005. "The Dilemma of Recognition: Administrative Categories and Cultural Diversity." *Theory and Society* 34(2): 137–69.

Diani, Mario. 1990. "The Italian Ecology Movement: From Radicalism to Moderation." In *Green Politics One*, ed. W. Rüdig, 153–76. Carbondale: Southern Illinois University Press.

DiMaggio, Paul J. 1983. "State Expansion and Organizational Fields." In *Organization Theory and Public Policy*, ed. Richard H. Hall and Robert E. Quinn, 147–61. Beverly Hills: Sage.

———. 1988. "Interest and Agency in Institutional Theory." In *Institutional Patterns and Organizations: Culture and Environment*, ed. L. G. Zucker, 3–22. Cambridge, Mass.: Ballinger.

———, and Walter W. Powell. 1983. "The Iron Cage Revisited: Institutional Isomorphism and Collective Rationality in Organizational Fields." *American Sociological Review* 48(2): 147–60.

————, and Walter W. Powell. 1991. "The Iron Cage Revisited: Institutional Isomorphism and Collective Rationality." In *The New Institutionalism in Organizational Analysis*, ed. Walter W. Powell and Paul J. DiMaggio, 63–82. Chicago: University of Chicago Press.

Dobratz, Betty A. 2001. "The Role of Religion in the Collective Identity of the White Racialist Movement." *Journal for the Scientific Study of Religion* 40:287–301.

Dorado, Silvia. 2005. "Institutional Entrepreneurship, Partaking, and Convening." *Organization Studies* 26(3): 385–414.

Dorsey, Michael. 2007. "Climate Knowledge and Power: Tales of Septic Tanks, Weather Gods, and Sagas for Climate (In)justice." *Capitalism, Nature, Socialism* 18(2): 7–21.

Downs, Anthony. 1957. *An Economic Theory of Democracy*. New York: Harper & Row.

Dranove, David. 2008. *The Economic Evolution of American Health Care*. Princeton: Princeton University Press.

Drentia, Patricia, and Jennifer L. Moren-Cross. 2005. "Social Capital and Social Support on the Web: The Case of an Internet Mother Site." *Sociology of Health and Illness* 27(7): 920–43.

Dreyfuss, Robert, and Peter Stone. 1996. "Medikill: Golden Rule Insurance has Lavished Campaign Funds on Gingrich and the GOP in order to Promote its Medical Savings Account Scheme—And Destroy Medicare. *Mother Jones*, January/February, 1–8.

Dugan, Kimberly B. 2005. *The Struggle Over Gay, Lesbian, and Bisexual Rights: Facing Off in Cincinnati*. New York: Routledge.

Dunn, Jennifer L. 2004. "The Politics of Empathy: Social Movements and Victim Repertoires." *Sociological Focus* 37:235–50.

Echols, Alice. 1989. *Daring to Be Bad: Radical Feminism in America, 1967–1975*. Minneapolis: University of Minnesota Press.

Eckenwiler, Lisa. 1999. "Pursuing Reform in Clinical Research: Lessons from Women's Experience." *Journal of Law, Medicine & Ethics* 27(2): 158–88.

Eckman, Anne K. 1998. "Beyond 'the Yentl Syndrome': Making Women Visible in Post-1990 Women's Health Discourse." In *The Visible Woman: Imaging Technologies, Gender, and Science*, ed. P. A. Treichler, L. Cartwright, and C. Penley, 130–68. New York: New York University Press.

Einwohner, Rachel L. 2002. "Bringing the Outsiders In: Opponents' Claims and the Construction of Animal Rights Activists' Identity." *Mobilization: The International Journal of Research in Social Movements, Protest, and Contentious Politics* 7:253–68.

Eisenberg, David, Kessler Ronald, Foster, Cindy, Norlock, Frances, Calkins, David, and Thomas Delbanco. 1993. Unconventional Medicine in the United States: Prevalence, costs, and patterns of use. *New England Journal of Medicine* 328:246–252.

————, ———— Roger Davis, Susan Ettner, Scott Appel, Sonja Wilkey, Maria Van Rompay, and Ronald Kessler. 1998. "Trends in Alternative Medicine Use in the United States, 1990–1997: Results of a Follow-Up National Survey." *Journal of American Medical Association* 280:1569–75.

Eisenberg, John B. 2005. *Using Terry: The Religious Right's Conspiracy to Take Away Our Rights*. New York: Harper-Collins.

———— 2005. "The Terri Schiavo Case: Following the Money." *Cal Law*, March 4.

Eisenbert, David, Ronald Kessler, Cindy Foster, Frances Norlock, David Calkins, and Thomas Delbanco. 1993. "Unconventional Medicine in the United States: Prevalence, Costs, and Patterns of Use." *New England Journal of Medicine* 328:246–52.

Elling, Richard C. 2004. "Administering State Programs: Performance and Politics." In *Politics in the American States: A Comparative Analysis*, ed. V. Gray and R. L. Hanson, 261–89. 8th ed. Washington, D.C.: CQ.

Ellingson, Stephen. 1995. "Understanding the Dialectic of Discourse and Collective Action: Public Debate and Rioting in Antebellum Cincinnati." *American Journal of Sociology* 101:100–44.

Environmental Health Coaltion. 2007. "EHC Executive Director Appointed to Landmark Greenhouse Gas Reductions Advisory Committee."

Epstein, Paul R. 2001. "Climate Change and Human Health." *The New England Journal of Medicine* 353:1433–36.

———, and Evan Mills, eds. 2005. *Climate Change Futures: Health, Ecological, and Economic Dimensions.* The Center for Health and the Global Environment, Harvard Medical School.

Epstein, Steven. [1996.] 1999. *Impure Science: AIDS, Activism, and the Politics of Knowledge.* Berkeley and Los Angeles: University of California Press.

———. 2001. "Biomedical Activism: Beyond the Binaries" Conference talk at the Annual Meeting of the Society for Social Studies of Science, Cambridge, Mass., November 1–4.

———. 2003a. "Inclusion, Diversity, and Biomedical Knowledge Making: The Multiple Politics of Representation." In *How Users Matter: The Co-Construction of Users and Technology,* ed. N. Oudshoorn and T. Pinch, 173–90. Cambridge, Mass.: MIT Press.

———. 2003b. "Sexualizing Governance and Medicalizing Identities: The Emergence of 'State-Centered' LGBT Health Politics in the United States." *Sexualities* 6(2): 131–71.

———. 2004. "Bodily Differences and Collective Identities: The Politics of Gender and Race in Biomedical Research in the United States." *Body and Society* 10(2–3): 183–203.

———. 2006. "Institutionalizing the New Politics of Difference in U.S. Biomedical Research: Thinking across the Science/State/Society Divides." In *The New Political Sociology of Science: Institutions, Networks, and Power,* ed. S. Frickel and K. Moore, 327–50. Madison: University of Wisconsin Press.

———. 2007a. *Inclusion: The Politics of Difference in Medical Research.* Chicago: University of Chicago Press.

———. 2007b. "Patient Groups and Health Movements." In *The Handbook of Science and Technology Studies,* ed. E. J. Hackett, O. Amsterdamska, M. Lynch, and J. Wajcman, 499–539. Cambridge: MIT Press.

———. 2008. "The Rise of 'Recruitmentology': Clinical Research, Racial Knowledge, and the Politics of Inclusion and Difference." *Social Studies of Science* 38(5): 739–70.

———. 2009. "Beyond the Standard Human?" in *Standards and Their Stories: How Quantifying, Classifying, and Formalizing Practices Shape Everyday Life,* Martha Lampland and Susan Leigh Star, eds. (Ithaca, NY: Cornell University Press): 35–53.

Evans, John. 2002. *Playing God? Human Genetic Engineering and the Rationalization of Public Bioethical Debate.* Chicago: University of Chicago Press.

Evans, Peter B. 2002. *Livable Cities? Urban Struggles for Livelihood and Sustainability.* Berkeley and Los Angeles: University of California Press.

Evans, Sara. 1979. *Personal Politics: The Roots of Women's Liberation in the Civil Rights Movement and the New Left.* New York: Knopf.

Ewick, Patricia, and Susan Silbey. 2003. "Narrating Social Structure: Stories of Resistance Legal Authority." *American Journal of Sociology* 108 (May): 1328–72.

Fahy, Joe. 2008. "Health Care Dispute Brings Problems: Physicians Will Have to Pay More For Malpractice Insurance, Gov. Rendell Warns." *Post-Gazette,* March 28.

Families USA. 2008. "McCain versus Obama: Key Health Plan Differences." http://www.familiesusa.org/election-2008/mccain-vs-obama-health-plan.html. Accessed November 15.

Fantasia, Rick. 1989. *Cultures of Solidarity: Consciousness, Action, and Contemporary American Workers*. Berkeley and Los Angeles: University of California Press.

Farhang, Sean, and Ira Katznelson. 2005. "The Southern Imposition: Congress and Labor in the New Deal and Fair Deal." *Studies in American Political Development* 19:1–30.

"FDA Debunks Myth of Too-Few-Women-in-Clinical-Trials." 1992. *PMA Newsletter*, October 19, 2–3.

"Fed Up With Insurance, Thousands Nationwide Champion Medicare for All." 2008. *Registered Nurse*, June, 4–5.

Feldberg, Georgina D. 1995. *Disease and Class: Tuberculosis and the Shaping of Modern North American Society*. New Brunswick: Rutgers University Press.

Feldman, Jeffrey. 2007. *Framing the Debate. Famous Presidential Speeches and How Progressives Can Use Them to Change the Conversation (and Win Elections)*. New York: Ig Publishing.

Ferrara, Peter J. 1995. "Gingrich Can Avert GOP Disaster over Medicare." *Wall Street Journal*, May 9, A20.

Ferree, Myra Marx. 2003. "Resonance and Radicalism: Feminist Framing in the Abortion Debates of the United States and Germany." *American Journal of Sociology* 109(2): 304–44.

———, William Anthony Gamson, Jurgen Gerhards, and Dieter Rucht. 2002. *Shaping Abortion Discourse: Democracy and the Public Sphere in Germany and the United States*. New York: Cambridge University Press.

Filene, Peter G. 1998. *In the Arms of Others: A Cultural History of the Right-to-Die Movement in America*. Chicago: I.R. Dee.

Fischer, Frank. 2000. *Citizens, Experts, and the Environment: The Politics of Local Knowledge*. Durham, N.C.: Duke University Press.

Fleischer, Doris, and Frieda Zames. 2000. *The Disability Rights Movement: From Charity to Confrontation*. Philadelphia: Temple University Press.

Flexner, A. 1910. "Medical Education in the United States and Canada: A Report to the Carnegie Foundation for the Advancement of Teaching." Bulletin No. 4. New York: Carnegie Foundation.

Flam, Helena, and Debra King, eds. 2005. *Emotions and Social Movements*. New York: Routledge.

Fligstein, Neil. 1991. "The Structural Transformation of American Industry: An Institutional Account of the Causes of Diversification in the Largest Firms, 1919–1979." In *The New Institutionalism in Organizational Analysis*, ed. Walter W. Powell and Paul J. DiMaggio, 311–36. Chicago: University of Chicago Press.

———. 1998. "Fields, Power, and Social Skill: A Critical Analysis of The New Institutionalisms." Paper presented at Hamburg University, October, 1997.

Food and Drug Administration. 1993. "Guidelines for the Study and Evaluation of Gender Differences in the Clinical Evaluation of Drugs." *Federal Register* 58 (139): 39406–16.

Foucault, Michel. 1977. *Discipline and Punish: The Birth of the Prison*. New York: Vintage.

———. 1980. *Power/Knowledge: Selected Interviews and Other Writings 1972–1977*. New York: Pantheon.

———. 1980. *The History of Sexuality, Volume One: An Introduction*. New York: Vintage.

Fox, Patrick. 1989. "From Senility to Alzheimer's Disease: The Rise of the Alzheimer's Disease Movement." *Milbank Quarterly* 67(1): 58–102.

Fowler-Brown, Angela, Giselle Corbie-Smith, Joanne Garrett, Nicole Lurie. 2007. "Risk of Cardiovascular Events and Death—Does Insurance Matter?" *Journal of General Internal Medicine* 22(4): 502–7.

Fraser, Nancy. 1997. *Justice Interruptus: Critical Reflections on the Postsocialist Condition*. New York: Routledge.

Freidson, Eliot. 1986. *Professional Power*. Chicago: University of Chicago Press.

Freire, Paolo. 1972. *The Pedagogy of the Oppressed*. Harmondsworth: Penguin.

Freudenberg, Nicholas and Urayoana Trinidad. 1992. The Role of Community Organizations in AIDS Prevention in Two Latino Communities in New York City. *Health Education Quarterly*. 19(2): 219–32.

Frickel, Scott. 2004a. "Building an Interdiscipline: Collective Action Framing and the Rise of Genetic Toxicology." *Social Problems* 51:269–87.

———. 2004b. *Chemical Consequences: Environmental Mutagens, Scientist Activism, and the Rise of Genetic Toxicology*. New Brunswick, N.J.: Rutgers University Press.

———. 2006. "When Convention Becomes Contentious: Organizing Science Activism in Genetic Toxicology." In *The New Political Sociology of Science: Institutions, Networks, and Power*, ed. S. Frickel and K. Moore, 185–214. Madison: University of Wisconsin Press.

———, and Neil Gross. 2005. "A General Theory of Scientific/Intellectual Movements." *American Sociological Review* 70:204–32.

———, and Kelly Moore, eds. 2005. *The New Political Sociology of Science: Institutions, Networks, and Power*. Madison: University of Wisconsin Press.

Friedland, Roger. Forthcoming. "Institution, Practice and Ontology: Towards A Religious Sociology." In *Ideology and Organizational Institutionalism, Research in the Sociology of Organizations*, ed. Renate Meyer et al.

———, and Robert R. Alford. 1991. "Bringing Society Back in: Symbols, Practices, and Institutional Contradictions." In *The New Institutionalism in Organizational Analysis*, ed. W. Walter Powell and Paul J. DiMaggio, 232–63. Chicago: Chicago University Press.

Futrell, Robert, and Pete Simi. 2004. "Free Spaces, Collective Identity, and the Persistence of U.S. White Power Activism." *Social Problems* 51(1): 16–42.

Galanter, Marc. 1974. "Why the 'Haves' Come Out Ahead: Speculations on the Limits of Legal Change." *Law and Society Review* 9:95–160.

Gale Research Company. 1955–2000. *Encyclopedia of Associations*, Vol. 1–36, *National Organizations*. Detroit: Gale Research.

Gale, Richard P. 1996. "Social Movements and the State: The Environmental Movement, Countermovement, and Government Agencies. *Sociological Perspectives* 29(2): 202–40.

Gamson, Joshua. 1989. "Silence, Death, and the Invisible Enemy: AIDS Activism and Social Movement 'Newness.'" *Social Problems* 36 (October): 351–67.

———. 1995. "Must Identity Movements Self-Destruct? A Queer Dilemma." *Social Problems* 42:390–407.

Gamson, William A. 1975. *The Strategy of Social Protest*. Homewood: Dorsey Press.

——— and Emilie Schmeidler. 1984. "Review: Organizing the Poor" *Theory and Society*. 13 (4):567–85. 1984.

———. 1990. *The Strategy of Social Protest*. Belmont, Calif.: Wadsworth.

———. 1992a. "The Social Psychology of Collective Action." In *Frontiers in Social Movement Theory*, ed. Aldon D. Morris and Carol McClurg Mueller, 53–76. New Haven, Conn.: Yale University Press.

———. 1992b. *Talking Politics*. Cambridge: Cambridge University Press.

———, and David S. Meyer. 1996. "Framing Political Opportunity." In *Comparative Perspectives On Social Movements: Political Opportunities, Mobilizing Structures, and Cultural Framings*, ed. Doug McAdam, John D. McCarthy, and Mayer N. Zald, 275–90. New York: Cambridge University Press.

Gateway Insurance Solutions. 2008. http://www.merchantcircle.com/blogs/Gateway. Insurance.Solutions.314–681–4743/2007/11/Health-Savings-Account-Growth-Continues/48051.

Geisel, Jerry. 2007. "HSA Contribution Limits Set to Increase." *AIG Passport*. Posted May 14, 2007, 12:43 PM. http://www.businessinsurance.com/cgi-bin/news,pl?newsId=10203.

General Accounting Office. 2003. "Alaska Native Villages: Most Are Affected by Flooding and Erosion, but Few Qualify for Federal Assistance." GAO Report number GAO-04–142.

Gerhardt, Uta. 1989. *Ideas about Illness: An Intellectual and Political History of Medical Sociology*. New York: New York University Press.

Geyman, John. 2005. "The Common Interest: Is It Time for National Health Insurance?" *Boston Review*, November/December, 8–11.

Ghaziani, Amin. 2008. *The Dividends of Dissent: How Conflict and Culture Work in Lesbian and Gay Marches on Washington*. Chicago: University of Chicago Press.

Gibbs, Lois. 2002. "Citizen Activism for Environmental Health: The Growth of a Powerful New Grassroots Movement." *The Annals of the American Academy of Political and Social Sciences* 584:97–109.

Giddens, Anthony. 1991. *Modernity and Self-Identity: Self and Society in the Late Modern Age*. Oxford: Blackwell.

Gieryn, Thomas F. 1999. *Cultural Boundaries of Science: Credibility on the Line*. Chicago: Chicago University Press.

Gieryn, Thomas F., George M. Bevins, and Stephen C. Zehr. 1985. "Professionalization of American Scientists: Public Science in the Creation/Evolution Trials." *American Sociological Review* 50(3): 392–409.

Gille, ZsuZsa, and Sean O'Riain. 2002. "Global Ethnography." *Annual Review of Sociology* 28:271–95.

Ginsburg, Faye. 1998. "Rescuing the Nation." In *Abortion Wars: A Half Century of Struggle, 1950–2000*, ed. R. Sollinger, 208–50. Berkeley and Los Angeles: University of California Press.

Ginsburg, Paul B., and Cara S. Lesser. 1999. "The View from Communities." *Journal of Health Politics, Policy & Law* 24(5): 1005–14.

Gitlin, Todd. 1980. *The Whole World is Watching*. Berkeley and Los Angeles: University of California Press.

Giugni, Marco. 1998. "Was It Worth the Effort? The Outcomes and Consequences of Social Movements." *Annual Review of Sociology* 24:371–93.

Giugni, Marco, Doug McAdam, and Charles Tilly, eds. 1999. *How Social Movements Matter*. Minneapolis: University of Minnesota Press.

Gladwell, Malcolm. 2005. "The Moral-Hazard Myth." *New Yorker*. 44–49.

Glaser, Barney, and Anselm Strauss. 1967. *The Discovery of Grounded Theory*. Chicago: Aldine.

Glass, Gregory E., James E. Cheek, Jonathan A. Patz, Timothy M. Shields, Timothy J. Doyle, Douglas A. Thoroughman, Darcy K. Hunt, Russell E. Enscore, Kenneth L. Gage, Charles Irland, C.J. Peters, and Ralph Bryan. 2000. "Using Remotely Sensed Data to Identify Areas at Risk for Hantavirus Pulmonary Syndrome." *Emerging Infectious Diseases* 6(3).

Goldfarb, Jeffrey C. 2006. *The Politics of Small Things: The Power of the Powerless in Dark Times*. Chicago: University of Chicago Press.

Goffman, Erving. 1961. *Asylums*. Garden City, N.Y.: Anchor Books.

———. 1974. *Frame Analysis: An Essay on the Organization of Experience*. New York: Harper Colophon Books.

Goldmann, Bonnie J. 1993. "A Drug Company Report: What Is the Same and What Is Changing with Respect to Inclusion/Exclusion of Women in Clinical Trials." *Food and Drug Law Journal* 48:169–74.

Goldsmith, Jeff. 1984. "Death of a Paradigm: The Challenge of Competition." *Health Affairs* 3(3): 5–19.

Goldstein, Michael. 1999. *Alternative Health Care: Medicine, Miracle, or Mirage?* Philadelphia: Temple University Press.

———. 2004. "The Persistence and Resurgence of Medical Pluralism." *Journal of Health Politics, Policy, and Law* 29:925–46.

———, Dennis Jaffe, Dale Garrell, and Ruth Ellen Berk. 1985. "Holistic Doctors: Becoming a Non-Traditional Medical Practitioner." *Urban Life* 14:317–44.

———, C. Sutherland, J. Wilson, and D. Jaffe. 1987. "Holistic Physicians: Implications for the Medical Profession." *Journal of Health and Social Behavior* 28:103–19.

Goldstone, Jack A. 1980. "The Weakness of Organization: A New Look at Gamson's *The Strategy of Social Protest.*" *American Journal of Sociology* 85:1017–42.

———. 2003. "Introduction: Bridging Institutionalized and Noninstitutionalized Politics." In *States, Parties, and Social Movements*, ed. J. A. Goldstone, 1–24. Cambridge, U.K.: Cambridge University Press.

Goodman, John. 1993. *Patient Power: The Free Market Alternative to Clinton's Health Plan.* Washington, D.C.: The Cato Institute.

———. 1995. Testimony of John C. Goodman, President, National Center for Policy Analysis, before the Health Subcommittee, Way and Means, House of Representatives (June 27): 50–51.

———. 2006. "Bush's Health Plan." http://www.john-goodman-blog.com.

———, and Richard Rahn. 1984. "Salvaging Medicare with an IRA." *Wall Street Journal* March 20, 1.

Goodnough, Abby. 2003a. "National Briefing South: Florida Legislature Enters Feeding Dispute." *New York Times*, October 21.

———. 2003b. "Governor of Florida Orders Woman Fed in Right-to-Die Case." *New York Times*, October 21.

———. 2003c. "Victory in Florida Feeding Case Emboldens the Religious Right." *New York Times*, October 23.

———. 2003d. "Spouse Fights New Law over Feeding Tube." *New York Times*, October 30.

———. 2003e. "Tube Is Removed in Florida Right-to-Die Case." *New York Times*, October 15.

——— 2003f. "Right-to-Die Battle Enters Its Final Days." *New York Times*, October 23.

——— 2004a. "Comatose Woman's Case Heard by Florida Court." *New York Times*, September 2.

——— 2004b. "Feeding Tube Law Is Struck Down in Florida Case." *New York Times*, September 24.

———. 2005a. "Protesters Hold Vigil for Schiavo at Hospice." *New York Times*, March 20.

———. 2005b. "US Judge Denies Feeding-Tube Bid in Schiavo's Case." *New York Times*, March 23.

———. 2005c. "Behind Life-and-Death Fight a Rift That Began Years Ago." *New York Times*, March 26.

———. 2005d. "In Two Friars Family Find Spiritual Support and More." *New York Times*, March 28.

———, and Adam Liptak. 2005. "Court Blocks Bid: New Schiavo Tactic by Governor Bush." *New York Times*, March 24.

Goodstein, Laurie. 2005. "Schiavo Case Highlights an Alliance between Catholics and Evangelicals." *New York Times*, March 24.

Goodwin, Jeff, James M. Jasper, and Francesca Polletta, eds. 2001. *Passionate Politics: Emotions and Social Movements*. Chicago: University of Chicago Press.

Gordon, Colin. 2003. *Dead on Arrival: The Politics of Healthcare in Twentieth-Century America*. Princeton: Princeton University Press.

Gottschalk, Marie. 1999. "The Elusive Goal of Universal Healthcare in the U.S.: Organized Labor and the Institutional Straightjacket on the Private Welfare State." *Journal of Policy History* 11(4): 367–98.

Gould, Deborah B. 2001. "Rock the Boat, Don't Rock the Boat, Baby: Ambivalence and the Emergence of Militant AIDS Activism." In *Passionate Politics: Emotions and Social Movements*, ed. Jeff Goodwin, James Jasper, and Francesca Polletta, 135–57. Chicago: University of Chicago Press.

Gould, Roger. 1991. "Multiple Networks and Mobilization in the Paris Commune, 1871." *American Sociological Review* 56 (December): 716–29.

Grady, Denise. 2005. "The Hard Facts behind a Heartbreaking Case." *New York Times*, June 19.

———. 2007. "Rise in Cases of West Nile May Portend an Epidemic." *New York Times*, July 26.

Granovetter, Mark. 1973. "The Strength of Weak Ties." *American Journal of Sociology* 78(6): 1360–80.

Grayson, Deborah R. 1999. "'Necessity Was the Midwife of Our Politics': Black Women's Health Activism in the 'Post'—Civil Rights Era (1980–1996)." In *Still Lifting, Still Climbing: Contemporary African American Women's Activism*, ed. K. Springer, 131–48. New York: New York University Press.

Greenberg, Gary. 1994. *The Self on the Shelf: Recovery Books and the Good Life*. New York: State University of New York Press.

Greenwald, Matthew. N.d. "A Brief Look at the Public Standing of the Life Insurance Business." American Council of Life Insurance publication, (c. 1970s), Folder 9–25, Committee for National Health Insurance Collection, Walter Reuther Library, Wayne State University.

Greenwood, Royston, and C. R. Hinings. 1993. "Understanding Strategic Change: The Contribution of Archetypes." *Academy of Management Journal* 36(5): 1052–81.

Greenwood, Royston, and C. R. Hinings. 1996. "Understanding Radical Organizational Change: Bringing Together the Old and New Institutionalism." *Academy of Management Review* 21:1022–54.

Greenwood, Royston, and C. R. Hinings. 1998. "Organizational Design Types, Tracks and the Dynamics of Strategic Change." *Organization Studies* 9(3): 293–316.

Greenwood, Royston, and Roy Suddaby. 2003. "Institutional Entrepreneurship and the Dynamics of Field Transformation." Presented to EGOS Colloquium, Lyon, France, July 11–13.

Greer, Scott L. 2007. *Nationalism and Self-Government: The Politics of Autonomy in Scotland and Catalonia*. Albany: State University of New York Press.

———, and Peter D. Jacobson. 2007. *Five Criteria for State Action*. Ann Arbor: University of Michigan, Department of Health Management and Policy.

——— and Peter D. Jacobson. 2010. "Health Policy and Federalism". *Journal of Health Politics Policy and Law*.

Griffin, Greg. 2007. "Consumer-Directed Health Plans Rise." *Denver Post*. www.denverpost.com/headlines/ci_5923235.

Groch, Sharon. 2001. "Free Spaces: Creating Oppositional Consciousness in the Disability Rights Movement." In *Oppositional Consciousness: The Subjective Roots of Social Protest*, ed. Jane J. Mansbridge and Aldon Morris, 65–98. Chicago: University of Chicago Press.

Grogan, Colleen M., and Michael K. Gusmano. 2007. *Healthy Voices, Unhealthy Silence: Advocacy and Health Policy for the Poor*. Washington, D.C: Georgetown University Press.

Gronbjerg, Kirsten. A. 1991. How Nonprofit Human Service Organizations Manage Their Funding Sources: Key Findings and Policy Implications. *Nonprofit Management and Leadership* 2(2):159–75.

Group Health Association of America. 1995. Statement of the Group Health Association of America for the Health Subcommittee, Way and Means, House of Representatives (June 27): 111–14.

Guigni, Marco G. 1998. "Was It Worth the Effort? The Outcomes and Consequences of Social Movements." *Annual Review of Sociology* 24:371–93.

Guillemin, Jeanne Harley, and Lynda Lytle Holmstrom. 1986. *Mixed Blessings: Intensive Care for Newborns*. New York: Oxford University Press.

Gujarati, Damodar N. 2003. *Basic Econometrics*. 4th ed. Boston: McGraw Hill.

Gusfield, Joseph R. 1975. "Categories of Ownership and Responsibility in Social Issues: Alcohol Abuse and Automobile Use." *Journal of Drug Issues* 5 (Fall): 285–303.

Guston, David. 1999. "Stabilizing the Boundary Between U.S. Politics and Science: The Role of the Office of Technology Transfer as a Boundary Organization." *Social Studies of Science* 29(1): 87–112.

Haas, Peter. 1992. "Introduction: Epistemic Communities and International Policy Coordination." *International Organization: Knowledge, Power, and International Policy Coordination* 46:1–35.

Hacker, Jacob S. 1997. *The Road to Nowhere: The Genesis of President Clinton's Plan for Health Security*. Princeton: Princeton University Press.

———. 2002. *The Divided Welfare State: The Battle over Public and Private Social Benefits in the United States*. New York: Cambridge University Press.

Hacker, Jacob. 2006. *The Great Risk Shift*. New York, NY: Oxford University Press

Haines, A., R. S. Kovats, D. Campbell-Lendrum, and C. Corvalan. 2006. "Climate Change and Human Health: Impacts, Vulnerability, and Mitigation." *The Lancet* 367(9528) 24:2101–9.

Haines, Herbert. H. 1996. *The Anti-Death Penalty Movement in America, 1972–1994*. New York: Oxford University Press.

Hall, Richard L., and Alan V. Deardorff. 2006. "Lobbying as Legislative Subsidy." *American Political Science Review* 1001(1): 69–84.

Hallfors, Denise, Hyunsan Cho, David Livert, and Charles Kadushin. 2002. Fighting Back against Substance Abuse: Are Community Coalitions Winning? *American Journal of Preventative Medicine* 23(4): 237–45.

Halpern, Sydney A. 2004. "Medical Authority and the Culture of Rights." *Journal of Health Politics, Policy and Law* 29 (August-October): 835–52.

Hambrick, Donald. 1994. "What If the Academy Mattered?" *Academy of Management Review* 19(11): 11–16.

Hamilton, Jean A. 1996. "Women and Health Policy: On the Inclusion of Females in Clinical Trials." In *Gender and Health*, ed. C. F. Sargent and C. Brettell, 292–325. Englewood Cliffs, N. J.: Prentice-Hall.

Hamm, Keith E., and Gary F. Moncrief. 2004. "Legislative Politics in the States." In *Politics in the American States: A Comparative Analysis*, ed. V. Gray and R. L. Hanson, 157–93. 8th ed. Washington, D.C.: CQ.

Hannan, Michael T. 1998. "Rethinking Age Dependence in Organizational Mortality: Logical Formalizations." *American Journal of Sociology* 104:85–123.

Hanson, Barbara. 1997. *Social Assumptions, Medical Categories*. Greenwich, Conn.: JAI Press.

Hanson, Russell. 1994. "Health-Care Reform, Managed Competition, and Subnational Politics." *Publius* 24(3): 49–68.

Haseltine, Florence B., and Beverly Greenberg Jacobson, eds. 1997. *Women's Health Research: A Medical and Policy Primer*. Washington, D.C.: Health Press International.

Hauptmeier, Marco, and Lowell Turner. 2007. "Political Insiders and Social Activists: Coalition Building in New York and Los Angeles." In *Labor in the New Urban Battlegrounds: Local Solidarity in a Global Economy*, ed. L. Turner and D. Cornfield. Ithaca, N.Y.: Cornell University Press.

Hays, R. Allen. 2001. *Who Speaks for the Poor? National Interest Groups and Social Policy*. New York: Routledge.

Heckler, Margaret M. 1985. "Report of the Secretary's Task Force on Black and Minority Health." Washington, D.C.: U.S. Department of Health and Human Services.

Heidenrich, Paul, and Mark McClellan. 2001. "Trends in Heart Attack Treatments and Outcomes, 1975–1995." In *Medical Care Output and Productivity*, ed. David M. Cutler, and Ernst R. Berndt. Chicago: University of Chicago Press.

Heinz, John P., Edward O. Laumann, Robert L. Nelson, and Robert H. Salisbury. 1993. *The Hollow Core: Private Interests in National Policy Making*. Cambridge, Mass.: Harvard University Press.

Helfgot, Joseph H. 1981. *Professional reforming: Mobilization for youth and the failure of social science*. Lexington, Mass: Lexington Books.

Hensel, B. 2004. "Harry Truman's Reluctance in Going Public for National Health Insurance." Paper presented at the Annual Meeting of the International Communication Association, New Orleans, May 27. Available at http://www.allacademic.com/meta/p113371_index.html. Accessed December 29, 2008.

Herbert, Bob. 2005. "Cruel and Unusual." *New York Times*, June 23.

Heron, Melonie P., Donna L. Hoyert, Jiaquan Xu, Chester Scott, and Betzaida Tejada-Vera. 2008. "Deaths: Preliminary Data for 2006." *National Vital Statistics Reports* 56(16): 1–51.

Hess, David J. 2004. "Medical Modernisation, Scientific Research Fields, and the Epistemic Politics of Health Social Movements." *Sociology of Health & Illness* 26(6): 695–709.

———. 2007. *Alternative Pathways in Science and Industry Activism, Innovation, and the Environment in an Era of Globalization*. Cambridge, MA: MIT Press.

Hilgartner, Steven, and Charles Bosk. 1988. "The Rise and Fall of Social Problems: A Public Arenas Model." *American Journal of Sociology* 94:53–78.

Hingson, Ralph W, Ronda C Zakocs, Timothy Heeren, Michael R Winter, David Rosenbloom, and William DeJong. 2005. Effects on Alcohol-Related Fatal Crashes of a Community-Based Initiative to Increase Substance Abuse Treatment and Reduce Alcohol Availability. *Injury Prevention* 11:84–90.

Hinsch, Katherine. 2005. *Bioethics and Public Policy: Conservative Dominance in the New Landscape*. Seattle: Women's Bioethics Project.

Hirschhorn, Larry. 2002. "Campaigning for Change." *Harvard Business Review* (July): 98–104.

Hjelle, Brian, and Gregory E. Glass. 2000. "Outbreak of Hantavirus Infection in the Four Corners Region of the United States in the Wake of the 1997–1998 El Niño Southern Oscillation." *The Journal of Infectious Diseases* 181:1569–73.

Hochschild, Arlie. 1983. *The Managed Heart: The Commercialization of Human Feeling*. Berkeley and Los Angeles: University of California Press.

Hoffman, Andrew J. 1999. "Institutional Evolution and Change: Environmentalism and the U.S. Chemical Industry." *Academy of Management Journal* 42(4): 351–71.

Hoffman, Beatrix. 2001. *The Wages of Sickness: The Politics of Health Insurance in Progressive America*. Chapel Hill: University of North Carolina Press.

———. 2003. "Health Care Reform and Social Movements in the United States." *American Journal of Public Health* 93 (January): 75–85.

———. 2004. "The False Promise of the Private Welfare State." *Journal of Policy History* 16(3): 268–73.

———. 2006a. "Tell Me Again: Why Is There No National Health Insurance in the United States?" *Journal of Health Politics, Policy, and Law* 31(4): 839–48.

———. 2006b. "Restraining the Health Care Consumer: The History of Deductibles and Co-Payments in U.S. Health Insurance." *Social Science History* 30(4) (Winter): 502–28.

———.[2003] 2008. "Health Care Reform and Social Movements in the United States." *American Journal of Public Health* S69–79. Originally published in *American Journal of Public Health* 93(2003): 75–85.

Hopper, Kim. 2003. *Reckoning with Homelessness*. Ithaca, N.Y.: Cornell University Press.

Horrigan, John B. 2008. "Home Broadband Adoption 2008 Report" Pew Internet and American Life. Available: http://www.pewinternet.org/pdfs/PIP_Broadband_2008.pdf.

Horwitz, Allan V., and Jerome C. Wakefield. 2007. *The Loss of Sadness: How Psychiatry Transformed Normal Sorrow into Depressive Disorder*. New York: Oxford University Press.

Houghton, J. T., Y. Ding, D. J.Griggs et al., eds. 2001. "Climate Change 2001: The Scientific Basis: Contribution of the Working Group I to the Third Assessment Report of the Intergovernmental Panel on Climate Change." Cambridge, U.K.: Cambridge University Press.

Hoover, Elizabeth, Phil Brown, Mara Averick, Agnes Kane, and Robert Hurt. 2008. "Teaching Small and Thinking Large: Effects of Including Social and Ethical Implications in an Interdisciplinary Nanotechnology Course." *Journal of Nano Education* 1:1–10.

Howard, Judith A., and Peter L. Callero. 1991. *The Self-Society Dynamic: Cognition, Emotion and Action*. New York: Cambridge University Press.

HSA for America. 2008. "Use of Health Savings Accounts up 35 Percent." Health Savings Account blog, August 23. http://www.health—savings—accounts.com/hsa-weblog-arch/2008/08/post_4.html#more.

Hughes, David, and Lesley Griffiths. 2003. "Going Public: References to the News Media in NHS Contract Negotiations." *Sociology of Health and Illness* 25:571–88.

Hughes, John R. and Anthony Liguori. 2000. A Critical View of PNIH Research Funding on Tobacco and Nicotine. *Nicotine and Tobacco Research* 2(2):117–20.

Hulse, Carl, and David D. Kirkpatrick. 2005. "Congress Passes and Bush Signs Schiavo Measures." *New York Times*, March 21.

Hunt, Scott A., and Robert D. Benford. 2004. "Collective Identity, Solidarity, and Commitment." In *The Blackwell Companion to Social Movements*, ed. David A. Snow, Sarah A. Soule, and Hans Peter Kriesi, 433–57. Malden, Mass.: Blackwell.

Industrial Areas Foundation (IAF). 1990. *50 Years Organizing for Change*. Franklin Square, N.Y.: Industrial Areas Foundation.

Ingham, Alan Jie Ma and Alistair Ulph. 2007. Climate change, mitigation and adaptation with uncertainty and learning. *Energy Policy* 35(11): 5354–5369.

Institute of Medicine. 2005. *Complementary and Alternative Medicine in the United States*. Washington, D.C., Institute of Medicine Press.

Ingram, Paul, and Hayagreeva Rao. 2004. "Store Wars: The Enactment and Repeal of Anti-Chain Store Legislation in America." *American Journal of Sociology* 110:446–87.

Israel, Barbara A, Amy J Schulz, Edith A Parker, and Adam B Becker. 1998. Review of Community-Based Research: Assessing Partnership Approaches to Improve Public Health. *Annual Review of Public Health* 19:173–202.

Israel, Barbara A., Eugenia Eng, Amy J. Schulz, and Edith A. Parker. 2005. *Methods in Community-Based Participatory Research for Health*. San Francisco: Jossey-Bass.

Jacobs, Lawrence R. 1993. "Health Reform Impasse: The Politics of American Ambivalence toward Government." *Journal of Health Politics, Policy and Law* 18(3): 629–55.

———, and Robert Shapiro. 2000. *Politicians Don't Pander: Political Manipulation and the Loss of Democratic Responsiveness*. Chicago: University of Chicago Press.

———, and Theda Skocpol. 2005. "Introduction." In *Inequality and American Democracy: What We Know and What We Need to Learn*, ed. Lawrence R. Jacobs and Theda Skocpol. New York: Russell Sage Foundation.

Jacobson, Peter D., and Rebecca L. Braun. 2007. "Let 1000 Flowers Wilt: The Futility of State-Level Health Care Reform." *University of Kansas Law Review* 55:1173–202.

Jaffe, Natalie. 1964. "Hundreds Attend Hearing for Aged." *New York Times*, January 19, 63.

Jarman, Holly. 2007. *Trading Lives: Democracy, Healthcare and Trade in Services*. Washington, D.C.: Americans for Democratic Action Education Fund.

Jaschik, Scott. 1990. "Report Says NIH Ignores Own Rules on Including Women in Its Research." *The Chronicle of Higher Education*, June 27, A27.

Jasper, James M. 2004. "A Strategic Approach to Collective Action: Looking for Agency in Social Movement Choices." *Mobilization: The International Journal of Research in Social Movements, Protest, and Contentious Politics* 9(1): 1–16.

———. 2006. *Getting Your Way: Strategic Dilemmas in Social Life*. Chicago: University of Chicago Press.

Jellinek, Paul S. and Ruby P. Hearn. 1991. Fighting drug abuse at the local level. *Issues in Science and Technology* 7(4): 78–84.

Jenkins, J. Craig and Craig M Eckert. 1986. Channeling Black Insurgency: Elite Patronage and Professional Social Movement Organizations in the Development of the Black Movement. *American Sociological Review* 51:812–29.

Jenkins, J. C., and C. Perrow. 1977. "Insurgency of the Powerless: Farm Worker Movements (1946–1972)." *American Sociological Review* 42:249–67.

Jenness, Valerie. 1995. "Social Movement Growth, Domain Expansion, and Framing Processes: The Case of Violence against Gays and Lesbians as a Social Problem." *Social Problems* 42(1): 145–70.

———. 1999. "Managing Differences and Making Legislation: Social Movements and the Racialization, Sexualization, and Gendering of Federal Hate Crime Law in the U.S., 1985–1998." *Social Problems* 46(4): 548–71.

———, and Ryken Grattet. 2001. *Making Hate a Crime: From Social Movement to Law Enforcement*. New York: Russell Sage Foundation.

Jessup. M. M. 1997. "Legitimacy and the Decline of the 1920s Ku Klux Klan. Research on Social Movements." *Conflict and Change* 20:103–50.

Joffe, Carole E., Tracy A. Weitz, and Chris L. Stacey. 2004. "Uneasy Allies: Pro-Choice Physicians, Feminist Health Activists and the Struggle for Abortion Rights." *Sociology of Health & Illness* 26(6): 775–96.

Johnson, D. 1990. "Schiavo Case Highlights an Alliance Between Catholics and Evangelicals." *New York Times*, July 31.

Johnston, Hank, and Bert Klandermans, eds. 1995. *Social Movements and Culture*. Minneapolis: University of Minnesota Press.

Johnson, Roberta Ann. 1983. "Mobilizing the Disabled." In *Social Movements of the Sixties and Seventies*, ed. Jo Freeman, 82–100. New York: Longmans.

Johnson, Steven. 2006. *The Ghost Map*. New York: The Penguin Group.

Johnson, Tracy, and Elizabeth Fee. 1994. "Women's Participation in Clinical Research: From Protectionism to Access." In *Women and Health Research: Ethical and Legal Issues of*

Including Women in Clinical Studies, ed. A. C. Mastroianni, R. Faden, and D. Federman, 1–10. Washington, D.C.: National Academy Press.

Jonsen, Albert. 1998. *The Birth of Bioethics*. New York: Oxford University Press.

Jost, Timothy. 2007. *Health Care at Risk: A Critique of the Consumer-Driven Movement*. Durham, N.C.: Duke University Press.

———, and Mark Hall. 2005. "The Role of State Regulation in Consumer-Driven Health Care." *American Journal of Law and Medicine* 31:395–418.

Judkins, Bennett M. 1983. "Mobilization of Membership: The Black and Brown Lung Movements." In *Social Movements of the Sixties and Seventies*, ed. Jo Freeman, 35–51. New York: Longmans.

Kaiser Family Foundation. 2006. "Employer Health Benefits: 2006 Survey of Findings." Menlo Park, Calif.: Henry J. Kaiser Family Foundation. Available at http://www.kff.org/insurance/7527/upload/7528.pdf.

Kaiser Commission on Medicaid and the Uninsured. 2008. "The Uninsured and the Difference Health Insurance Makes."Available at http://www.kff.org/uninsured/1420.cfm.

Kaminer, Wendy. 1992. *I'm Dysfunctional, You're Dysfunctional: The Recovery Movement and Other Self-Help Fashions*. Reading, Mass.: Addison-Wesley.

Kaptchuk, Ted, and David Eisenberg. 2001. "Varieties of Healing, 1: Medical Pluralism in the United States." *Annals of Internal Medicine* 135:189–95.

Kasper, Anne S., and Susan J. Ferguson. 2002. *Breast Cancer: Society Shapes an Epidemic*. London: Palgrave Macmillan.

Katz, Alfred H. 1993. *Self-Help in America: A Social Movement Perspective*. New York: Twayne.

Katz, Michael B. 1989. *The Underserving Poor: From the War on Poverty to the War on Welfare*. New York: Pantheon Books.

Katzenstein, Mary Fainsod. 1996. "The Spectacle of Life and Death: Feminist and Lesbian/Gay Politics in the Military." In *Gay Rights, Military Wrongs: Political Perspectives on Lesbians and Gays in the Military*, ed. C. A. Rimmerman, 229–47. New York: Garland Publishing.

———. 1998. *Faithful and Fearless: Moving Feminist Protest Inside the Church and Military*. Princeton, N.J.: Princeton University Press.

———, and Judith Reppy. 1999. "Introduction: Rethinking Military Culture." In *Beyond Zero Tolerance: Discrimination in Military Culture*, ed. M. F. Katzenstein and J. Reppy, 1–21. Lanham: Rowman & Littlefield.

Kaufert, Patricia A. 1998. "Women, Resistance and the Breast Cancer Movement." In *Pragmatic Women and Body Politics*, ed. M. Lock and P. A. Kaufert, 1–21. Cambridge, U.K.: Cambridge University Press.

Keck, Margaret, and Kathryn Sikkink. 1998. "Transnational Advocacy Networks in the Movement Society." In *The Social Movement Society*, ed. David Meyer and Sidney Tarrow. Lanham, Md.: Rowman & Littlefield.

Kemper, Theodore. 2001. "A Structural Approach to Social Movement Emotions." In *Passionate Politics: Emotions and Social Movements*, ed. Jeff Goodwin, James M. Jasper, and Francesca Polletta, 58–73. Chicago: University of Chicago Press.

Keen, Justin, Donald Light, and Nicholas Mays. 2001. *Public-Private Relations in Health Care*. London: The Kings Fund.

Keller, Morton. 1963. *The Life Insurance Enterprise, 1885–1910: A Study in the Limits of Corporate Power*. Cambridge, Mass.: Harvard/Belknap.

Kellogg, Katherine. 2007. "Inside Countermobilization: Resisting Social Movement Reform in a Professional Organization." Paper presented at the Conference on Social Movements and Health Institutions, Ann Arbor, Mich.

Kennedy, Edward. 1972. *In Critical Condition: The Crisis in America's Health Care*. New York: Simon and Schuster.

Kennedy, John F. 1962. Address at a New York Rally in Support of the President's Program of Medical Care for the Aged, May 20. John T. Woolley and Gerhard Peters, The American Presidency Project [online]. Santa Barbara, CA: University of California (hosted), Gerhard Peters (database). Available from World Wide Web: http://www.presidency.ucsb.edu/ws/?pid=8669. Accessed November 1, 2008.

Kessler, Ronald, Roger Davis, David Foster, M. I. Van Rompay, E. E. Walters, S. A. Wilkey, T. J. Kaptchuk, and D. M. Eisenberg. 2001. "Long Term Trends in the Use of Complementary and Alternative Medical Therapies in the United States." *Annals of Internal Medicine* 135:262–68.

Khan, A. S., R. F. Khabbaz, L. R. Armstrong, R. C. Holman, S. P. Bauer, J. Graber, T. Strine, G. Miller, S. Reef, J. Tappero, P. E. Rollin, S. T. Nichol, S. R. Zaki, R. T. Bryan, L. E. Chapman, C. J. Peters, and T. G. Ksiazek. 1996. "Hantavirus Pulmonary Syndrome: The First 100 US Cases." *Journal of Infectious Diseases* 173(6): 1297–303.

Khurana, Rakesh, and Christopher Marquis. 2006. "Diagnosing and Dissolving Our 'Translation Gap.'" *Journal of Management Inquiry*, 15(4): 406–9.

Kimport, Katrina. 2005. "The Campaign to Make Emergency Contraception Available Over-the-Counter: The Role of Gender in Framing Contests." MA thesis, University of California, Santa Barbara.

King, Nicholas B. 2004. "The Scale Politics of Emerging Diseases." *Osiris*, 2nd ser., 19:62–76.

Kingsbury, John A. 1937. "Health Insurance in a National Health Program." *Proceedings of the National Conference of Social Work* 64 (1937): 485. Quoted in Monte M. Poen, *Harry S. Truman Versus the Medical Lobby*. Columbia: University of Missouri Press, 1979.

Kinney, P. L., M. Aggarwal, M. E. Northridge, N. A. Janssen, and P. Shepard. 2000. "Airborne Concentrations of PM (2.5) and Diesel Exhaust Particles on Harlem Sidewalks: A Community-Based Pilot Study." *Environmental Health Perspectives* 108(3): 213–18.

Kirkpatrick, David D. 2005. "Conservatives Invoke Case in Fund-Raising Campaigns." *New York Times*, March 25.

———, and John Schwartz. 2005. "List of Schiavo Donors will be Sold to Direct-Marketing Firm." *New York Times*, March 29.

———, and Sheryl G. Stolberg. 2005. "How a Family's Cause Reached the Halls of Congress." *New York Times*, March 21.

Kitchener, Martin. 1998. "Quasi-Market Transformation: An Institutionalist Approach to Change in UK Hospitals." *Public Administration* 76(1): 73–96.

———, and Charlene Harrington. 2004. "The U.S. Long-Term Care Field: A Dialectic Analysis of Institutional Dynamics." *Journal of Health & Social Behavior* 45:87–101.

Klandermans, Bert, and Marga de Weerd. 2000. "Group Identification and Political Protest." In *Self, Identity, and Social Movements*, ed. S. Stryker, T. Owens, and R. White, 68–90. Minneapolis: University of Minnesota Press.

Klaus, Alisa. 1993. *Every Child a Lion: The Origins of Maternal and Infant Health Policy in the United States and France, 1890–1920*. Ithaca, N.Y.: Cornell University Press.

Klawiter, Maren. 1999. "Racing for the Cure, Walking Women, and Toxic Touring: Mapping Cultures of Action within the Bay Area Terrain of Breast Cancer." *Social Problems* 46(1): 104–26.

———. 2004. "Breast Cancer in Two Regimes: The Impact of Social Movements on Illness Experience." *Sociology of Health and Illness* 26 (September): 845–74.

———. 2008. *The Biopolitics of Breast Cancer*. Minneapolis: University of Minnesota Press.

Kleidman, Robert, and Thomas R. Rochon. 1997. "Dilemmas of Organization in Peace Campaigns." In *Coalitions and Political Movements: The Lessons of the Nuclear Freeze*, ed. T. R. Rochon and D. S. Meyer, 47–60. Boulder, Colo.: Lynne Rienner.

Klein, Jennifer. 2003. *For All These Rights: Business, Labor, and the Shaping of America's Public-Private Welfare State*. Princeton, N.J.: Princeton University Press.

Klein, Naomi, and Verta Taylor. 2007. "Emotions and Social Movements." Paper presented at the Annual Meetings of the American Sociological Association, New York, N.Y.

Kleiner, Art. 1996. *The Age of Heretics: Heroes, Outlaws, and the Forerunners of Corporate Change*. New York: Doubleday.

Klinenberg, Eric. 2002. *Heatwave: A Social Autopsy of Disaster in Chicago*. Chicago: University of Chicago Press.

Knorr Cetina, Karen. 1999. *Epistemic Cultures: How the Sciences Make Knowledge*. Cambridge, Mass.: Harvard University Press.

Kohl, Herbert. 2005. *She Would Not Be Moved: How We Tell the Story of Rosa Parks and the Montgomery Bus Boycott*. New York: New Press.

Kolata, Gina. 1990. "N.I.H. Neglects Women, Study Says." *New York Times*, June 19.

Kornblut, Arlene. 2005. "After Signing Schiavo Law, Bush Says, 'It Is Wisest to Err on the Side of Life." *New York Times*, March 22.

Koopmans, Ruud and Susan Olzak. 2004. "Medical Authority and the Culture of Rights." *Journal of Health Politics, Policy and Law* 29 (August–October): 835–52.

Kovats, R. Sari, Diarmid Campbell-Lendrum, and Franziska Matthies. 2005. "Climate Change and Human Health: Estimating Avoidable Deaths and Disease." *Risk Analysis* 25(6): 1409–18.

Kozinets, Robert, and Jay Handelman. 2004. "Adversaries of Consumption: Consumer Movements, Activism and Ideology." *Journal of Consumer Research* 3:691–704.

Kraig, Robert. 2004. *Woodrow Wilson and the Lost World of the Oratorical Statesman*. College Station: Texas A&M Press.

Kriesi, Hans Peter. 1996. "The Organizational Structure of New Social Movements in a Political Context." In *Comparative Perspectives on Social Movements: Political Opportunities, Mobilizing Structures, and Cultural Framings*, ed. Doug McAdam, John D. McCarthy, and Mayer N. Zald, 152–84. New York: Cambridge University Press.

Krimsky, Sheldon. 2000. *Hormonal Chaos: The Scientific and Social Origins of the Environmental Endocrine Hypothesis*. Baltimore: Johns Hopkins University Press.

Kroll-Smith, Steve, Philip Brown, and Valerie Gunter. 2000. *Illness and the Environment: A Reader in Contested Medicine*. New York: New York University Press.

Kroll-Smith, Steve, and Worth Lancaster. "Bodies, Environments, and a New Style of Reasoning." *Annals of the American Academy of Political and Social Science* 584:203–12.

Kuntz, Phil. 1995. "Golden Rule Insurance Takes Lead in Advocating MSAs as Way of Controlling Health Care Costs." *Wall Street Journal*, May 15.

Lantz, Paula M., and Karen M. Booth. 1998. "The Social Construction of the Breast Cancer Epidemic." *Social Science and Medicine* 46(7): 907–18.

Larana, Enrique, Hank Johnston, and Joseph Gusfield, eds. 1994. *New Social Movements: From Ideology to Identity*. Philadelphia: Temple University Press.

"Lauds NMA Doctors on Medicare Stand." 1965. *Chicago Daily Defender*, August 19, 10.

Lawrence, Thomas B., Monika I. Winn, and P. Devereaux Jennings. 2001. "The Temporal Dynamics of Institutionalization." *Academy of Management Review* 26:624–44.

Lawrence, Thomas B., and Roy Suddaby. 2006. "Institutions and Institutional Work." In *The Sage Handbook of Organizational Studies*, ed. Stuart Clegg, Cynthia Hardy, Thomas B. Lawrence, and Walter R. Nord. Thousand Oaks, Calif.: Sage.

Leblebici, Hussein, Gerald Salancik, Ann Copay, and Tom King. 1991. "Institutional Change and the Transformation of Inter-organizational Fields: An Organizational History of the U.S. Radio Broadcasting Industry." *Administration Science Quarterly* 36(3): 333–64.

Lerner, Barron H. 2006. *When Illness Goes Public: Celebrity Patients and How We Look at Medicine*. Baltimore: Johns Hopkins University Press.

Levesque, William R. 2002. "Schiavo Case Doctor Target of Complaint." *St. Petersberg Times*, October 22.

Lewin, K. 1951. *Field Theory in Social Science: Selected Theoretical Papers*. New York: Harper & Row.

Lessor, Roberta. 1984a. "Occupational Health Policy: Addressing Personal Troubles or Social Problems?" *Occupational Health Nursing* 32:146–50.

———. 1984b. "Social Movements, the Occupational Arena and Changes in Career Consciousness: The Case of Women Flight Attendants." *Journal of Occupational Behaviour* 5:37–51.

———. 1985. "Consciousness of Time and Time for the Development of Consciousness: Health Awareness Among Women Flight Attendants." *Sociology of Health and Illness* 7:191–213.

———, Nancyann Cervantes, Nadine O'Connor, Jose Balmaceda, and Richardo Asch. 1993. "An Analysis of Social and Psychological Characteristics of Women Volunteering to Become Oocyte Donors." *Fertility and Sterility* 59:65–71.

Lidwell, William, Kristina Holden, and Jill Butler. 2003. *Universal Principles of Design*. Gloucester, Mass.: Rockport Publishers.

Light, Donald W. 1993. "Escaping the Traps of Postwar Western Medicine: How to Maximize Health and Minimize Expenses." *European Journal of Public Health* 3 (August): 281–89.

Lindsay, D. Michael. 2006. "Elite Power: Social Networks within American Evangelicalism." *Sociology of Religion* 67(3): 207–27.

Link, Bruce G., and Jo Phelan. 1995. "Social Conditions as Fundamental Causes of Disease." *Journal of Health and Social Behavior* 35 (extra issue): 80–94.

Lipset, Seymour Martin. 1996. *American Exceptionalism: A Double-Edged Sword*. New York: W.W. Norton.

Lipsky, Michael and Steven Rathgeb Smith. 1989. Nonprofit organizations, government, and the welfare State. *Political Science Quarterly* 104, no. 4:625–49.

Loehr, Jim, and Tony Schwartz. 2003. *The Power of Full Engagement*. New York: Free Press.

Loh, Penn, and Jodi Sugerman-Brozan. 2002. "Environmental Justice Organizing for Environmental Health: Case Study on Asthma and Diesel Exhaust in Roxbury, Massachusetts." *Annals of American Academy of Political and Social Science* 584:110–24.

Lopez, Steven Henry. 2004. *Reorganizing the Rust Belt: An Inside Study of the American Labor Movement*. Berkeley and Los Angeles: University of California Press.

Lorber, Judith. 1984. *Women Physicians: Careers, Status, and Power*. New York: Tavistock.

Lown, Bernard. 2007. "The Commodification of Health Care." *PNHP Newsletter* (Spring): 40–44.

Luker, Kristin. 1984. *Abortion and the Politics of Motherhood*. Berkeley: University of California Press.

Lunbeck, Elizabeth. 1994. *The Psychiatric Persuasion: Knowledge, Gender, and Power in Modern America*. Princeton, N.J.: Princeton University Press.

Lyman, Rick. 2005a. "As Legal Moves Dwindle in the Schiavo Case, the Focus Returns to Governor Bush." *New York Times*, March 27.

———. 2005b. "Schiavo in Her Last Hours, Father Says amid Appeals." *New York Times*, March 26.

Macklin, Ruth. 2006. "The New Conservatives in Bioethics: Who Are They and What Do They Seek?" *Hastings Center Report* 36(1): 34–43.

Madar, Olga M. 1976. "Discrimination against Women in Current Health Insurance Programs." Speech at Women's Leadership Rally, March, Folder 31–1, Committeee on National

Health Insurance Collection, Walter Reuther Library, Wayne State University, Detroit, Mich.

Maguire, Steve, Cynthia Hardy, and Thomas B. Lawrence. 2004. "Institutional Entrepreneurship in Emerging Fields: HIV/ADIS Treatment Advocacy in Canada." *Organization* 11(5): 689–711.

Maino D. M., J. Kofman, M. F. Flynn, and L. Lai. 1994. "Ocular Manifestations of Sotos Syndrome." *Journal of the American Optometric Association* 65(5): 339–46.

Manley, Marc, William. Lynn, Roselyn Payne. Epps, Donna. Grande, Tom. Glynn, and Donald. Shopland. 1997. The American Stop Smoking Intervention Study for Cancer Prevention: An overview. *Tobacco Control* 6 Suppl 2:S5–11.

Marcus, George E. 1995. "Ethnography In/Of the World System: The Emergence of Multi-Sited Ethnography." *Annual Review of Anthropology* 24:95–118.

Markides, Costas. 2007. "In Search of Ambidextrous Professors." *Academy of Management Journal*, Editor's Forum on Research with Relevance to Practice 50(4): 762–68.

Markowitz, Gerald, and David Rosner. 1991. "Seeking Common Ground: The History of Labor and Blue Cross." *Journal of Health Politics, Policy, and Law* 16(4):695–718.

Marmor, Theodore. 2000. *The Politics of Medicare*. New York: Aldine de Gruyter.

———. 2007. "Commentary: Medicare's Politics." *Journal of Health Politics, Policy and Law* 32(2): 307–15.

Marmot, Michael. 2001. "Inequalities in Health." *New England Journal of Medicine* 345(2): 12–17.

M.artin, John Levi. 2003. "What is Field Analysis?" *American Journal of Sociology* 109:1–49.

Marullo, Sam. 1996. "Frame Changes and Social Movement Contraction: U.S. Peace Movement Framing After the Cold War." *Sociological Inquiry* 66(1): 1–28.

Massey, Douglas S. 2007. *Categorically Unequal: the American Stratification System*. New York: Russell Sage Foundation.

Mayer, Brian, Phil Brown, and Meadow Linder. 2002. "Moving Further Upstream: From Toxics Reduction to the Precautionary Principle." *Public Health Reports* 117:574–86.

Mayer, Brian, Phil Brown, and Laura Senier. 2008. "Health, Labor, and the Environment." Paper presented at the Annual Meeting of the American Sociological Association, August 2.

Mayes, R. 2004. *Universal Coverage: The Elusive Quest for National Health Insurance*. Ann Arbor: University of Michigan Press.

Mayes, Rick. 2005. *Universal Coverage: The Elusive Quest for National Health Insurance*. Ann Arbor: University of Michigan Press.

McAdam, Doug. 1982. *Political Process and the Development of Black Insurgency*. Chicago: University of Chicago Press.

———. 1988a. "Micromobilization Ccontexts and Recruitment to Activism." *International Social Movement Research* 1:125–54.

———. 1988b. *Freedom Summer*. Oxford: Oxford University Press.

———. 1995. "'Initiator' and 'Spin-Off' Movements: Diffusion Processes in Protest Cycles." In *Repertoires and Cycles of Collective Action*, ed. M. Traugott, 217–39. Durham, N.C.: Duke University Press.

———. 1999. *Political Process and the Development of Black Insurgency, 1930–1970*. 2nd ed. Chicago: University of Chicago Press.

———, John D. McCarthy, and Mayer N. Zald. 1986. "Introduction: Opportunities, Mobilizing Structures, and Framing Processes: Toward a Synthetic, Comparative Perspective on Social Movements." In *Comparative Perspectives in Social Movements*, ed. Doug McAdam, John D. McCarthy, and Mayer N. Zald, 1–20. Cambridge: Cambridge University Press.

————, John D. McCarthy, and Mayer N. Zald. 1996. *Comparative Perspectives on Social Movements: Political Opportunities, Mobilization Structures, and Cultural Framing.* Cambridge, U.K.: Cambridge University Press.

————, and W. Richard Scott. 2005. "Organizations and Movements." In *Social Movements and Organization Theory*, ed. G. F. Davis, D. McAdam, W. R. Scott, and Meyer N. Zald, 4–41. New York: Cambridge University Press.

————, Sidney Tarrow, and Charles Tilly. 2001. *Dynamics of Contention.* Cambridge: Cambridge University Press.

McCally, Michael. 2002. "Medical Activism and Environmental Health." *Annals of the American Academy, AAPSS* 584:145–58.

McCammon, Holly, and Karen Campbell. 2002. "Allies on the Road to Victory: Coalition Formation between the Suffragists and the Women's Christian Temperance Union." *Mobilization: The International Journal of Research in Social Movements, Protest, and Contentious Politics* 7(3): 231–51.

McCammon, Holly, Karen Campbell, Ellen Granberg, and Christine Mowrey. 2001. "How Movements Win: Gendered Opportunity Structures and U.S. Women's Suffrage Movements, 1866 to 1919." *American Sociological Review* 66(1): 49–70.

McCanne, Don. 2006. "Single Payer vs. HSA Exchange." Debate on KPBS Radio, San Diego, Calif., March.

McCarthy, John D. 1996. "Constraints and Opportunities in Adopting, Adapting, and Inventing." In *Comparative Perspectives on Social Movements: Political Opportunities, Mobilizing Structures, and Cultural Framings*, ed. Doug McAdam, John D. McCarthy, and Mayer N. Zald, 141–51. Cambridge: Cambridge University Press.

———— and Mark Wolfson. 1992. Consensus Movements, Conflict Movements, and the Cooptation of Civic and State Infrastructures. In *frontiers in social movement theory*, eds. Morris, Aldon D. and Carol McClurg Mueller, 273–97. New Haven: Yale Univesity Press.

————, and Mark Wolfson. 1996. "Resource Mobilization by Local Social Movement Organizations: Agency, Strategy, and Organization in the Movement Against Drinking and Driving." *American Sociological Review* 61(6): 1070–88.

————, and Mayer N. Zald. 1973. *The Trend of Social Movements in America: Professionalization and Resource Mobilization.* Morristown, N.J.: General Learning Press.

————, and Mayer N. Zald. 1977. "Resource Mobilization and Social Movements: A Partial Theory." *The American Journal of Sociology* 82(6): 1212–41.

————, and Mayer N. Zald. 1987. "Resource Mobilization and Social Movements: A Partial Theory." In *Social Movements in an Organizational Society*, ed. Mayer N. Zald and John D. McCarthy, 15–47. New Brunswick, N.J.: Transaction Books.

————, and Mayer N. Zald. 2001. "The Enduring Vitality of the Resource Mobilization Theory of Social Movements." In *Handbook of Sociological Theory*, ed. J. Turner, 533–65. New York: Kluwer Academic.

McCormick, Sabrina. 2007. "Democratizing Science Movements: A New Framework for Contestation." *Social Studies of Science* 37:609–23.

———— 2009. *No Family History: The Environmental Links to Breast Cancer.* New York, NY: Rowman and Littlefield.

————, Phil Brown, and Stephen Zavestoski. 2003. "The Personal Is Scientific, the Scientific Is Political: The Public Paradigm of the Environmental Breast Cancer Movement." *Sociological Forum* 18(4): 545–76.

————, and Maryhelen D'Ottavi. 2001. "Fibromyalgia." National Women's Health Network Publication. Spring.

McFarland, Ross A. 1953. *Human Factors in Air Transportation: Occupational Health and Safety.* New York: McGraw-Hill.

McGee, Glenn. 2006. Panel II. *The Future of Progressive Bioethics. In Bioethics and Politics: Past, Present, and Future*. Washington, D.C., Center for American Progress. Available at www.americanprogress.org/transcriptforbioethicsconference.

McGovern, Theresa M., Martha S. Davis, and Alma M. Gomez. 1992. *Citizen Petition*. New York: HIV Law Project of the AIDS Service Center.

McIntosh, J. 1993. "Postpartum Depression: Women's Help-Seeking Behaviour and Perceptions of Cause." *Journal of Advanced Nursing* 18(2): 178–84.

The——— and P. Martens. 2002. "Global Environmental Changes: Anticipating and Assessing Risks to Health." In *Environmental Change: Climate and Health*, P. Martens and A. J. McMichael eds. Cambridge University Press: Cambridge, England.

Meckel, Richard A. 1990. *Save the Babies: American Public Health Reform and the Prevention of Infant Mortality*. Baltimore: Johns Hopkins University Press.

Melucci, Alberto. 1989. *Nomads of the Present: Social Movements and Individual Needs in Contemporary Society*. Philadelphia: Temple University Press.

———. 1995. "The Process of Collective Identity." In *Social Movements and Culture*, ed. Hank Johnston and Bert Klandermans, 41–63. Minneapolis: University of Minnesota.

———. 1996. *Challenging Codes: Collection Action in the Information Age*. Cambridge: Cambridge University Press.

Merton, Vanessa. 1993. "The Exclusion of Pregnant, Pregnable, and Once-Pregnable People (a.k.a. Women) from Biomedical Research." *American Journal of Law and Medicine* 19(4): 369–451.

Meyer, Cheryl L., and Michelle Oberman. 2001. *Mothers who Kill Their Children: Understanding the Acts of Moms from Susan Smith to the "Prom Mom."* New York: New York University Press.

Meyer, David S. 2004. "Protest and Political Opportunities." *Annual Review of Sociology* 30:125–45.

———, Valerie Jenness, and Helen M. Ingram, eds. 2005. *Routing the Opposition: Social Movements, Public Policy, and Democracy*. Minneapolis: University of Minnesota Press.

———, and Suzanne Staggenborg. 1996. "Movements, Countermovements, and the Structure of Political Opportunity." *American Journal of Sociology* 101(6): 1628–60.

———, and Sidney Tarrow, eds. 1998. *The Social Movement Society: Contentious Politics for a New Century*. Boulder: Rowman & Littlefield.

———, and Nancy Whittier. 1994. "Social Movement Spillover." *Social Problems* 41(2): 277–98.

Meyerson, Deborah. 2003. *Tempered Radicals: How Everyday Leaders Inspire Change at Work*. Boston: Harvard Business School Press.

———, and Maureen Scully. 1995. "Tempered Radicalism and the Politics of Ambivalence and Change." *Organization Science* 6(5): 585–600.

Milden, Susan, and Daniel Stokols. 2004. "Physician's Attitudes and Practices Regarding Complementary and Alternative Medicine." *Behavioral Medicine* 30:73–82.

Miller, Clark. 2001. "Hybrid Management: Boundary Organizations, Science Policy, and Environmental Governance in the Climate Regime." *Science, Technology, and Human Values* 26(4): 478–500.

Minkler, Meredith. 2005. *Community organizing and community building for health*. New Brunswick, NJ: Rutgers University Press.

Minkler, Meredith and Nina Wallerstein. 2005. Improving Health through Community Organization and Community Building: A Health Education Perspective. In *Community Organization and Community Building for Health*, ed. Minkler, Meredith, 26–50. New Brunswick and London: Rutgers.

Mintel. 2007. "Health Savings Account Enrollees Predicted to Rise to 30 Million by 2009." http://home.businesswire.com/portal/site/google/index.jsp?ndmVie.

Mishler, Eliot. 1981. "Viewpoint: Critical Perspectives on the Biomedical Model." In *Social Contexts of Health, Illness, and Patient Care*, ed. Eliot Mishler, 1–19. Cambridge: Cambridge University Press.

Moore, Kelly. 1996. "Organizing Integrity: American Science and the Creation of Public Interest Organizations, 1955–1975." *American Journal of Sociology* 101:1592–627.

———. 1999. "Political Protest and Institutional Change: The Anti–Vietnam War Movement and American Science." In *How Social Movements Matter*, ed. M. Giugni, D. McAdam, and C. Tilly, 97–118. Minneapolis: University of Minnesota Press.

Morello-Frosch, Rachel. 2008. Report to Richmond City Permitting Council on Proposed Changes in Refinery Operations. Unpublished document.

———, Manuel Pastor Jr., James L. Sadd, Carlos Porras, and Michele Prichard. 2005. "Citizens, Science, and Data Judo: Leveraging Secondary Data Analysis to Build a Community-Academic Collaborative for Environmental Justice in Southern California." In *Methods in Community-Based Participatory Research for Health*, ed. Barbara A. Israel, Eugenia Eng, Amy J. Schulz, and Edith A. Parker, 371–92. San Francisco: Jossey-Bass.

———, Stephen Zavestoski, Phil Brown, Rebecca Gasior Altman, Sabrina McCormick, and Brian Mayer. 2006. "Embodied Health Movements: Responses to a 'Scientized' World." In *The New Political Sociology of Science: Institutions, Networks, and Power*, ed. Kelly Moore and Scott Frickel. Madison: University of Wisconsin Press.

Moreno, Jonathan, and Sam Berger. 2007. "Biotechnology and the New Right: Neoconservatism's Red Menace." *American Journal of Bioethics* 7(10): 7–13.

Morgan, M. Granger, Robin Cantor, William C. Clark, Ann Fisher, Henry D. Jacoby, Anthony C. Janetos, Ann P. Kinzig, Jerry Melillo, Roger B. Street, and Thomas J. Wilbanks. 2005. "Learning from the U.S. National Assessment of Climate Change Impacts." *Environmental Science and Technology* 39(23): 9023–32.

Morgen, Sandra. 2002. *Into Our Own Hands: The Women's Health Movement in the United States, 1969–1990*. New Brunswick, N.J.: Rutgers University Press.

Morone, James A., and Lawrence R. Jacobs, eds. 2005. *Healthy, Wealthy, and Fair: Healthcare and the Good Society*. New York: Oxford University Press.

Morrill, Calvin, Mayer N. Zald, and Hayagreeva Rao. 2003. "Covert Political Conflict in Organizations: Challenges from Below." *Annual Review of Sociology* 29:391–415.

Morrison, Linda J. 2005. *Talking Back to Psychiatry: The Psychiatric Consumer/Survivor/Ex-Patient Movement*. London and New York: Routledge.

Moser, Susanne. 2007. "In the Long Shadows of Inaction: The Quiet Building of a Climate Protection Movement in the United States." *Global Environmental Politics* 7(2): 124–45.

Moynihan, Daniel Patrick. 1969. *Maximum Feasible Misunderstanding; Community Action in the War on Poverty*. New York: Free Press.

Multi-Society Task Force on Persistent Vegetative State. 1994. "Medical Aspects of the Persistent Vegetative State [in two parts]." *New England Journal of Medicine* 330(1499–508): 1572–79.

Muncy, Robyn. 2008. "Coal-Fired Reforms: Social Citizenship, Dissident Miners, and the Great Society." Unpublished paper in the author's possession.

Murphy, Michelle. 2004. "Liberation through Control in the Body Politics of U.S. Radical Feminism." In *The Moral Authority of Nature*, ed. L. Daston and F. Vidal, 331–55. Chicago: University of Chicago Press.

Myers, Daniel J., and Daniel Cress, eds. 2004. *Authority in Contention: Research in Social Movements, Conflict and Change*. Vol. 25, *Research in Social Movements, Conflict, and Change*, ed. Daniel J. Myers and Daniel M. Cress. Oxford: JAI Press.

Nadel, Mark V. 1990. "Statement of Mark V. Nadel before the Subcommittee on Health and the Environment, Committee on Energy and Commerce." Washington, D.C.: House of Representatives, U.S. General Accounting Office.

———. 1992. "Women's Health: FDA Needs to Ensure More Study of Gender Differences in Prescription Drug Testing." Washington, D.C.: U.S. House of Representatives General Accounting Office.

Nagel, Joane. 1994. "Constructing Ethnicity: Creating and Recreating Ethnic Identity and Culture." *Social Problems* 41(1):152–76.

Namako, Tom. 2007. "Health Plan B." *Citypaper*, September 18.

Narrigan, Deborah, Jane Sprague Zones, Nancy Worcester, and Maxine Jo Grad. 1997. "Research to Improve Women's Health: An Agenda for Equity." In *Women's Health: Complexities and Differences*, ed. S. B. Ruzek, V. L. Olesen, and A. E. Clarke, 551–79. Columbus: Ohio State University Press.

Nash, Denis, Farzad Mostashari, Annie Fine, James Miller, Daniel O'Leary, Kristy Murray, Ada Huang, Amy Rosenberg, Abby Greenberg, Margaret Sherman, Susan Wong, Grant L. Campbell, John T. Roehrig, Duane J. Gubler, Wun-Ju Shieh, Sherif Zaki, Perry Smith, Marcelle Layton. 2001. "The Outbreak of West Nile Virus Infection in the New York City Area in 1999." *New England Journal of Medicine* 344(24): 1807–14.

Nathanson, Constance A. 1999. "Social Movements as Catalysts for Policy Change: The Case of Smoking and Guns." *Journal of Health Politics, Policy and Law* 24(3): 421–88.

———. 2003. "The Skeptic's Guide to a Movement for Universal Health Insurance." *Journal of Health Politics, Policy and Law* 28(2–3): 443–71.

———. 2007. *Disease Prevention as Social Change: The State, Society, and Public Health in the United States, France, Great Britain, and Canada*. New York: Russell Sage Foundation.

National Alliance on Mental Illness. 2007. http://www.nami.org. Accessed February 6.

"National Call to Action: A Movement to End Child Abuse and Neglect." 2007. Community Networks of Authentic Voices. A Plan to Mobilize Communities to Prevent Child Abuse. http://www.volunteermatch.org/about/.

National Center for Complementary and Alternative Medicine. 2008. http://nccam.nih.gov/about/budget/institute-center.htm. Accessed February 22.

National Center for Health Statistics. 1999. *Health. United States, 1999, with Health and Aging*. Chartbook. Hyattsville.

National Commission on the Observance of International Women's Year. 1978. Document 41: "Plank 14: Insurance." From *The Spirit of Houston: The First National Women's Conference*, 60–62. Washington, D.C.: U.S. Government Printing Office. Available at http://womhist. alexanderstreet.com/dp59/doc41.htm. Accessed November 18.

National Institutes of Health. 2007. "NIH Roadmap for Medical Research. Re-Engineering the Clinical Research Enterprise: Translational Research.". http://nihroadmap.nih.gov/clinical-research/overcview-translational.asp.

Newman, Maria. 2005. "Governor Bush's Role Is Ended in Feeding Tube Dispute." *New York Times*, January 25.

New State Ice v. Liebmann, 285 US 262, 311 (1932) (J. Brandeis, dissenting). New York Times Subject Index 1955–2000.

Noonan, Rita K. 1995. "Women against the State: Political Opportunities and Collective Action Frames in Chile's Transition to Democracy." *Sociological Forum* 19:81–111.

Norgaard, Kari. 2006. "Denial, Privilege and Global Environmental Justice: The Case of Global Climate Change." Paper presented at American Sociological Association Meeting, Atlanta Hilton Hotel, Atlanta, Ga.

Nyman, John A. 2003. *The Theory of Demand for Health Insurance*. Stanford, CA: Stanford University Press.

Oakley, Ann. 1979. "A Case of Maternity: Paradigms of Women as Maternity Cases." *Signs: Journal of Women in Culture and Society* 4 (Summer): 607–31.

Obama-Biden 2008. "HealthCare." www.barackobama.com/issues/healthcare. Accessed November 15.

Oberman, Michelle, and Cheryl Meyer. 2008. *When Mothers Kill: Interviews from Prison*. New York: New York University Press.

O'Connor, Alice. 2001. *Poverty Knowledge: Social Science, Social Policy, and the Poor in Twentieth-Century U. S. History*. Princeton, N.J.: Princeton University Press.

Oliver, J. Eric. 2006. *Fat Politics: The Real Story Behind America's Obesity Epidemic*. New York: Oxford University Press. Oliver-Smith, Anthony. 1996. "Anthropoligical Research on Hazards and Disasters." *Annual Review of Anthropology* 25:303–28.

Olson, Mancur. 1965. *The Logic of Collective Action: Public Goods and the Theory of Groups*. Cambridge, Mass.: Harvard University Press.

O'Neill, M. S., S. Hajat, A. Zanobetti, M. Ramirez-Aguilar, and J. Schwartz. 2005. "Impact of Control for Air Pollution and Respiratory Epidemics on the Estimated Associations of Temperature and Daily Mortality." *International Journal of Biometeorology* 50(2): 121–29.

O'Rourke, Dara, and Gregg P Macey. 2003. "Community Environmental Policing: Assessing New Strategies of Public Participation in Environmental Regulation." *Journal of Policy Analysis and Management* 22:383–414.

Ottinger, Gwen. 2007. "Buckets of Resistance: Standards and the Effectiveness of Citizen Science." Unpublished manuscript.

Owcharenko, Nina, and Robert Moffit. 2006. "The Massachusetts Health Plan: Lessons for the States." Backgrounder #1953. The Heritage Foundation, July 18.

Palmer, Peter. 1997. *The Courage to Teach: Exploring the Inner Landscape of a Teacher's Life*. San Francisco: Jossey Bass.

Parents Anonymous Research Profile. 2005. http://www.parentsanonymous.org/pahtml/pubPubs.html. Accessed January 20.

Parker, Cindy. 2007. Personal communication. Newark, N.J.

Parks, Bradley C., and J. Timmons Roberts. 2006. "Globalization, Vulnerability to Climate Change and Perceived Injustice." *Society and Natural Resources* 19:337–55.

Parsons, Talcott. 1951. *The Social System*. New York: Free Press.

Patterson, Mary Jane. 1976. "Health Security: What It Is." Speech at Women's Leadership Rally, March, Folder 31–1, Committee on National Health Insurance Collection, Walter Reuther Library, Wayne State University, Detroit, Mich.

Patz, Jonathan A., Michael A. McGeehin, Susan M. Bernard, Kristie L. Ebi, Paul R. Epstein, Anne Grambsch, Duane J. Gubler, Paul Reiter, Isabelle Romieu, Joan B. Rose, Jonathan M. Samet, and Julie Tartanj. 2000. "The Potential Health Impacts of Climate Variability and Change for the United States: Executive Summary of the Report of the Health Sector of the U.S. National Assessment." *Environmental Health Perspectives* 108(4): 367–76.

Pauly, Mark V. 1968. "The Economics of Moral Hazard: Comment." *American Economic Review* 53:531–37.

Pear, Robert. 2008. "Women Buying Health Policies Pay a Penalty." *New York Times*, October 29.

Peele, Stanton M. 1989. *The Diseasing of America: Addiction Treatment Out of Control*. Lexington, Mass.: D.C. Heath.

Peindl, K. S., K. L. Wisner, K. L. E. J. Zolnik, and B. H. Hanusa. 1995. "Effects of Postpartum Depression on Family Planning International." *Journal of Psychiatry Medicine* 25(3): 291–300.

Pennsylvania Healthcare Cost Containment Council. 2007. *Critical Condition: the State of Healthcare in Pennsylvania*.

Perlin, Michael L. 1997. "'The Borderline Which Separated You from Me': The Insanity Defense, the Authoritarian Spirit, the Fear of Faking, and the Culture of Punishment." *Iowa Law Review* 82:1375–426.

Petryna, Adriana. 2002. *Life Exposed: Biological Citizens After Chernobyl*. Princeton, NJ: Princeton University Press.

Pettigrew, Andrew. 1998. "Success and Failure in Corporate Transformation Initiatives." In *Information Technology and Organizational Transformation*, ed. R. D. Galliers and W. R. J. Baets, 271–89. Chichester: Wiley.

Pettit, Jethro. 2004. "Climate Justice: A New Social Movement for Atmospheric Rights." *IDS Bulletin Institute of Development Studies* 35(3): 102.

Pfohl, Stephen J. 2003. "The 'Discovery' of Child Abuse." In *Health and Health Care as Social Problems*, ed. Peter Conrad and Valerie Leiter, 69–86. Lanham, Md.: Rowman & Littlefield.

Phelan, Jo, and Bruce G. Link. 2005. "Controlling Disease and Creating Disparities: A Fundamental Cause Perspective." Special issue, *Journal of Gerontology* 60B:27–33.

Physicians' Working Group for Single-Payer National Health Insurance. 2003. "Proposal of the Physicians' Working Group for Single-Payer National Health Insurance." *Journal of the American Medical Association* 290(6): 798–805.

Pierson, Pauland Theda Skocpol, eds. 2007. *The Transformation of American Politics: Activist Government and the Rise of Conservatism*. Princeton, N.J.: Princeton University Press.

Pieterse, Jan Nederveen. 2008. *Is There Hope for Uncle Sam? Beyond the American Bubble*. London and New York: Zed Books.

Pitts, Victoria. 2004. "Illness and Internet Empowerment: Writing and Reading Breast Cancer in Cyberspace." *Health* 2(2).

Piven, Frances Fox and Richard A. Cloward. 1971. *Regulating the Poor: The Functions of Public Welfare*. New York: Pantheon Books.

Piven, Frances F., and Richard A. Cloward. 1979. *Poor People's Movements: Why They Succeed, How They Fail*. New York: Random House/Vintage Books.

Plsek, Paul, Jo Bibby, and Elaine Whitby. 2007. "Practical Methods for Extracting Explicit Design Rules Grounded in the Experience of Organizational Managers." *Journal of Applied Behavioral Science* 43(1): 153–70.

Poen, Monte S. 1996. *Harry S. Truman vs. the Medical Lobby: The Genesis of Medicare*. Columbia: University of Missouri Press.

Polletta, Francesca. 2002. *Freedom is an Endless Meeting: Democracy in American Social Movements*. Chicago: University of Chicago Press.

———. 2004. "Culture in and Outside Institutions." In *Authority in Contention*. Vol. 25, Research in Social Movements, Conflicts and Change, ed. D. J. Myers and D. M. Cress, 161–83. New York: Elsevier.

———, and James M. Jasper. 2001. "Collective Identity and Social Movements." *Annual Review of Sociology* 27:283–305.

Polsky, Andrew J. 1991. *The Rise of the Therapeutic State*. Princeton, N.J.: Princeton University Press.

Porter, Lyman, and Lawrence McKibbin. 1988. *Management Education and Development: Drift or Thrust into the 21st Century?* New York: McGraw-Hill.

Portnoy, Barry, Jennifer Miller, Kathryn Brown-Huamani, and Emily DeVoto. 2007. Impact of the National Institutes of Health Consensus Development Program on stimulating National Institutes of Health-funded research, 1998 to 2001. *International Journal of Technology Assessment in Health Care* 23(3): 343–48.

Poumadere, Marc, Claire Mays, Sophie Le Mer, and Russell Blong. 2005. "The 2003 Heat Wave in France: Dangerous Climate Change Here and Now." *Risk Analysis* 25(6): 1483–94.

Powell, Thomas J. 1994. "Introduction." In *Understanding the Self-Help Organization*, ed. Thomas J. Powell, 1–20. Thousand Oaks, Calif.: Sage Publications.

———. 1987. *Self-Help Organizations and Professional Practice*. Silver Spring, Md.: National Association of Social Workers.

Prejan, Michelle R. 2006. "Texas Law Made This Mad Woman Sane." *Houston Law Review* 42:1487–522.

Preves, Sharon. 2005. "Out of the O.R. and into the Streets: Exploring the Impact of Intersex Media Activism." *Cardozo Journal of Law and Gender* 12 (Fall): 247–88.

Primmer, Lesley. 1997. "Women's Health Research: Congressional Action and Legislative Gains: 1990–1994." In *Women's Health Research: A Medical and Policy Primer*, ed. F. B. Haseltine and B. G. Jacobson. Washington, D.C.: Health Press International.

Progressive States Network. 2007. "Nation's Most Comprehensive Health Plan Approved in Wisconsin Senate." *Stateside Dispatch*, June 28.

Public Health Service Task Force on Women's Health Issues. 1985. "Women's Health: Report of the Public Health Service Task Force on Women's Health Issues: Volume 1." *Public Health Reports* 100(1): 73–106.

Quadagno, Jill. 1992. "Social Movements and State Transformation: Labor Unions and Racial Conflict in the War on Poverty." *American Sociological Review* 57(5): 616–34.

———. 1994. *The Color of Welfare: How Racism Undermined the War on Poverty*. New York: Oxford University Press.

——— 2000. "Promoting Civil Rights through the Welfare State: How Medicare Integrated Southern Hospitals." *Social Problems* 47:68–89.

———. 2004. "Why the United States Has No National Health Insurance: Stakeholder Mobilization Against the Welfare State, 1945–1996." Extra issue, *Journal of Health and Social Behavior* 45:25–44.

———. 2005. *One Nation, Uninsured: Why the U.S. Has No National Health Insurance*. New York: Oxford University Press.

Raeburn, Nicole C. 2004. *Changing Corporate America from the Inside Out: Lesbian and Gay Workplace Rights*. Minneapolis: University of Minnesota Press.

Ragin, Charles. 1999. "Using Qualitative Comparative Analysis to Study Causal Complexity." *Health Services Research* 34(5): 1225–39.

Rao, Hayagreeva. 1994. "The Social Construction of Reputation: Certification Contests, Legitimation, and the Survival of Organizations in the American Automobile Industry, 1895–1912." *Strategic Management Journal* 15:29–44.

———. 2009. *Market Rebels: How Activists Make or Break Radical Innovations*. Princeton, N.J.: Princeton University Press.

———, Calvin Morrill, and Mayer N. Zald. 2000. "Power Plays: How Social Movements and Collective Action Create New Organizational Forms." *Research in Organizational Behavior* 22:236–82.

Rapp, Rayna. 1999. *Testing Women, Testing the Fetus: The Social Impact of Amniocentesis in America*. New York: Routledge.

——, Deborah Heath, and Karen-Sue Taussig (2001) "Genealogical Dis-Ease: Where Hereditary Abnormality, Biomedical Explanation, and Family Responsibility Meet," in S. Franklin and S. McKinnon (eds), *Relative Values: Reconfiguring Kinship Studies* (Durham, N.C.: Duke University Press): 384–409.

Rapping, Elayne. 1996. *The Culture of Recovery: Making Sense of the Self-Help Movement in Women's Lives*. Boston: Beacon Press.

Rateliff, Charles R. 1995. Testimony of Charles R. Rateliff, Senior Vice President, Benefits Administration and Risk Management, Wal-Mart Stores, Inc. before the Health Subcommittee, Way and Means, House of Representatives (June 27): 80–81.

Ray, Raka. 1999. *Fields of Protest: Women's Movements in India*. Minneapolis: University of Minnesota Press.

Rayside, David. 1998. *On the Fringe: Gays and Lesbians in Politics*. Ithaca, N.Y.: Cornell University Press.

Reay, Trish, and C. R. Hinings. 2005. "The Recomposition of an Organizational Field: Health Care in Alberta." *Organization Studies* 26(3): 351–84.

Rehbein, Kathleen, Sandra Waddock, and Samuel Graves. 2004. "Understanding Shareholder Activism: Which Corporations Are Targeted?" *Business and Society* 43(3): 239–67.

Resnick, Phillip J. 1969. "Child Murder by Parents: A Psychiatric Review of Filicide." *American Journal of Psychiatry* 126:325–33.

Rice, John Steadman. 1996. *A Disease of One's Own: Psychotherapy, Addiction, and the Emergence of Co-Dependency*. New Brunswick: Transaction Publishers. Rieff, David. 1991. "Victims All? Recovery, Co-Dependency, and the Art of Blaming Somebody Else." *Harper's Magazine*, October, 49–56.

Riessman, Frank, and David Carroll. 1995. *Redefining Self-Help: Policy and Practice*. San Francisco: Jossey-Bass.

Roberts, J. Timmons, and Melissa M. Toffolon-Weiss. 2001. *Chronicles from the Environmental Justice Frontline*. New York: Cambridge University Press.

Roberts, Pat. 1995. Testimony of Rep. Pat Roberts (R-KS) before the Health Subcommittee, Way and Means, House of Representatives (June 27): 13–14.

Roche, Terence. 2005. "Are HSAs a New Big Thing?" *What Counts Newsletter*, Federal Home Loan Bank of Seattle, December. http://www.fhlbsea.com/WhatCounts/Issues/200512/Article2.

Rochon, Thomas, and Daniel Mazmanian. 1993. "Social Movements and the Policy Process." *Annals of the American Academy of Political and Social Science* 528:75–87.

Rohlinger, Deana. 2002. "Framing the Abortion Debate: Organizational Resources, Media Strategies, and Movement-Countermovement Dynamics." *Sociological Quarterly* 43(4): 479–507.

Roosevelt, Franklin D. 1938. Franklin D. Roosevelt to Josephine Roche, July 15. John T. Woolley and Gerhard Peters, The American Presidency Project [online]. Santa Barbara: University of California (hosted), Gerhard Peters (database). Available from http://www.presidency.ucsb.edu/ws/?pid=15519. Accessed November 1, 2008.

Rosen, George. 1958. *A History of Public Health*. New York: MD Publications.

Rosenbaum, Marcy, Nicole Nisly, Kristi Ferguson, and Evan Kligman. 2002. "Academic Physicians and Complementary and Alternative Medicine: An Institutional Survey" *American Journal of Medical Quality* 17:3–9.

Rosenberg, Charles E. 2007. *Our Present Complaint: American Medicine, Then and Now*. Baltimore: Johns Hopkins University Press.

Rosenthal, Elisabeth. 2005. "A Most Personal Test for the Church's Rules." *New York Times*, March 27.

Rosner, David. 1982. *A Once Charitable Enterprise: Hospitals and Health Care in Brooklyn and New York, 1885–1915*. Cambridge: Cambridge University Press.

———— and Gerald Markowitz. 1987. *Dying for Work: Workers' Safety and Health in Twentieth-Century America*. Indianapolis: Indiana University Press.

Rosser, Sue V. 1994. *Women's Health—Missing from U.S. Medicine*. Bloomington: Indiana University Press.

Rothman, David. 1991. *Strangers at the Bedside: A History of How Law and Bioethics Transformed Medical Decision Making*. New York: Basic Books.

Rothman, Franklin Daniel, and Pamela E. Oliver. 1999. "From Local to Global: The Anti-Dam Movement in Southern Brazil, 1979–1992." *Mobilization: The International Journal of Research in Social Movements, Protest, and Contentious Politics* 4:41–58.

Rothstein, William. 1985. *American Physicians in the Nineteenth Century: From Sects to Science*. Baltimore: Johns Hopkins University Press.

Rousselle, Robert. 1985. "Healing Cults in Antiquity: The Dream Cures of Asclepius and Epidaurus." *Journal of Psychohistory* 12:339–52.

Rowley, Tim, and Mihnea Moldoveanu. 2003. "When Will Stakeholder Groups Act? An Interest- and Identity-Based Model of Stakeholder Group Mobilization." *Academy of Management Review* 28:204–19.

Rucht, Dieter. 1996. "The Impact of National Contexts on Social Movement Structures: A Cross-Movement and Cross-National Comparison." In *Comparative Perspectives on Social Movements: Political Opportunities, Mobilizing Structures, and Cultural Framings*, ed. Doug McAdam, John D. McCarthy, and Mayer N. Zald, 185–204. Cambridge: Cambridge University Press.

Ruggie, Mary. 2004. *Marginal to Mainstream: Alternative Medicine in America*. New York: Cambridge University Press.

Rupp, Leila J. 1997. *The Worlds of Women: The Makings of an International Women's Movement*. Princeton, N.J.: Princeton University Press.

————, and Verta Taylor. 1987. *Survival in the Doldrums: The American Women's Rights Movement, 1945 to the 1960s*. New York: Oxford University Press.

Ruzek, Sheryl Burt. 1978. *Feminist Alternatives to Medical Control*. New York: Praeger.

Ruzek, Jennifer, Edward O'Neil, Renee Williard, and Rebecca W. Rimel. Trends in U.S. Funding for Biomedical Research. 1996. San Francisco, UCSF Center for the Health Professions.

Rynes, Sara. 2007. "Carrying Sumantra Ghoshal's Torch: Creating More Positive, Relevant, and Ecologically Valid Research." *Academy of Management Journal*, Editor's Forum on Research with Relevance to Practice 50(4): 745–47.

————, Jean Bartunek, and Richard Daft. 2001. "Across the Great Divide: Knowledge Creation and Transfer Between Practitioners and Academics." *Academy of Management Journal* 44:340–55.

Sachs, Jeffrey, and Pia Malaney. 2002. "The Economic and Social Burden of Malaria." *Nature* 415:680–85.

Saguy, Abigail C., and Rene Aimeling. 2005. "Fat Devils and Moral Panics: News Reporting on Obesity Science." Paper presented at American Sociological Association Meetings, Philadelphia, Pa., August 15.

Saguy, Abigail C., and Kevin W. Riley. 2005. "Weighing Both Sides: Morality, Mortality, and Framing Contests over Obesity." *Journal of Health Politics, Policy and Law* 30:869–921.

Salamon, Lester M. 2003. *The Resilient Sector: The State of Nonprofit America*. Washington D.C.: Brookings Institution Press.

Salmon, Matt. 1995. Testimony of Rep. Matt Salmon (R-AZ) before the Health Subcommittee, Way and Means, House of Representatives (June 27): 17–19.

Samuelson, Jean. 1995. Testimony of Jean Samuelson, Director of Benefit Services at Cornell University and Board Member of Employers Council on Flexible Compensation, before the Health Subcommittee, Way and Means, House of Representatives (June 27): 72–79.

Sanders, Lisa. 2006. "Heart Ache: Medical Issues Can Get Complicated When It Comes to Matters of the Heart." *New York Times Magazine*, June 18, 27–28.

Scandlen, Greg. 1995. Testimony of Greg Scandlen, Executive Director, Council for Affordable Health Insurance, before the Health Subcommittee, Way and Means, House of Representatives (June 27): 108–9.

Scandlen, Greg. 2000. "Defined Contribution Health Insurance." *Policy Backgrounder No. 154*. National Center for Policy Analysis.

Schaeffer, Francis A., and C. Everett Koop. 1979. *Whatever Happened to the Human Race?* Old Tappan, N.J.: Revell.

Scheff, Thomas, and Suzanne Retzinger. 1991. *Emotions and Violence: Shame and Rage in Destructive Conflicts*. Lanham, Md.: Lexington Books.

Schiebinger, Londa. 1999. *Has Feminism Changed Science?* Cambridge, Mass.: Harvard University Press.

Schlafly, Phyllis. 1996. "MSAs Are the Republicans Best Issue." Eagle Forum, April 18 www.eagleforum.org/column/1996/arp96/4–18–96.html.

Schlozman, Kay L., Sydney Verba, and Henry E. Brady. 1999. "Civic Participation and the Equality Problem." In *Civic Engagement in American Democracy*, ed. Theda Skocpol and Morris P. Fiorina, 427–59. Washington, D.C.: The Brookings Institution; New York: Russell Sage Foundation.

Schneiberg, Marc, and Elisabeth Clemens. 2006. "The Typical Tools for the Job: Research Strategies in Institutional Analysis." *Sociological Theory* 3:195–227.

Schneiberg, Marc, and Michael Lounsbury. 2008. "Social Movements and Institutional Analysis." In *The Handbook of Organizational Institutionalism*, ed. Royston Greenwood, Christine Oliver, Kerstin Sahlin-Andersson, and Roy Suddaby, 650–72. London: Sage.

Schneiberg, Marc, and Michael Lounsbury. 2009. "Social Movements and Neo-Institutional Theory: Analyzing Path Creation and Change." In *Handbook of Institutional Theory*, ed. R. Greenwood, C. Oliver, S. Sahlin-Andersson and R. Suddaby. Thousand Oaks: Sage.

Schneiberg, Marc, and Sarah Soule. 2005. "Institutionalization as a Contested Multilevel Process: The Case of Rate Regulation in American Fire Insurance." In *Social Movements and Organization Theory*, ed. Gerald F. Davis, Doug McAdam, W. Richard Scott, and Mayer N. Zald, 122–61. New York: Cambridge University Press.

Schneiberg, Marc, Marissa King, and Thomas Smith. 2008. "Social Movements and Organizational Form: Cooperative Alternatives to Corporations in the American Insurance, Dairy, and Grain Industries." *American Sociological Review* 73:635–67.

Schneider, Carl E. 2005. "Hard Cases and the Politics of Righteousness." *Hastings Center Report* 35(3): 24–27.

Schrock, Douglas, Daphne Holden, and Lori Reid. 2004. "Creating Emotional Resonance: Interpersonal Emotion Work and Motivational Framing in a Transgender Community." *Social Problems* 5:61–81.

Schwartz, John. 2005. "Neither 'Starvation' Nor the Suffering It Connotes Applies to Schiavo, Doctors Say." *New York Times*, March 25.

Schwartz, Mildred. 2002. "Factions and the Continuity of Political Challengers." In *Social Movements: Identity, Culture, and the State*, ed. David S. Meyer, Belinda Robnett, and Nancy Whittier, 157–71. New York: Oxford University Press.

Scott, Amy, and Scott Tong. 2005. "Under the Influence." Four-part series produced by National Public Radio and The Economist, June 2–3, 2005. Available at http://marketplace.publicradio.org/features/under_the_influence/.

Scott, W. Richard. 1994. "Conceptualizing Organizational Fields: Linking Organizations and Societal Systems." In *Systemrationalitat und partialintereresse [systems rationality and partial interests]*, ed. M. Hans-Ulrich Derlien, M. Uta Gerhadt, and F. W. Scharpf, 203–21. Baden-Baden: Nomos Verlagsgesellschaft.

———. 2001. *Institutions and Organizations*. Thousand Oaks: Sage.

———. 2003. *Organizations: Rational, Natural, and Open Systems*. 5th ed. Thousand Oaks: Sage.

———. 2008. *Institutions and Organizations: Ideas and Interests 3rd ed*. Thousand Oaks: Sage.

———, and John W. Meyer. 1992. "The Organization of Societal Sectors." In *Organizational Environments*, ed. John W. Meyer and W. Richard Scott, 129–53. Newbury Park, Calif.: Sage.

———, Martin Ruef, Peter J. Mendel, and Carol A. Caronna. 2000. *Institutional Change and Healthcare Organizations: From Professional Dominance to Managed Care*. Chicago: University of Chicago Press.

Scott, Wilbur J. 1990. "PTSD in DSM-III: A Case in the Politics of Diagnosis and Disease." *Social Problems* 37 (August): 294–310.

Senier, Laura, Brian Mayer, and Phil Brown. 2005. "Boston Public Schools Green Cleaners Project: Pilot Program Assessment." Report to Massachusetts Committee on Occupational Safety and Health and Boston Urban Asthma Coalition.

Senier, Laura, Rebecca Gasior Altman, Rachel Morello-Frosch, and Phil Brown. 2006. "Research and Action for Environmental Health and Environmental Justice: A Report on the Brown University Contested Illnesses Research Group." *Collective Behavior and Social Movements Newsletter* (American Sociological Association).

Senier, Laura, Brian Mayer, Phil Brown, and Rachel Morello-Frosch. 2007. "School Custodians and Green Cleaners: New Approaches to Labor-Environment Coalitions." *Organization and Environment* 20:304–24.

Seo, Myeong-Gu, and W. E. Douglas Creed. 2002. "Institutional Contradictions, Praxis and Institutional Change." A Dialectic Perspective. *Academy of Management Review* 27(1): 222–47.

Sewell Jr., William H. 1992. "A Theory of Structure: Duality, Agency, and Transformation." *American Journal of Sociology* 99:1–29.

Shapiro, Eve. 2004. "Trans'cending Barriers: Transgender Organizing on the Internet." *Journal of Gay and Lesbian Social Services: Special Issue on Strategies for Gay and Lesbian Rights Organizing* 16(3/4): 165–79.

Shapiro, Joseph. 1994. *No Pity: People with Disabilities Forging a New Civil Rights Movement* New York: Random House.

Shortell, Stephen, M. Robin, R. Gillies, K. M. Erickson, and John. B. Mitchell. 2000. *Remaking Health Care in America: The Evolution of Organized Delivery Systems*. San Francisco: Jossey-Bass.

Shostak, Sara. 2004. "Environmental Justice and Genomics: Acting on the Futures of Environmental Health." *Science as Culture* 13:539–62.

"Signing of Medicare Bill Hailed by NMA Head." 1965. *The Chicago Defender*, August 7.

Simonds, Wendy. 1996. *Abortion at Work: Ideology and Practice in a Feminist Clinic*. New Brunswick: Rutgers University Press.

Sims, Benjamin. 2007. "Things Fall Apart: Disaster, Infrastructure, and Risk." *Social Studies of Science* 37(1): 93–95.

Skocpol, Theda. 1991. "Targeting within Universalism: Politically Viable Policies to Combat Poverty in the United States." In *The Urban Underclass*, ed. Christopher Jencks and Paul E. Peterson, 411–36. Washington, D.C.: Brookings Institute.

————. 1992. *Protecting Soldiers and Mothers: the Political Origins of Social Policy in the United States*. Cambridge, Mass.: Harvard University Press.

————. 1997. *Boomerang: Healthcare Reform and the Turn Against Government*. 2nd ed. New York: W.W. Norton.

Skrentny, John David. 2002. *The Minority Rights Revolution*. Cambridge, Mass.: Harvard University Press.

Smelser, Neil. 1962. *Theory of Collective Behavior*. New York: Free Press.

Smith, Brad. 2005. "Schiavo Tapes Offer Powerful but Misleading Evidence." *Tampa Tribune*, March 20.

Smith, Steven Rathgeb, and Michael Lipsky. 1993. *Nonprofits for Hire: The Welfare State in the Age of Contracting*. Cambridge, Mass.: Harvard University Press.

Smith-Lovin, Lynn. 1990. "Emotion as the Confirmation and Disconfirmation of Identity." In *Research Agendas in the Sociology of Emotions*, ed. Theodore D. Kemper, 238–70. Albany: State University of New York Press.

————. 1995. "The Sociology of Affect and Emotion." In *Sociological Perspectives of Social Psychology*, ed. Karen S. Cook, Gary Alan Fine, and James S. House. Boston: Allyn & Bacon.

————, and David R. Heise. 1988. *Analyzing Social Interaction: Advances in Affect Control Theory*. New York: Gordon and Breach Science Publishers.

Smith-Rosenberg, Carroll. 1972. "The Hysterical Woman: Sex Roles and Role Conflict in Nineteenth-Century America." *Social Research* 39 (Winter): 652–78.

Snow, David A. 2001. "Collective Identity and Expressive Forms." In *International Encyclopedia of the Social and Behavioral Sciences*, ed. Neil Smelser and Paul D. Baltes. Oxford, U.K.: Pergamon Press.

————. 2004a. "Framing Processes, Ideology, and Discursive Fields." In *The Blackwell Companion to Social Movements*, ed. D.A. Snow, S. A. Soule, and H. P. Kriesi, 380–412. Oxford, U.K.: Blackwell Publishing.

————. 2004b. "Social Movements as Challenges to Authority: Resistance to an Emerging Conceptual Hegemony." In *"Authority in Contention,"* special issue, *Research in Social Movements, Conflicts, and Change*, ed. Daniel J. Myers and Daniel M. Cress, 3–25. New York: Elsevier.

————. 2008. "Elaborating the Discursive Contexts of Framing: Discursive Fields and Spaces." *Studies in Symbolic Interaction* 30: 3–28.

————, and Robert D. Benford. 1988. "Ideology, Frame Resonance, and Participant Mobilization." In *From Structure to Action: Social Movement Participation across Cultures*, ed. B. Klandermans, H. P. Kriesi, and S. Tarrow. Greenwich, Conn.: JAI.

————, and Robert D. Benford. 1992. "Master Frames and Cycles of Protest." In *Frontiers in Social Movement Theory*, ed. Aldon D. Morris and Carol McClurg Mueller, 133–55. New Haven, Conn.: Yale University Press.

————, and Catherine Corrigall-Brown. 2005. "Falling on Deaf Ears: Confronting the Prospect of Non-Resonant Frames. In *Rhyming Hope and History: Activism and Social Movement Scholarship*, 222–38. Minneapolis: University of Minnesota Press.

————, D. Cress, L. Downey, and A. Jones. 1998. "Disrupting the Quotidian: Reconceptualizing the Relationship between Breakdown and the Emergence of Collective Action." *Mobilization: The International Journal of Research in Social Movements, Protest, and Contentious Politics* 3:1–22.

————, and Doug McAdam. 2000. "Identity Work Processes in the Context of Social Movements: Clarifying the Identity/Movement Nexus." In *Self, Identity, and Social Movements*, ed. S. Stryker, T. Owens, and R. White, 41–67. Minneapolis: University of Minnesota Press.

———, E. Burke Rochford, Stephen K. Worden, and Robert D. Benford. 1986. "Frame Alignment Processes, Micromobilization, and Movement Participation." *American Sociological Review* 51(4): 464–81.

———, Sarah A. Soule, and Hans Peter Kriesi, ed. 2004. *The Blackwell Companion to Social Movements*. Oxford: Blackwell.

Sombart, Werner. 1976. *Why Is There No Socialism in the United States?* Trans. Patricia M. Hocking and C.T. Husbands. 1906. Reprint, White Plains, N.Y.: International Arts and Sciences Press.

Sommer, David. 2002a. "Doctors Testify: She Will Not Improve." *Tampa Tribune*, October 23.

———. 2002b. "Judge: Unhook Schiavo's Tube." *Tampa Tribune*, November 23.

Soule, Sarah A., Doug McAdam, John McCarthy, and Yang Su. 1999. "Protest Events: Cause or Consequence of State Action? The U.S. Women's Movement and Federal Congressional Activities, 1956–1979." *Mobilization: The International Journal of Research in Social Movements, Protest, and Contentious Politics* 4 (Fall): 239–56.

Spicer, Andre. 2006. "Resistance for Change." *Organization* 13(3): 455–58.

Spinelli, Margaret G. 2003. "The Promise of Saved Lives: Recognition, Prevention, and Rehabilitation." In *Infanticide: Psychosocial and Legal Perspectives on Mothers Who Kill*, ed. Margaret G. Spinelli, 235–56. Arlington, Va.: American Psychiatric Publishing, Inc.

———. 2005. "Infanticide: Contrasting Views." *Archives of Women's Mental Health* 8(1): 1434–816.

Sridhar, Devi. 2005. "Inequality in the United States Health Care System." United Nations Human Development Report Office: Occasional Paper 36.

Staggenborg, Suzanne. 1986. "Coalition Work in the Pro-Choice Movement: Organizational and Environmental Opportunities and Obstacles." *Social Problems* 33:374–90.

———. 1991. *The Pro-Choice Movement: Organization and Activism in the Abortion Conflict*. New York: Oxford University Press.

———. 1993. "Critical Events and the Mobilization of the Pro-Choice Movement." *Research in Political Sociology* 6:319–45.

———. 2002. "The 'Meso' in Social Movement Research." In *Social Movements: Identity, Culture, and the State*, ed. David S. Meyer, Belinda Robnett, and Nancy Whittier, 124–40. New York: Oxford University Press.

———, and Verta Taylor. 2005. "Whatever Happened to the Women's Movement?" *Mobilization: The International Journal of Research in Social Movements, Protest, and Contentious Politics* 10(1): 37–52.

Stanford, Jim. 2008. "Radical Economics and Social Change Movements: Strengthening the Links Between Academics and Activists." *Review of Radical Political Economics* 40:205.

Star, Susan Leigh, and James R. Griesemer. 1989. "Institutional Ecology, 'Translations' and Boundary Objects: Amateurs and Professionals in Berkeley's Museum of Vertebrate Zoology, 1907–1939." *Social Studies of Science* 19:387–420.

Starr, Paul. 1982. *The Social Transformation of American Medicine*. New York: Basic Books.

———. 1995. "What Happened to Health Care Reform?" *The American Prospect* 20 (Winter): 20–31.

Steinberg, Marc. 1999. "The Talk and Back Talk of Collective Action: A Dialogic Analysis of Repertoires of Discourse among Nineteenth-Century English Cotton Spinners." *American Journal of Sociology* 105 (November): 736–80.

Stevens, Rosemary. 1989. *In Sickness and in Wealth: American Hospitals in the Twentieth Century*. New York: Basic Books.

Stolberg, Sheryl G. 2003a. "A Collision of Disparate Forces May Be Reshaping American Law." *New York Times*, March 31.

————. 2003b. "The Schiavo Case: Legislators with Medical Degrees Offer Opinions on Schiavo Case." *New York Times*, March 23.

Stone, Deborah. 2001. *Policy Paradox: The Art of Political Decision Making*. New York: W.W. Norton.

Strach, Patricia. 2007. *All in the Family: The Private Roots of American Public Policy*. Stanford: Stanford University Press.

Strang, David, and Dong-Il Jung. 2005. "Organizational Change as an Orchestrated Social Movement: Determinants and Implications of Recruitment to a 'Quality Initiative.'" In *Social Movements and Organization Theory*, ed. G. F. Davis, D. McAdam, W. R. Scott, and M. Zald, 208–309. Cambridge: Cambridge University Press.

Strickland, Stephen P. 1972. *Politics, Science, and Dread Disease: A Short History of United States Medical Research Policy*. Cambridge, Mass.: Harvard University Press.

Stryker, Robin. 2000. "Legitimacy Processes as Institutional Politics: Implications for Theory and Research in the Sociology of Organizations." *Research in the Sociology of Organizations*, 17:179–223.

————. 2002. "A Political Approach to Organizations and Institutions." In *Research in the Sociology of Organizations*, ed. M. Lounsbury and M. Ventresca, 171–93. Oxford: JAI Press.

Stryker, Sheldon. 1987. "The Vitalization of Symbolic Interactionism." *Social Psychology Quarterly* 50:83–94.

Substance Abuse and Mental Health Services Administration. 2006. Strategic prevention framework state incentive grant program (Short Title: SPF SIG) (Initial Announcement). Catalogue of Federal Domestic Assistance (CFDA) No.: 93.243 [SP-06-002].

Summers, Judith. 1989. *Soho: A History of London's Most Colourful Neighborhood*. Bloomsbury, London: Trafalgar Square.

Sundberg, Mikaela. 2007. "Parameterization as Boundary Objects on the Climate Arena." *Social Studies of Science* 37(3): 473–88.

Swenson, Peter, and Scott L. Greer. 2002. "Foul Weather Friends: Big Business and Healthcare Reform in the 1990s in Historical Perspective." *Journal of Health Politics, Policy and Law* 27(4): 605–38.

Swidler, Ann. 1995. "Cultural Power and Social Movements." In *Social Movements and Culture*, ed. H. Johnston and B. Klandermans, 25–40. Minneapolis: University of Minnesota Press.

Szaz, Andrew. 1994. *Ecopopulism: Toxic Waste and the Movement for Environmental Justice*. Minneapolis: University of Minnesota Press.

Szreter, Simon. 2002. Rethinking McKeown: The Relationship between Public Health and Social Change. *American Journal of Public Health* 92(5):722–25.

————. 2003. The population health approach in historical perspective. *American Journal of Public Health* 93, no. 3:421–31.

Talley, Colin. 2004. "The Combined Efforts of Community and Science: American Culture, Patient Activism, and the Multiple Sclerosis Movement in the United States." In *Emerging Illnesses and Society: Negotiating the Public Health*, ed. R. M. Packard, P. J. Brown, R. L. Berkelman, and H. Frumkin, 39–70. Baltimore: Johns Hopkins University Press.

Tanner, Michael. 2008. "A Fork in the Road: Obama, McCain 2000 and Health Care." Cato Institute Briefing Paper, July 29. Washington, D.C.: Cato Institute.

Tarrow, Sidney. 1994. *Power in Movement: Social Movements, Collective Action, and Mass Politics in the Modern State*. Cambridge: Cambridge University Press.

————. 1998. *Power in Movement: Social Movements and Contentious Politics*. Cambridge: Cambridge University Press.

Taubes, Gary. 2007. "Unhealthy Science." *New York Times Magazine*, September 16, 52–59, 74, 78, 90.

Taylor, Verta. 1989. "Social Movement Continuity: The Women's Movement in Abeyance." *American Sociological Review* 54:761–75.

———. 1995a. "Watching for Vibes: Bringing Emotions into the Study of Feminist Organizations." In *Feminist Organizations: Harvest of the New Women's Movement*, ed. Myra Marx Ferree and Patricia Yancey Martin, 223–33. Philadelphia: Temple University Press.

———. 1995b. "Self-Labeling and Women's Mental Health: Postpartum Illness and the Reconstruction of Motherhood." *Sociological Focus* 28 (August): 23–47.

———. 1996. *Rock-a-by Baby: Feminism, Self-Help, and Postpartum Depression.* New York: Routledge.

———. 2000a. "Emotions and Identity in Women's Self-Help Movements." In *Self, Identity, and Social Movements*, ed. S. Stryker, T. Owens, and R. White, 271–99. Minneapolis: University of Minnesota Press.

———. 2000b. "Mobilizing for Change in a Social Movement Society." *Contemporary Sociology* 29 (January): 219–30.

———, and Leila J. Rupp. 1993. "Women's Culture and Lesbian Feminist Activism: A Reconsideration of Cultural Feminism." *Signs: Journal of Women in Culture and Society* 19:32–61.

———, and Leila J. Rupp. 2002. "Loving Internationalism: The Emotion Culture of Transnational Women's Organizations, 1888–1945." *Mobilization: The International Journal of Research in Social Movements, Protest, and Contentious Politics* 7(2): 125–44.

———, and Nella Van Dyke. 2004. "'Get Up, Stand Up': Tactical Repertoires of Social Movements." In *The Blackwell Companion to Social Movements*, ed. David A. Snow, Sarah A. Soule, and Hans Peter Kriesi, 262–93. Oxford: Blackwell.

———, and Marieke Van Willigen. 1996. "Women's Self-Help and the Reconstruction of Gender: The Postpartum Support and Breast Cancer Movements." *Mobilization: The International Journal of Research in Social Movements, Protest, and Contentious Politics* 1 (September): 122–44.

———, and Nancy Whittier. 1992. "Collective Identity in Social Movement Communities: Lesbian Feminist Mobilization." In *Frontiers in Social Movement Theory*, ed. Aldon D. Morris and Carol McClurg Mueller, 104–29. New Haven and London: Yale University Press.

Tenenbaum, David. 1998. "Northern Overexposure." *Environmental Health Perspectives*, A64–A69.

———. 2005. "Arctic Climate: The Heat Is On." *Environmental Health Perspectives* 113(2): 91A.

Tesh, Sylvia N. 2000. *Uncertain Hazards: Environmental Activists and Scientific Proof.* Ithaca, N.Y.: Cornell University Press.

"The Horrible Herb Show." 1976. *Time*, September 13. www.time.com. Accessed November 20.

The Multi-Society Task Force on Persistent Vegetative State. 1994. Medical aspects of the persistent vegetative state [in two parts]. *New England Journal of Medicine* 330:1499–1508, 1572–1579.

"They Are All Afraid of Herb the Horrible." 1972. *Time*, July 10. www.time.com. Accessed November 20.

Thornton, Patricia H., Candace Jones, and Kenneth Kury. 2005. "Institutional Logics and Institutional Change in Organizations: Transformation in Accounting, Architecture and Publishing." *Research in the Sociology of Organizations* 23:125–70.

Tickner, Joel. 2002. "The Precautionary Principle and Public Health Trade-Offs: Case Study of West Nile Virus." *Annals of the American Academy of Political and Social Science* 584:69–79.

Tilly, Charles. 1978. *From Mobilization to Revolution*. Reading, PA: Addison Wesley.

———. 1979. "Repertoires of Contention in America and Britain: 1750–1820." In *The Dynamics of Social Movements*, ed. Mayer Zald and John McCarthy, 126–55. Cambridge, Mass.: Winthrop.

———. 1984. "Social Movements and National Politics." In *Statemaking and Social Movements*, ed. C. Bright and S. Harding, 297–317. Ann Arbor: University of Michigan Press.

———. 1993. "Contentious Repertoires in Great Britain, 1758–1834." *Social Science History* 17:253–80.

———. 1998. "From Interactions to Outcomes in Social Movements." In *How Movements Matter*, ed. M. Giugni, Doug McAdam, and Charles Tilly. Minneapolis: University of Minnesota Press.

Tomes, Nancy. 1998. *The Gospel of Germs: Men, Women, and the Microbe in American Life*. Cambridge, Mass.: Harvard University Press.

Toner, Robin. 1995. "Gingrich Vows Total Review of Medicare for Cost Savings." *New York Times*, January 31.

Touraine, Alan. 1981. *The Voice and the Eye: An Analysis of Social Movements*. Cambridge: Cambridge University Press.

Townley, Barbara. 2002. "The Role of Competing Rationalities in Institutional Change." *Academy of Management Journal* 45(1): 163–79.

"Transcript of President's News Conference on Foreign and Domestic Matters." 1964. *New York Times*, April 26, 64.

Treadway, Jack. 2005. *Elections in Pennsylvania: A Century of Partisan Conflict in the Keystone State*. University Park: Pennsylvania State University Press.

Treichler, Paula A., Lisa Cartwright, and Constance Penley, ed. 1998. *The Visible Woman: Imaging Technologies, Gender, and Science*. New York: New York University Press.

Tuohy, Carolyn. 1999. *Accidental Logics: The Dynamics of Change in the Health Care Arena in the United States, Britain, and Canada*. New York: Oxford University Press.

Turner, Bryan. 2004. *The New Medical Sociology: Social Forms of Health and Illness*. New York: Norton.

Turner, Lowell, and Daniel Cornfield, eds. 2007. *Labor in the New Urban Battlegrounds: Local Solidarity in a Global Economy*. Ithaca, N.Y.: Cornell University Press.

United States Congress. House of Representatives Committee on Way and Means, Subcommittee on Health. H.R. 1818, The Family Medical Savings and Investment Act: Hearing. 104th Cong., 1st sess., 1–140.

United States Department of the Treasury. 2006. *Health Savings Accounts and Other Tax-Favored Health Plans*. IRS Publication 969.

United States Global Research Program 2000. "Climate Change and a Global City: An Assessment of the Metropolitan East Coast Region." Washington, D.C.

United States National Commission on AIDS. 1992. "The Challenge of HIV/AIDS in Communities of Color." Washington, D.C.: U.S. Government Printing Office.

Useem, Bert, and Mayer N. Zald. 1982. "From Pressure Group to Social Movement: Organizational Dilemmas of the Effort to Promote Nuclear Power." *Social Problems* 30:144–56.

Unselman, J., and J. McKlveen. 1975. "Radiation Exposures Aboard Commercial Aircraft." *Health Physics* 29:881–83.

van Aken, Joan E. 2004. "Actionable Knowledge, Produced by Action Research, Informed by the Approach of the Design Sciences." Presentation to the Academy of Management Symposium: Is Design Science Better at Creating Actionable Research and Knowledge than Action Research Is? New Orleans, August 6–11.

Van de Ven, Andrew. 2007. *Engaged Scholarship: A Guide for Organizational and Social Research*. New York: Oxford University Press.

———, and Paul Johnson. 2006. "Knowledge for Theory and Practice." *Academy of Management Review* 31(4): 802–21.

Van Dyke, Nella, Sarah A. Soule, and Verta A. Taylor. 2004. "The Targets of Social Movements: Beyond a Focus on the State." *Research in Social Movements, Conflict and Change* 25:27–51.

Van Dyke, Nella, Sarah A. Soule, and Rebecca Widom. 2001. "The Politics of Hate: Explaining Variation in the Incidence of Anti-Gay Hate Crime." *Research in Political Sociology: The Politics of Social Inequality* 9 (February): 33–56.

Viswanathan, Meera, Alice Ammerman, Eugenia Eng, Gerald Garlehner, Kathleen N. Lohr, Derek Griffith, Scott Rhodes et al. 2004. Community-Based Participatory Research: Assessing the Evidence. *Evid.Rep.Technol.Assess.(Summ.)*, no. 99:1–8.

Wagenaar, Alexander. C., Darin. J. Erickson, Eileen. M. Harwood, and Patrick. M. O'Malley. 2006. Effects of State Coalitions to Reduce Underage Drinking: A National Evaluation. *American Journal of Preventive Medicine* 31(4):307–15.

Wagner, David. 1997. *The New Temperance: The American Obsession with Sin and Vice*. Boulder, Colo.: Westview Press.

Walker Jr., Jack L. 1991. *Mobilizing Interest Groups in America: Patrons, Professions, and Social Movements*. Ann Arbor: University of Michigan Press.

Wallace, Michael B. and Paul Hurlstone. 2003. Federal Funding of Endoscopic Research in the United States: 1972–2002. *Gastrointestinal Endoscopy* 58(6): 831–835.

Walsh, Edward J. 1988. *Democracy in the Shadows: Citizen Mobilization in the Wake of the Accident at Three Mile Island*. New York: Greenwood Press.

Warren, John R., and Elaine M. Hernandez. 2007. "Did Socioeconomic Inequalities in Morbidity and Mortality Change in the United States Over the Course of the Twentieth Century?" *Journal of Health and Social Behavior* 48 (December): 335–51.

Watanabe, Myrna E. 1995. "From Internal Guidelines to the Law." *The Scientist*, March 6.

Watson, Wilbur H. 1999. *Blacks in the Profession of Medicine in the United States: Against the Odds*. New Brunswick: Transaction.

Weil, Alan. 2008. "How Far Can States Take Health Reform?" *Health Affairs* 27(3): 736–47.

Weisman, Carol S. 1998. *Women's Health Care: Activist Traditions and Institutional Change*. Baltimore: John Hopkins University Press.

———. 2000. "Breast Cancer Policymaking." In *Breast Cancer: Society Shapes an Epidemic*, ed. A. S. Kasper and S. J. Ferguson, 213–43. New York: St. Martin's.

Weiss, Rick. 2005. "Conservatives Draft a 'Bioethics Agenda' for President." *Washington Post*, March 8.

Weitzman, Elissa. R., Toben. F. Nelson, Hang. Lee, and Henry. Wechsler. 2004. Reducing drinking and related harms in college: evaluation of the "A Matter of Degree" program. *American Journal of Preventive Medicine* 27(3): 187–96.

Wenner, David. 2007. "Rendell's Health Plan Draws Fire from Panel." *Patriot News*, May 15.

Werner, Ben. 2007. "Blue Cross Banks on Health Savings Plans." *The State.com*. http://www.thestate.com/mid/thestate/business/16812989.

Wertz, Richard W., and Dorothy C. Wertz. 1989. *Lying-In: A History of Childbirth in America*. New Haven, Conn.: Yale University Press.

West, Candace. 1984. *Routine Complications: Troubles with Talk Between Doctors and Patients*. Bloomington: Indiana University Press.

Westen, Drew. 2007. *The Political Brain: The Role of Emotion in Deciding the Fate of the Nation*. New York: Public Affairs.

White, Barbara J., and Edward J. Madara. 2002. *The Self-Help Sourcebook: Finding and Forming Mutual Aid Self-Help Groups*. 7th ed. Denville, N.J.: New Jersey Self-Help Clearinghouse.

White, William L. 1998. *Slaying the Dragon: The History of Addiction Treatment and Recovery in America*. Illinois: Chestnut Health Systems/Lighthouse Institute.

Whittier, Nancy. 1995. *Feminist Generations: The Persistence of the Radical Women's Movement*. Philadelphia: Temple University Press.

———. 1997. "Political Generations, Micro-Cohorts, and the Transformation of Social Movements." *American Sociological Review* 62(5):760–78.

———. 2001. "Emotional Strategies: The Collective Reconstruction and Display of Oppositional Emotions in the Movement Against Child Sexual Abuse." In *Passionate Politics: Emotions and Social Movements*, ed. Jeff Goodwin, James M. Jasper and Francesca Polletta, 233–50. Chicago: University of Chicago Press.

———. 2002. "Meaning and Structure in Social Movements." In *Social Movements: Identity, Culture, and the State*, ed. David S. Meyer, Belinda Robnett, and Nancy Whittier, 289–309. New York: Oxford University Press.

———. 2007. "The Politics of Visibility: Coming Out and Individual and Collective Identity." Paper presented at Collective Behavior and Social Movement Workshop on Movement Cultures, Strategies, and Outcomes, Hofstra University, Long Island, N.Y.

———. 2009. *Healing for Justice: The Politics of Child Sexual Abuse*. Oxford and New York: Oxford University Press.

———. Forthcoming. "The Politics of Visibility: Coming Out and Individual and Collective Identity." In *Strategy in Action: Movements and Social Change*, ed. Jeff Goodwin et al.

Wholey, Douglas R., Jon B. Christianson, Debra A. Draper, Cara S. Lesser, and Lawton R. Burns. 2004. "Community Responses to National Healthcare Firms." *Journal of Health and Social Behavior* 45 (Extra Issue):118–35.

Widener, Patricia. 2007. "Oil Conflict in Ecuador." *Organization and Environment* 20:84–105.

Wilensky, Harold L. 2002. *Rich Democracies: Political Economy, Public Policy, and Performance*. Berkeley and Los Angeles: University of California Press.

Williams, Rhys H. 2004. "The Cultural Contexts of Collective Action." In *The Blackwell Companion to Social Movements*, ed. D. A. Snow, S. A. Soule and H. P. Kriesi, 91–115. Malden, MA: Blackwell Publishing.

Willie, Charles V. et al., eds. 1995. *Mental Health, Racism, and Sexism*. Pittsburgh and London: University of Pittsburgh Press.

Wilogren, Jodi. 1999. "New York City Mosquito Control is Weak and Late, Experts Say." *New York Times*, September 8.

Wisconsin Citizen Action. 2007. *Healthy Wisconsin: Your Choice Your Plan*.

Wolch, Jennifer R. 1996. "Community-Based Human Service Delivery." *Housing Policy Debate* 7:649–71.

Wojcik, Joanne. 2007. "Large Employers Lead in HSA Adoption." Podcast posted April 2, 2007, 2:52 PM. http://www.businessinsurance.com/cgi-bin/news,pl?newsId=9899.

Wolfson, Mark. 2001. *The Fight Against Big Tobacco: The Movement, the State, and the Public's Health*. New York: Aldine de Gruyter.

Wolfson, Mark, Eun-Young Song, Barbara Alvarez Martin, Kimberly Wagoner, Cindy Miller, Debbie Pleasants, Rebecca Nieberg, L Kaltenbach, Beth Reboussin, Kristie Long Foley, J Preisser, and Sheryl Hulme. National evaluation of the Enforcing Underage Drinking Laws Randomized Community Trial: Year 2 report. 2006. Winston-Salem, NC, Wake Forest University School of Medicine.

"Women's Health Research: Prescription for Change." 1991. Annual Report. Washington, D.C.: Society for the Advancement of Women's Health Research.

Worden, Amy. 2007. "Rendell Gives Insuring All a New Push." *Philadelphia Inquirer*, October 3.

World Health Organization. 2003. *Climate Change and Human Health—Risks and Responses. Summary.*

Wright, John R. 1990. "Contributions, Lobbying, and Committee Voting in the U.S. House of Representatives." *American Political Science Review* 84(2): 417–38.

Wuthnow, Robert. 1994. *Sharing the Journey: Support Groups and America's New Quest for Community*. New York: Free Press.

Yeaton, W. H. 1994. "The Development and Assessment of Valid Measures of Service Delivery to Enhance Inference in Outcome-Based Research. Measuring Attendance at Self Attendance of Self-Help Group Meetings: New Methods in Mental Health Research." *Journal of Consulting Clinical Psychology* 62(4): 686–94.

Young, Michael P. 2002. "Confessional Protest: The Religious Birth of U.S. National Social Movements." *American Sociological Review* 67 (October): 660–88.

Zakocs, Ronda. C. and Erika. M. Edwards. 2006. What Explains Community Coalition Effectiveness?: A Review of the Literature. *American Journal of Preventive Medicine* 30 (4):351–61.

Zakocs, Ronda. C. and Sarah. Guckenburg. 2007. What coalition factors foster community capacity? Lessons learned from the Fighting Back Initiative. *Health Education and Behavior* 34(2):354–75.

Zald, Mayer N. 2005. "The Strange Career of an Idea and Its Resurrection: Social Movements in Organizations." *Journal of Management Inquiry* 14:57–66.

———, and R. Ash. 1966. "Social Movement Organizations: Growth, Decay, and Change." *Social Forces* 44:327–40.

———, and Michael Berger. 1978. "Social Movements in Organizations: Coup d'Etat, Bureaucratic Insurgency, and Mass Movements." *American Journal of Sociology* 83(4): 823–61.

———, and John D. McCarthy. 1975. "Organizational Intellectuals and the Criticism of Society." Social Service 49(3):344–62.

———, Calvin Morrill, and Hayagreeva Rao. 2002. "How Do Social Movements Penetrate Organizations? Environmental Impact and Organizational Response." Paper presented at Conference on Social Movement and Organization Theory, Ann Arbor, Mich.

———, Calvin Morrill, and Hayagreeva Rao. 2005. "The Impact of Social Movements on Organizations." In *Social Movements and Organization Theory*, ed. G. F. Davis, D. McAdam, W. R. Scott, and M. N. Zald, 253–79. Cambridge: Cambridge University Press.

———, and Bert Useem. 1987. "Movement and Countermovement Interaction: Mobilization, Tactics, and State Involvement." In *Social Movements in an Organizational Society*, ed. Mayer N. Zald and John D. McCarthy, 247–71. New Brunswick: Transaction.

Zavestoski, Stephen, Phil Brown, Meadow Linder, Brian Mayer, and Sabrina McCormick. 2002. "Science, Policy, Activism and War: Defining the Health of Gulf War Veterans." *Science, Technology, & Human Values* 27(2): 171–205.

———, Phil Brown, Sabrina McCormick, et al. 2004. "Illness Experience and Patient Activism: Gulf War–Related Illnesses and other Medically Unexplained Physical Symptoms." *Social Science and Medicine* 58(1): 161–76.

———, Rachel Morello-Frosch, Phil Brown, Brian Mayer, Sabrina McCormick, and Rebecca Gasior Altman. 2004. "Embodied Health Movements and Challenges to the Dominant Epidemiological Paradigm." *Research in Social Movements, Conflict, and Change* 25:253–78.

Zoller, Heather M. 2007. "Resistance Leadership: The Overlooked Potential in Critical Organization and Leadership Studies." *Human Relations* 60(9): 1331–60.

Zota, Ami R., Ruthann A. Rudel, Rachel Morello-Frosch and Julia G. Brody. 2008. "Elevanted House Dust and Serum Concentrations of PBDEs in California: Unintended Consequences of Furniture Flammability Standards?" *Environmental Science and Technology, 42* (21): 8158–8164.

Index